THE BROWN FOUNDATION, INC., PLAZA

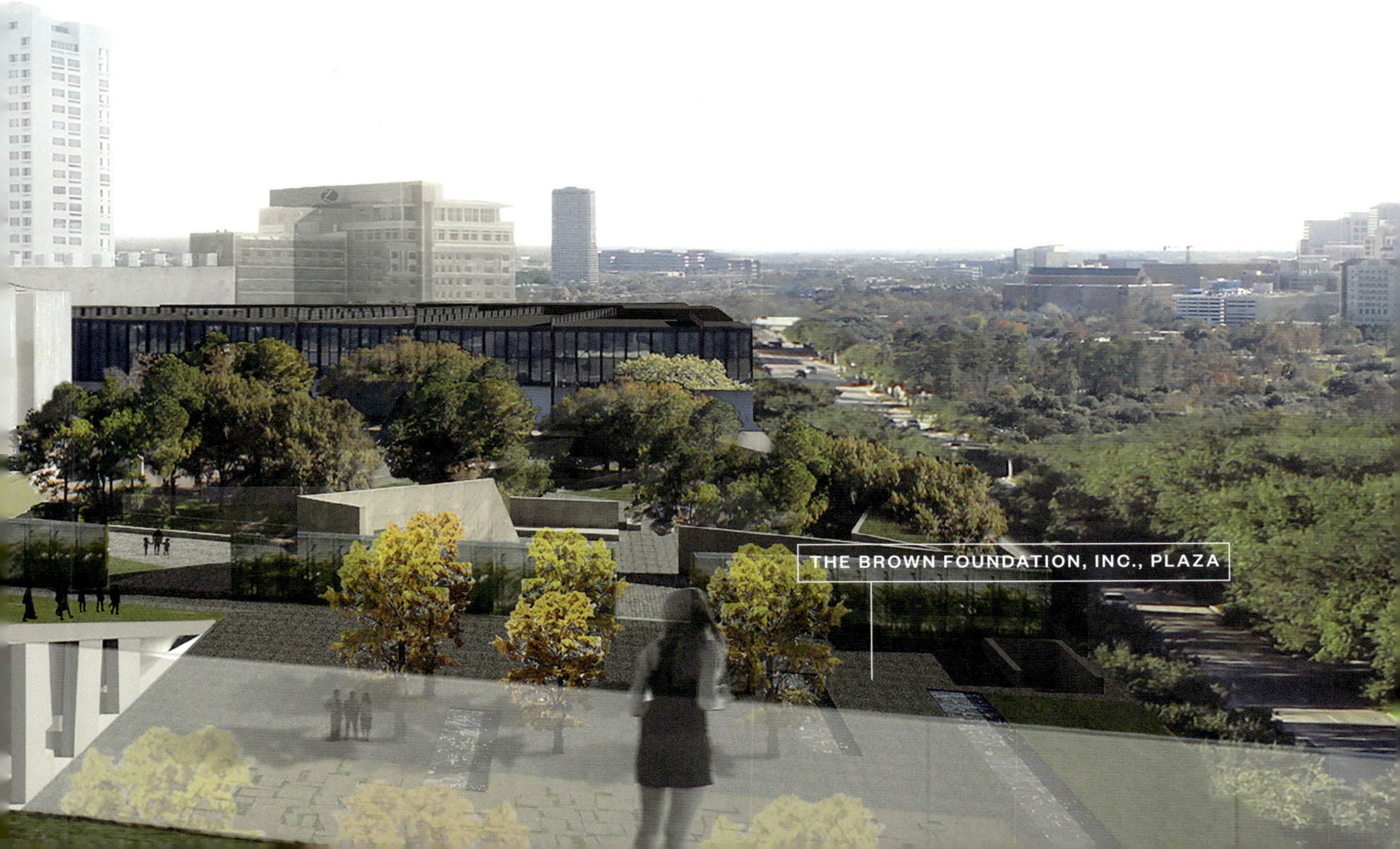

HOUSTON'S HUB FOR ALL THINGS CULTURAL

A MASTER PLAN FOR THE MUSEUM OF FINE ARTS, HOUSTON

Gary Tinterow

With contributions by
David Bomford, Alison de Lima Greene,
Joseph Havel, Marian Luntz,
Mari Carmen Ramírez, Cindi Strauss,
Anne Wilkes Tucker, and Dena M. Woodall

THE MUSEUM OF FINE ARTS, HOUSTON

100 copies of this publication were printed by Puritan Press, Inc. in May 2015.

Publisher in Chief: Diane Lovejoy

Book jacket and design by Phenon Finley-Smiley

Library of Congress Cataloging-in-Publication Data

Museum of Fine Arts, Houston.
    Houston's hub for all things cultural / Gary Tinterow ; with contributions by David Bomford, Alison de Lima Greene, Joseph Havel, Marian Luntz, Mari Carmen Ramírez, Cindi Strauss, Anne Wilkes Tucker, and Dena M. Woodall.
        pages cm
    Summary: "This book focuses on the campus redevelopment and new buildings for the Museum of Fine Arts, Houston, as well as on a new way of presenting the permanent collections of art created after 1900. Featured are notable works from Asia, Africa, Europe, Latin America, and the United States"— Provided by publisher.
    ISBN 978-0-89090-179-3
    I. Museum of Fine Arts, Houston. 2. Art—Texas—Houston. I. Tinterow, Gary. Building on a vision. II. Title.
    N576.H7A83 2013
    708.164'1411—dc23
    2013034236

Gary Tinterow is Director of the Museum of Fine Arts, Houston.

The following members of the Museum's staff contributed to this volume:

David Bomford is Conservation Director.

Alison de Lima Greene is Curator of Modern and Contemporary Art and Special Projects.

Joseph Havel is Director of the Glassell School of Art.

Marian Luntz is Curator of Film and Video.

Mari Carmen Ramírez is the Wortham Curator of Latin American Art and the Director of the International Center for the Arts of the Americas.

Cindi Strauss is the Sara and Bill Morgan Chair of Decorative Arts, Craft, and Design and Assistant Director, Programming.

Anne Wilkes Tucker is the Gus and Lyndall Wortham Curator of Photography.

Dena M. Woodall is Associate Curator of Prints and Drawings.

Cover: Stephen Holl Architects, 2013. Computer rendering of a nighttime view of the new Nancy and Rich Kinder Building.

Inside front cover: Stephen Holl Architects, 2014. Computer rendering of a view of the Fayez S. Sarofim Campus from the BBVA Roof Garden of the Glassell School of Art.

Page 4: Architectural model for the expanded Fayez S. Sarofim Campus of the Museum of Fine Arts, Houston.

Inside back cover: Detail of aerial view of the Museum of Fine Arts, Houston, 1926.

CONTENTS

Art after 1900
Highlights from the Modern and Contemporary Collections of
the Museum of Fine Arts, Houston

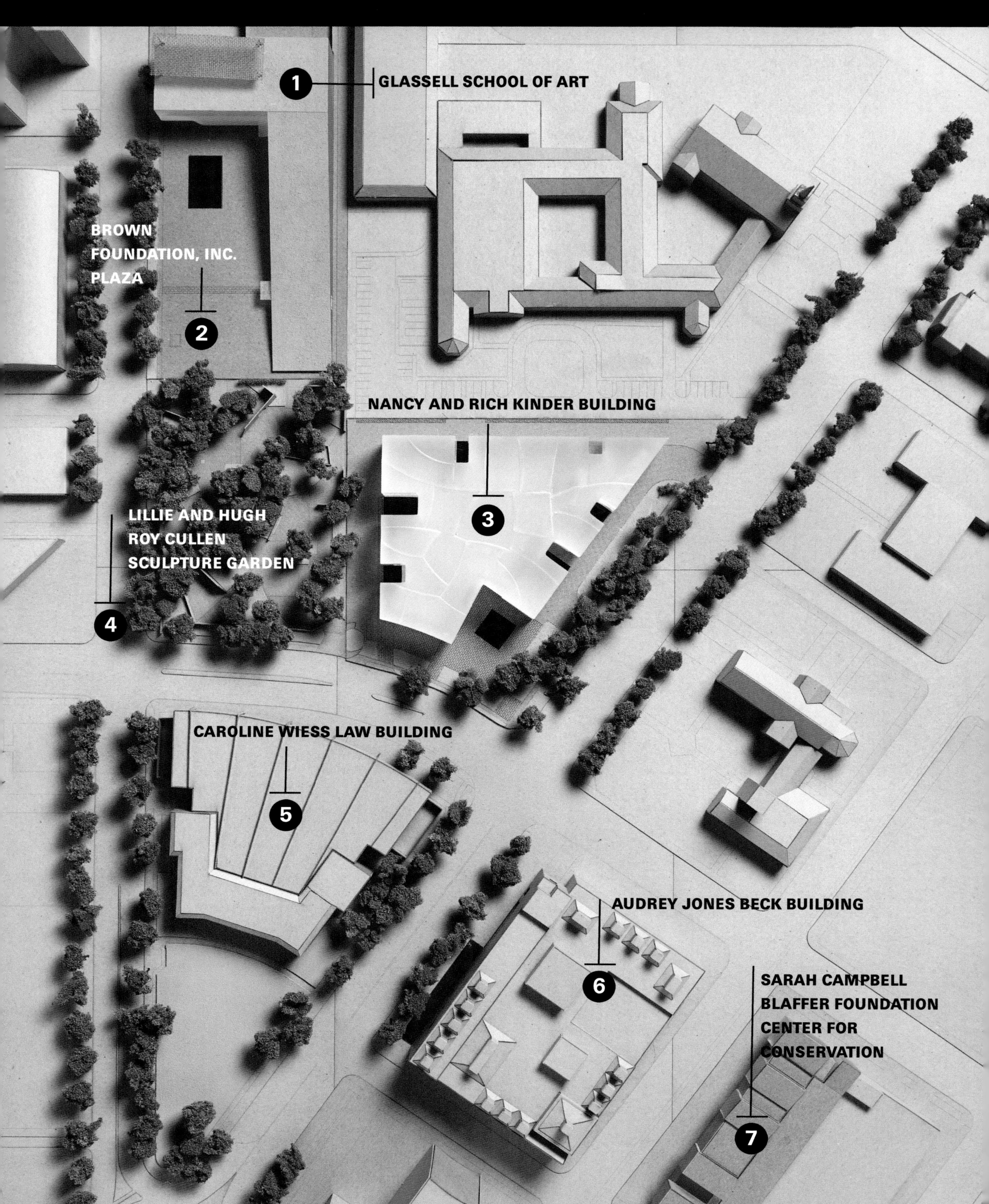
1 GLASSELL SCHOOL OF ART
BROWN FOUNDATION, INC. PLAZA
2
NANCY AND RICH KINDER BUILDING
3
LILLIE AND HUGH ROY CULLEN SCULPTURE GARDEN
4
CAROLINE WIESS LAW BUILDING
5
AUDREY JONES BECK BUILDING
6
SARAH CAMPBELL BLAFFER FOUNDATION CENTER FOR CONSERVATION
7

FOREWORD

PREFACIO

Forward-looking. Entrepreneurial. Dynamic. Diverse. These qualities define Houston's present and its future. The Museum of Fine Arts, Houston, embraces these essential values and is positioned to play a central role in what the city will become.

The Museum is at the most important crossroads of its history, set to embark on a dynamic project with Steven Holl Architects to unify its campus and to create essential new spaces for the public to engage with art, educational programs, and performances. The redevelopment project will enhance the Museum's ability to fully engage our visitors, and will renew the public's experience of this city, with 14 acres of art, green space, and pedestrian walkways in the heart of the Museum District—a destination point for the people of Houston, and visitors to Houston from around the world.

This specially published volume provides an overview of the Museum's plans for a new Glassell School of Art and sculpture plaza, a new center for conservation, and the project's centerpiece – a new building for modern and contemporary art, a facility that will greatly expand our capacity for educational and outreach programs. Together, these three buildings along with the existing Caroline Wiess Law Building, Audrey Jones Beck Building, and Lillie and Hugh Roy Cullen Sculpture Garden, will be known as the Fayez S. Sarofim Campus. These pages only begin to address the scope, depth, and quality of the works of art in the Museum's modern and contemporary collections—touchstones of humanity that the Museum will convey to future generations. They also offer a glimpse of the extraordinary spaces that architects Steven Holl and Chris McVoy have developed in reimagining, with the Museum's leadership, the public's experience of the Museum and its role in the life of Houston. But, taken together, we hope they convey the ambition, the beauty, and the resonance of a project that will transform not only the Museum, but the city of Houston, and will serve as a beacon of Houston's remarkable civic culture.

Progresista. Emprendedor. Dinámico. Diverso. Estos son los atributos que definen el presente y el futuro de la ciudad de Houston. El Museum of Fine Arts, Houston acepta estos valores y se encuentra en condiciones de desempeñar un papel medular en el desarrollo de la ciudad.

El Museo se encuentra en la encrucijada más importante de su historia, listo para lanzar un proyecto dinámico en colaboración con Steven Holl Architects cuyo objetivo consiste en unificar el recinto de la institución y crear nuevos espacios esenciales donde el público podrá apreciar obras de arte, programas instructivos y representaciones de diversos tipos. Con este proyecto de renovación el Museo estará en mejores condiciones de recibir al público y reactivar su interacción con la ciudad con casi 6 hectáreas de arte, espacio verde y senderos peatonales en pleno centro del Distrito Museológico—un destino deseable tanto para los residentes de la ciudad de Houston como para los que la vienen a visitar de todas partes del mundo.

Esta publicación ha sido creada especialmente para dar una perspectiva general de los planes del Museo: una nueva Escuela de Arte Glassell, un nuevo Centro de Conservación y el eje fundamental del proyecto—un nuevo edificio para arte moderno y contemporáneo, instalación que aumentará considerablemente nuestra capacidad para ofrecer programas docentes y comunitarios. Estas páginas apenas logran expresar el alcance, la profundidad y la calidad de las obras que forman parte de las colecciones de arte moderno y contemporáneo del Museo. Permiten vislumbrar los espacios extraordinarios que los arquitectos y la dirección del Museo han propuesto al re-imaginar tanto el Museo como el papel que desempeña dicha institución en la vida de la ciudad de Houston. Pero esperamos que sirvan para transmitir la ambición, la belleza, y la resonancia de un proyecto que transformará no sólo al Museo sino a la metrópolis que lo rodea y que servirá de modelo de la extraordinaria cultura cívica de la ciudad de Houston.

Richard D. Kinder
Chairman of the Board of Trustees

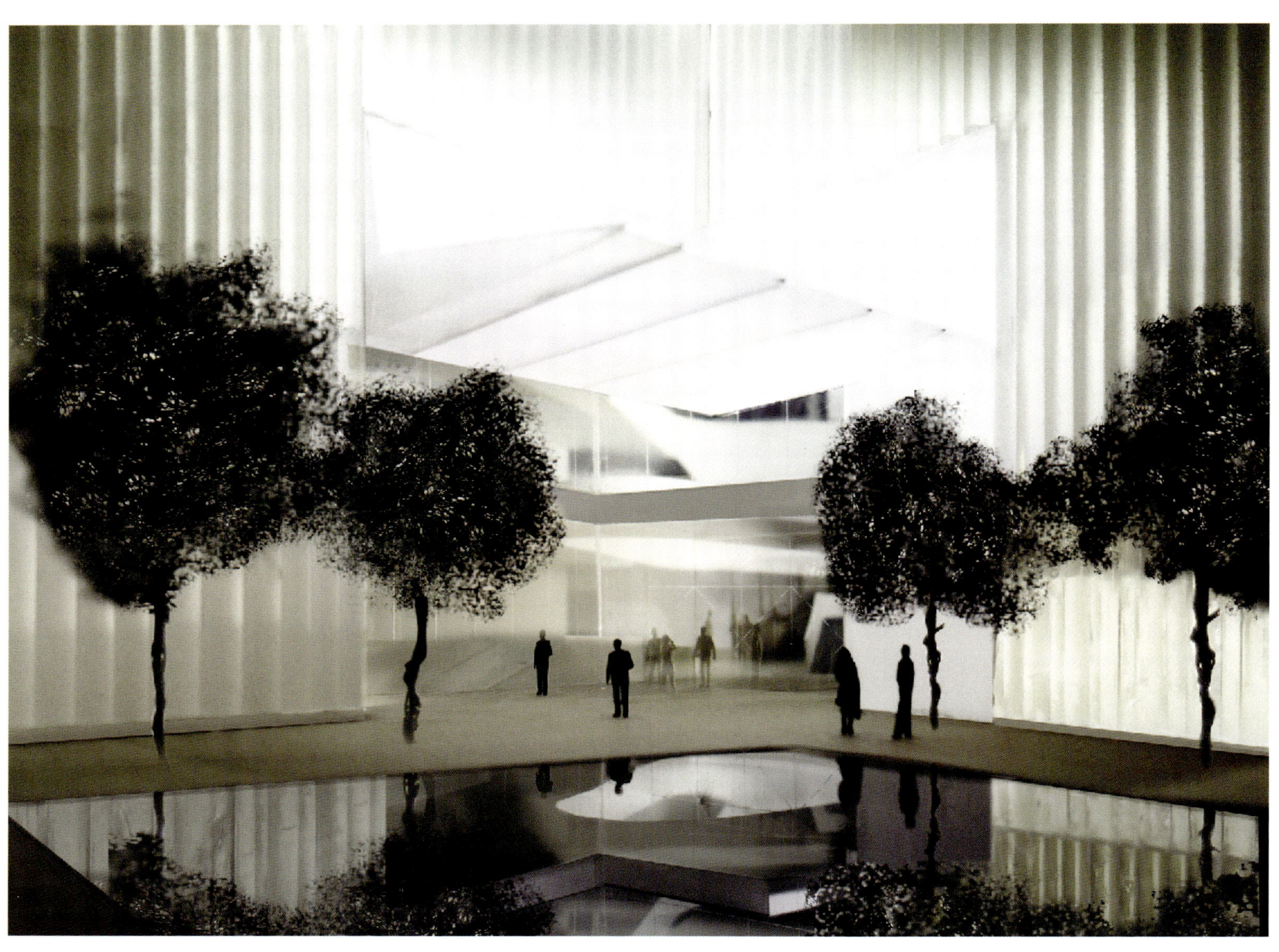

Stephen Holl Architects, 2014.
Computer rendering of view into the
Cornelia and Meredith Long Atrium
from the Entrance Court to the
Nancy and Rich Kinder Building.

BUILDING ON A VISION
Houston's Hub for All Things Cultural

GARY TINTEROW

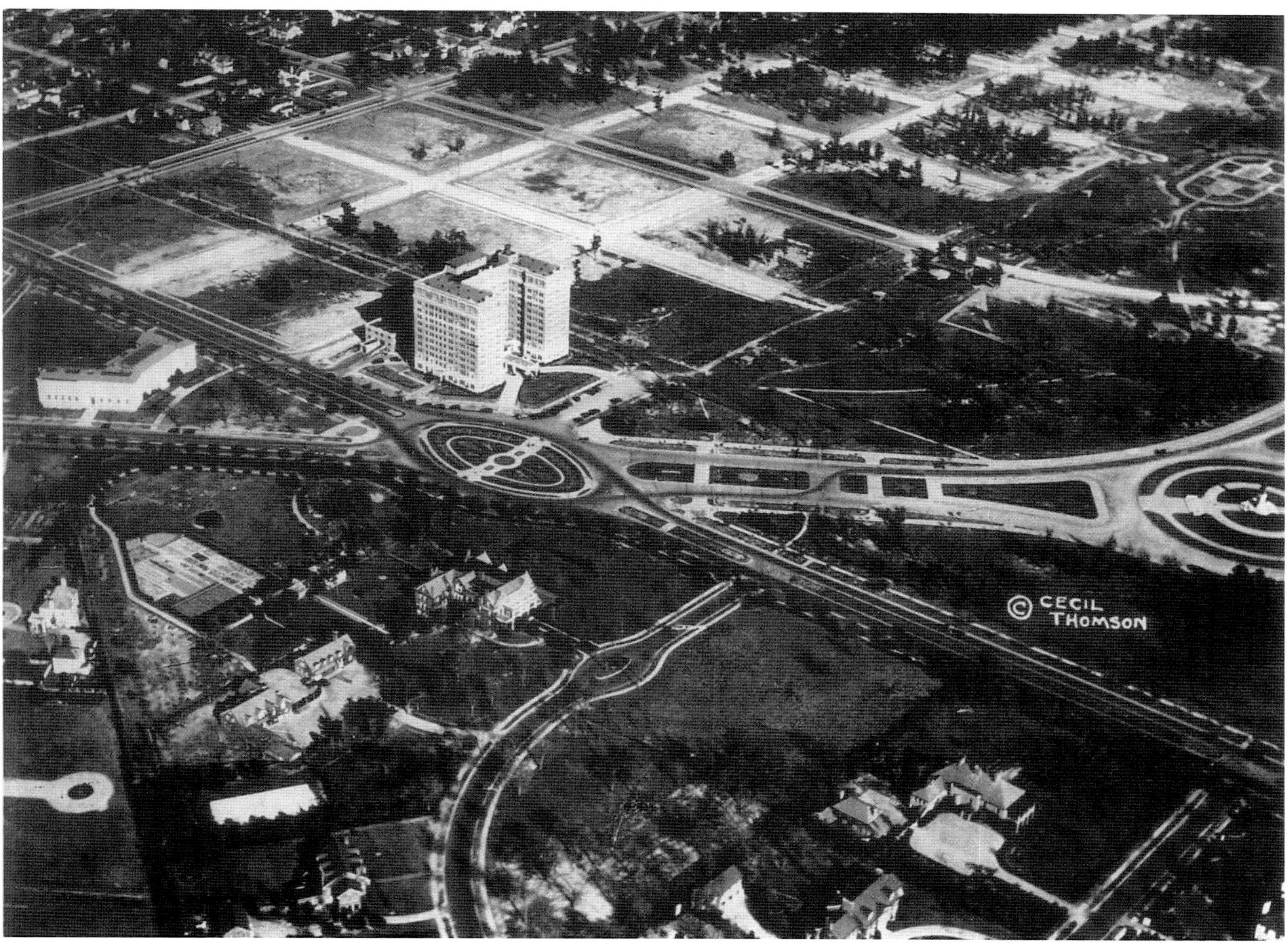

Aerial view of The Museum of Fine Arts, Houston, with flanking wings, 1926. From the Collection of the Museum of Fine Arts, Houston, Archives.

In 1916, J. S. Cullinan, founder of Texaco Oil Company, renewed discussions between the Art League of Houston, the City of Houston, and the estate of George R. Hermann to acquire a triangle of land just north of Hermann Park, the Rice Institute, and Shadyside, the residential development that Cullinan had recently created.

A more auspicious site for a museum of art could hardly have been imagined. Forming the intersection of Houston's two urban grids— the northeast/southwest diagonal of Main Street and the central business district, and the cardinal North-South-East-West grid of the rest of the city— this triangle pointed to the Sunken Garden— now Mecom Fountain—that announced the stately entrance to Hermann Park, providing the first glimpse of the precinct of art, education, recreation, and recuperation that would soon become home to many of Houston's chief charitable institutions: The Museum of Fine Arts, Rice Institute (now Rice University), Hermann Park and Zoo, and Hermann Memorial Hospital, the lynchpin of the future Texas Medical Center.

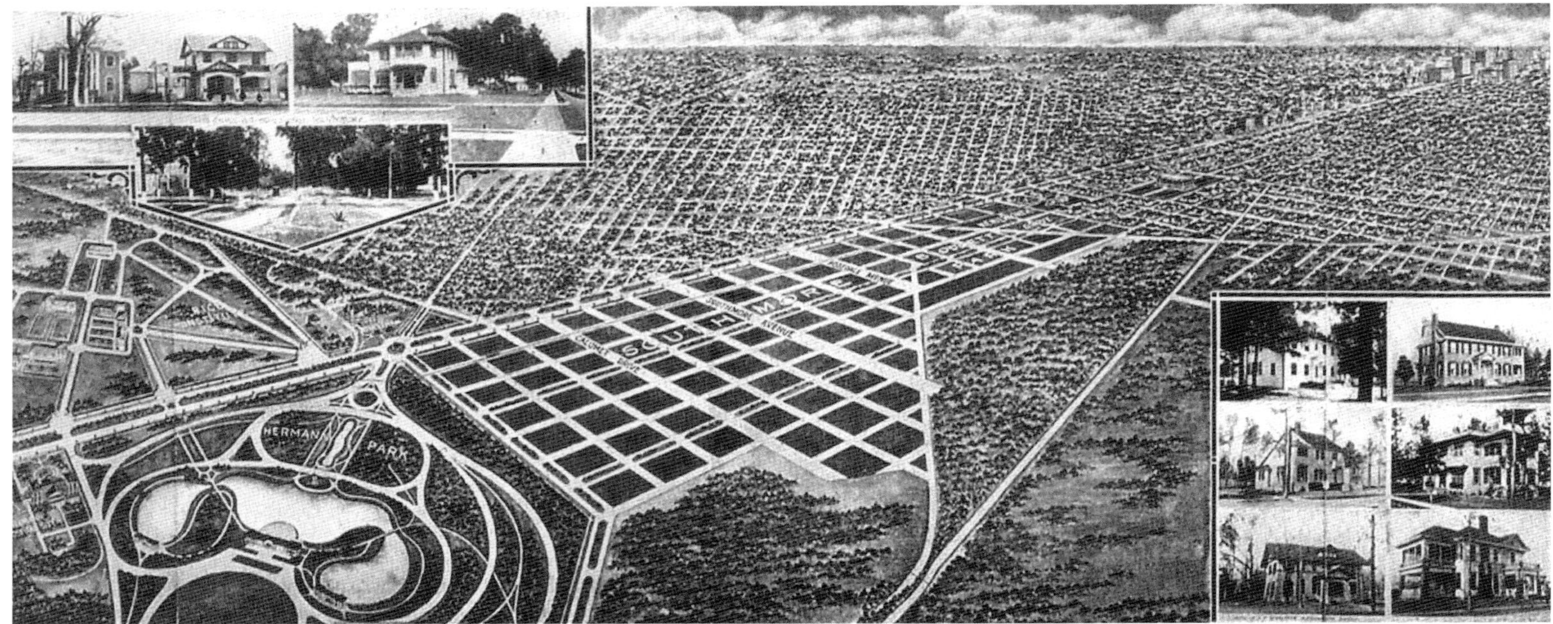

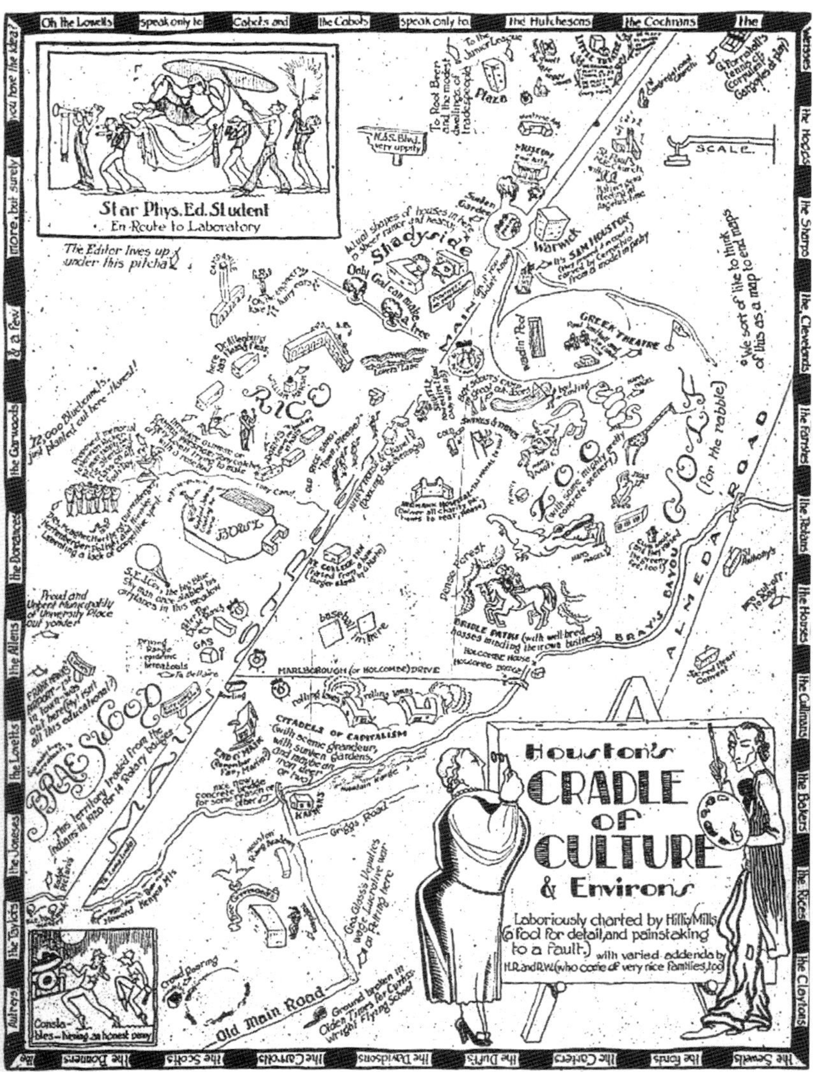

Cullinan prevailed upon the city fathers to retain George Kessler, a prominent urban planner who had made his reputation in St. Louis and Kansas City, to conceive a grand extension to Main Street, providing elegant esplanades adorned with hundreds of live oaks. By the time the Museum of Fine Arts opened in 1924, designed by architects William Ward Watkin and Ralph Adams Cram, the area south of the intersection of Bissonnet Street with Montrose Boulevard and South Main Street was known as the Cradle of Culture.

Since then, succeeding generations of Trustees of the Museum of Fine Arts have acted with foresight and acumen to grow the initial 1¼-acre plot to a 14-acre campus ennobled by buildings and gardens by outstanding architects and designers: Kenenth Franzheim, Ludwig Mies van der Rohe, Isamu Noguchi, S.I. Morris, Carlos Jiménez, and Rafael Moneo. Now, nearly a century after J.S. Cullinan secured our site, we stand poised to complete the campus with a third museum building for art after 1900; a new building reuniting the Glassell Junior School and the Glassell Studio School under one roof; and a new Center for Conservation.

Designed by Steven Holl Architects, our reconceived campus will fully develop the value of our extraordinary location, at the heart of Houston's Cradle of Culture, to fulfill the original promise of Cullinan, the city fathers, and the lady founders of the Art League of Houston to create a vibrant cultural center. Their enlightened vision called for enriching the lives of all people, providing opportunities for education and inspiration to the citizens of the entire region.

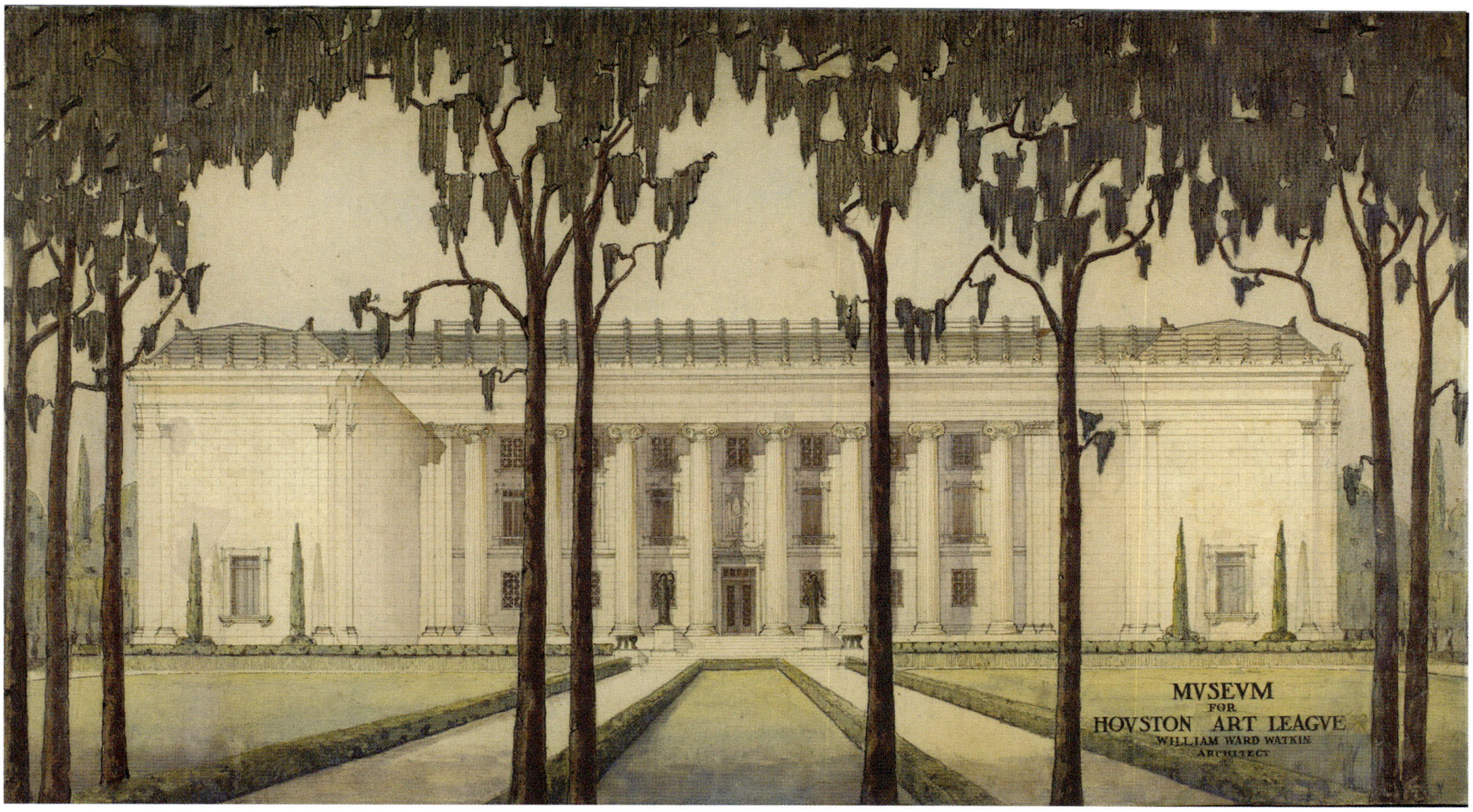

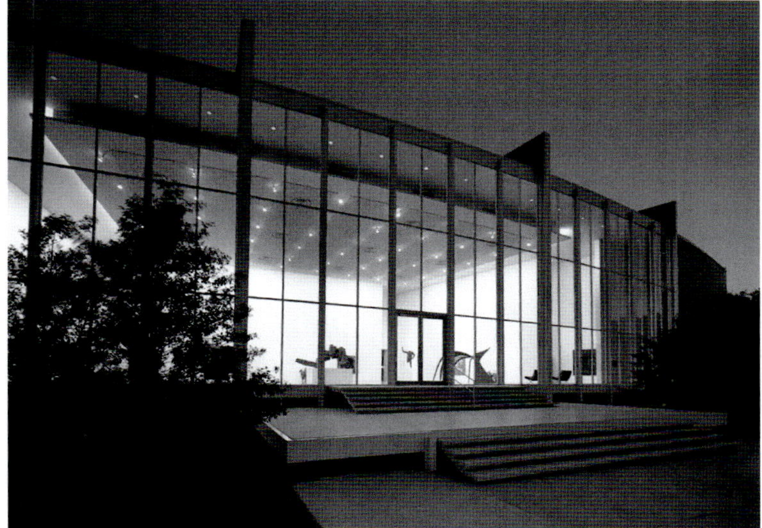

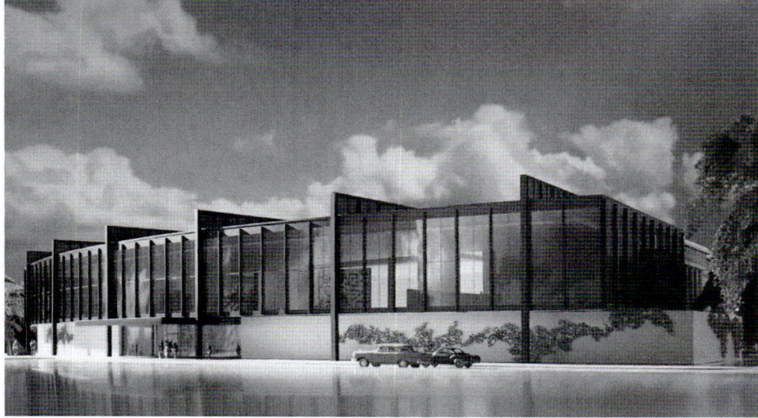

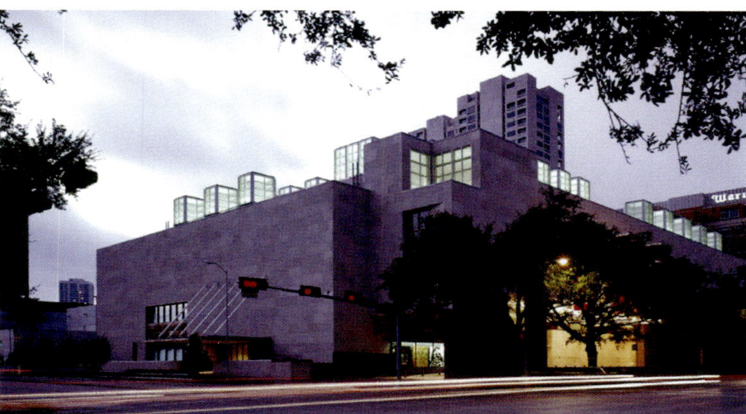

Opposite, top: Aerial perspective of Main Boulevard Photo: Cecil Thomson. From the Cecil Thomson Collection at the Albert and Ethel Herzstein Library, The University of Texas at Austin.

Opposite, bottom: "Houston's Cradle of Culture and Environs," from *Houston Gargoyle* 5, May 1, 1932, page 11.

Top: Preliminary rendering of The Museum of Fine Arts, Houston, exterior, south facade, c. 1921. From the Collection of the Museum of Fine Arts, Houston, Archives.

Above, left: Cullinan Hall, north facade by night, with installation of works from the Museum's permanent collections, c. 1967. Photo: Balthazar Korab. From the Collection of the Museum of Fine Arts, Houston, Archives.

Above, right: Model of Brown Pavilion showing entrance canopy and ivy-covered walls, 1969. Photo: Hedrich-Blessing. From the Collection of the Museum of Fine Arts, Houston, Archives.

Right: The Audrey Jones Beck Building. Photo: © 2000 Aker/Zvonkovic Photography L.L.P. All Rights Reserved.

Right: Model of the Lillie and
Hugh Roy Cullen Sculpture Garden, 1983.
Photo: Paul Hester, Hester + Hardaway
Photographers. From the Collection of the
Museum of Fine Arts, Houston, Archives.

Below: Stephen Holl Architects, 2014.
Computer rendering of view from the
Cornelia and Meredith Long Atrium
into Restaurant and Water Garden,
Nancy and Rich Kinder Building.

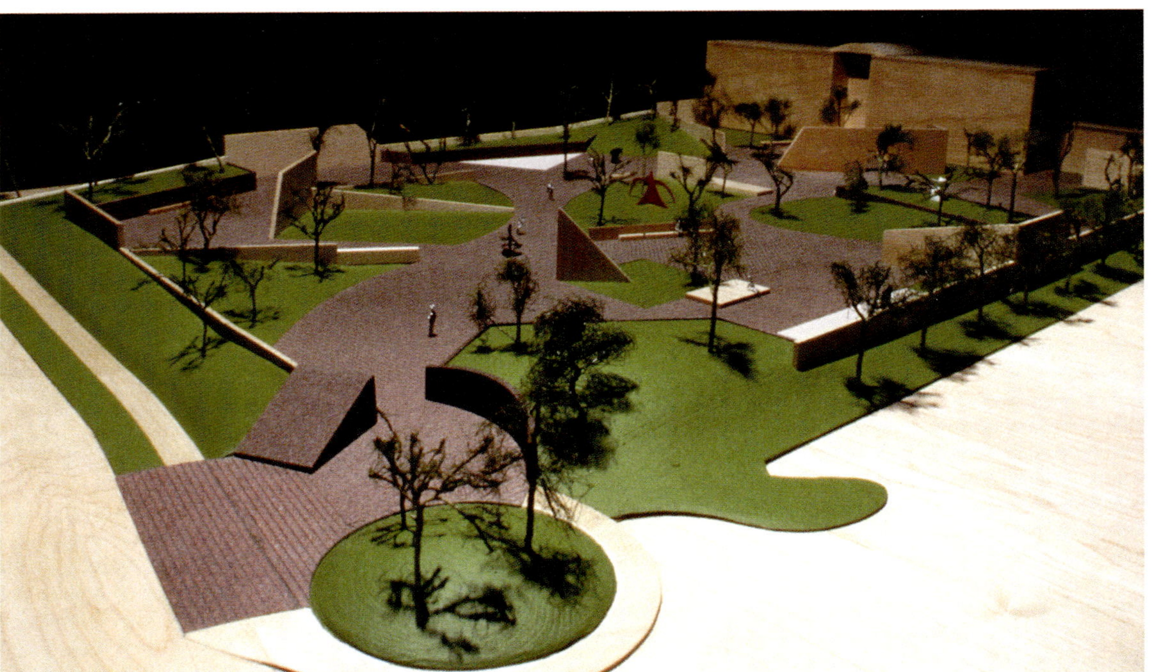

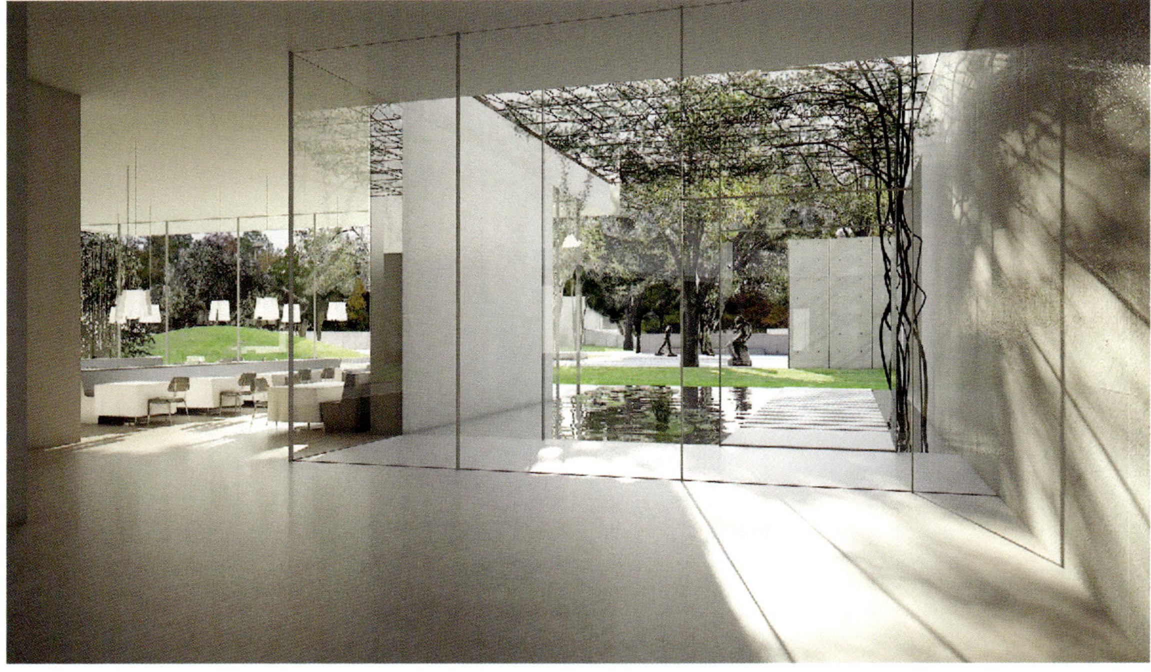

Following the cues established by urban planner George Kessler and William Ward Watkin, who created the street plan for the immediate neighborhood, our new campus will be an urban oasis designed to facilitate pedestrian enjoyment of the small city blocks shaded by the century-old live oaks for which our Museum District is famous. A new underground garage with more than 400 parking spaces will free the street, sidewalks, and plazas for visitors to enjoy outdoor displays of art and sculpture, performances, and video projections. Providing a complementary contrast to the opaque limestone facades of the Mies and Moneo buildings, Holl's structures will be transparent at street level, inviting visitors and passersby to enter and to engage with our programs and our extraordinarily rich, varied, and still largely little-known collections of twentieth- and twenty-first-century art. Whether through one of the seven small gardens that punctuate the new Museum building, or through new paths that will link Noguchi's Lillie and Hugh Roy Cullen Sculpture Garden with the new restaurant and café, or through the new public plaza on Montrose Boulevard designed for special art installations and projections, visitors will find a porous and welcoming campus, encouraging informal strolling while also providing the full range of amenities that our visitors from both near and far will require.

Improved crosswalks will encourage the public to explore neighboring institutions, from the Contemporary Art Museum and the Children's Museum to the Museum of Natural Science and Hermann Park. Families will be able to begin their journey at the Museum of Fine Arts, Houston, park in our underground garage, and then spend the entire day on foot in the Museum District, visiting the most extensive cultural district in the center of the country, emerging refreshed, inspired, and reinvigorated.

The Museum's integrated new facilities will enable us to fully realize our destiny as the vibrant cultural hub for creativity and discovery that Houston's founders envisioned. We will be a primary destination for cultural tourism for adults and children alike. Not only during the day, but at night as well: business people downtown, employees of and

visitors to the Texas Medical Center, students at the Glassell School as well as neighboring families and members of the university communities will drop in after work to attend an exhibition or a program, to see a film or a favorite work of art, to dine or snack, knowing that they can always count on something to be happening at the Museum of Fine Arts. We will become Houston's crossroads, a place where our city's diverse communities encounter each other, generate energy, build relationships, and share ideas.

The Museum of Fine Arts is perfectly positioned to become one of the top encyclopedic art museums in the world and the best of its kind in America. With these three new facilities, our programs, acquisitions, and staff will reach the pinnacle of their potential; we will be recognized even more so than we are today as a leader among museums, not just as a repository for marvelous art, handsomely installed in fine galleries, but as one of the most beautiful and inspiring museums in the world; a place, for our visitors, of continual wonder and self-discovery; a place, for the staff, of creativity, innovation, and accomplishment; a beacon of integrity and inclusiveness; the crown jewel of Houston.

In the following pages, you will find further details about our campus redevelopment and new Museum buildings, as well as about our collections of modern and contemporary art. We have selected notable works that span chronological, cultural, and geographic categories. Art from Asia, Africa, Europe, Latin America, and the United States comes together in innovative juxtapositions that anticipate the revelatory experiences in store for visitors to the Museum of Fine Arts—Houston's hub for all things cultural.

A HUB FOR CULTURAL ACTIVITIES

With the redevelopment of the campus of the Museum of Fine Arts, Houston, there will be an even greater hub for cultural activities for people of all ages. The Museum's extensive offerings of programs will span the globe and will touch multiple corners of creativity—from lectures by famous art-world experts to art-making workshops for families; from screenings of classic Hollywood films to "meet the director" private events; from behind-the-scenes programs with contemporary art critics to studio classes with practicing artists; and from opening-night previews of major exhibitions to intimate evenings with the Museum's Director.

Every day, every night: The Museum of Fine Arts is Houston's hub for all things cultural.

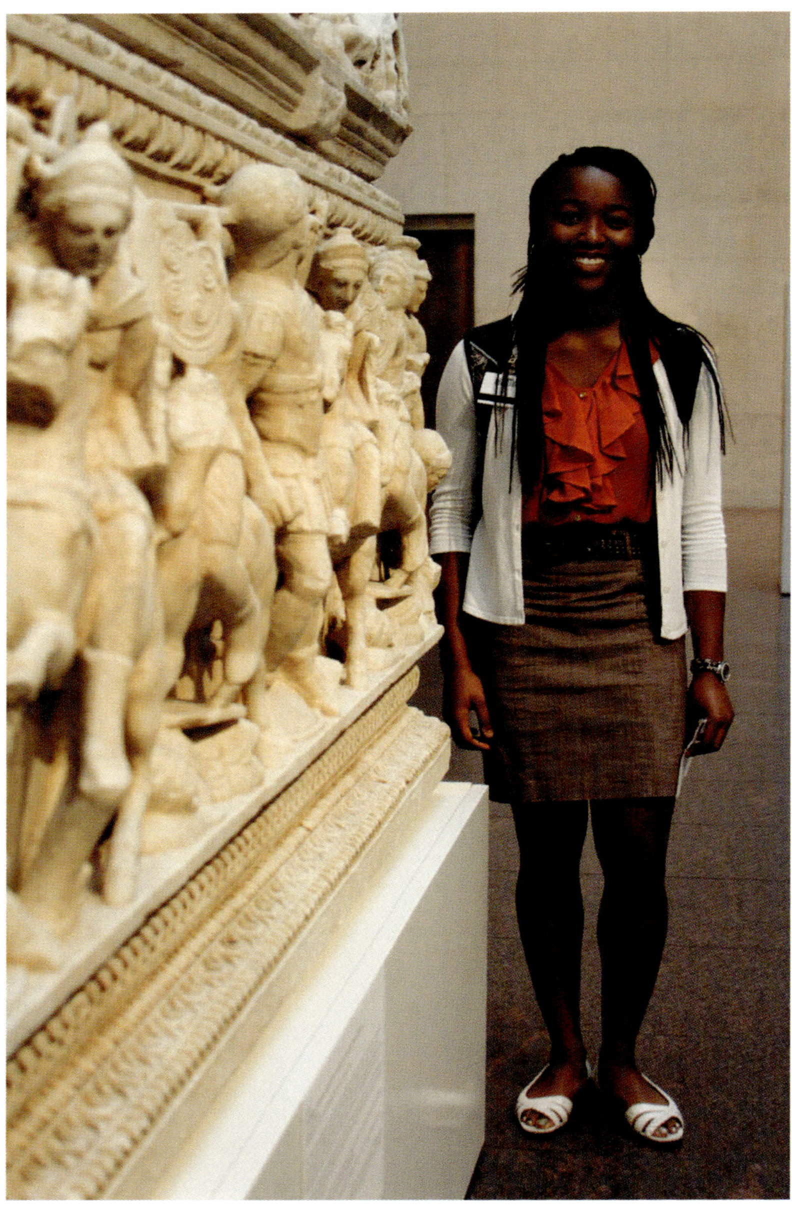

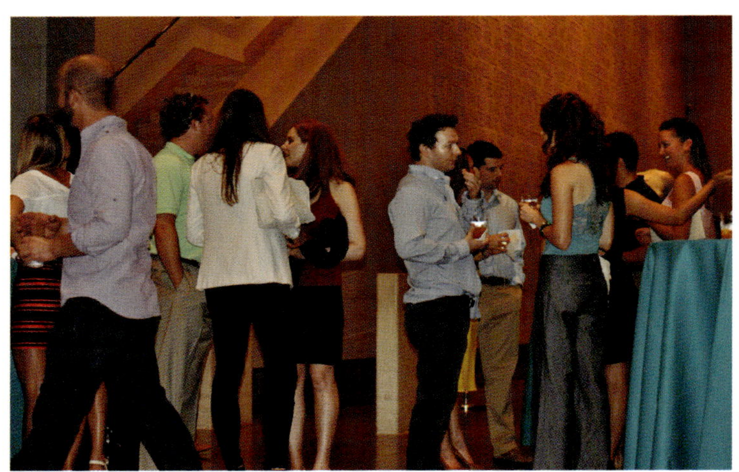

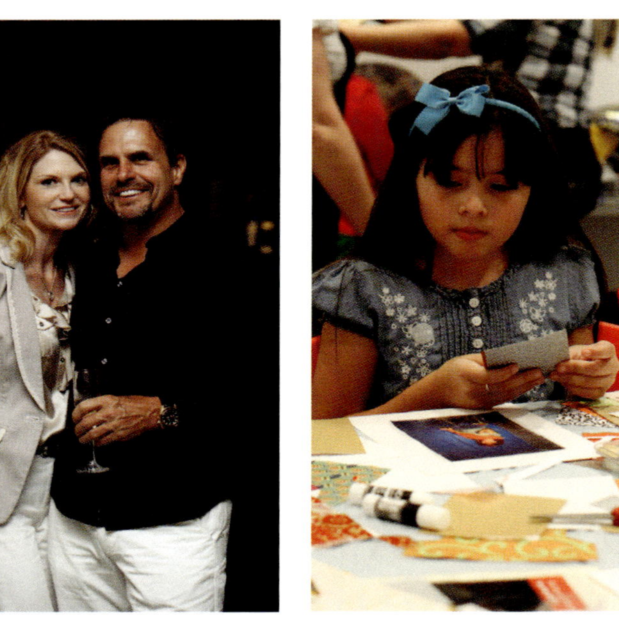

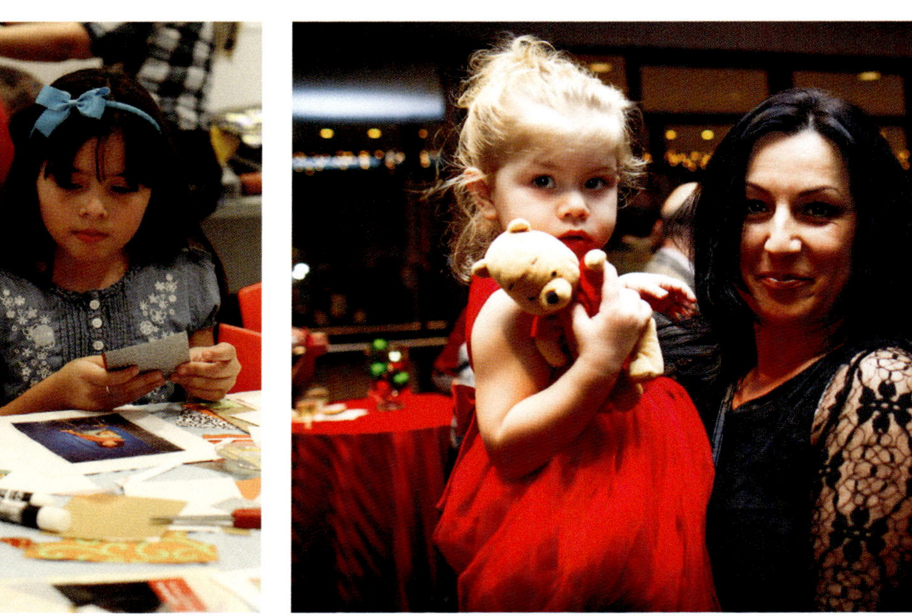

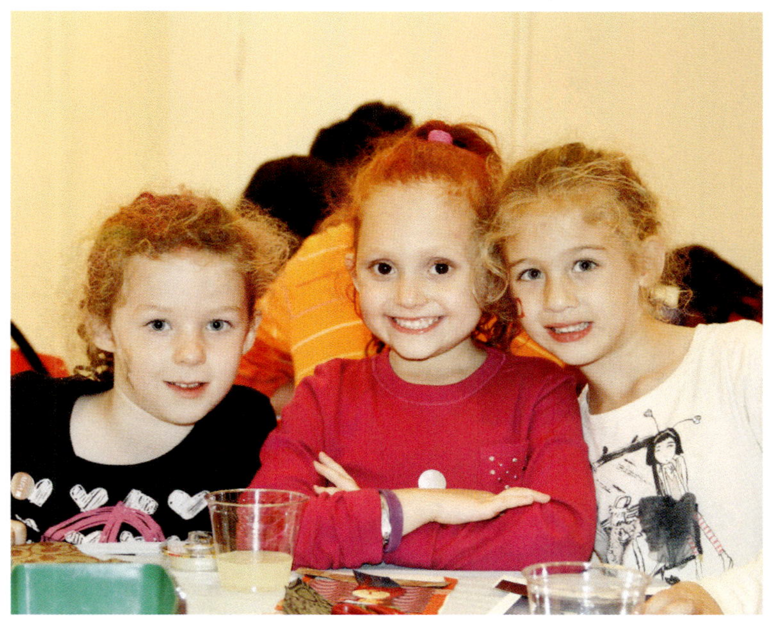
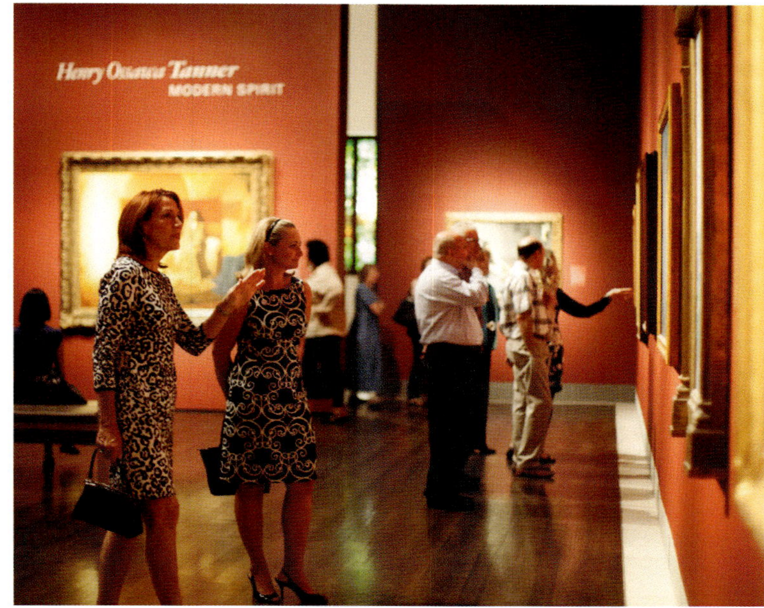
Henry Ossawa Tanner
MODERN SPIRIT

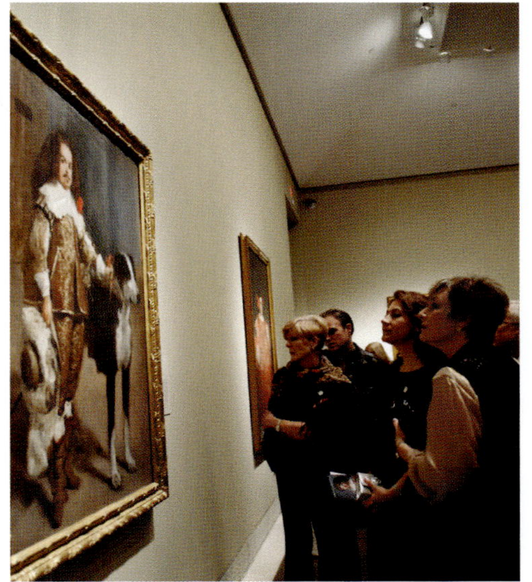
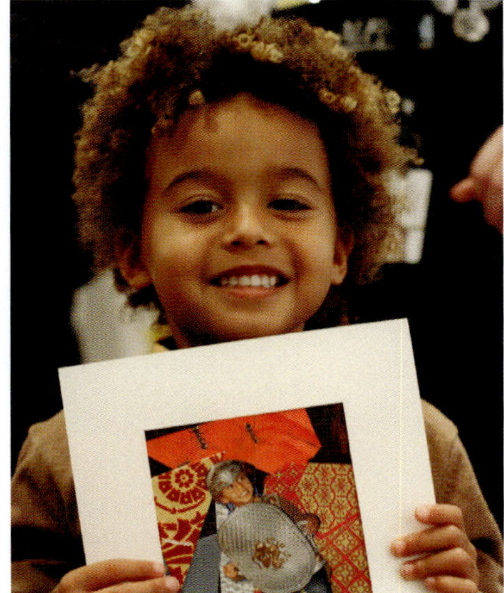
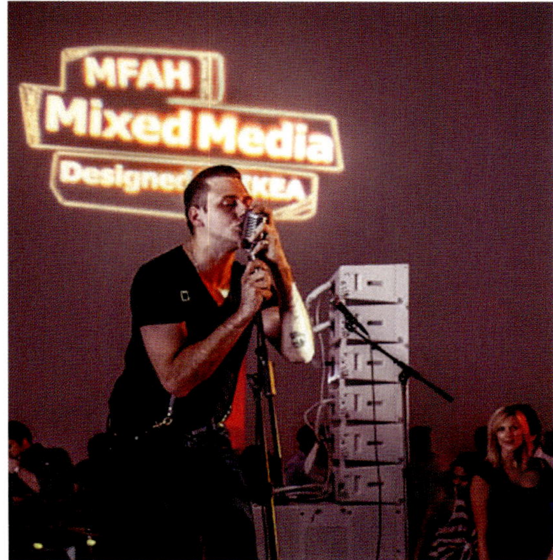
MFAH
Mixed Media
Designed by IKEA

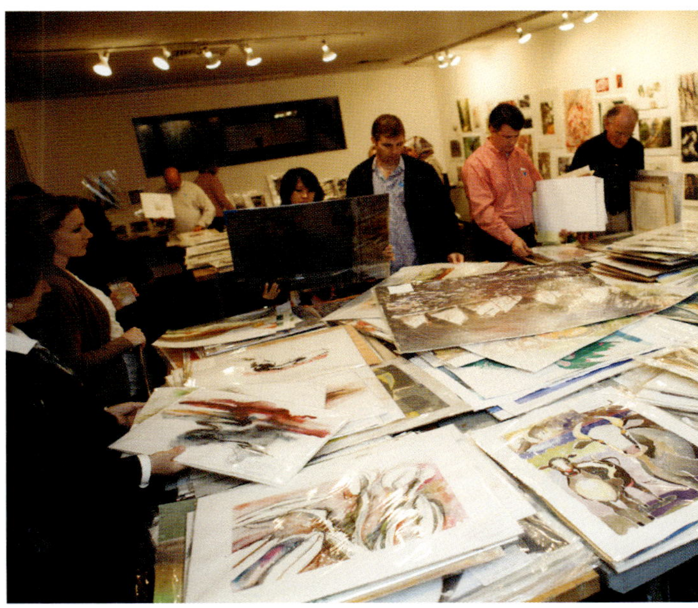
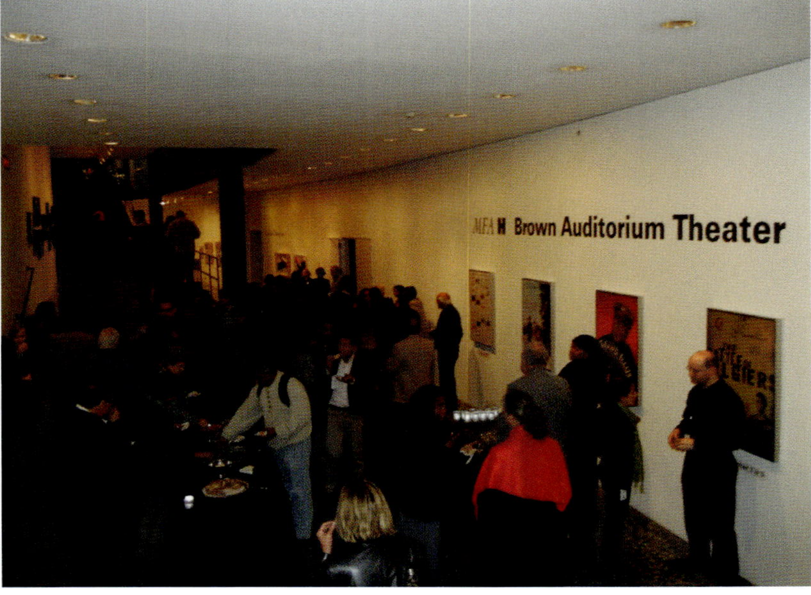
MFA H Brown Auditorium Theater

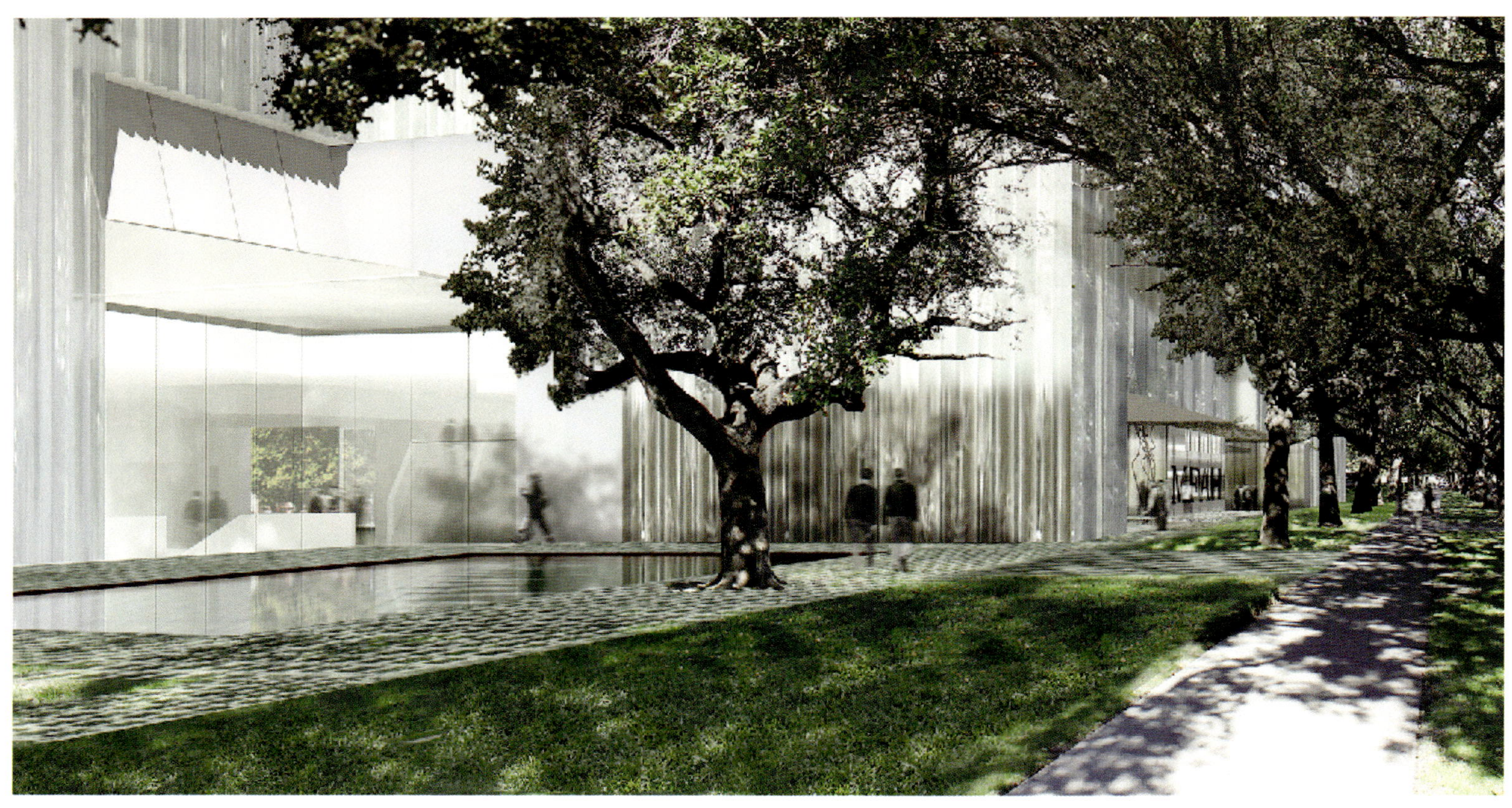

Above: Stephen Holl Architects 2014.
Computer rendering of view down Main Street
with new Nancy and Rich Kinder Building.

Right: Steven Holl. Watercolor of early design
for new Museum building and the Glassell
School of Art, 2011.

THE NEW BUILDINGS OF THE FAYEZ S. SAROFIM CAMPUS, AN URBAN CAMPUS DEVOTED TO ARTS AND CULTURE

CINDI STRAUSS

In 2009, the Museum of Fine Arts, Houston, launched a search for an architect to design a new building for art created after 1900. A leadership committee comprised of Peter C. Marzio, director; Gwendolyn H. Goffe, associate director of finance; Willard Holmes, associate director of administration; Amy Purvis, associate director of development; and Kathleen Jameson, assistant director, programming worked with the long-range planning committee of the Museum's Board of Trustees to review the work of fifty international architects. In 2010, upon Dr. Jameson's resignation, Cindi Strauss was appointed assistant director, Programming and joined the leadership committee. Ten architects were interviewed before the committees reached a final short list of three firms. The Trustees made extensive visits to see the built projects by these firms, as well as heard presentations in Houston that took place under the leadership of the Museum's new Director, Gary Tinterow, and that, with the advice of Joseph Havel, director of the Glassell School of Art, included their ideas for the Museum's campus redevelopment. Steven Holl Architects was unanimously chosen by the Trustees in January 2012 for the commission of the new buildings.

World-renowned and award-winning architect Steven Holl established his eponymous architectural firm in 1976. With offices in New York and Beijing, Holl, along with Senior Partner Chris McVoy, has realized architectural works in the United States and overseas, specializing in museums, educational facilities, residences, and master planning. For the Museum of Fine Arts, Houston, Holl and McVoy have designed two new buildings, a plaza, and parking garages as well as their attendant connections to the Lillie and Hugh Roy Cullen Sculpture Garden and the Caroline Wiess Law Building.

For the approximately 165,000-square-foot Nancy and Rich Kinder Building to house art after 1900, Holl and McVoy have designed a luminous translucent glass structure that will feature an open lobby, new galleries, education spaces, an auditorium, and facilities for fine and casual dining. Majestic Live Oak trees will surround the building on two sides with the contiguous verdant landscape of the Cullen Sculpture Garden providing a link to the new Glassell School of Art and the new Brown Foundation, Inc. Plaza. Steven Holl said that the design is "much more than an inspiring new

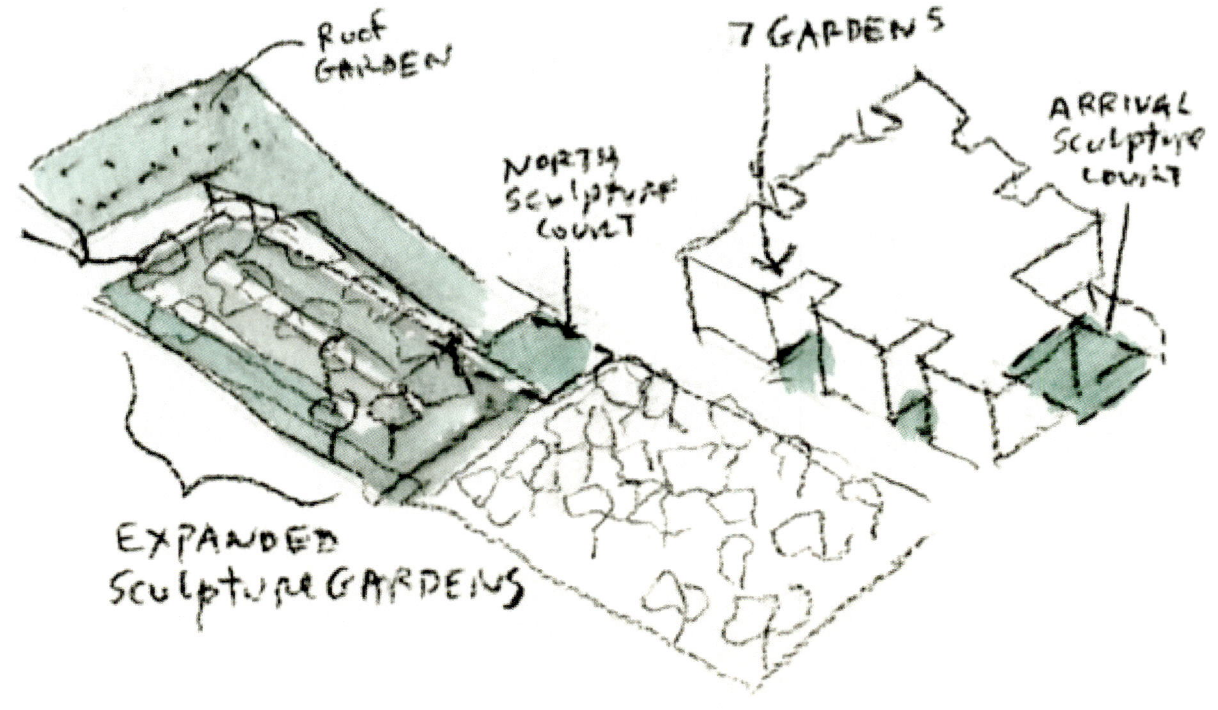

museum pavilion, we are developing a cohesive campus for the Museum of Fine Arts, Houston."

Holl and McVoy's designs incorporate five strategies that were developed in response to the Museum's needs and site. The overarching goal of the architects is to create *An Integral Campus Experience* by unifying and connecting the larger campus. For the new Museum building, they have envisioned a porous structure with seven gardens that penetrate the perimeter of the building and slice through three levels of facade (*Porosity: Seven Gardens/ Social Space*). The largest garden court, at the corner of Bissonnet and Main streets, will be a primary entry point for pedestrians arriving from the Audrey Jones Beck and Caroline Wiess Law buildings. The

overall design for the new Museum building is described by Holl and McVoy as *Architecture: Complementary Contrast*, a strategy that takes into account the differences and complementary nature between their translucent glass facade and the materials used for the Museum's two other exhibition buildings–stone (1924, by William Ward Watkin), steel and glass (1958 and 1974, by Ludwig Mies van der Rohe) for the Caroline Wiess Law Building, and stone (2000, by Raphael Moneo) for the Audrey Jones Beck Building. As Chris McVoy remarked, "The expansion brings the new and existing buildings into an integral arts campus unified by the lush landscape of Houston; fusing art, architecture, and landscape." Holl and McVoy have provided two levels of galleries and

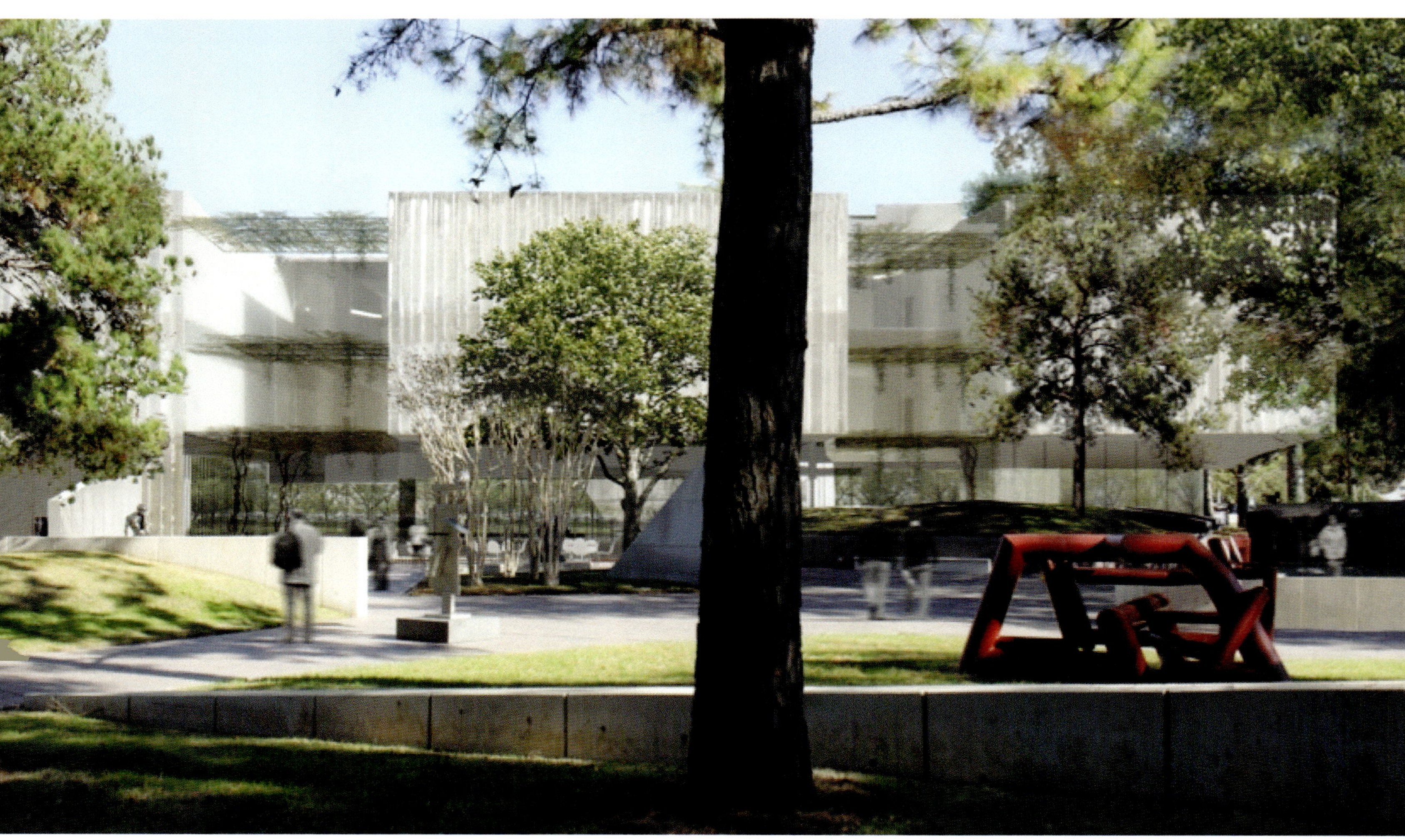

Steven Holl Architects, 2013. Computer rendering of conceptual design for exterior of new Museum building, looking from the Lillie and Hugh Roy Cullen Sculpture Garden.

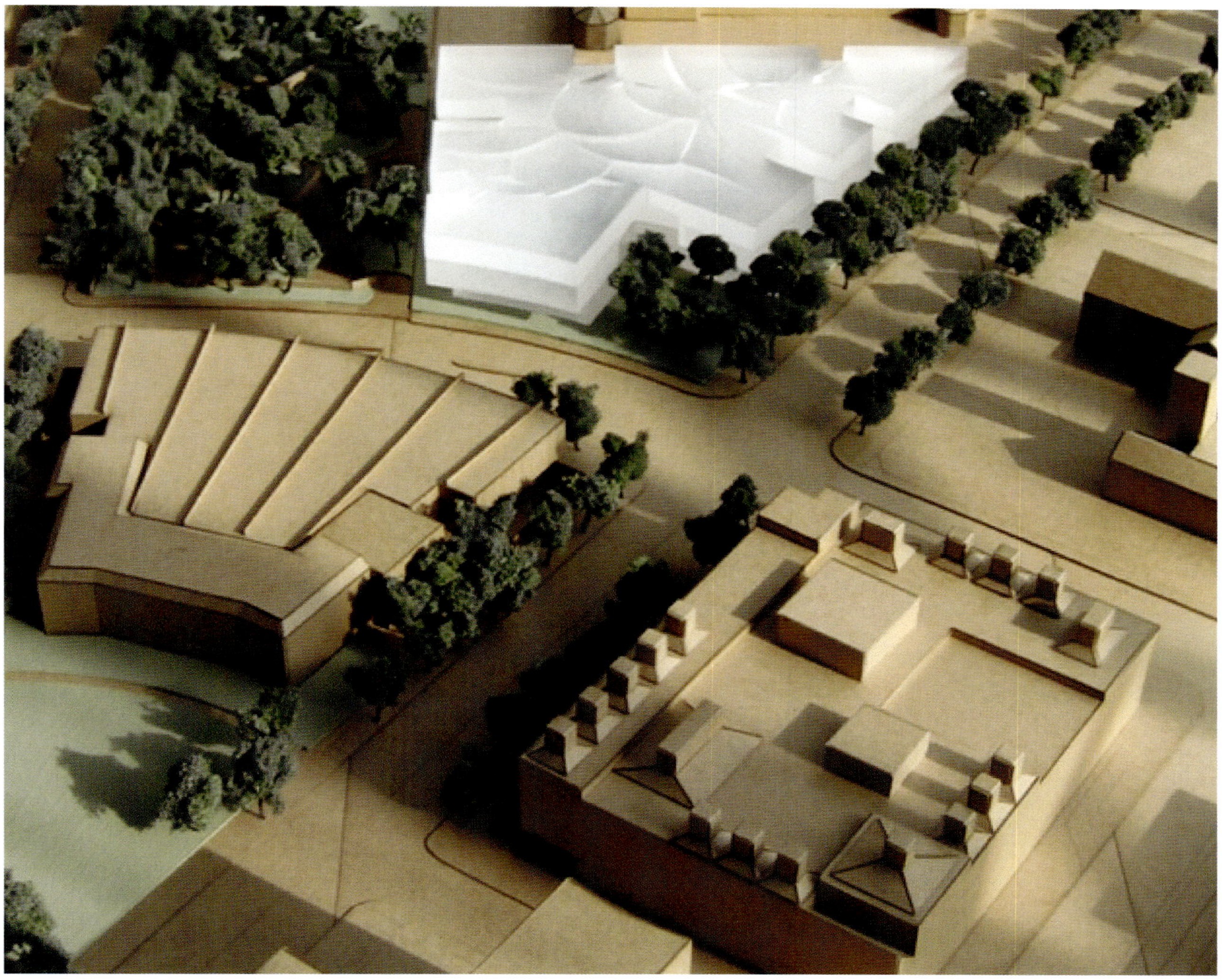

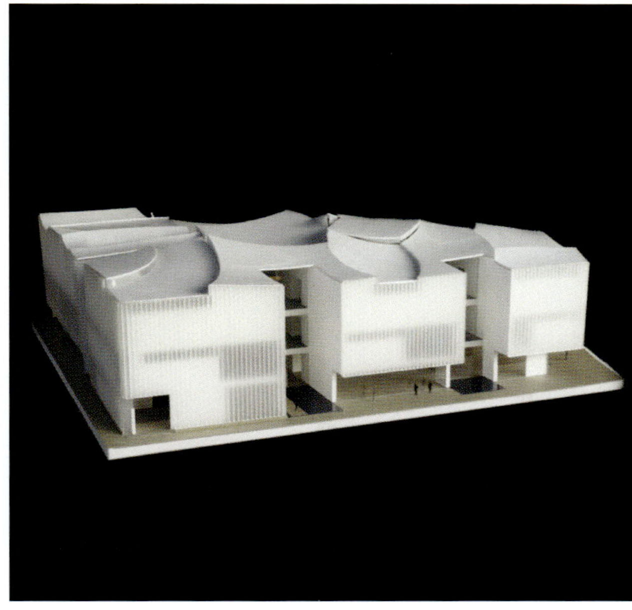

Top: Detail of architectural model for the
expanded Fayez S. Sarofim Campus of
the Museum of Fine Arts, Houston.

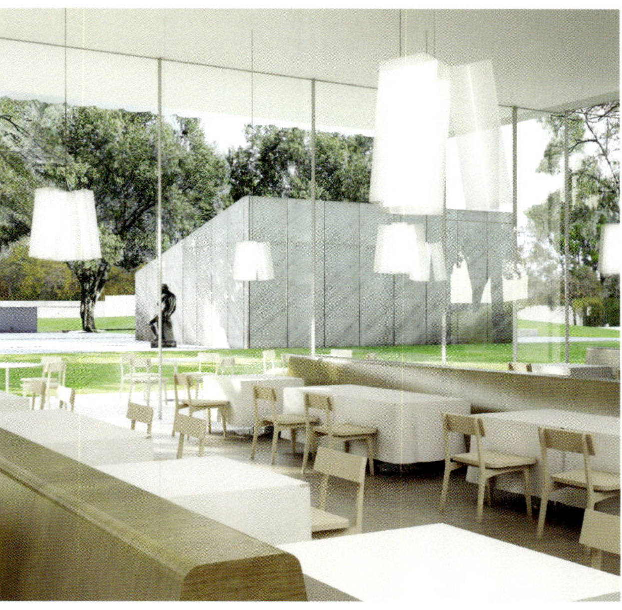

Bottom, left: Steven Holl Architects, 2014.
Model of Nancy and Rich Kinder Building.

Bottom, right: Steven Holl Architects, 2014.
Computer rendering of conceptual design
for the new restaurant.

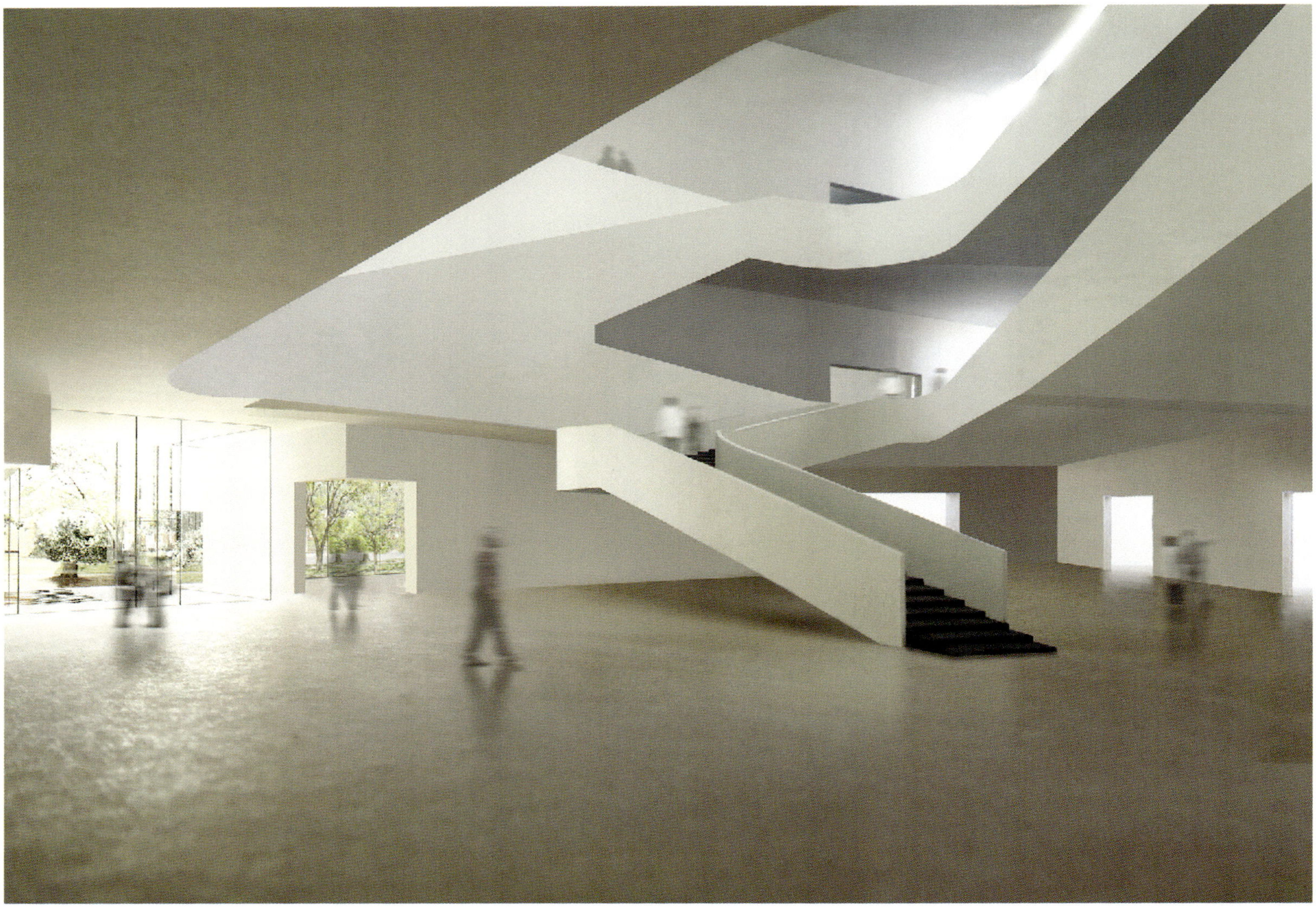

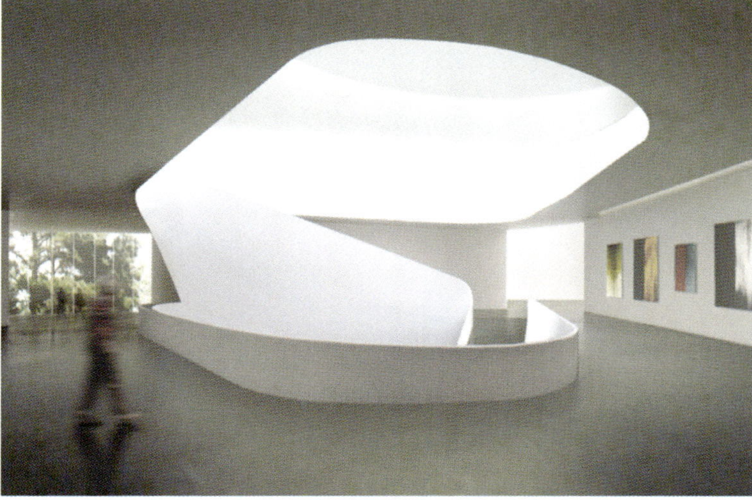

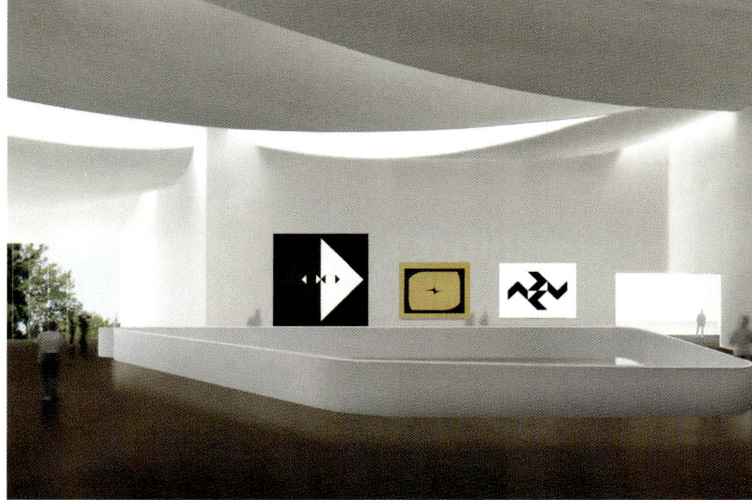

Top: Steven Holl Architects, 2014. Computer rendering of Cornelia and Meredith Long Atrium, Nancy and Rich Kinder Building.

Bottom, left and right:
Steven Holl Architects, 2013. Computer renderings of conceptual design of forum galleries in the Nancy and Rich Kinder Building.

Far right:
Steven Holl Architects, 2013. Computer renderings of conceptual design of forum galleries in the Nancy and Rich Kinder Building.

a central gallery forum in the new building that are flexible and visitor-friendly as part of their strategy *Circulation: Gallery Rooms and Open Flow.* As visitors ascend the stairs or elevators through the central forum, they will be surrounded by art. Galleries feature generous spaces for art in all media and are designed to accommodate the Museum's permanent collections as well as temporary exhibitions. Top-floor galleries will have the coved ceilings that are a signature of Holl's designs and will be partially illuminated through a roof membrane that will emit diffused natural light and a soft glow at night (*Light: Luminous Canopy*). And a highlight of the building will be a double-height gallery intended for large-scale works of art.

North of the Cullen Sculpture Garden will be Holl and McVoy's new 80,000-square-foot building for the Glassell School of Art. During the architect search process, the possibility of building a new Glassell School was discussed by the long-range planning committee with the shortlisted architects and ultimately endorsed by the trustees. Holl's design for the new Glassell School reunites the studio and junior classrooms under one roof,

allowing the school to provide expanded curricula and superior facilities for its students (see pp. 27–31). Of tremendous excitement is the planned BBVA Roof Garden, a sloping green walkway that rises from the ground to a terrace on top of the Glassell School of Art, which is sure to be a new destination in the Museum District for socialization. An education court that is connected to the new Museum building by an underground tunnel is also included in the plans for the new Glassell School. The close connection between education at the Glassell School and the new Museum building will provide enhanced opportunities for programming and visitor experiences.

Holl and McVoy's design for the new campus expansion also includes the Brown Foundation, Inc. Plaza, which will connect the new Glassell School of Art with the Cullen Sculpture Garden. In addition to serving as a social space, the Brown Foundation, Inc. Plaza, complete with water features and trees, allows for new exhibition and programming possibilities, thereby further enlivening the campus with sculpture, performances, or video projects.

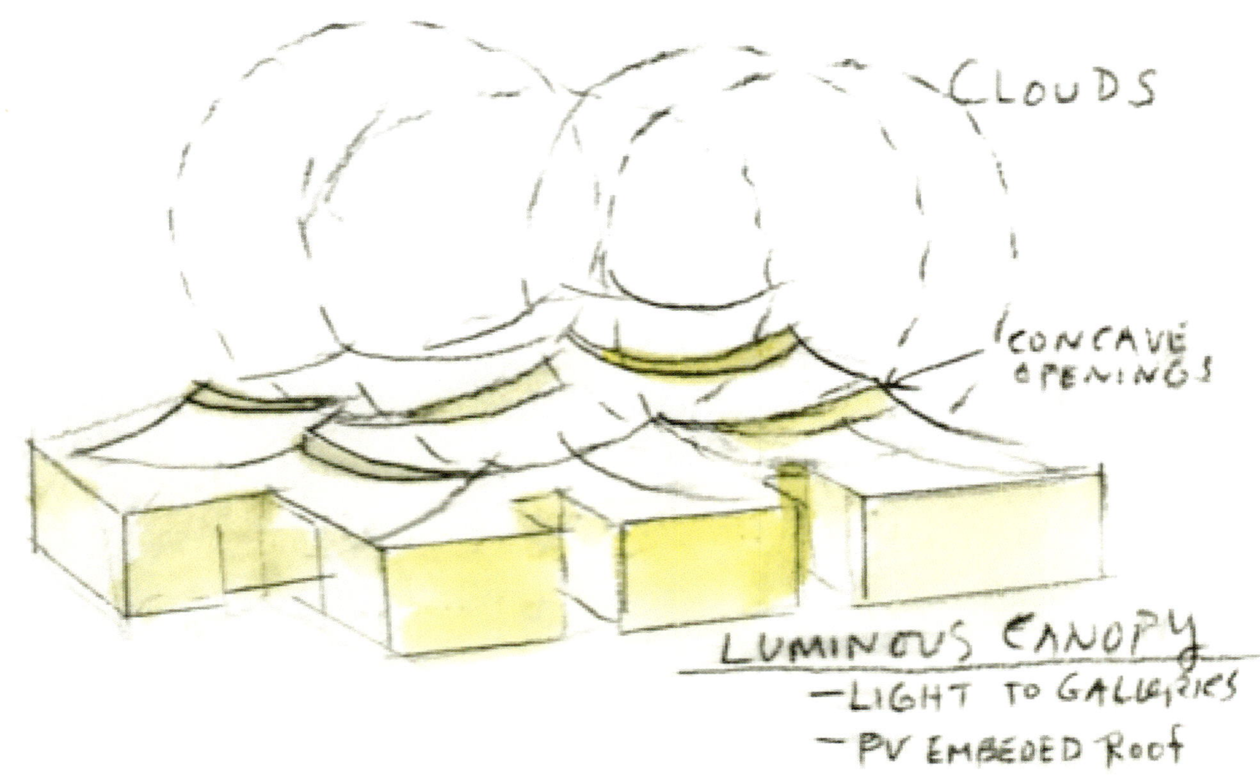

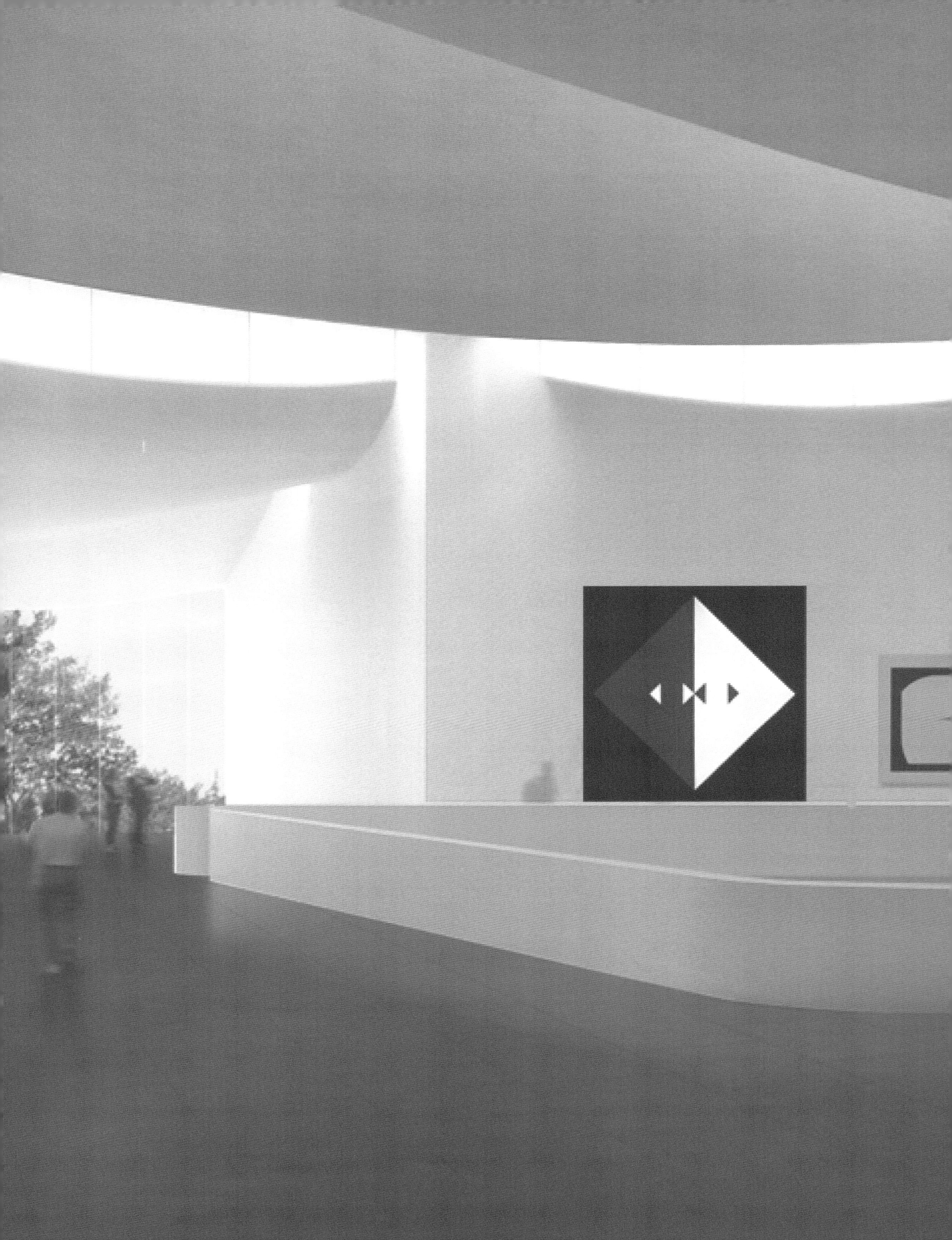

A NEW WAY OF PRESENTING ART

MARI CARMEN RAMÍREZ

Over the last three decades, the twentieth- and twenty-first-century art collections of the Museum of Fine Arts, Houston, grew at an unprecedented pace. The exponential growth of these collections is attributed to the generosity of the institution's trustees and patrons, as well as to the establishment in 1992 of a restricted fund—the Caroline Wiess Law Accessions Endowment—for the acquisition of works from this period. Resulting from gifts and direct purchases, at present these collections make up roughly 56 percent of the Museum's overall holdings. Cutting across traditional categories such as media and/or culture, this dramatic expansion encompasses modern and contemporary photography, film and video, prints and drawings, and decorative arts and design, as well as European, American, Latin American, and Asian painting, sculpture, and new media. The remarkable increase in the scope and depth of these holdings, however, sharply contrasts with the limited amount of space currently available in the Museum's footprint to show them at any given time.

With the exception of American art from the first half of the twentieth century, there are no permanent galleries reserved for the display of modern and contemporary art on the Museum's campus. This fact alone more than justifies the need for a third building that will focus on art created after 1900 from Europe, the United States, Latin America, and Asia. The new Nancy and Rich Kinder Building will be designed by the internationally prominent architecture firm of Steven Holl Architects. Yet there are many additional reasons that call for such an ambitious enterprise. The lack of gallery space for modern and contemporary art significantly curtails the Museum's ability to fulfill its mission as an encyclopedic museum dedicated to collecting, displaying, and educating audiences about the art of our time. Moreover, the surge in modern and

contemporary art as a worldwide phenomenon has been accompanied by a strong demand for engagement by the Museum's increasingly young and diverse audiences. To continue to both respond to and satisfy these demands, the Museum must be able to display its modern and contemporary collections as part of the story of universal art.

And yet, the construction of this additional facility is only part of the solution for countering the invisibility in the Museum's galleries of the twentieth- and twenty-first-century art collections. At the core of this enterprise lies a major challenge: How will the institution use its new space to exhibit artworks that tell, for the first time, the multiple stories that make up the complex history of art? In other words, what criteria should guide the display of these heterogeneous collections in the new Nancy and Rich Kinder Building for modern and contemporary art?

As part of a comprehensive initiative to address these fundamental questions, an interdisciplinary and cross-cultural team of the Museum's curators began meeting in 2009 to debate core issues and possible formats for displaying the collections. This curatorial team comprises Anne Wilkes Tucker and Yasufumi Nakamori (photography), Alison de Lima Greene (modern and contemporary art), Cindi Strauss (modern and contemporary decorative arts and design), and Mari Carmen Ramírez and Michael Wellen (Latin American art). Barry Walker, curator of prints and drawings, served on the team until his death in 2012. The team's discussions coincided with and were informed by a major reassessment of permanent-collection displays taking place in art museums worldwide. Indeed, during this same period, the repercussions of cultural and political trends such as globalization and multiculturalism significantly altered how museums—whether encyclopedic or focused on modern and/or contemporary art—go about conceiving and organizing exhibitions and collection displays. The acknowledged obsolescence of aesthetic canons—combined with the increasingly interactive, socially engaged, and interdisciplinary production associated with contemporary art—has stimulated a search for alternative exhibition formats that depart from the traditional chronological and/or geographic presentations of artists and movements.

Moving away from time-based models, major museums in Europe, the United States, and Asia have adopted comparative or thematic frameworks for their presentations. Rather than a passing fad or trend, this approach has taken hold, and it is ideally suited to meeting the needs of today's technologically literate and interconnected society. Indeed, current data supports that museum audiences experience the world in ways that are less about compartmentalized knowledge, seamlessly unfolding through time, and more about a vivid network, connecting and intersecting with its own skein.

In this context, the curatorial team's first priority was to thoroughly review the history, special features, and specific needs of the Museum's collections of modern and contemporary art. Throughout its 113-year history, the Museum of Fine Arts, Houston—like many American museums that developed outside of the central aegis of New York—pursued a sui generis, and often pioneering, approach to collecting modern and contemporary art. This approach was not strictly regional, nor did it always reflect the tastes or collecting patterns of the leading artistic centers. Indeed, this off-centric approach cuts across the institution's high moments of collection expansion, from the 1950s until today, led by visionary directors such as James Johnson Sweeney (1961–67), Philippe de Montebello (1969–74), William Agee (1974–82), Peter C. Marzio (1982–2010), and, more recently, Gary Tinterow (2012–), thus shaping the collections and curatorial departments that focus on modern and contemporary art.

Similarly, the Museum of Fine Arts, Houston, was the first museum to hire two prize-winning architects, Ludwig Mies van der Rohe and Rafael Moneo, for the expansion of its campus in 1957

and 2000, respectively, and to commission Isamu Noguchi to create the magnificent Lillie and Hugh Roy Cullen Sculpture Garden.

Additionally, the extensive photography holdings reflect both the mainstream history of this medium as well as the Museum's bold strategy to collect in previously unconventional areas. The Museum proactively acquired photographic works by artists from Eastern Europe, Asia, and Latin America.

In decorative arts and design, the Museum was one of the first institutions, after the Museum of Modern Art in New York, to focus on contemporary design as a distinct collecting area and to respect the field of crafts as fine art. The Museum also exhibited avant-garde art from the Czech Republic and contemporary art from Africa, Asia, and Latin America long before other arts institutions in the United States or elsewhere ventured into these terrains. Since its establishment in 2001, the Museum's Latin American art department has set out to collect paradigmatic pieces by well-known artists as well as others little known outside of their countries of origin. This process not only has contributed to the legitimization of Latin American art on the global stage but also has set new standards for institutional and private collecting in this area.

Such a daring spirit also characterizes significant gifts and acquisitions that have enhanced the Museum's collections. Caroline Wiess Law's magnificent bequest of early and midcentury modern masterpieces forms a critical segment of the Museum's collections, as does the Edward R. Broida bequest. Other landmarks within the Museum's collection of art after 1900 include the Target Collection of American Photography, the Peter Blum Edition Archive of prints and related preparatory materials, and the Robert Frank Collection and Archive of film. Equally, a number of key collections have substantially augmented the range and depth of modern and contemporary art at the Museum: The Manfred Heiting Collection of photography; the Helen Williams Drutt Collection and the Garth Clark and Mark Del Vecchio Collection, each of decorative arts and design; and the Adolpho Leirner Collection of Brazilian Constructive Art. Throughout this

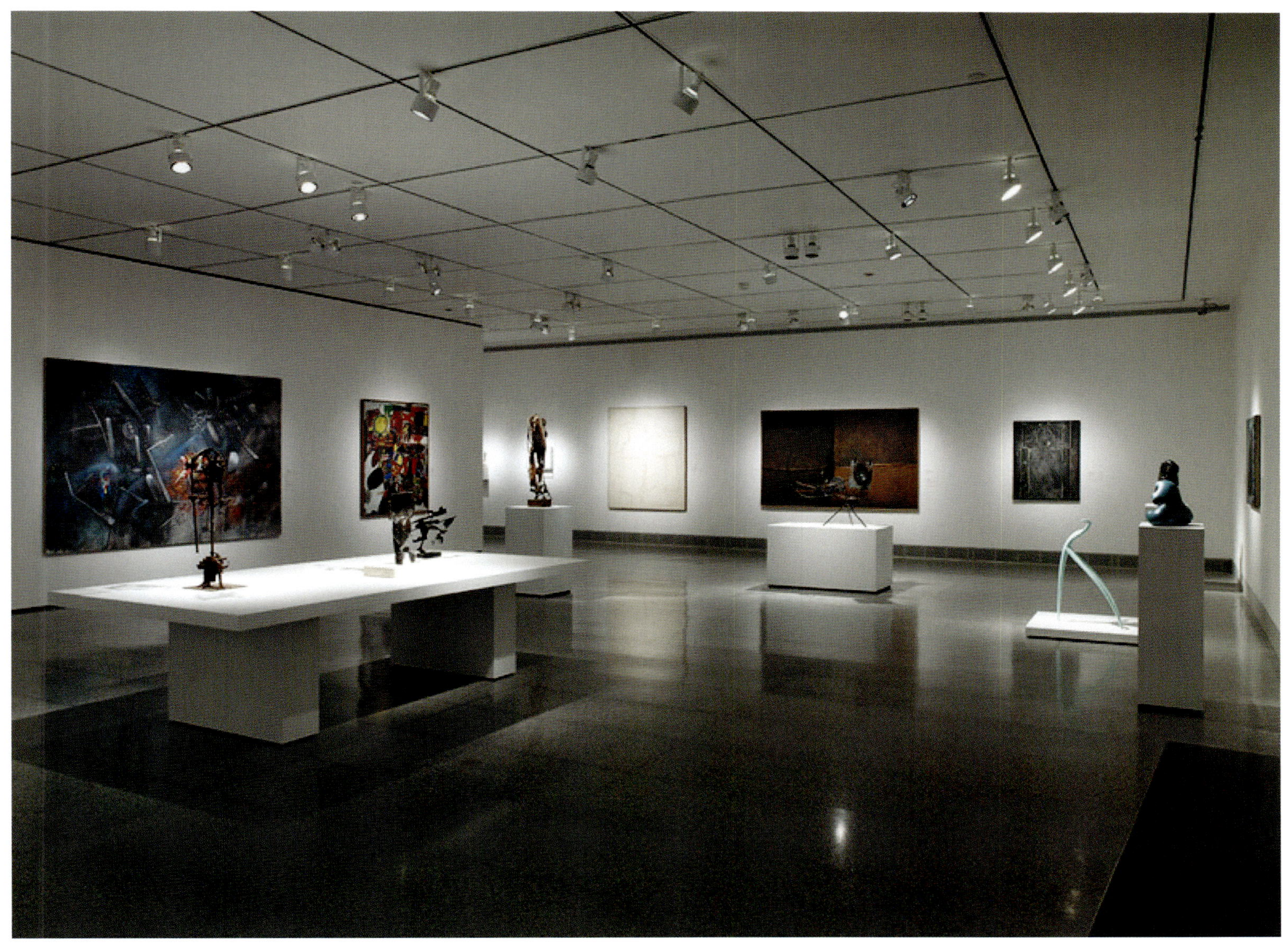

Installation view of *The Abstract Impulse:
Selections from the Modern and Contemporary
Collections,* presented at the Museum in 2013.

process, the Museum strove to articulate a compelling narrative of modern and contemporary art while at the same time staying ahead of the global collecting curve. From the outset, the cross-departmental team posed the following questions: How could the Museum present these heterogenous and highly idiosyncratic collections in a brand-new way, all the while distinguishing the Museum from its counterparts? How could the permanent-collection displays combine works by artists from Europe, the United States, Latin America, and

Asia, without losing the specificities of their individual manifestations? How could objects in different media be placed in formal and conceptual dialogues with each other? The lack of permanent-display galleries for twentieth-century art led the institution early on to adopt a thematic approach based on periodic rotations. It is precisely the flexibility of this approach that is guiding the curatorial strategy for representing "what is permanent" in the new building.

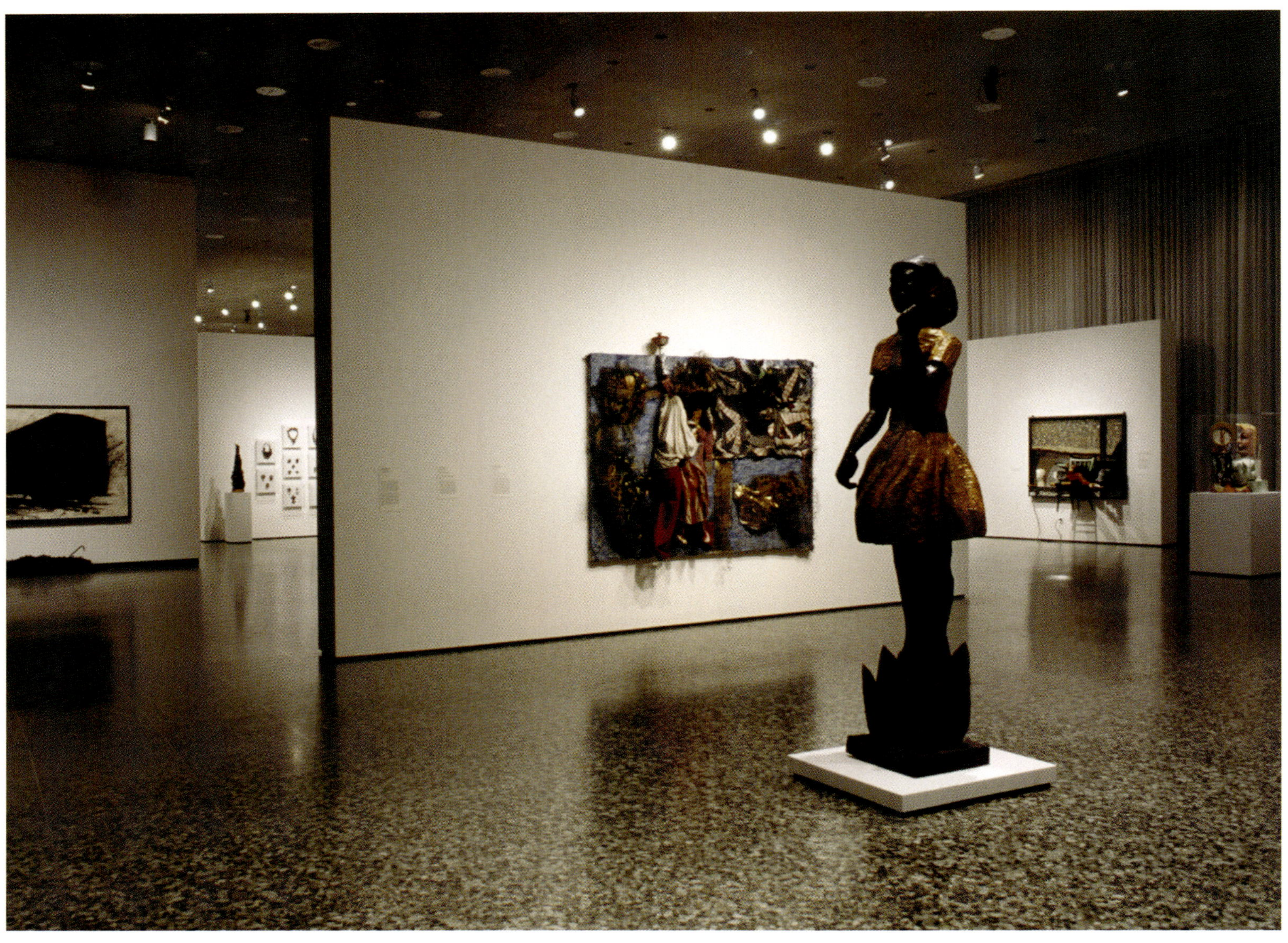

Since 2000, the Museum's curators have carefully tested this approach in a series of experimental exhibitions and installations that focus on the modern and contemporary collections. These shows include *The Passionate Adventure of the Real: Collage, Assemblage, and the Object in 20th-Century Art* (2003) and *The Past Made Present: Contemporary Art and Memory* (2006). Following and expanding on these initial experiments, recent permanent-collection installations such as *Color into Light:*

Selections from the MFAH Collection (2008) brought together artists from Europe, the United States, and Latin America in formal and conceptual juxtapositions of their work that challenged established histories of Abstract Expressionism, Color Field Painting, and Kinetic art, among others. In the Latin American area, the "constellation model" introduced by the 2004 exhibition *Inverted Utopias: Avant-Garde Art in Latin America* inspired the strategy for displaying works in *Brought to Light:*

An installation view of *The Passionate Adventure of the Real: Collage, Assemblage, and the Object in 20th-Century Art,* presented in 2003.

Recent Accessions in Latin American Art (2005) and *North Looks South: Building the Permanent Collection* (2009). This curatorial model condenses, rather than illustrates, themes or historic sensibilities. Key developments or singular visions are presented to expose and illuminate the relationships or nexuses among artists, their works, and the specific contexts in which they were produced. More recently, *The Abstract Impulse: Selections from the Modern and Contemporary Collections* (January–May 2013) both condensed and expanded the curatorial team's insights into this process. This exhibition was, indeed, the first one to fully test both the new, integrated format as well as the team-based approach toward collection displays. The curators assembled a broad range of objects that dissolve the boundaries of media, geography, and time, illustrating the twentieth- and twenty-first-century artist's eternal longing for abstraction as the basis for creation.

As explored in these exhibitions, the non-canonic model proposed for the new building consists of a two-pronged approach that takes into account cross-cultural dialogue and the integration of media. On one hand, a large suite of galleries will center on a general narrative that brings together modern and contemporary art from Europe and the United States in a bountiful dialogue with concurrent manifestations from Latin America and Asia, or elsewhere. On the other hand, these galleries will be complemented by focus galleries devoted to specific artists, movements, or media represented in the Museum's collections in depth. In this way, the Museum will be able to engage both well- and lesser-known accounts of these artists and movements. In each case, however, collection displays will not only present works from different cultures and time periods but will also integrate works in different media (photography, film, painting, sculpture, prints and drawings, decorative arts and design, and new media) across the curatorial departments.

One of the chief benefits of this two-pronged approach is that the resulting installations will present persuasive arguments for a new way of looking at art. Further, the installations will serve as catalysts, inspiring the active participation of the Museum's visitors. Moreover, such an approach to the display of the Museum's collections of twentieth- and twenty-first-century art will undoubtedly strengthen the Museum's leadership position worldwide.

Permanent collections are among a museum's most prized assets. The collections not only justify a museum's existence; they define it for posterity. The range and depth of the modern and contemporary collections of the Museum of Fine Arts, Houston, deserve to be on an equal footing with the ancient, Pre-Columbian, European, and American art collections, all of which have long been on permanent display in the Caroline Wiess Law and Audrey Jones Beck buildings. The display of the modern and contemporary holdings, in turn, will reflect the same trailblazing spirit that has guided the institution's extraordinary history. The installations in the proposed new building also have the potential to elevate the Museum's national and international standing, situating it among the finest museums with modern and contemporary art collections in the world.

For all of these reasons, the Museum of Fine Arts, Houston, is convinced that, with a new building, comes an unparalleled opportunity. The Museum is empowered and uniquely poised to tell a *different story*. As in the past, visitors will discover installations that are fresh, engaging, innovative, and intellectually challenging. The new displays promise to raise the bar further, facilitating a completely new way of seeing and interacting with some of the greatest art produced in the twentieth- and twenty-first centuries.

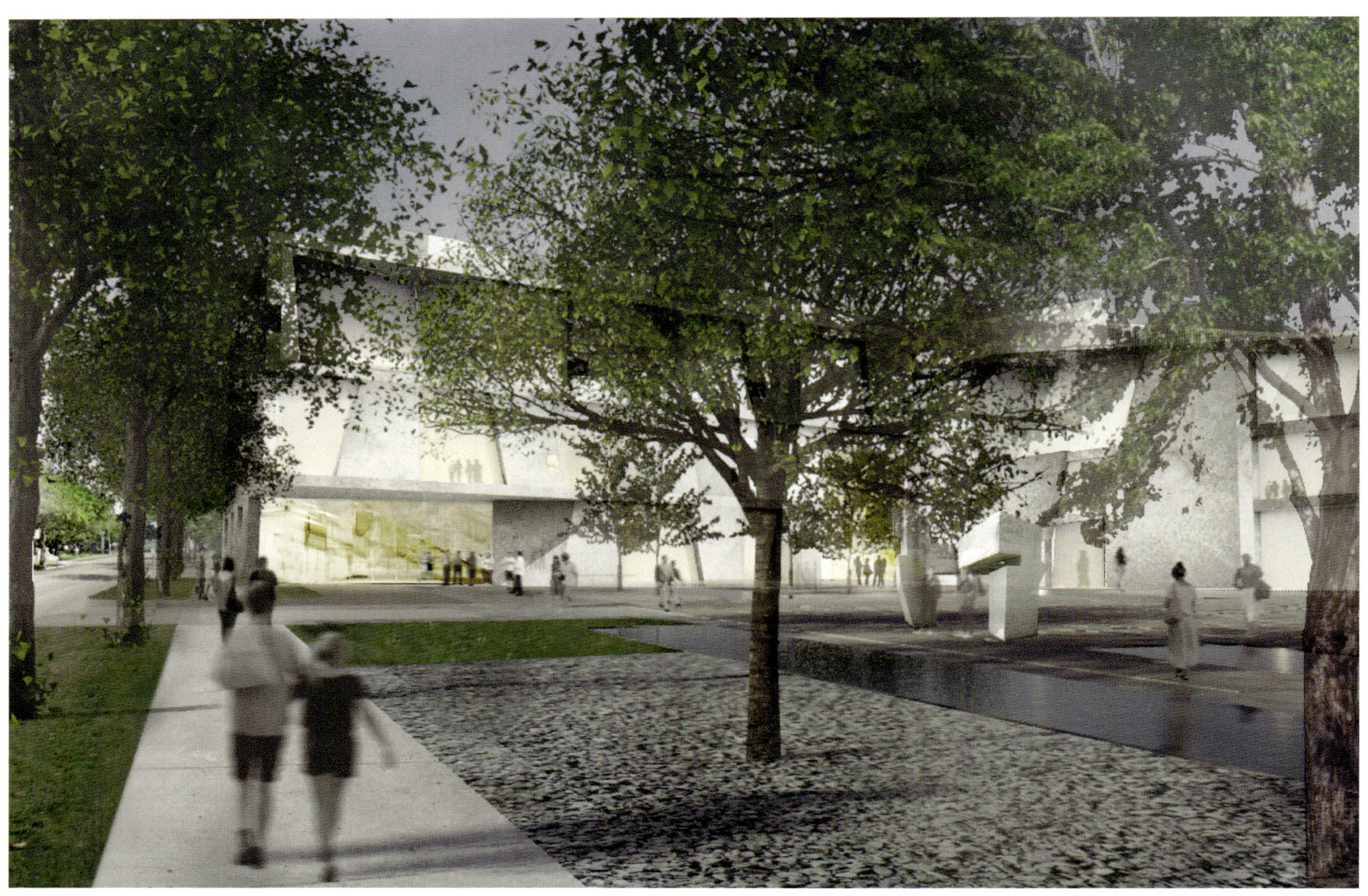

Steven Holl Architects, 2014. Computer rendering of the new Glassell School of Art and Brown Foundation, Inc. Plaza.

THE GLASSELL SCHOOL OF ART

JOSEPH HAVEL

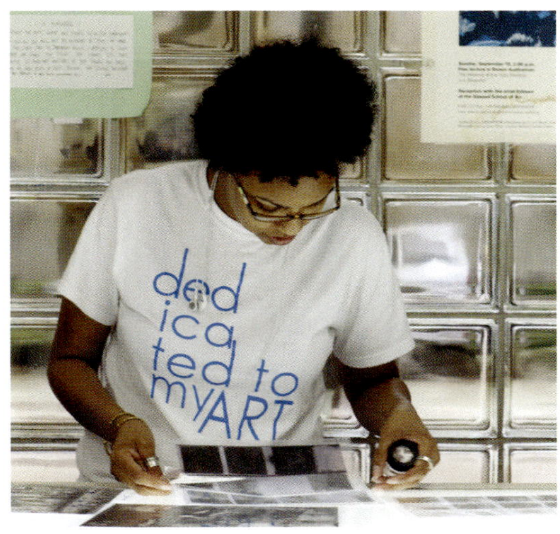

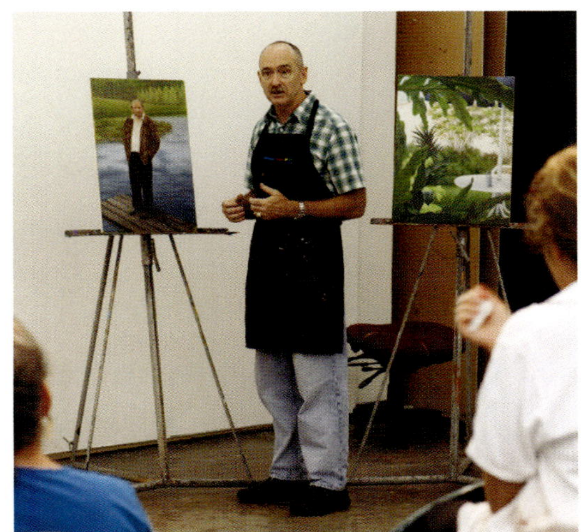

The Glassell School of Art offers a variety of classes, workshops, and educational opportunities for students diverse in age, interest, skill level, and need. Now in its eighty-seventh year, the Glassell School is one of the oldest museum schools in the country. The following highlights exemplify both the magnitude of the school's programming and the commitment of the Museum of Fine Arts, Houston, to provide a premier educational experience for adults and children.

The Glassell School of Art Studio School offers courses in art history and studio art for adults ages 18 and older. Studio courses and workshops are presented in a variety of media, including painting, watercolor, printmaking, photography, ceramics, sculpture, digital media, and jewelry, as well as in art theory. Students enrolled at the Studio School have diverse backgrounds and skill levels. Classes may be taken at the student's leisure, or for an in-depth, Certificate of Achievement program, or for undergraduate credit through the University of St. Thomas in Houston. In 2012–2013, enrollment at the Studio School was approximately 2,750 students, of which 160 were registered at the University of St. Thomas. Studio School students are accustomed to taking rigorous classes, and they also enjoy a robust schedule of lectures, exhibitions, and other activities that culminate in an annual juried student exhibition, which is held each spring. Art-history offerings include general surveys as well as specific subjects that focus often on the Museum's exhibitions and permanent collections.

The Core Program at the Glassell School of Art has earned an international reputation for cultivating the highest level of vanguard practice in contemporary art. Many distinguished artists have participated in the program, and the Core alumni group is exceptionally strong. The Core Program provides a nine-month postgraduate residency for

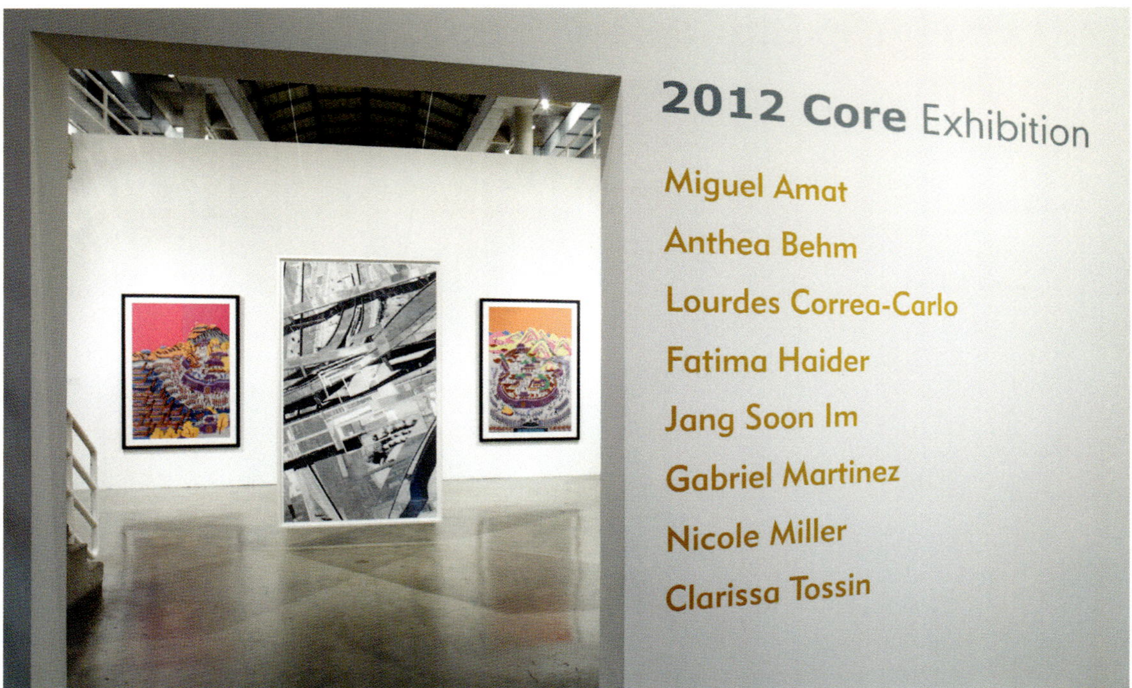

artists and critical writers; the residency may be renewed for two terms. Participants are provided studio or office space in the Glassell Studio School building, a stipend, and access to all of the school's equipment and facilities. Residents benefit from the rich environment of the Museum's campus as well as from the opportunity to interact with curators and other museum professionals. The Core residents also have borrowing privileges at the Museum's Hirsch Library and at Rice University's Fondren Library. A distinguished roster of artists, critics, curators, and art historians is invited each year to lecture, to lead seminars, and to conduct studio visits and individual reviews with the critical writers.

Every March, the Core artists mount an exhibition of their work created while in residence. This annual exhibition is accompanied by the Core Yearbook, which serves both as a catalogue for the artists and a publishing platform for the Core critical writers. During their second year, the Core writers have an opportunity to curate an exhibition for the Studio School's gallery.

The Junior School of the Glassell School of Art offers year-round art classes and workshops for children ages 4 to 18. In 2012–2013, enrollment was 3,800 students, including 130 who received scholarships. Some of these scholarships are awarded in recognition of talent through programs such as the sketching competition; others are based on need, thus ensuring access to art education for young people in Houston's diverse communities. Classes range in subject—from promoting family experience and familiarity with art, such as in toddler/parent workshops, to providing pre-professional school training and portfolio development, such as in advanced courses for students ages 15 to 18.

As part of an extensive outreach effort to Houston's communities, the Junior School has developed partnerships with various groups and schools, including the home-school network, Post Oak High School, and the Presbyterian School.

The expansion of the Museum's campus will include a new building for the Glassell School of Art. This development will have an enormous impact on the quality of the school's programming, the breadth of its services, and the broader integration of the school's activities into the Museum's program across campus. Presently, the Junior School is housed in a building at the farthest northwest corner of the campus, which inhibits

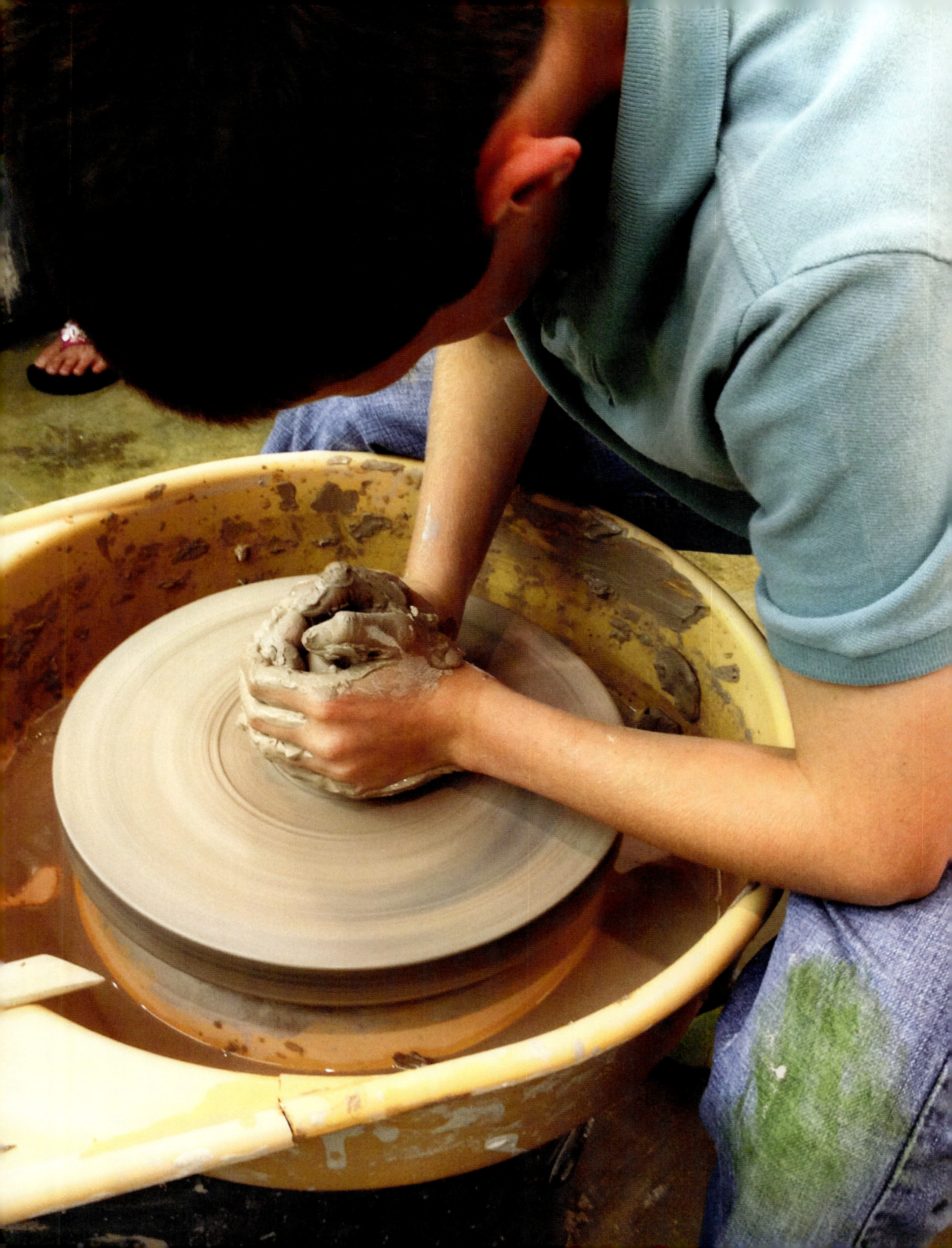

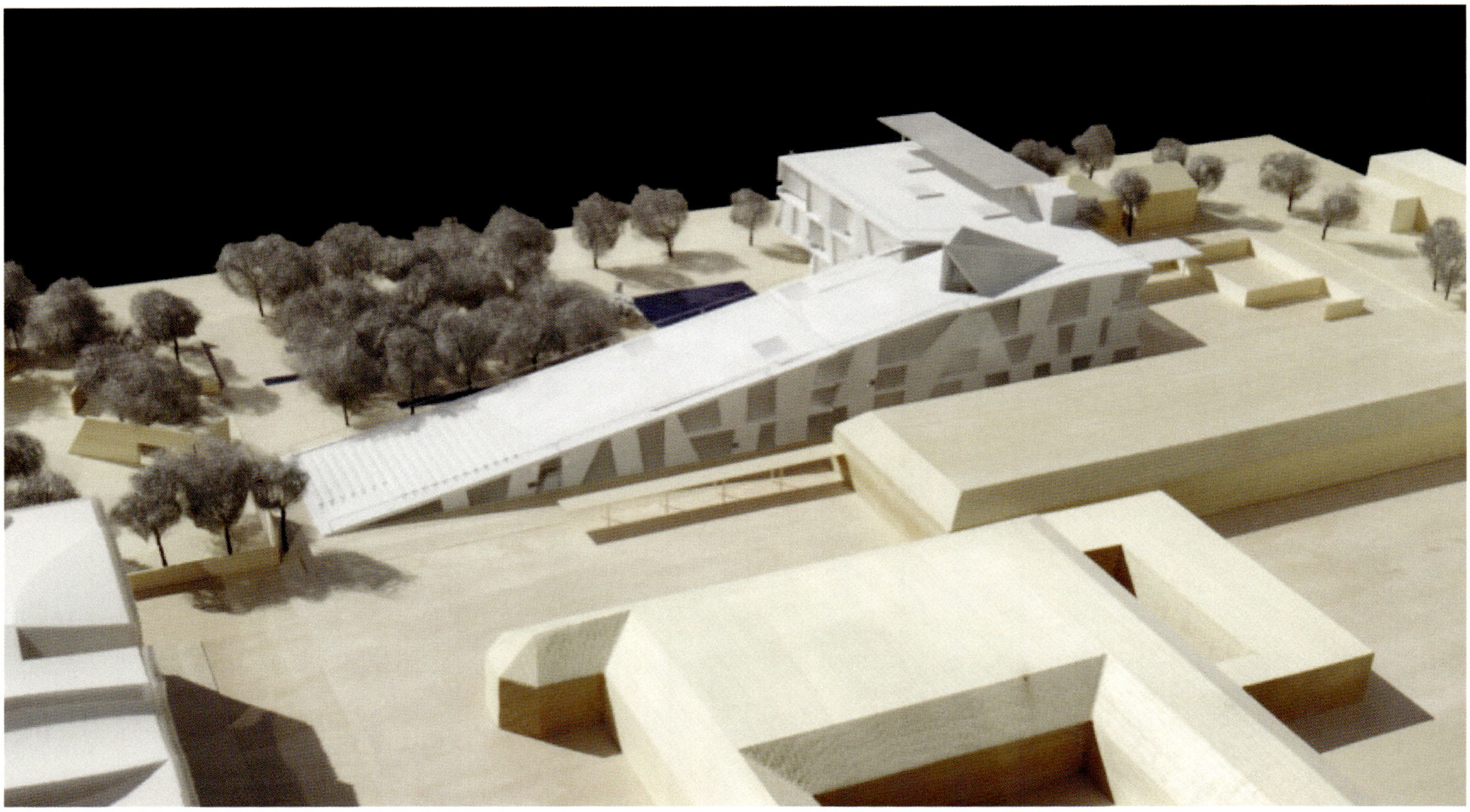

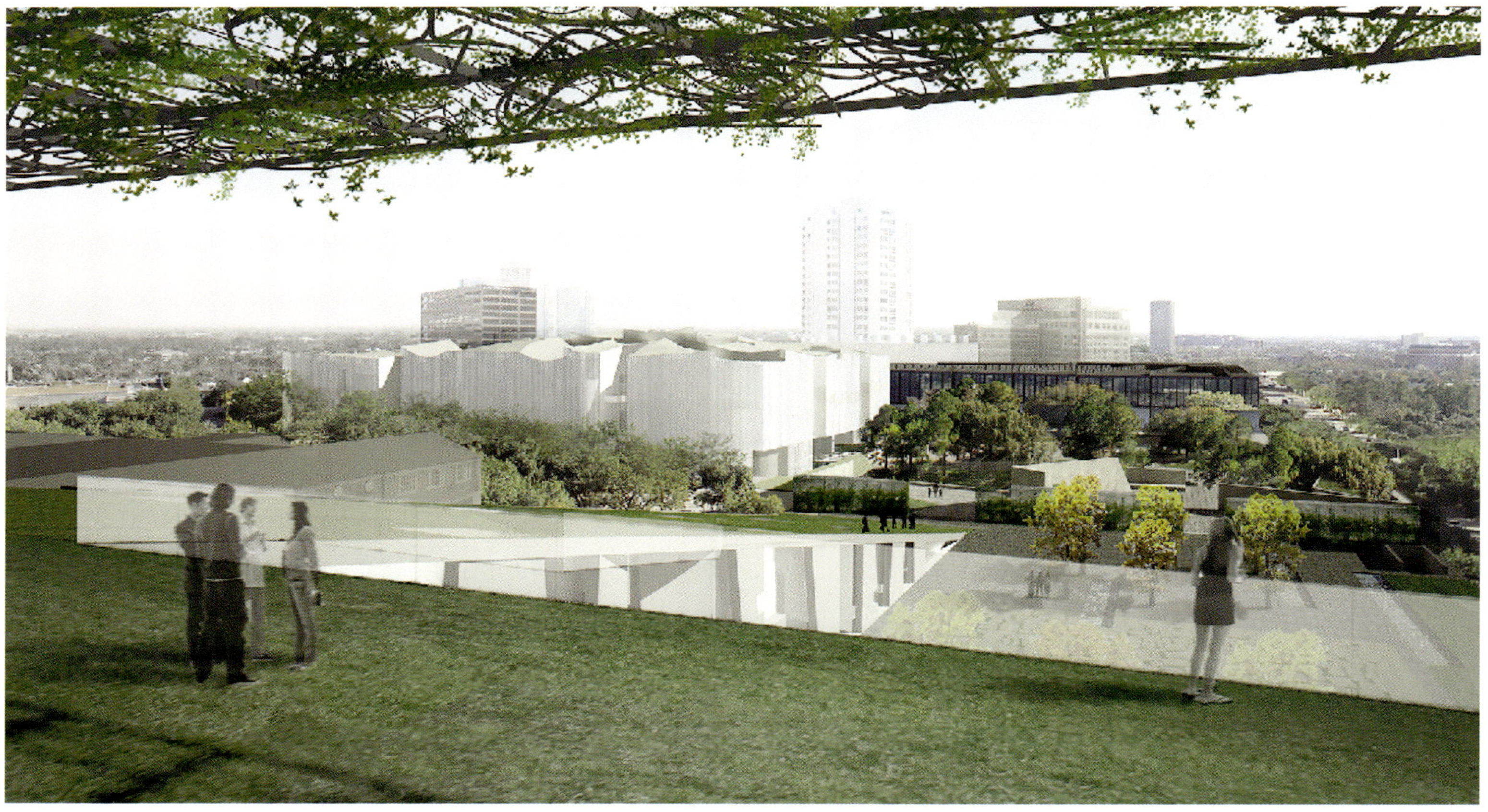

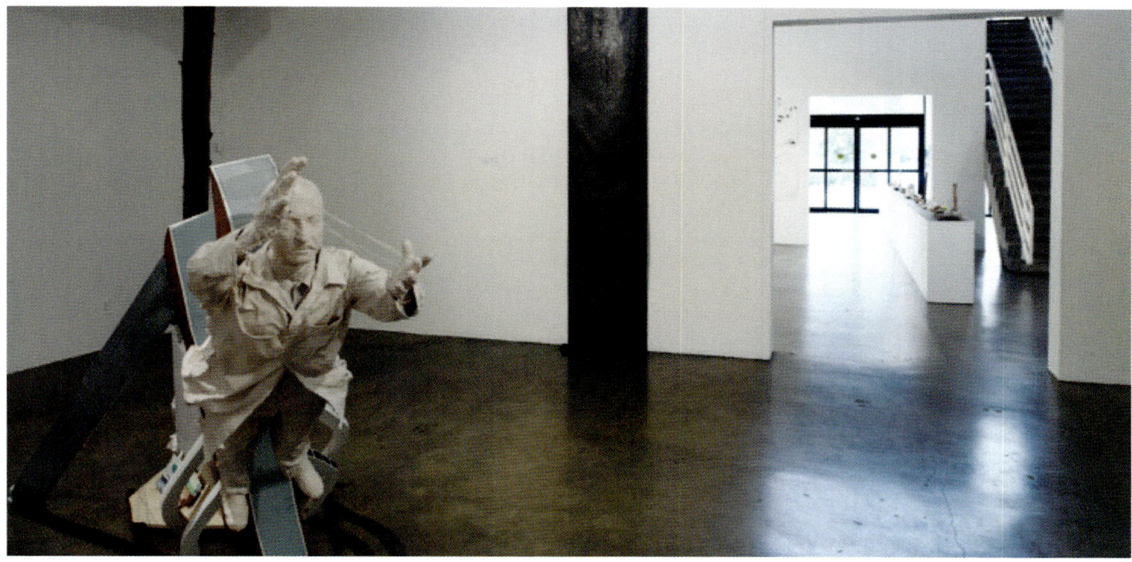

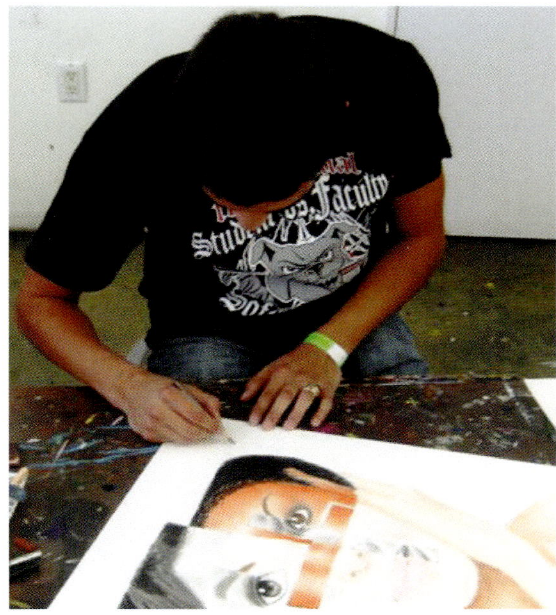

easy, convenient access to the Museum's galleries. The consolidation of all Glassell School programs in one building, located in close proximity to the Museum's galleries, and with a direct connection by underground tunnels, will make for a seamless experience of both seeing and making art.

Furthermore, the development of facilities that provide the best in current digital technologies will enable the Glassell School not only to honor traditional media, but also to be at the forefront of creating images that define contemporary culture. The Glassell School, as it stands now, has reached maximum capacity in all of its programs and must turn away individuals who wish to participate in certain classes. The expanded square footage will allow for growth that corresponds to the dynamic expansion of Houston. Finally, the Glassell School's beautiful, light-filled building, designed by Steven Holl Architects, will be both extremely functional and a beacon that represents the creative force of culture aligned harmoniously with the Museum's new, luminous building for art created after 1900.

Opposite, top: Detail of architectural model for the Glassell School of Art and expanded Fayez S. Sarofim Campus of the Museum of Fine Arts, Houston.

Opposite, bottom: Steven Holl Architects, 2014. View from the BBVA Roof Garden on the new building for the Glassell School of Art, looking south toward the new Nancy and Rich Kinder Building, the Lillie and Hugh Roy Cullen Sculpture Garden, and the Caroline Wiess Law Building.

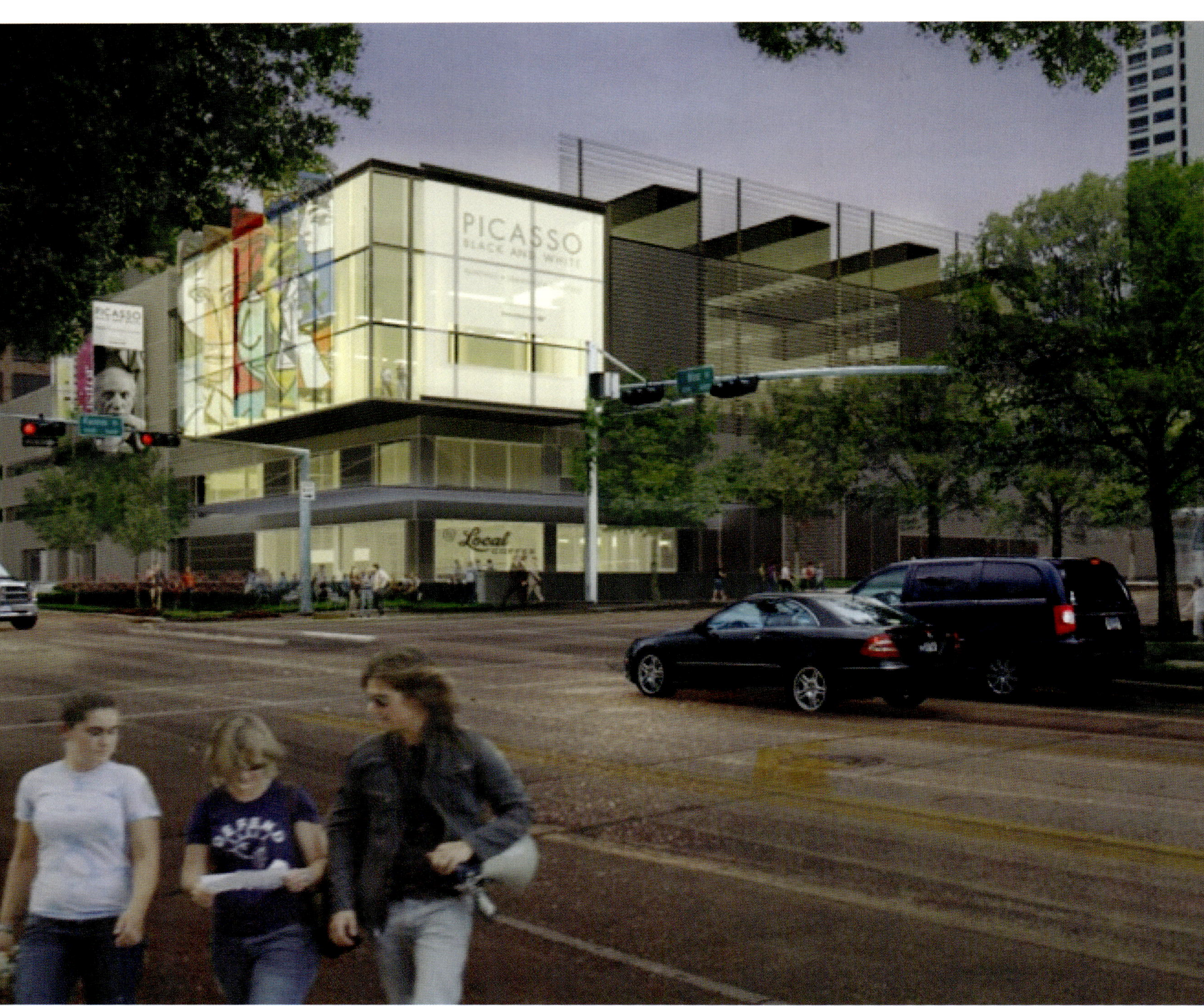

Above: Lake/Flato Architects, 2013.
Computer rendering of the Sarah Campbell
Blaffer Foundation Center for Conservation.

Opposite: Lake/Flato Architects, 2013.
Sketches of the Sarah Campbell Blaffer
Foundation Center for Conservation.

THE SARAH CAMPBELL BLAFFER FOUNDATION CENTER FOR CONSERVATION

DAVID BOMFORD

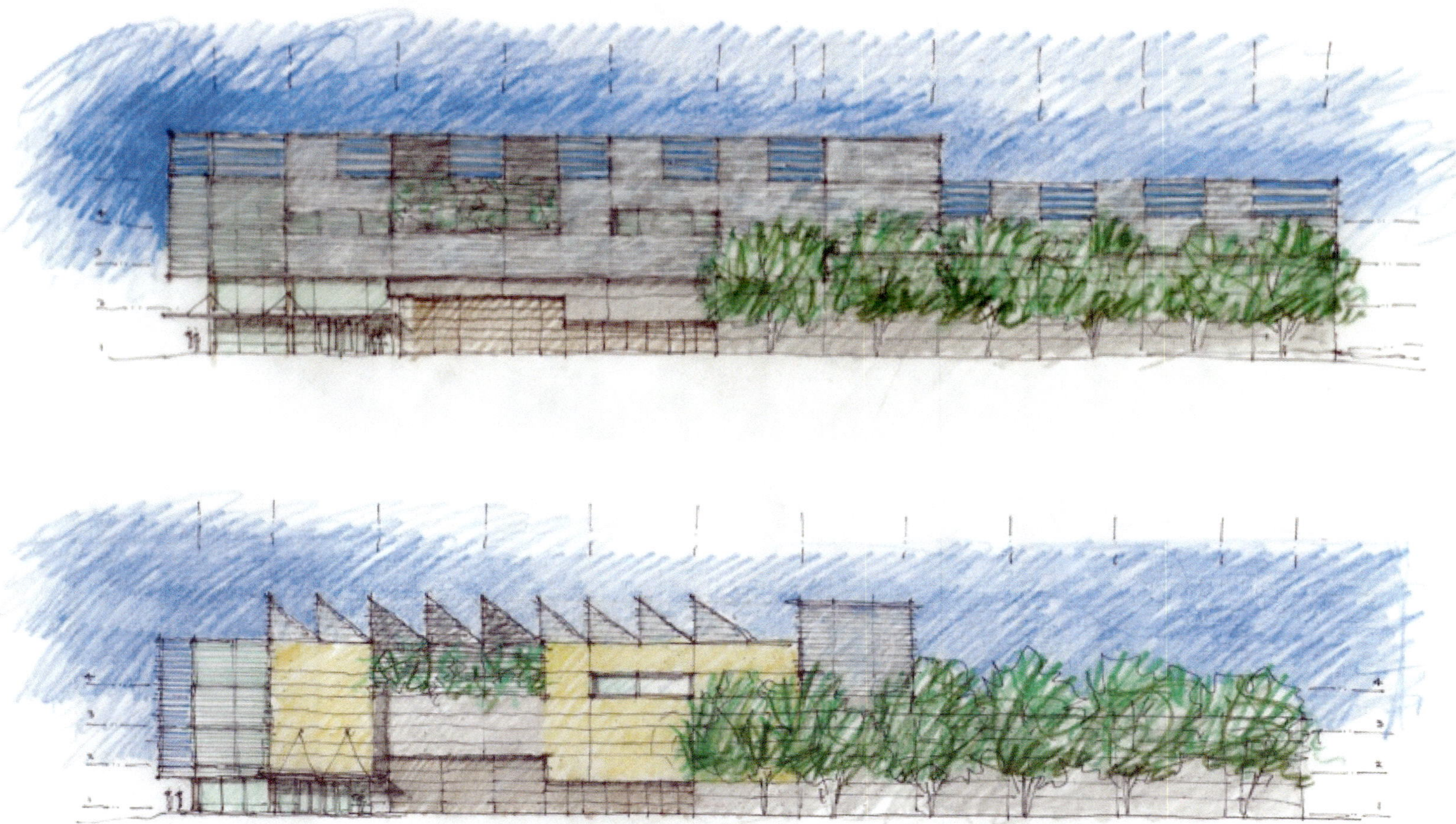

Conservation is central to the mission of the Museum of Fine Arts, Houston: to preserve and display the permanent collections for present and future generations. In addition, fundamental technical research on artworks places them in their material and historical contexts. Curators, academic art historians, conservators, and scientists collaborate to explore the ways in which works were made and their subsequent histories; they look at questions of authenticity and attribution; they consider the ethics and aesthetics of conservation and restoration. This thrilling, combined scholarly endeavor is at the heart of all museum life, and the new Sarah Campbell Blaffer Foundation Center for Conservation at the Museum of Fine Arts, Houston, will be where these specialists meet and discuss the objects in their care.

The Museum's conservation team is one of the finest in the country. The expertise of its conservators covers all aspects of the Museum's world-class encyclopedic collections and is divided into five departments: paintings, decorative arts, sculpture and textiles, works on paper, and photographs. At present, the existing conservation laboratories and studios are housed in two locations: in the Audrey Jones Beck Building, on the Museum's main campus, and in the Rosine Building, three miles north of the campus. These facilities have served the

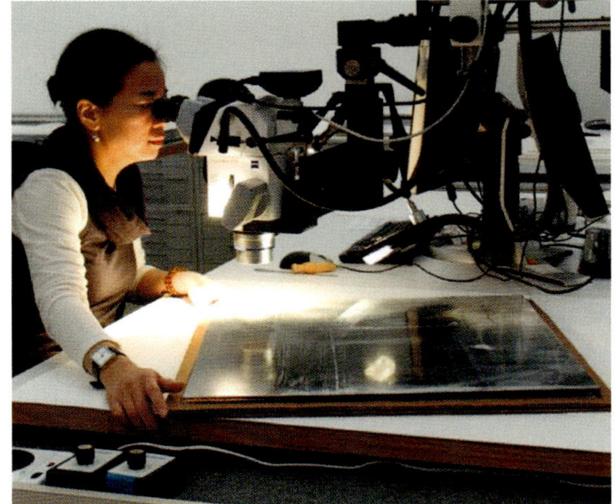

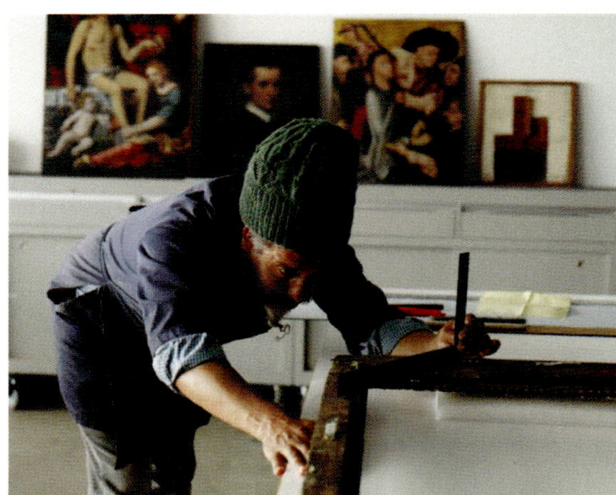

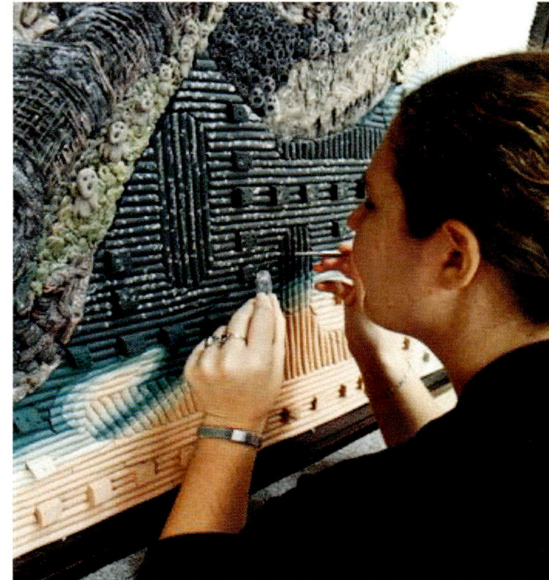

Above: Members of the Museum's conservation team at work.

conservation department well for the past twenty years, but they were always intended as only temporary solutions to the problem of not having a centralized space for conservation initiatives.

Now, there is a marvelous and exciting opportunity to bring the entire conservation operation together in a new, state-of-the-art facility on the Museum's campus. The new Center for Conservation will be a highly visible presence, adjacent to the Beck Building, and will add a luminous dimension to the extraordinary group of buildings that make up the Museum of Fine Arts, Houston.

The Center will be built above the west side of the Museum's Visitor Center and parking garage, transforming these two facilities that are located on Fannin Street. The two-story Center will provide spacious light-filled studios, laboratories, workrooms, and offices, in which conservation and research will be carried out to the highest standards of professional practice.

The Museum's Trustees have chosen Lake/Flato Architects to build the Center. The lightweight structure above the Visitor Center and garage will have a cantilevered bay window projecting forward on Binz and Fannin streets, bringing in light while giving pedestrians visual access to the critical role that conservation plays at the Museum.

The Center's projecting bay, which recalls Ludwig Mies van der Rohe's Law Building, will create a welcoming lantern that frames the east side of the Museum campus. Also, the architectural character of the Center will complement the Beck Building: a delicate metal sunshade scrim will hover above the existing heavy precast base of the garage. Further, by repurposing the lobby floor of the Visitor Center and garage into a sidewalk café, the Museum will create an animated urban presence on Fannin Street.

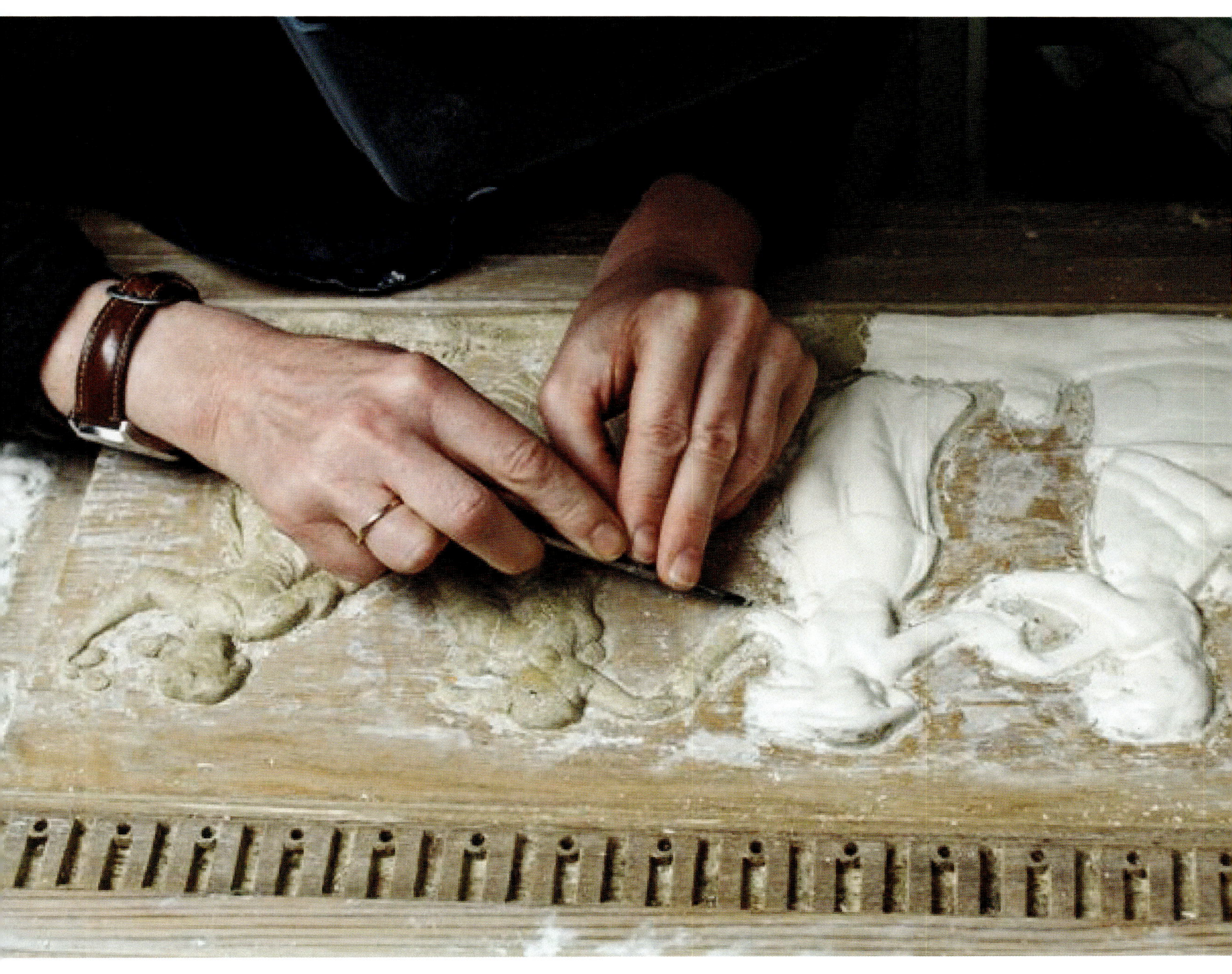

MODERN AND CONTEMPORARY ART

ALISON DE LIMA GREENE

From its first annual exhibitions of local artists to its current reach across six continents, engaging the art of our times has been central to the mission of the Museum of Fine Arts, Houston. Works by Aristide Maillol and Diego Rivera were among the first acquisitions for the permanent collections in the 1920s, and over the following decade important works on paper introduced such artists as Pablo Picasso, Henri Matisse, Paul Klee, Emil Nolde, and Yasuo Kuniyoshi to Houston audiences. Further gifts of works by Frederic Remington, Native American art, and the Straus Collection of European paintings gave the Museum's holdings authority in the 1940s, with such masterpieces as Paul Cézanne's portrait of his wife and Matisse's *Meditation (Portrait of Lorette)* establishing a strong foundation for future growth in modern art. However, it was not until the mid-1950s, more than half a century after the founding charter of the Museum of Fine Arts, Houston, that Modernism and contemporary art came together to shape the institution's future. Ushering in this new era was Nina Cullinan's 1953 landmark pledge to underwrite a major addition, "designed by an architect of outstanding reputation and wide experience." Within six months Ludwig Mies van der Rohe was named the architect of a new master plan. Cullinan Hall, the core segment of Mies's proposal, was inaugurated in 1954, offering a dramatic *tabula rasa* for a radical reappraisal of the Museum's collections program.

Cullinan's and Mies's ambitions for Houston were quickly matched by James Johnson Sweeney, who served as the Museum's director from 1961 to 1967. With extraordinary support from the Museum's trustees, Sweeney built a foundational collection of twentieth-century European art, ranging from Constantin Brancusi, Piet Mondrian, and Picasso, to Corneille, Eduardo Chillida, Niki de Saint Phalle, and Jean Tinguely, among others. New developments in American art were embraced as well, with signal works by Alexander Calder, Robert Motherwell, Jackson Pollock, Mark Rothko, Lee Bontecou, and Claes Oldenburg bringing fresh currents to Houston. By the end of Sweeney's tenure, the modern and contemporary collection could claim more than sixty major works by twentieth-century artists.

Today the Museum's modern and contemporary collection numbers more than 1,400 objects, expanding upon Sweeney's worldview and dedication to excellence. Particular collection strengths in American postwar art lie in the areas of Abstract Expressionism and the New York School, Color Field Painting, later developments in Pop art, the New Image movement of the 1970s and 1980s, as well as the more independent developments of the Postmodernist era. Several artists are represented in exceptional depth, including Jackson Pollock, Franz Kline, Philip Guston, Jasper Johns, Robert Rauschenberg, Kenneth Noland, Frank Stella, Nan Goldin, and James Turrell, among others. At the same time compelling works by Forrest Bess, John Biggers, Louise Nevelson, Agnes Martin, Alice Neel, Donald Judd, Sol LeWitt, Jennifer Bartlett, Luis Jimenez, Ed and Nancy Kienholz, Thornton Dial, Sr., Mel Chin, Rackstraw Downes, Sherrie Levine, Roni Horn, Bill Viola, Jennifer Steinkamp, Fred Wilson, Nick Cave, and numerous Texas artists relate a broader narrative of American art over the past six decades.

The Museum's European holdings complement American strengths. Following the first generation of the Paris avant-garde, Surrealism is introduced with works by Joan Miró, Yves Tanguy, Alberto Giacometti, and René Magritte. Works representing postwar developments range from the CoBrA, Zero, and Nouveau Réaliste associations of artists, to such individuals as Joseph Beuys, Gerhard Richter, Anselm Kiefer, Richard Long, Rebecca Horn, Christian Boltanski, Francesco Clemente, Rachel Whiteread, Damien Hirst, and Simon Starling. Additionally, artists based in Africa, Asia, the Middle East, and Latin America have created cross-cultural dialogues both within the department and with the Museum's other curatorial areas. Of particular note are works by Malick Sidibé, William Kentridge, Yinka Shonibare, Do Ho Suh, Lee Bul, Yoshitomo Nara, Monir Sharoudy Farmanfarmaian, Zhang Huan, Lucio Fontana, Matta, Tunga, and Alfredo Jaar, which connect individual histories with global concerns.

The Core Program at the Glassell School of Art has a special chapter within the Museum's collections. Former Core Fellows Julie Mehretu, Shahzia Sikander, Jeff Elrod, Amy Blakemore, Trenton Doyle Hancock, Leslie Hewitt, Nicola Costantino, Leandro Erlich, and Clarissa Tossin are among the many artists who launched their professional careers at the Museum of Fine Arts, Houston, establishing new legacies for generations to come.

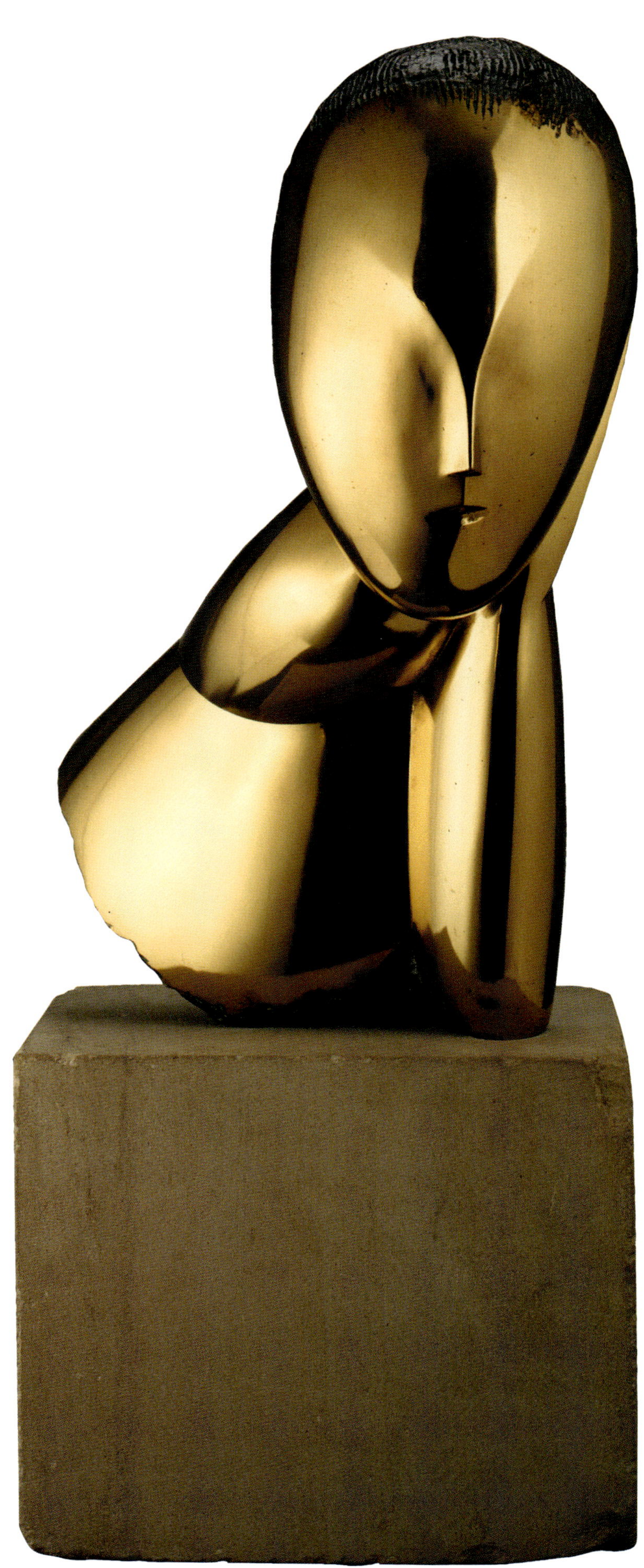

CONSTANTIN BRANCUSI | French,
born Romania, 1876–1957
A Muse, 1917
Polished bronze
19 5/8 x 11 11/16 x 9 5/8 in. (49.8 x 29.7 x 24.4 cm)
Museum purchase funded by
Mrs. Herman Brown and
Mrs. William Stamps Farish
62.1

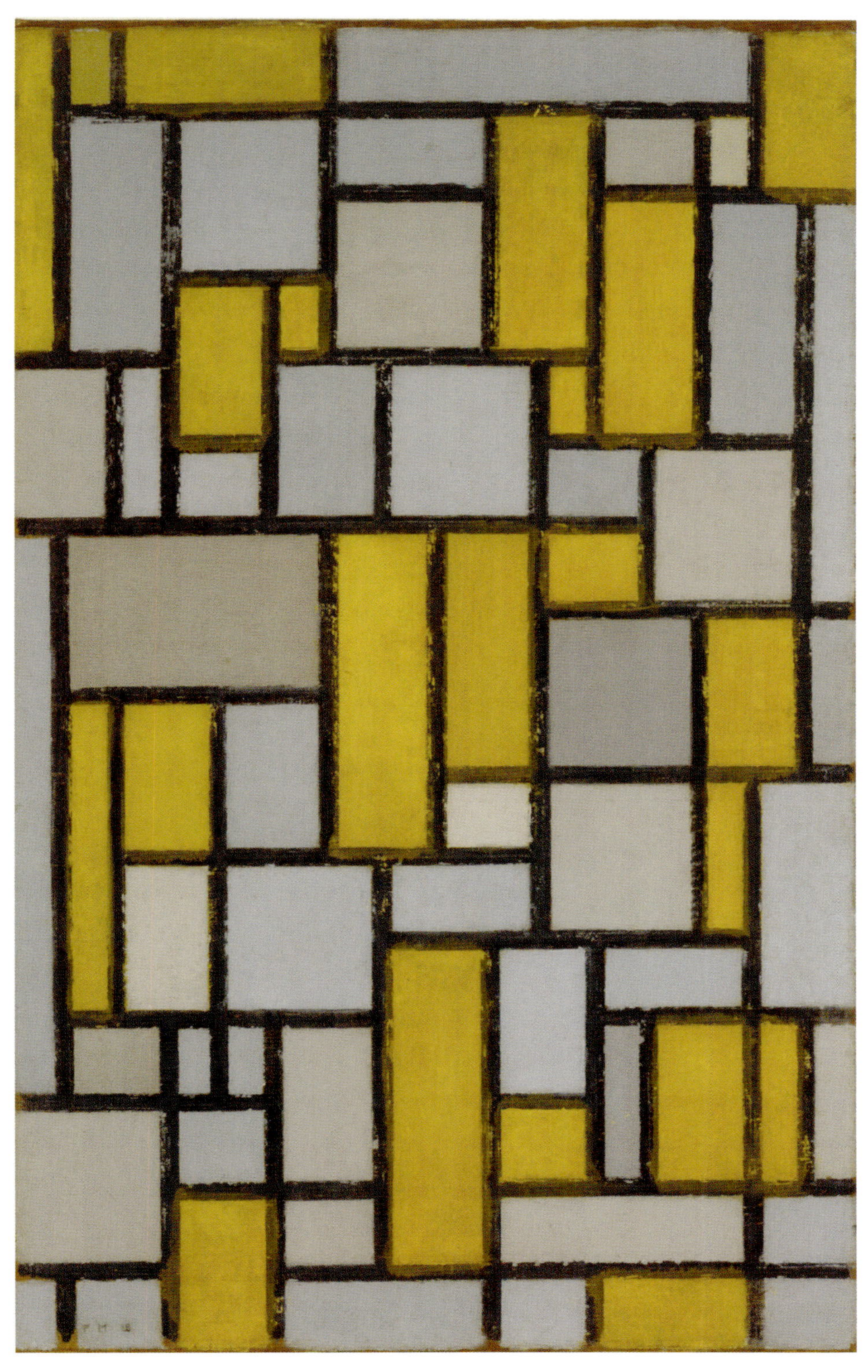

PIET MONDRIAN | Dutch, 1872–1944
Composition with Grid #1, 1918
Oil on canvas
31 9/16 x 19 5/8 in. (80.2 x 49.8 cm)
Gift of Mr. and Mrs. Pierre Schlumberger
63.16

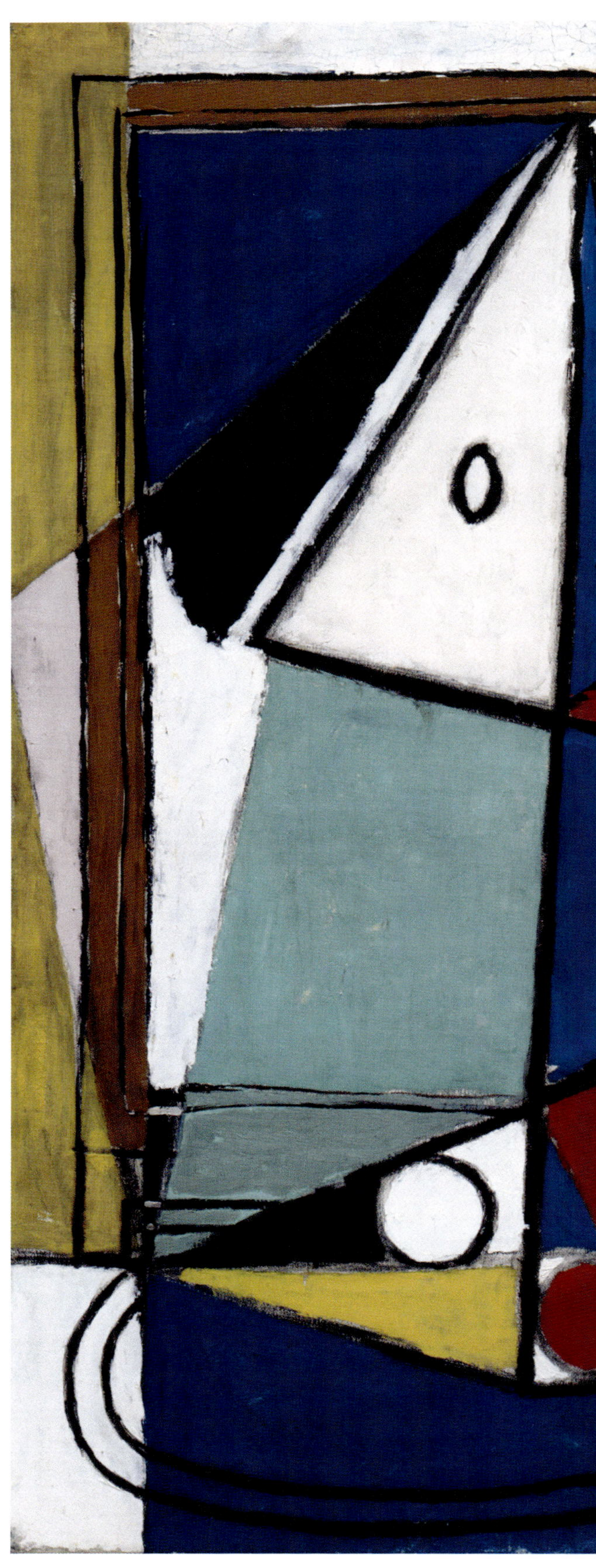

PABLO PICASSO | Spanish, 1881–1973
Two Women in Front of a Window, 1927
Oil on canvas
Canvas or panel: 38 1/2 x 51 1/2 in. (97.8 x 130.8 cm)
Gift of Mr. and Mrs. Theodore N. Law
64.17

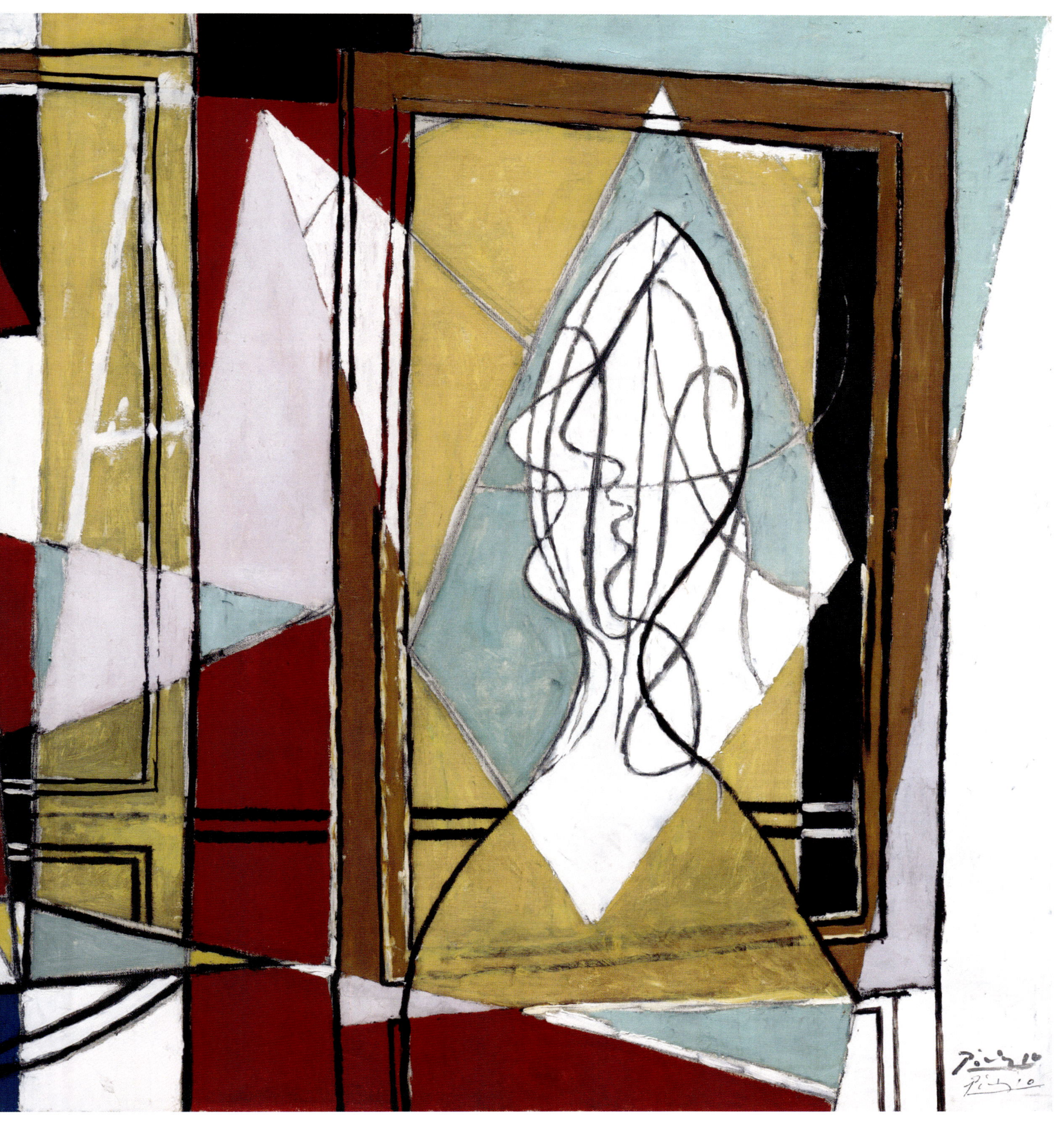

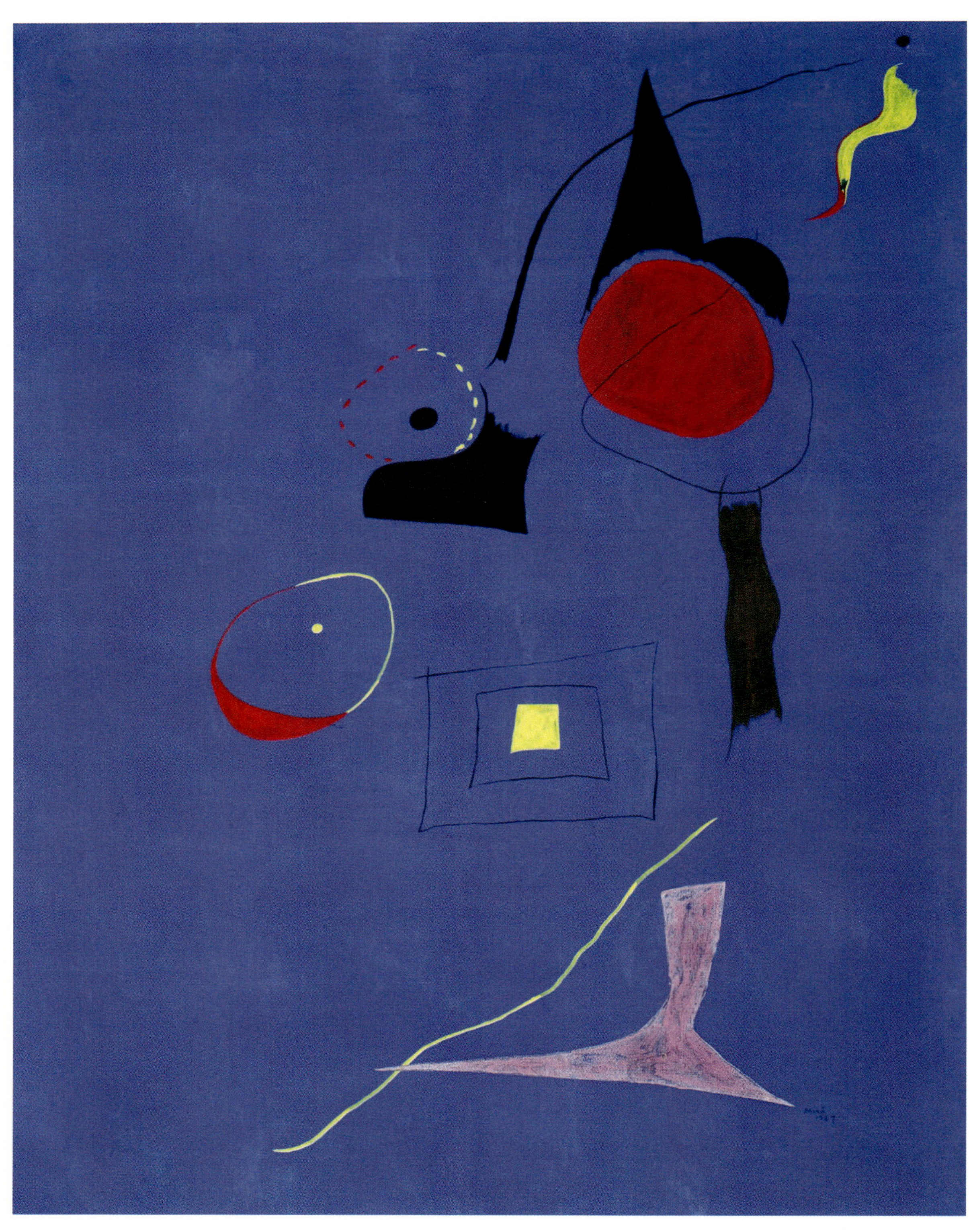

JOAN MIRÓ | Spanish, 1893–1983
Painting (Circus), 1927
Peinture (Cirque)
Oil on canvas
45 1/2 x 33 1/4 in. (115.6 x 84.5 cm)
Bequest of Caroline Wiess Law
2004.45

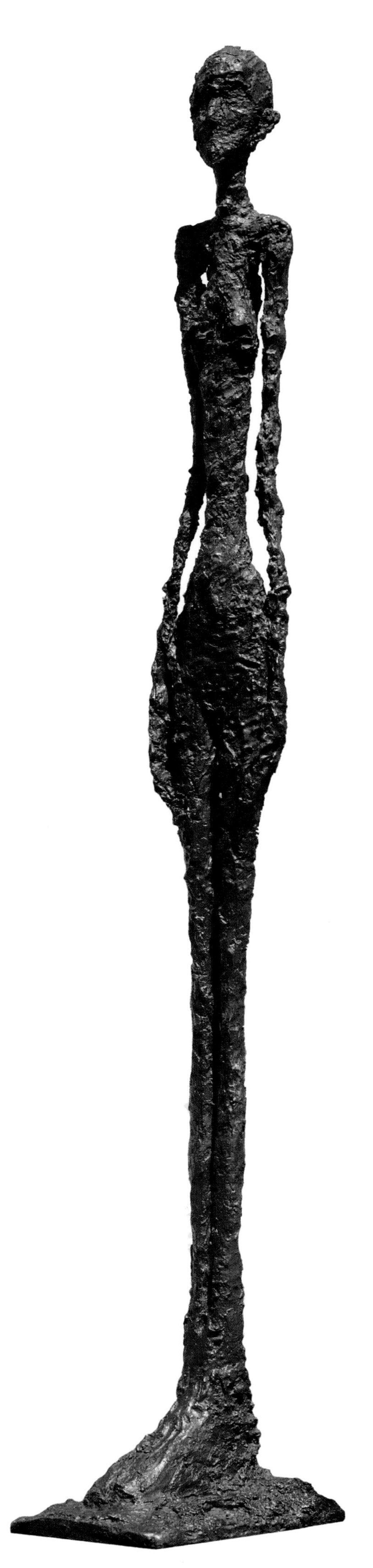

ALBERTO GIACOMETTI | Swiss, 1901–1966
Large Standing Woman I, 1960
Bronze
105 1/2 x 12 7/8 x 19 3/4 in. (268 x 32.7 x 50.2 cm)
Museum purchase funded
by the Brown Foundation
Accessions Endowment Fund
86.397

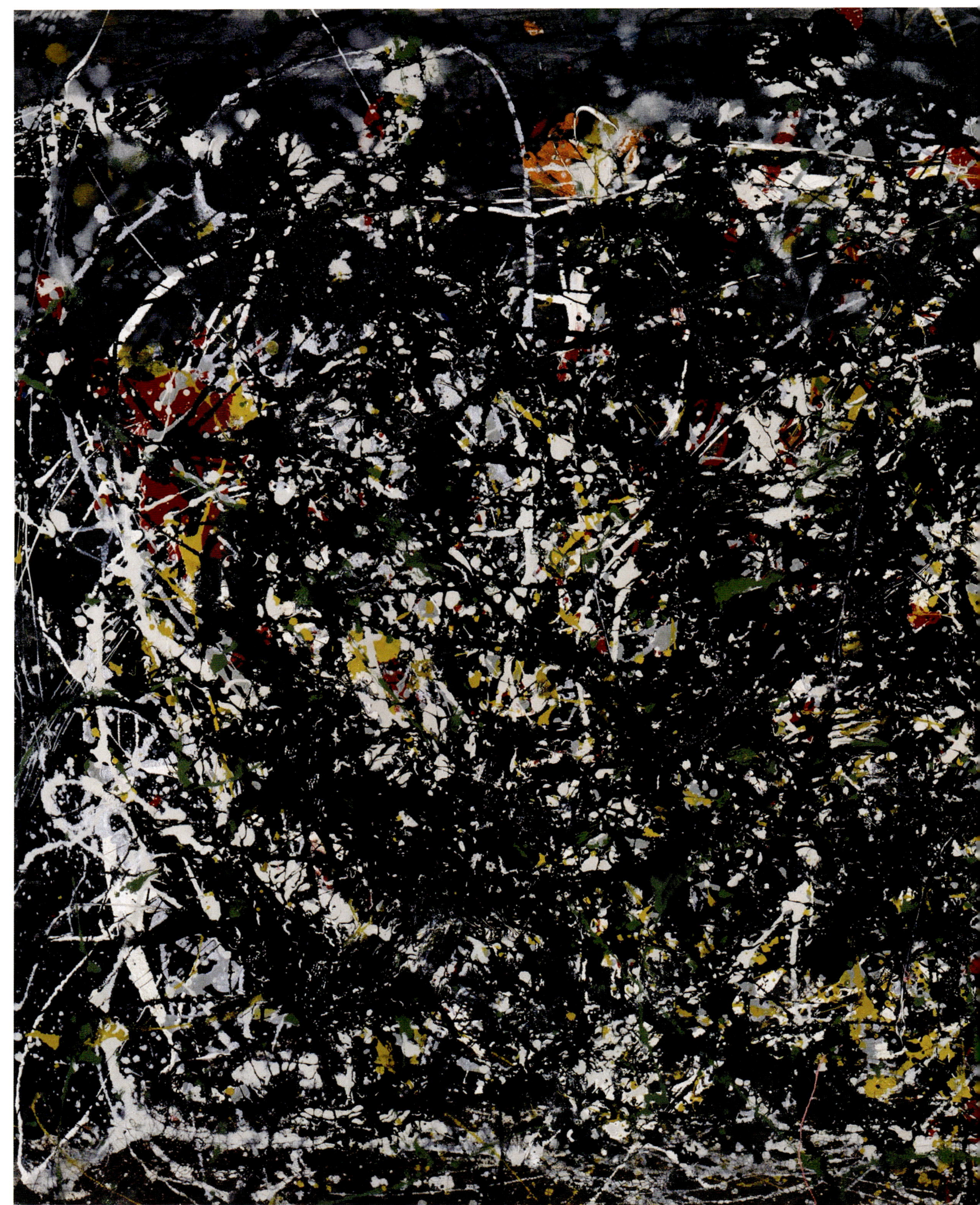

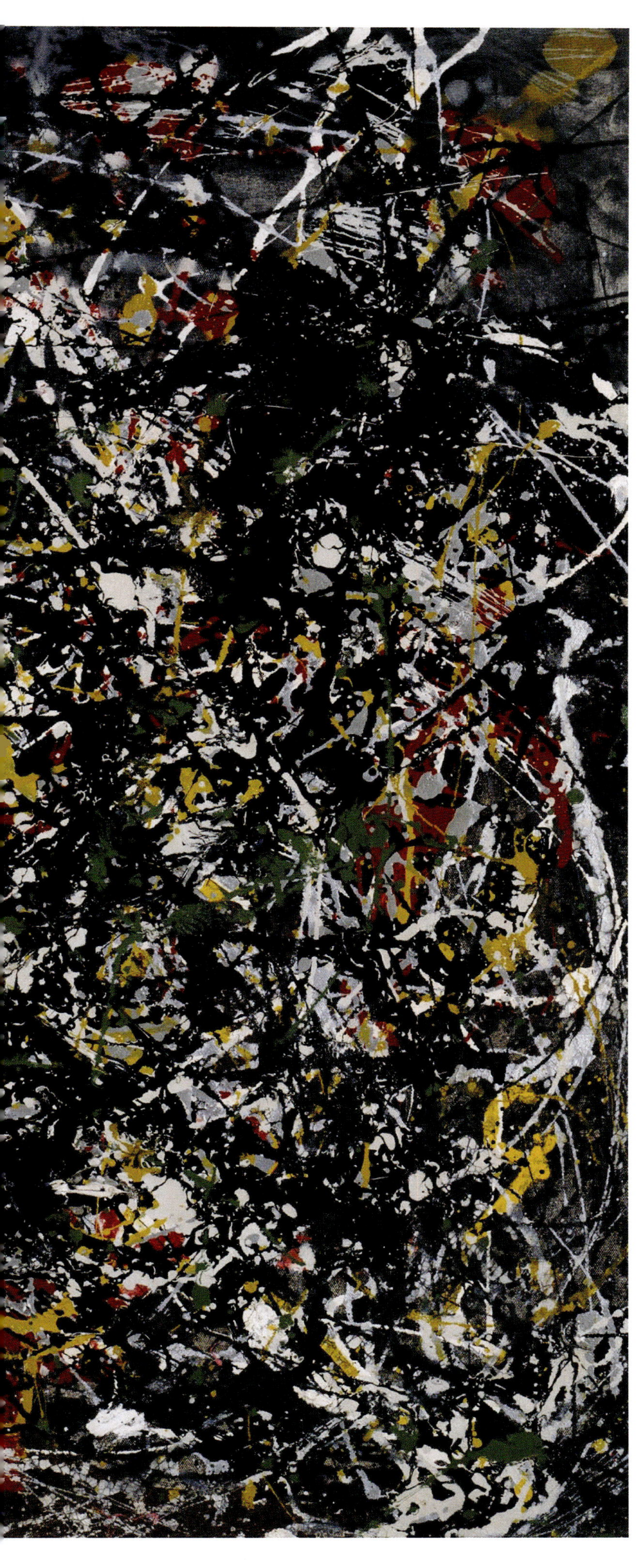

JACKSON POLLOCK | American, 1912–1956
Number 6, 1949
Duco and aluminum paint on canvas
Canvas: 44 3/16 x 54 in. (112.3 x 137.2 cm)
Museum purchase funded by
D. and J. de Menil
64.36

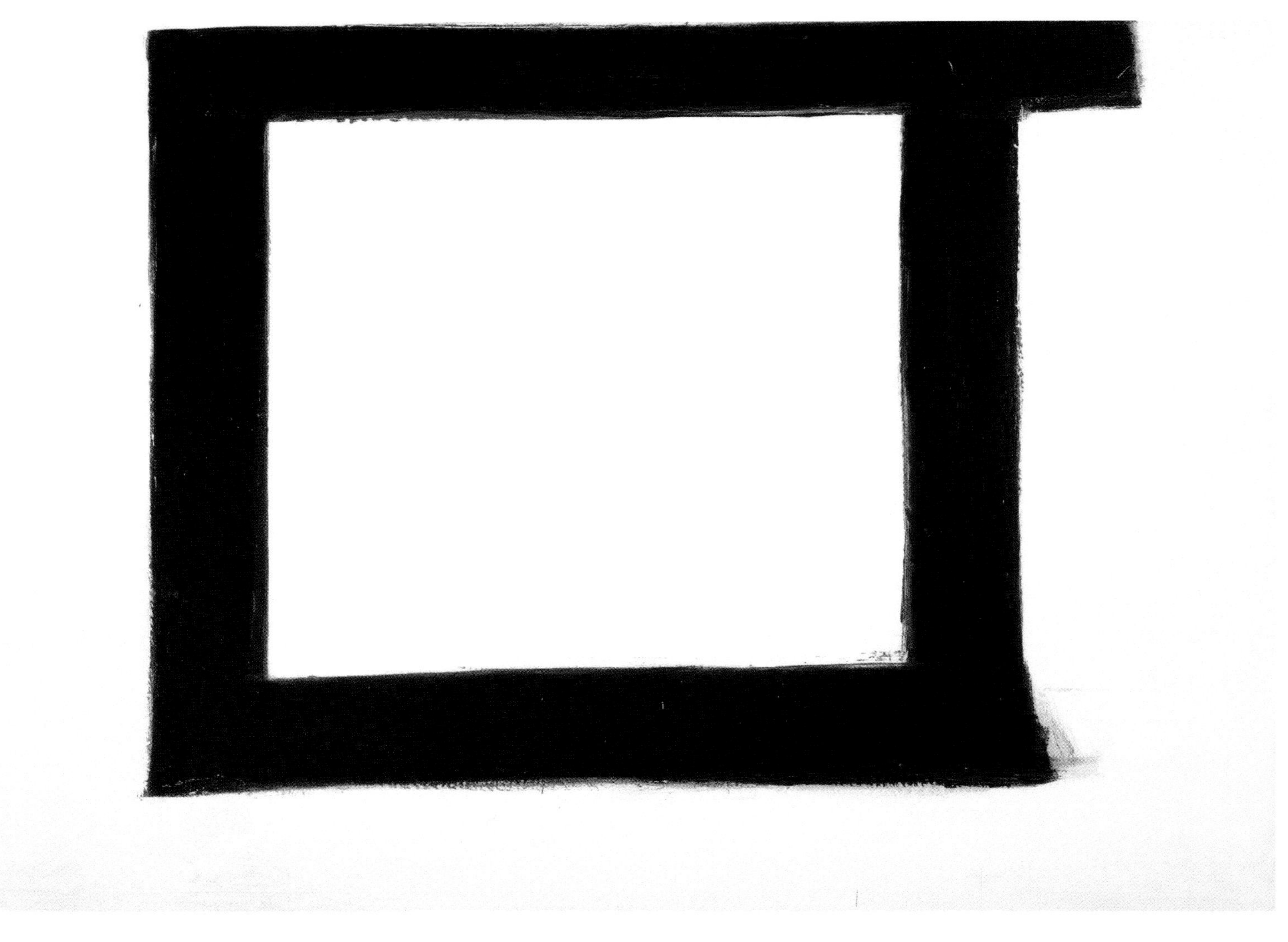

FRANZ KLINE | American, 1910–1962
Wotan, 1950
Oil on canvas mounted on Masonite
Canvas: 55 x 79 5/16 in.
Museum purchase, by exchange
80.120

ADOLPH GOTTLIEB | American, 1903–1974
Penumbra, 1959
Oil on linen
Canvas: 90 x 72 in. (228.6 x 182.9 cm)
Bequest of Caroline Wiess Law
2004.19

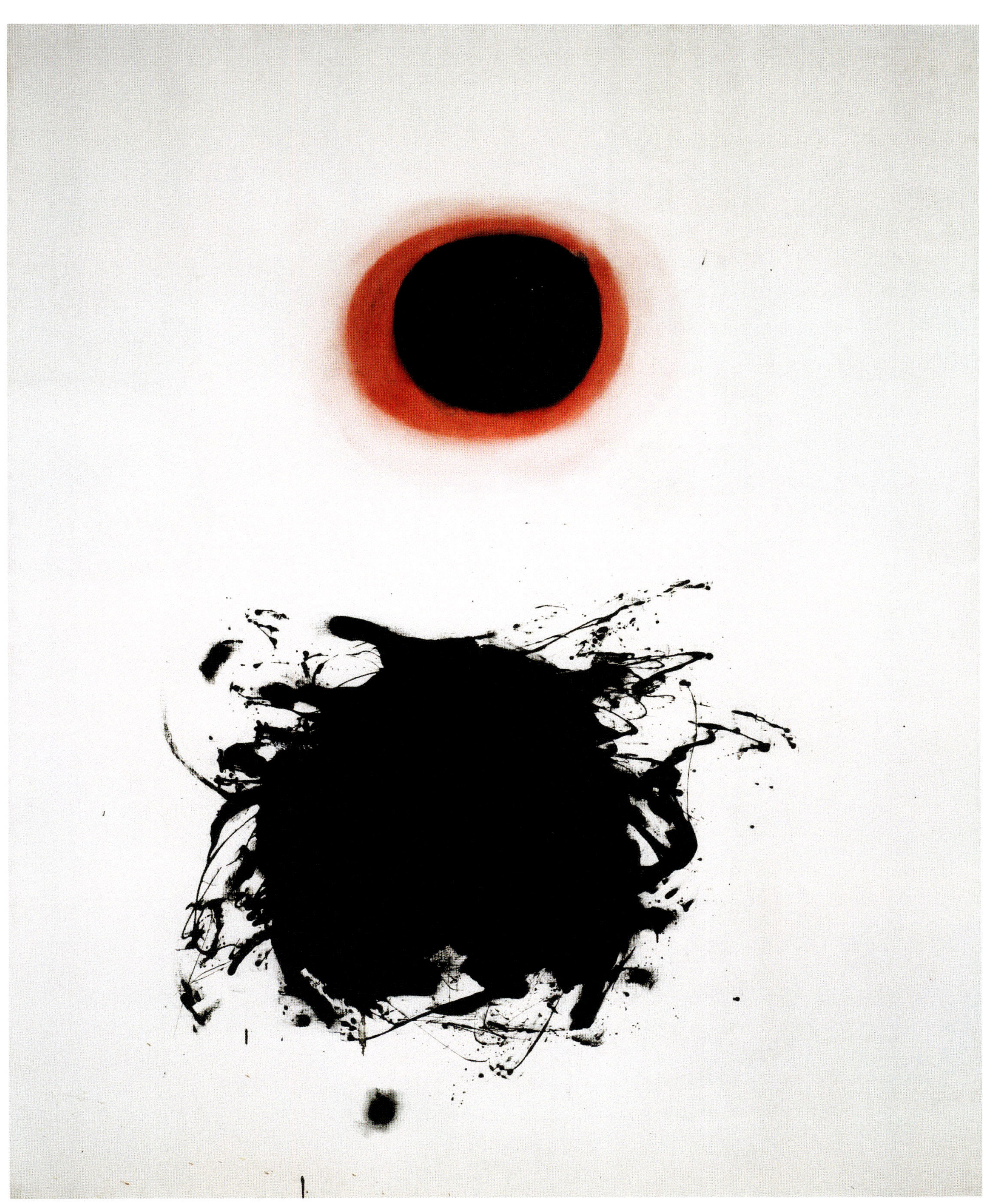

LUCIO FONTANA | Italian, born Argentina, 1899–1968
Concetto Spaziale, Attese [Spatial Concept, Waiting], 1960
Water-based paint on canvas
49 1/2 x 39 5/8 in. (125.7 x 100.6 cm)
Bequest of Caroline Wiess Law
2004.15

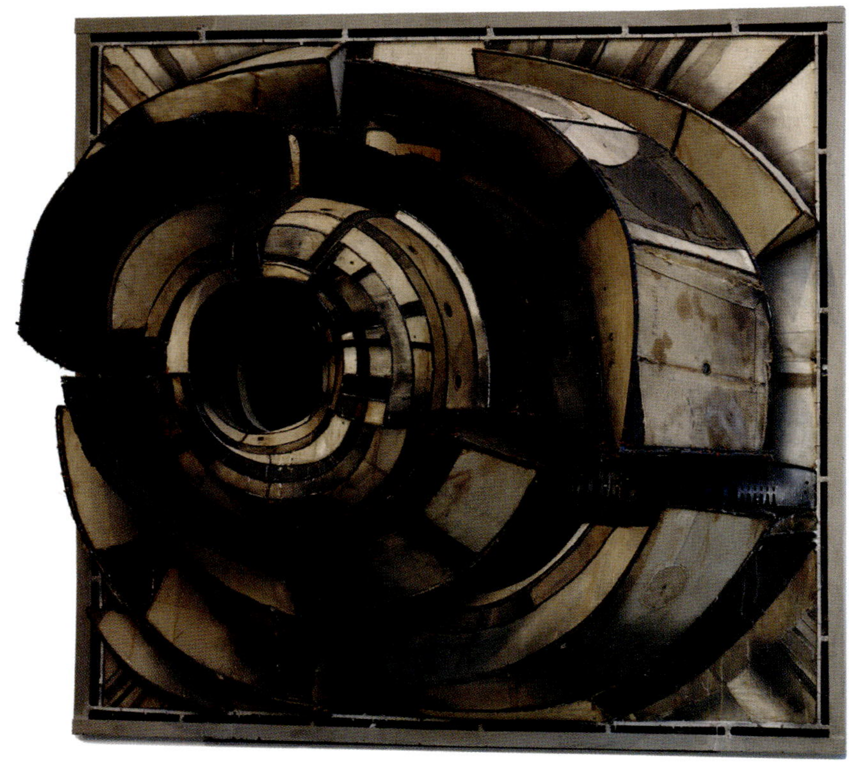

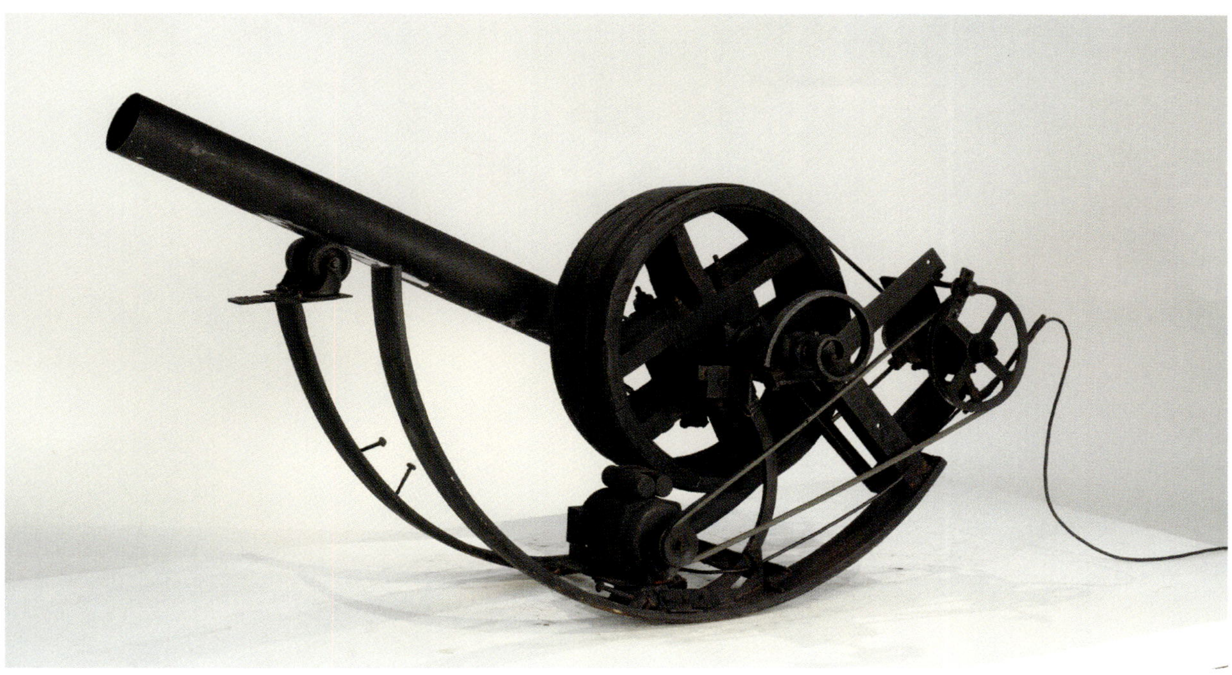

Top:
LEE BONTECOU | American, born 1931
Untitled, 1962
Welded steel, epoxy, canvas, fabric,
saw blade, and wire
68 x 72 x 30 in. (172.7 x 182.9 x 76.2 cm)
Gift of D. and J. de Menil
62.45

JEAN TINGUELY | Swiss, 1925–1991
La Bascule VII, 1967
Mixed media: Iron rocker bars, wood fly-wheel,
steel tube, rubber V-belt, and electric motor
48 1/4 x 32 1/4 x 80 1/2 in.
(122.56 x 81.92 x 204.47 cm)
Gift of the artist
68.44

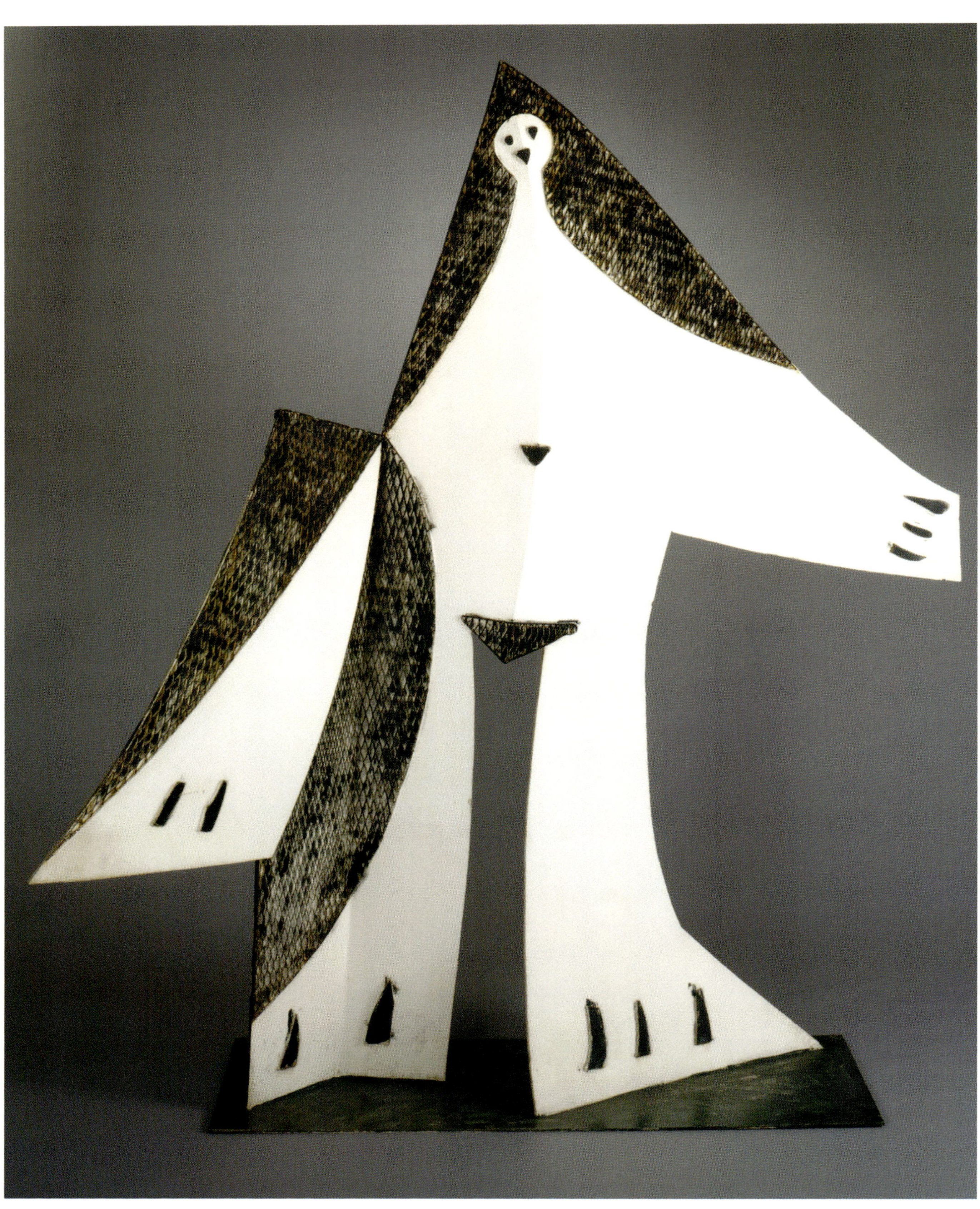

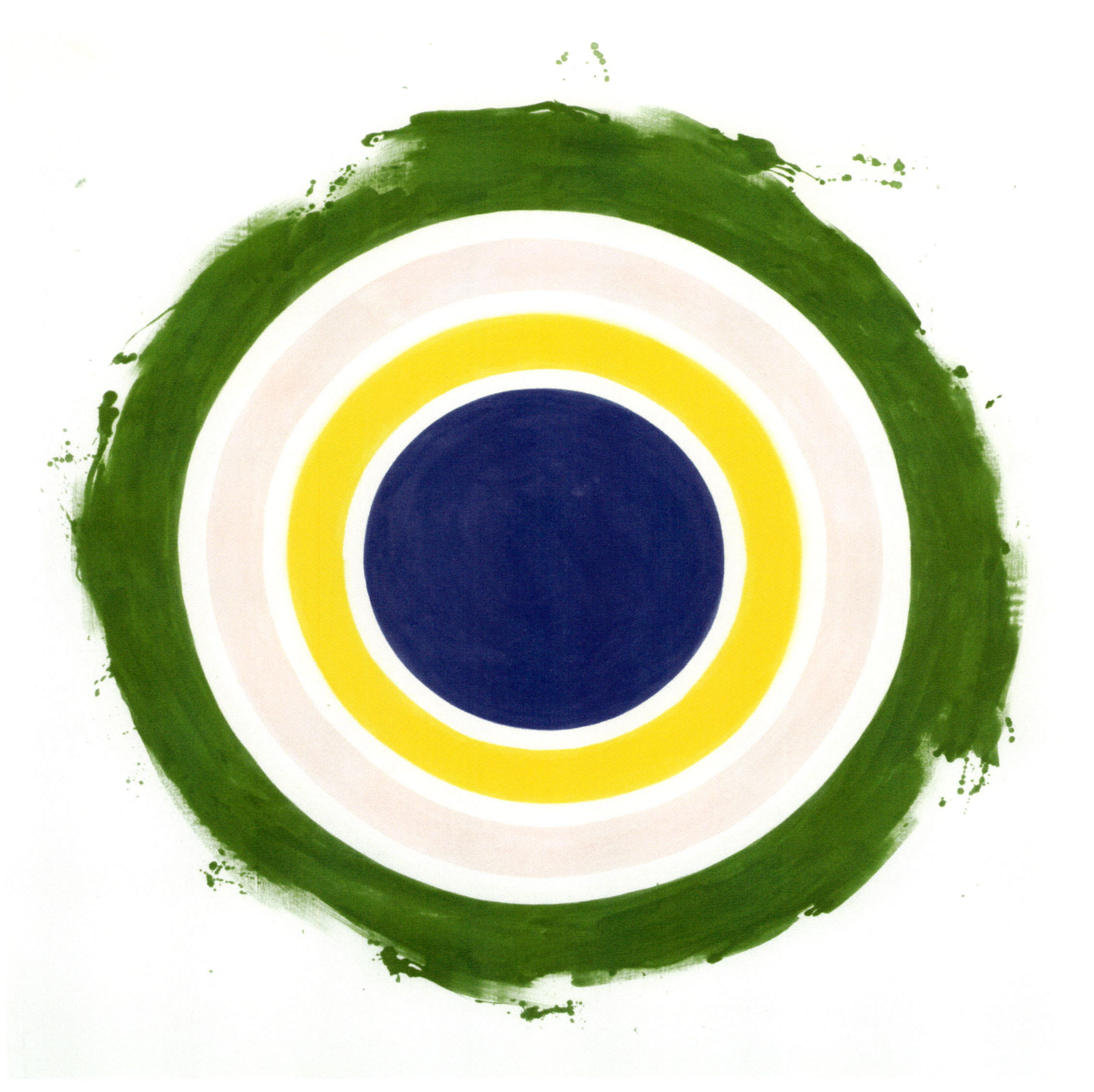

PABLO PICASSO | Spanish, 1881–1973
Woman with Outstretched Arms, Cannes 1961
Painted iron and metal sheeting
70 5/16 x 61 9/16 x 28 9/16 in.
(178.6 x 156.4 x 72.5 cm)
Gift of the Esther Florence Whinery Goodrich
Foundation
66.15

KENNETH NOLAND | American, 1924–2010
Half, 1959
Acrylic on canvas
68 5/8 x 68 5/8 in. (174.3 x 174.3 cm)
Museum purchase
74.260

FRANK STELLA | American, born 1936
Palmito Ranch, 1961
Acrylic on canvas
Canvas: 77 x 77 in. (195.6 x 195.6 cm)
Museum purchase funded by the
Caroline Wiess Law Accessions Endowment
Fund and the artist in memory of
Peter C. Marzio
2011.543

ANTHONY CARO | English, born 1924
Orangerie, 1969
Painted steel
Overall: 88 1/2 x 64 x 91 in.
(224.8 x 162.6 x 231.1 cm)
Museum purchase funded by
the Caroline Wiess Law Accessions
Endowment Fund
2012.195

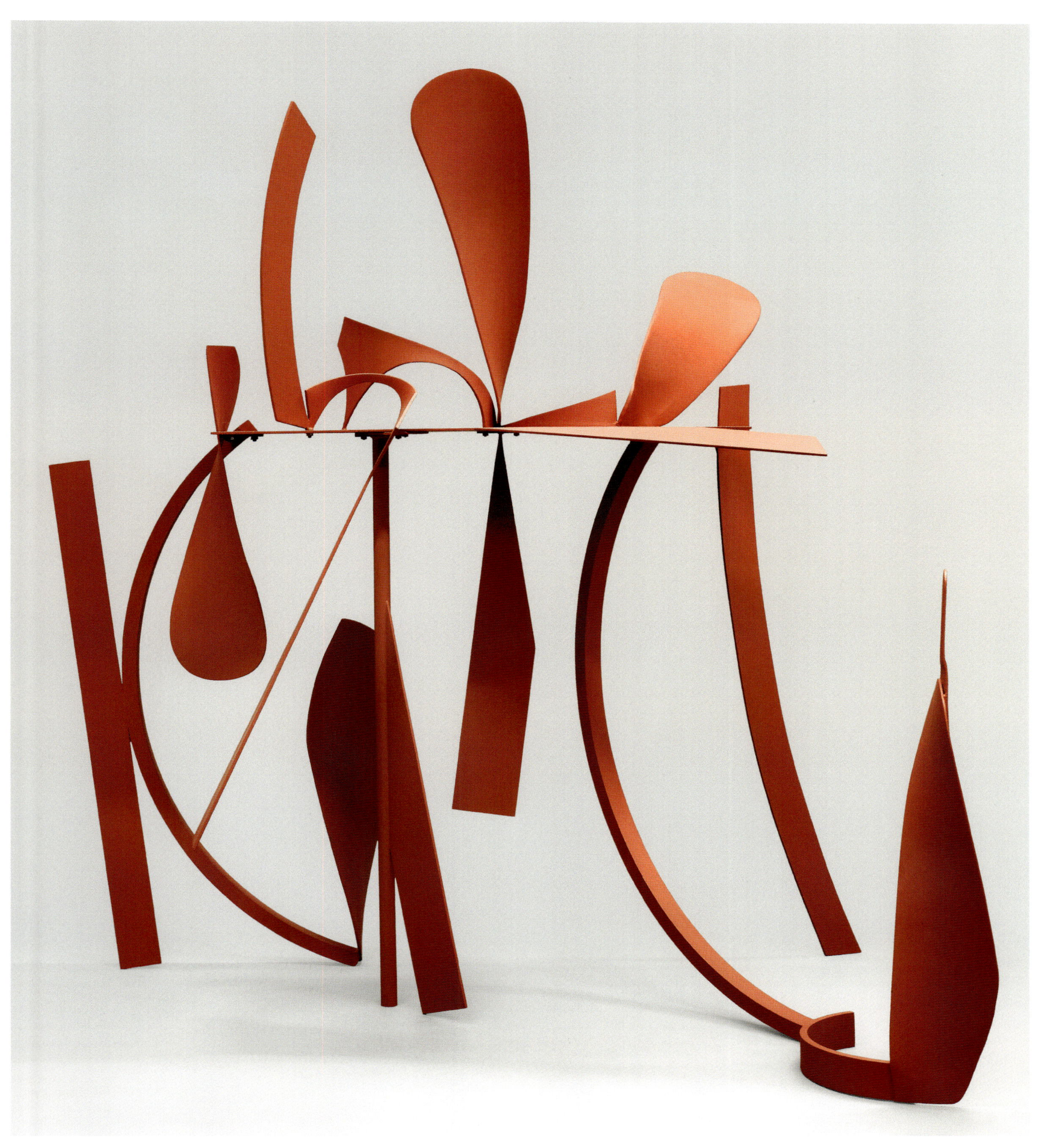

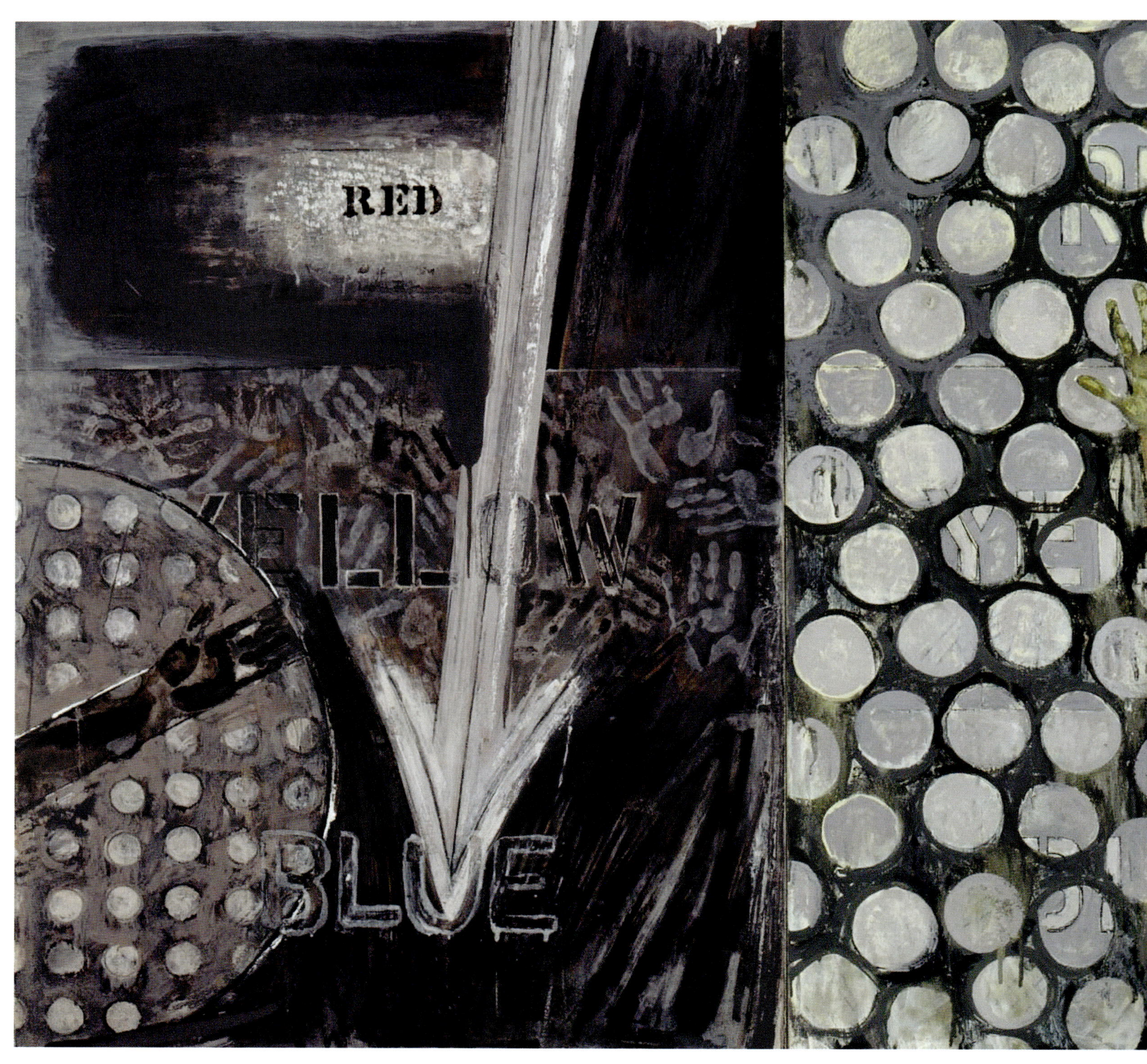

RED
YELLOW
BLUE

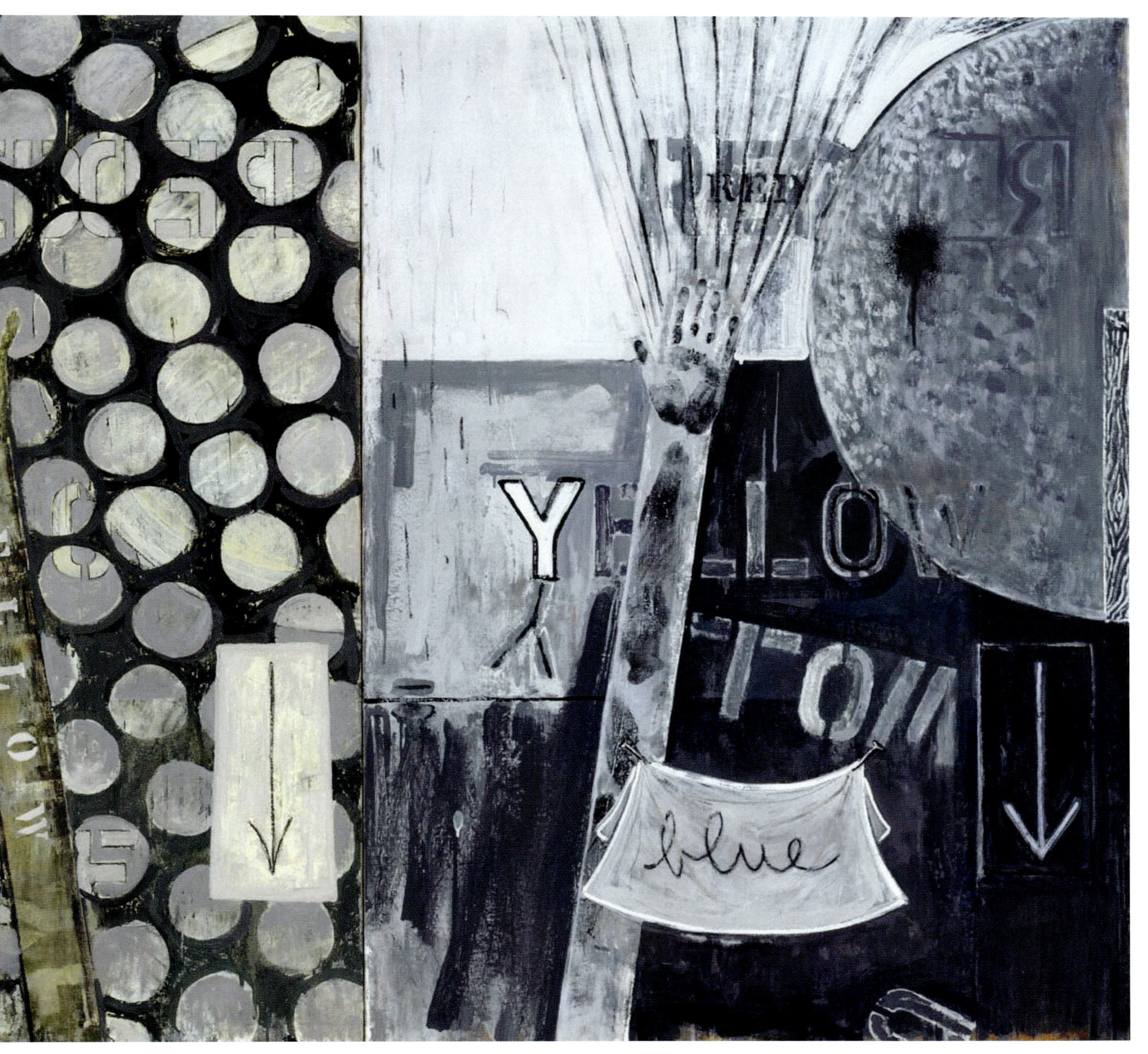

JASPER JOHNS | American, born 1930
Untitled (Red, Yellow, Blue), 1984
Encaustic on three canvas panels
Overall: 55 1/4 x 118 1/2 in. (140.3 x 301 cm)
Canvas or panel (each):
55 1/4 x 39 1/2 in. (140.3 x 100.3 cm)
Museum purchase funded by
The Brown Foundation, Inc.
2000.421

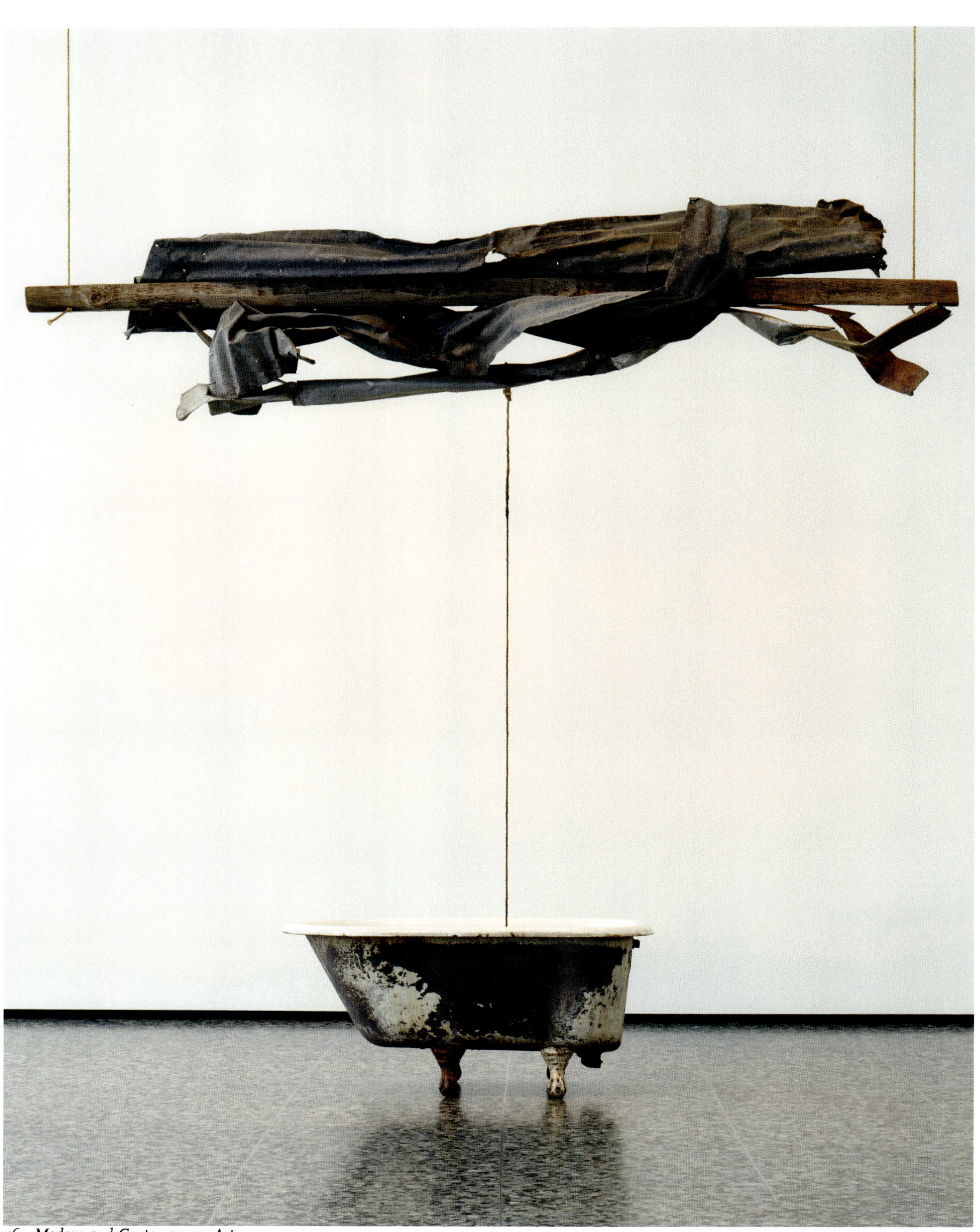

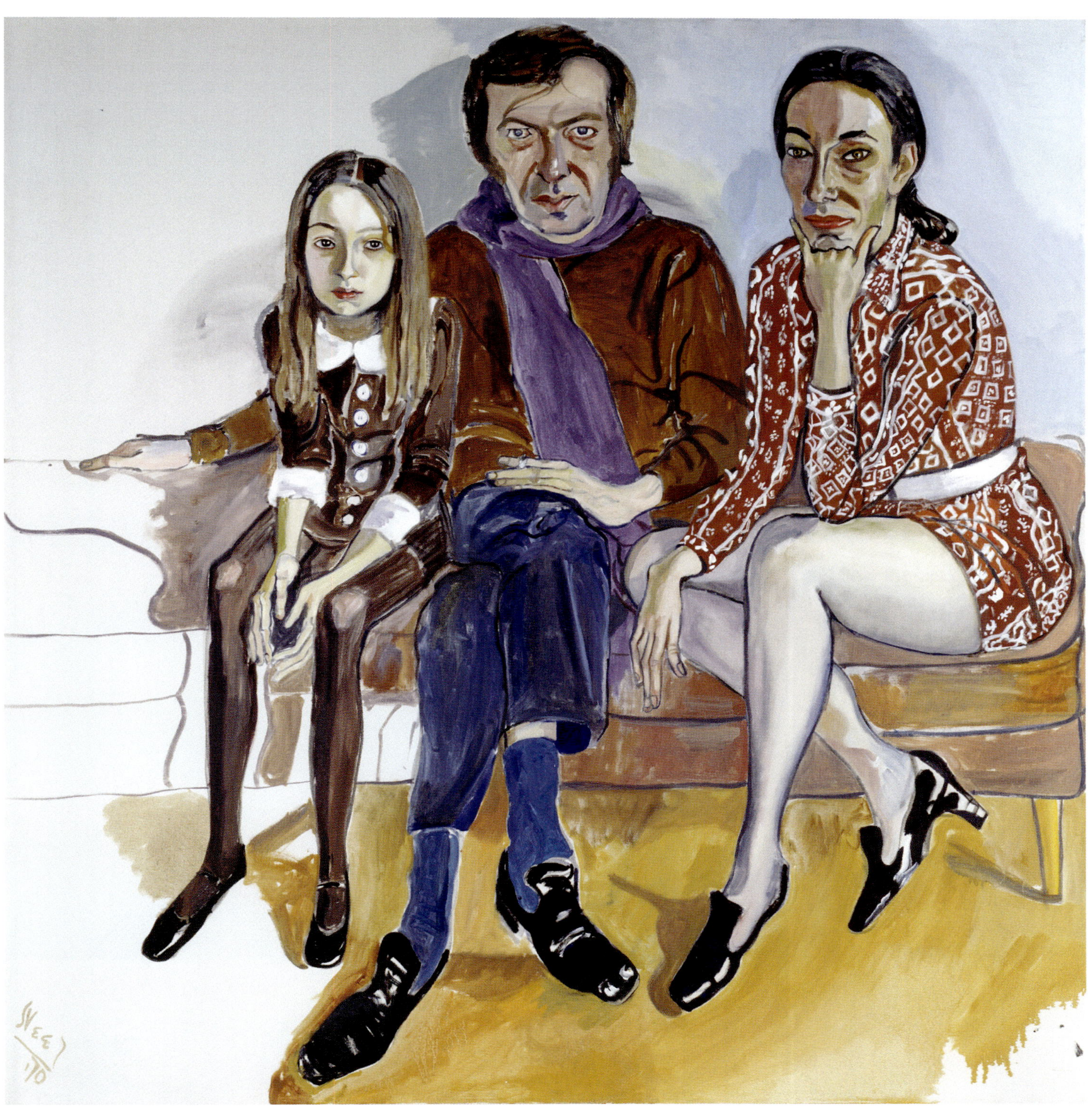

ROBERT RAUSCHENBERG | American, 1925–2008
Sor Aqua (Venetian), 1973
Wood, metal, rope, glass jug, and
water-filled bathtub
118 x 118 x 41 in. (299.7 x 299.7 x 104.1 cm)
Museum purchase funded by
the Caroline Wiess Law Foundation
2002.4.A,.B

ALICE NEEL | American, 1900–1984
The Family (John Gruen, Jane Wilson and Julia), 1970
Oil on canvas
Canvas: 60 1/4 x 58 in. (153 x 147.3 cm)
Museum purchase funded by
the Caroline Wiess Law Accessions
Endowment Fund
2011.224

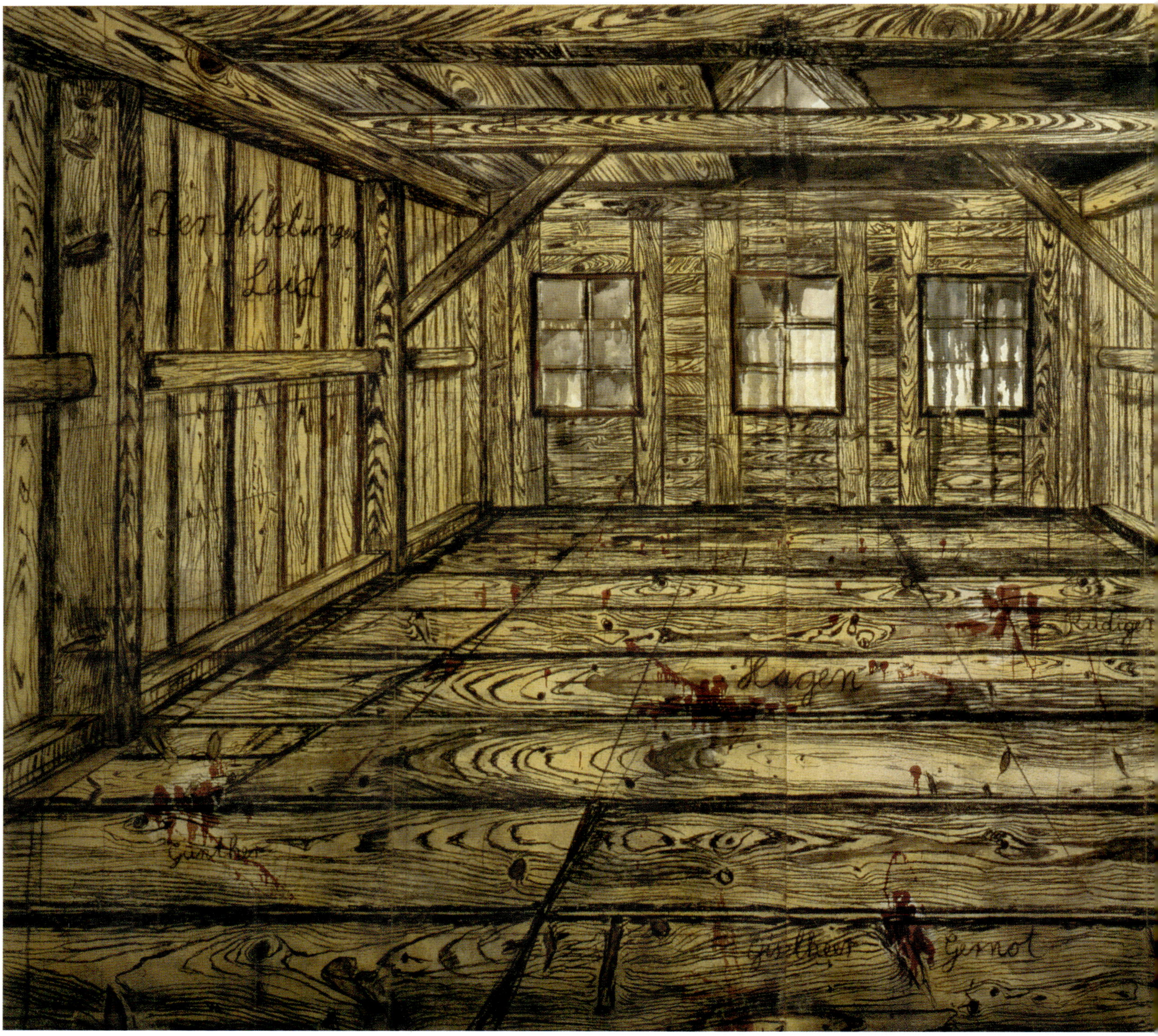

ANSELM KIEFER | German, born 1945
The Sorrow of the Nibelungen
[Der Nibelungen Leid], 1973
Oil on charcoal on burlap
118 1/4 x 173 1/4 in. (300.3 x 440 cm)
Museum purchase funded by
Caroline Wiess Law
98.52

RICHARD LONG | British, born 1945
Ring of Flint, 1996
English flint
Overall: 240 in. diameter (609.6 cm)
Museum purchase funded by
The Brown Foundation, Inc.
97.167.1

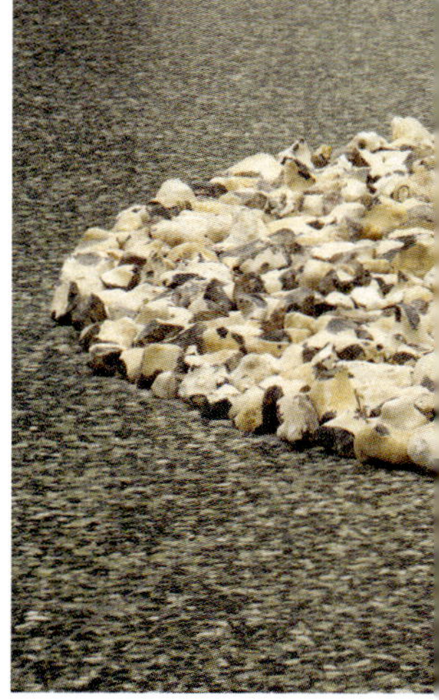

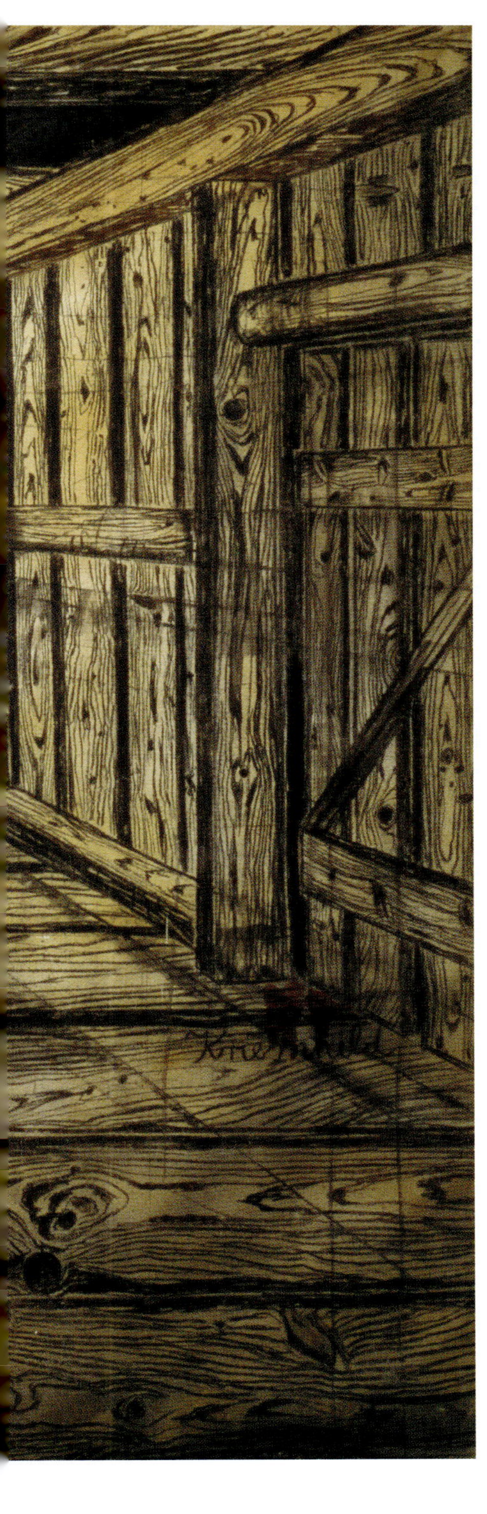

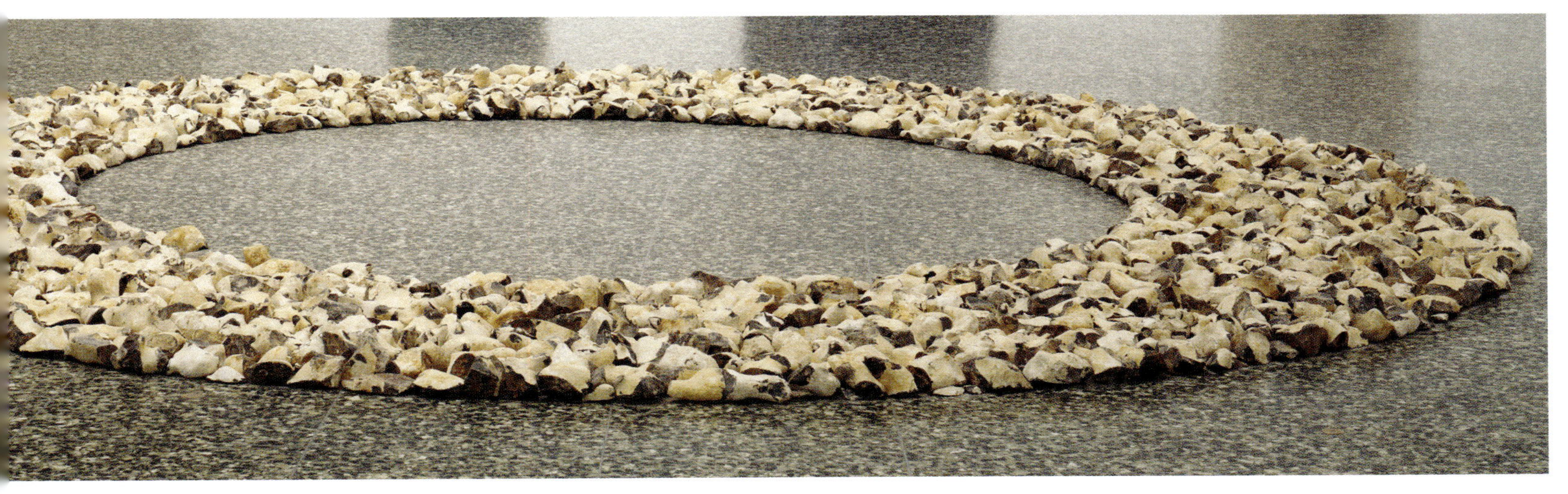

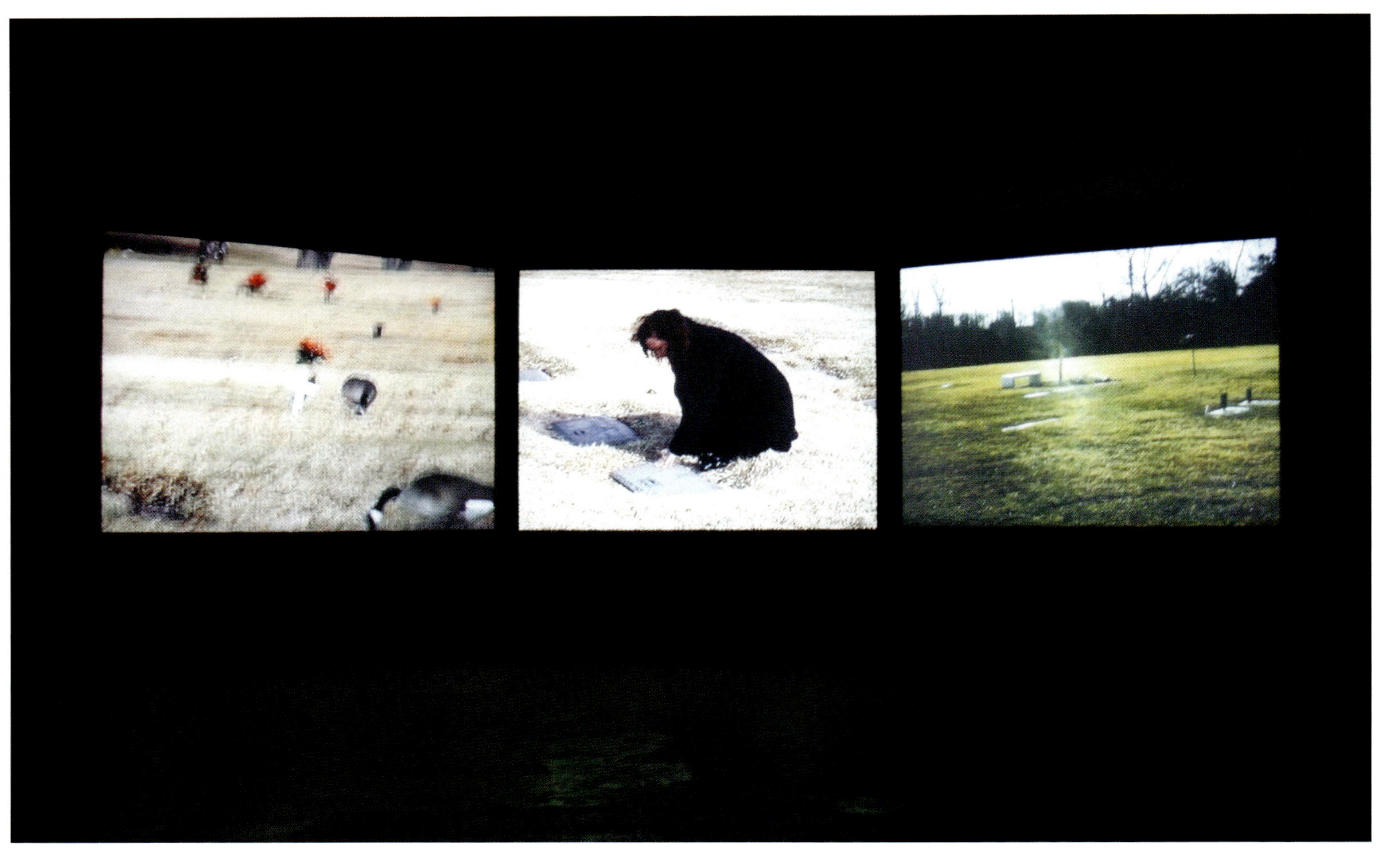

NAN GOLDIN | American, born 1953
Sisters, Saints, and Sibyls, 2004
39 minutes, 3-screen DVD projection
40 min. multi-media 3-screen projection,
with 18 tracks of sound
Joint acquisition of The Museum of Fine Arts,
Houston, and the Solomon R. Guggenheim
Foundation, funded by Nina and Michael Zilkha
in honor of Frances and Peter C. Marzio
2007.495.A–.C

YINKA SHONIBARE | English, born 1962
The Sleep of Reason Produces Monsters (Africa), 2008
Chromogenic print mounted on aluminum, ed. #3/5
Image: 72 x 49 1/2 in. (182.9 x 125.7 cm)
Museum purchase funded by Cecily E. Horton; the Caroline Wiess Law
Accessions Endowment Fund; bequest of Edward R. Broida and
Eva K. Kitchen, both by exchange; Bettie Cartwright; Chris Urbanczyk,
with matching funds provided by Chevron; and the Wolff-Toomin
Foundation in memory of Edward Oppenheimer, Jr. and
Adolph Horwitz, and in honor of Lester Marks
2012.339

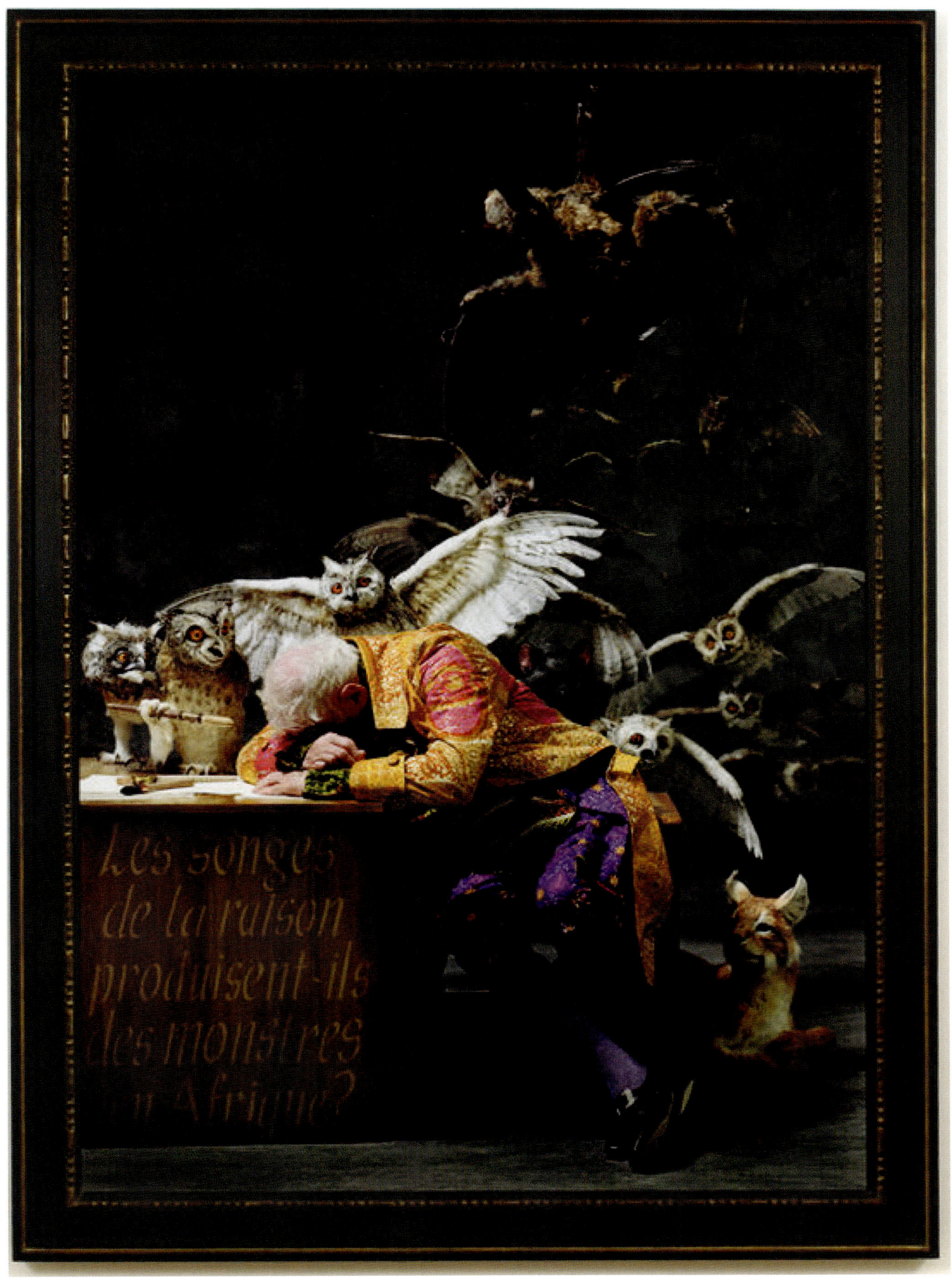

Les songes
de la raison
produisent-ils
des monstres
en Afrique?

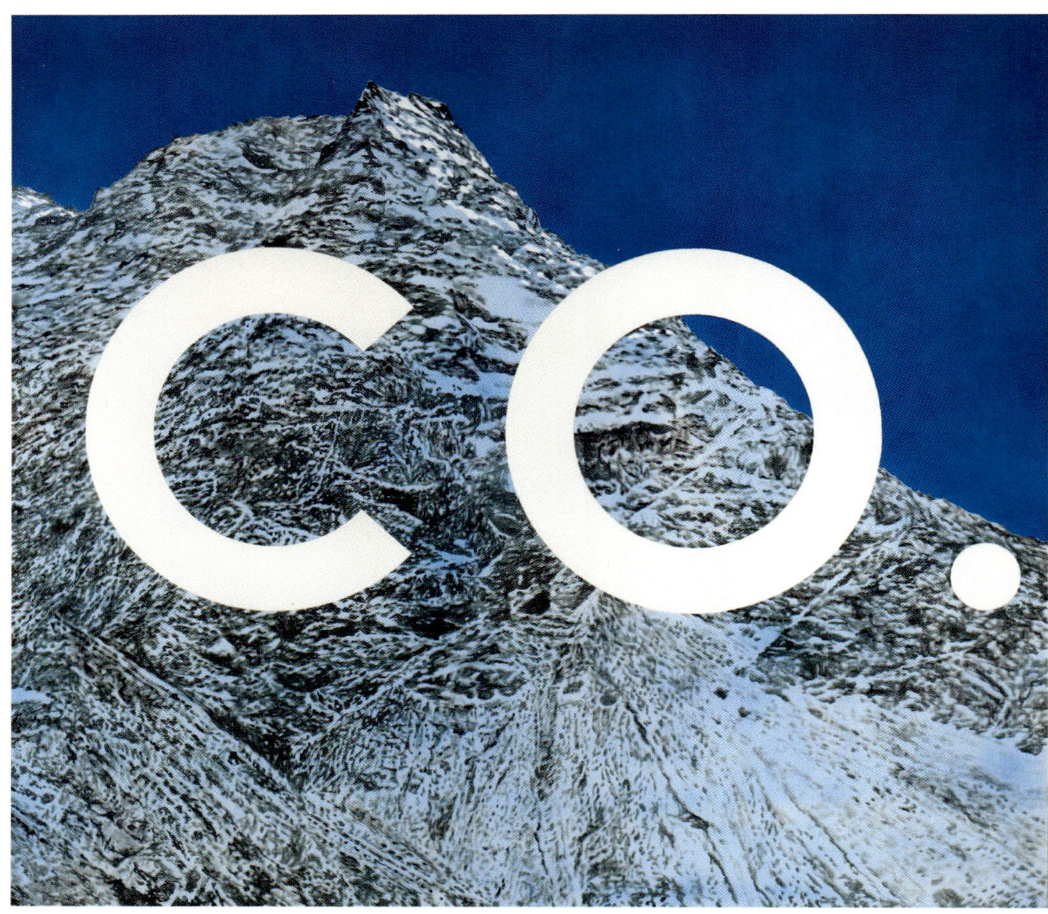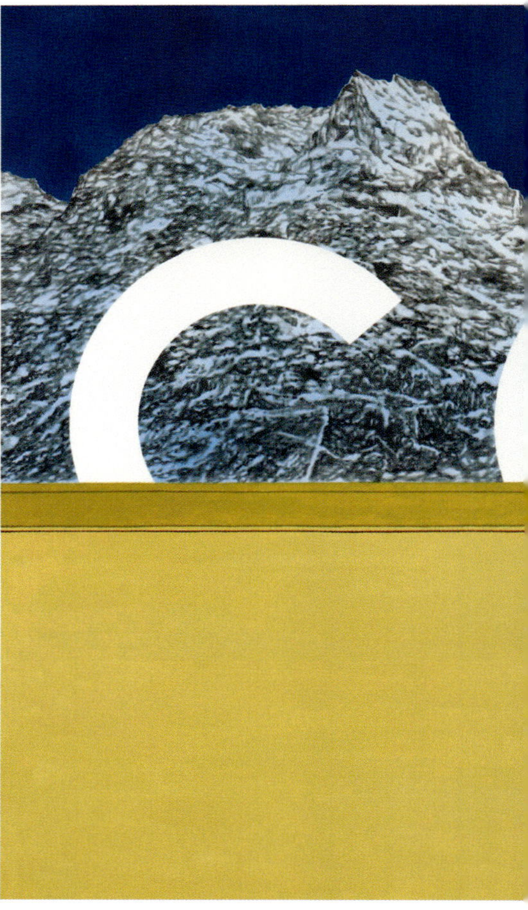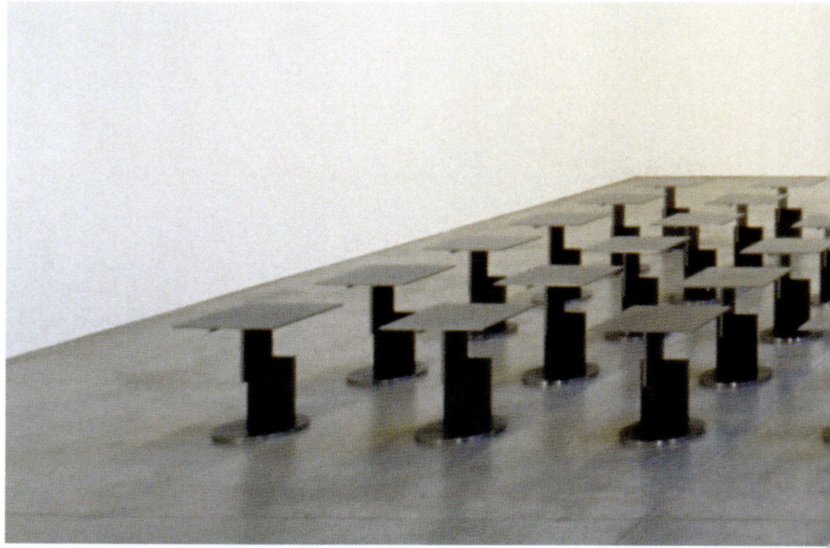

ED RUSCHA | American, born 1937
Untitled (#1) and *Untitled (#2)*, 2007–8
Acrylic on canvas
Each: 64 x 72 in. (162.6 x 182.9 cm)
Museum purchase funded by the
Caroline Wiess Law Accessions Endowment Fund
2008.110.A,.B

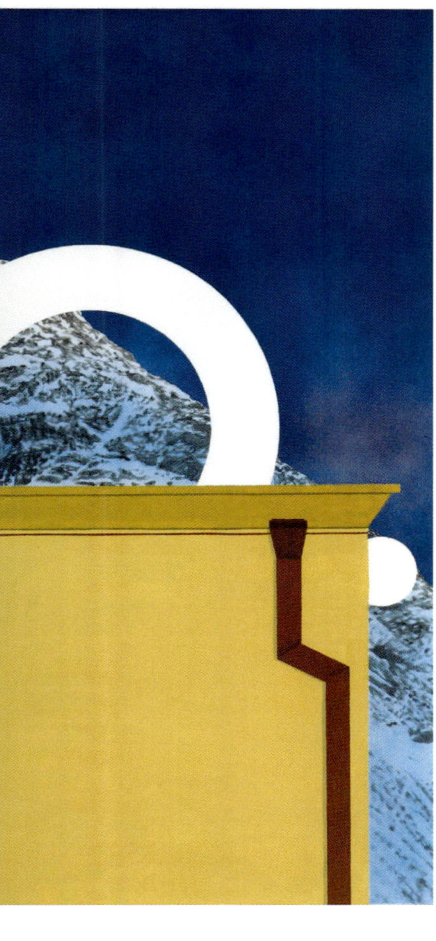

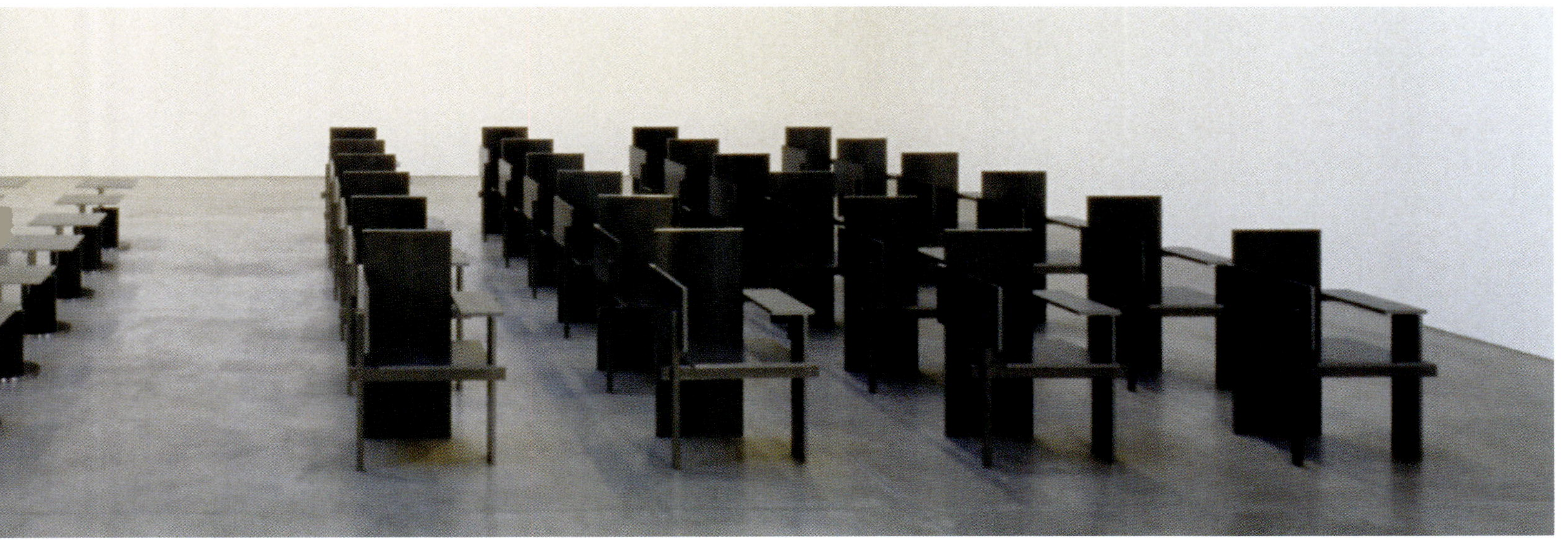

SHERRIE LEVINE | American, born 1947
and **JOOST VAN OSS** | Dutch, born 1956
"Sculpture II" and *"Sculpture III,"* 1999
Rolled steel: 24 chairs and 24 tables
Overall installation variable
Each chair: 42 x 30 x 23 in. (106.7 x 76.2 x 58.4 cm)
Each table: 24 x 20 x 20 in. (61 x 50.8 x 50.8 cm)
Gift of Jeanne and Michael Klein
2005.1401

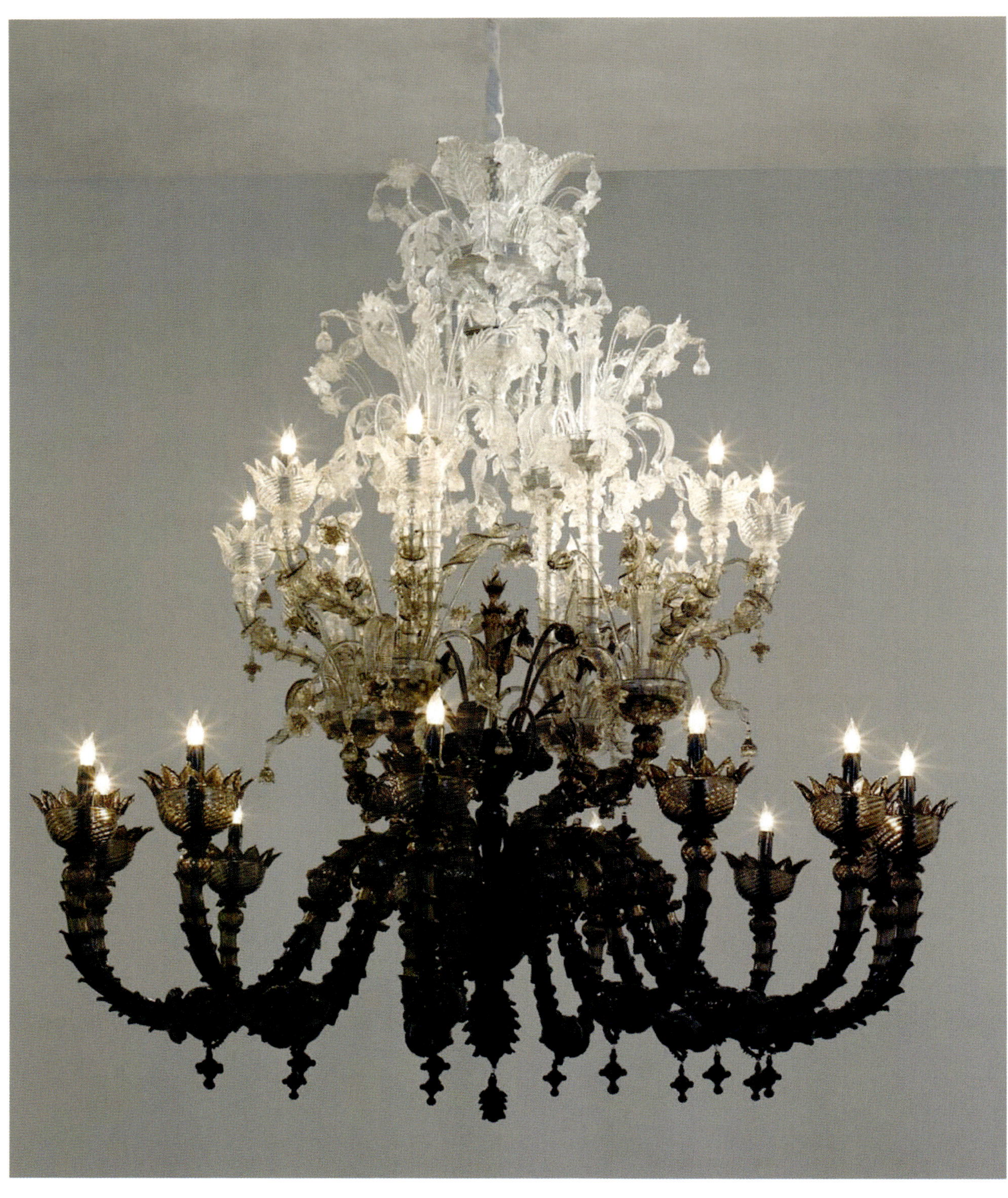

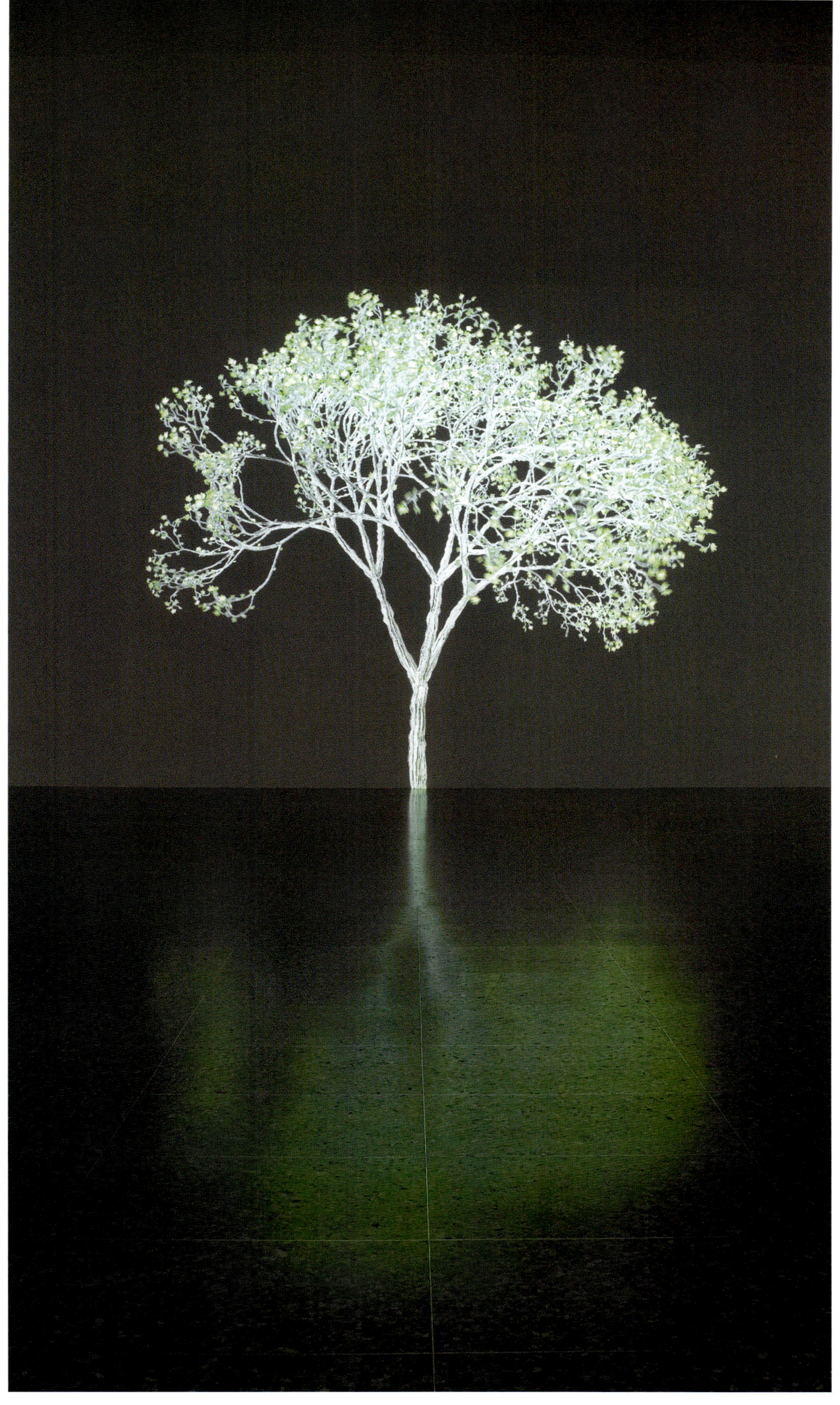

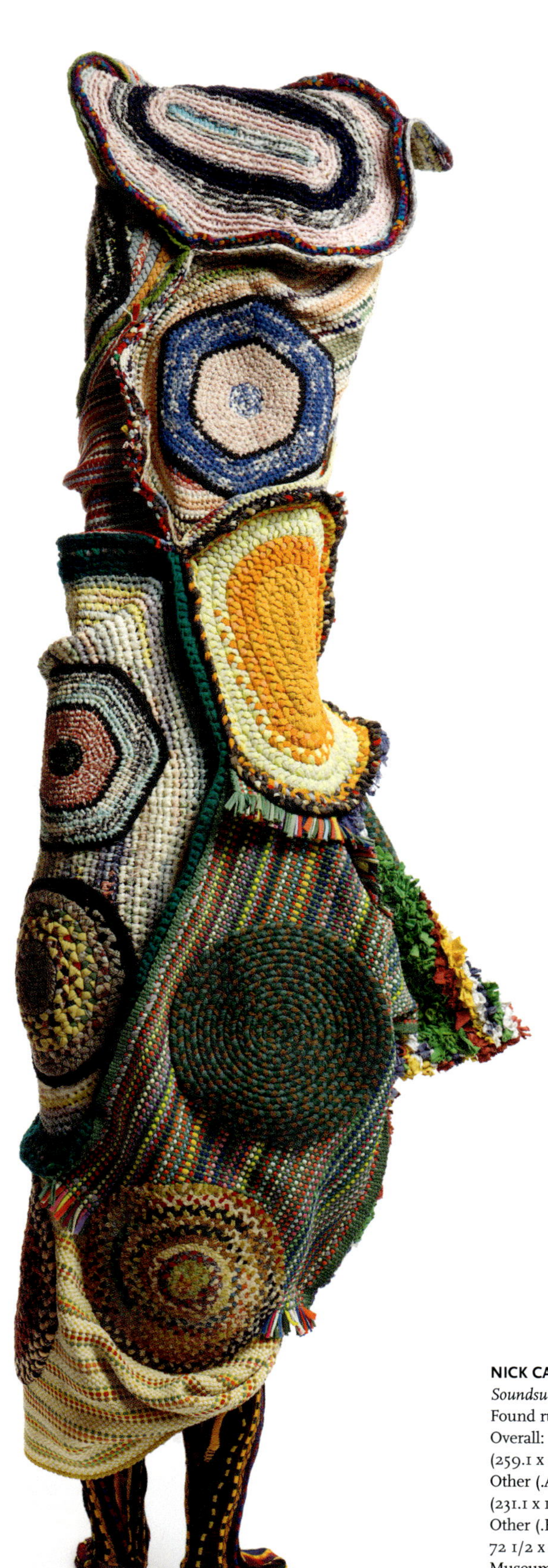

NICK CAVE | American, born 1959
Soundsuit, 2011
Found rugs and mixed media
Overall: 102 x 40 x 23 in.
(259.1 x 101.6 x 58.4 cm)
Other (.A–rug suit): 91 x 40 x 23 in.
(231.1 x 101.6 x 58.4 cm)
Other (.B–mannequin & leggings):
72 1/2 x 24 x 18 in. (184.2 x 61 x 45.7 cm)
Museum purchase funded by
Barbara and Michael Gamson
in memory of Peter C. Marzio
2011. 870

DO HO SUH | Korean, born 1962
Karma, 2003
Urethane paint on fiberglass and resin
Overall: 153 1/2 x 118 x 291 in.
(389.9 x 299.7 x 739.1 cm)
Museum purchase with funds provided by
the Caroline Wiess Law Accessions
Endowment Fund
2008.536

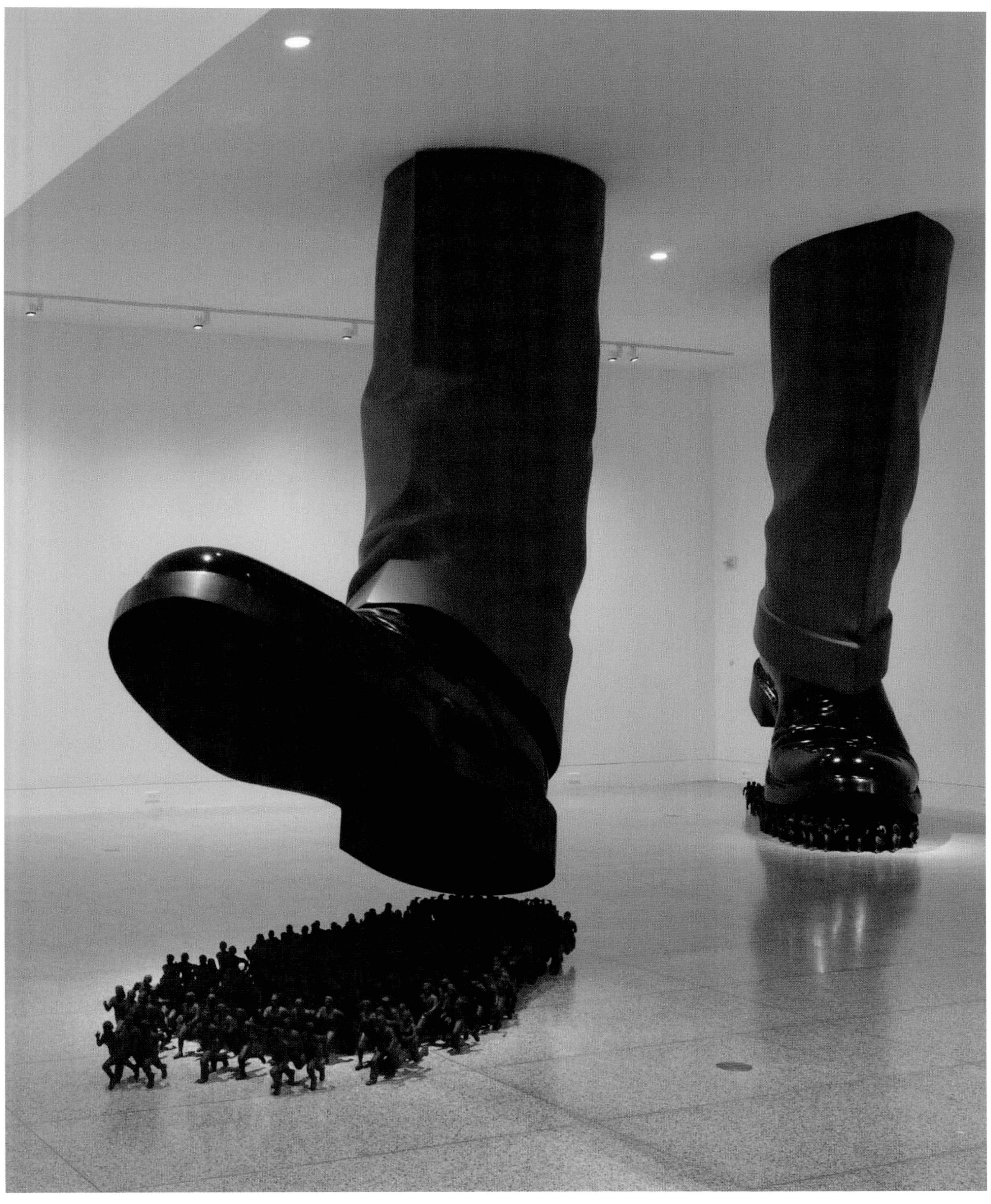

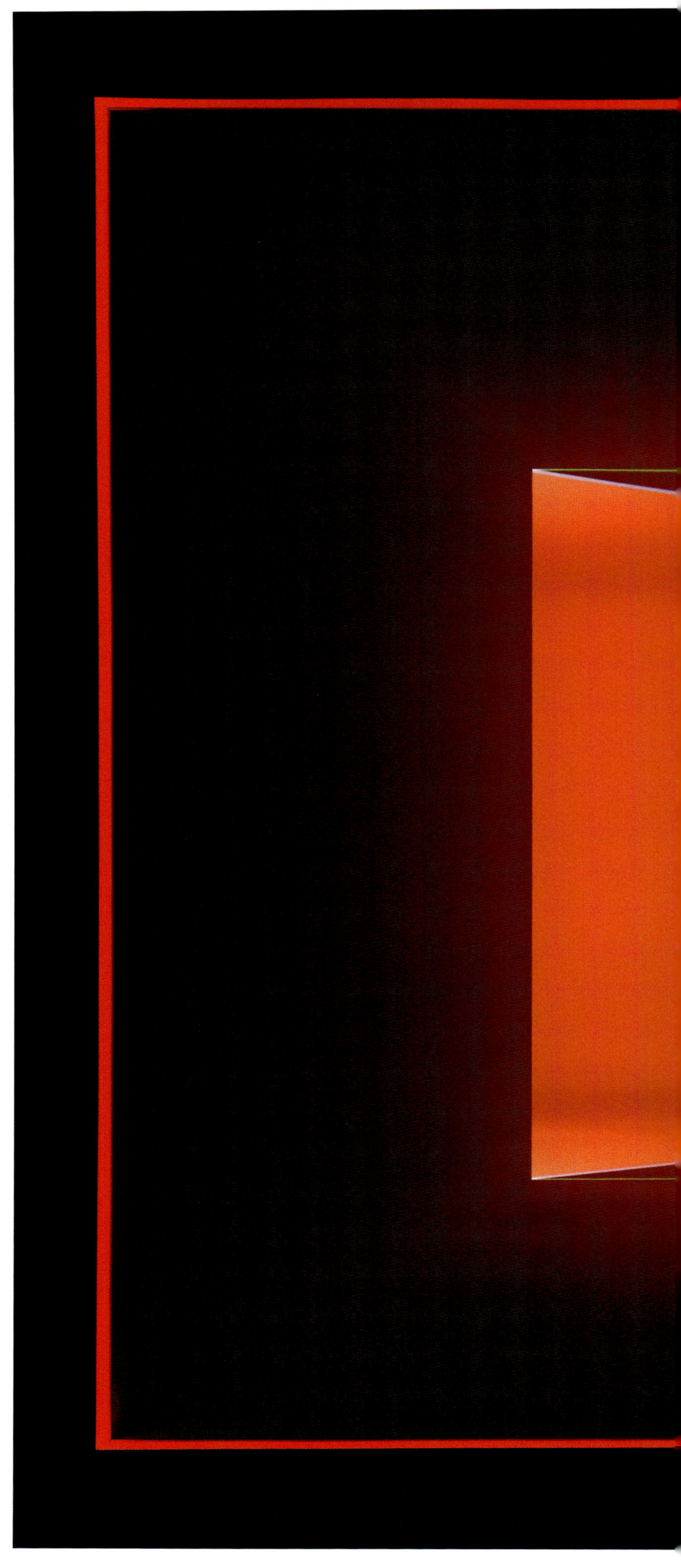

JAMES TURRELL | American, born 1943
Caper, Salmon to White: Wedgework, 2000
LED and fluorescent light
Museum purchase funded by the estate of
Isabel B. Wilson in memory of Peter C. Marzio
2011.646

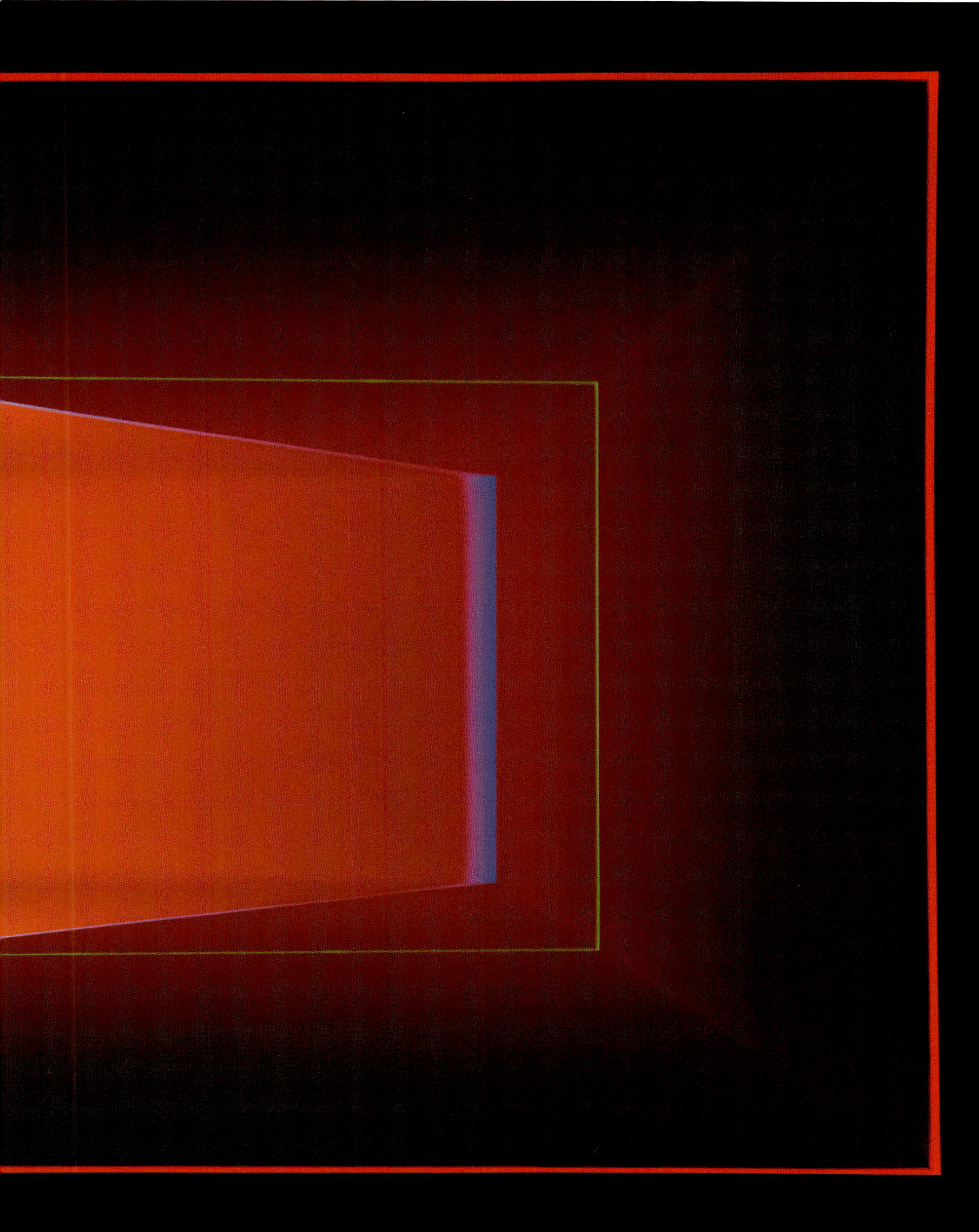

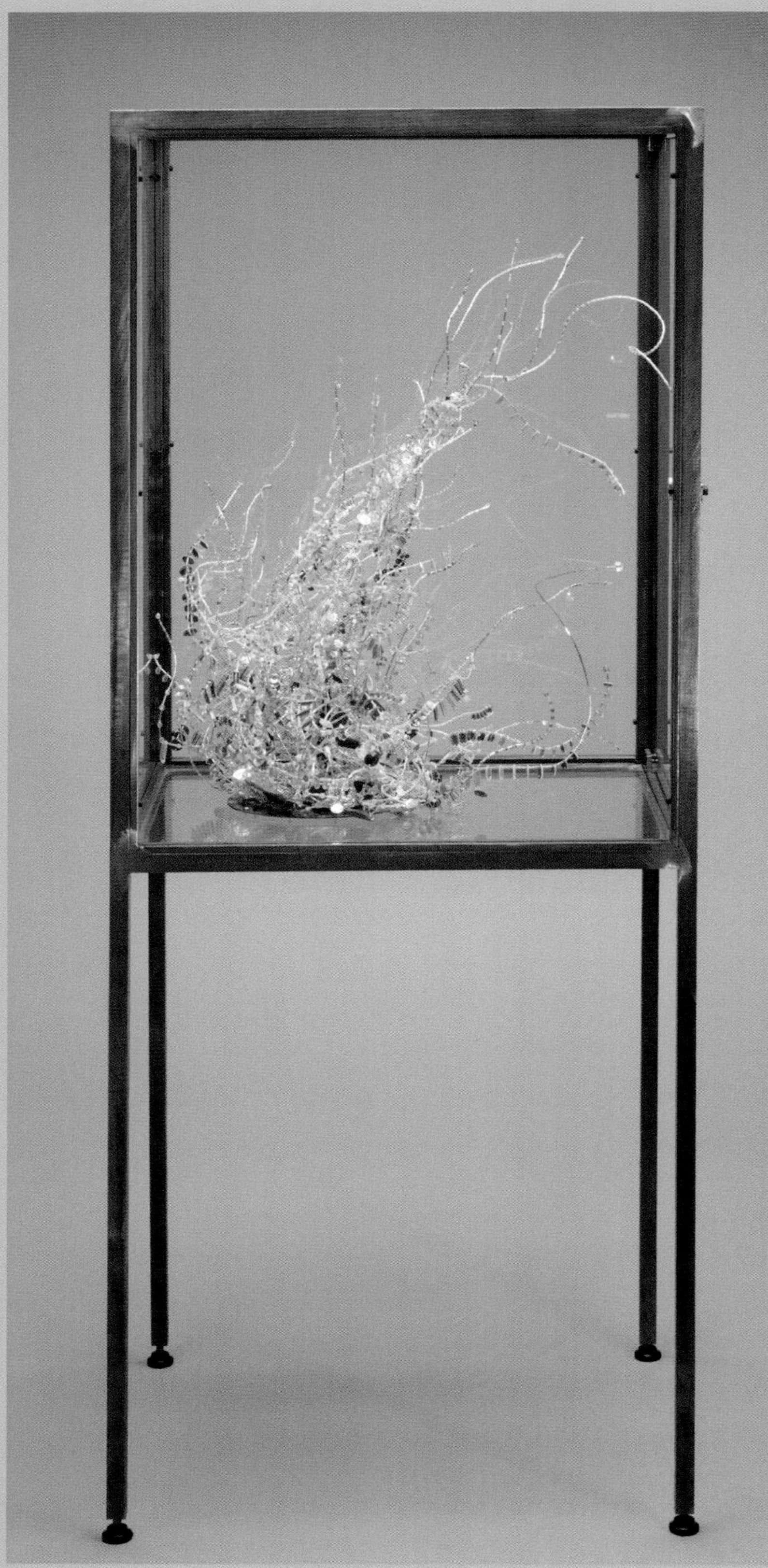

LIGHT AND COLOR

In the second half of the seventeenth century, Isaac Newton proved through a series of experiments that white light can be broken down into a full spectrum of colors, and that the reverse is possible as well. Two hundred years later, light took on a new role in art with the invention of photography, as light on film can be both the means of making the artwork and its subject.

The interdependent relationship of light and color and the roles they play in art continue to fascinate modern and contemporary artists. For some, such as the painter Hans Hofmann, color could create light in his canvases. For others, including Carlos Cruz-Diez and James Turrell, light itself becomes a palpable medium.

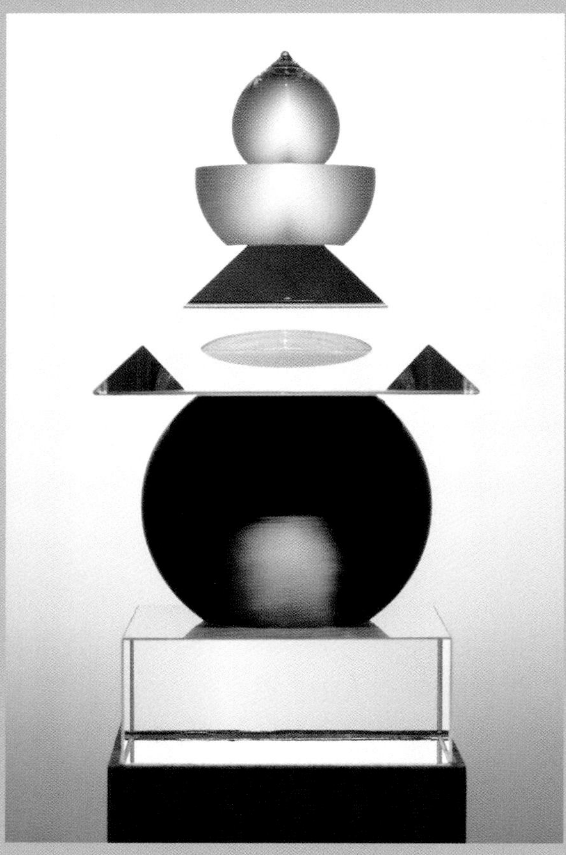

LEE BUL | Korean, born 1964
Untitled, 2004
Wire, crystal, beads and mixed media
25 x 26 1/2 x 20 in. (63.5 x 67.3 x 50.8 cm)
Overall with vitrine: 59 3/4 x 19 3/4 x 23 5/8 in. (151.8 x 50.2 x 59.9 cm)
Museum purchase funded by Mrs. Chong-Ok Matthews
2004.206

HIROSHI SUGIMOTO | Japanese, born 1948
Pagoda 409, Tyrrhenian Sea, Priano, 1994, 2011
From the series *Five Elements*
Optical glass (low-dispersion photographic lens glass), black-and-white film
(gelatin silver on polyester film toned with gold chloride), unknown hyper-clear
silicone adhesive, cypress wood pedestal with black finished steel base
Overall: 6 x 3 x 3 in. (15.2 x 7.6 x 7.6 cm)
Museum purchase funded by the Friends of Asian Art, Chris Urbanczyk,
and Chevron
2012.262

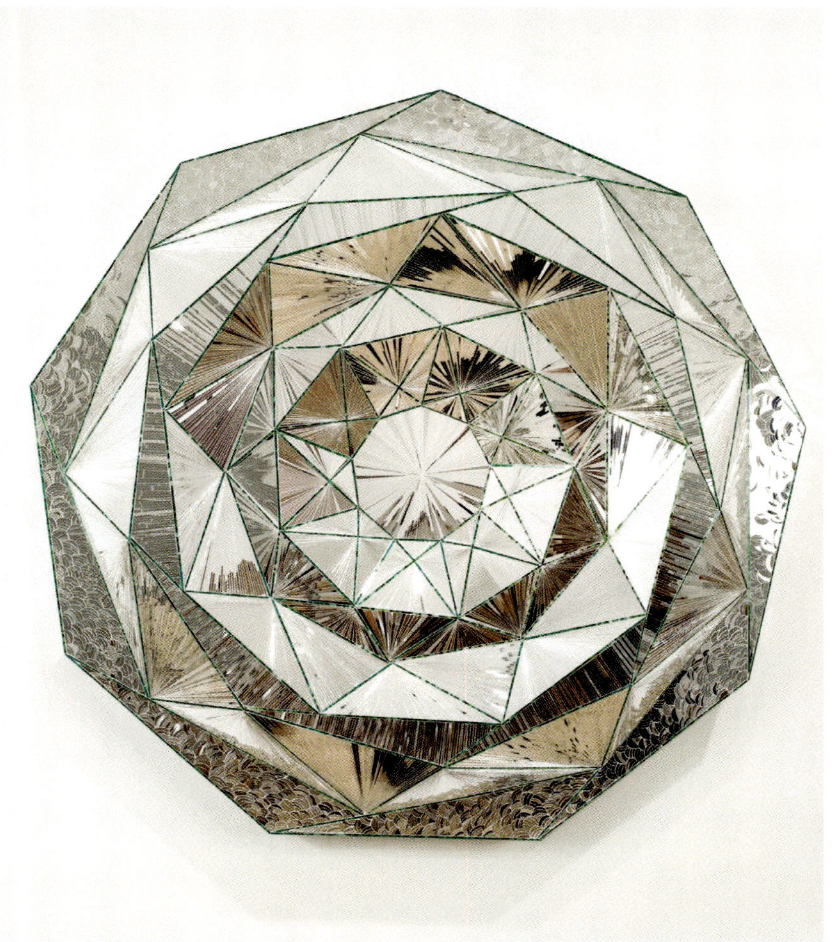

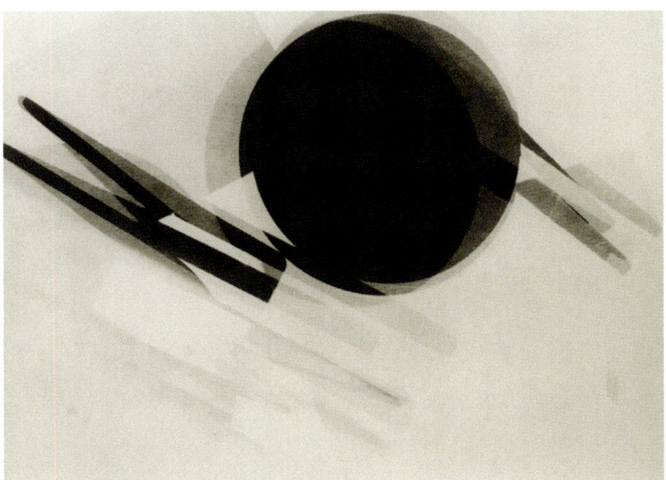

MONIR FARMANFARMAIAN | Iranian, born 1923/24
Nonagon, 2011
Mirror and reverse glass painting on plaster and wood
Overall: 45 5/8 x 46 1/2 x 5 1/2 in. (115.9 x 118.1 x 14 cm)
Museum purchase funded by the Caroline Wiess Law
Accessions Endowment Fund
2013.97

JAMES TURRELL | American, born 1943
Meeting, 1989–90
From: *First Light*
Printed by Peter Kneubühler, Zürich, Switzerland, Published by
Peter Blum Edition/Blumarts, Inc., New York
Aquatint
Plate: 39 3/16 x 27 5/16 in. (99.5 x 69.4 cm)
Sheet: 42 7/16 x 29 13/16 in. (107.8 x 75.7 cm)
The Peter Blum Edition Archive, 1980–1994,
Museum purchase funded by the Alice Pratt Brown Museum Fund
96.39.1

LÁSZLÓ MOHOLY-NAGY | American, born Austria-Hungary, 1895–1946
Fotogramm, 1926
Gelatin silver print, photogram
Image: 8 5/16 x 11 1/16 in. (21.1 x 28.1 cm) Sheet: 8 3/4 x 11 9/16 in. (22.3 x 29.4 cm)
Museum purchase funded by the Caroline Wiess Law Accessions
Endowment Fund, The Manfred Heiting Collection
2002.1691

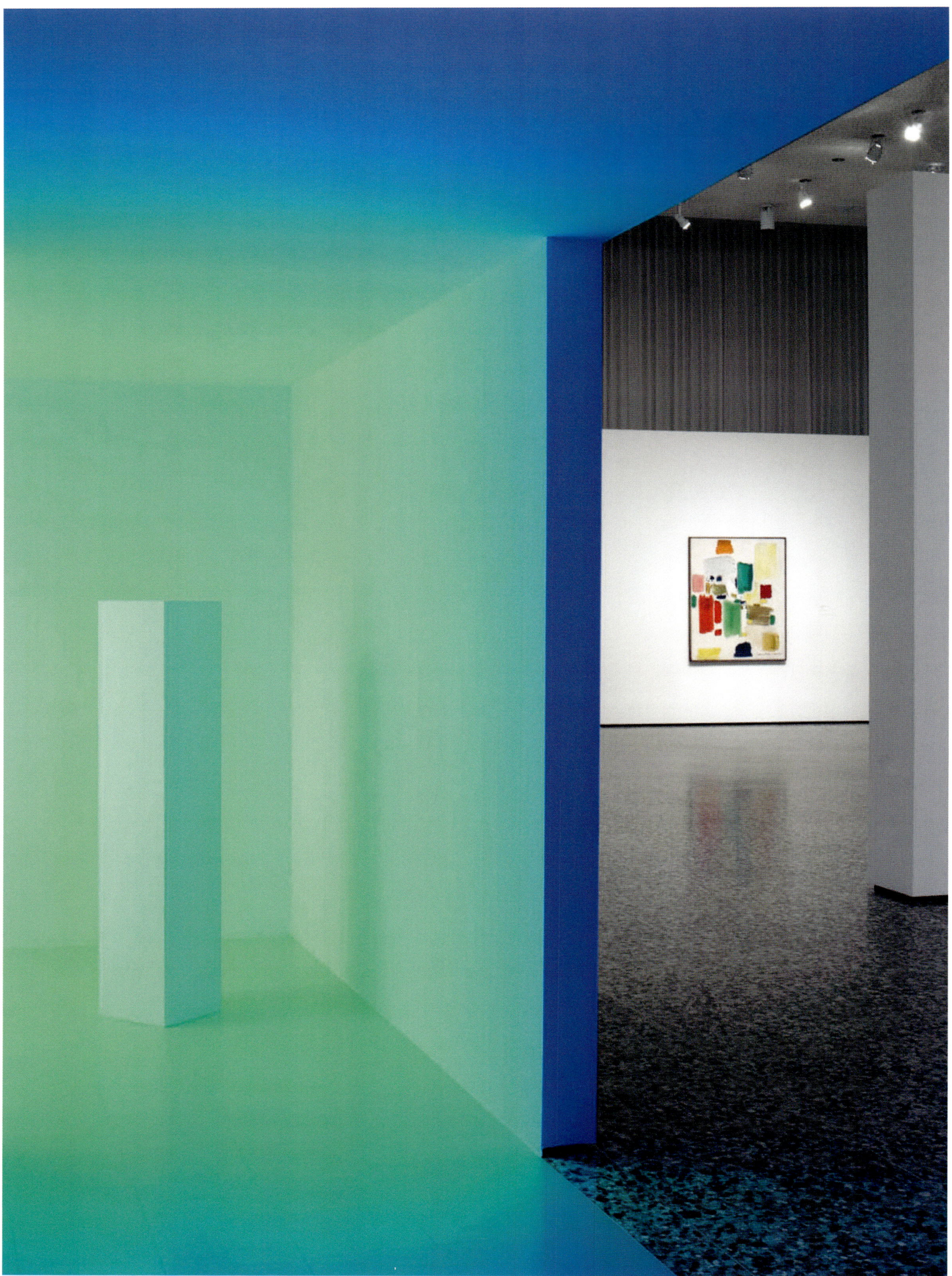

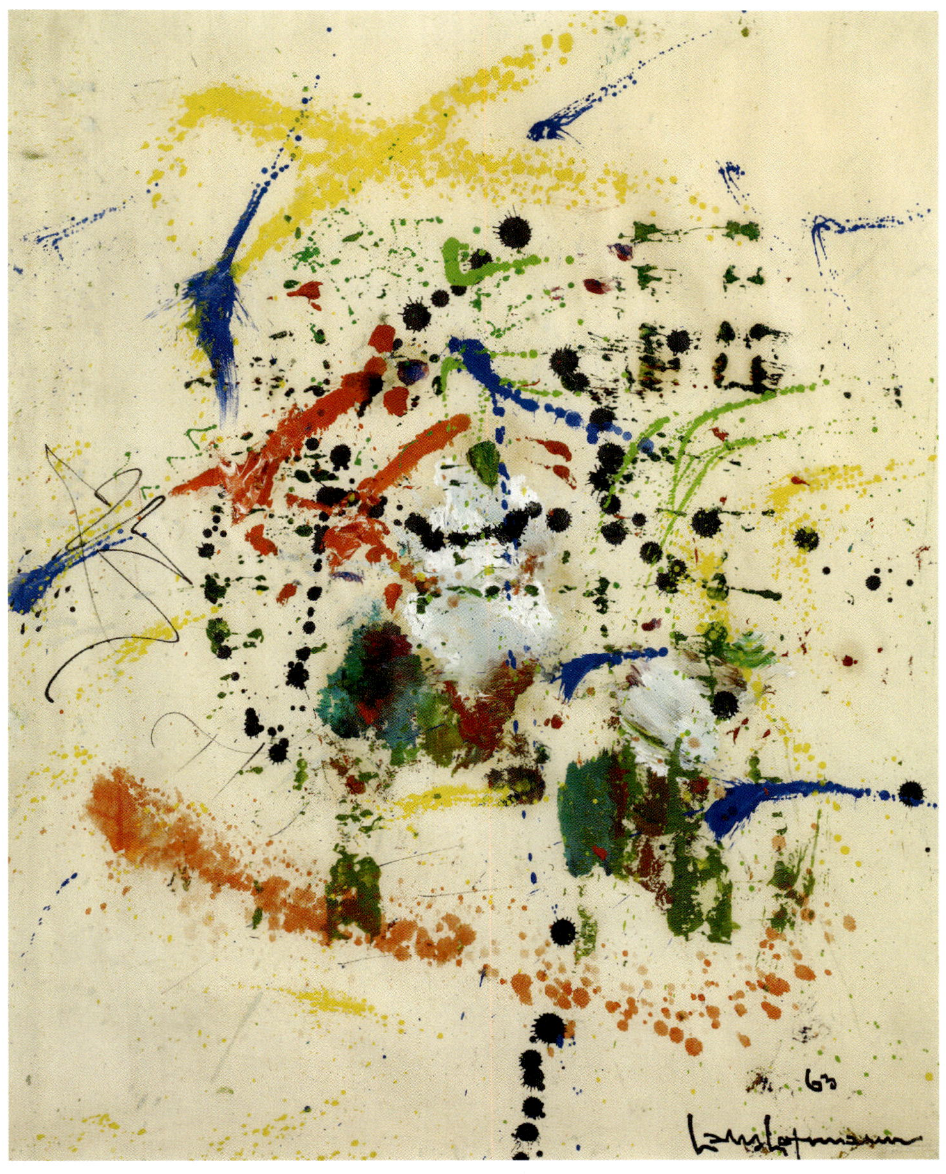

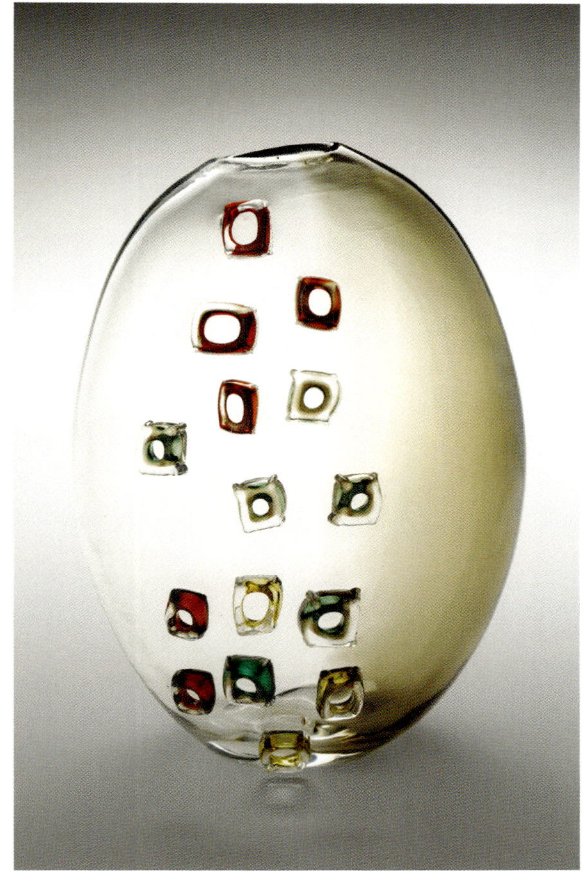

Installation view of *Color into Light: Selections from the MFAH Collection,* presented at the Museum in 2008.

HANS HOFMANN | American, born Germany, **1880–1966**
Untitled, 1963
Oil on paper
Sheet: 29 x 22 3/4 in. (73.7 x 57.8 cm)
Gift of Isabel B. Wilson
2004.1472

ALFREDO BARBINI | Italian, born 1912
Vase, c. 1965
Blown glass
11 1/4 x 8 x 7 in. (28.6 x 20.3 x 17.8 cm)
Gift of Curtis B. Wolff
2006.1343

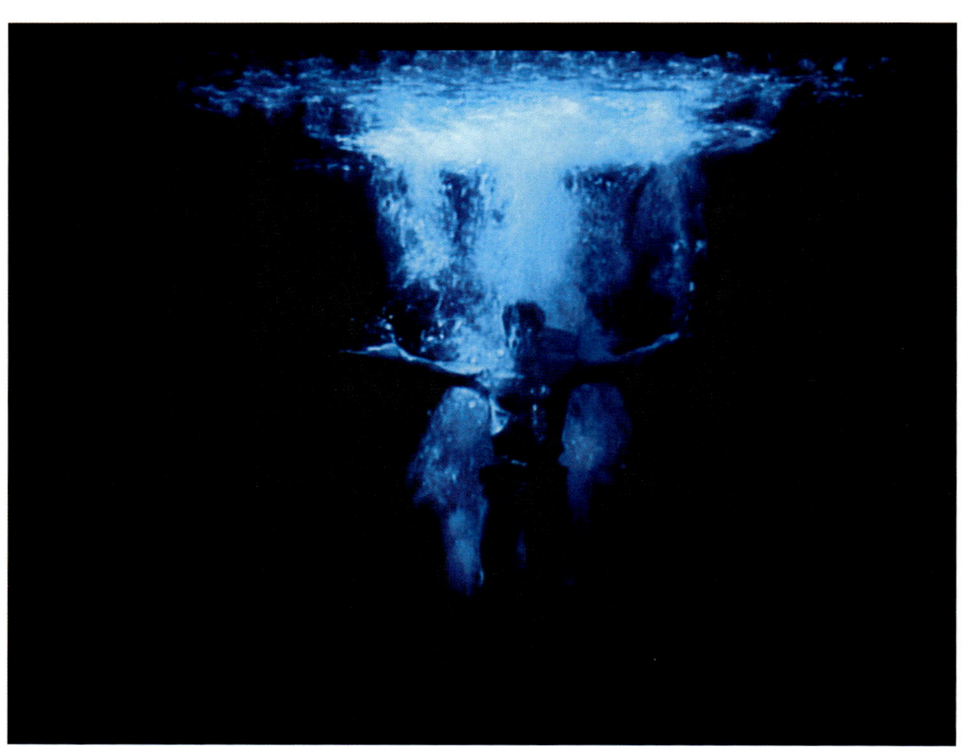

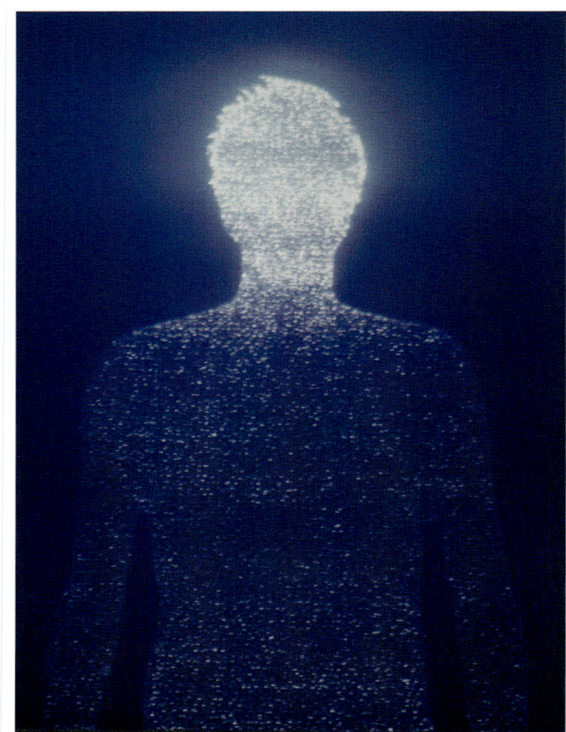

BILL VIOLA | American, born 1951
Ascension, 2000
Single-channel color video and stereo-sound installation,
10-minute continuous loop
Video (color, sound), 10 minutes, edition 3/3
Museum purchase funded by Nina and Michael Zilkha
in honor of Fayez Sarofim on the occasion of their tenth
wedding anniversary
2001.152

CHRISTOPHER BUCKLOW | British, born 1957
Guest, 25,000 Solar Images [AF], 5:03 pm, 10th October 1995, 1995
Silver dye bleach print, photogram
Sheet (visible): 38 1/2 x 28 3/4 in. (97.8 x 73 cm)
Museum purchase funded by Photo Forum 2002,
The Manfred Heiting Collection
2002.2990

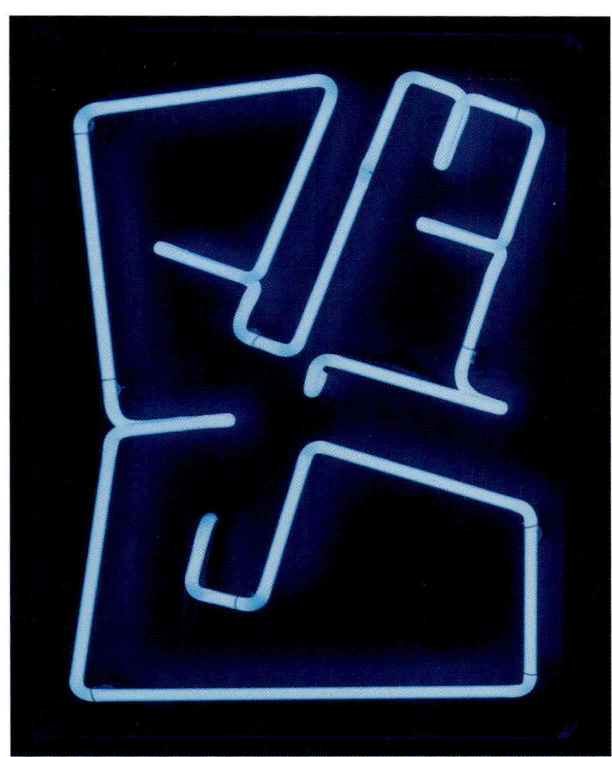

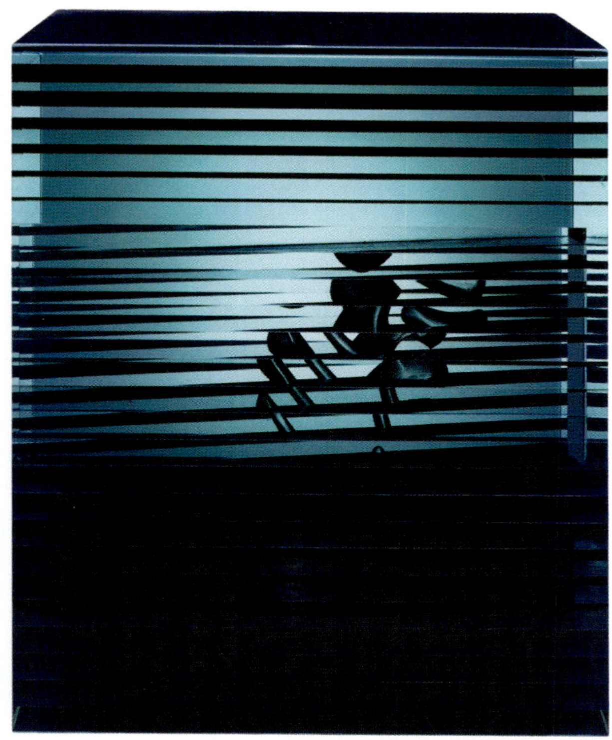

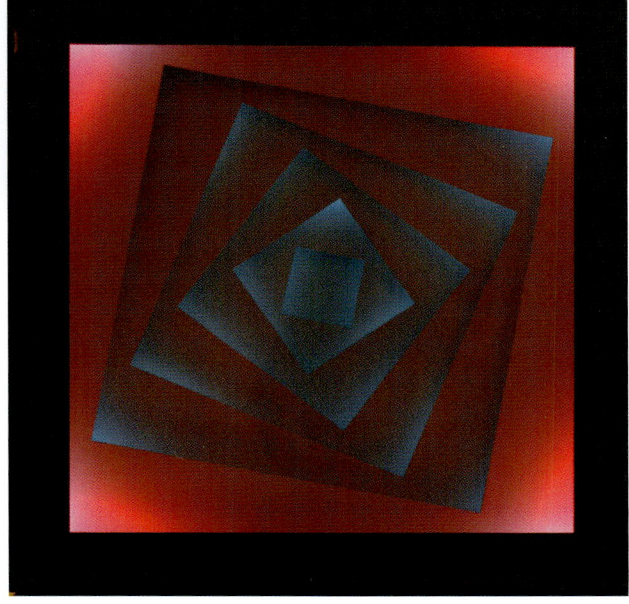

GYULA KOSICE | Argentinean, born 1924
Estructura lumínica Madí 6
[Luminescent Madí Structure No. 6], 1946
Neon gas, Plexiglas, and wood box
23 5/8 x 19 5/8 x 4 3/4 in. (60 x 50 x 12 cm)
Museum purchase funded by
the Caroline Wiess Law Accessions
Endowment Fund
2004.1655

BOHUMIL ELIÁS | Czech, 1937–2005
Inhabitant of Blue, 2002
Overall: 10 3/8 x 8 3/4 x 7 1/8 in. (26.4 x 22.2 x 18.1 cm)
Gift of Barry Friedman, Ltd.
2002.449

GREGORIO VARDÁNEGA | Argentinean, 1923–2007
Espaces Chromatiques Carrées en Spirale
[Chromatic Spaces Turning in a Spiral], 1968
Plexiglas, light bulbs, and motor
Overall: 39 3/4 x 39 3/8 x 18 1/8 in. (101 x 100 x 46 cm)
Museum purchase funded by the
Latin Maecenas
2010.173

LATIN AMERICAN ART

MARI CARMEN RAMÍREZ

Since the establishment of the Latin American Art Department and the International Center for the Arts of the Americas, in 2001, the Museum of Fine Arts, Houston, has been systematically and aggressively collecting art from Mexico, Central and South America, and the Caribbean, as well as works by Latino artists in the United States. During this period, more than 547 works in all media have been acquired through gifts or purchases. These works complement existing holdings in photography, works on paper, decorative arts, painting, and sculpture, some of which entered the Museum as early as the 1930s. Taken together, the total number of works in the Latin American art collection, as of the press date of this publication, numbers 1,941.

With the exception of notable examples of the production of early-twentieth-century masters such as David Alfaro Siqueiros, Manuel Álvarez Bravo, Xul Solar, Armando Reverón, Joaquín Torres-García, Matta, and Maria Martins, the general strength of the Latin American art holdings lies in post-World War II artists and movements. At least three conceptual and/or stylistic nuclei can be detected within this time period: 1, Constructive art from Argentina, Brazil, Venezuela, and Uruguay; 2, 1960s Neo-Figurative and Pop Art tendencies; and, 3, contemporary art and new media.

The cornerstone of the Museum's Constructive art holdings is the Adolpho Leirner Collection of Brazilian Constructive Art, acquired in 2007. This world-renowned collection consists of more than one hundred extraordinary examples by Concrete and Neo-Concrete groups that flourished in São Paulo and Rio de Janeiro between 1950 and 1965. Featured prominently in the Leirner Collection is the innovative production by the leaders of these two groups—Waldemar Cordeiro, Lygia Clark, and Hélio Oiticica—as well as a representation of works by independent artists such as Mira Schendel, Alfredo Volpi, and Milton Dacosta, among many others. Expanding on these holdings, there are iconic examples of the Argentinean Madí Art Group (Gyula Kosice and Rhod Rothfuss), the School of the South (Gonzalo Fonseca, Julio Alpuy, Francisco Matto, and José Gurvich), Gego (Gertrud Goldschmidt), and a large ensemble of light- and water-activated Kinetic works by Paris-based Latin American artists (Jesús Soto, Carlos Cruz-Diez, Julio Le Parc, Gregorio Vardánega, Marta Boto, Antonio Asís, and Luis Tomasello). Gyula Kosice's *La ciudad hidroespacial* [Hydrospatial City] (1946–72) stands out as a highlight of the Kinetic art ensemble.

The iconoclastic production of the 1960s, in turn, is represented by experimental sculpture and painting by such innovators as Antonio Berni, León Ferrari, Luis Felipe Noé, Alberto Heredia, Luis Benedit, Víctor Grippo, Beatriz González, and Juan Carlos Distéfano. In contemporary art and new media, the Museum has pursued a vast array of large-scale sculptures and installations by cutting-edge artists such as Cildo Meireles, Tunga, Alfredo Jaar, Regina Silveira, Carmela Gros, Oscar Muñoz, Teresa Margolles, Miguel Angel Ríos, Daniel Joseph Martinez, Gabriel de la Mora, Liliana Porter, and Carlos Runcie Tanaka.

The Latin American Art Department has also pursued innovative partnerships that expanded the scope of the permanent collections. In 2011, the Museum established an accessions fund with Fundación Gego, Caracas, to acquire works from Venezuela, Colombia, Central America, and the Caribbean. The Caribbean Art Fund has allowed the Museum to gather a broad range of innovative works in all media by artists born in these countries after 1960. Among the artists are Roberto Obregón, José Gabriel Fernández, Juan Iribarren, Johana Calle, and Tanya Bruguera. Through the Caribbean Art Fund, the Museum has also made significant inroads in developing an outstanding collection of video installations by leading exponents of this medium, such as Javier Tellez, José Alejandro Restrepo, Miguel Angel Rojas, Magdalena Fernández, and Oscar Muñoz.

Further complementing the Museum's Latin American art collection is the Partners in Art Program. Through this initiative, the Museum has established multiyear partnerships with collectors and artists' estates that allow it to research, exhibit, and publish their holdings in exchange for managing, storing, caring for, and preserving them on a long-term basis. Productive collaborations have been formed with Fundación Gego, Caracas (2003–); Fundación Cruz-Diez, Houston (2008–); The Brillembourg Capriles Collection (2009); and, most recently, the Oscar Ascanio Estate (2011).

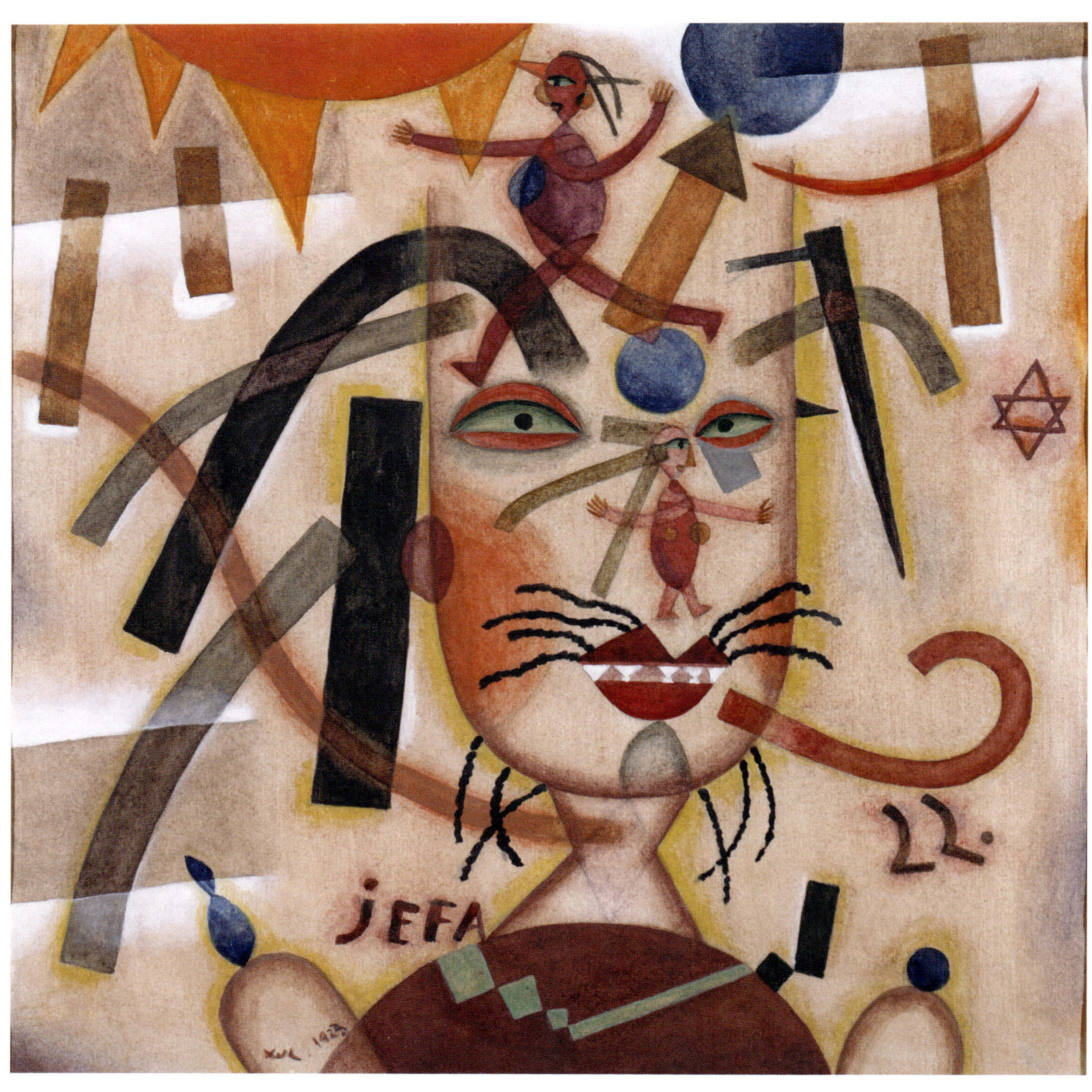

ALEJANDRO XUL SOLAR | Argentinean, 1887–1963
Jefa [Patroness], 1923
Watercolor on paper, set on cardboard
Sheet: 10 1/8 x 10 1/8 in. (25.7 x 25.7 cm)
Museum purchase funded by the 2005
Latin American Experience Gala and Auction
2005.343

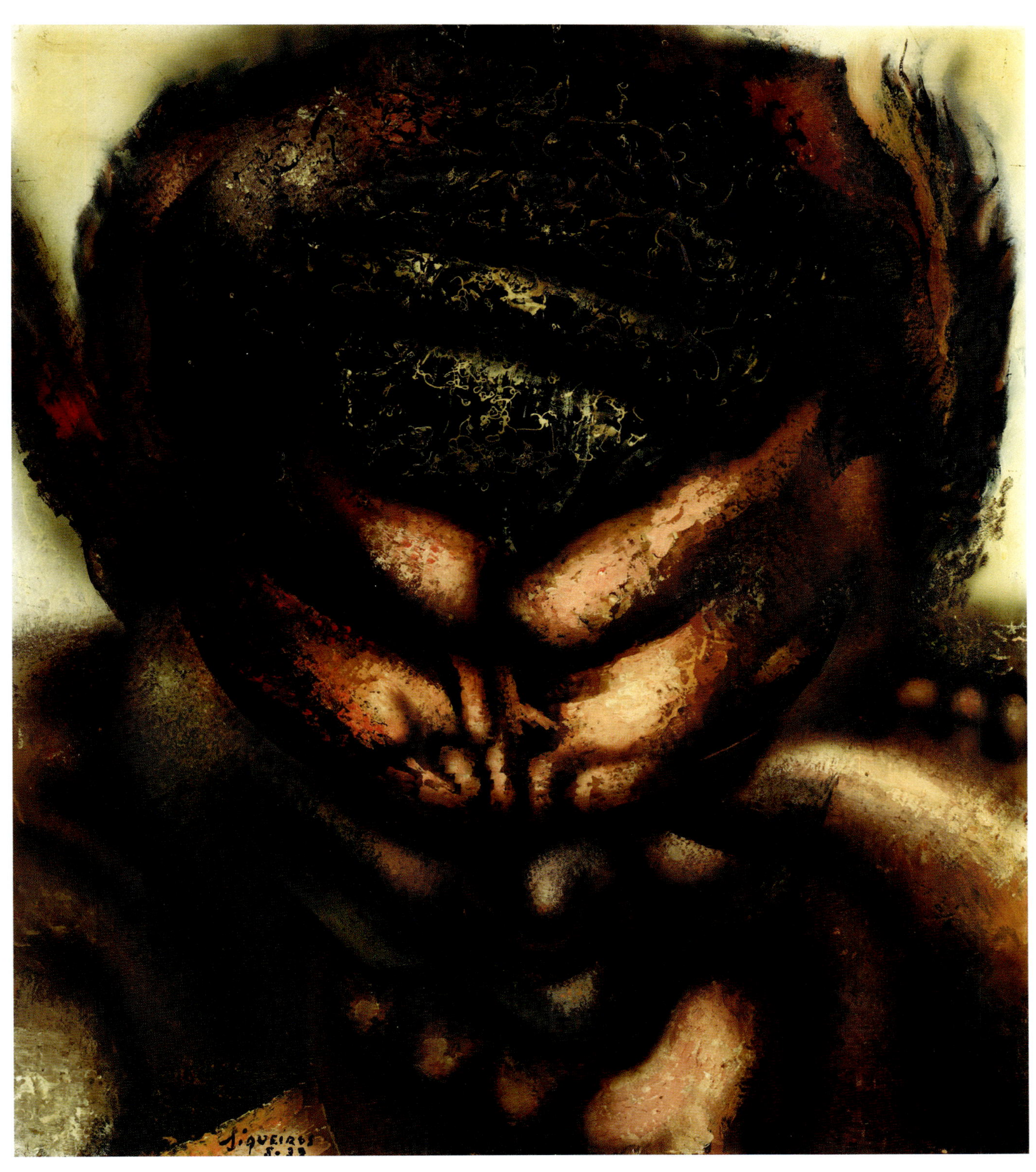

DAVID ALFARO SIQUEIROS | Mexican, 1896–1974
Concentration (Head of a Boy)
[Cara de niño (Concentración)], 1939
Piroxylene on Masonite
Canvas or panel: 27 1/2 x 23 15/16 x 1/4 in.
(69.9 x 60.8 cm)
Museum purchase funded by
the Agnes Cullen Arnold
Accessions Endowment Fund
2010.9

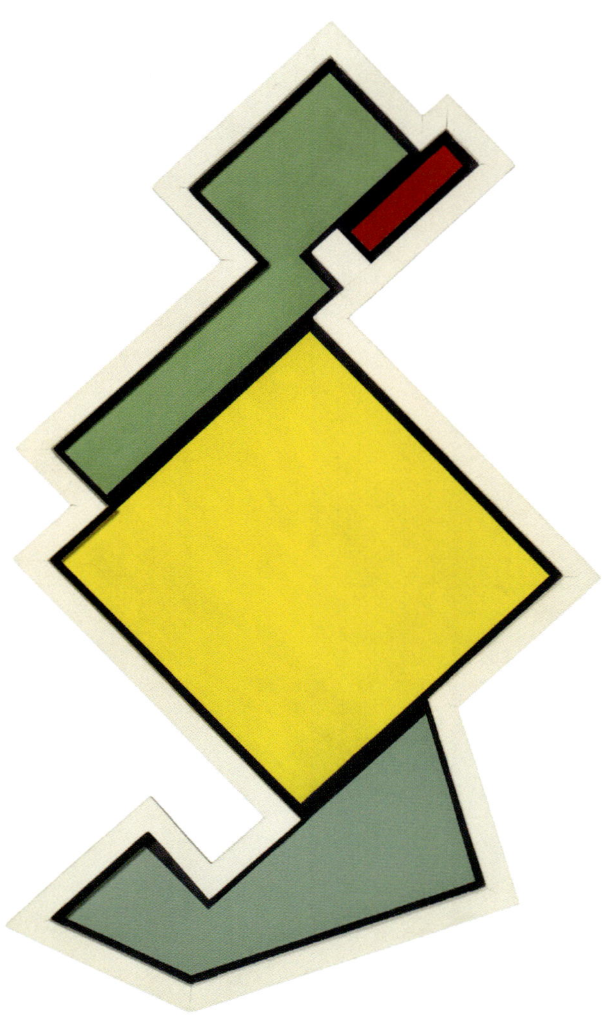

RHOD ROTHFUSS | Uruguayan, 1920–1969
Composición Madí
[Madí composition], 1948
Enamel on wood
40 3/4 x 35 1/4 in. (103.5 x 89.5 cm)
Museum purchase funded by the
Caroline Wiess Law Accessions Endowment Fund
2004.1658

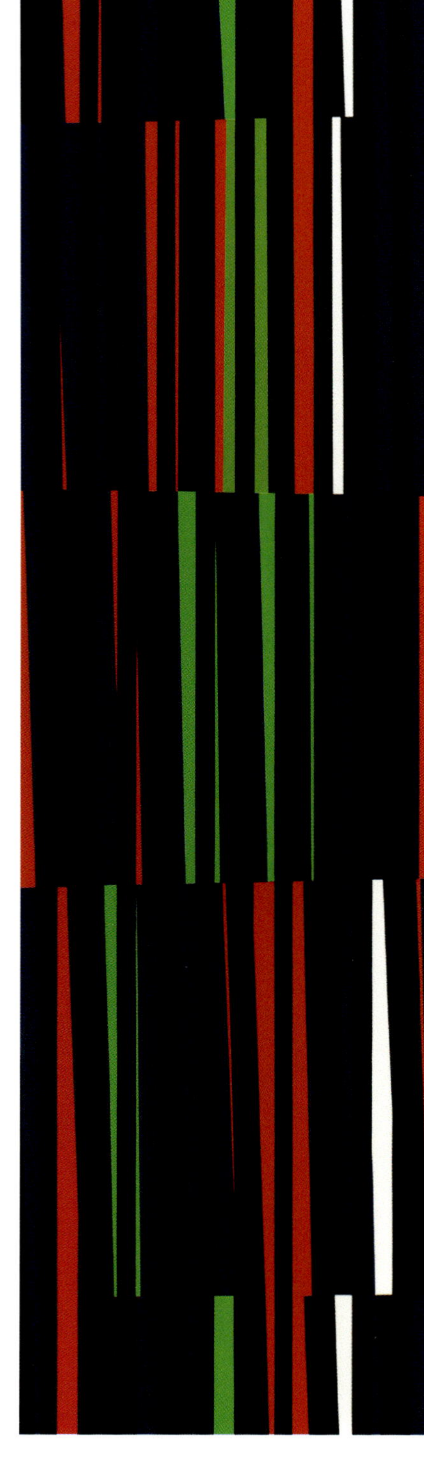

ALEJANDRO OTERO | Venezuelan, 1921–1990
Coloritmo No. 43 [Rhythmicolor No. 43],
from the *Coloritmos* series, 1960
Duco paint on wood
78 7/8 x 21 3/8 x 1 in. (200.4 x 54.3 x 2.5 cm)
Museum purchase funded by the Latin Maecenas
2004.61

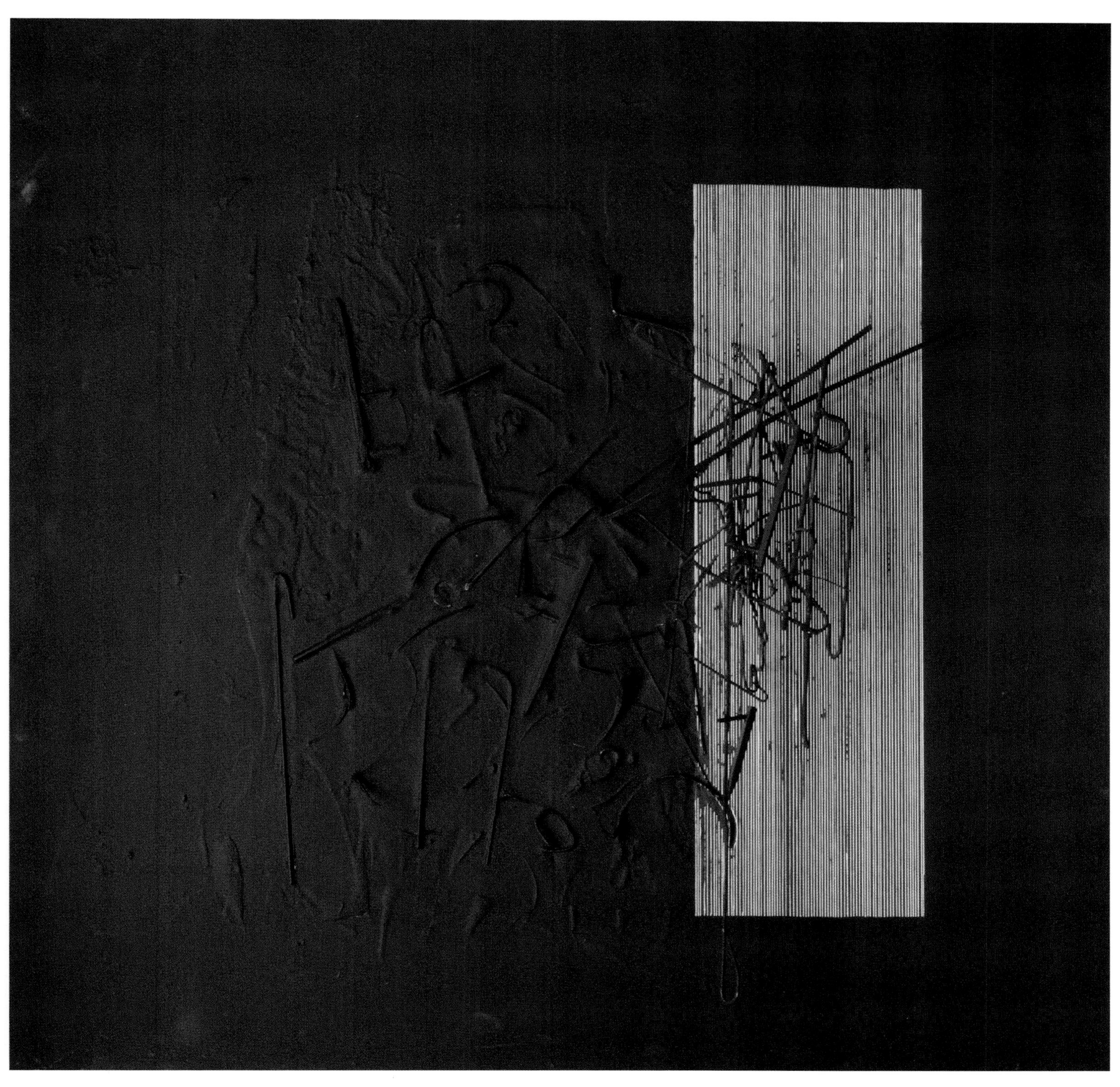

JESÚS RAFAEL SOTO | Venezuelan, 1923–2005
Sin título [Untitled], 1959
Painted wood and metal on canvas
Canvas or panel: 39 3/4 x 39 3/8 x 1 3/4 in.
(101 x 100 x 4.4 cm)
Museum purchase funded by the
Caroline Wiess Law Accessions Endowment Fund
2004.2213

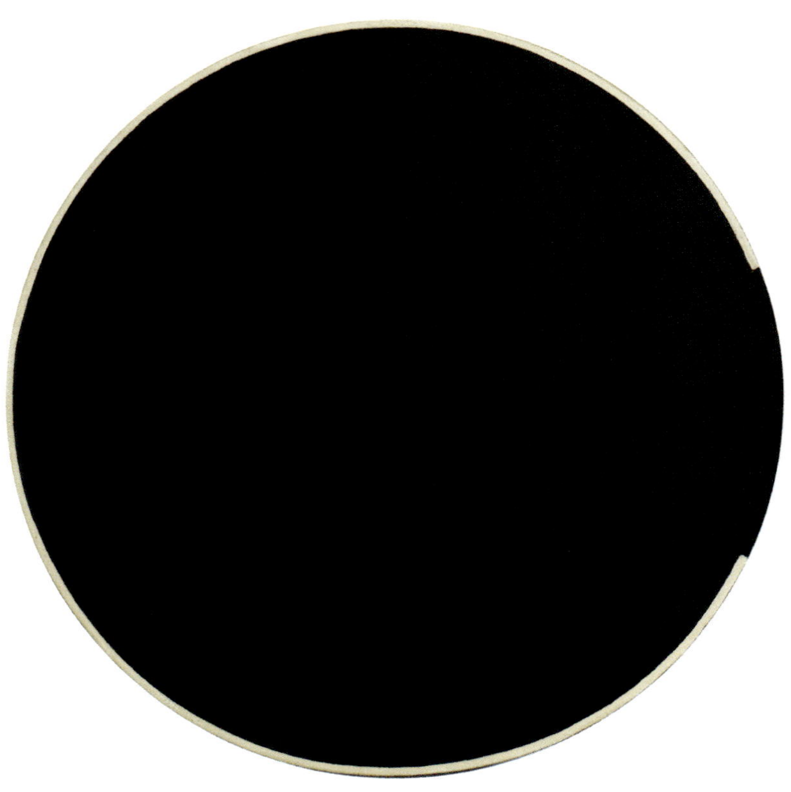

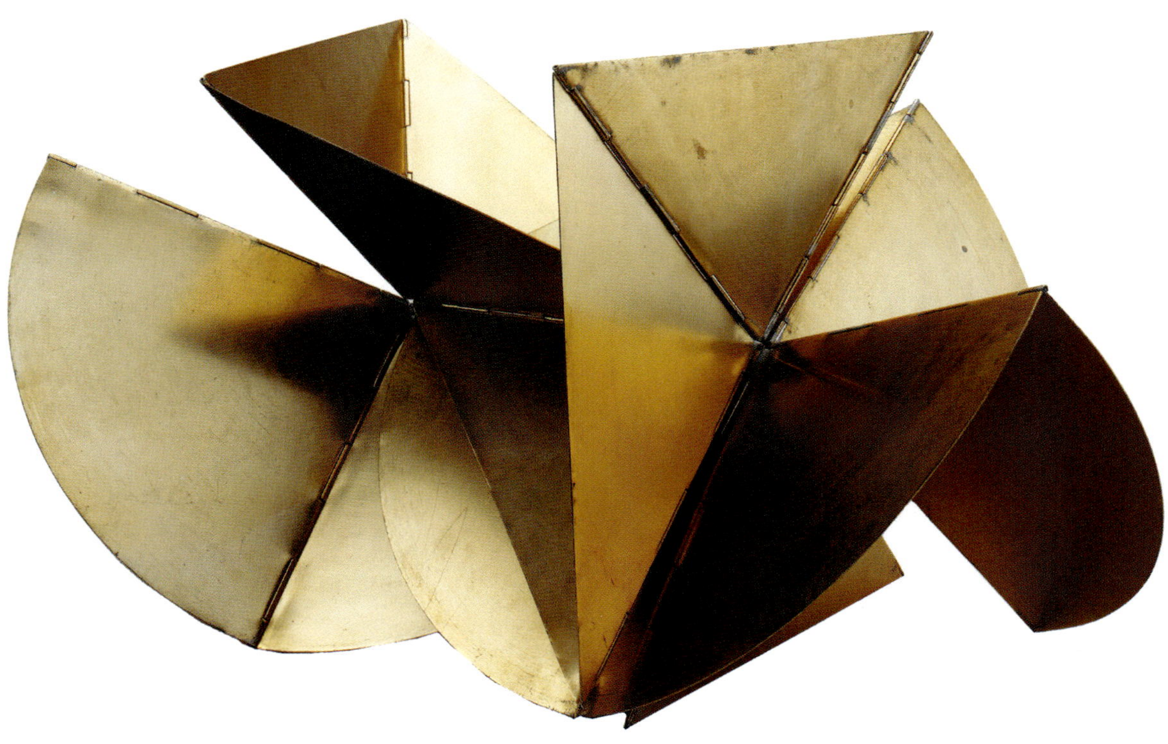

LYGIA CLARK | Brazilian, 1920–1988
Bicho (Máquina) [Critter (Machine)], 1962
Anodized aluminum
(variable): 21 x 35 1/2 x 21 1/2 in.
(53.3 x 90.2 x 54.6 cm)
The Adolpho Leirner Collection of Brazilian
Constructive Art, Museum purchase funded by
the Caroline Wiess Law Accessions
Endowment Fund
2005.470

LYGIA CLARK | Brazilian, 1920–1988
Ovo [Egg], 1959
Industrial paint on wood
Panel: 13 in. diameter (33 cm)
The Adolpho Leirner Collection of Brazilian
Constructive Art, Museum purchase funded by
the Caroline Wiess Law Accessions
Endowment Fund
2007.13

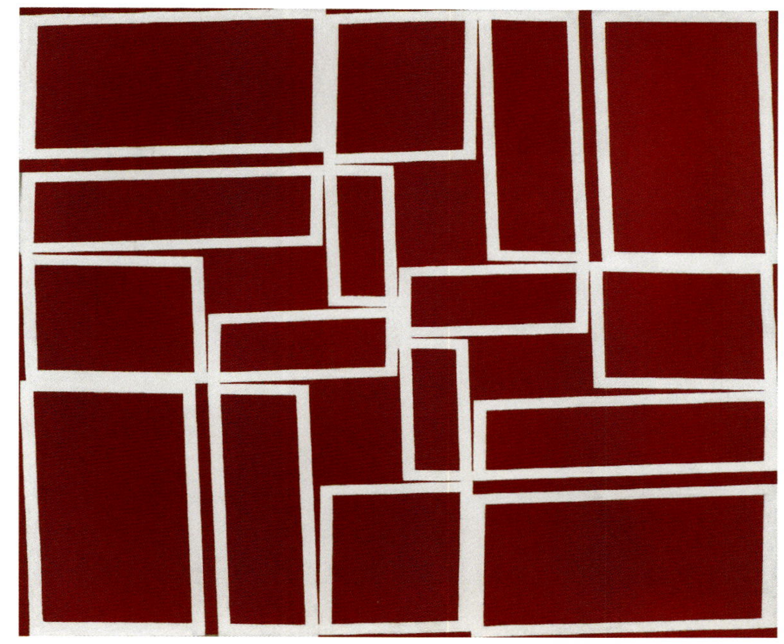

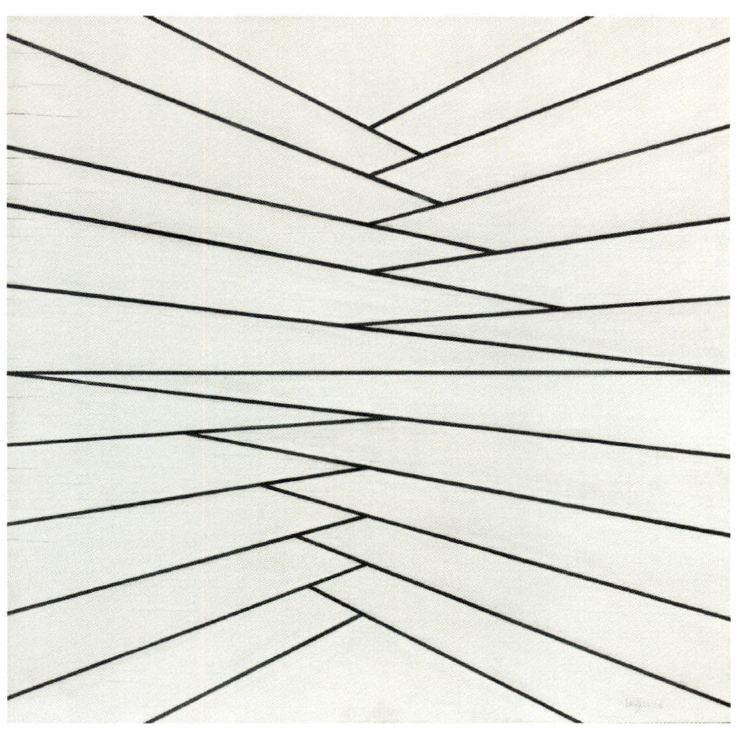

WALDEMAR CORDEIRO | Brazilian, born Italy,
1925–73
Idéia visível [Visible Idea], 1956
Industrial latex paint on plywood
laminate panel
39 1/2 x 39 9/16 in. (100.3 x 100.5 cm)
The Adolpho Leirner Collection of Brazilian
Constructive Art, Museum purchase funded by
the Caroline Wiess Law Accessions
Endowment Fund
2007.15

HÉLIO OITICICA | Brazilian, 1937–1980
Vermelho cortando o branco, 1958
[Red Going through White]
Oil on canvas
20 1/8 x 23 5/8 in. (51.1 x 59.9 cm)
The Adolpho Leirner Collection of Brazilian
Constructive Art, Museum purchase funded by
the Caroline Wiess Law Accessions
Endowment Fund
2007.20

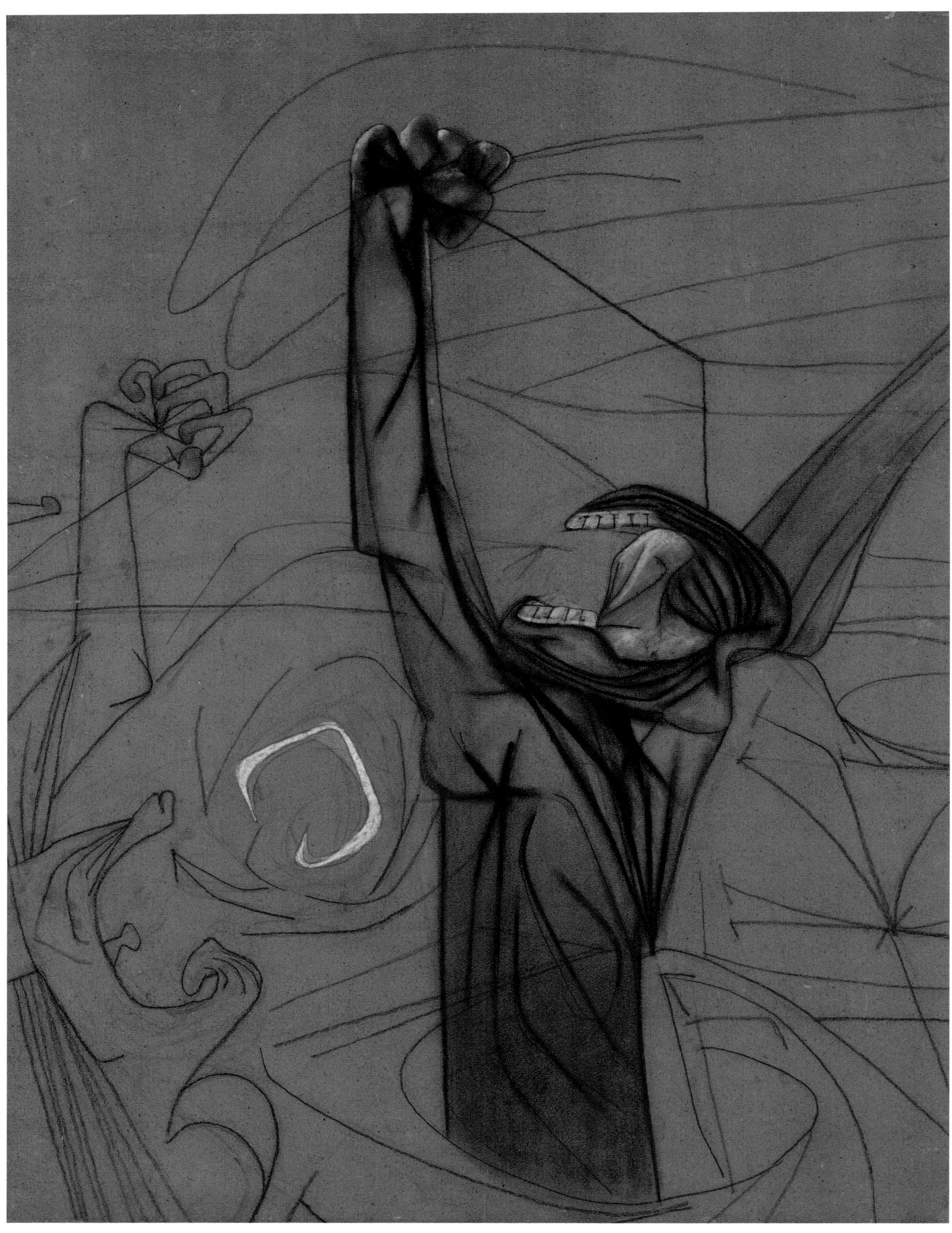

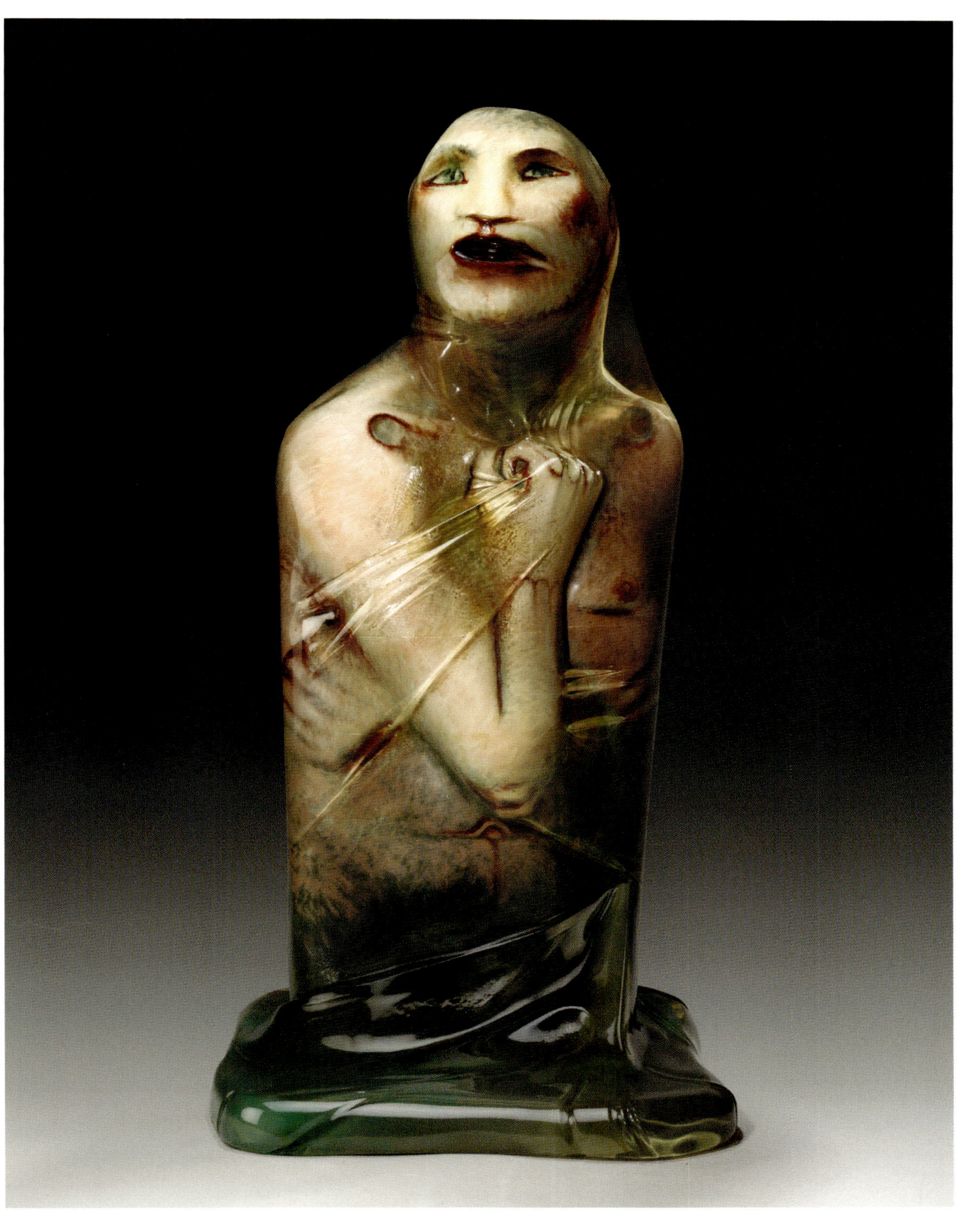

MATTA | Chilean, 1911–2002
La Pipe (pour 120 Journées du Marquis de Sade)
[The Pipe (for 120 Days by the Marquis de Sade)],
1943–45
Pastel on paper, laid on cardboard
Sight: 44 x 34 in. (111.8 x 86.4 cm)
Museum purchase funded by "One Great Night
in November, 2012" and the Caroline Wiess Law
Accessions Endowment Fund
2012.561

JUAN CARLOS DISTÉFANO | Argentinean,
born 1933
Telaraña [Spider Web], 1974–75
Fiberglass-reinforced polyester,
cast polyester, and enamel epoxy
Overall: 43 1/2 x 22 x 25 3/4 in.
(110.5 x 55.9 x 65.4 cm)
Jorge and Marion Helft Collection,
Museum purchase funded by
the Caroline Wiess Law
Accessions Endowment Fund
2011.1066

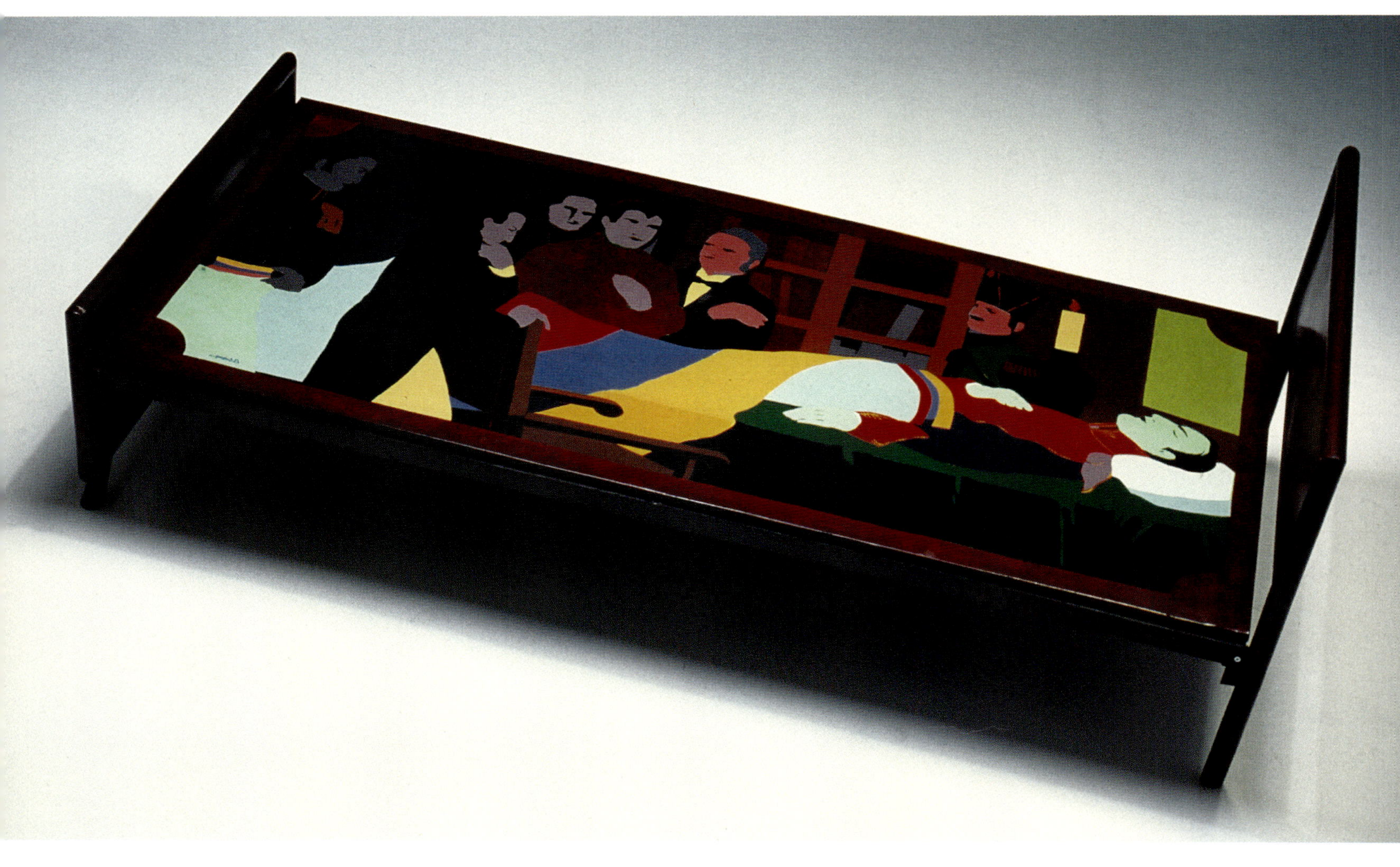

BEATRIZ GONZÁLEZ | Colombian, born 1938
Mutis por el foro (cama) [Stage Rear (A Bed)], 1973
Enamel on metal sheet joint on metal furniture
47 1/4 x 96 1/2 x 35 1/2 in. (120 x 245 x 90 cm)
Museum purchase funded by the Caroline Wiess Law
Accessions Endowment Fund, Leslie and Brad Bucher,
Karol Kreymer and Robert Card, M.D., Anne and
John C. Moriniere, and the Latin Maecenas
2005.1728

LUIS FELIPE NOÉ | Argentinean, born 1933
Nuestro Señor de cada día
[Our Daily Father], 1964
Mixed media on canvas
Overall: 102 1/4 x 76 1/4 x 4 1/2 in.
(259.7 x 193.7 x 11.4 cm)
Jorge and Marion Helft Collection,
Museum purchase funded by
the Caroline Wiess Law Accessions
Endowment Fund
2011.1072

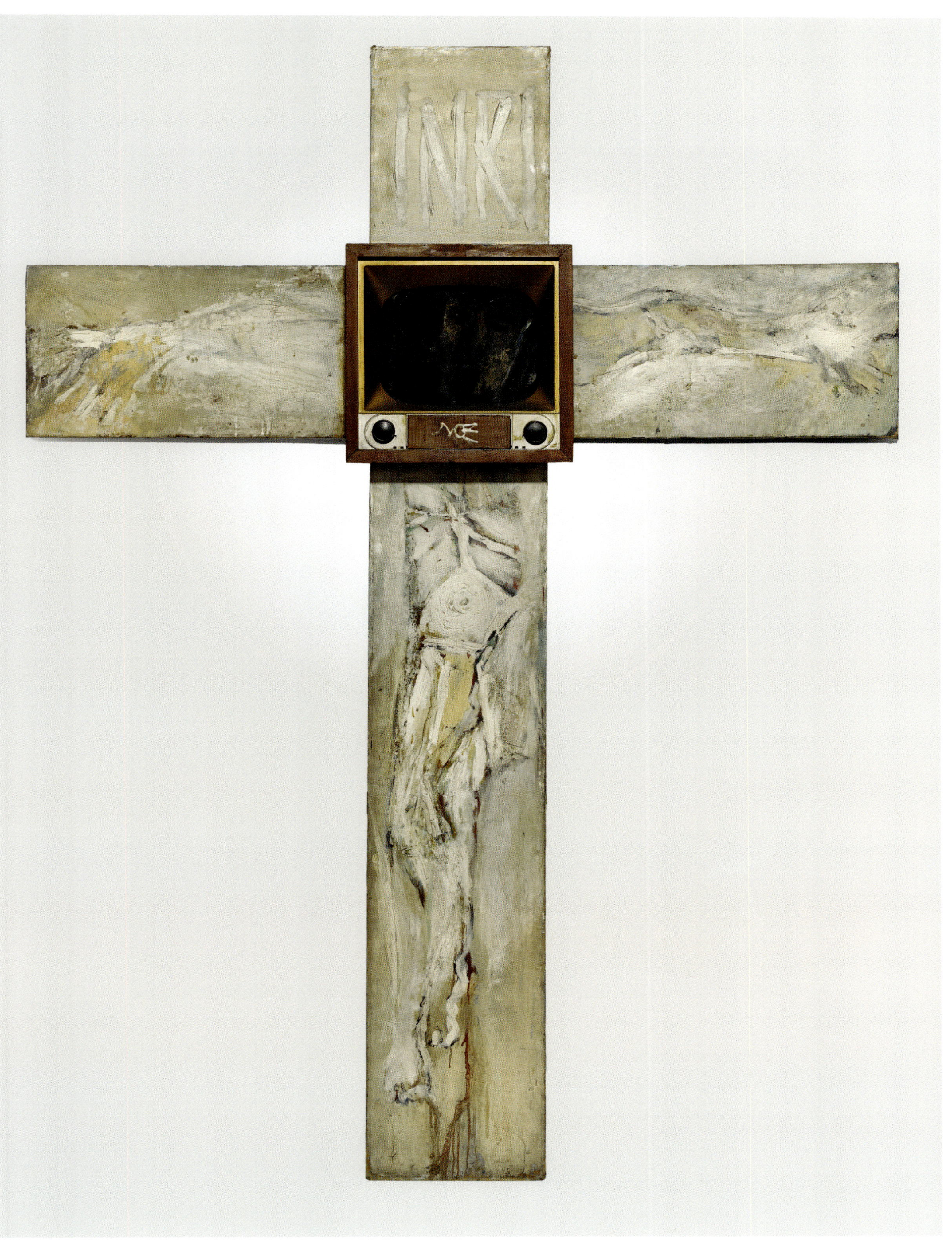

INRI

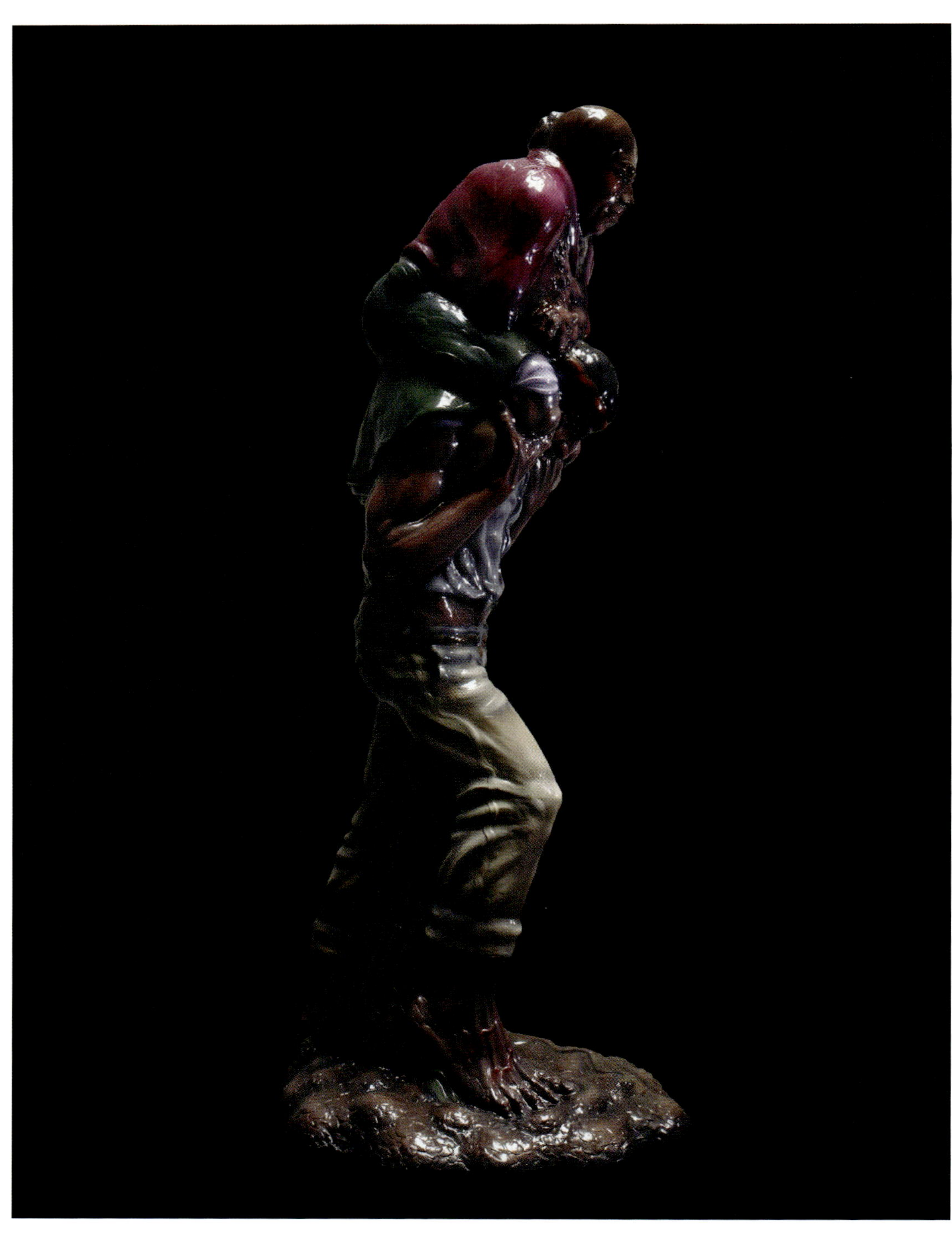

LUIS JIMÉNEZ | American, 1940–2006
Border Crossing, 1989
Fiberglass with urethane finish
Overall: 127 x 34 x 54 in. (322.6 x 86.4 x 137.2 cm)
Museum purchase funded by the Caroline Wiess Law
Accessions Endowment Fund
2010.1758

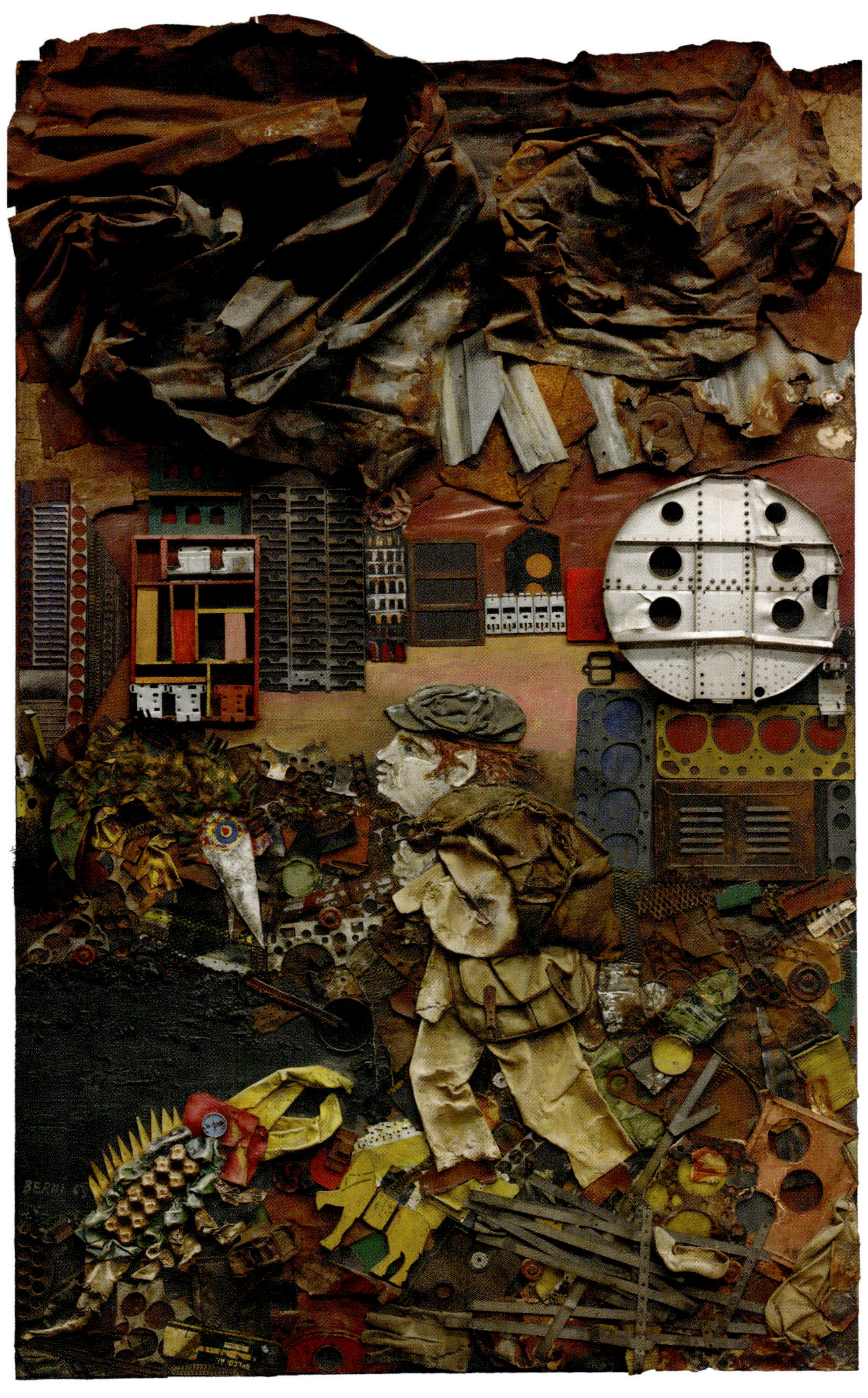

ANTONIO BERNI | Argentinean, 1905–1981
Juanito va a la Ciudad [Juanito Goes to the City], 1963
Wood, paint, industrial trash, cardboard, scrap metal,
and fabric assemblage on board
129 x 79 x 15 in. (327.7 x 200.7 x 38.1 cm)
Museum purchase funded by
the Caroline Wiess Law Accessions Endowment Fund
2007.1167

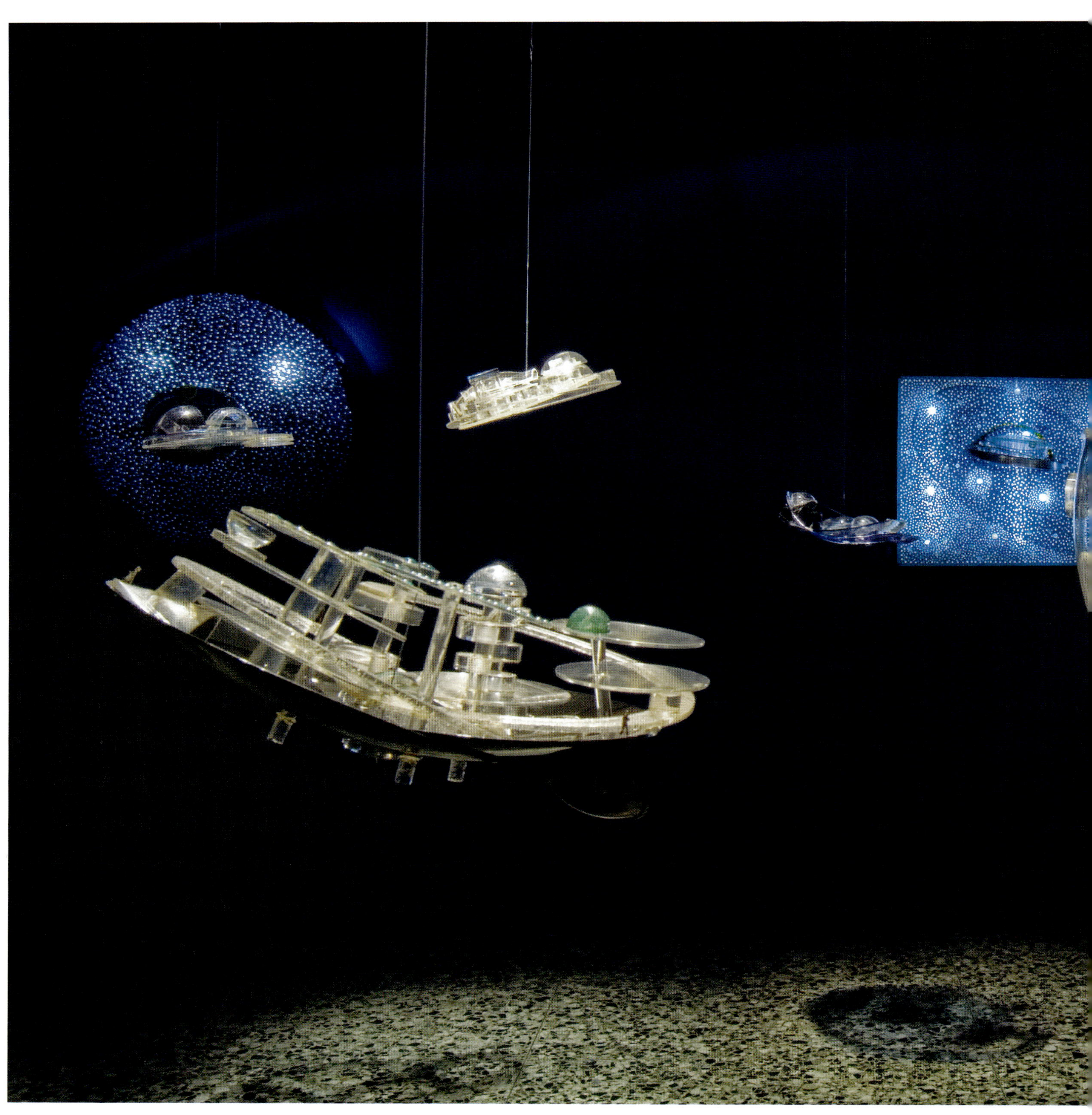

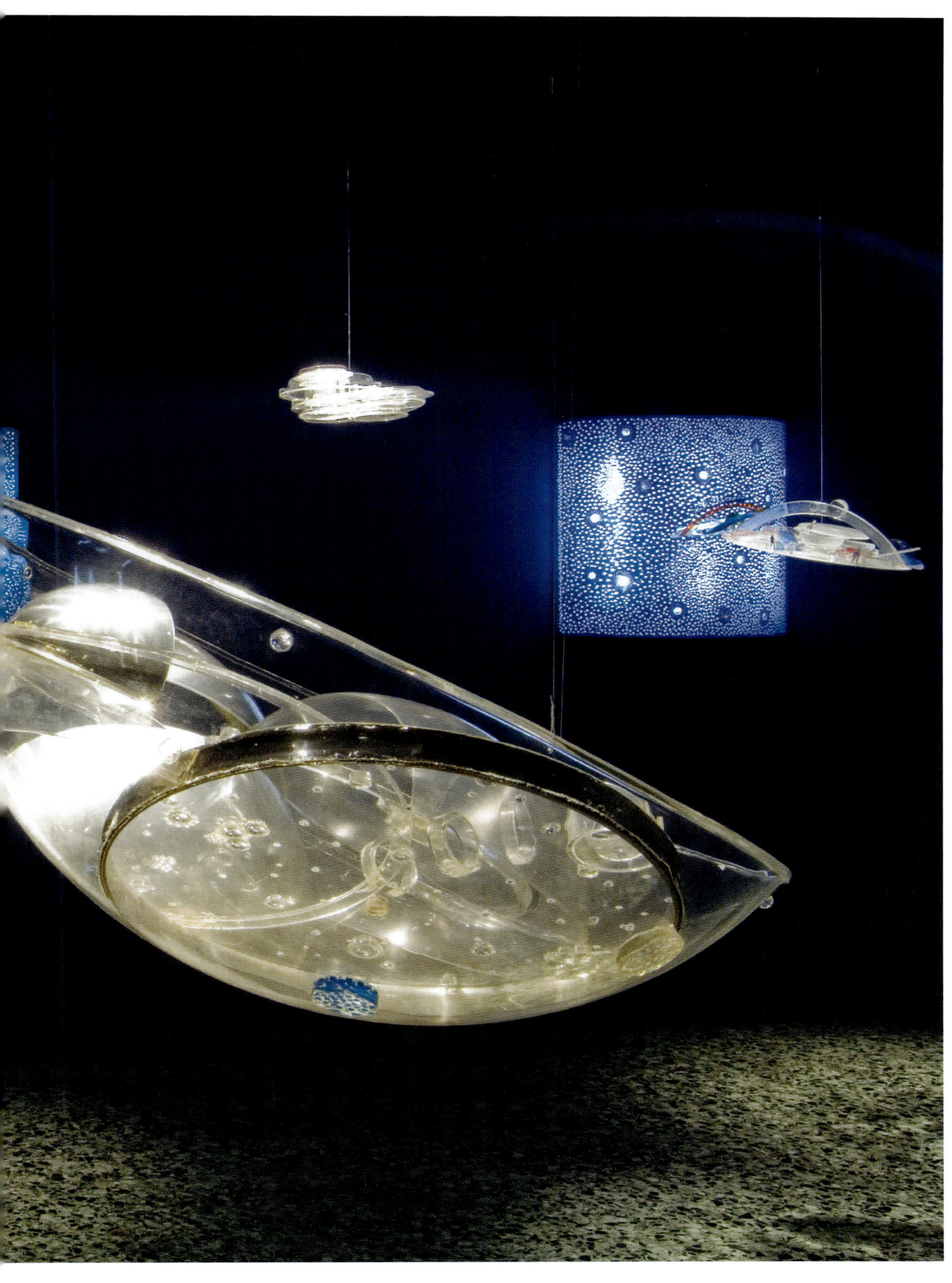

GYULA KOSICE | Argentinean, born 1924
La ciudad hidroespacial
[The Hydrospatial City], 1946–72
Acrylic, Plexiglas, paint, and light
Variable dimensions
Museum purchase funded by
the Caroline Wiess Law Accessions
Endowment Fund
2009.29.1–.47

CARLOS CRUZ-DIEZ | Venezuelan, born 1923
Cromosaturación [Chromosaturation], 1965/2004
Three chromo-cubicles
(fluorescent light with blue, red, and green filters)
Overall (minimum ceiling height):
96 x 362 x 204 in. (243.8 x 919.5 x 518.2 cm)
Overall (each cubicle): 120 x 120 in. (304.8 x 304.8 cm)
Gift of the Cruz-Diez Foundation at the
Museum of Fine Arts, Houston
2009.464

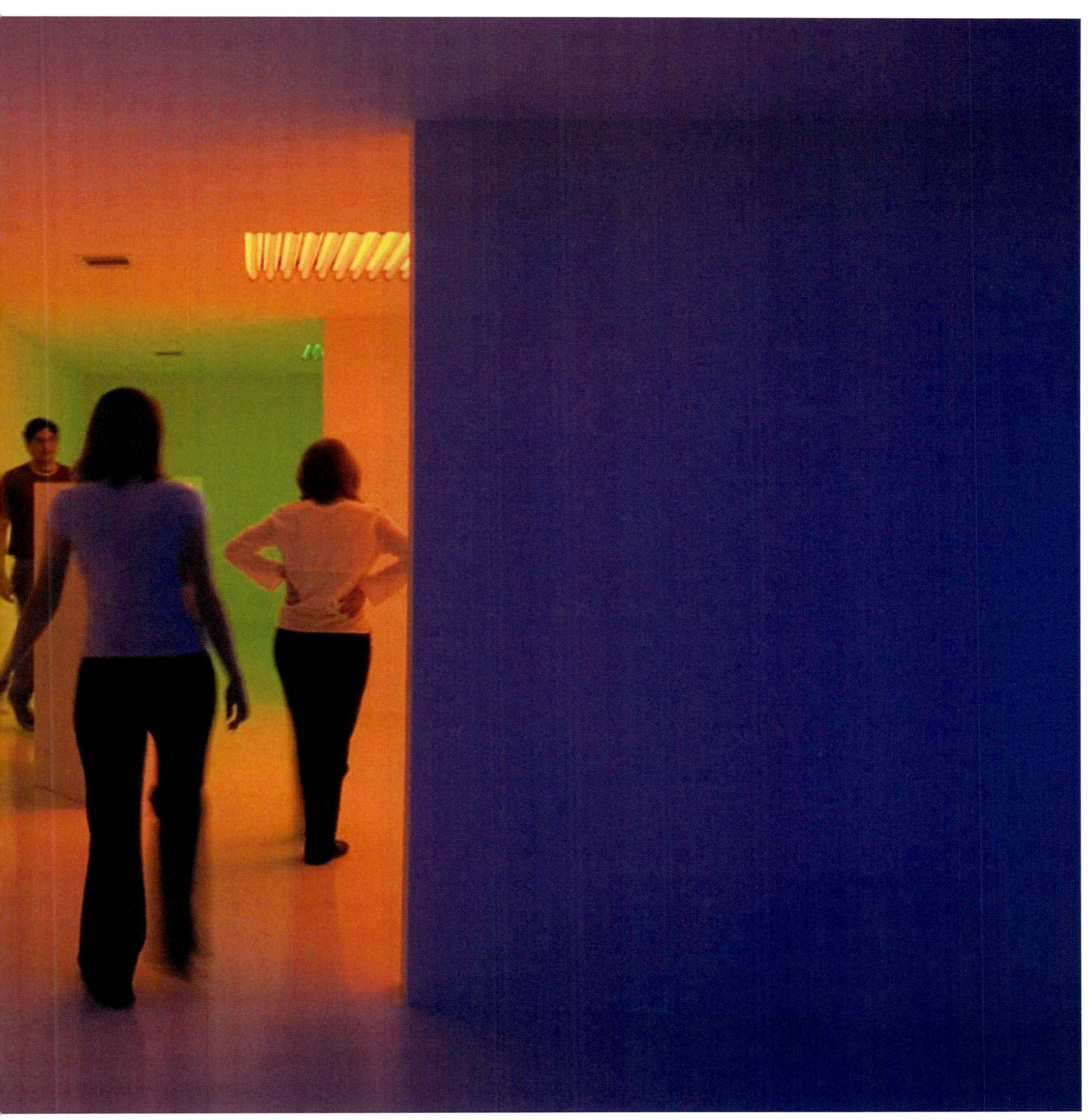

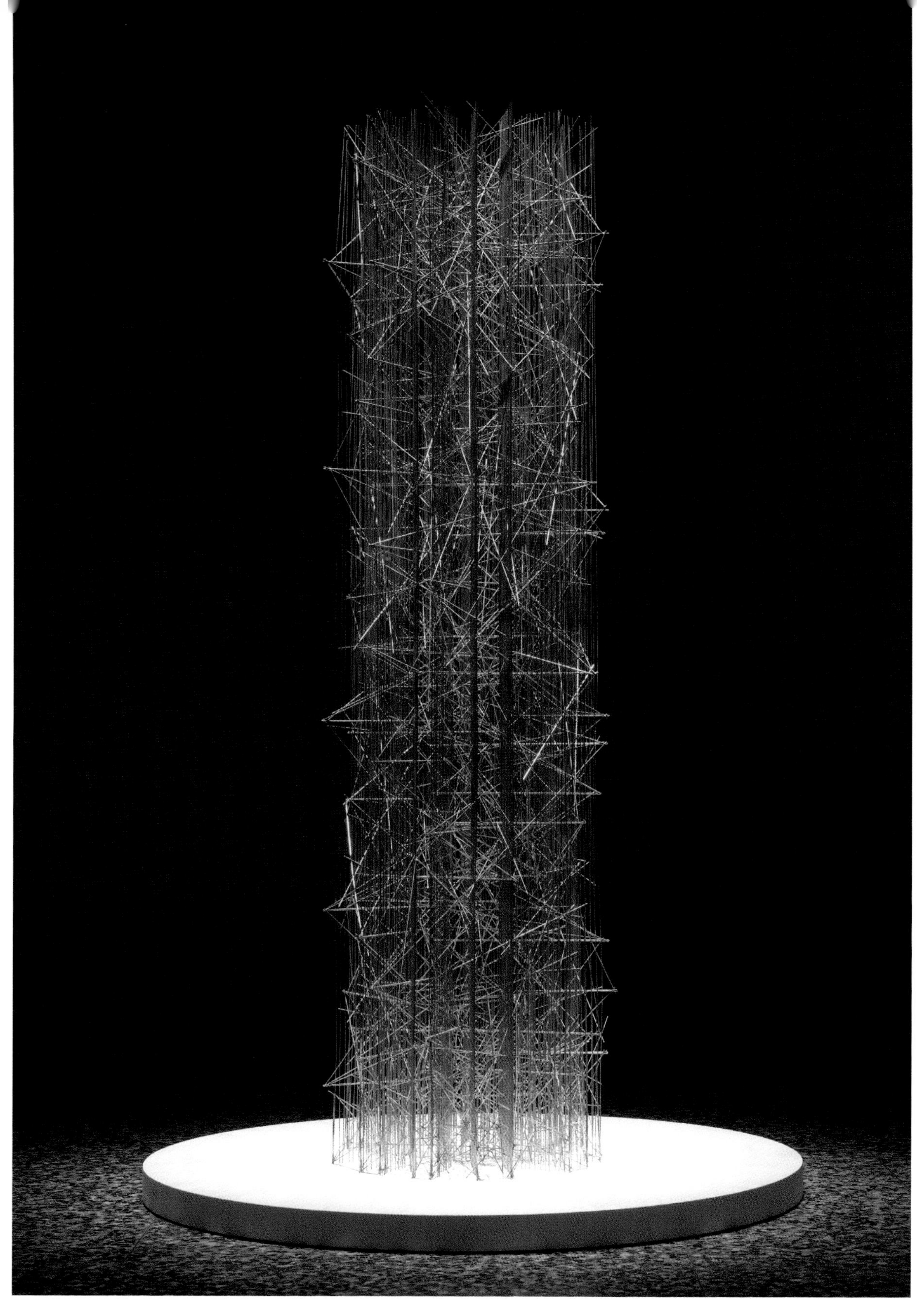

LEÓN FERRARI | Argentinean, 1920–2013
Untitled, 1979–81
Stainless steel
120 x 32 x 34 in. (304.8 x 81.3 x 86.4 cm)
Museum purchase funded by the
Caroline Wiess Law Accessions
Endowment Fund
2010.1761

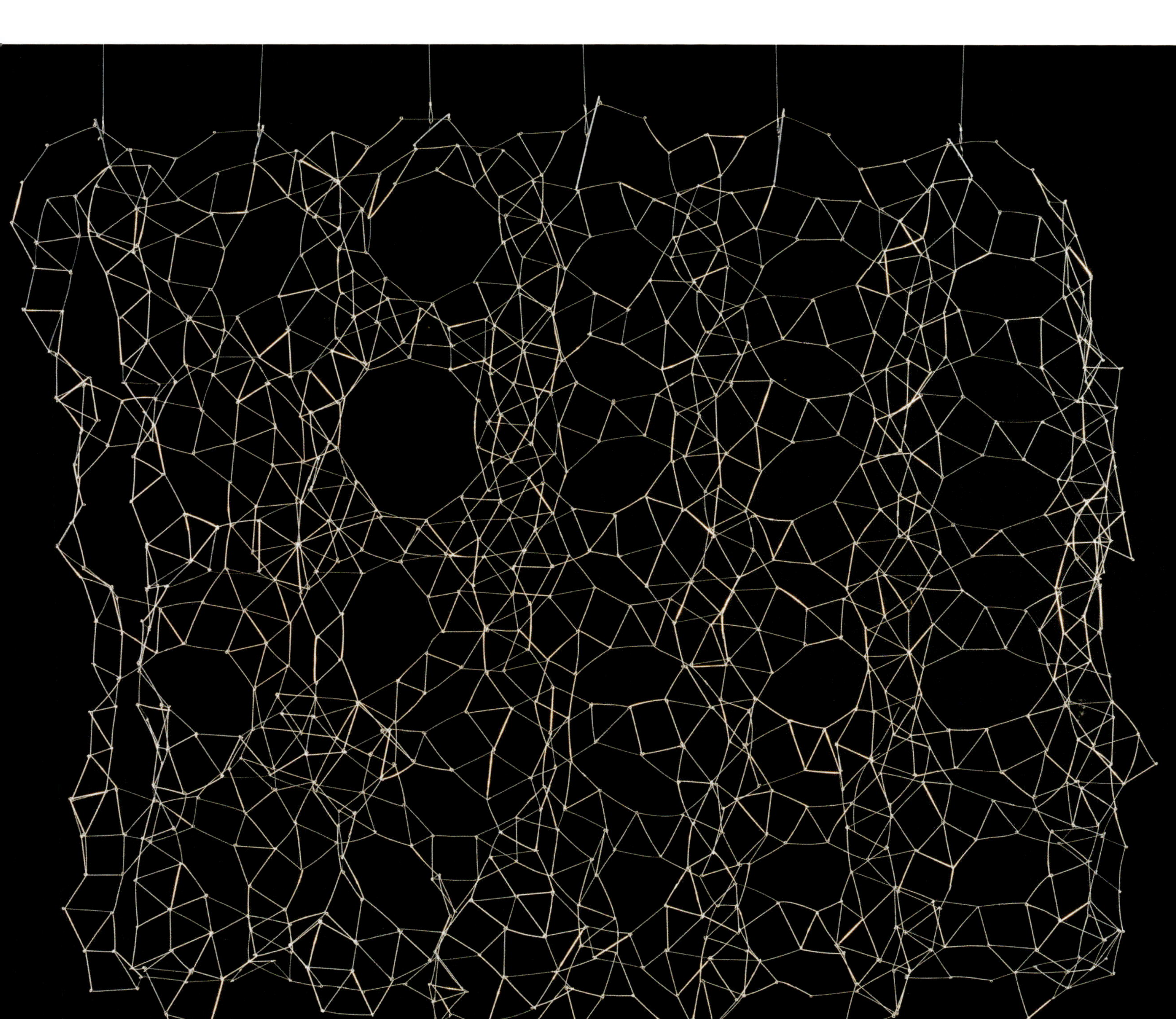

GEGO (GERTRUD GOLDSCHMIDT) | Venezuelan,
born Germany, 1912–1994
Reticulárea, 1975
Stainless steel wire
Overall: 82 11/16 x 102 3/8 x 7 7/8 in. (210 x 260 x 20 cm)
Gift of AT&T
2002.165

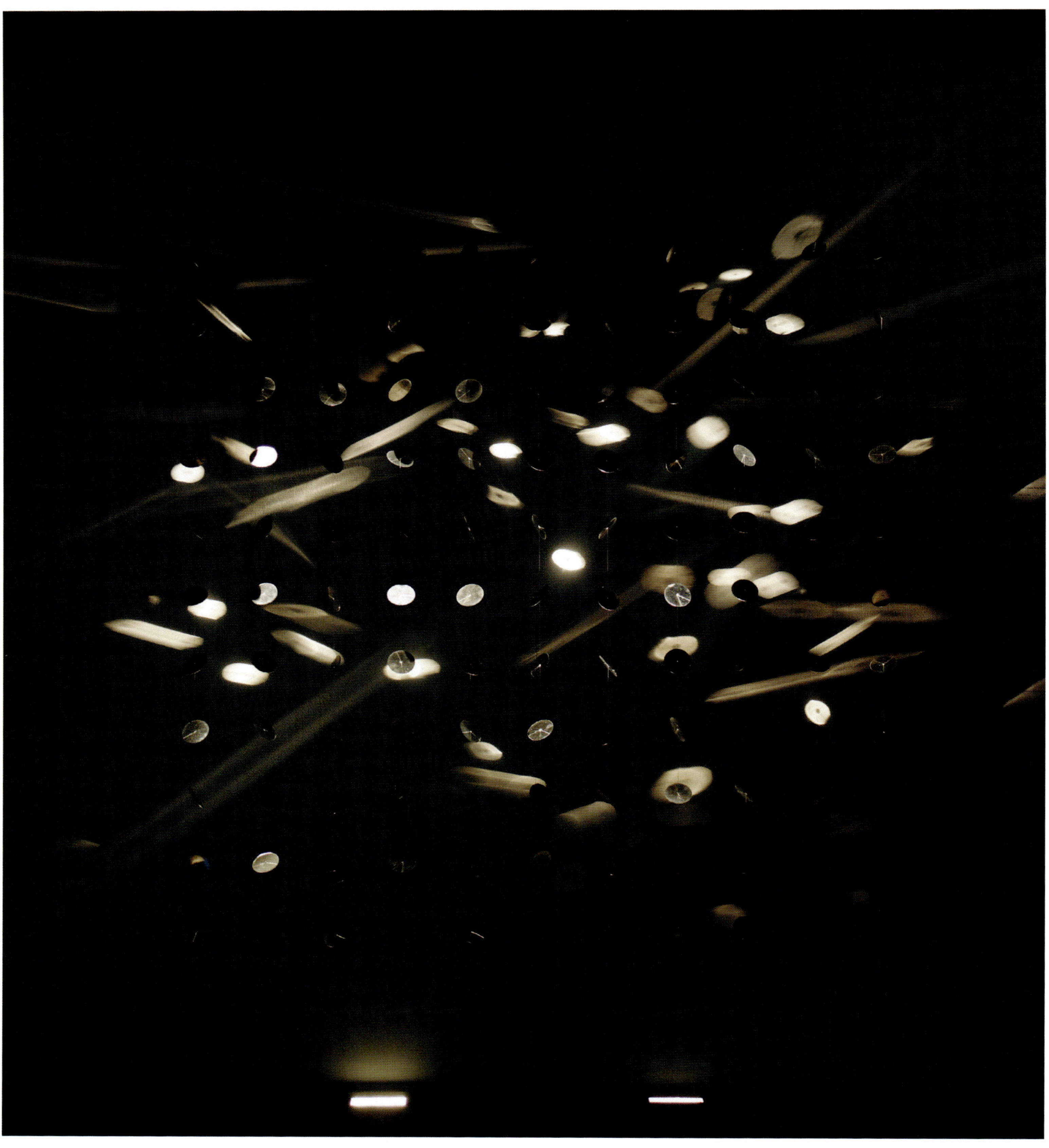

JULIO LE PARC | Argentinean, born 1928
Continuel-lumiére mobile, 1960–66
Hanging metallic elements and spotlights
Overall: 86 5/8 x 78 3/4 x 11 5/8 in.
(220 x 200 x 30 cm)
Museum purchase with funds provided by the
2005 Latin American Experience Gala and
Auction, and the Latin Maecenas
2005.321

MIRA SCHENDEL | Brazilian, 1919–1988
Variantes [Variants], 1977
93 monotypes
Variable dimensions
Museum purchase funded by the
Caroline Wiess Law Accessions
Endowment Fund
2004.1701.1–.93

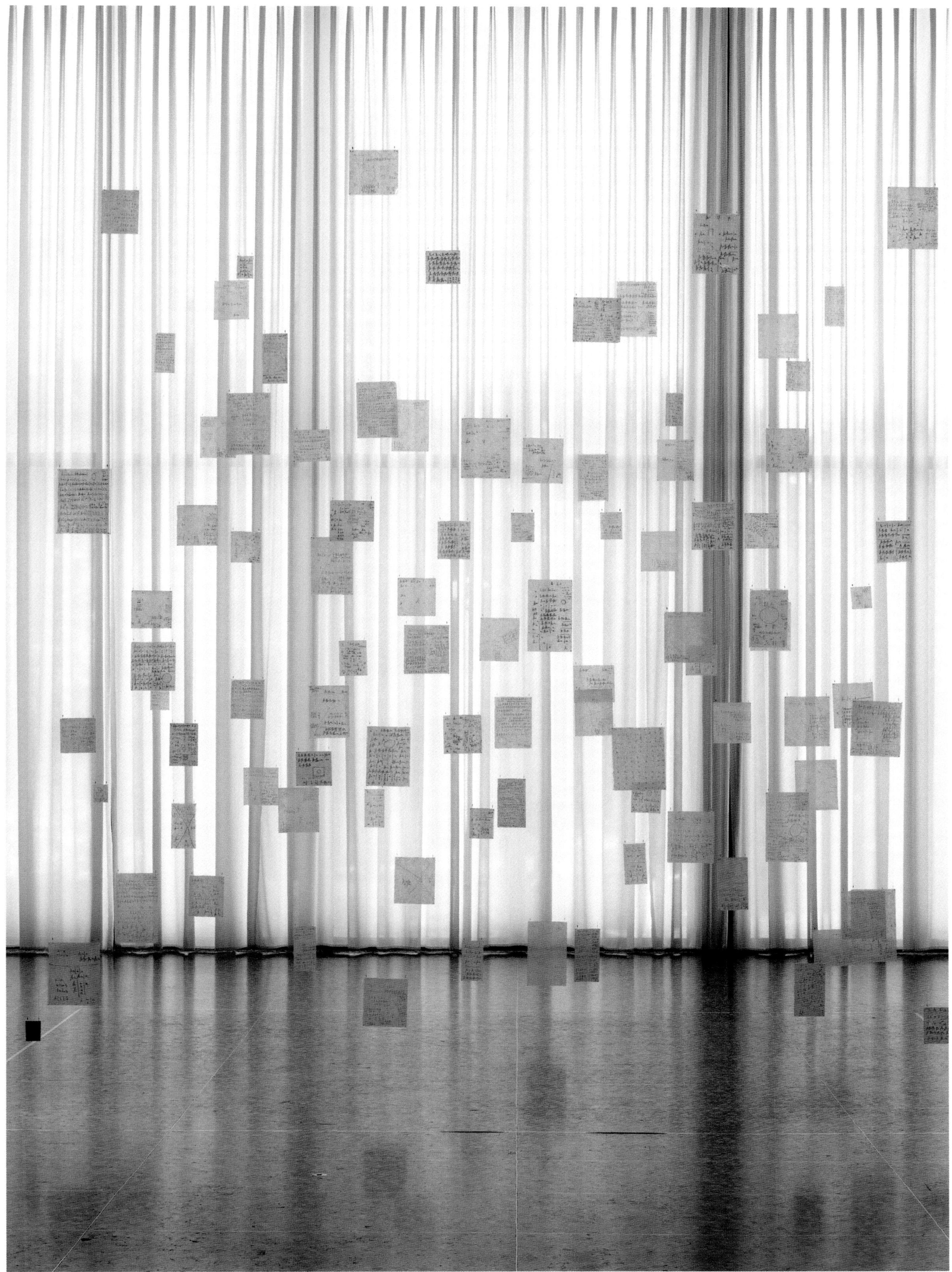

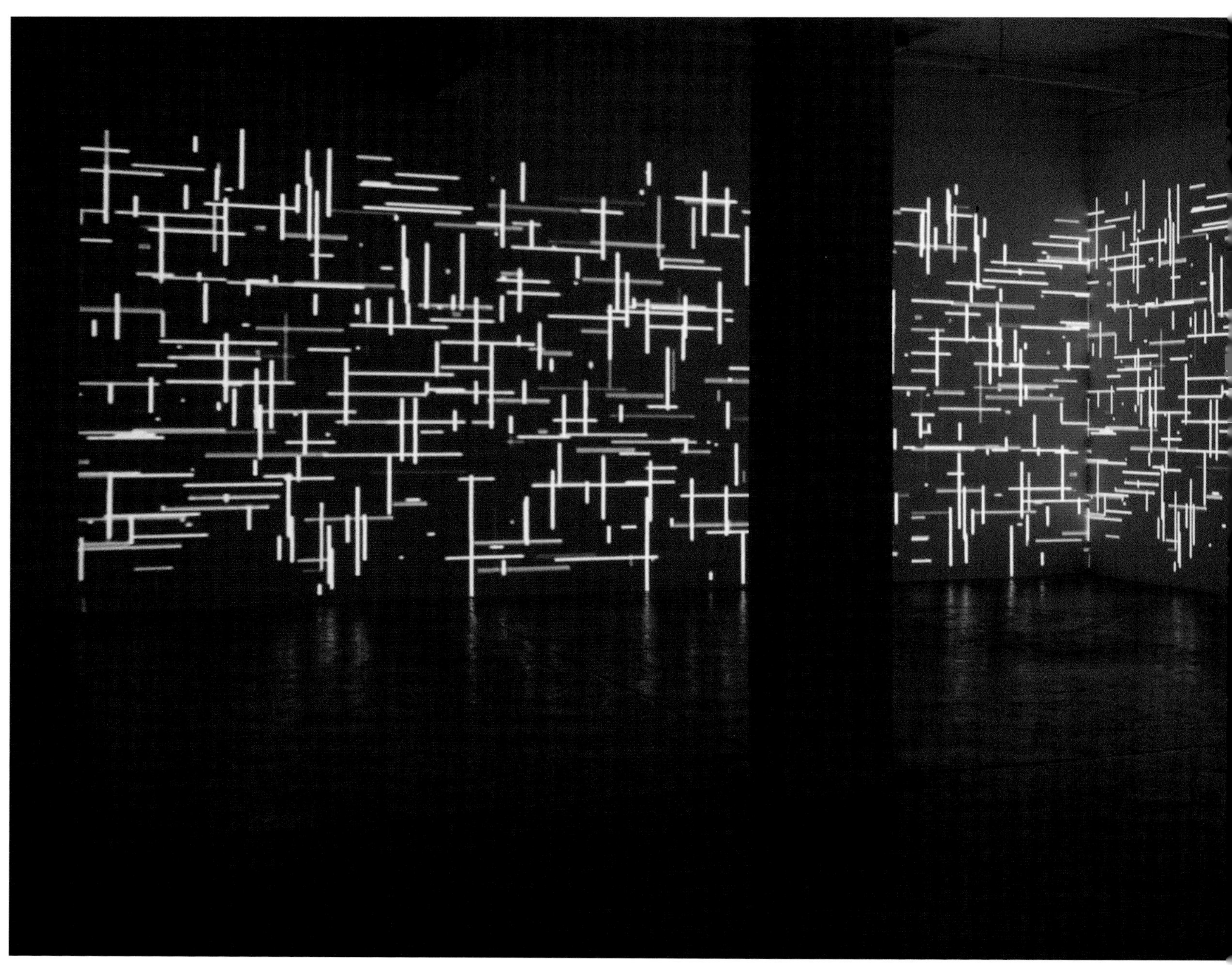

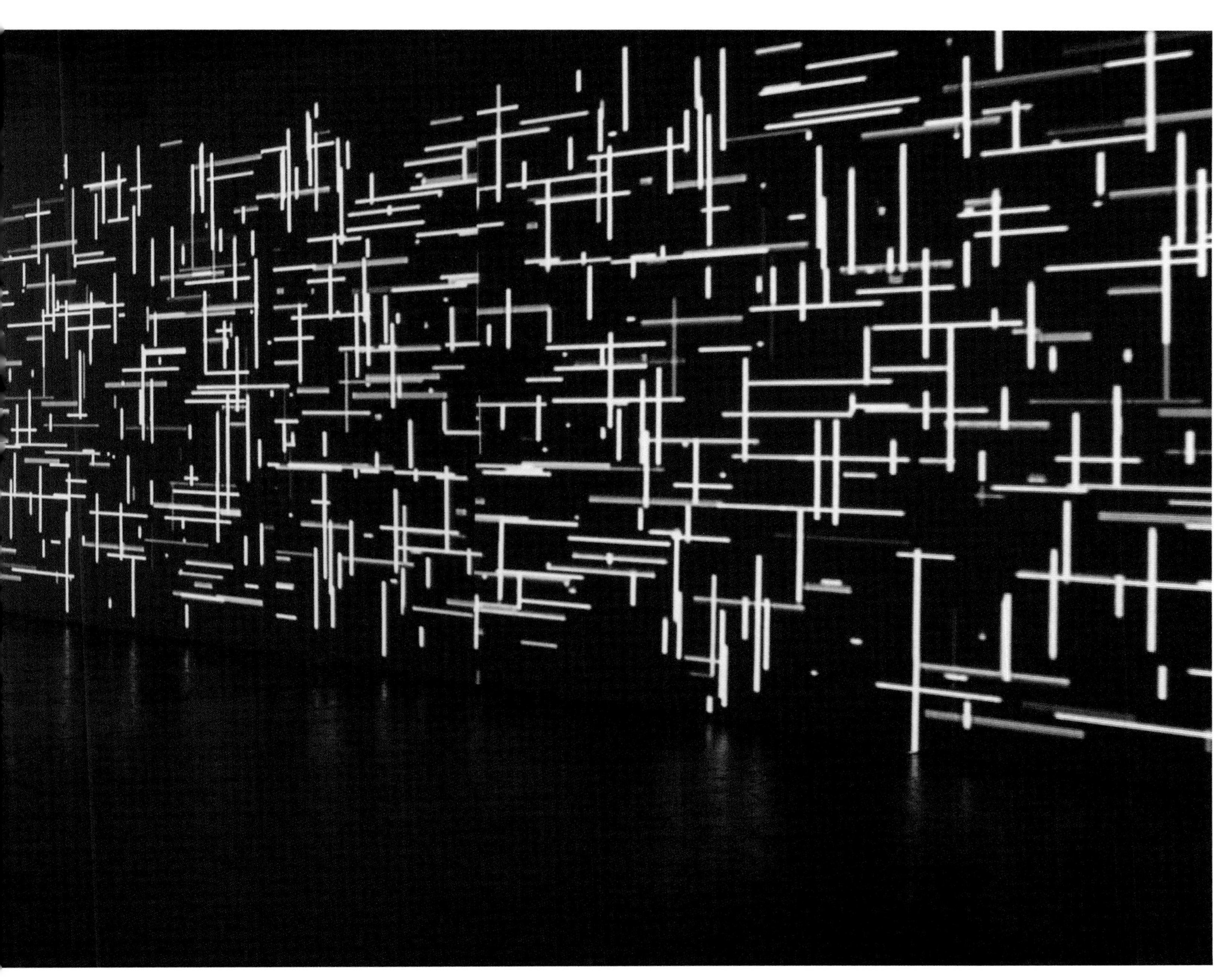

MAGDALENA FERNÁNDEZ | Venezuelan, born 1964
Digital animation by Marcelo D'Orazio,
sound effects by Perpetuum Jazzile
2iPM009, 2009
Video, ed. # 2/3
Duration: 1 minute, 56 seconds
Museum purchase funded by the Caribbean
Art Fund and the Caroline Wiess Law
Accessions Endowment Fund
2012.84

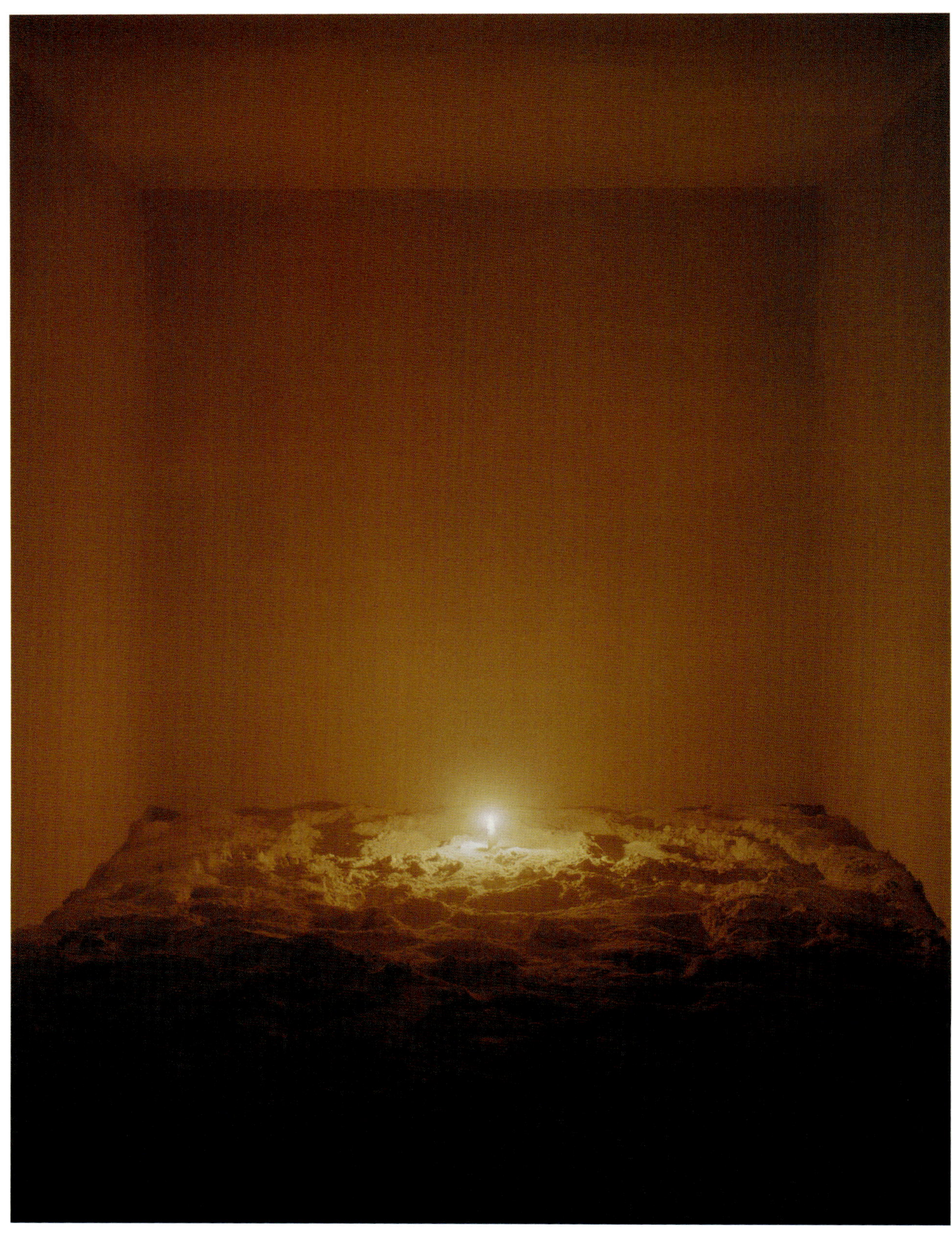

CILDO MEIRELES | Brazilian, born 1948
Volátil [Volatile], 1980–94
Wood, ash, candle, and essence
Overall: 137 13/16 x 275 9/16 x 354 5/16 in.
(350 x 700 x 900 cm)
Gift of Diane and Bruce Halle from
the Thomarie Foundation, in honor of Peter C. Marzio
2010.48

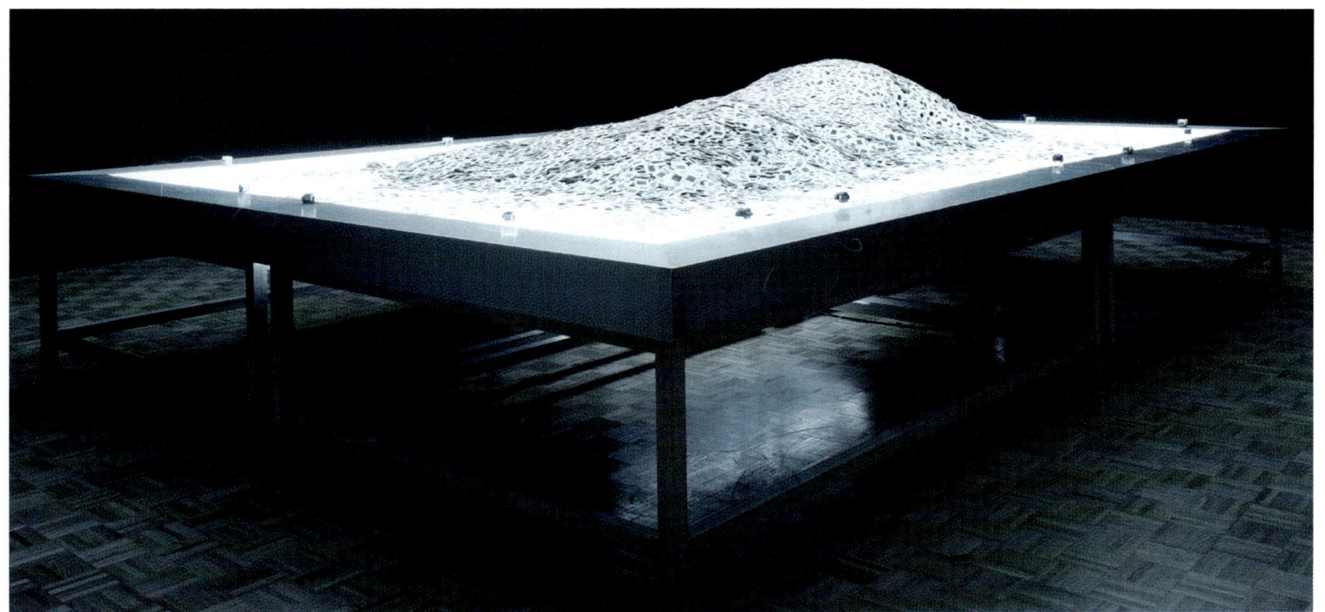

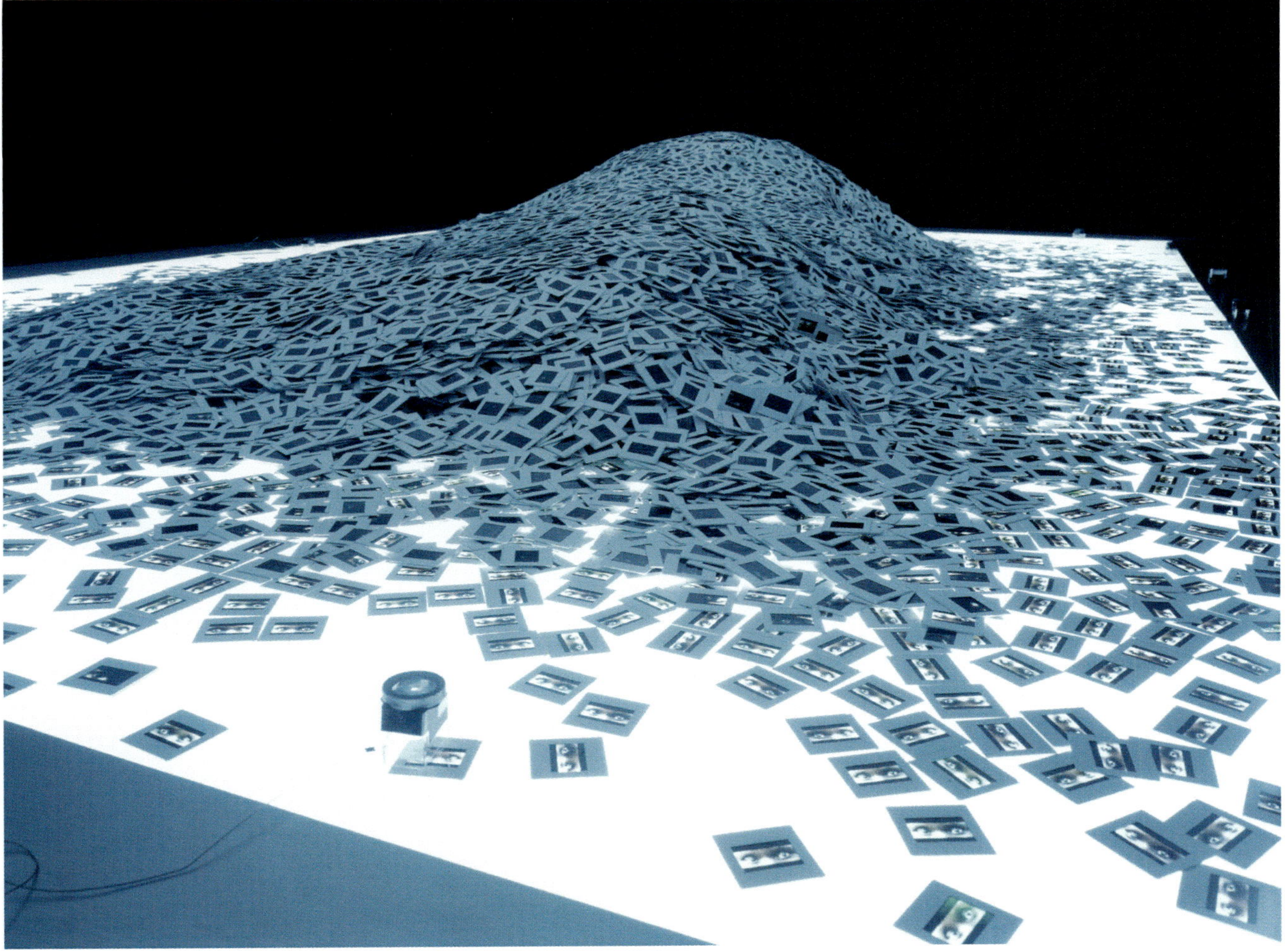

ALFRED JAAR | Chilean, born 1956
The Eyes of Gutete Emerita, 1996
100,000 slides, light table, magnifiers,
and illuminated wall text
Table: 216 3/4 x 143 x 36 in.
(550.5 x 363.2 x 91.4 cm)
Text: 180 x 6 in. (457.2 x 15.2 cm)
Museum purchase funded by the Latin
Maecenas, the Caroline Wiess Law Foundation,
the Bruce T. Halle Family Foundation,
Stewart and Gigi Shapiro, Joan Morgenstern,
and Alice C. Simkins
2004.138

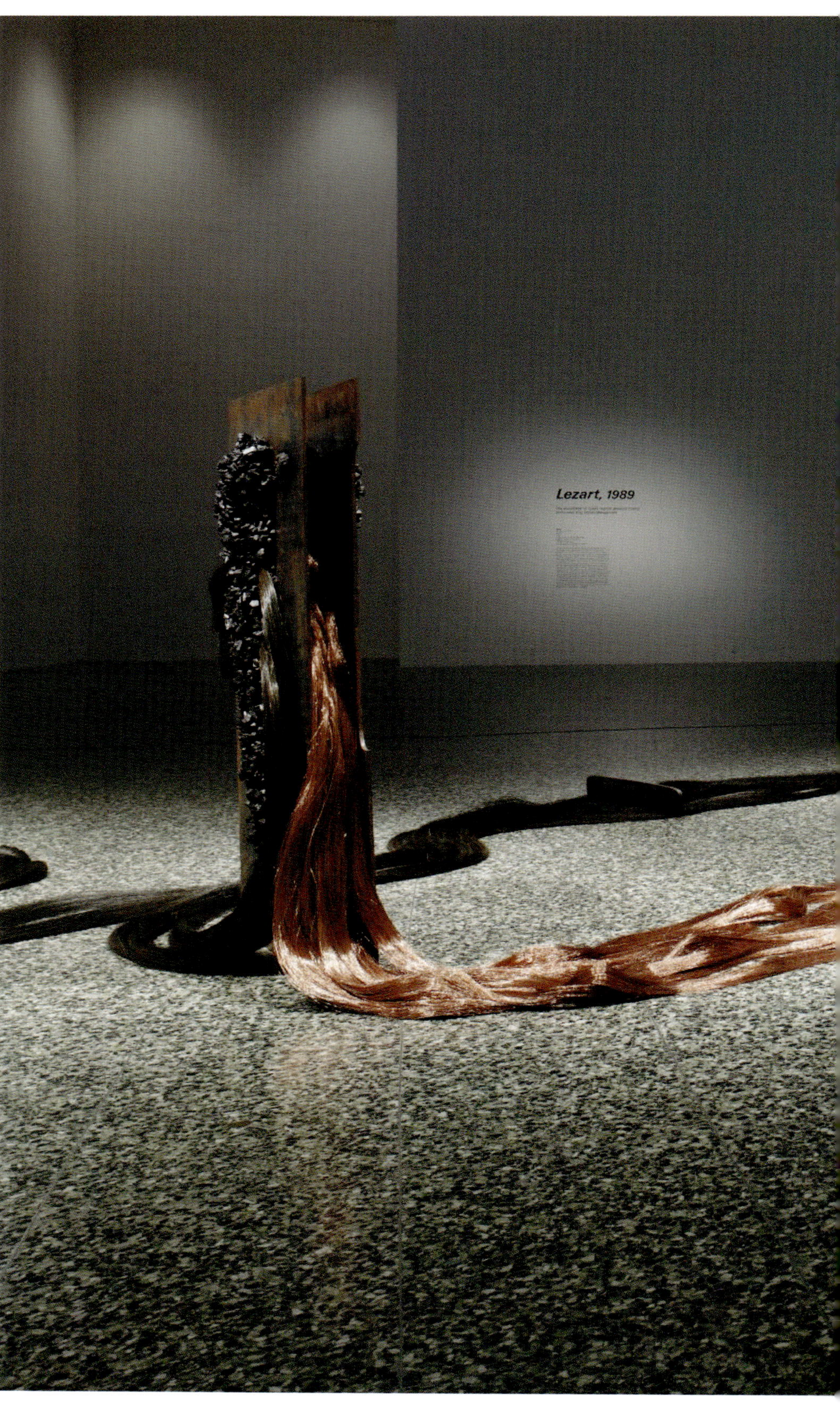

TUNGA | Brazilian, born 1952
Lezart, 1989
Iron, copper, magnets, and embroidered silk
Overall: 196 7/8 x 315 x 137 3/4 in. (500.1 x 800.1 x 349.9 cm)
Museum purchase funded by the
Caroline Wiess Law Accessions Endowment Fund
2009.572

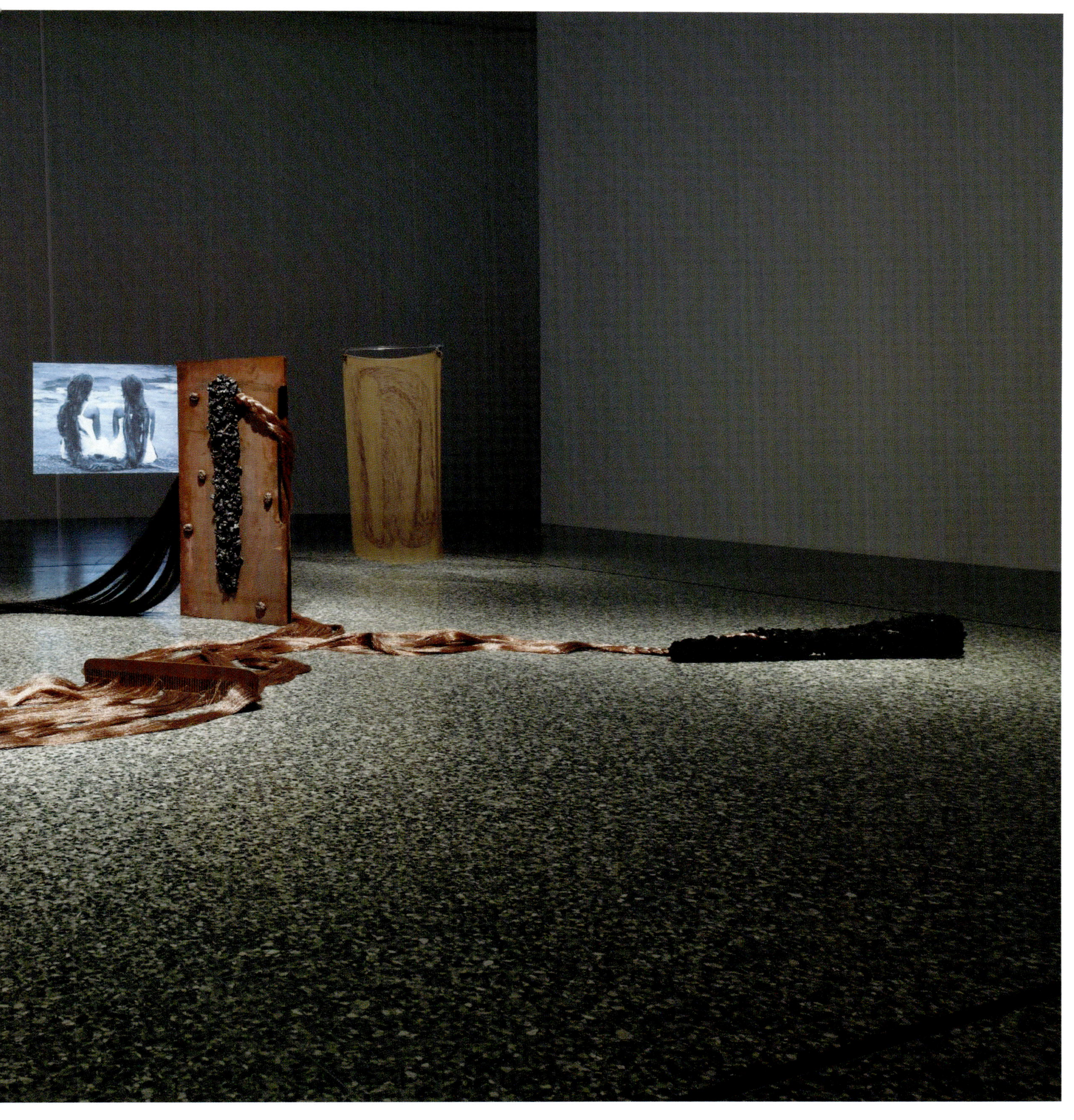

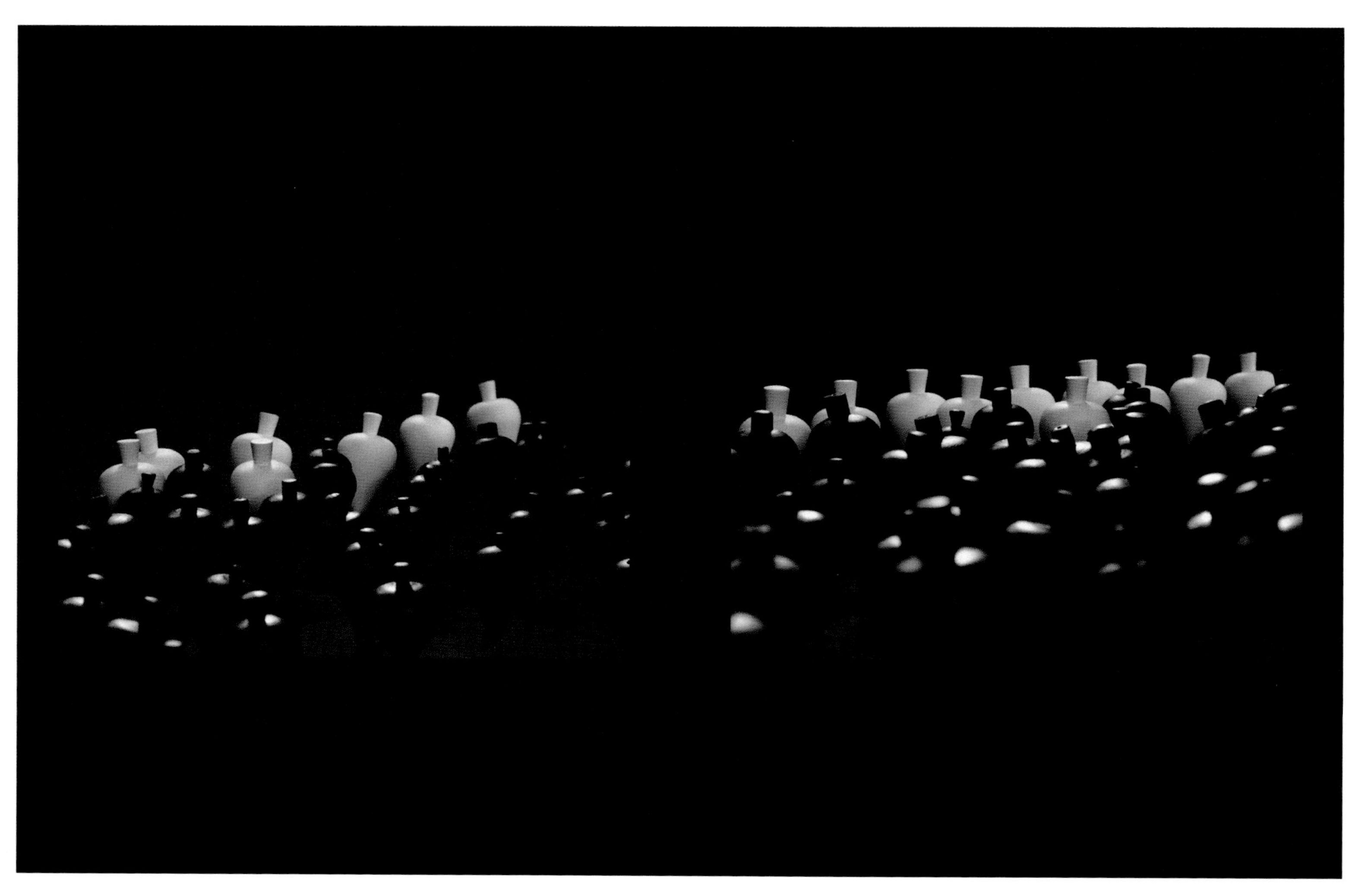

MIGUEL ÁNGEL RIOS | Argentinean, born 1943
On the Edge, 2007
Two-channel video wall projection, 4 min., 23 sec.
Center image: 9 x 14 in. (22.9 x 35.6 cm)
Left: 4 x 6 in. (10.2 x 15.2 cm)
Museum purchase funded by
the Caroline Wiess Law
Accessions Endowment Fund
2010.171

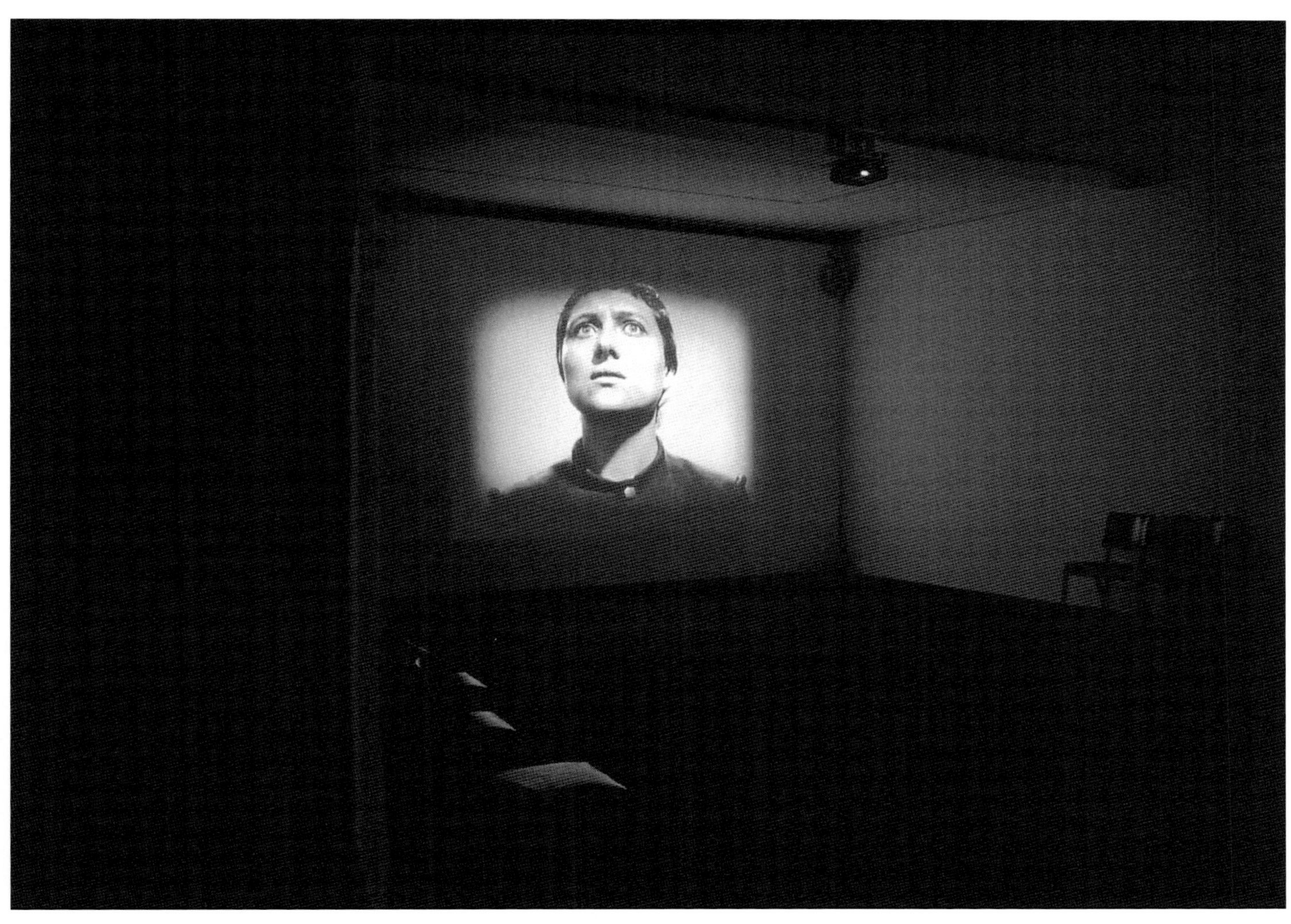

JAVIER TÉLLEZ | Venezuelan, born 1969
La passion de Jeanne d'Arc
[The Passion of Joan of Arc (Rozelle Hospital)],
ed. 2/5, 2005
Two BETACAM projections, 2 DVDs, and
3 velvet curtains
Video 1: 97 min, 25 sec
Video 2: 40 min, 55 sec
Curtain 1: 120 x 180 in. (304.8 x 457.2 cm)
Gift of Diane and Bruce Halle
from the Thomarie Foundation
2012.511

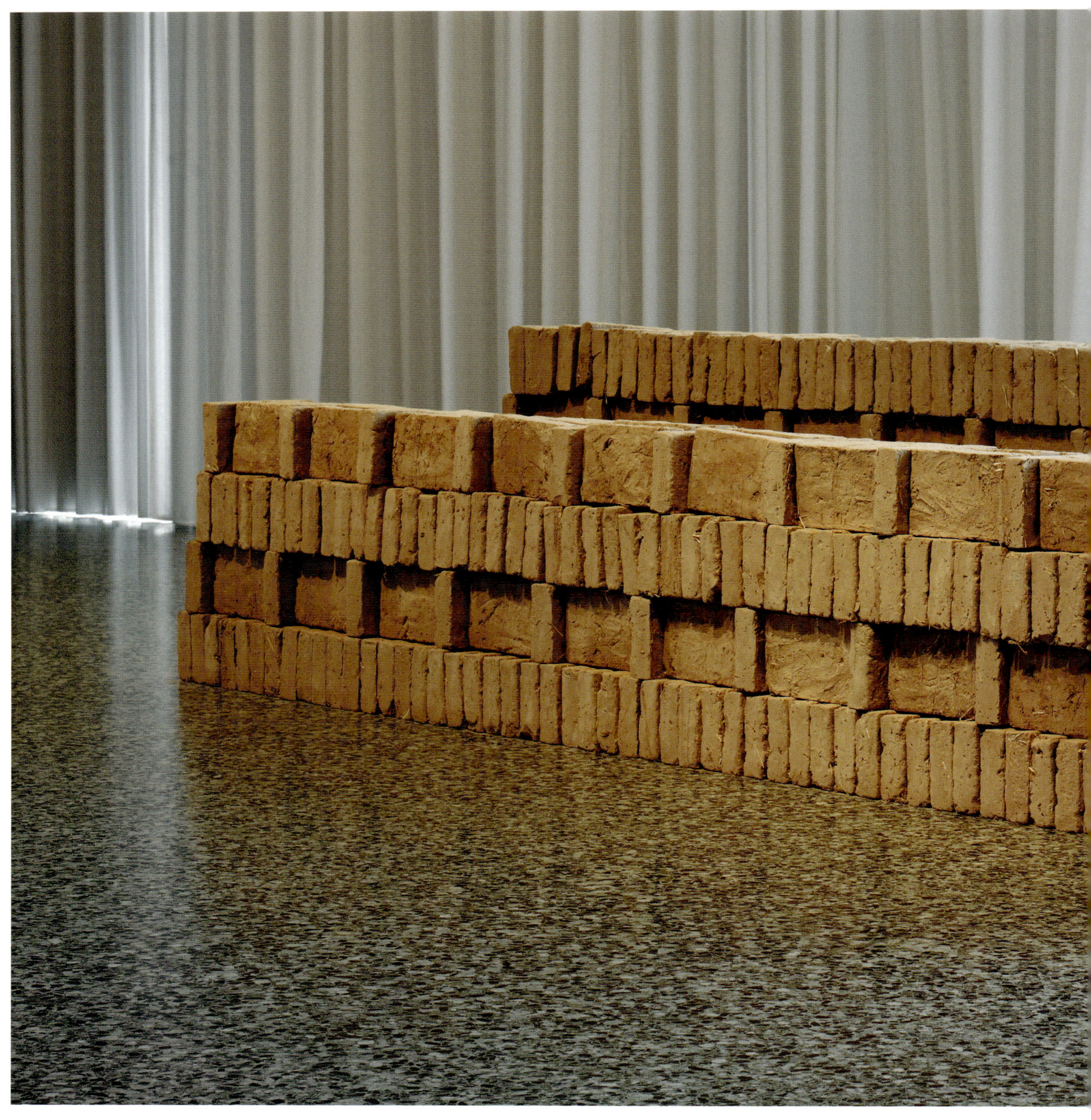

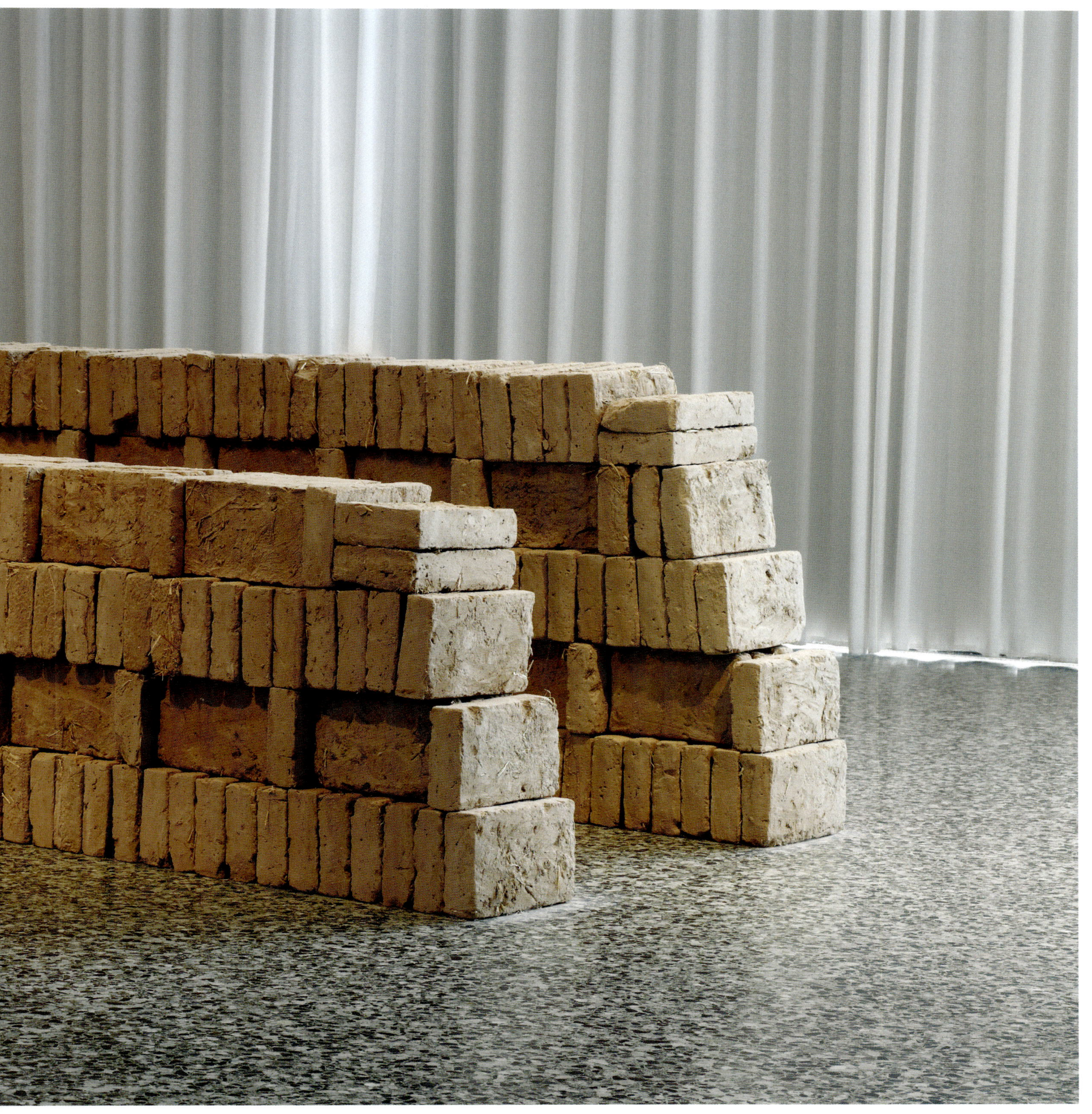

TERESA MARGOLLES | Mexican, born 1963
Lote bravo, 2005
400 mud bricks
Variable dimensions
Museum purchase with funds provided by the 2007 Latin American
Experience Gala and Auction, Mary and Roy Cullen, Sofia Adrogué,
P.C. and Sten Gustafson, Celina and Alfredo Brener, Brad and Leslie Bucher,
Eduardo and Eugenia Grüneisen, Bruce and Diane Halle, Gonzalo Parodi,
and Robert J. Card M.D. and Karol Kreymer in honor of Gilbert Vicario
2007.1855

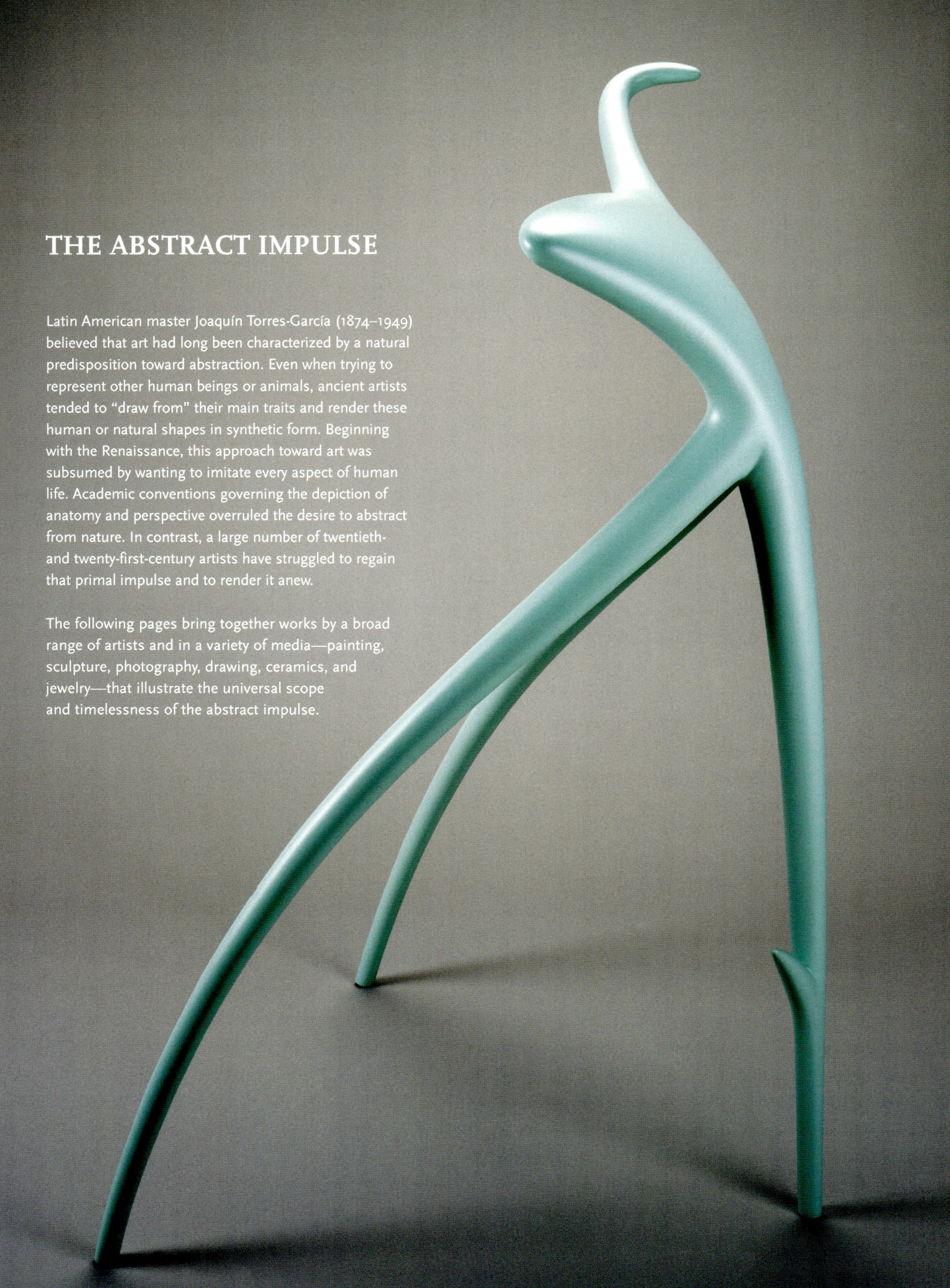

THE ABSTRACT IMPULSE

Latin American master Joaquín Torres-García (1874–1949) believed that art had long been characterized by a natural predisposition toward abstraction. Even when trying to represent other human beings or animals, ancient artists tended to "draw from" their main traits and render these human or natural shapes in synthetic form. Beginning with the Renaissance, this approach toward art was subsumed by wanting to imitate every aspect of human life. Academic conventions governing the depiction of anatomy and perspective overruled the desire to abstract from nature. In contrast, a large number of twentieth- and twenty-first-century artists have struggled to regain that primal impulse and to render it anew.

The following pages bring together works by a broad range of artists and in a variety of media—painting, sculpture, photography, drawing, ceramics, and jewelry—that illustrate the universal scope and timelessness of the abstract impulse.

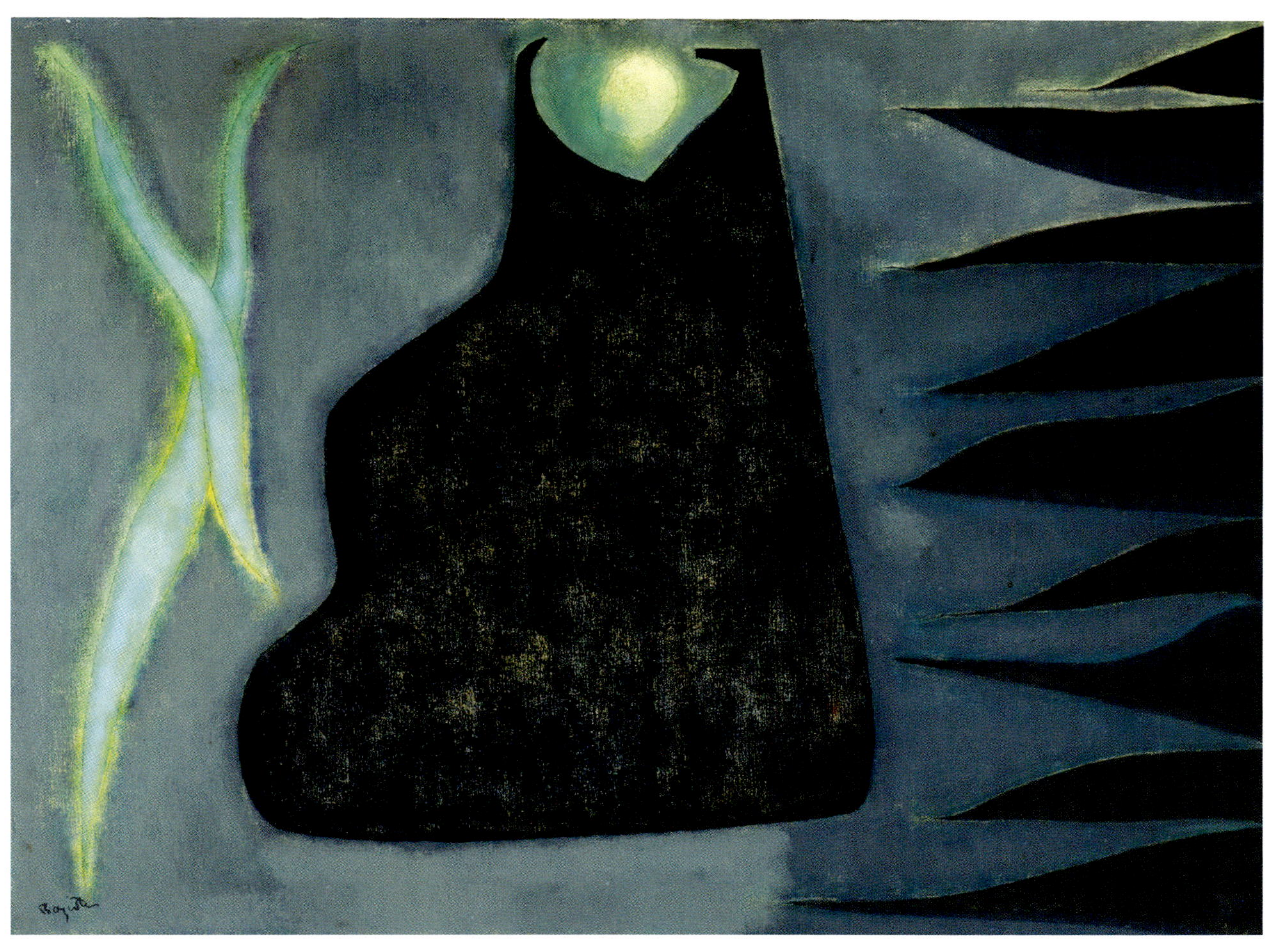

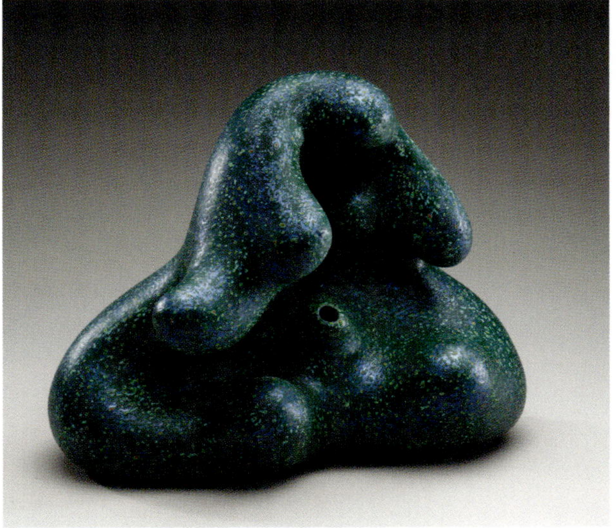

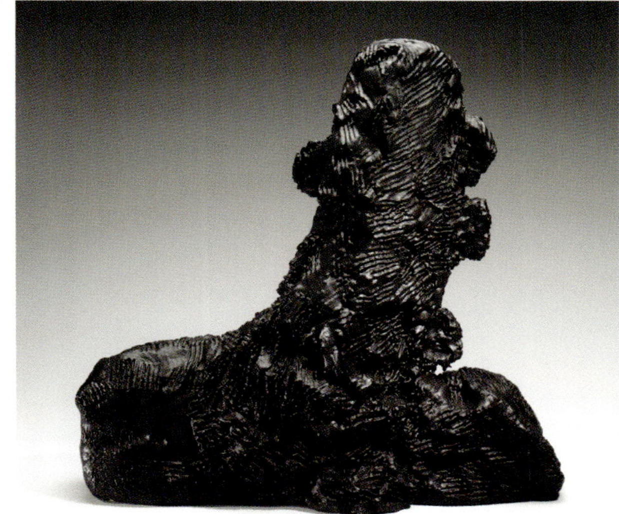

DESIGNED BY PHILIPPE STARCK | French, born 1949
Manufactured by Vitra
W. W. Stool, designed 1990, made 1996
Aluminum and paint
38 1/16 x 22 in. (96.7 x 55.9 cm)
Museum purchase funded by B. N. Woodson in honor of
Grace, Olivia, and Cate at
"One Great Night in November, 1996"
96.1711

WILLIAM BAZIOTES | American, 1912–1963
Trance, 1953
Oil on canvas
35 15/16 x 47 3/4 in. (91.3 x 121.3 cm)
Museum purchase funded by the
Caroline Wiess Law Accessions Endowment Fund
2000.429

KEN PRICE | American, 1935–2012
Bumps, 1999
11 1/2 x 14 1/4 x 9 1/4 in. (29.2 x 36.2 x 23.5 cm)
Bequest of Edward R. Broida
2007.662

JAMES BROWN | American, 1951
Stabat Mater Black, 1988
Stoneware
Overall: 22 1/2 x 22 x 10 1/4 in. (57.2 x 55.9 x 26 cm)
Garth Clark and Mark Del Vecchio Collection,
museum purchase funded by the Caroline Wiess Law
Accessions Endowment Fund
2007.777

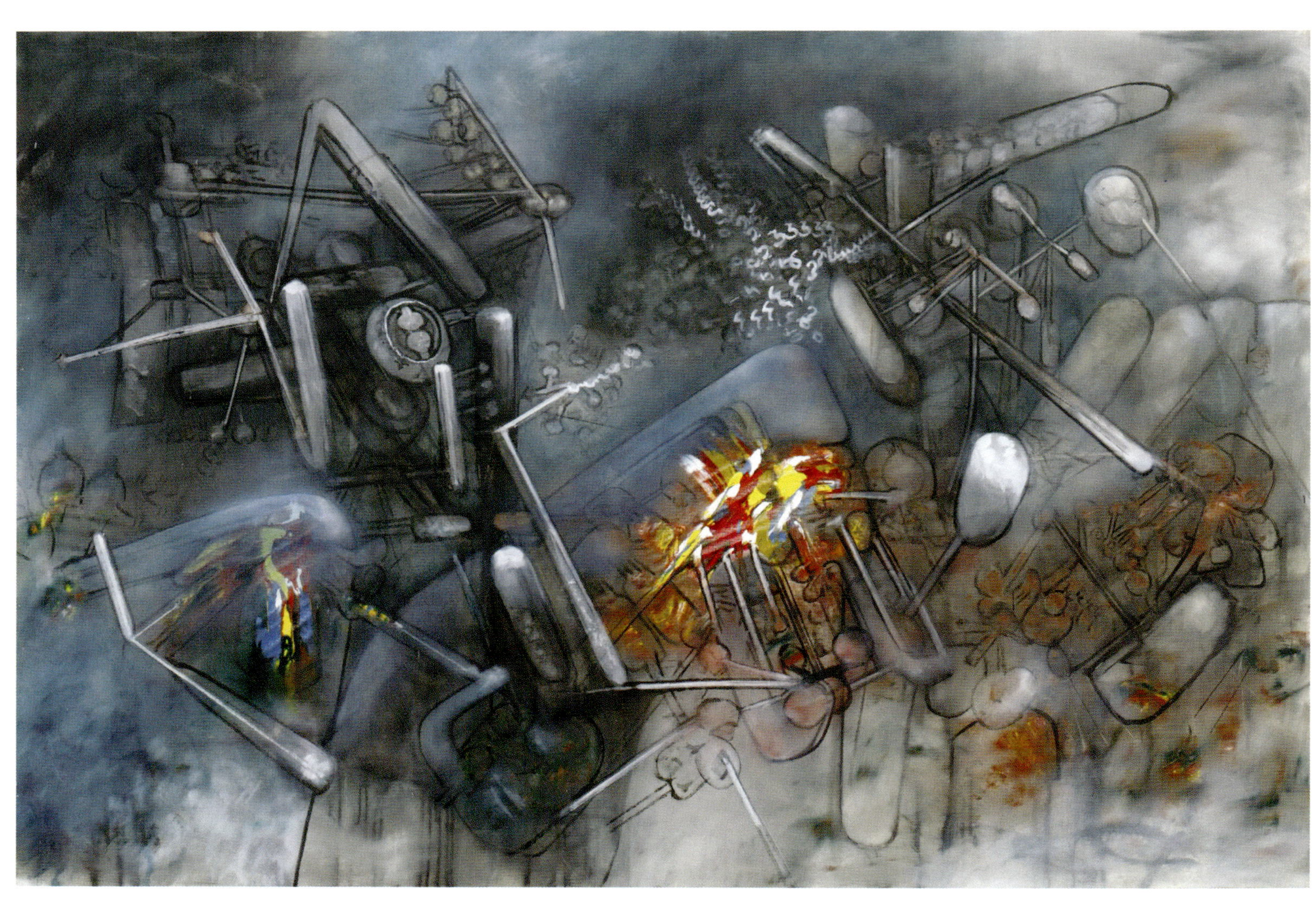

MATTA | Chilean, 1911–2002
26, c. 1963
from the series *The Space of the Species*
Oil on canvas
79 x 115 1/2 in. (200.7 x 293.37 cm)
Gift of D. and J. de Menil
64.37

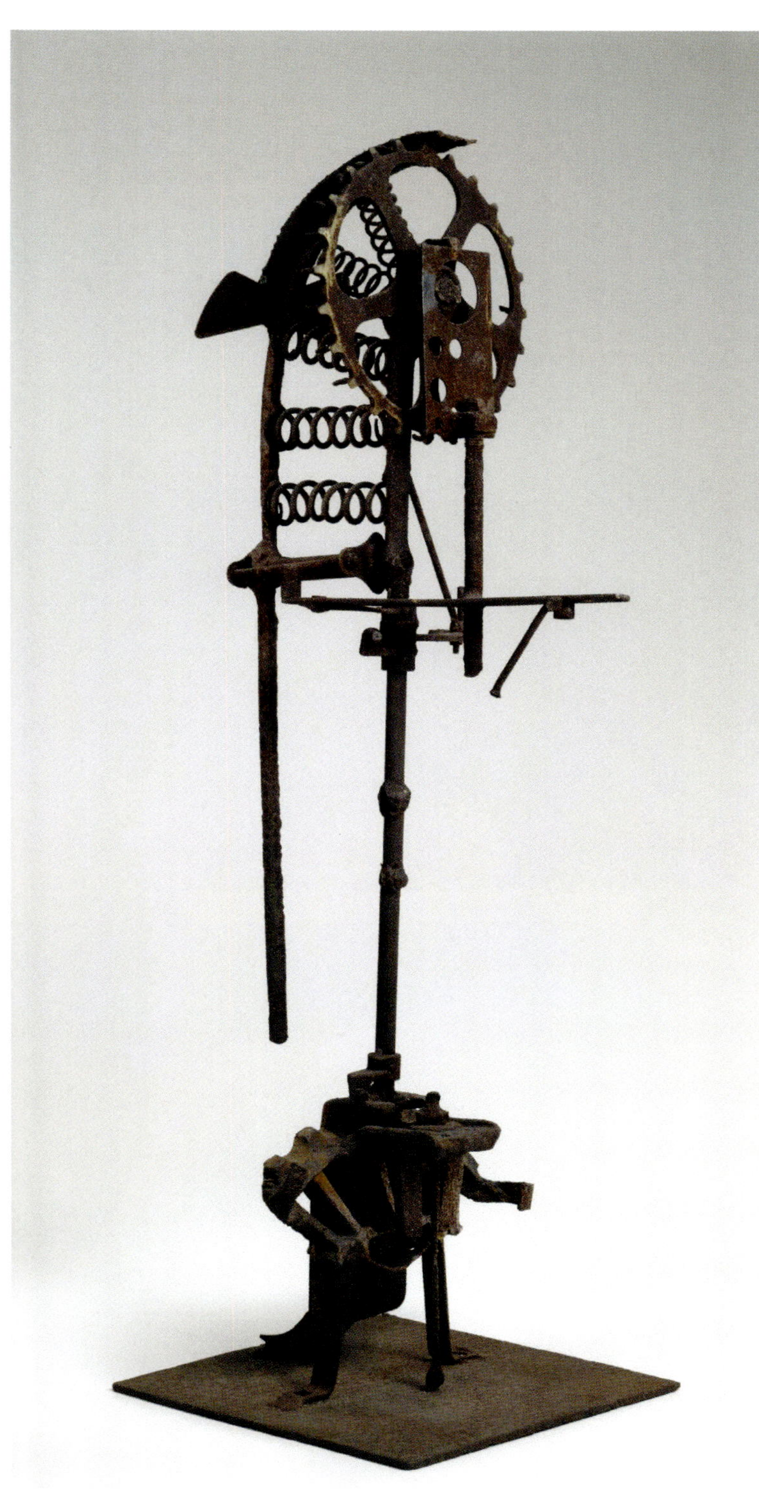

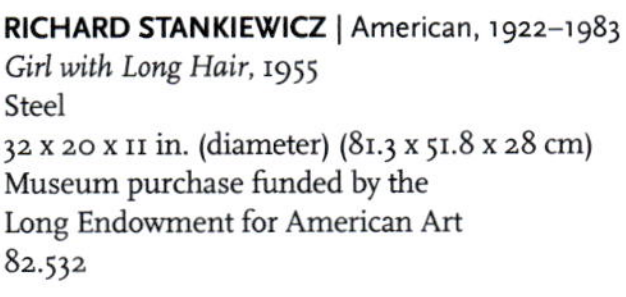

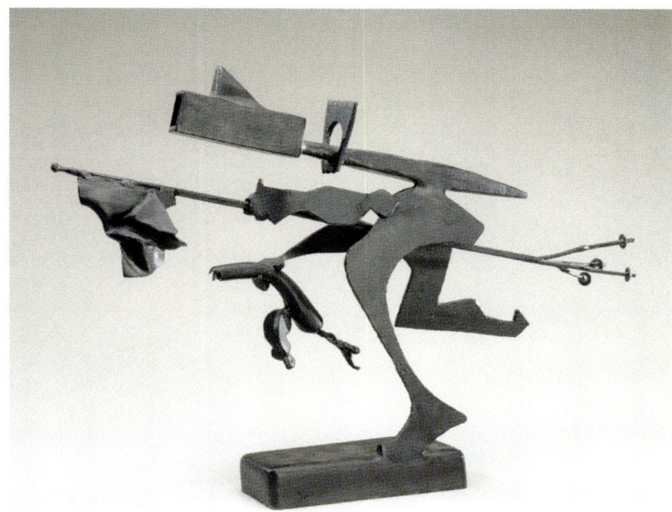

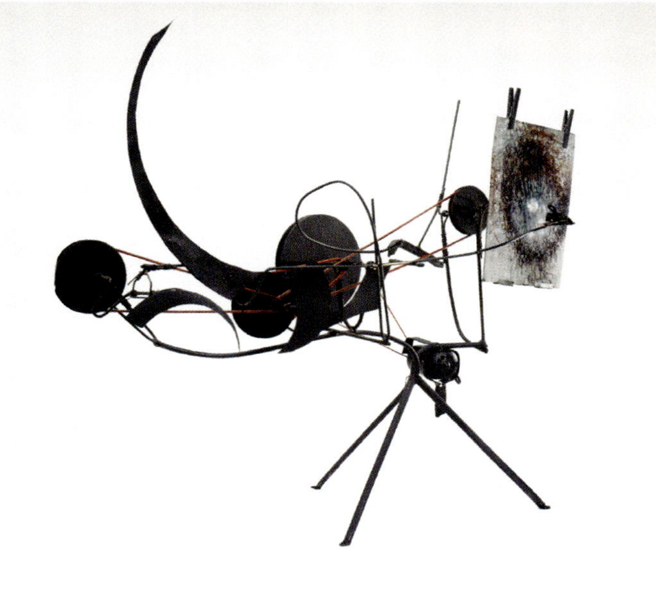

RICHARD STANKIEWICZ | American, 1922–1983
Girl with Long Hair, 1955
Steel
32 x 20 x 11 in. (diameter) (81.3 x 51.8 x 28 cm)
Museum purchase funded by the
Long Endowment for American Art
82.532

DAVID SMITH | American, 1906–1965
War Spectre, 1944
Painted steel
14 1/2 x 22 5/8 x 6 3/4 in.(36.8 x 57.4 x 17.1 cm)
Museum purchase
78.58

JEAN TINGUELY | Swiss, 1925–1991
Méta-matic No. 9, 1958
Round rubber belt, steel rods, painted sheet
metal, wire wooden pulleys, two clothes pins,
and electric motor
35 1/2 x 56 5/8 x 14 1/4 in. (90.2 x 143.8 x 36.2 cm)
Gift of D. and J. de Menil
65.16

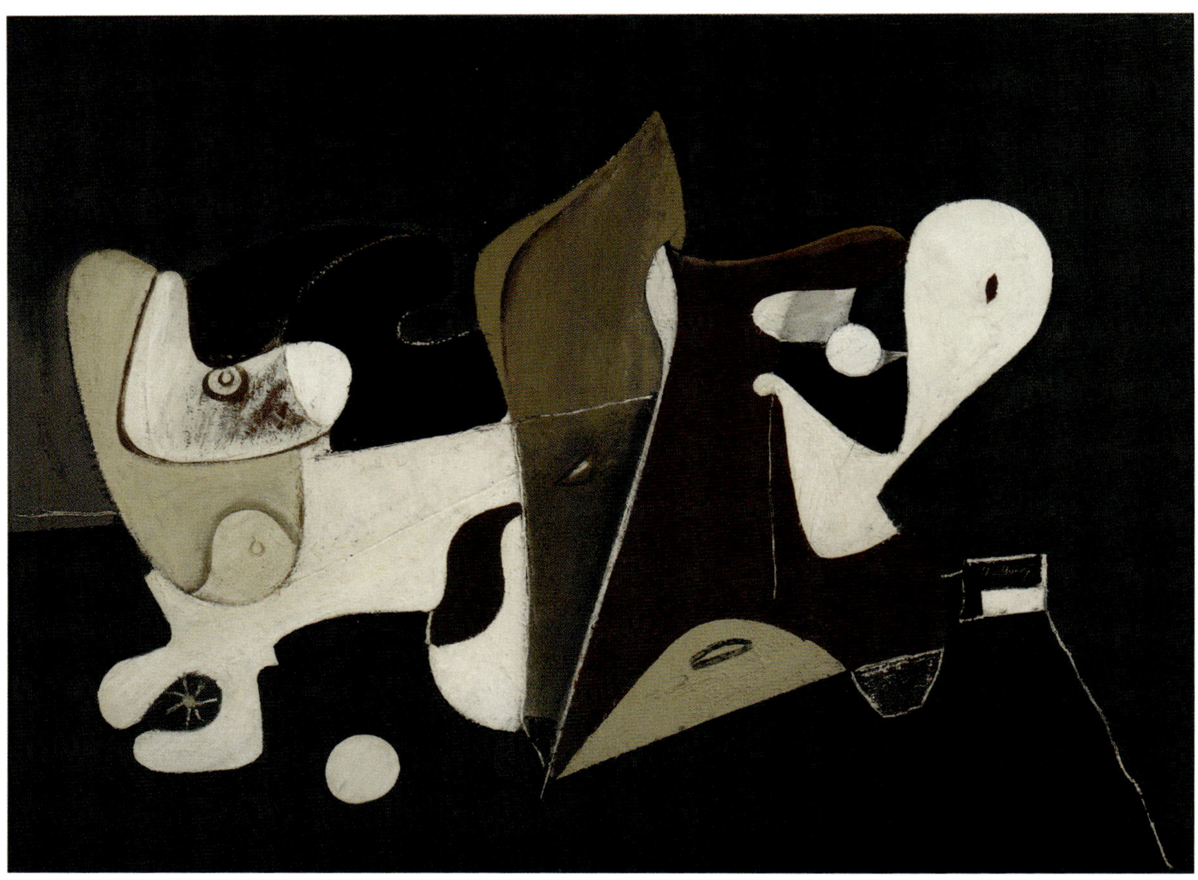

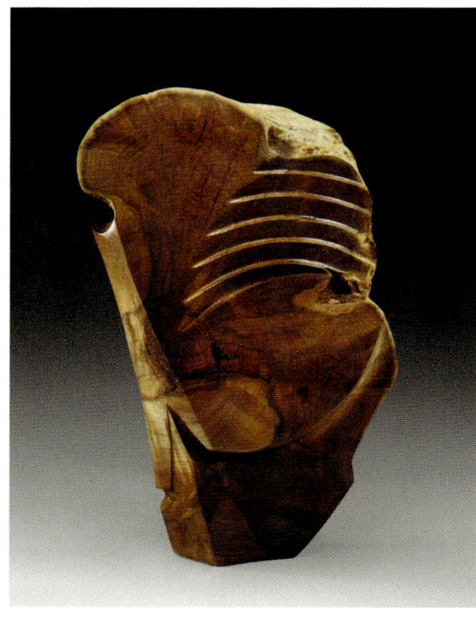

ARSHILE GORKY | American, born Armenia, 1904–1948
Nightime, Enigma and Nostalgia, c. 1933–34
Oil on canvas mounted onto panel
Canvas: 36 x 47 7/8 in. (91.4 x 121.6 cm)
Museum purchase with funds provided by
the Caroline Wiess Law
Accessions Endowment Fund
2005.1157

STONEY LAMAR | American, born 1951
A Man of Gaaaad, 1995
Maple
18 1/2 x 12 1/2 x 7 in. (47 x 31.8 x 17.8 cm)
Gift of John and Robyn Horn
2008.461

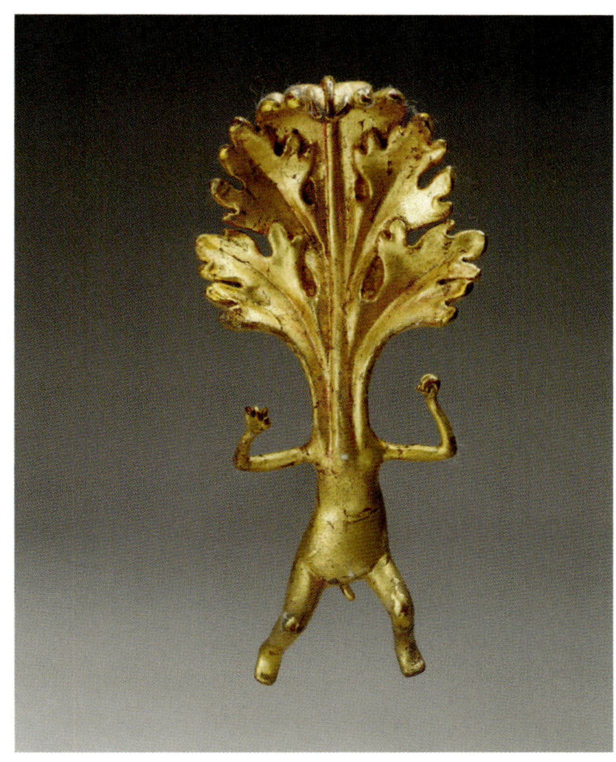

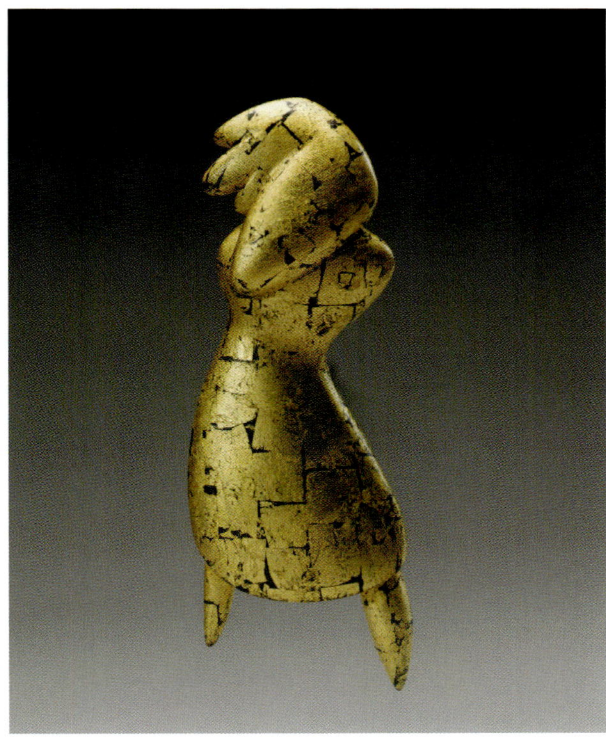

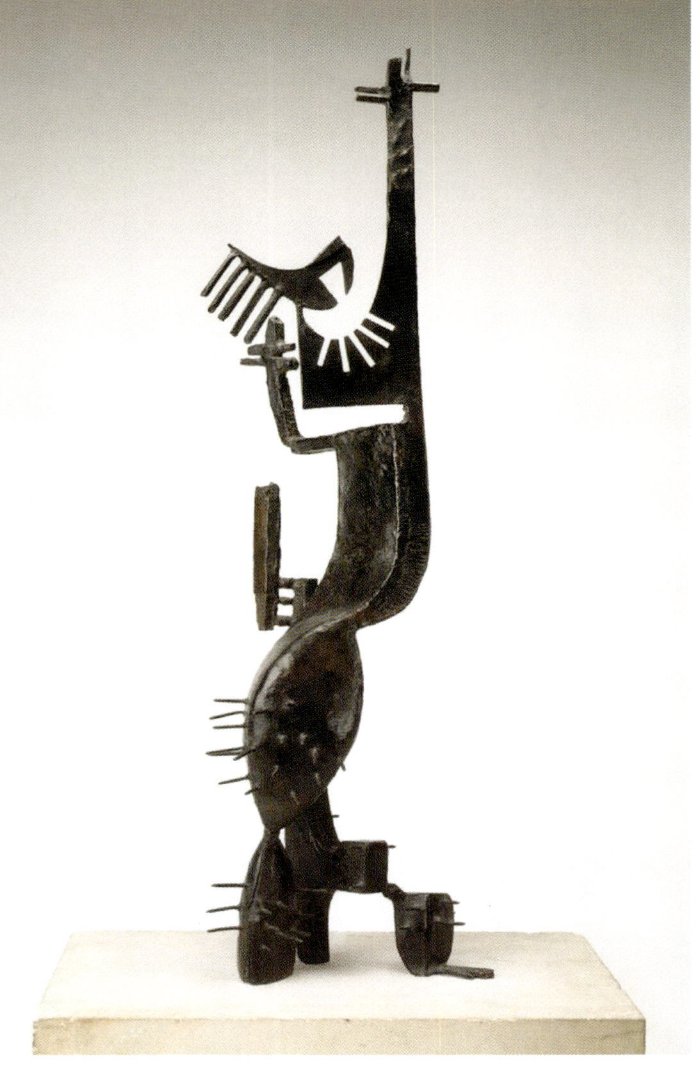

BRUCE METCALF | American, born 1949
Wood Brooch #109, 1995
23k gold leaf, paint, maple wood, copper,
and brass
4 3/8 x 2 x 3/4 in. (11.1 x 5.1 x 1.9 cm)
Helen Williams Drutt Collection,
Museum purchase funded by the
Caroline Wiess Law Foundation
2002.3964

BRUCE METCALF | American, born 1949
"Wood Pin #3" Brooch, 1987
23k gold leaf, oak wood, and maple wood
5 x 2 x 1 in. (12.7 x 5.1 x 2.5 cm)
Helen Williams Drutt Collection,
Museum purchase funded by the
Caroline Wiess Law Foundation
2002.3962

JULIO GONZÁLEZ | Spanish, 1876–1942
Cactus Woman, 1939–40 / cast posthumously
Bronze
30 15/16 x 10 3/8 x 7 5/8 in. (78.6 x 26.3 x 19.3 cm)
Base: 2 1/2 x 18 1/8 x 10 1/4 in. (6.4 x 46 x 26 cm)
Museum purchase
73.27

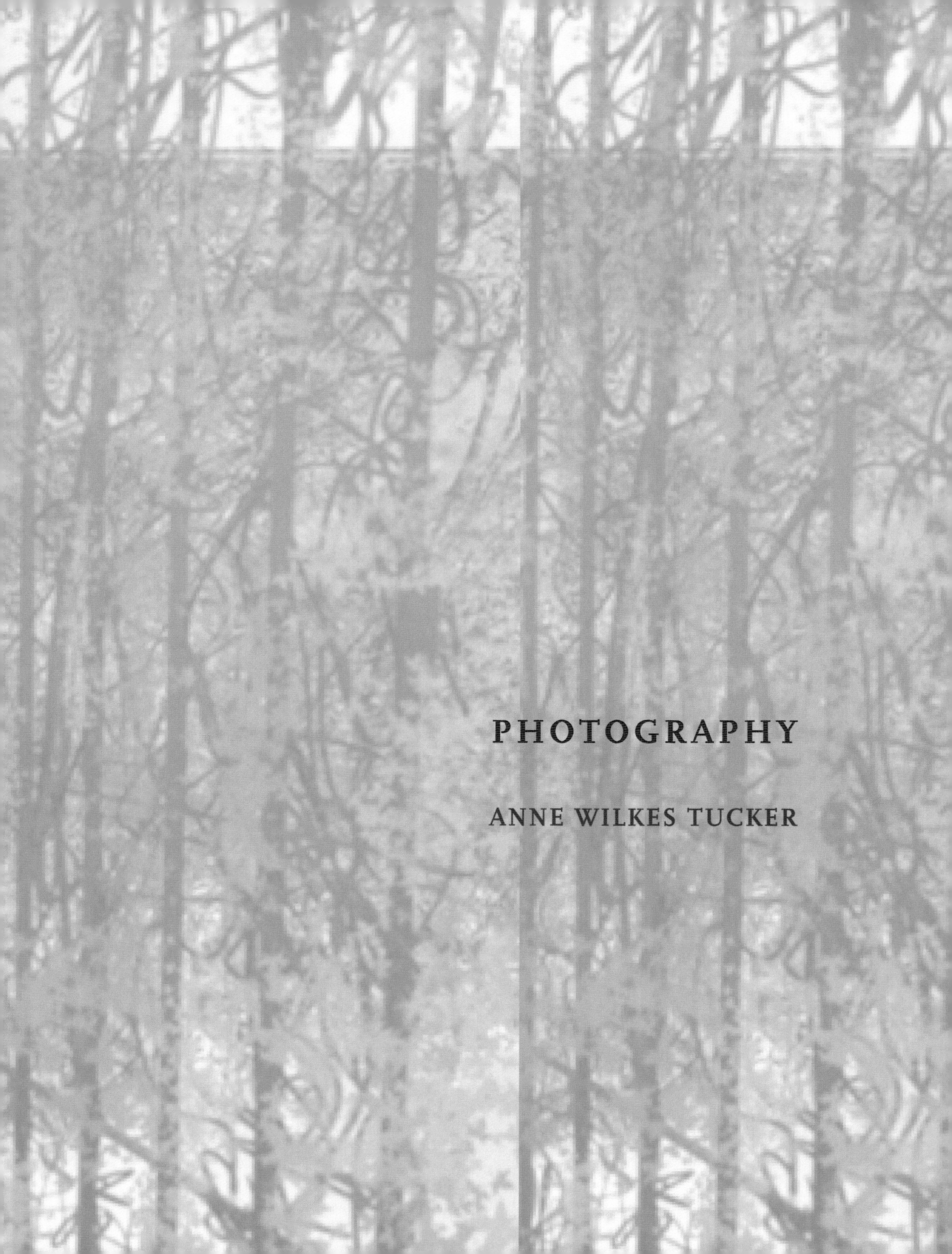

PHOTOGRAPHY

ANNE WILKES TUCKER

Images in the Museum's photography collection were made on all seven continents between 1840 and the present, but the strengths of the collection are works made in the United States and Europe in the twentieth and twenty-first centuries. Most of the images featured in this book were made for fine-art exhibitions by photographers who considered themselves to be artists, such as Paul Strand and Cindy Sherman. Others were made for major publications such as *Life* and *Vogue* magazines by photojournalists and portraitists who also considered themselves to be artists; among this group are W. Eugene Smith and Irving Penn. The collection's images reflect major aesthetic movements, including the particular brand of American Modernism that evolved around the photographer and gallerist Alfred Stieglitz, as well as practitioners in Modernist circles from other regions of the United States, Czechoslovakia, France, Germany, and Mexico. Within the Modern tradition, the collection includes major divisions of thought and practice: Dada by the collagist Hannah Höch, Surrealism by Man Ray, Group f'64 by Imogen Cunningham, and the Bauhaus School by László Moholy-Nagy.

Each image selected here represents depth in the collection, both in other works by that photographer as well as by their contemporaries. For instance, Jaromír Funke was an important photographer, theorist, and writer about photography in Czechoslovakia in the first half of the twentieth century, as was his colleague Josef Sudek, whose career is also well represented in the Museum's collection, along with several hundred other photographs made by Czech photographers in the twentieth century. There are more than sixty photographers whose holdings at the Museum range from thirty to several hundred photographs covering the full range of their rich careers. For instance, the Museum owns a complete set of Robert Frank's historic series titled The Americans, as well as the original maquette for the book on that series and many other photographs made by Frank before and

subsequent to the publication of *The Americans* in 1959, up through the twenty-first century. The Museum also collects Frank's films (see pp. 147–48). Similarly, the Museum has collected nearly complete sets of three major series by Diane Arbus, as well as most of the prints in W. Eugene Smith's major essay *Country Doctor*, published by *Life* magazine in 1948. The collection also includes photographs from each of the types of photographs made by Irving Penn during his prolific and influential career: portrait, still life, fashion, nude studies, and his work with experimental techniques.

There is a relationship between depth in the Museum's collection of works by certain artists and having prepared early or midcareer retrospective exhibitions by that artist, such as the representation of the career of Richard Misrach. Works were also purchased from historical surveys shown at the Museum, including the exhibitions *Czech Modernism 1900–1945* (in 1999) and *The History of Japanese Photography* (in 2003). In-depth holdings of August Sander and rare early works by Bernd and Hilla Becher came to the Museum with the acquisition of the Manfred Heiting Collection. Works by Asian photographers are often acquired in consultation with the Museum's Asian Art Department. Finally, the Photography Department continues to identify and collect the works of young photographers whose talent undoubtedly will continue to evolve and mature. Equally, the Museum collects major works by established artists who work increasingly in multiple media.

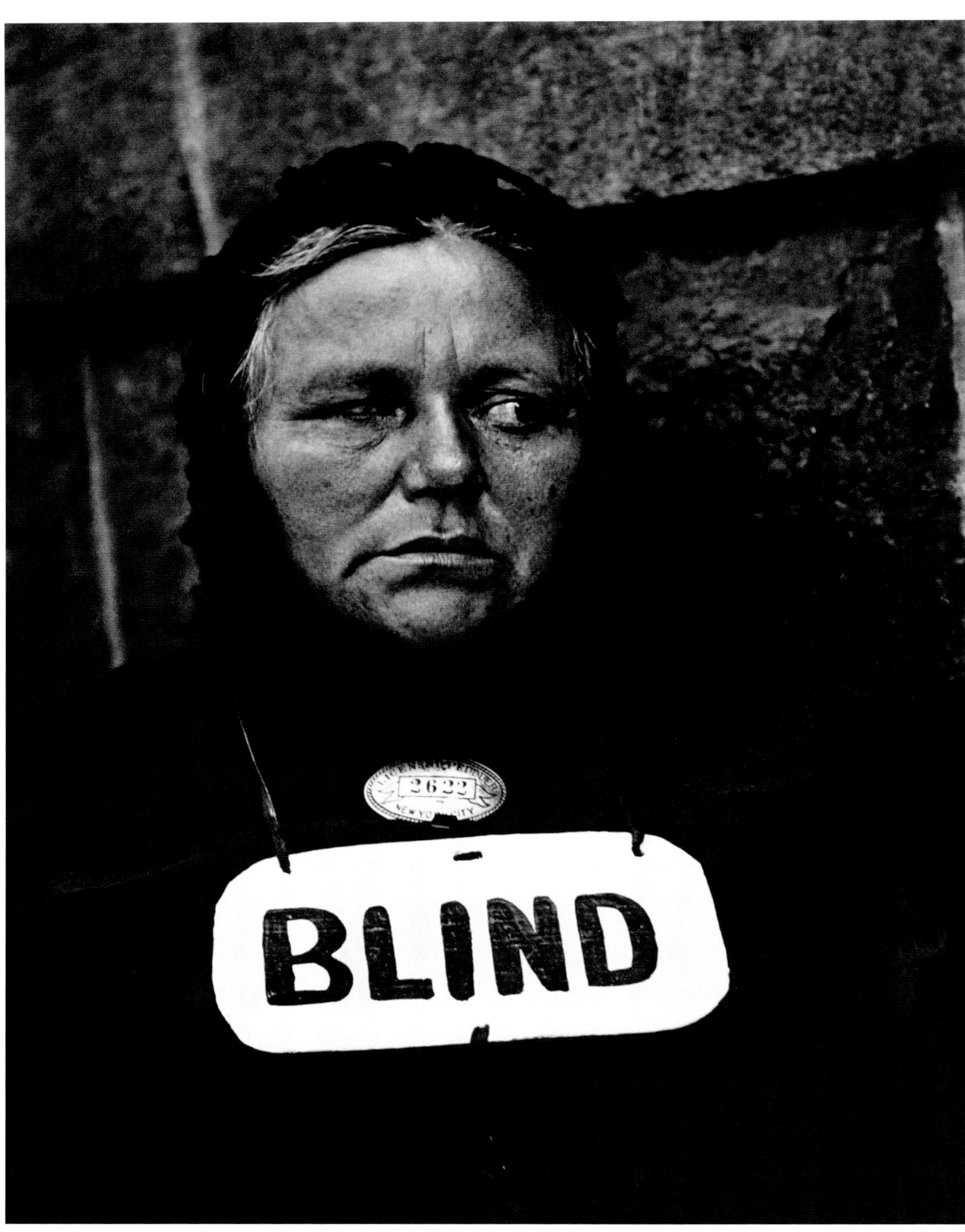
2622
BLIND

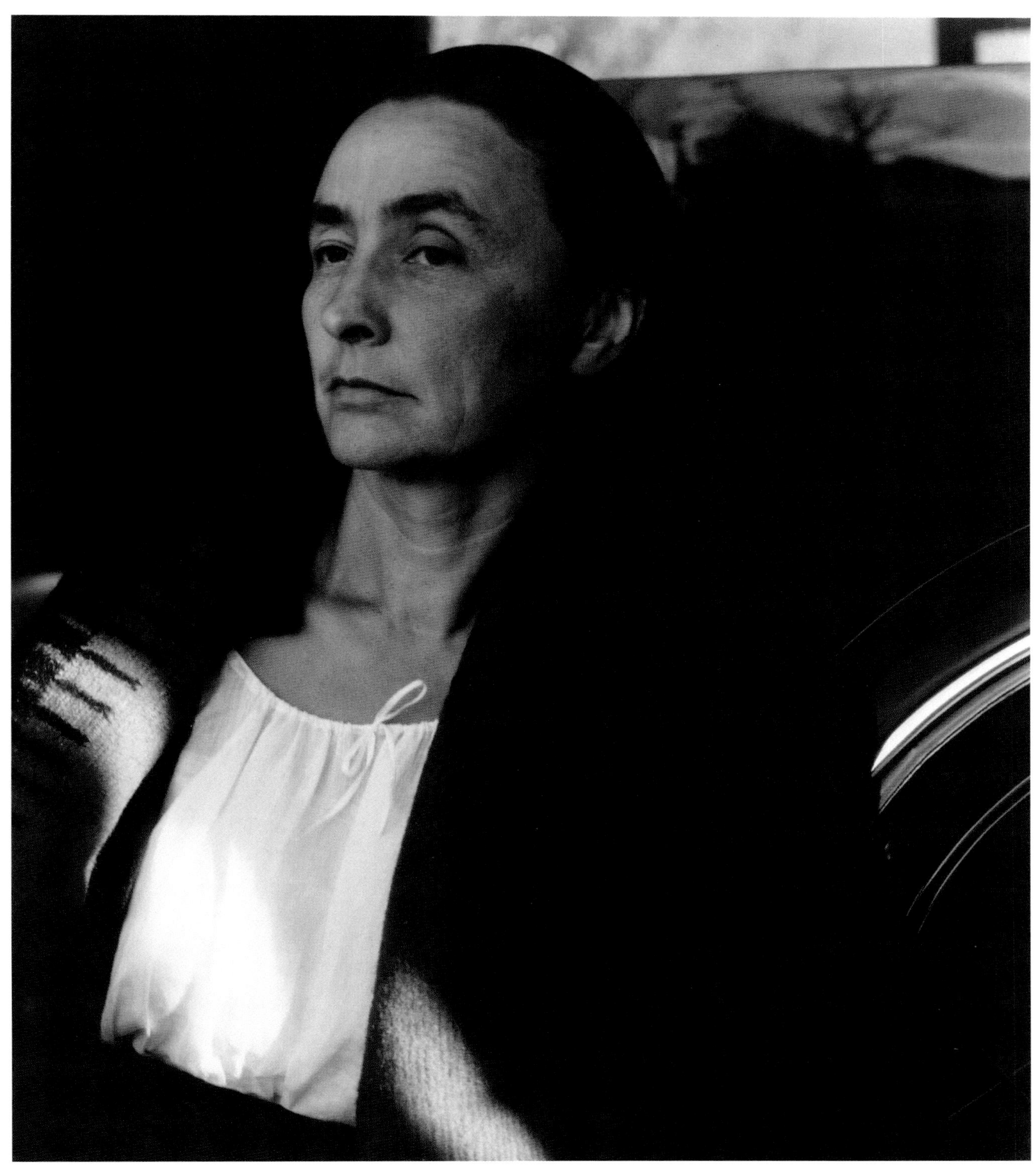

PAUL STRAND | American, 1890–1976
Blind Woman, New York, 1916
Gelatin silver print
Image: 12 7/8 x 9 13/16 in. (32.8 x 24.9 cm)
Mount: 13 1/2 x 10 7/16 in. (34.3 x 26.5 cm)
Gift of Manfred Heiting,
The Manfred Heiting Collection
2004.677

ALFRED STIEGLITZ | American, 1864–1946
Georgia O'Keeffe, 1933
Gelatin silver print
Image/Sheet: 8 3/4 x 7 1/2 in. (22.2 x 19.1 cm)
Mount: 20 9/16 x 15 11/16 in. (52.2 x 39.9 cm)
The Target Collection of American Photography,
Museum purchase funded by Target Stores
78.63

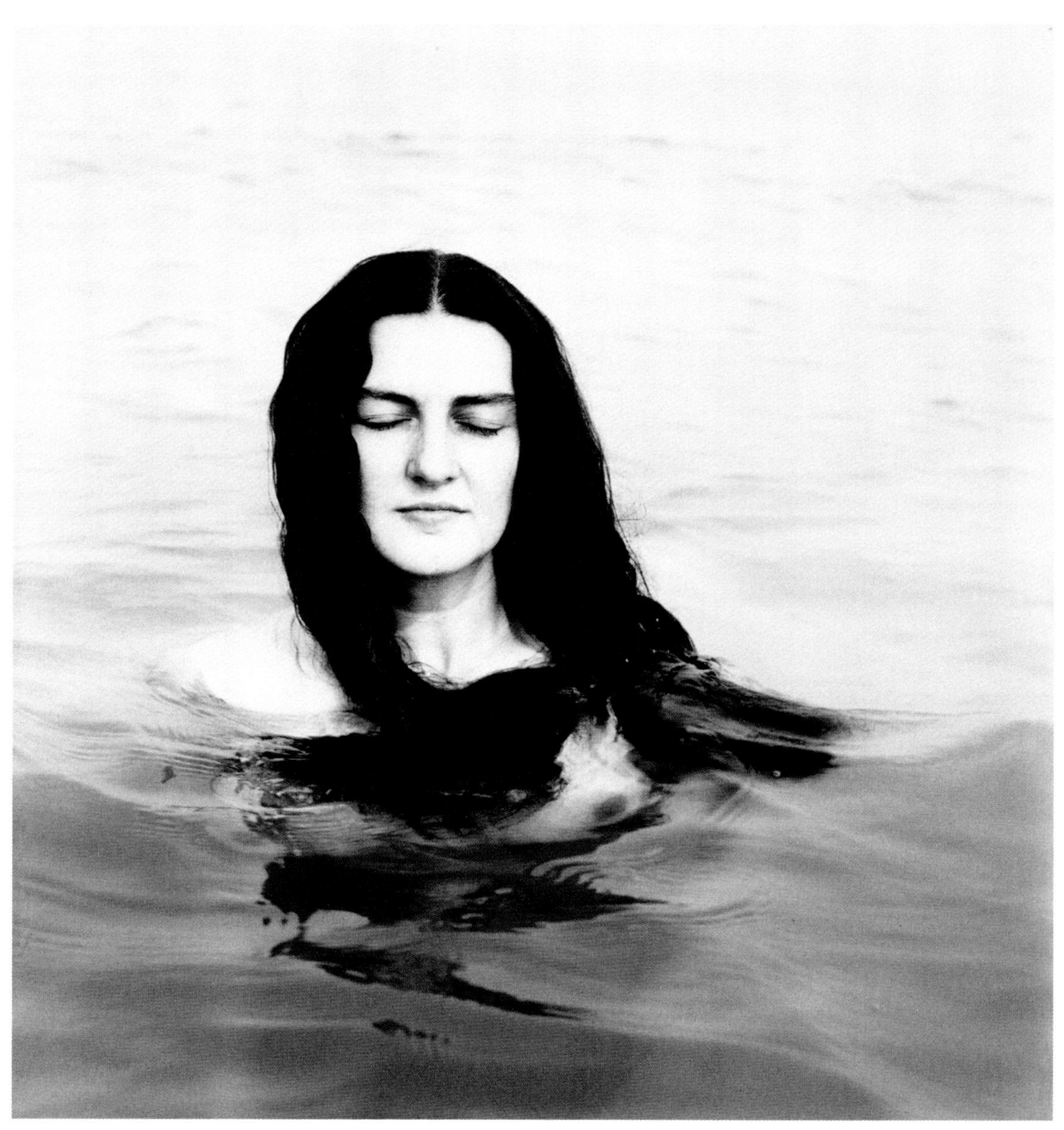

HARRY CALLAHAN | American, 1912–1999
Eleanor, Chicago, 1949
Gelatin silver print
Image: 10 x 9 3/8 in. (25.4 x 23.8 cm)
Sheet: 13 7/8 x 11 in. (35.2 x 27.9 cm)
Museum purchase
75.579

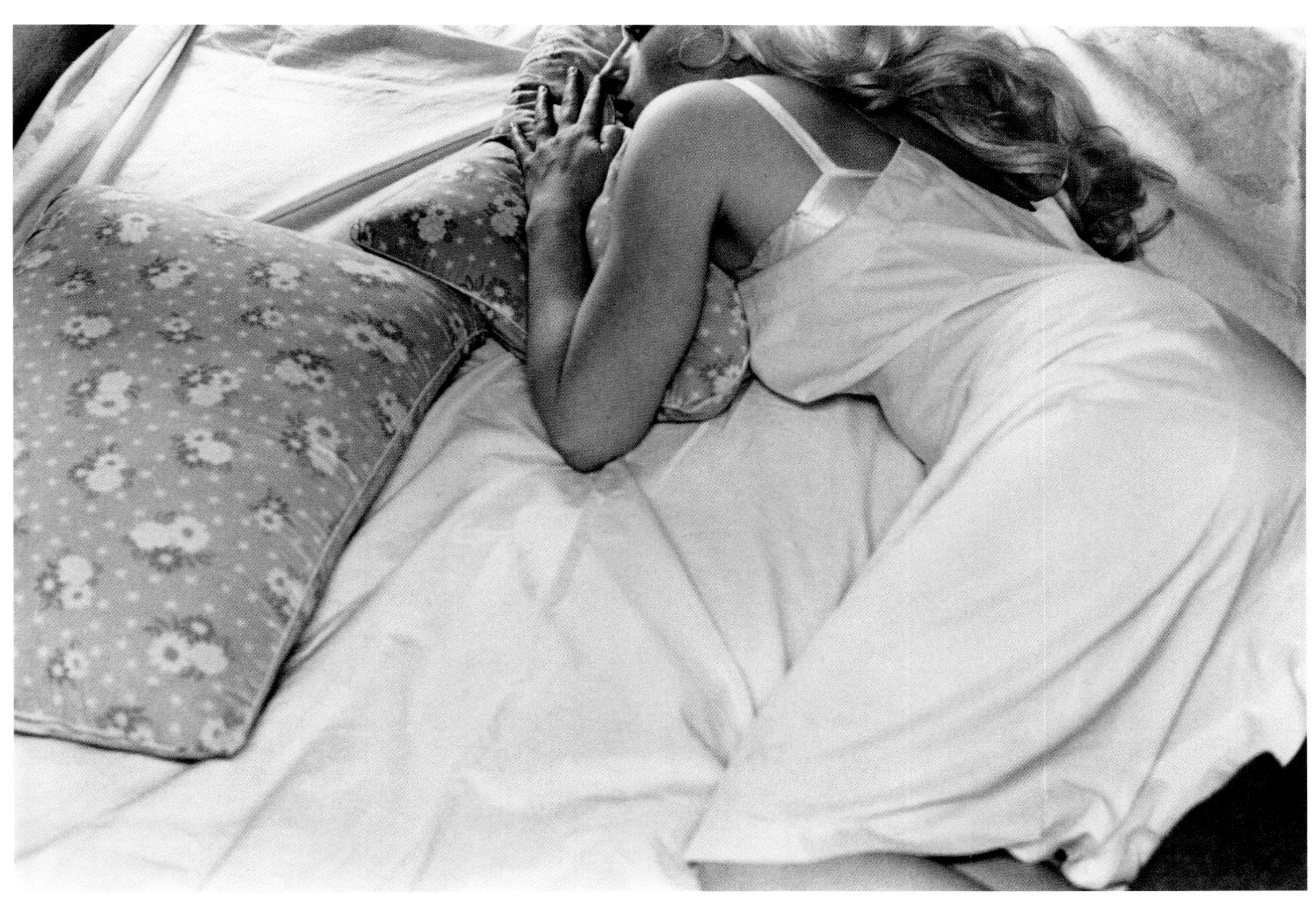

CINDY SHERMAN | American, born 1954
Untitled Film Still #52, 1979
Gelatin silver print, edition 9/10
Image: 6 1/2 x 9 7/16 in. (16.5 x 24 cm)
Sheet: 8 x 9 15/16 in. (20.3 x 25.3 cm)
Museum purchase funded by the Karen
and Eric Pulaski Philanthropic Fund of the
Houston Jewish Community Foundation
2001.206

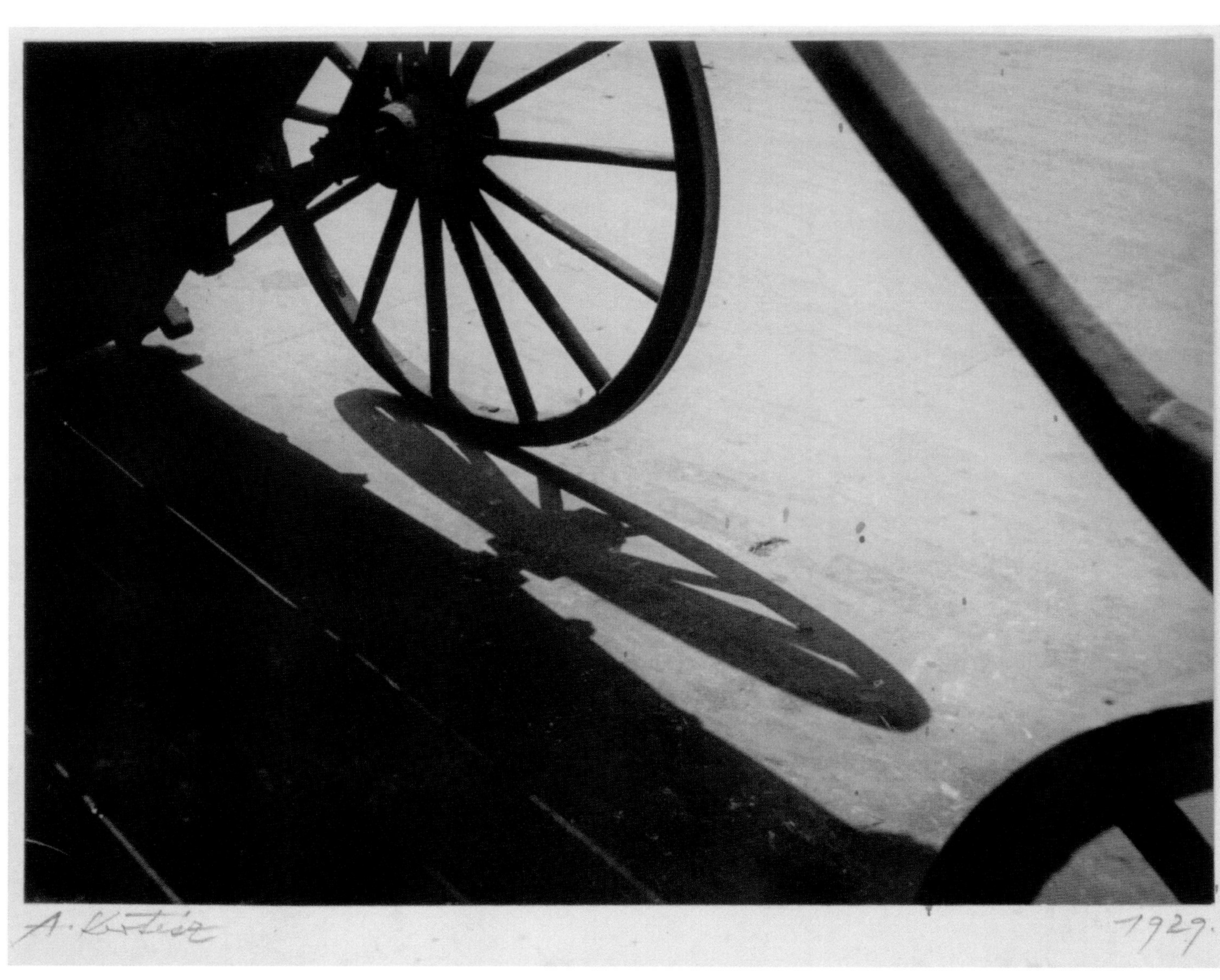

ANDRÉ KERTÉSZ | American,
born Hungary, 1894–1985
In Les Halles, 1929
Gelatin silver print
Image/Sheet: 6 5/8 x 8 3/4 in. (16.8 x 22.2 cm)
Mount: 12 5/8 x 11 5/8 in. (32 x 29.5 cm)
Museum purchase funded by the
Brown Foundation Accessions
Endowment Fund
88.13

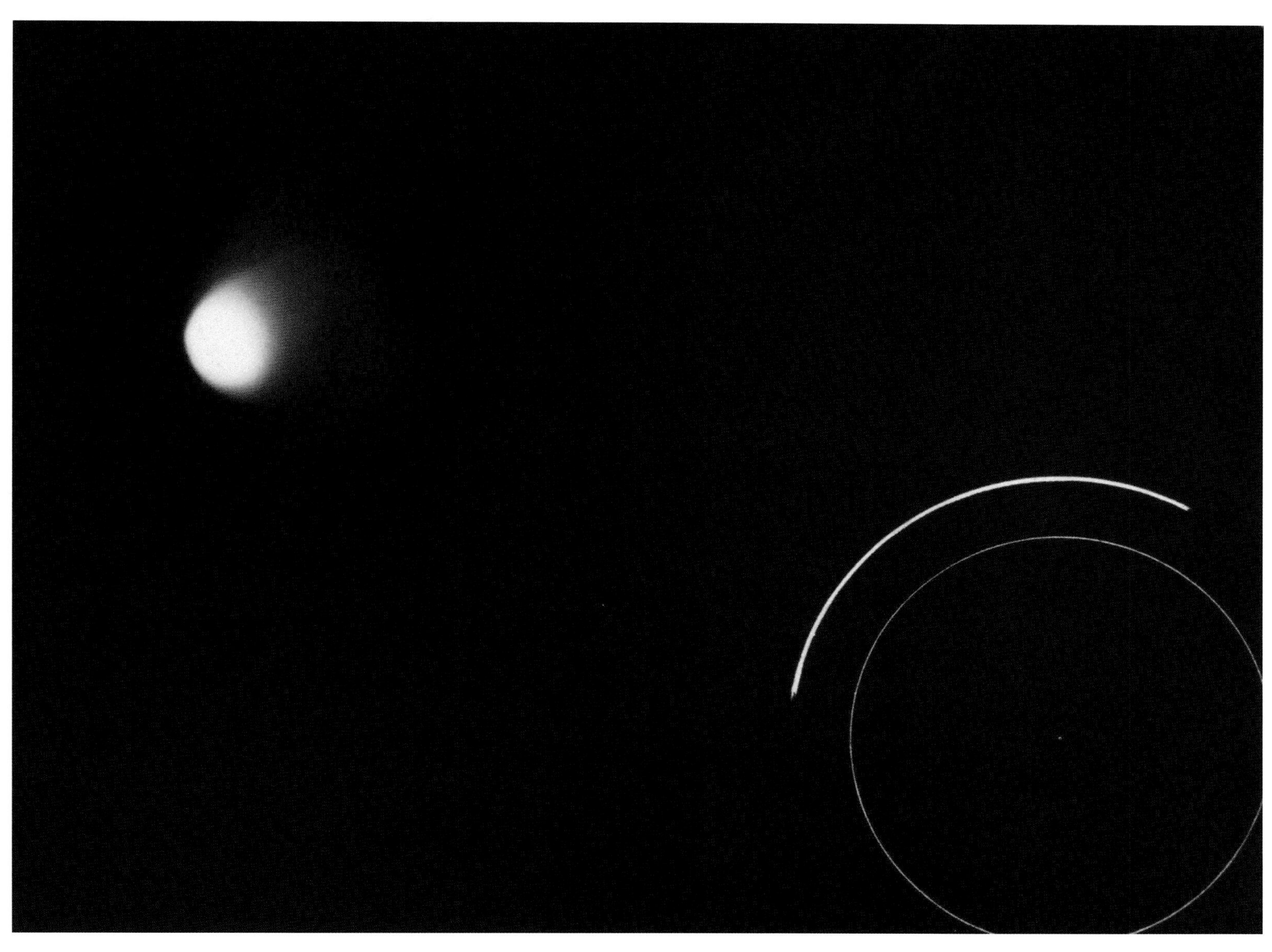

LÁSZLÓ MOHOLY-NAGY | American,
born Austria-Hungary, 1895–1946
Untitled, 1925–28
Gelatin silver print, photogram
Image/Sheet: 7 x 9 5/16 in. (17.8 x 23.7 cm)
Museum purchase funded by the
S. I. Morris Photography Endowment
84.246

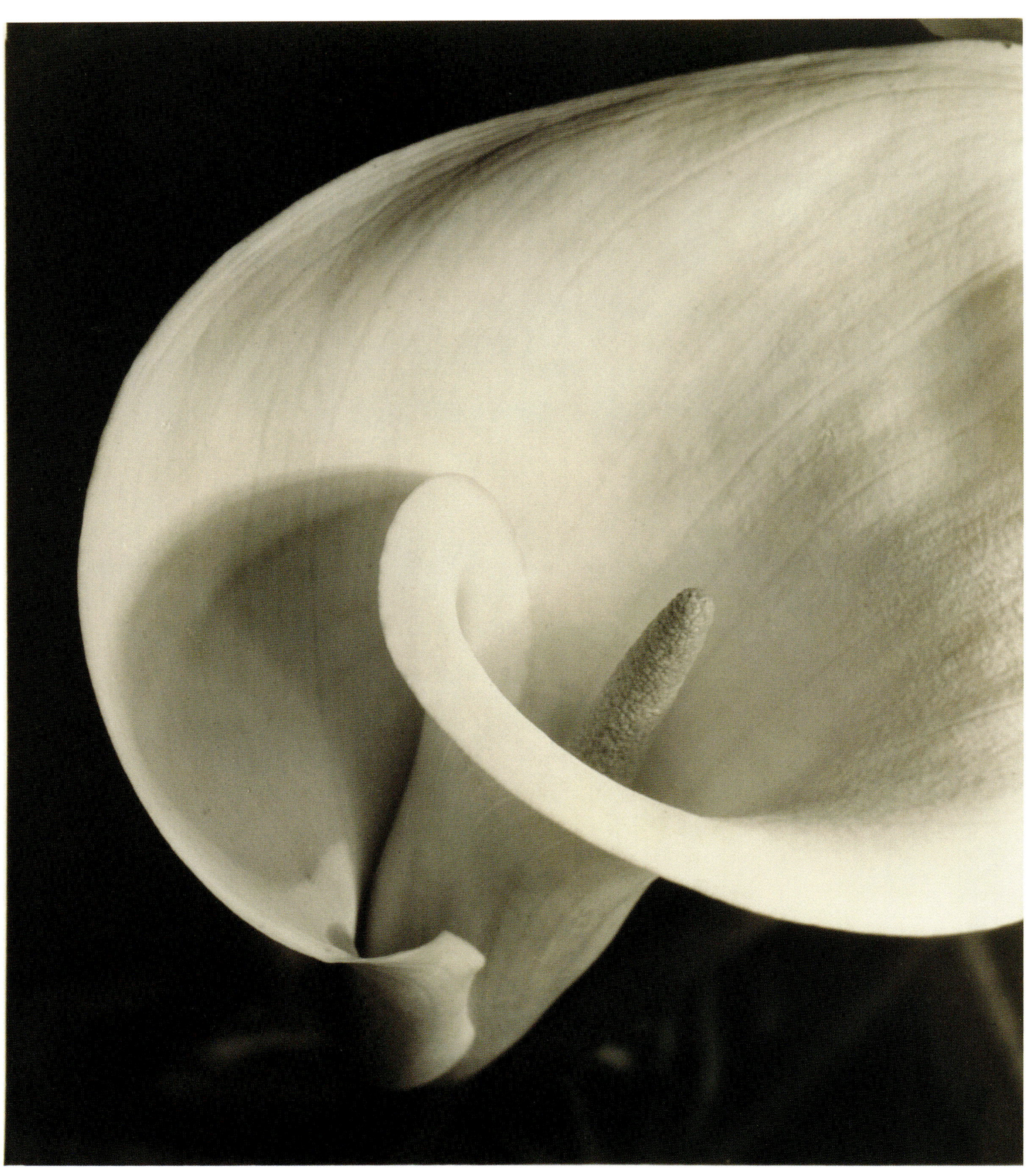

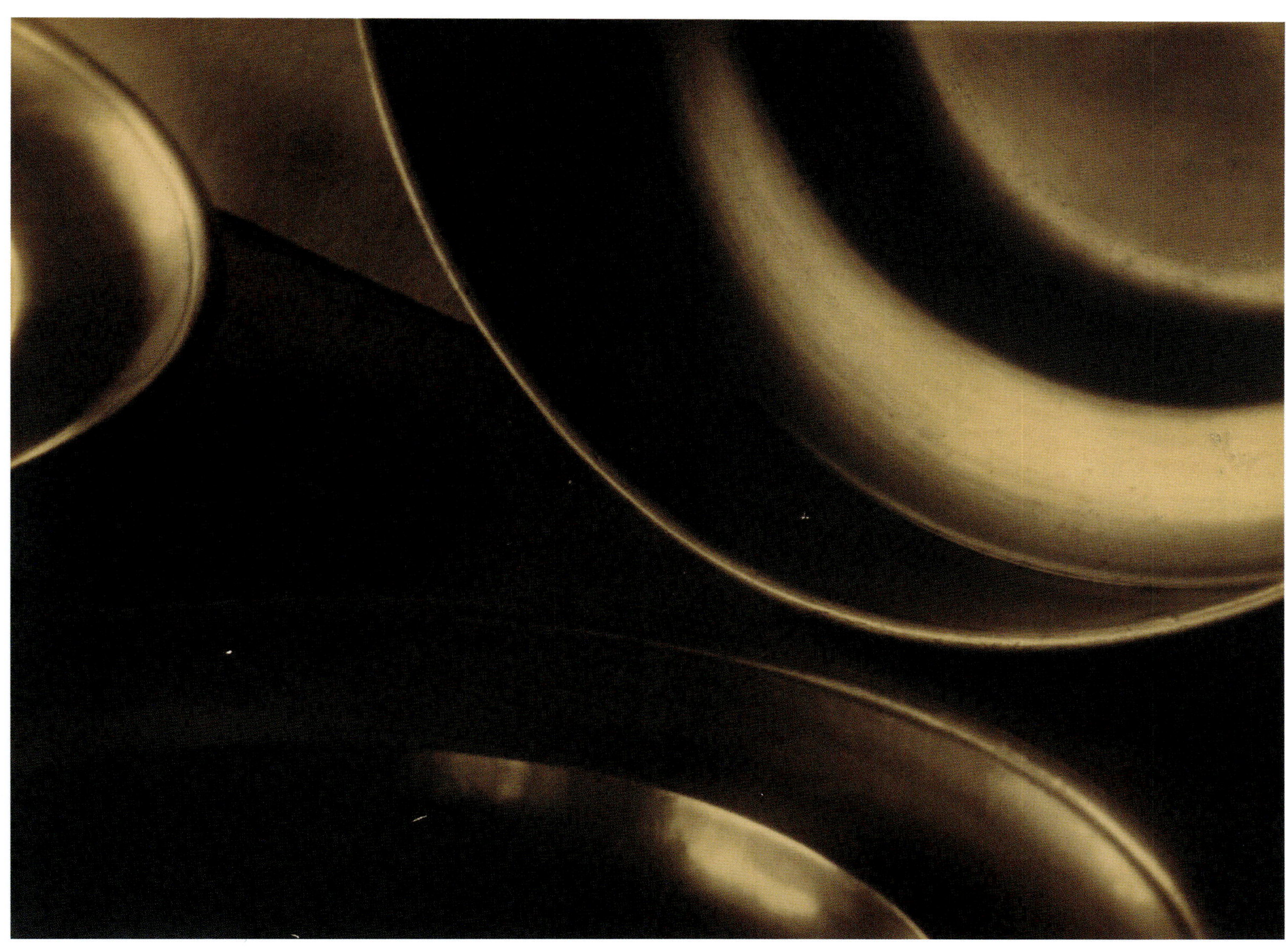

IMOGEN CUNNINGHAM | American, 1883–1976
Calla, c. 1925
Gelatin silver print
Image: 10 5/8 x 9 1/8 in. (26.9 x 23.2 cm)
Sheet: 13 15/16 x 10 7/8 in. (35.4 x 27.6 cm)
Museum purchase funded by the
Alice Pratt Brown Museum Fund as a
matching gift to the donations of Gay Block
2000.345

JAROMÍR FUNKE | Czech, 1896–1945
Composition, 1923
Gelatin silver print
Image/Sheet: 8 5/8 x 11 9/16 in. (21.9 x 29.4 cm)
Mount: 12 3/8 x 16 1/16 in. (31.4 x 40.8 cm)
Museum purchase funded by the
Prospero Foundation
84.95

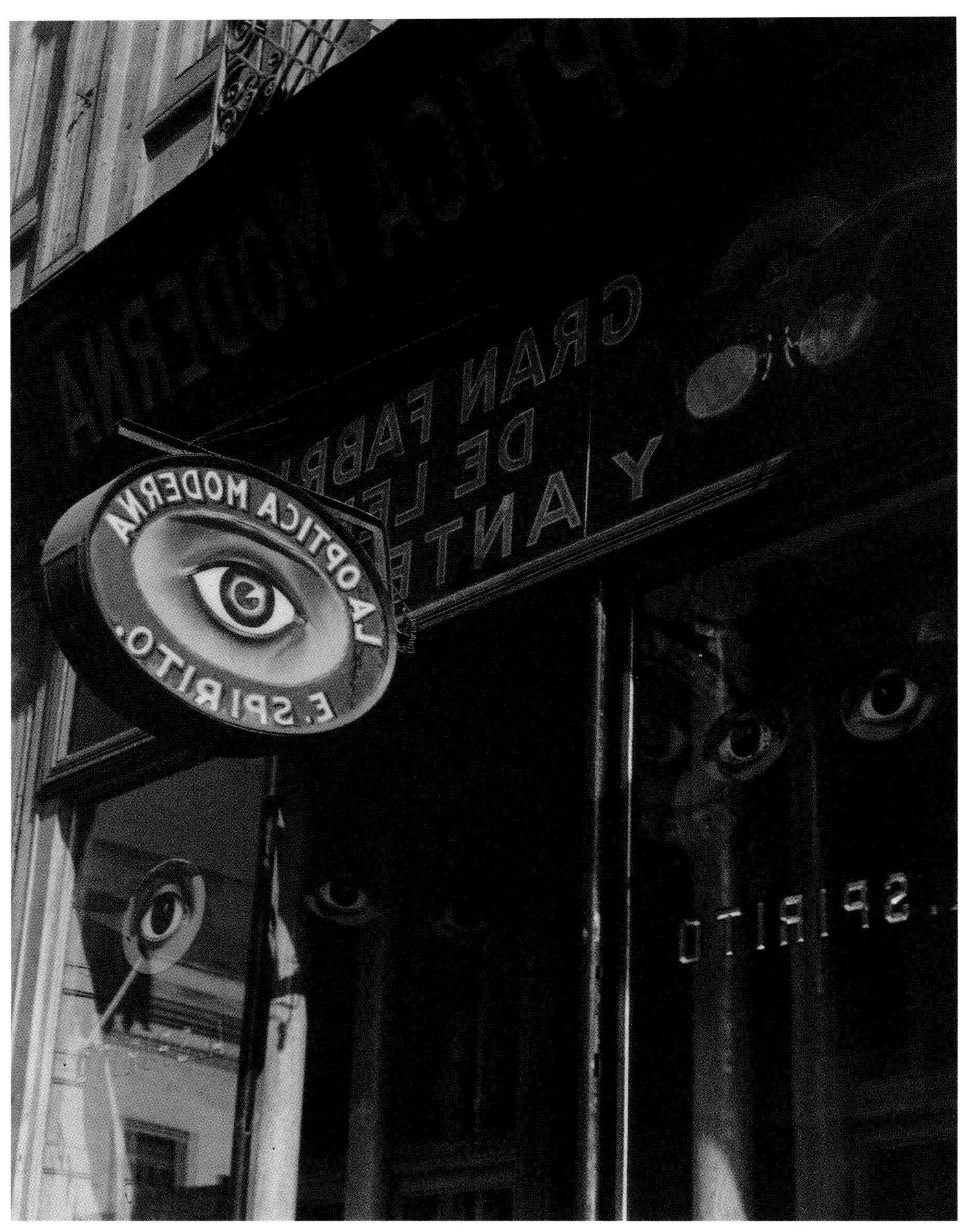

MANUEL ÁLVAREZ BRAVO | Mexican, 1902–2002
Paràbola òptica [Optical Parable], 1931
From the portfolio *Fifteen Photographs by
Manuel Alvarez Bravo*, 1974
Gelatin silver print, printed 1974, ed. #44/75
Image/Sheet: 9 1/4 x 7 1/16 in. (23.5 x 17.9 cm)
Mount: 19 11/16 x 14 3/4 in. (50 x 37.5 cm)
Museum purchase funded by the Lynch Foundation
87.123.1

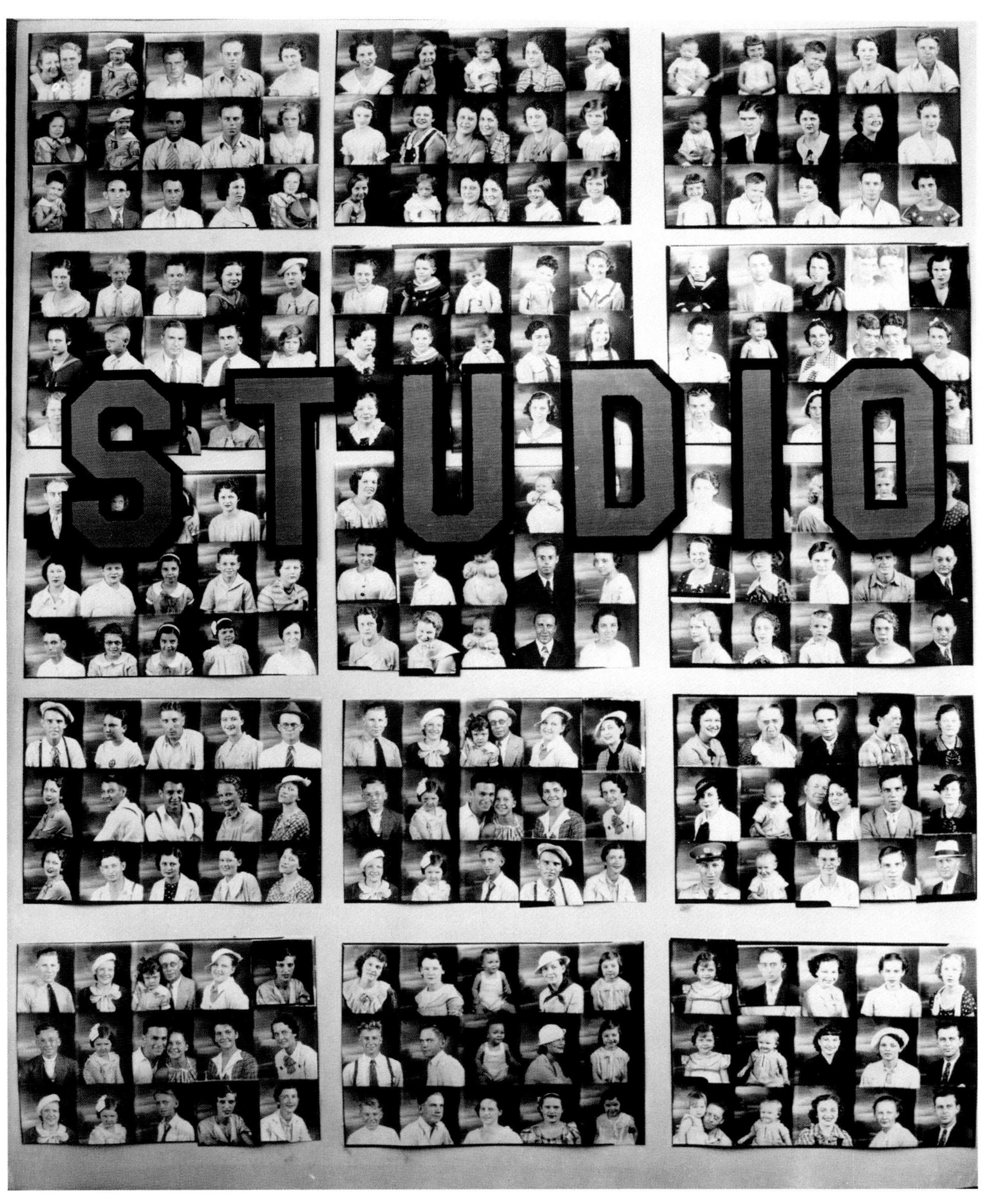

WALKER EVANS | American, 1903–1975
Penny Picture Display, Savannah, 1936
Gelatin silver print
Image: 9 3/8 x 7 5/8 in. (23.8 x 19.3 cm)
Sheet: 9 15/16 x 8 in. (25.3 x 20.3 cm)
Museum purchase funded by the
Caroline Wiess Law Accessions
Endowment Fund,
The Manfred Heiting Collection
2002.972

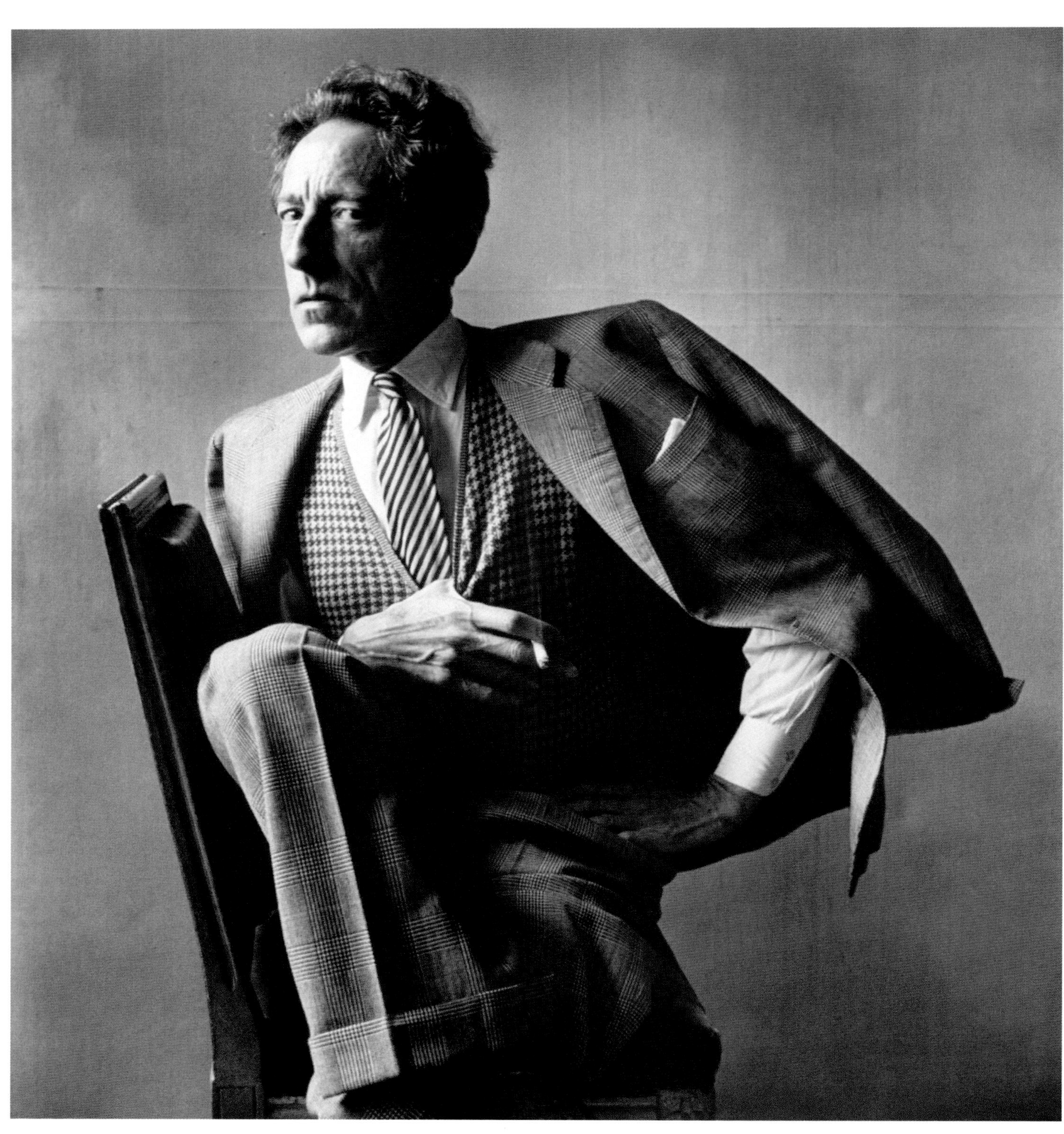

IRVING PENN | American, 1917–2009
Jean Cocteau, July 26, 1948
Gelatin silver print
Image: 10 15/16 x 10 3/16 in. (27.8 x 25.9 cm)
Sheet: 10 15/16 x 10 3/16 in. (27.8 x 25.9 cm)
Mount: 14 7/8 x 10 15/16 in. (37.8 x 27.8 cm)
The Sonia and Kaye Marvins Portrait
Collection, Museum purchase funded by
Sonia and Kaye Marvins
84.276

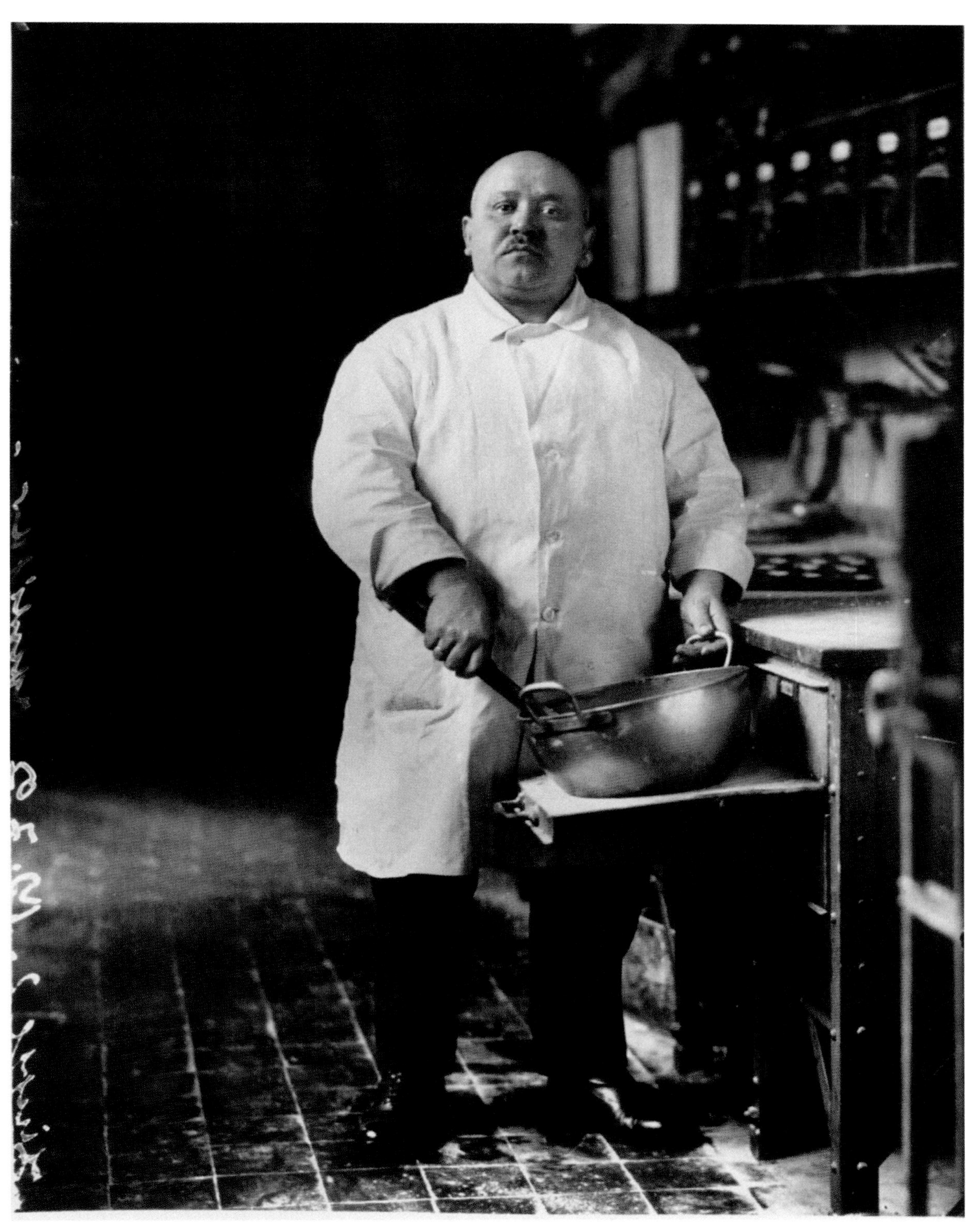

AUGUST SANDER | German, 1876–1964
Pastry Cook, 1928
From *Group 2, The Skilled Tradesman;*
Portfolio 8, The Master Craftsman,
People of the 20th Century
Gelatin silver print, printed by
Gunther Sander, 1980
Image: 10 7/16 x 8 1/8 in. (26.5 x 20.6 cm)
Sheet: 10 7/8 x 8 15/16 in. (27.6 x 22.7 cm)
The Allan Chasanoff Photographic Collection
91.1056

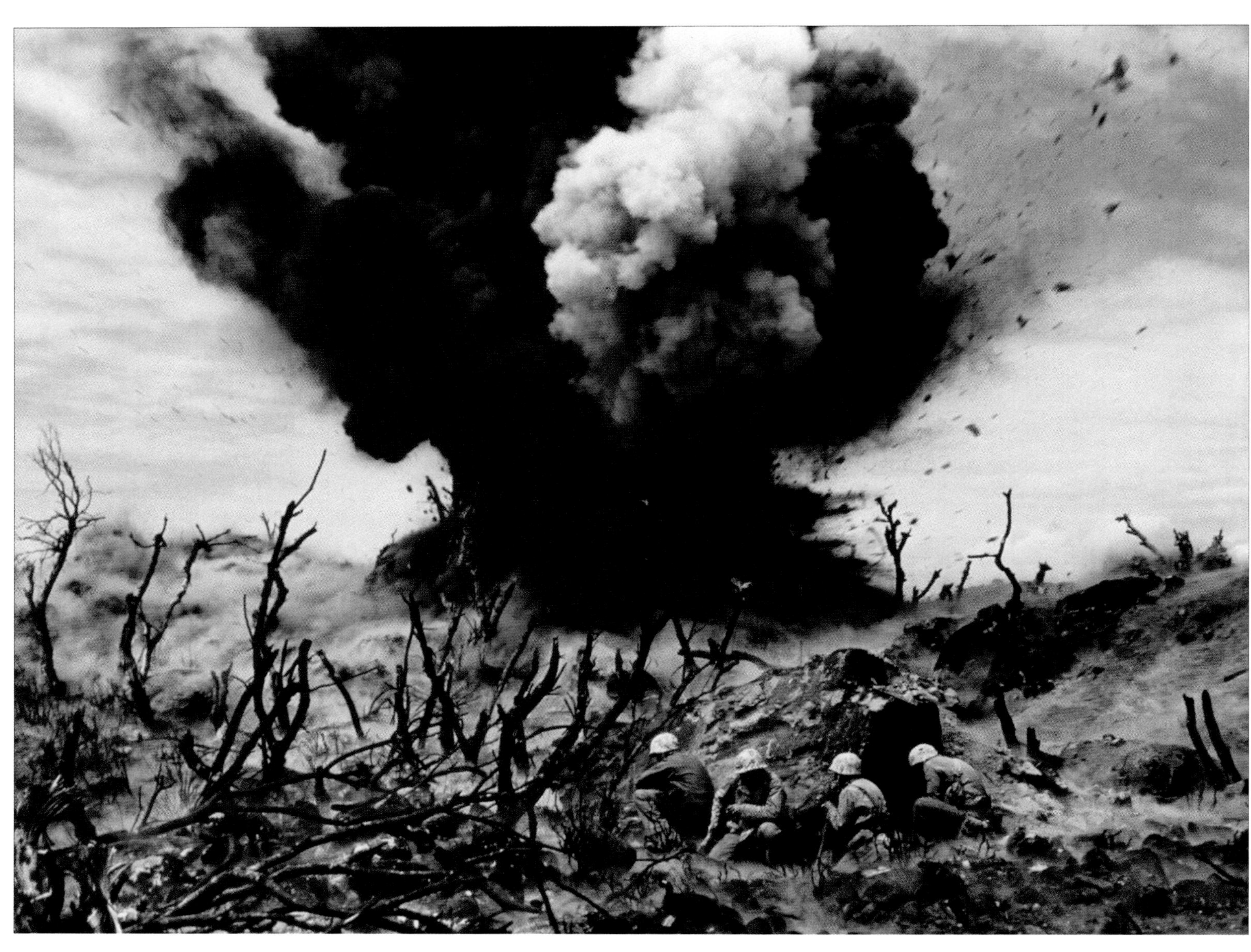

W. EUGENE SMITH | American, 1918–1978
Marine Demolition Team Blasting Out a Cave
on Hill 382, Iwo Jima, 1945
From the photo essay *Iwo Jima*
Gelatin silver print
Image: 10 1/2 x 13 7/16 in. (26.6 x 34.2 cm)
Sheet: 19 1/2 x 15 7/8 in. (49.5 x 40.3 cm)
Museum purchase funded by the
S. I. Morris Photography Endowment,
The Manfred Heiting Collection
2002.2298

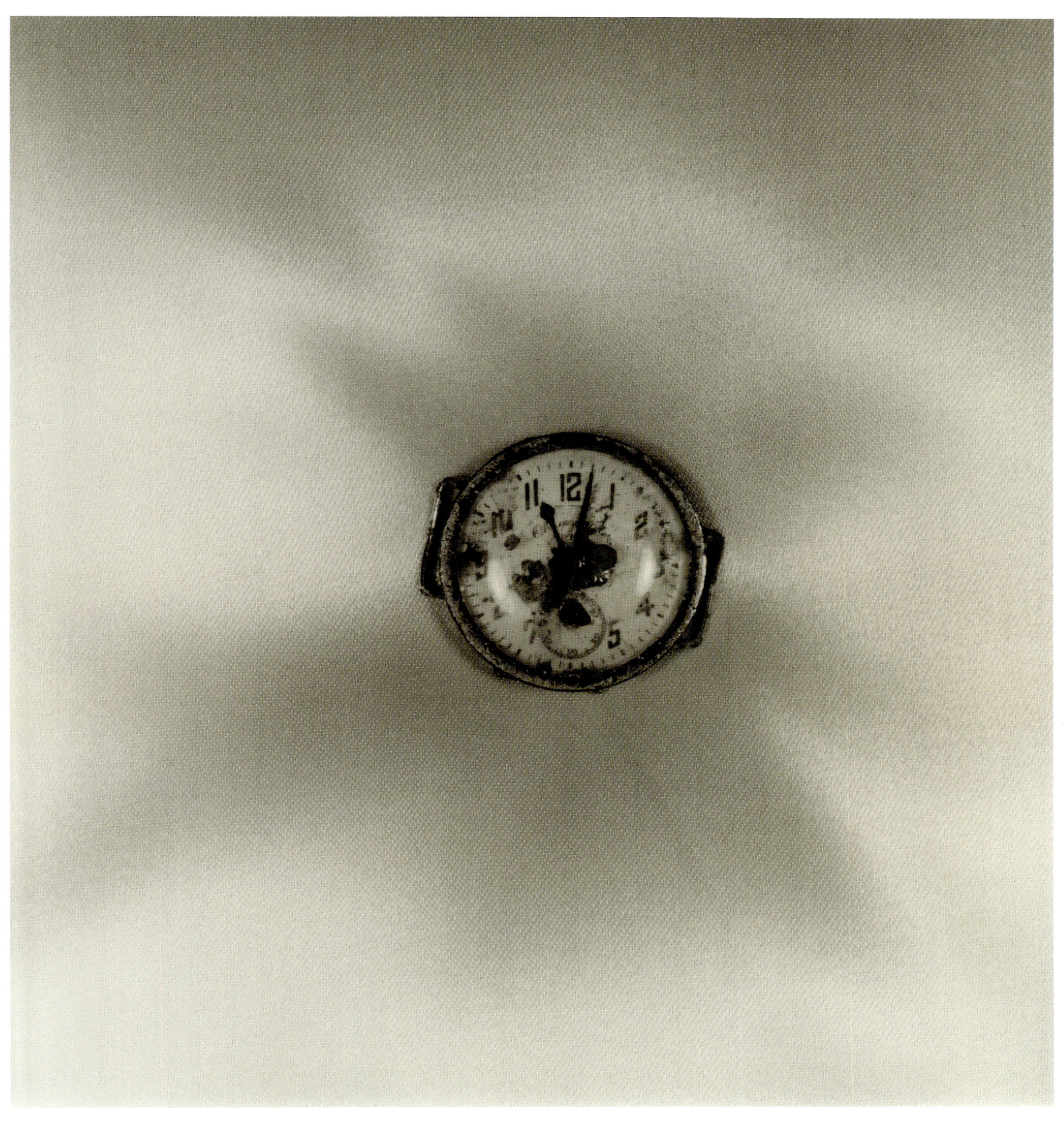

TŌMATSU SHŌMEI | Japanese, 1930–2012
*Atomic Bomb Damage: Wristwatch Stopped
at 11:02, August 9, 1945*, 1961
Gelatin silver print, printed 1969
Image: 13 3/16 x 13 13/16 in. (33.5 x 35.1 cm)
Museum purchase funded by
Janice and Robert C. McNair at
"One Great Night in November, 2010,"
in honor of the birth of their grandson,
Robert Daniel McNair, and in the hope that
during his lifetime there will be peace
2011.243

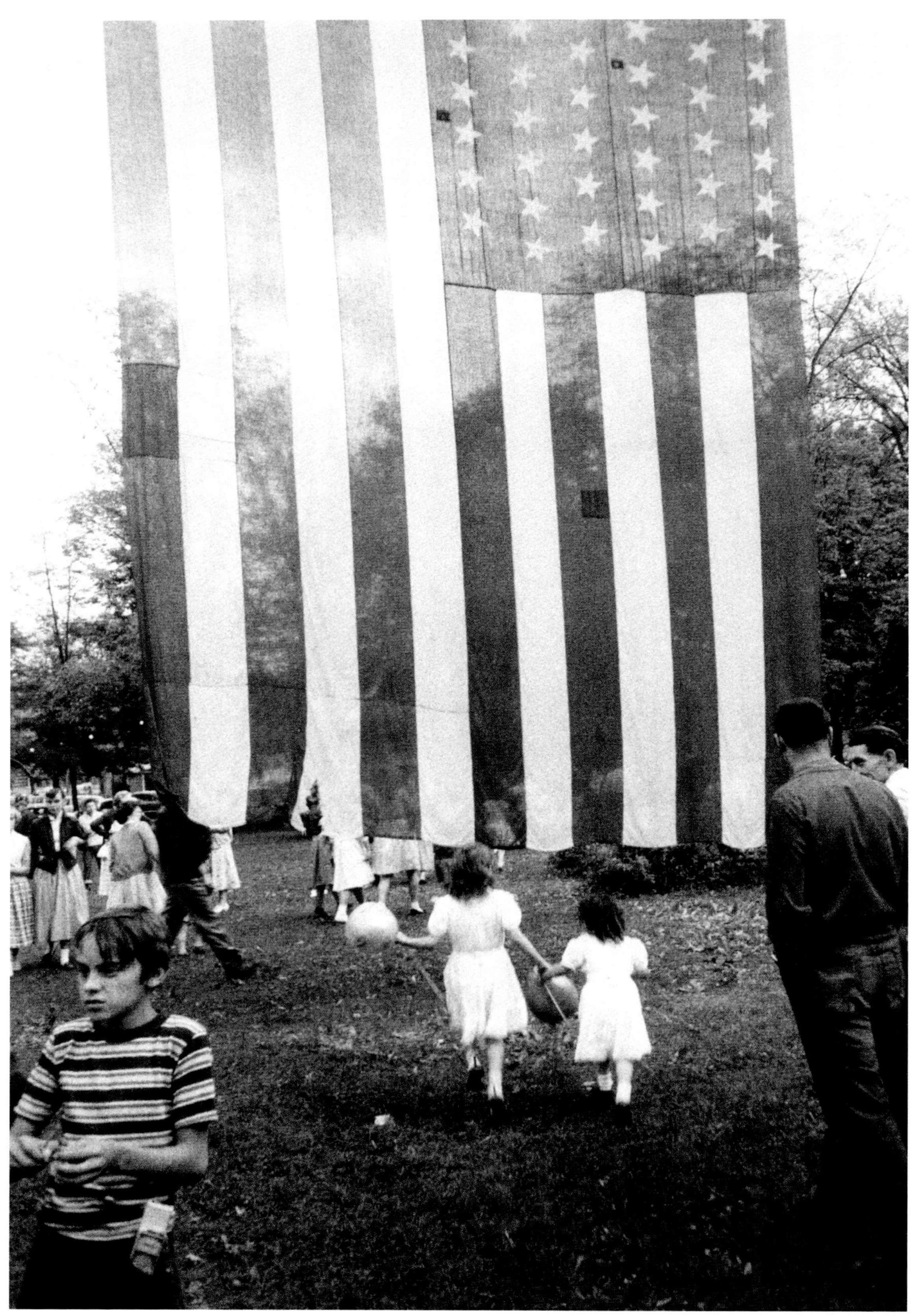

ROBERT FRANK | American, born Switzerland, 1924
Fourth of July, Jay, New York, 1955
from the series The Americans
Gelatin silver print
Image: 11 15/16 x 8 in. (30.3 x 20.3 cm)
Sheet: 13 7/8 x 10 15/16 in. (35.3 x 27.8 cm)
The Target Collection of American Photography,
Museum purchase funded by Target Stores
82.500

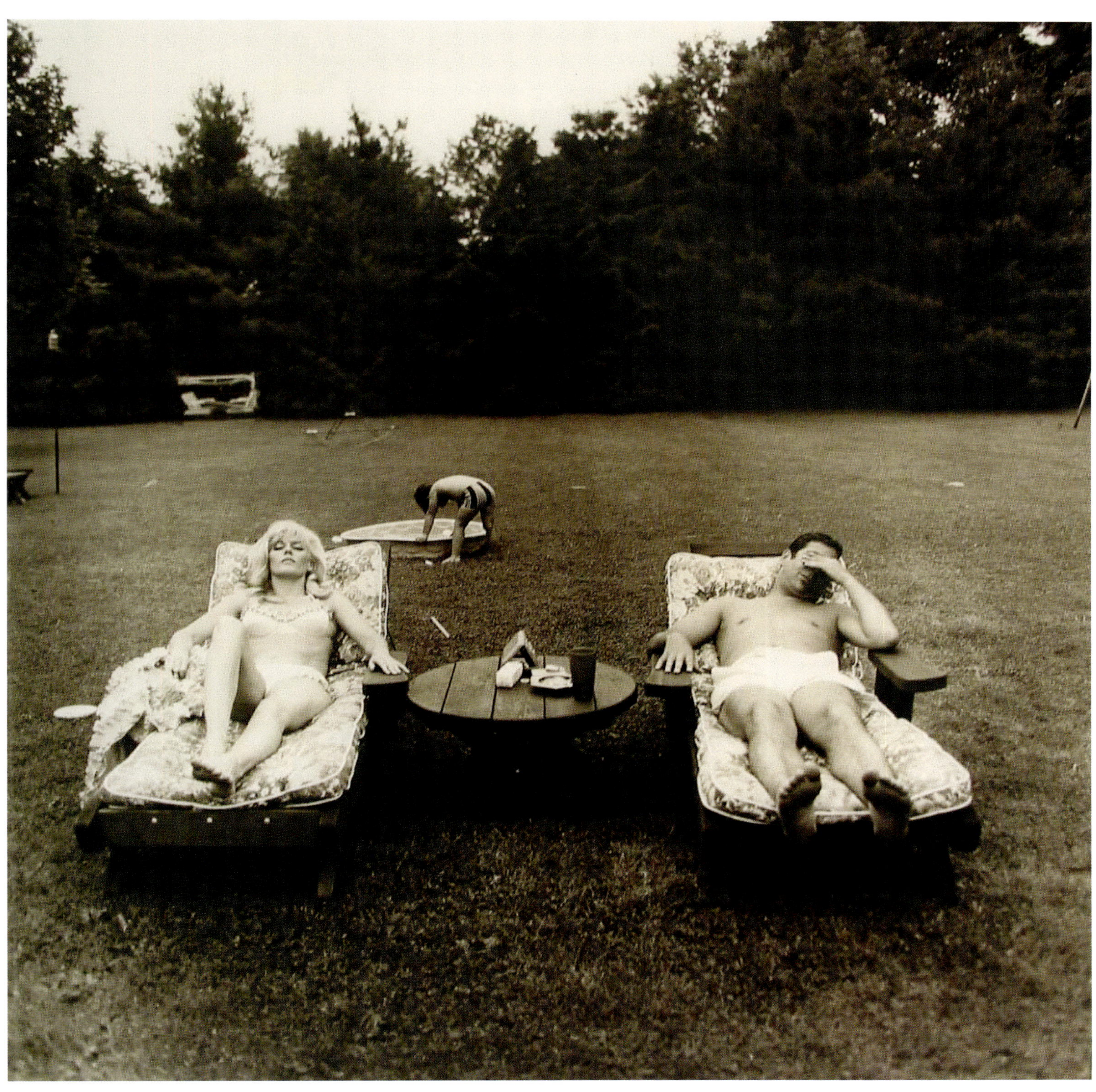

DIANE ARBUS | American, 1923–1971
A Family on the Lawn One Sunday, 1968
From the portfolio
A Box of Ten Photographs, 1973
Gelatin silver print, printed posthumously by
Neil Selkirk, 1973, ed. #8/50
Image: 15 1/8 x 15 1/8 in. (38.4 x 38.4 cm)
Sheet: 19 7/8 x 15 7/8 in. (50.5 x 40.3 cm)
Museum purchase funded by Gay Block
in memory of Eric Alexander, by exchange
2004.1524

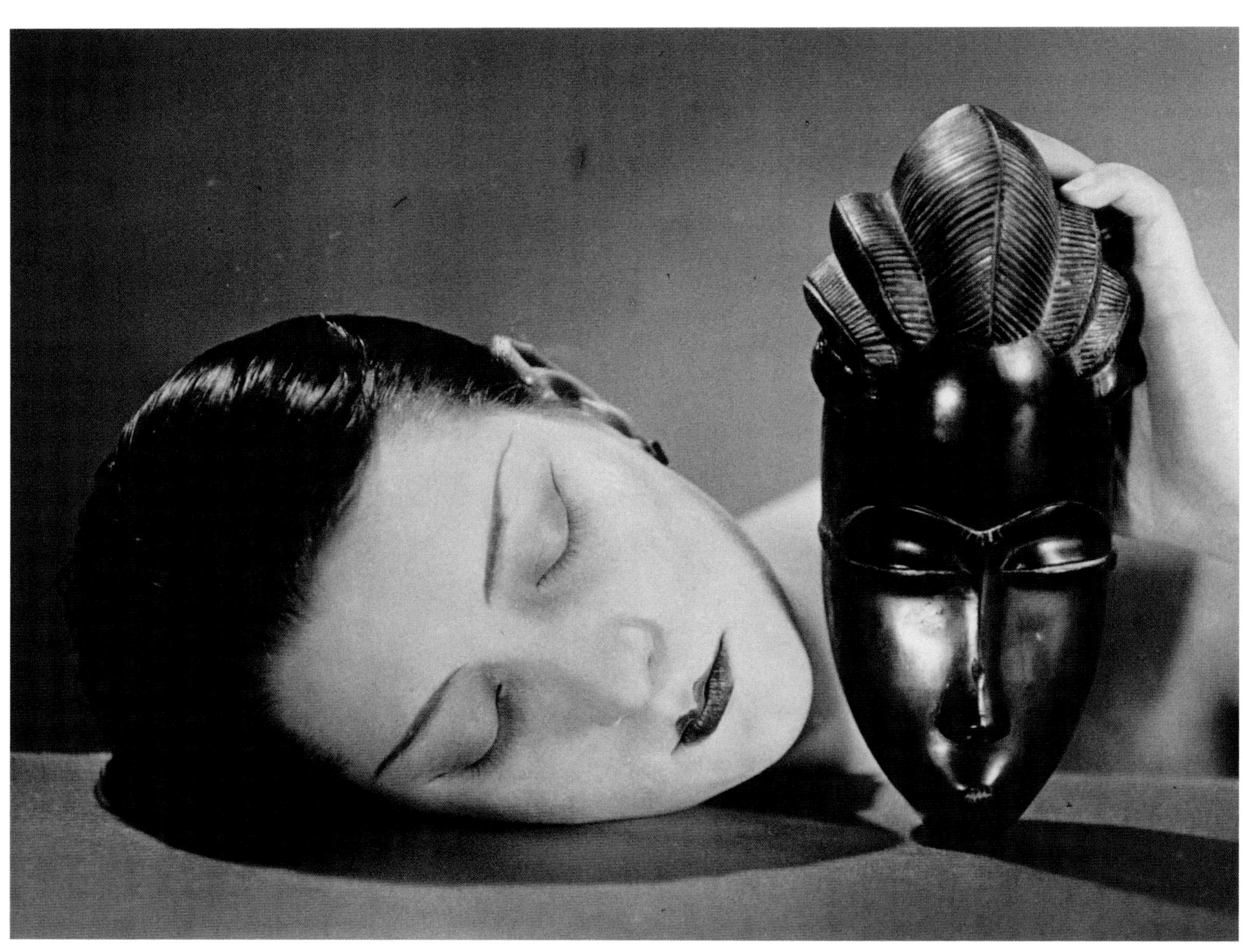

MAN RAY (BORN EMMANUEL RUDNITZKY)
American, 1890–1976
Kiki, Noire et Blanche, 1926
Gelatin silver print
Image: 7 x 9 1/8 in. (17.8 x 23.2 cm)
Sheet: 7 x 9 3/8 in. (17.8 x 23.8 cm)
Museum purchase funded by the
Caroline Wiess Law Accessions Endowment
Fund, The Manfred Heiting Collection
2002.1577

HANNAH HÖCH | German, 1889–1978
Broken, 1925
Halftone collage
Image (irregular): 5 7/8 x 4 7/16 in. (14.9 x 11.3 cm)
Sheet: 8 5/16 x 6 1/4 in. (21.1 x 15.9 cm)
Museum purchase funded by the
Brown Foundation Accessions Endowment Fund
89.377

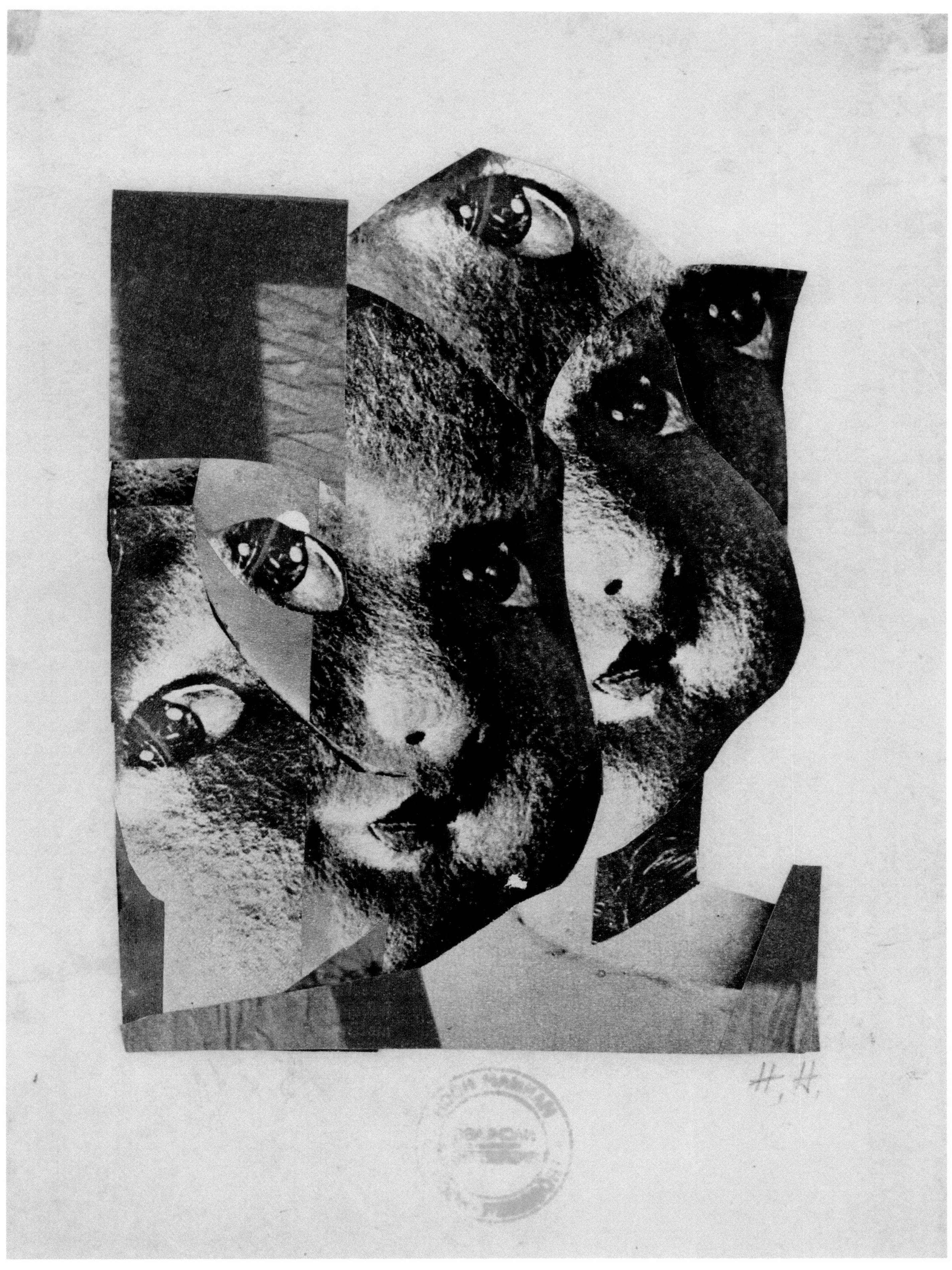

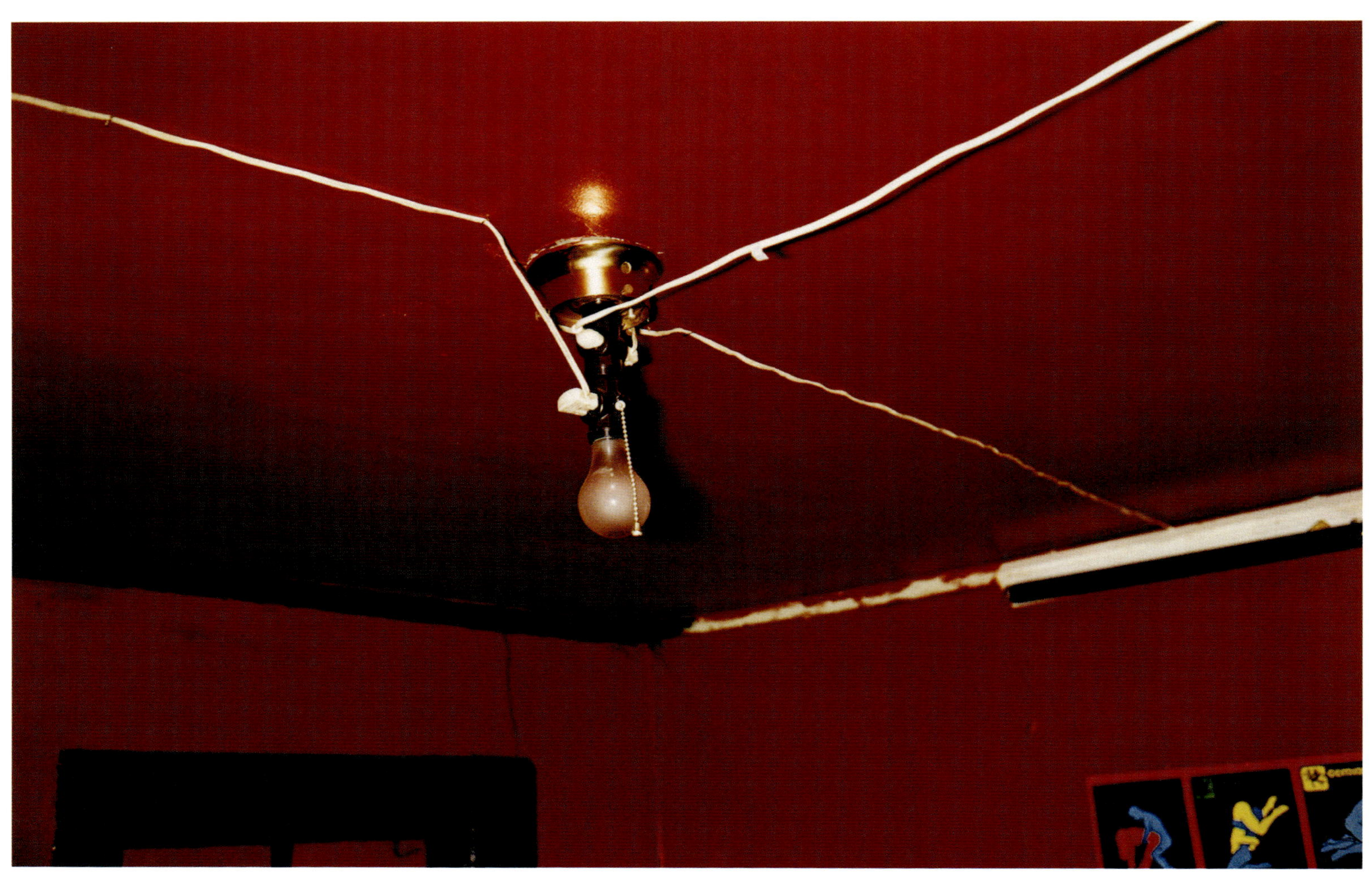

WILLIAM EGGLESTON | American, born 1939
Red Ceiling, 1973
Dye imbibition print
Image: 11 7/8 x 18 3/8 in. (30.2 x 46.7 cm)
Sheet: 15 1/4 x 20 5/8 in. (38.7 x 52.4 cm)
Gift of Caroline Huber and Walter Hopps
in honor of Anne Wilkes Tucker
99.563

RICHARD MISRACH | American, born 1949
Playboy #38, 1990–91
From the series *Desert Canto XI: The Playboys*
Chromogenic print
Image: 23 1/8 x 18 5/16 in. (58.7 x 46.5 cm)
Sheet: 23 15/16 x 20 in. (60.8 x 50.8 cm)
Museum purchase funded by Photo Forum 2003,
The Manfred Heiting Collection
2002.1670

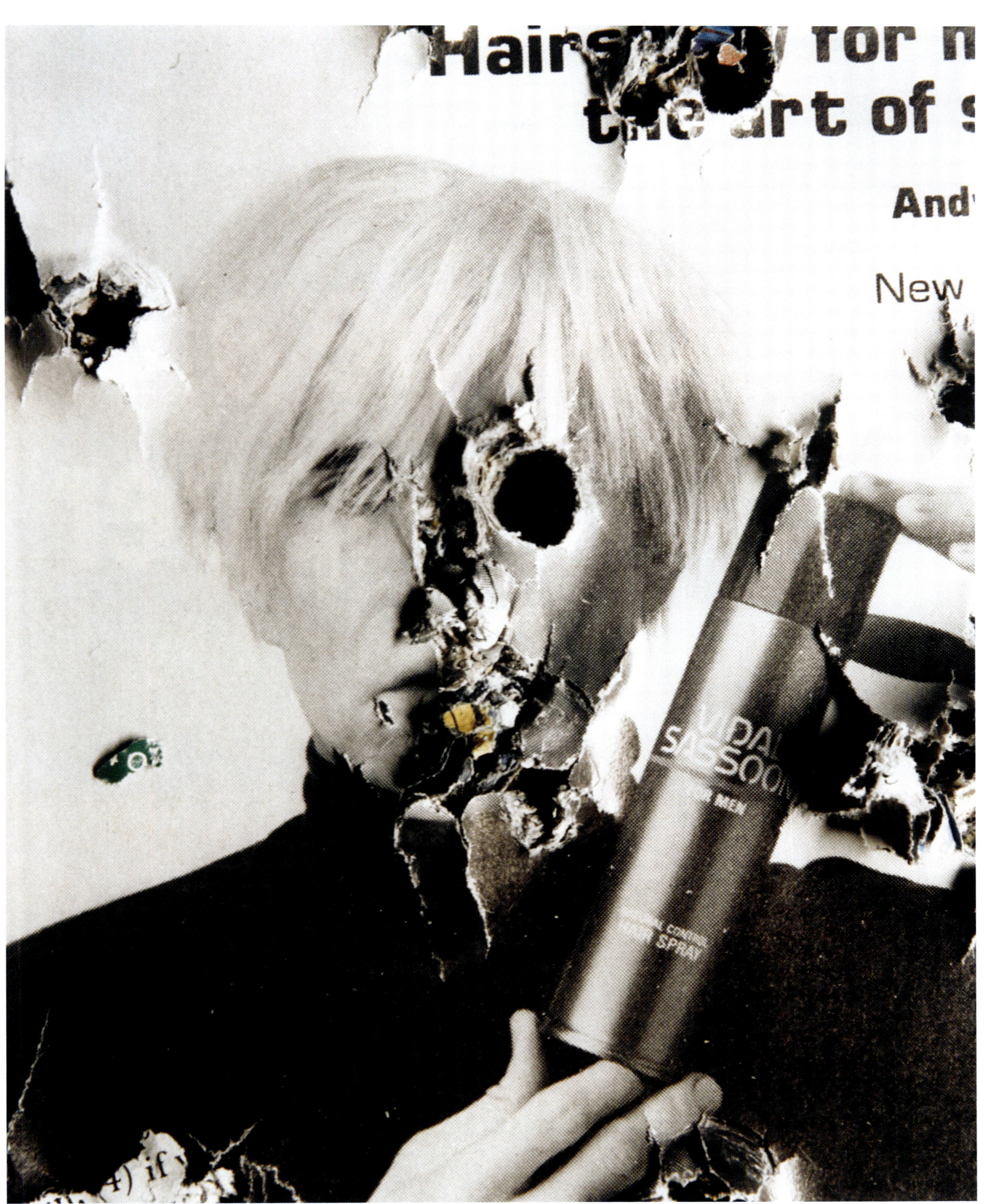
Hairspray for m
the art of s
And
New
VIDAL
SASSOON
FOR MEN
CONTROL
SPRAY

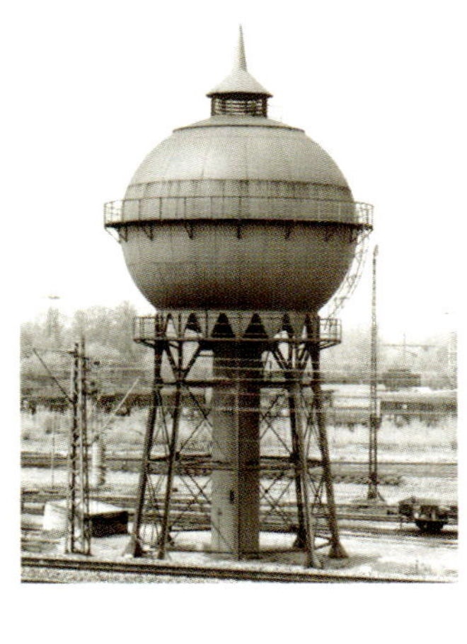 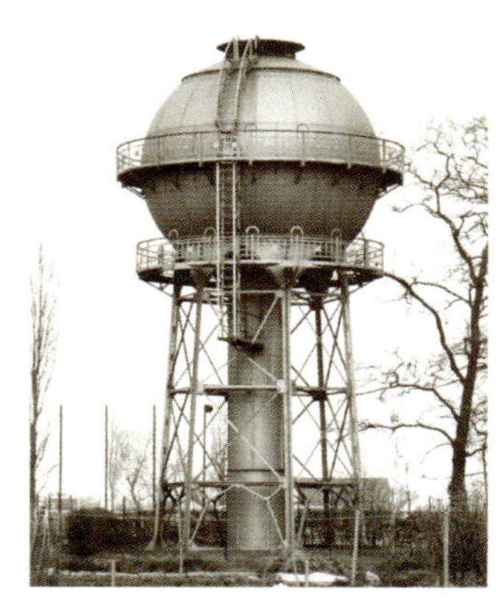 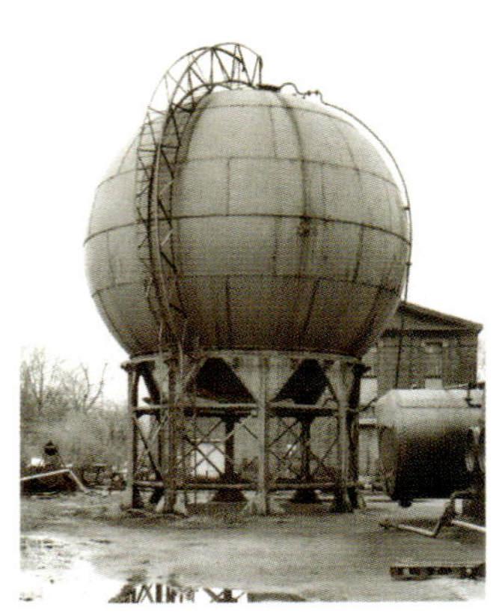

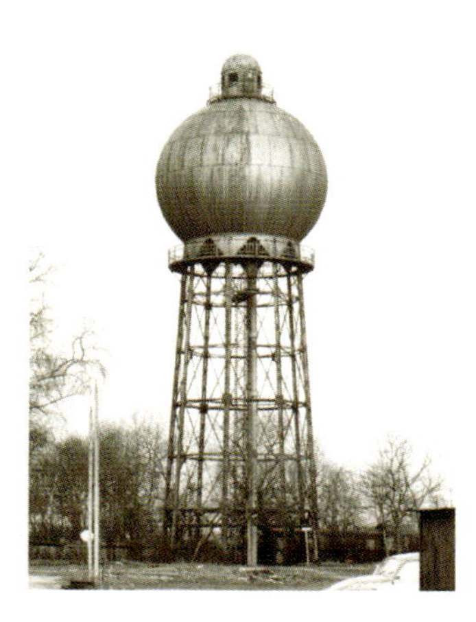 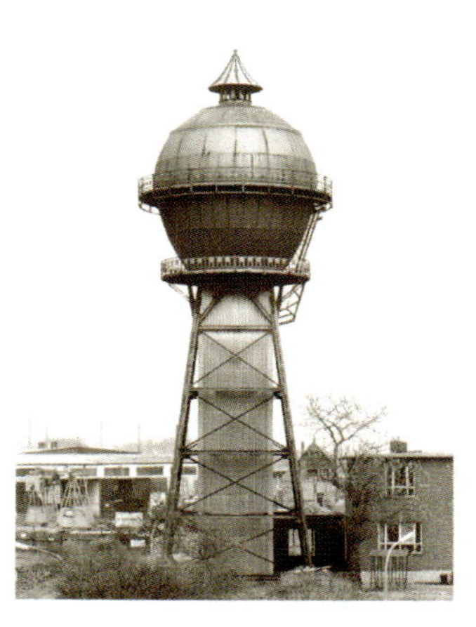 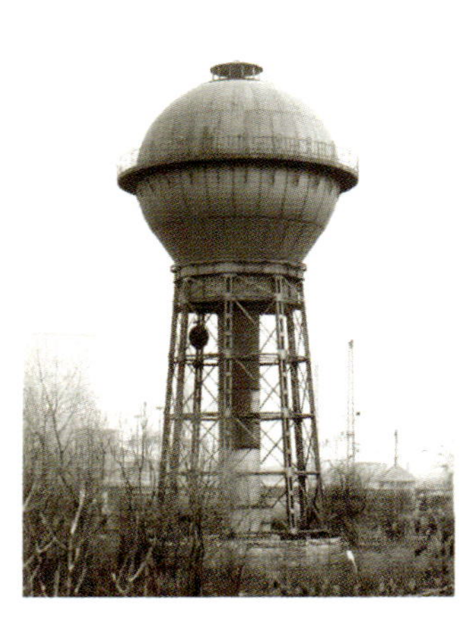

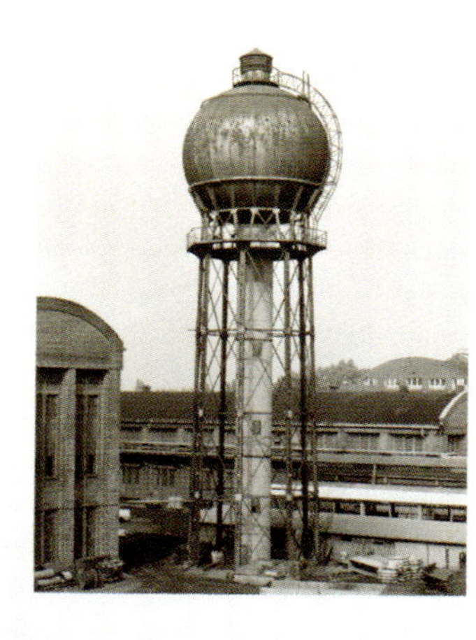 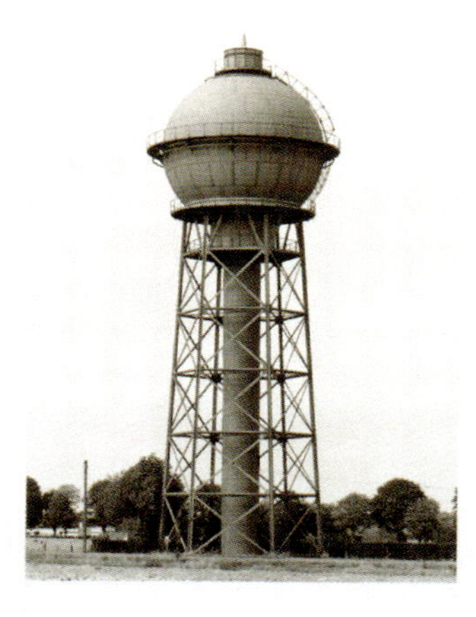 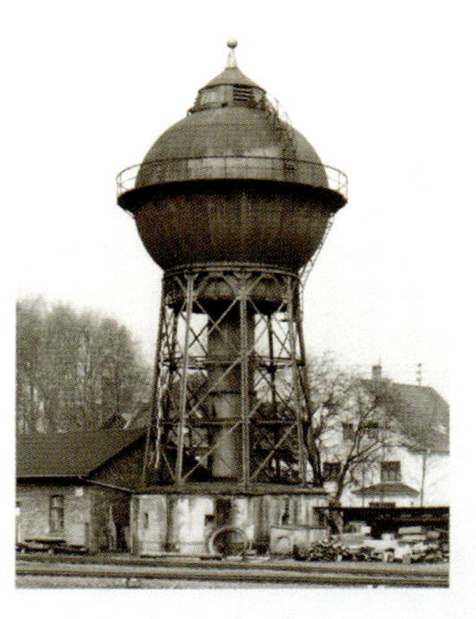

BERND BECHER | German, 1931–2007
and **HILLA BECHER** | German, born 1934
Water Towers, 1980
Gelatin silver prints
Overall: 61 1/4 x 49 1/4 in. (155.6 x 125.1 cm)
Image (Each): 15 15/16 x 12 in. (40.5 x 30.5 cm)
Museum purchase funded by
Louisa Stude Sarofim
82.575.A–.I

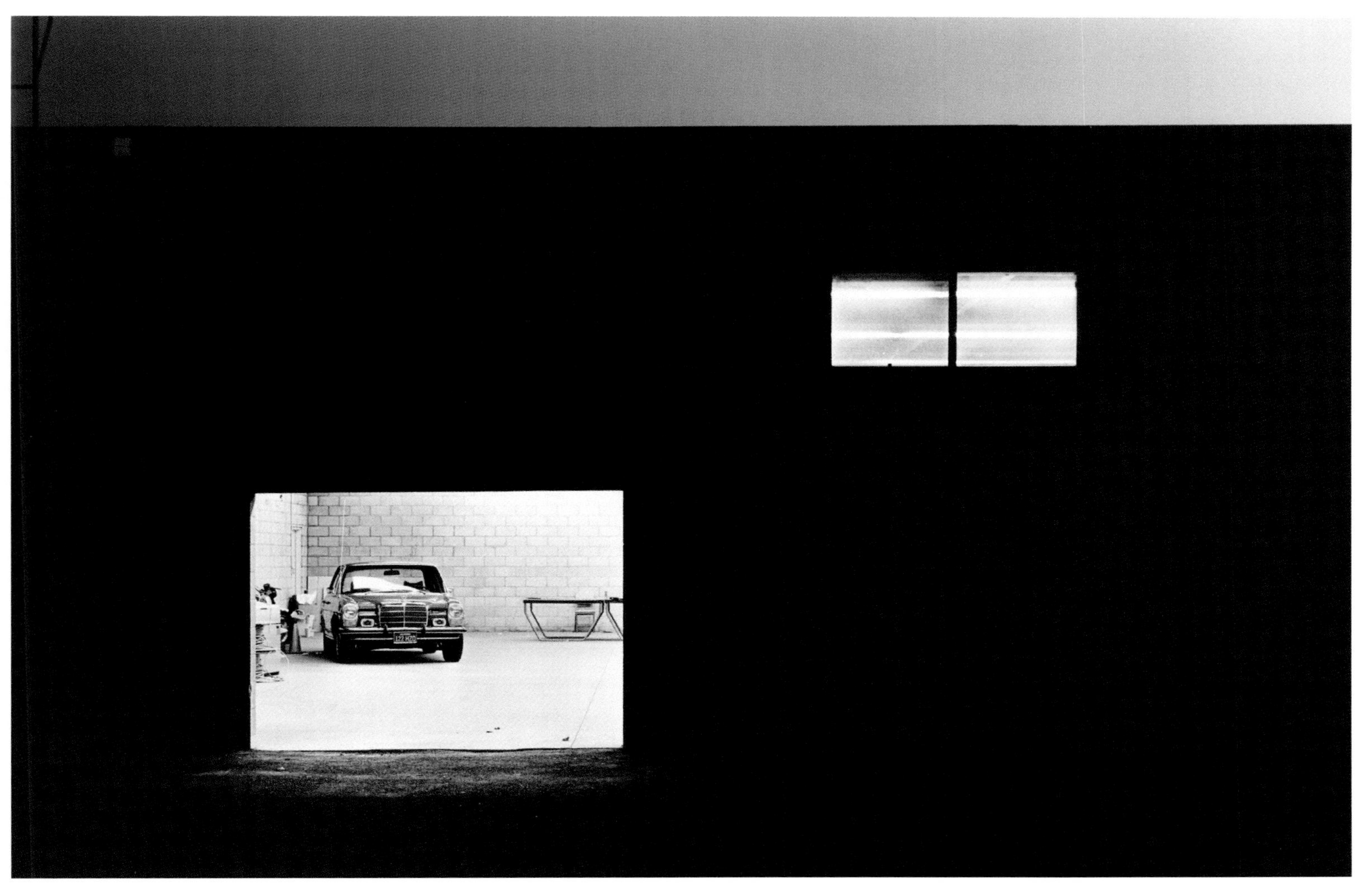

LEWIS BALTZ | American, born 1945
North Wall, Automated Marine International,
1641 McGaw, Irvine, 1974
From the series *The New Industrial Parks*
near Irvine, California
Gelatin silver print, ed. #10/21
Image: 6 x 9 in. (15.2 x 22.9 cm)
Sheet: 7 15/16 x 9 15/16 in. (20.2 x 25.2 cm)
Museum purchase funded by
the National Endowment for the Arts
and by Gamma Phi Beta
75.39.16

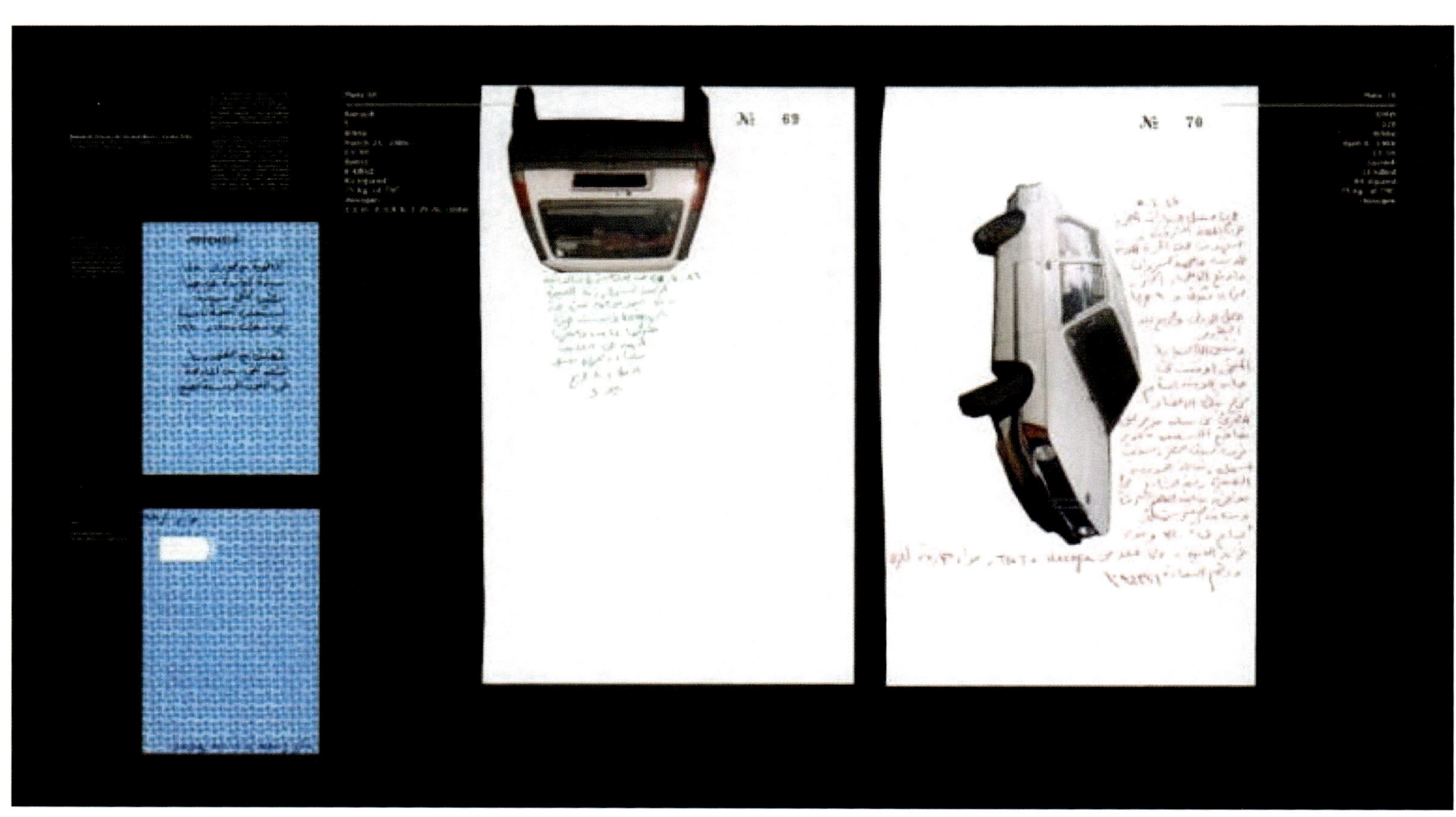

WALID RAAD | Lebanese, born 1967
*Notebook Volume 38: Already Been in a
Lake of Fire (Plates 69–70),* 1991/2003
Inkjet print, ed. #2/3
Sheet: 44 x 78 1/4 in. (111.8 x 198.8 cm)
Museum purchase funded by the
S. I. Morris Photography Endowment
2012.36

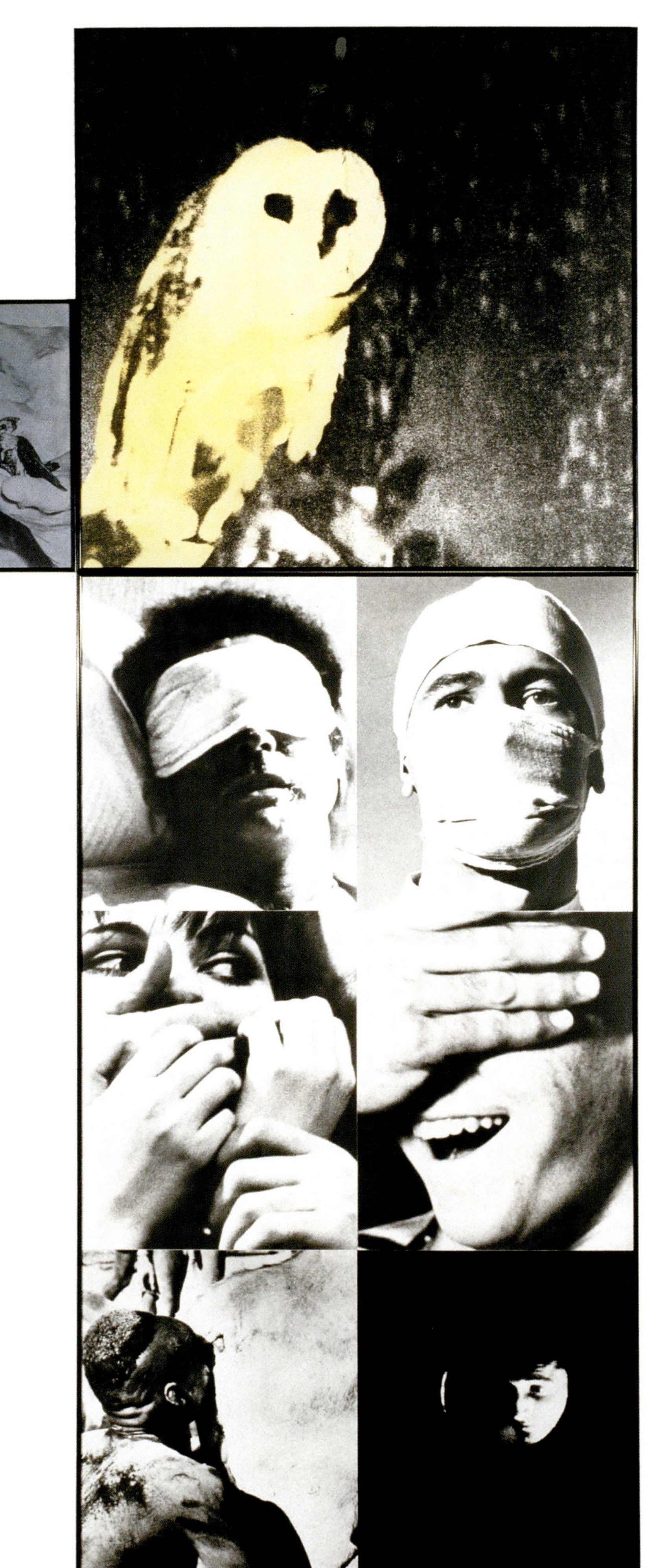

JOHN BALDESSARI | American, born 1931
Minerva (With Old and New Truths), 1987
Gelatin silver prints with applied color
92 1/2 x 48 1/2 in. (235 x 123.2 cm)
Museum purchase funded by the
Agnes Cullen Arnold Endowment Fund
89.116

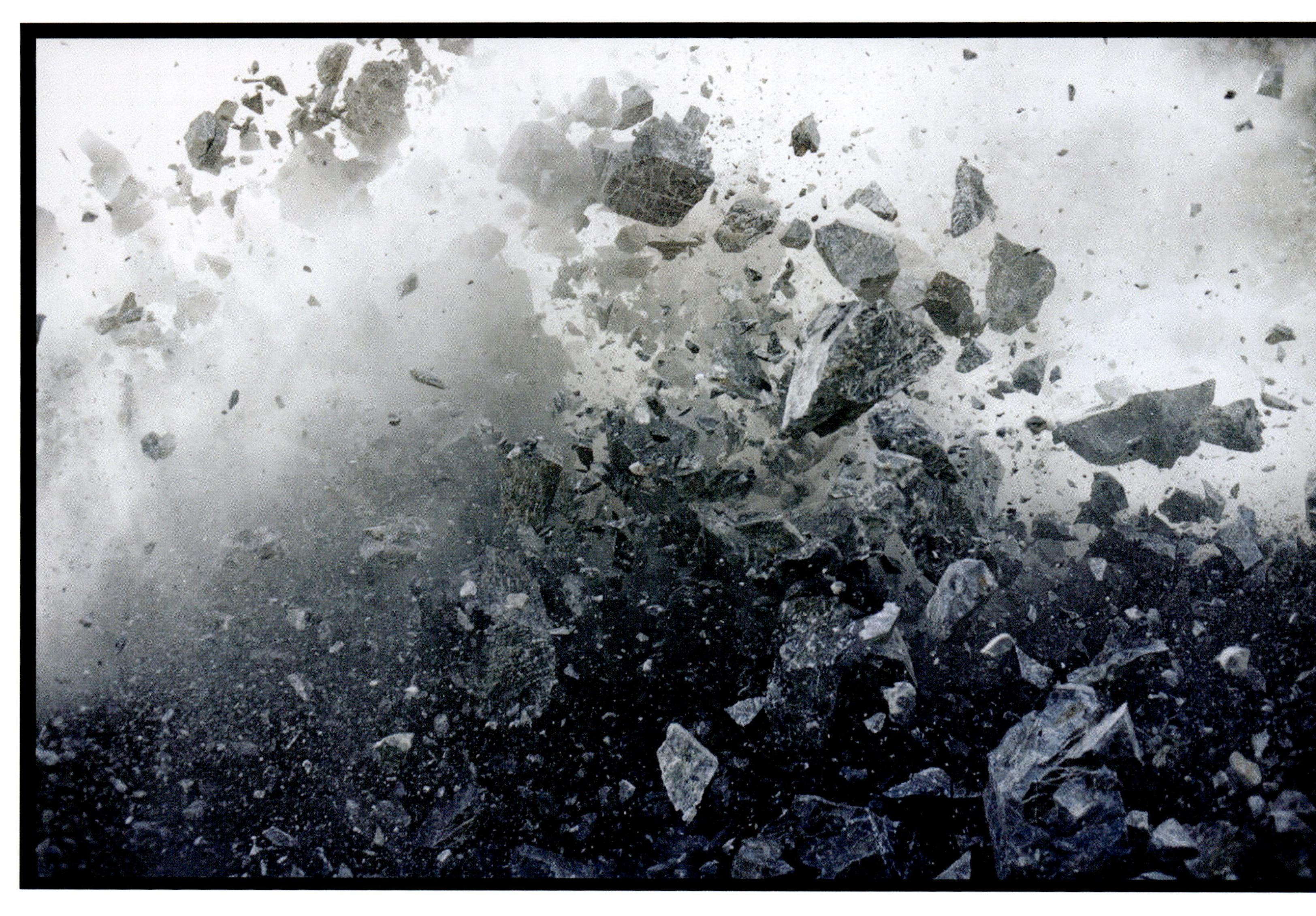

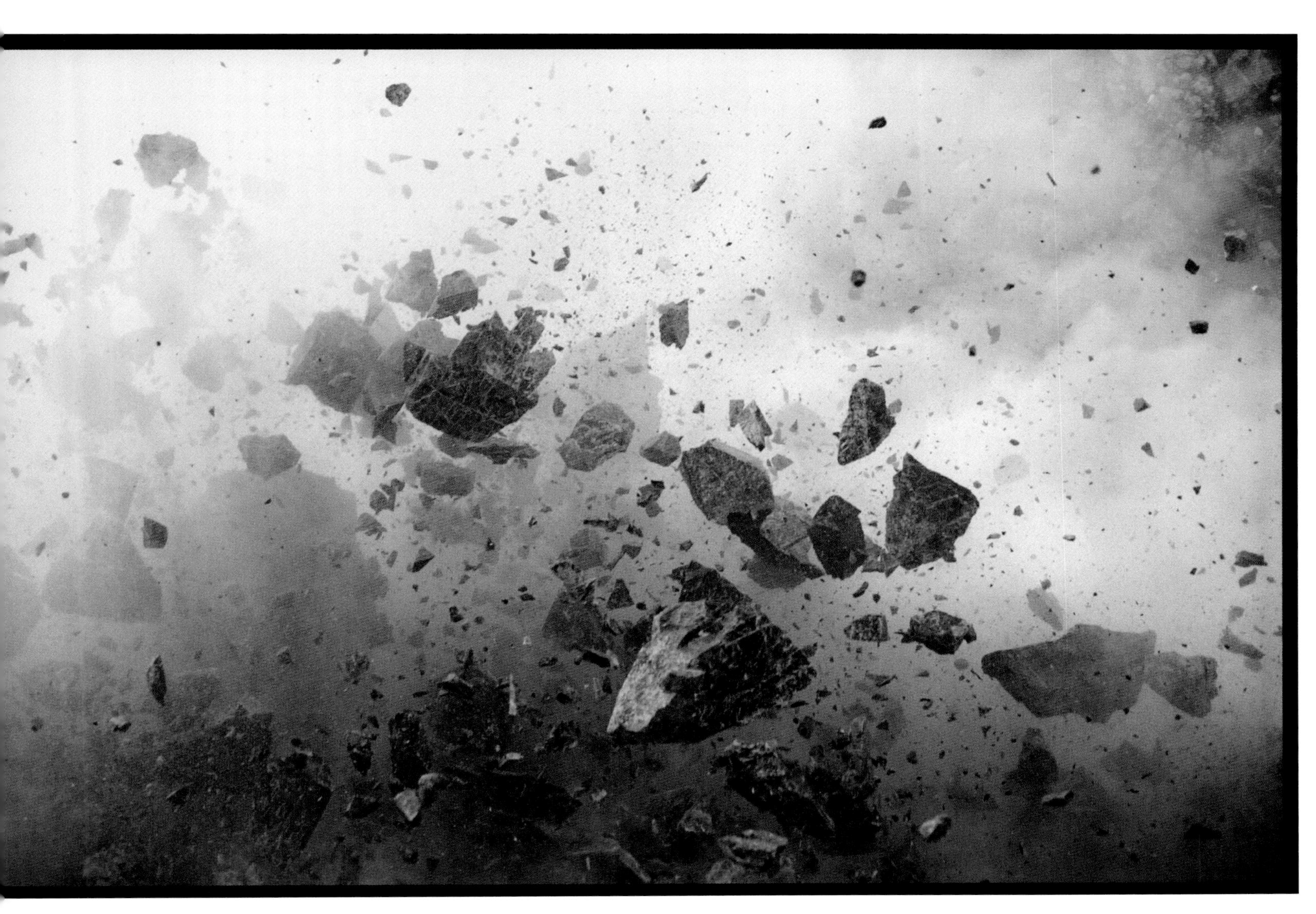

HATAKEYAMA NAOYA | Japanese, born 1958
Blast, 2005
Chromogenic prints, diptych, edition of 7
Overall (framed): 40 x 119 1/2 x 2 in.
(101.6 x 303.5 x 5.1 cm)
Museum purchase funded by the
S. I. Morris Photography Endowment
2008.531.A,.B

ASSEMBLAGE AND COLLAGE

Assemblage, coined from the words "assemble" and "collage," became an increasingly important aspect of contemporary art in the 1950s and 1960s as artists challenged traditional conventions of painting and sculpture. In 1960, the French critic Pierre Restany captured the spirit of the time when he proposed that assemblage could lead to a "new realism of pure sensibility . . . and finally, once again, poetry."

Like collage, assemblage uses found materials and telling juxtapositions to create fresh associations. Whether working with common objects on a monumental scale or more intimately with a jeweler's eye, artists have used assemblage to engage with the full spectrum of contemporary life, from the everyday to the sublime.

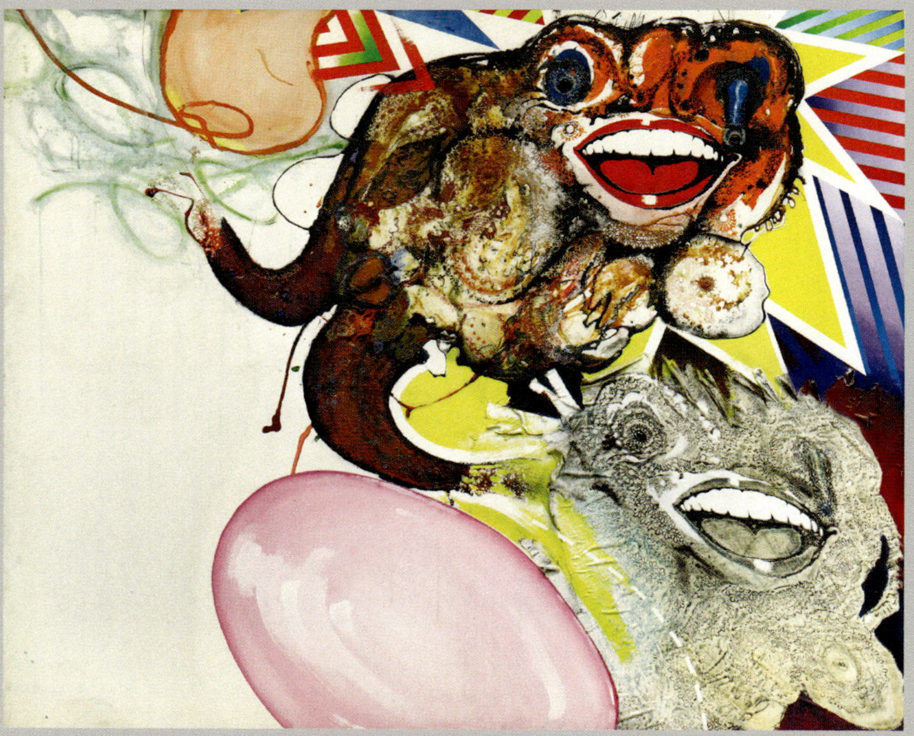

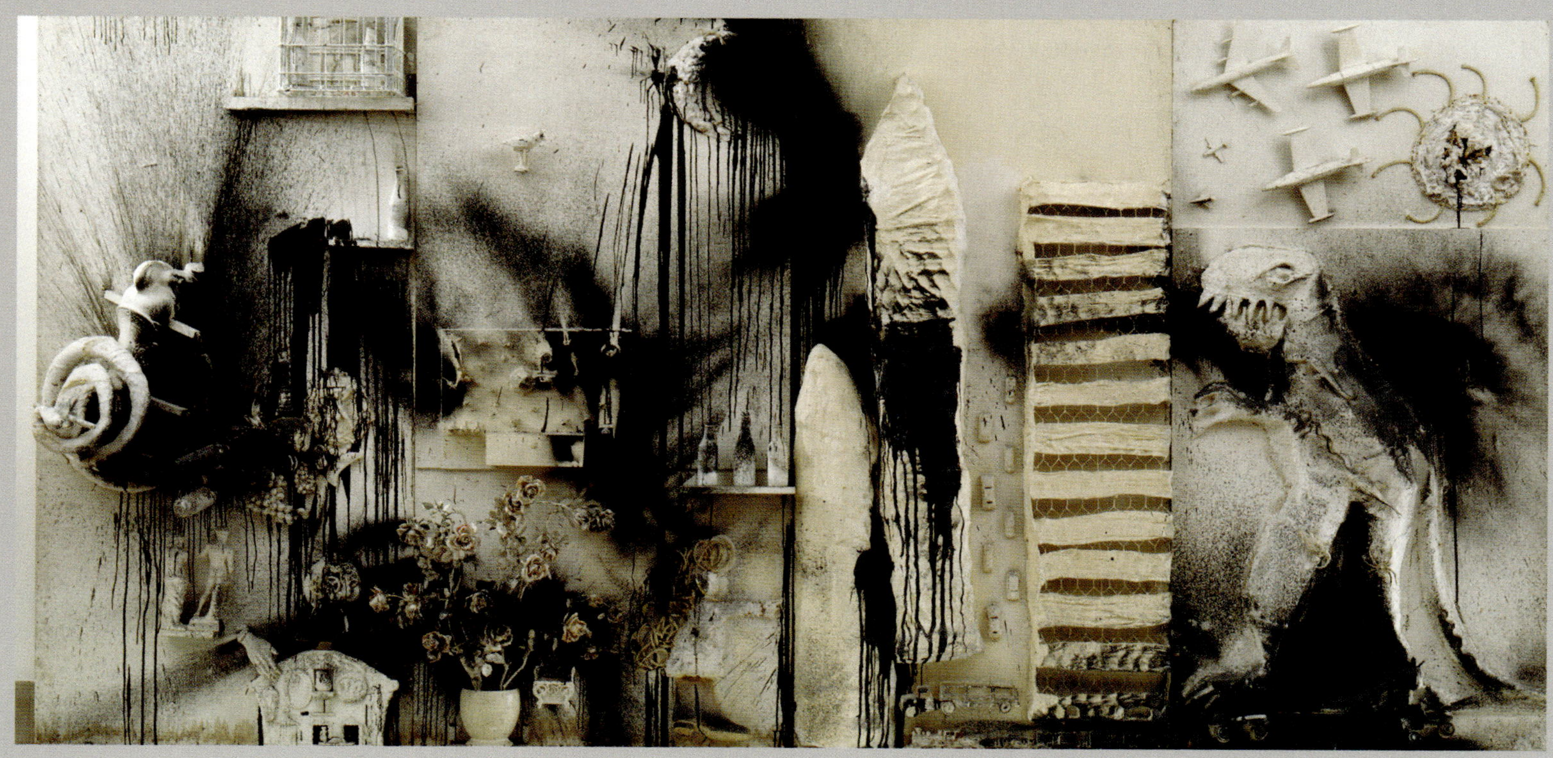

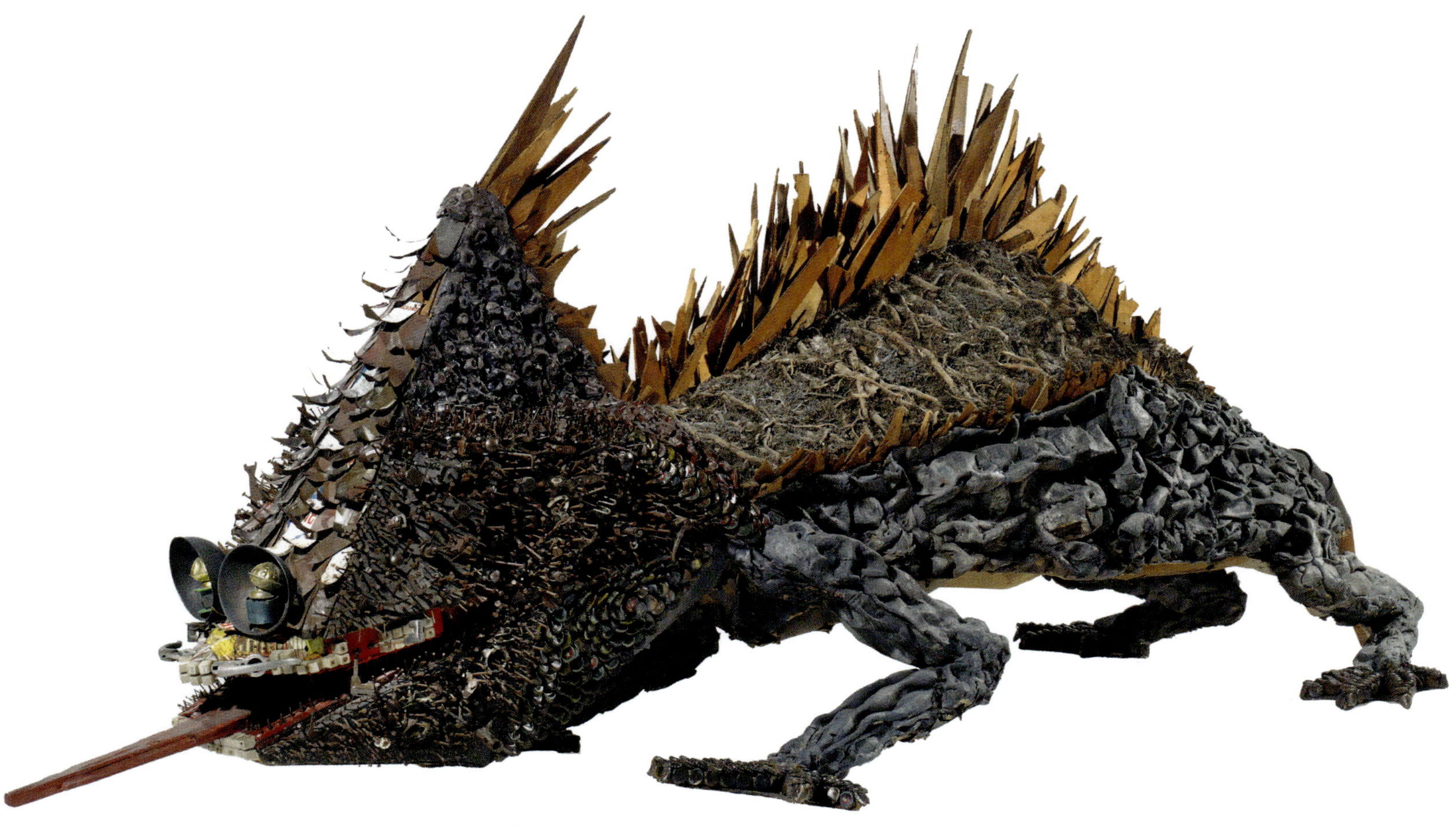

JORGE DE LA VEGA | Argentinean, 1930–1971
Images, 1966
Oil and collage on canvas
Canvas or panel: 63 7/8 x 77 1/4 in.
(162.2 x 196.2 cm)
Jorge and Marion Helft Collection,
Museum purchase funded by the
Caroline Wiess Law Accessions
Endowment Fund
2011.1064

NIKI DE SAINT-PHALLE | French, 1930–2002
Gorgo in New York, 1962
Mixed media
Overall [assembled]: 95 3/4 x 193 x 19 1/2 in.
(243.205 x 490 x 49.53 cm)
Each panel: 95 3/4 x 48 1/4 in.
(243.205 x 122.555 cm)
Gift of D. and J. de Menil
62.47

ANTONIO BERNI | Argentinean, 1905–1981
La sordidez [Sordidness], c. 1964
From the series *Cosmic Monsters*
Wood, steel, iron, aluminum, cardboard, plastic,
roots, nails and enamel
50 3/4 x 47 1/4 x 157 1/2 in. (129 x 120 x 400 cm)
with platform
Museum purchase funded by the
Caroline Wiess Law Foundation
2004.1536

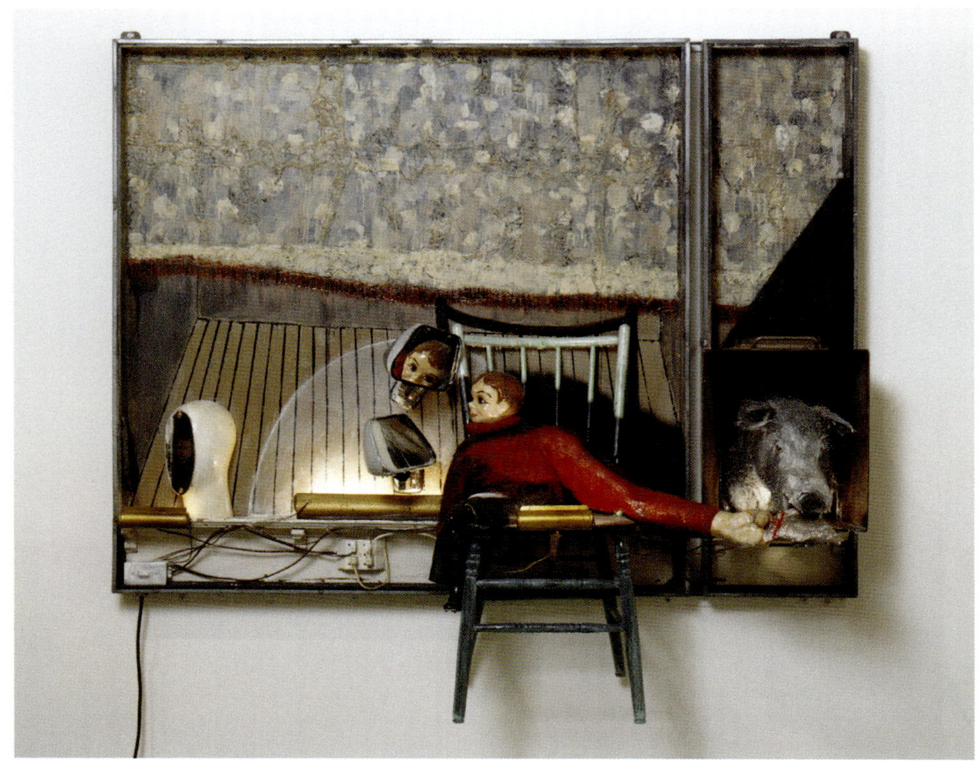

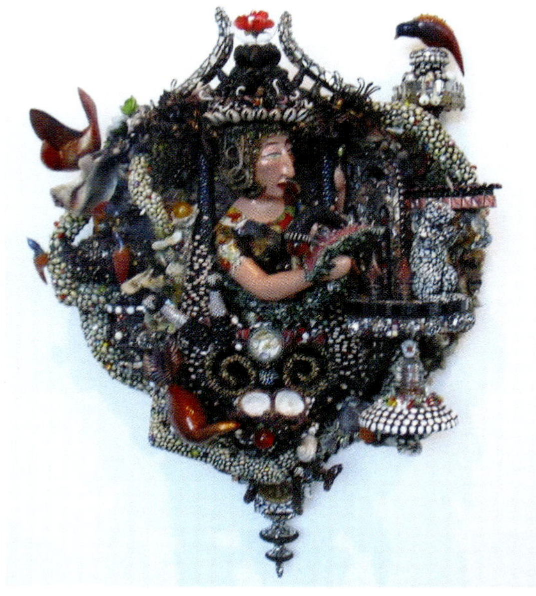

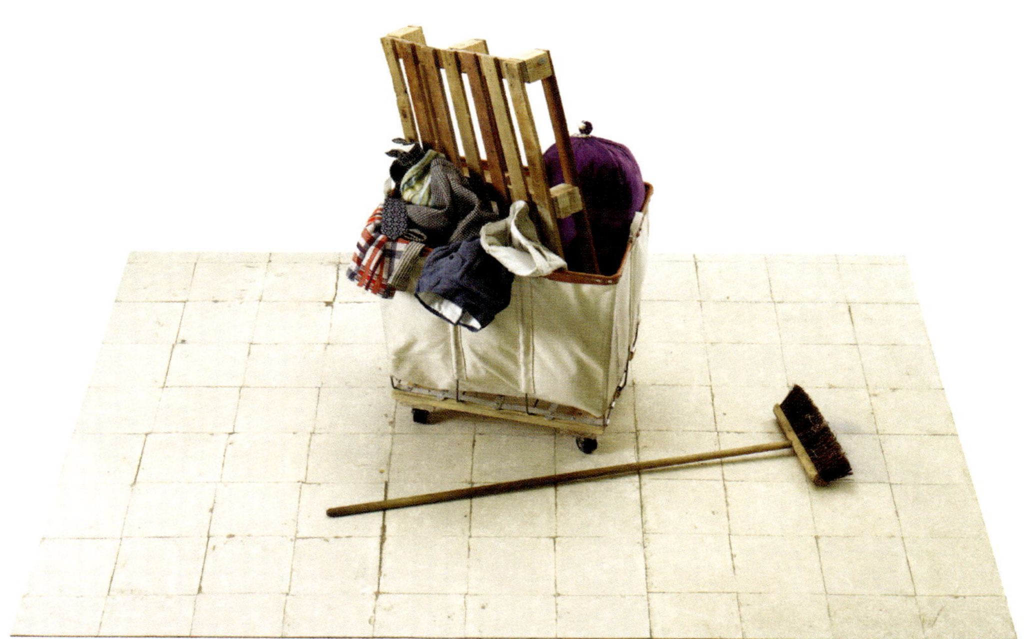

EDWARD KIENHOLZ | American, 1927–1994
NANCY REDDIN KIENHOLZ | American, born 1943
Feedin' the Hog, 1993–94
Mixed media assemblage with electric lights
5 x 73 x 21 3/4 in. (165.1 x 185.4 x 55.2 cm)
Museum purchase funded by the
Caroline Wiess Law Accessions
Endowment Fund
95.326

CHARLES LEDRAY | American, born 1960
Untitled (Men's Suits), 2009
Laundry cart contents: purple satin bag; clear, white, and black hangers
made from alumilite clear cast resin and galvanized steel wire; six pairs of
trousers, one shirt, two neckties made from various fabrics. Laundry bag
with nylon cord, alumilite toggles, fabric, thread, stuffed with fabric.
Palette: wood, nails, glue, wood stain, dirt.
Cart: wood frame with woven aluminum strips, 1/8 inch ungalvanized steel
rod, clear acrylic spray coating, canvas, thread, vinyl, aluminum rivets,
dirt and newspaper ink.
Broom: wood handle and housing with bristles.
Floor: linoleum backed with canvas.
Overall: 27 3/4 x 55 x 40 in. (70.5 x 139.7 x 101.6 cm)
Overall (.A, Laundry cart): 27 3/4 x 17 3/8 x 15 1/2 in. (70.5 x 44.1 x 39.4 cm)
Overall (.B, Broom): 31 1/4 x 8 5/8 x 2 5/8 in. (79.4 x 21.9 x 6.7 cm)
Overall (.C, Linoleum flooring): 55 x 40 in. (139.7 x 101.6 cm)
Gift of Nina and Michael Zilkha in honor of Joseph Havel
2010.221

JUDY ONOFRIO | American, born 1939
Woman with Large Flower, 1995
Wood, glass, shell, printed tin, glass beads, mirror, chain
Overall: 56 x 44 x 21 1/2 in. (142.2 x 111.8 x 54.6 cm)
Gift of Matthew and Claudia Drutt
2004.1971

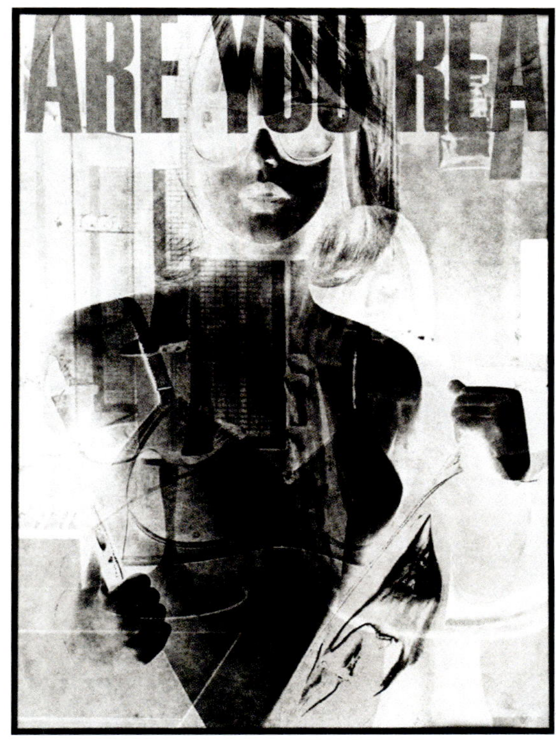

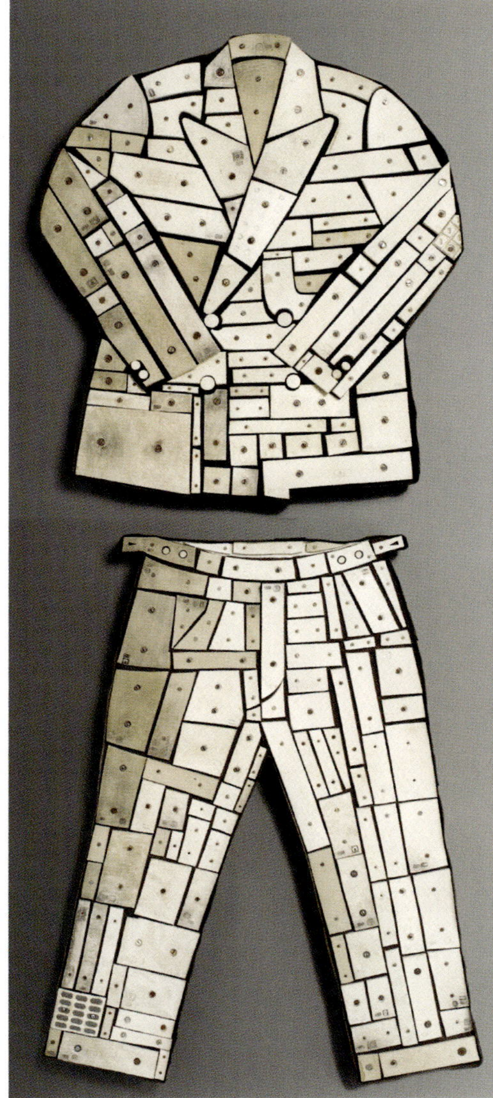

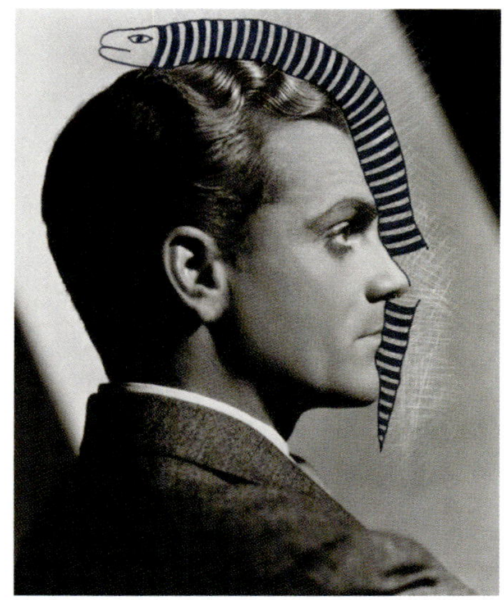

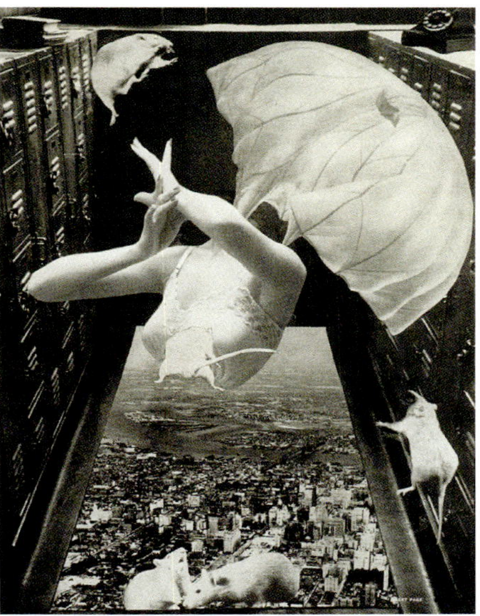

ROBERT HEINECKEN | American, 1931–2006
Utitled, 1968
From the Series *Are You Rea #1*
Gelatin silver print
Image: 11 1/16 x 7 15/16 in. (28.1 x 20.1 cm)
Sheet: 11 5/16 x 8 3/16 in. (28.8 x 20.8 cm)
Mount: 14 1/16 x 11 in. (35.7 x 28 cm)
Gift of Manfred Heiting,
The Manfred Heiting Collection
2002.1287

PAUL ASTBURY | British, born 1945
Black Jacket, 1984
Work Trousers, 1984
From *Prisoner's Suit*
Ceramic, fabric, and wood
Overall (.1, Jacket): 33 x 29 x 2 3/4 in. (83.8 x 73.7 x 7 cm)
Overall (.2, Trousers): 42 1/2 x 33 x 3 in. (108 x 83.8 x 7.6 cm)
Garth Clark and Mark Del Vecchio
Collection, Museum purchase funded
by the Caroline Wiess Law Accessions
Endowment Fund
2007.755.1, .2

RAY JOHNSON | American, 1927–1995
James Cagney, 1933, 1988–92
Collage
Sheet: 8 x 6 1/2 in. (20.3 x 16.5 cm)
Mount: 10 1/4 x 8 1/4 in. (26 x 21 cm)
Museum purchase funded by the
Alvin S. Prints and Drawings Accessions Endowment Fund
2002.327

OKANOUE TOSHIKO | Japanese, born 1928
Falling, 1956
Collage
Image: 13 3/8 x 10 1/4 in. (34 x 26 cm)
Museum purchase funded by Joan Morgenstern, an anonymous
donor, and the Louisa Stude Sarofim Charitable Trust, courtesy of
Mary Lawrence Porter
2002.340

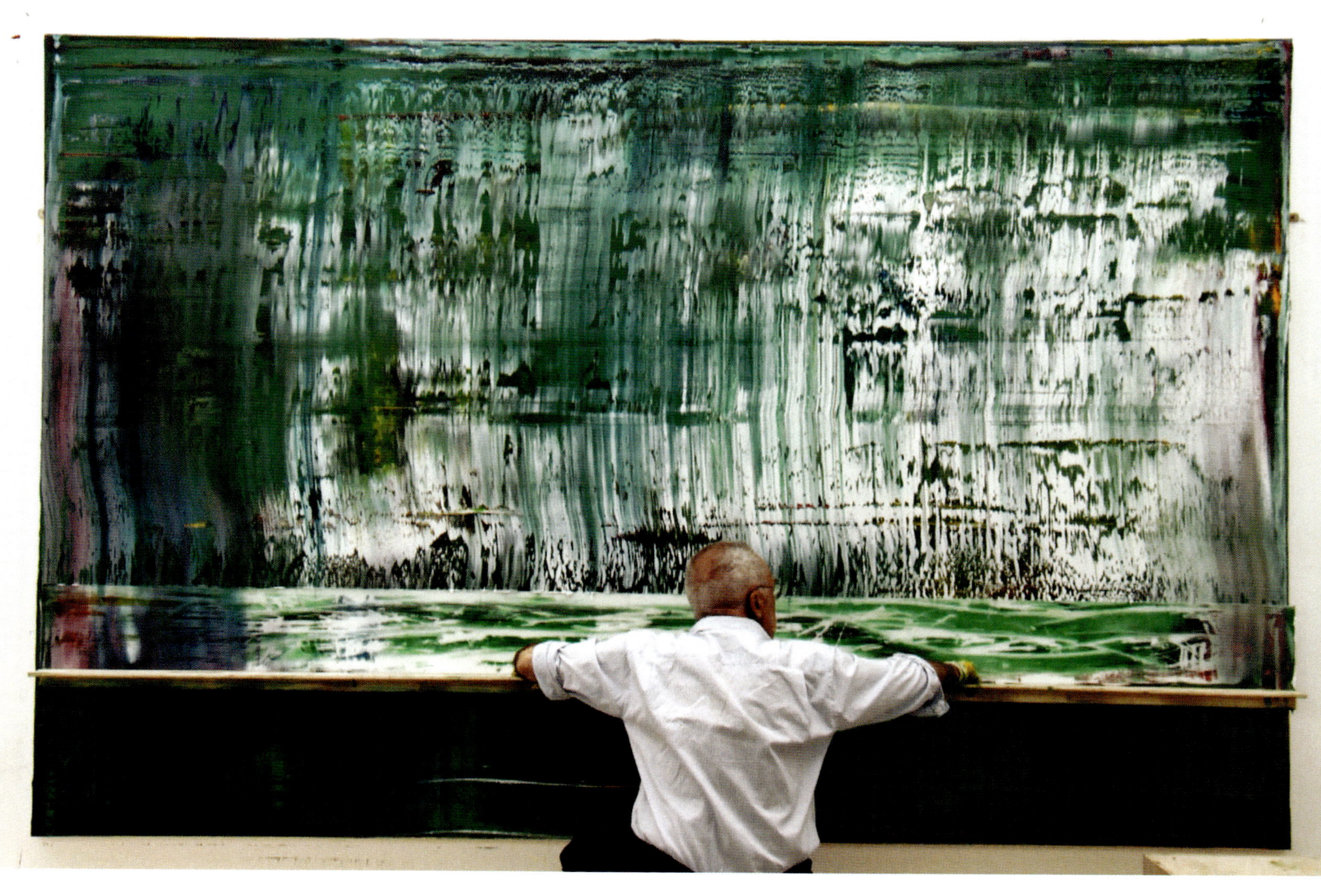

THE FILM PROGRAM

MARIAN LUNTZ

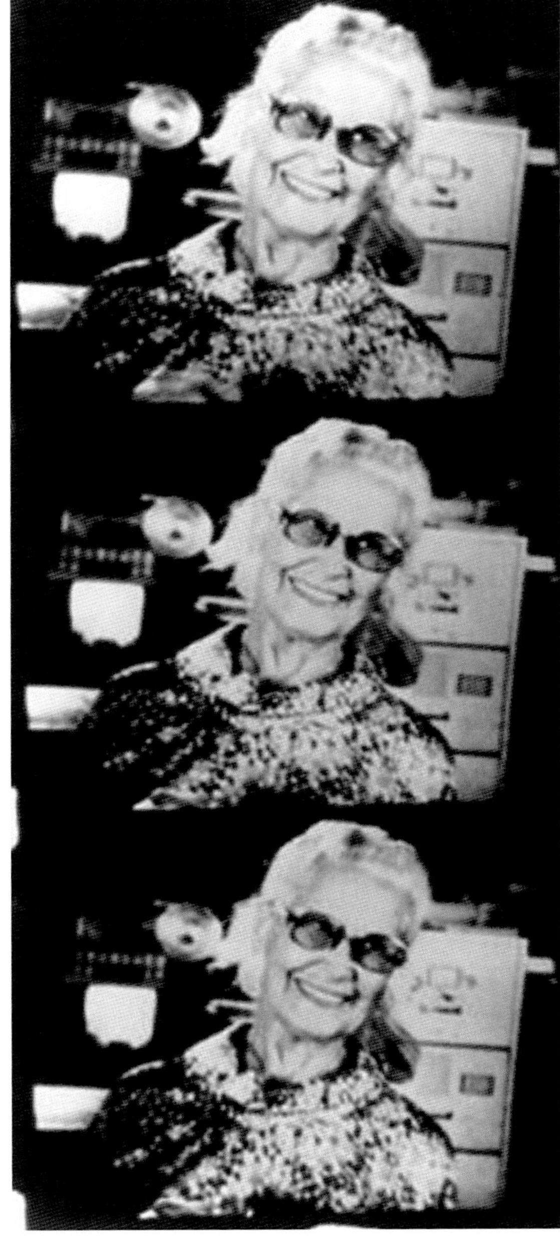

Since the late 1930s, the Museum of Fine Arts, Houston, has celebrated the art of cinema through its popular year-round film program. Audiences have flocked to the Museum's film theater, designed by Ludwig Mies van der Rohe, to see varied film offerings. The Museum is a popular destination for aficionados of classic and contemporary world cinema as well as for the general public.

More than two hundred screenings are scheduled annually, many featuring introductions and post-film discussions and conversations with noted filmmakers, critics, and scholars. Guests in recent years have included filmmakers Wes Anderson and Richard Linklater, actors Eva Marie Saint and Peter Fonda, musicians Debra Harry and Bun B, authors Nick Flynn and Justin Cronin, and journalist Adam Curtis. Museum visitors have the opportunity to enrich their knowledge of art and artists through films on contemporary art, and also through screenings that complement the Museum's dynamic exhibitions. This pro-gramming is enhanced by the superb quality of presentation: the Museum is committed to maintaining state-of-the-art projection, assuring a memorable and unparalleled viewing experience that inspires audience members to return often.

The diverse population of Houston is well served by the Museum's annual festivals of films from France, Iran, Turkey, and Latin America, among other countries. These much-anticipated surveys are exclusive opportunities to experience acclaimed

Opposite: Film still from *Gerhard Richter Painting*, directed by Corinna Belz.

Film still from *Energy and How to Get It*, directed by Robert Frank.

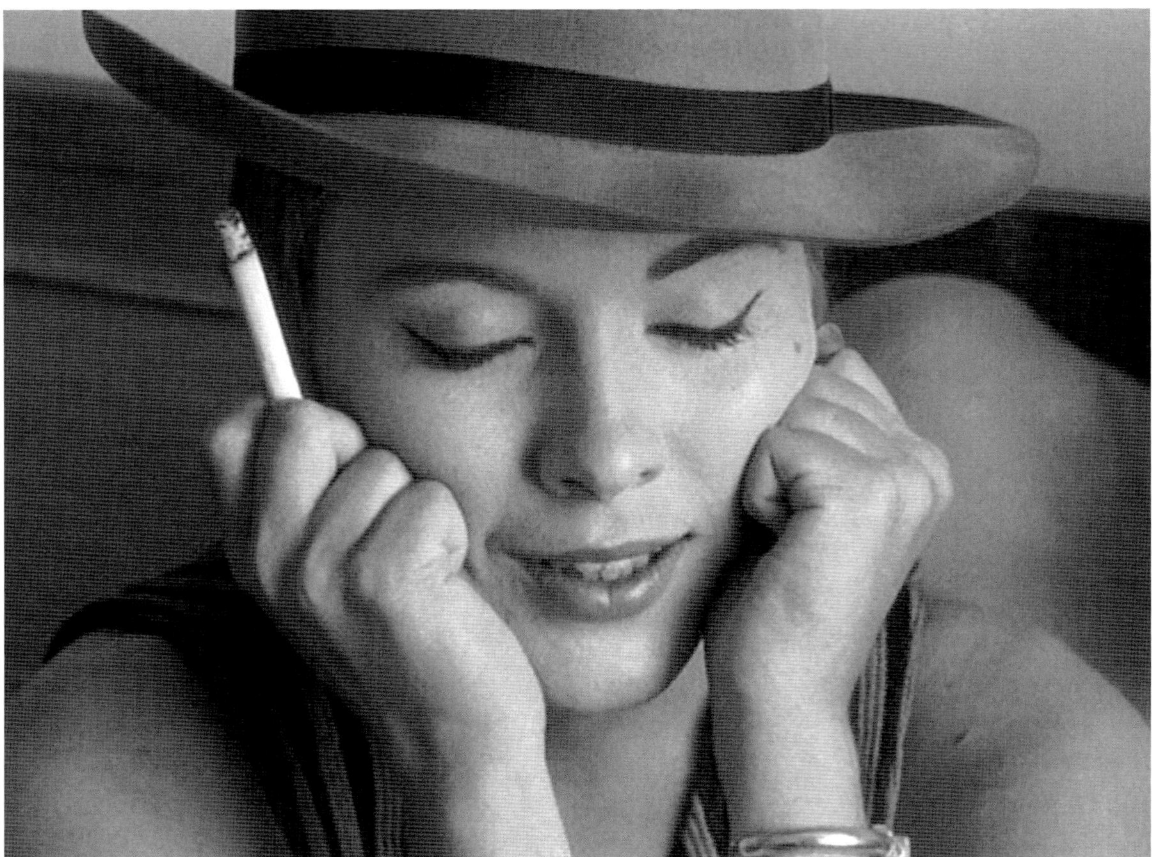

films that Houstonians would otherwise only read about in the national media. The Museum also partners with various organizations and collaborates with consulates to screen films of mutual interest to their audiences.

The addition of a second, state-of-the art theater will enable the Museum to offer an even wider selection of film and moving-image arts to visitors. The new theater will make the Museum more competitive, fulfilling a goal to schedule week-long runs of new films that previously could not open in Houston because of limited screens. Discussions are under way to add the Museum to the itinerary for acclaimed cultural programming such as The Metropolitan Opera Live in HD and the Great Art on Screen series. In addition, during the Museum's film festivals, the number of offerings could increase, with two different films screening simultaneously. Also envisioned in the new theater are film-and-discussion programs for school groups, special-interest groups, and community partners, and screenings of children's films that will appeal to families.

The Museum's film collection includes landmark films by artists such as Paul Strand, Charles Sheeler, and Fernand Léger. The Museum has served since the mid-1980s as the repository and distributor of films by the noted photographer Robert Frank. Since the 1990s, the Museum's modern and contemporary art, Latin American art, Asian art, and photography departments have also been collecting film, as well as video and digital work. Curated programs of these films will be scheduled in the new theater, acquainting visitors with the depth of the Museum's holdings in the moving-image arts.

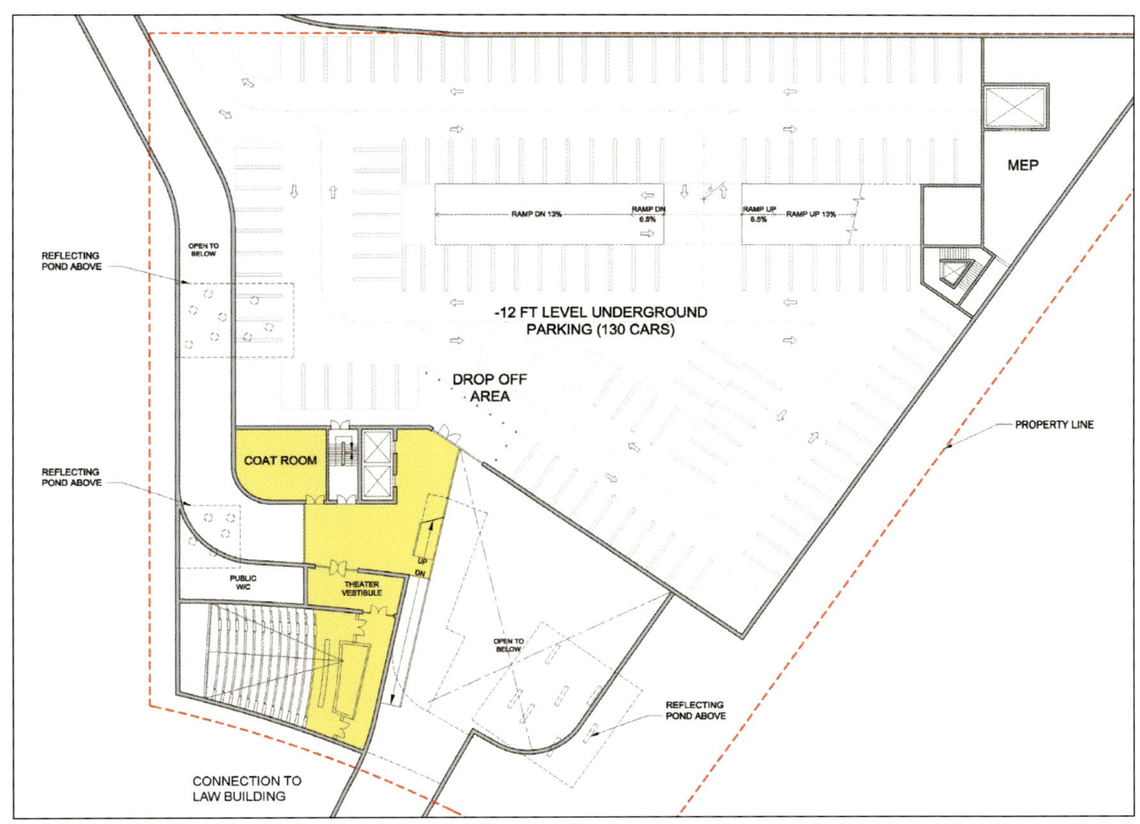

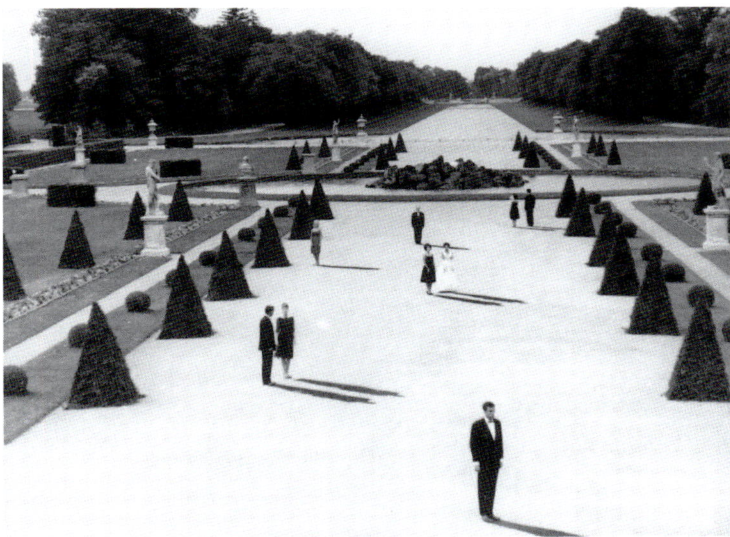

Opposite: Film still from *Breathless*, directed by Jean-Luc Godard.

Top: Steven Holl Architects, 2013. Conceptual plan for auditorium in the new Museum building.

Left: Film still from *Last Year at Marienbad*, directed by Alain Resnais. Photo courtesy Rialto Pictures.

PHOTO-BASED WORK

Photography is a tool, like any other medium or material
that artists choose to employ to convey an idea or effect.
In photo-based art, photographs can be one of multiple
mediums employed, such as the group of photographs
that Christian Boltanski surrounded with lights, wires, and
metal bread boxes, giving the impression of sacred halos
around the faces of ordinary children. Other artists work
against the properties for which photographs are best
known, such as clarity of detail. Oscar Muñoz literally
dissolved nine photographs, rescuing them just before the
images totally disappeared, similar to the way memories
break up and fade. Still another approach is to reinterpret
a famous photograph in a different medium, such as
Vik Muniz redrawing a famous photographic portrait of
Sigmund Freud in liquid chocolate and then photographing
the new image.

CHRISTIAN BOLTANSKI | French, born 1944
Monuments (La Fête du Pourim), 1989
Gelatin silver prints with metal biscuit boxes, and
light fixtures with bulbs
Dimensions variable
Each image/sheet: 15 3/4 x 11 7/8 in. (40 x 30.2 cm)
Each biscuit box: 2 3/8 x 9 1/8 x 8 1/2 in. (6 x 23.2 x 21.6 cm)
Museum purchase funded by the
Brown Foundation Accessions
Endowment Fund
89.284

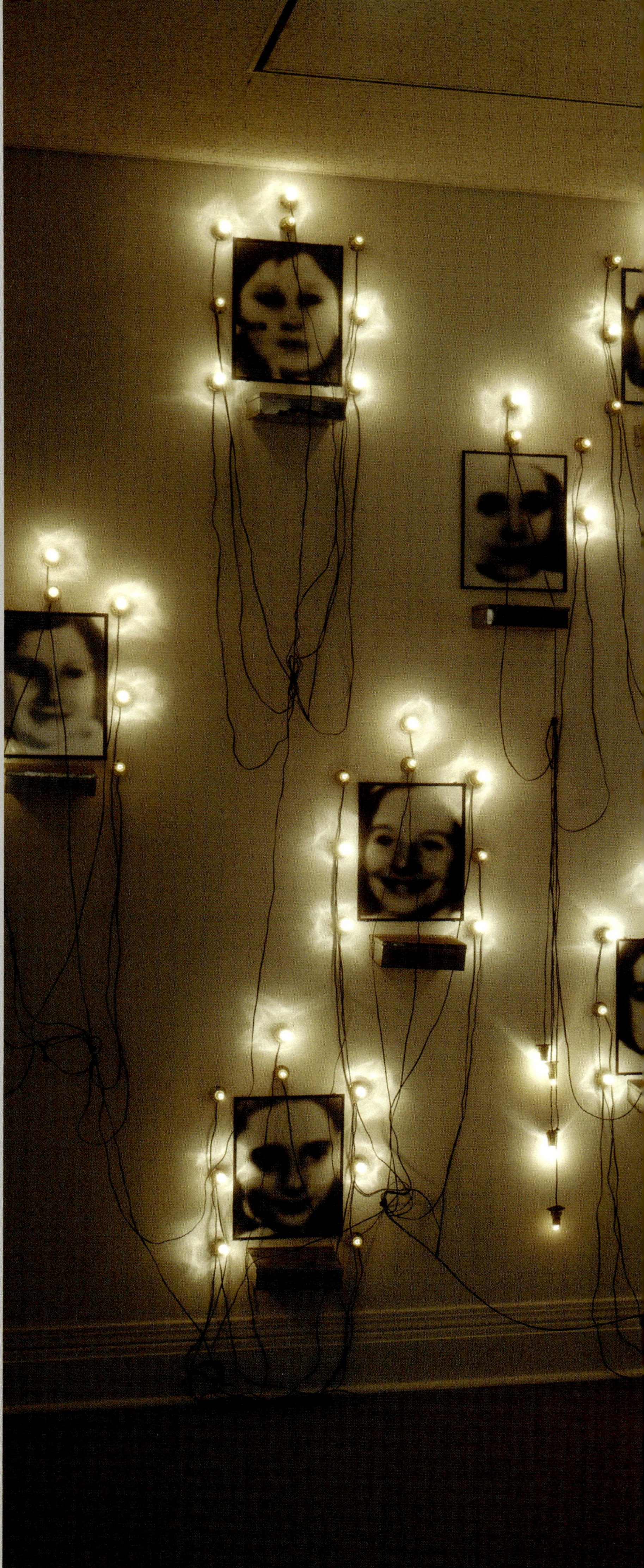

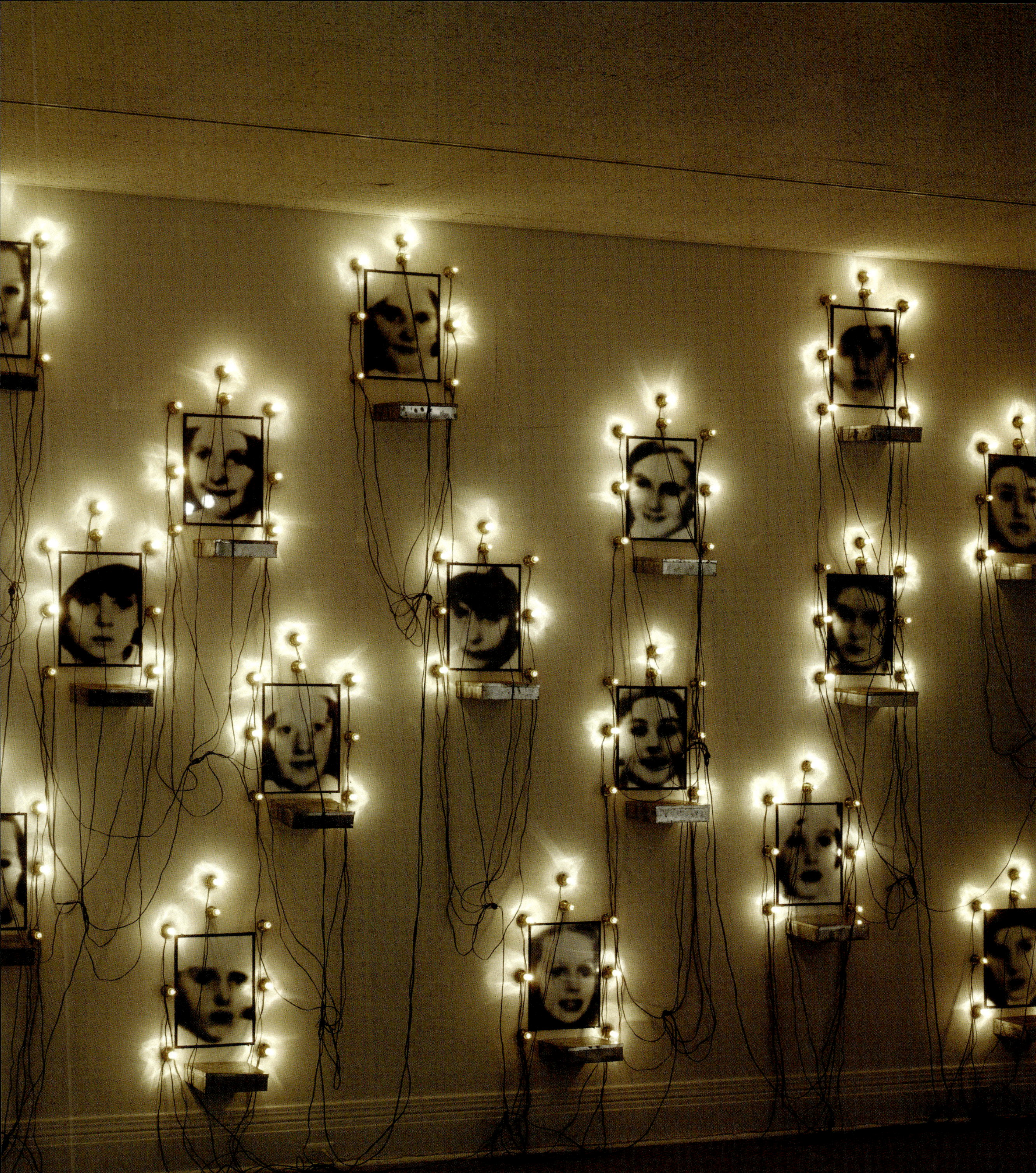

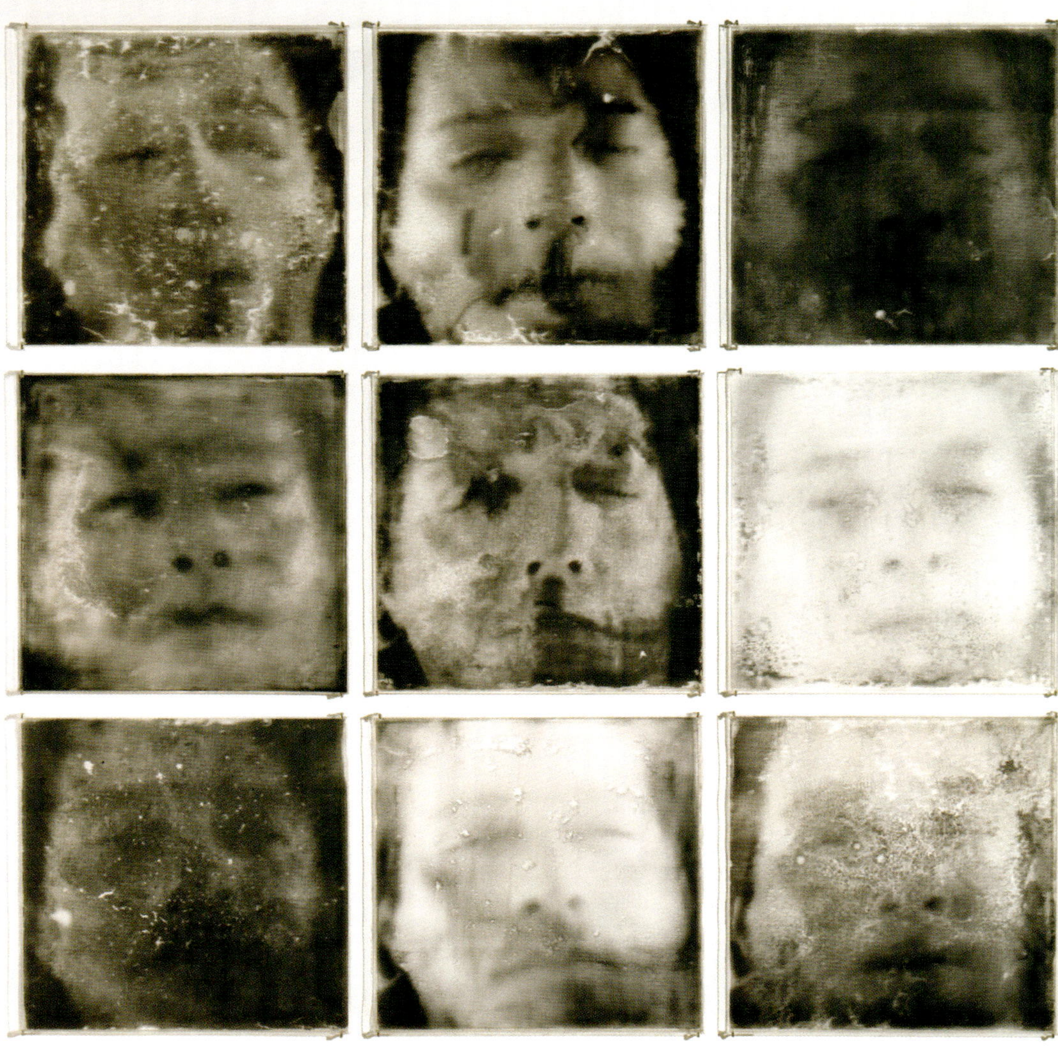

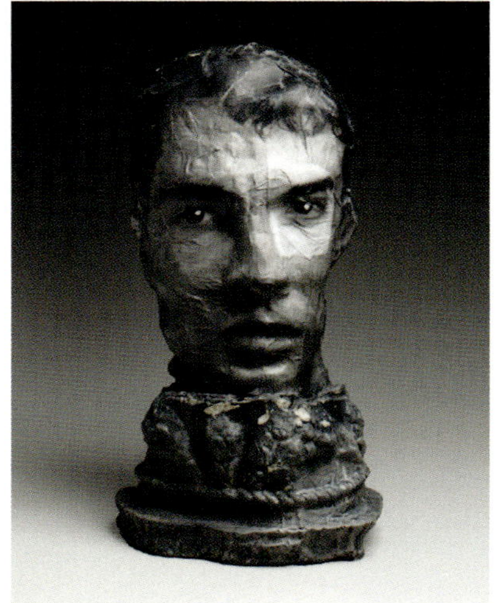

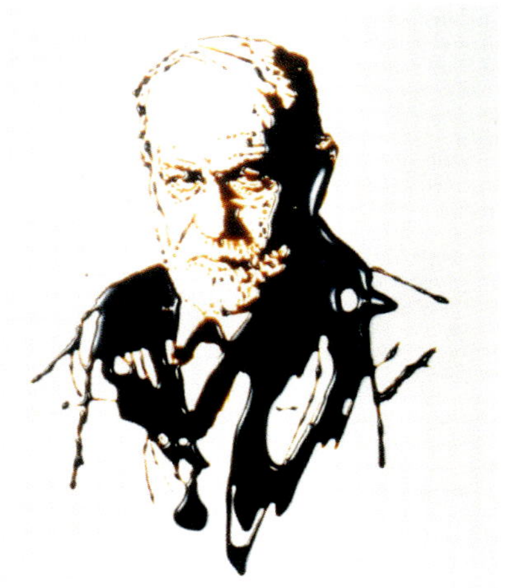

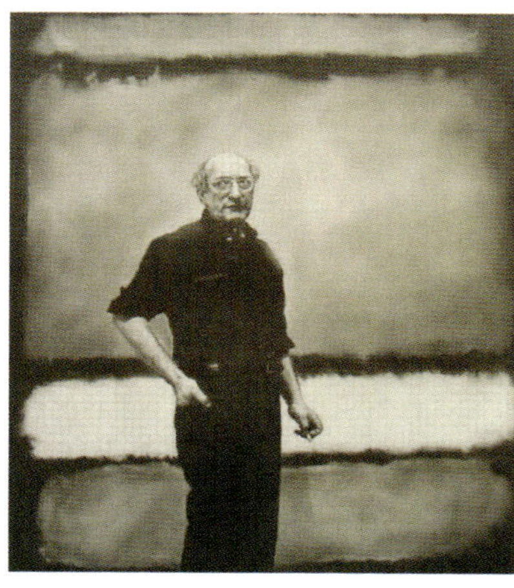

Above:
OSCAR MUÑOZ | Colombian, born 1951
Narcissos Secos, series de nueve
[Dry Narcissi, Series of Nine], 1999
Charcoal on Plexiglas
Overall: 86 x 86 in. (218.4 x 218.4 cm)
Each panel: 27 15/16 x 27 15/16 x 1 1/8 in.
(71 x 71 x 2.9 cm)
Museum purchase funded by Leslie and Brad Bucher,
Dr. Luis and Cecilia Campos, Mary and Roy Cullen,
Margaret C. and Louis Skidmore, Jr., Samuel F.
Gorman, Frank Ribelin, Frances and Peter C. Marzio,
Dr. and Mrs. Miguel Miro-Quesada, and Dr. Don
Baxter at the Latin Maecenas Gala Dinner, 2003
2003.316.A–I

Above, top right:
DOUG JECK | American, born 1963
Portrait of Claudio, 2006
Clay and mixed media
Overall: 12 1/4 x 6 3/8 x 5 in. (31.1 x 16.2 x 12.7 cm)
Garth Clark and Mark Del Vecchio Collection,
gift of Garth Clark and Mark Del Vecchio
2010.1672

VIK MUNIZ | Brazilian, born 1961
Sigmund, 1997–98
From the series *Pictures of Chocolate*
Silver dye bleach print
Image: 38 1/2 x 30 3/4 in. (96.3 x 76.9 cm)
Irregular sheet: 50 x 34 15/16 in. (125 x 87.3 cm)
Museum purchase funded by the
Houston-Galveston Psychoanalytic Institute
in honor of C. Glenn Cambor
99.294

DAN FISCHER | American, born 1977
Mark Rothko, 2002
Graphite on paper
22 1/2 x 15 in. (57.2 x 38.1 cm)
Gift of Barry Walker
2003.210

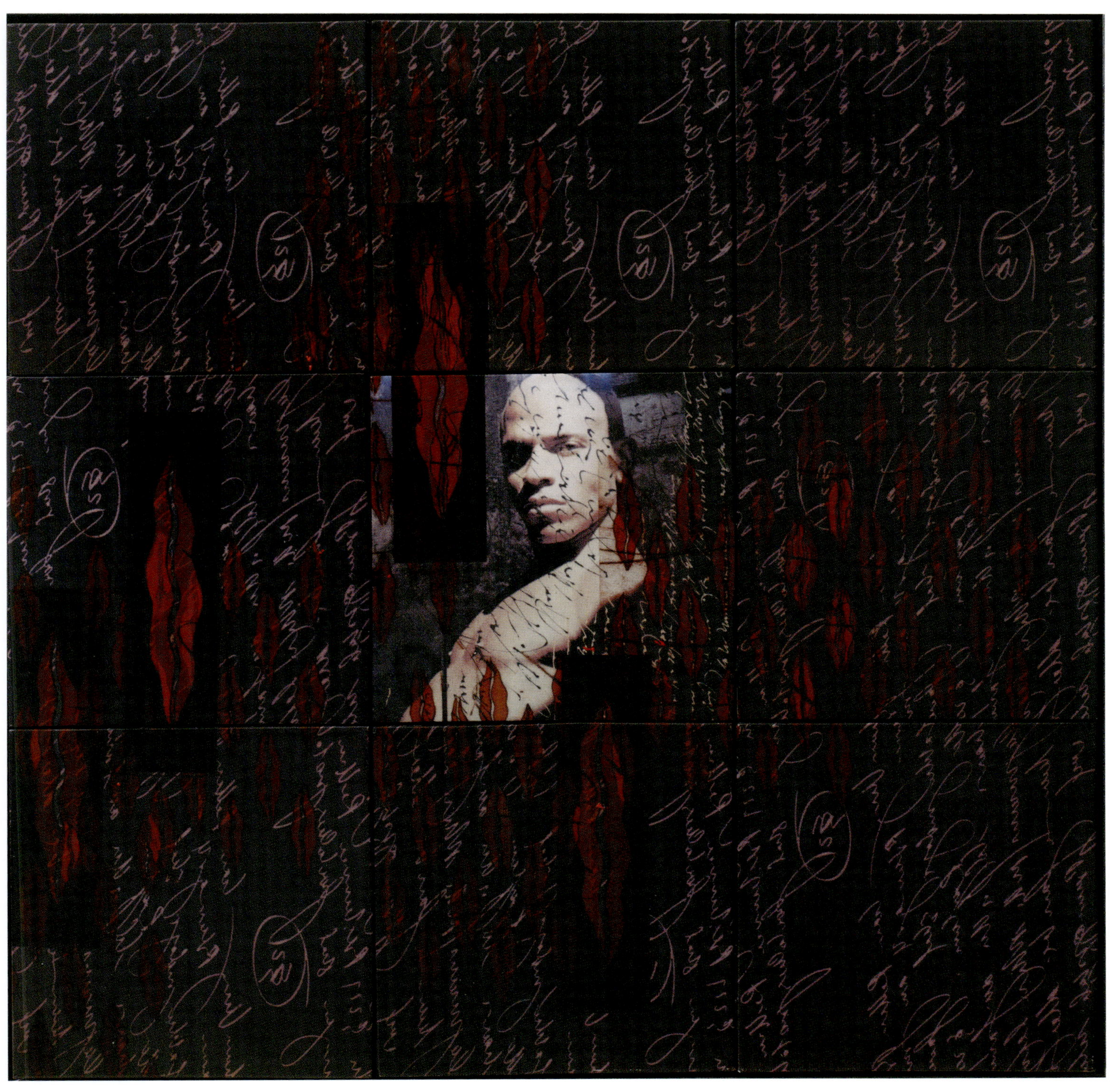

OLE LISLERUD | Norwegian, born South Africa 1950
Siyah Dudak, 2002
From the series *Metaphorical Portraits*
Porcelain and steel
Overall: 34 1/4 x 34 1/4 x 1 in. (87 x 87 x 2.5 cm)
Garth Clark and Mark Del Vecchio Collection,
gift of Garth Clark and Mark Del Vecchio
2007.944

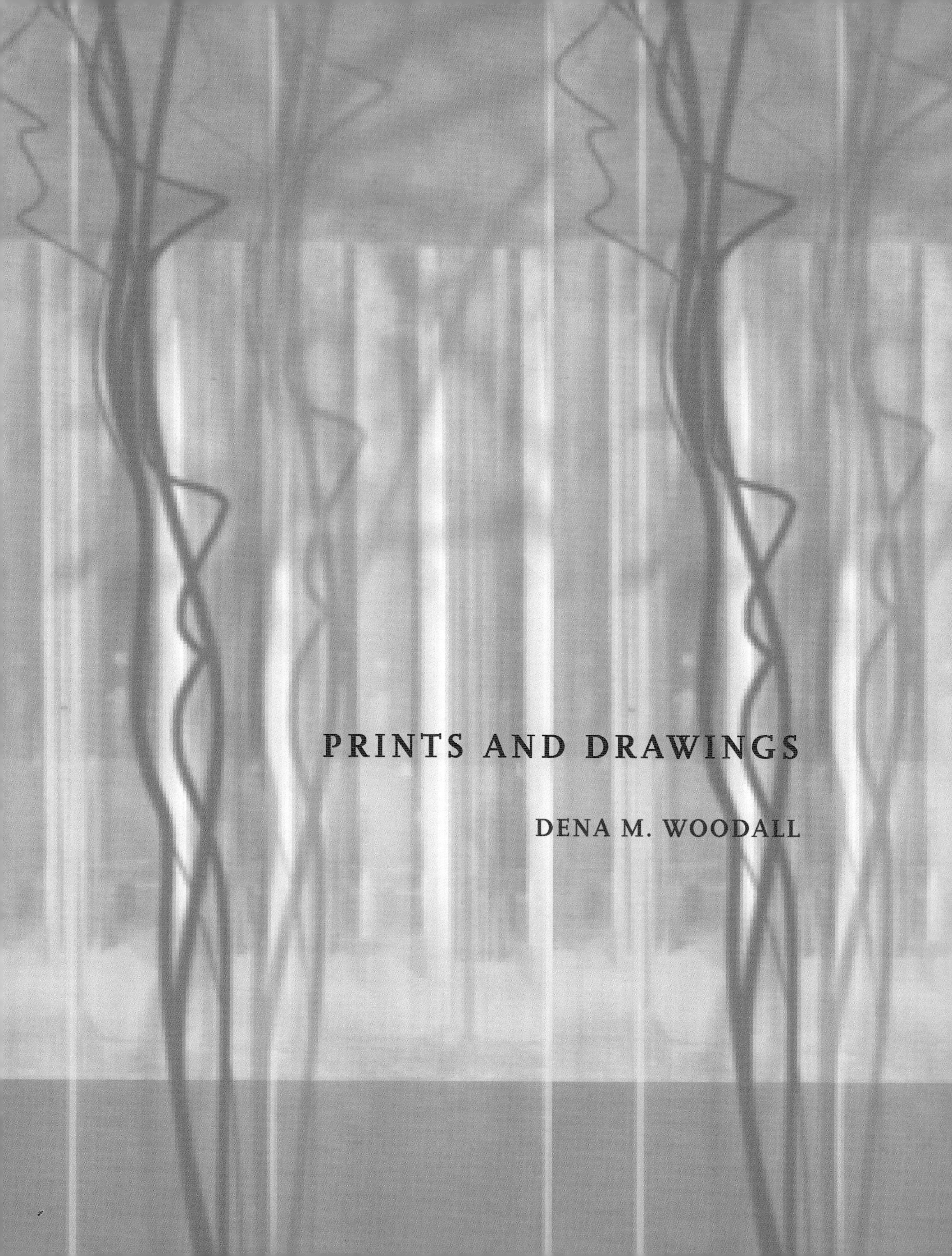
PRINTS AND DRAWINGS
DENA M. WOODALL

The Museum's encyclopedic collection of prints and drawings ranges from the Middle Ages to the present. It comprises more than 8,700 objects, including drawings, prints, watercolors, pastels, collages, paintings on paper, and printing matrices. The acquisition of works on paper began shortly after the Museum opened to the public in 1924. Throughout the 1930s, significant drawings and prints from the American Regionalists and the Mexican Muralists, such as Rockwell Kent, Diego Rivera, and José Clemente Orozco, entered the Museum. In 1939, Miss Ima Hogg donated a large number of works on paper from the early twentieth century. Prominent Expressionists and European Modernists, such as Henri Matisse, Franz Marc, Emil Nolde, Lyonel Feininger, and Pablo Picasso, were among the artists added. Paul Klee's watercolor, *Marjamshausen*, is an especially stellar work, with its buildings composed of colorful, variegated planes. Several important donors aided in the building of the collection throughout the years, including Oveta Culp Hobby, who, beginning in the 1980s, gave impressive drawings by Amedeo Modigliani, Picasso, and Joan Miró. A milestone occurred in 1991, when the Prints and Drawings Department was formally established. Peter C. Marzio, a former print curator who was then the Museum's director, hired Barry Walker to be the first curator of the department.

Approximately one-half of the collection was acquired after the department's inception, with the greatest number of works coming from the modern and contemporary eras. Simultaneous to the department's founding, collector Sue Rowan Pittman donated nearly forty graphic works by notable twentieth-century sculptors, such as Louise Nevelson, David Smith, Eduardo Chillida, Claes Oldenburg, and Eva Hesse. The collector's personal passion for modern and contemporary sculpture inspired this act of philanthropy, which in turn has led to the growth of one of the most important areas within the Prints and Drawings Department.

From the mid-1990s to the early 2000s, the Museum began acquiring noteworthy drawings by Abstract Expressionist painters, including Jackson Pollock, Robert Motherwell, and Arshile Gorky. In 1991, the Museum procured a remarkable group of nine sketchbook drawings by Pollock that shows his absorption of the European Modernists, yet depicts the beginning of his own visual aesthetic. The drawings complement the Museum's other holdings by Pollock: paintings on canvas and paper, drawings, and two of five extant sculptures, all demonstrating the breadth of the artist's career and making the Museum of Fine Arts, Houston, the repository of the most cohesive collection of Pollock's work in the world. In 2004, the Museum acquired *Nighttime, Enigma and Nostalgia,* which is considered to be the most outstanding drawing of Gorky's series of the same name. Showcasing the artist's working method, the drawing combines gestural marks, elaborated grids, biomorphic forms, and skeletal fish, and it forms a stunning pair with a painting from the same series in the Museum's collections.

The Museum also made a landmark acquisition, the Peter Blum Edition Archive, consisting of more than four hundred works created from 1980 to 1994 by contemporary American and European artists. This archive is a major resource for exploring the creative potential of printmaking, and it includes drawings and working proofs, along with the finished prints, portfolios, and books from esteemed artists. Among these artists are Louise Bourgeois, Alex Katz, Barbara Kruger, and James Turrell. The Museum has a complete record of many of the print projects, such as Eric Fischl's *Year of the Drowned Dog.*

The Museum's formidable holdings of Jasper Johns's work in all media underscore the artist's experimentation with his subject matter. Johns's conceptualization of an image is determined by reexamining motifs in a nonlinear process through paintings, sketches, finished drawings, and variable impressions in print form. His dynamic watercolor *Cicada* revisits the artist's painted imagery and mixes a finished drawing style with sketchy notations.

Other notable highlights in the Prints and Drawings Department include Julie Mehretu's monumental tour-de-force, twelve-panel etching; Vija Celmins's illusionistic yet abstracted intaglio print of a spiderweb; and a pared-down, austere triptych by Richard Diebenkorn, which summarizes the imagery in his celebrated Ocean Park series.

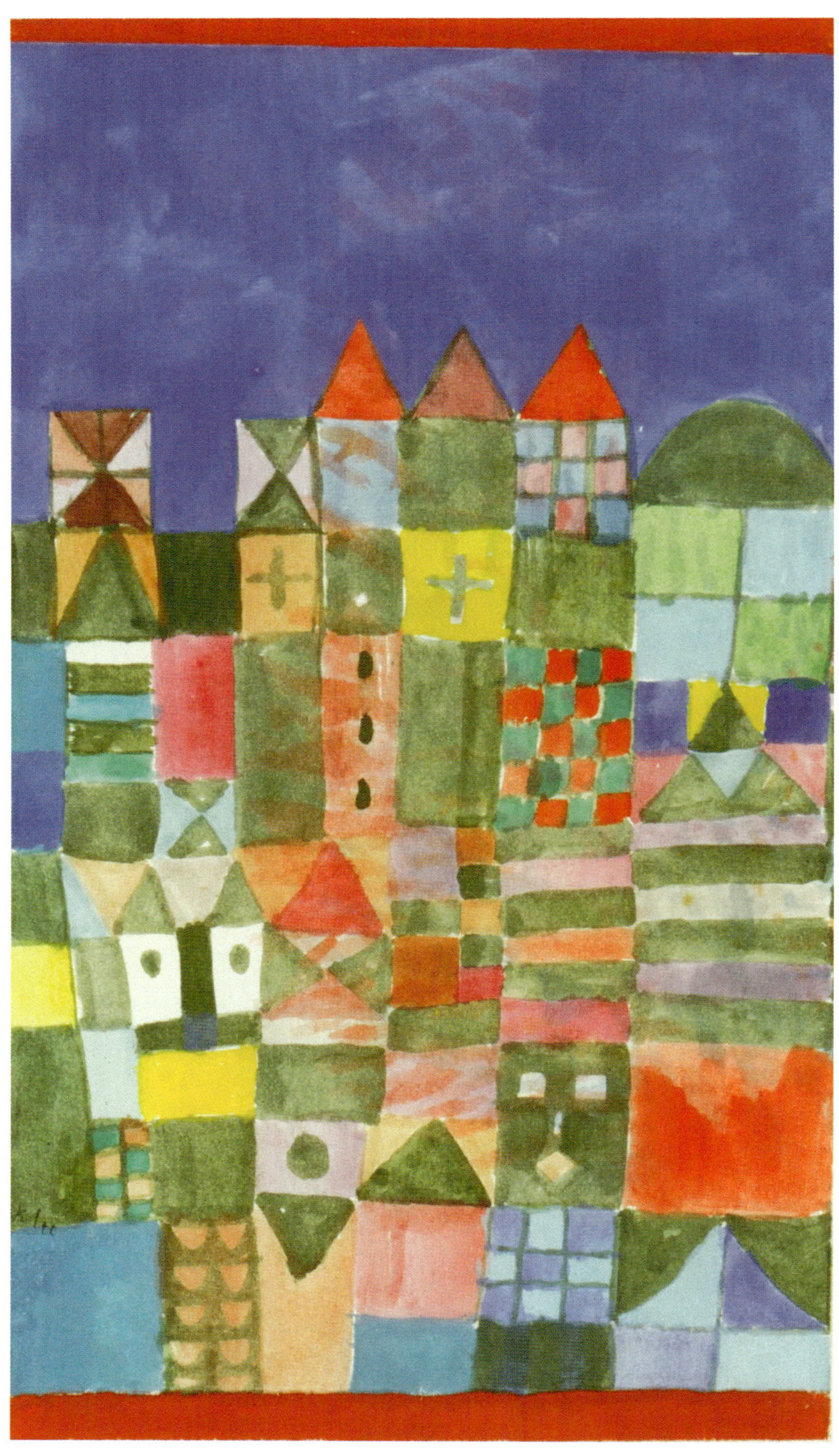

PAUL KLEE | Swiss, 1879–1940
Marjamshausen, 1928
Watercolor on paper
16 2/5 x 12 1/3 in. (41.7 x 31.4 cm)
Mat: 16 5/8 x 12 3/8 in. (42.2 x 31.4 cm)
Gift of Miss Ima Hogg
39.111

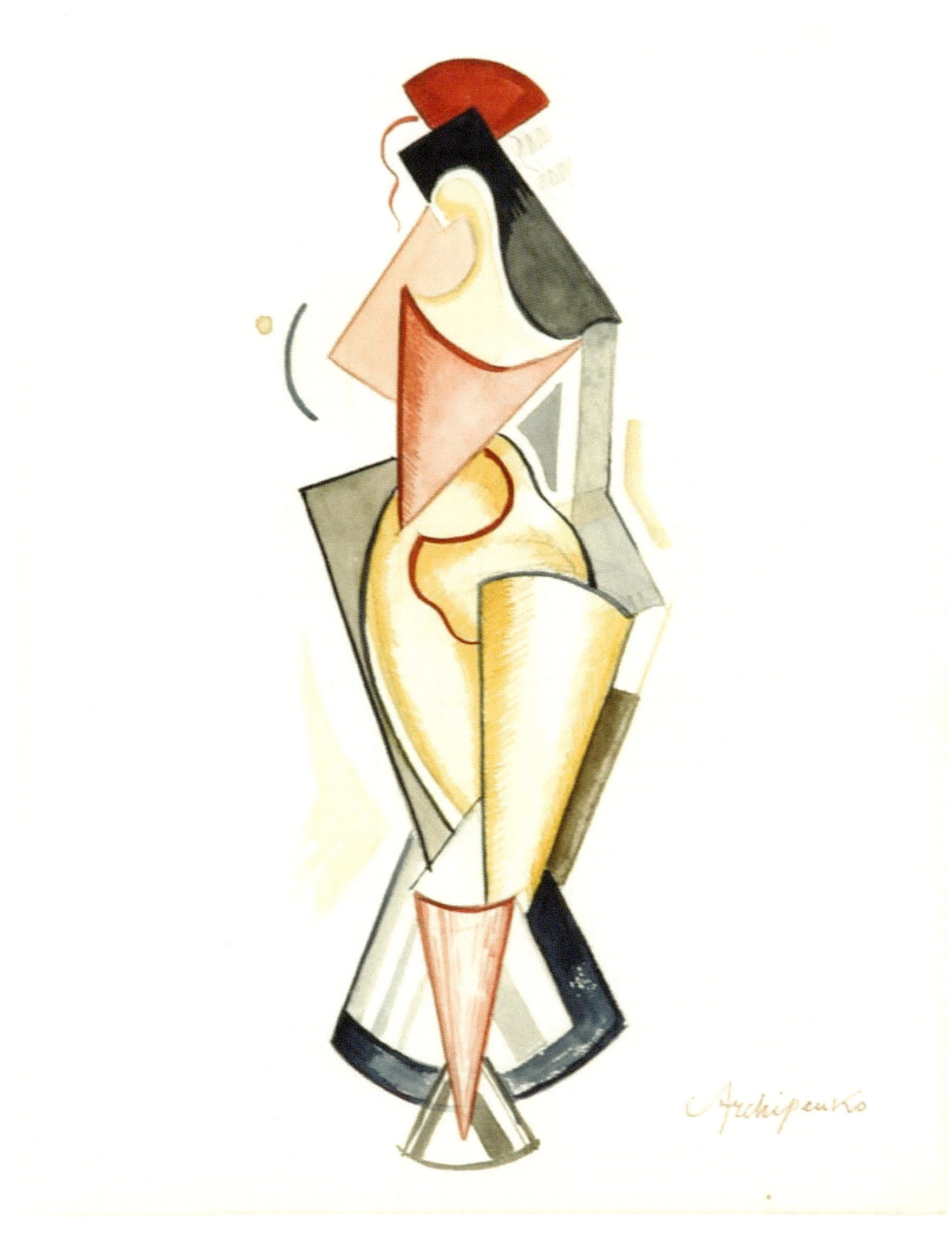

ALEXANDER ARCHIPENKO | American,
born Russia, 1887–1964
Frauen IV [Women IV], 1922
Watercolor and graphite on paper
11 1/16 x 8 3/8 in. (28.1 x 21.3 cm)
Museum purchase funded by the
Caroline Wiess Law
Accessions Endowment Fund
2009.1340

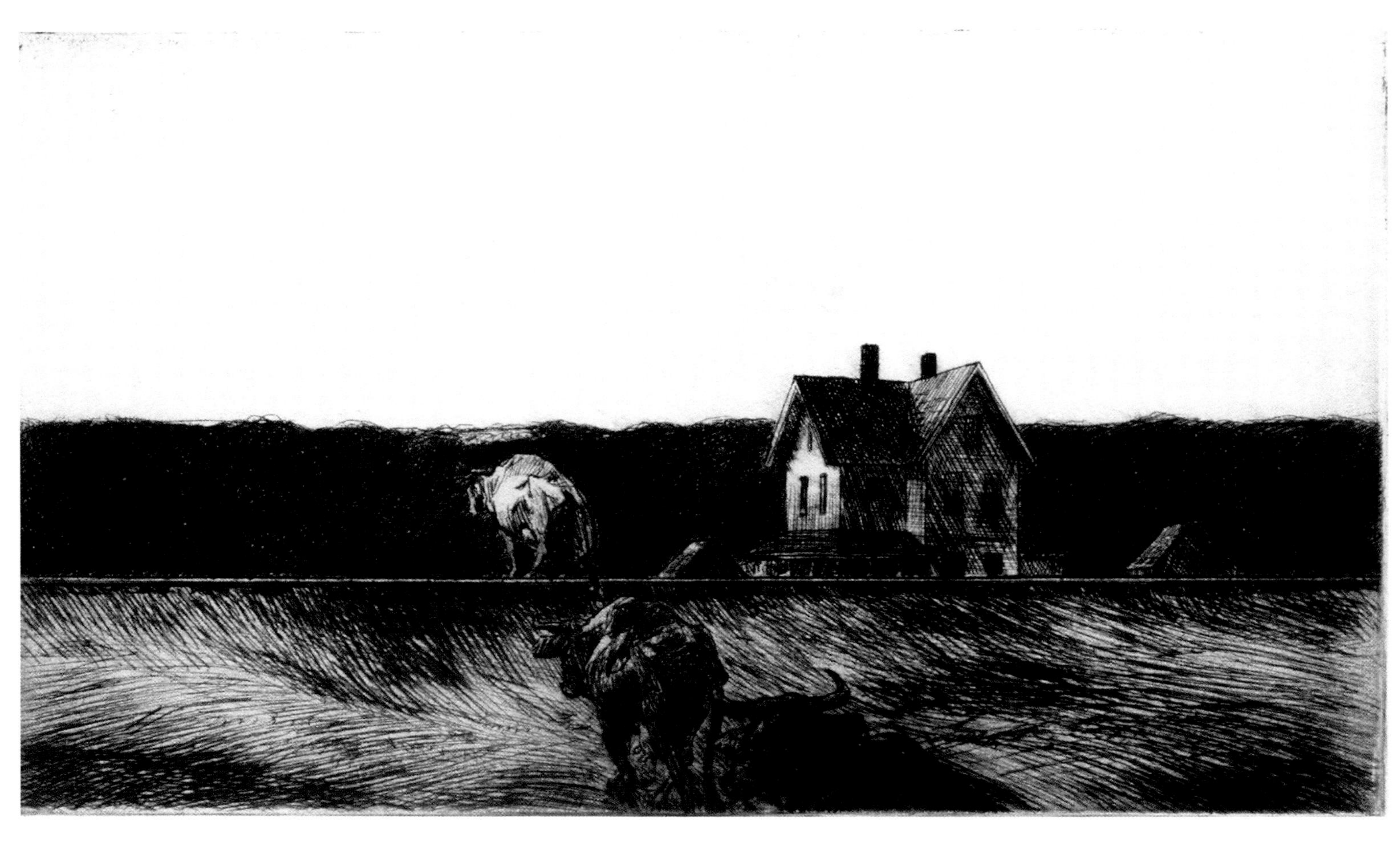

EDWARD HOPPER | American, 1882–1967
American Landscape, 1920
Etching
Plate: 7 5/16 x 12 7/16 in. (18.6 x 31.6 cm)
Sheet: 13 1/2 x 17 11/16 in. (34.3 x 44.9 cm)
Museum purchase funded by
Alan R. Buckwalter III, James R. Crane,
Thomas S. Glanville, Frank J. Hevrdejs,
Neil E. Kelley, John McVaney, Kane C. Weiner,
and Michael T. Willis in memory of
Kenneth Schnitzer at "One Great Night in
November, 1999"
99.483

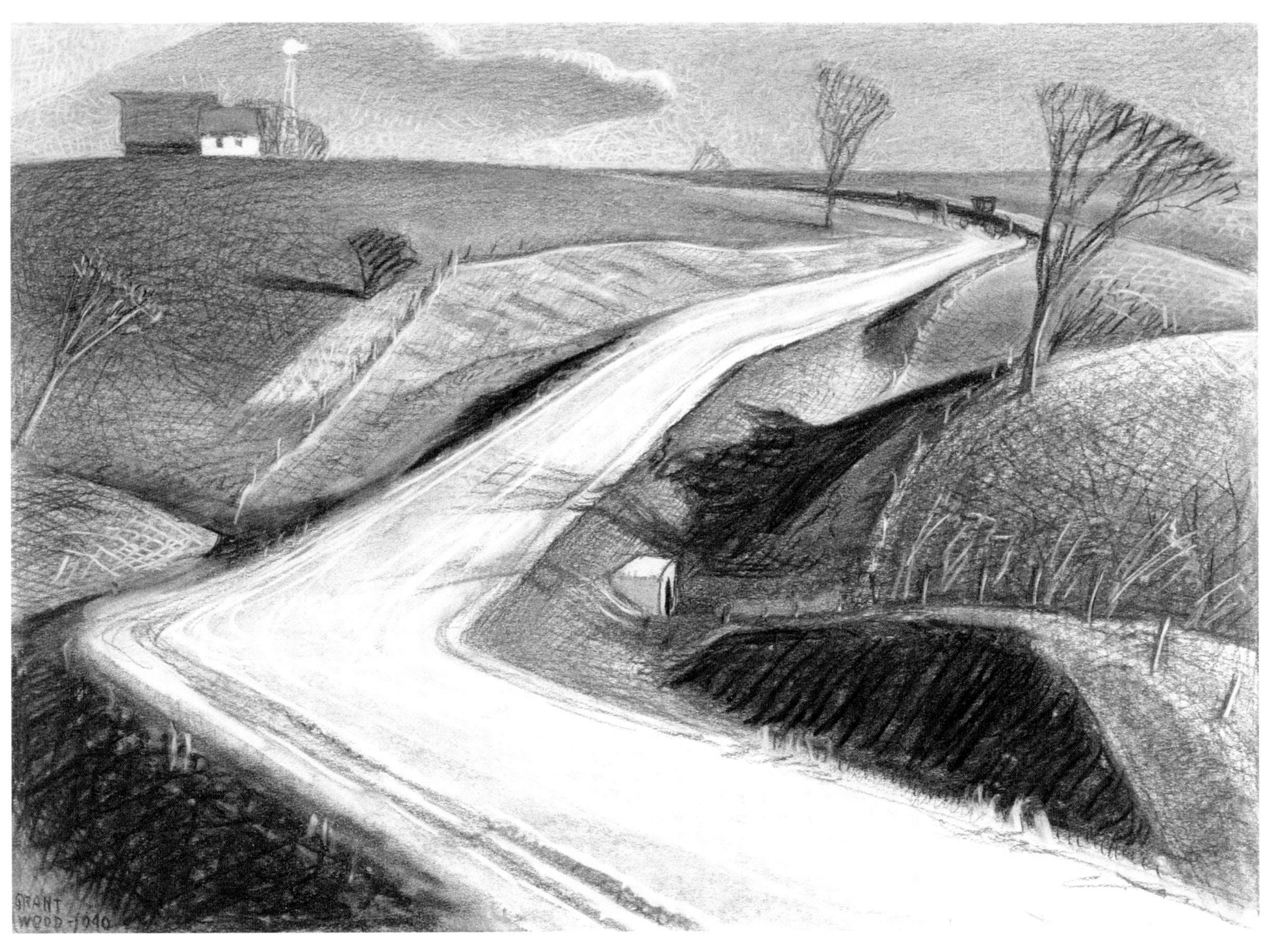

GRANT WOOD | American, 1891–1942
March, 1940
Charcoal on paper
18 1/8 x 24 1/8 in. (46 x 61.3 cm)
Gift of Dr. Jack Tausend in memory of
Mary Nesbit Tausend
2005.972

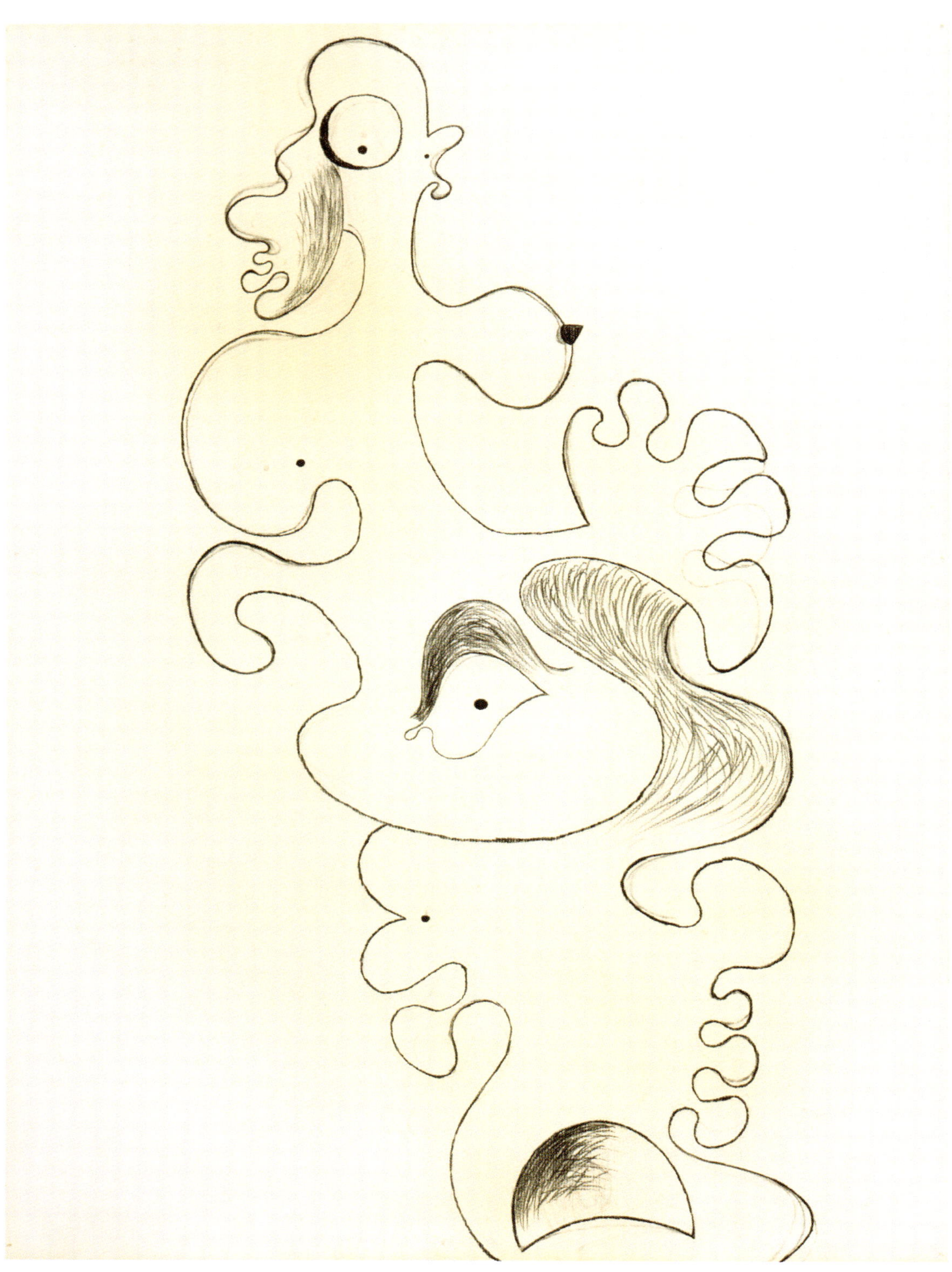

JOAN MIRÓ | Spanish, 1893–1983
Composition, 1930
Charcoal on paper
Sheet: 24 1/2 x 17 7/8 in. (62.2 x 45.5 cm)
Museum purchase funded by Oveta Culp Hobby
92.119

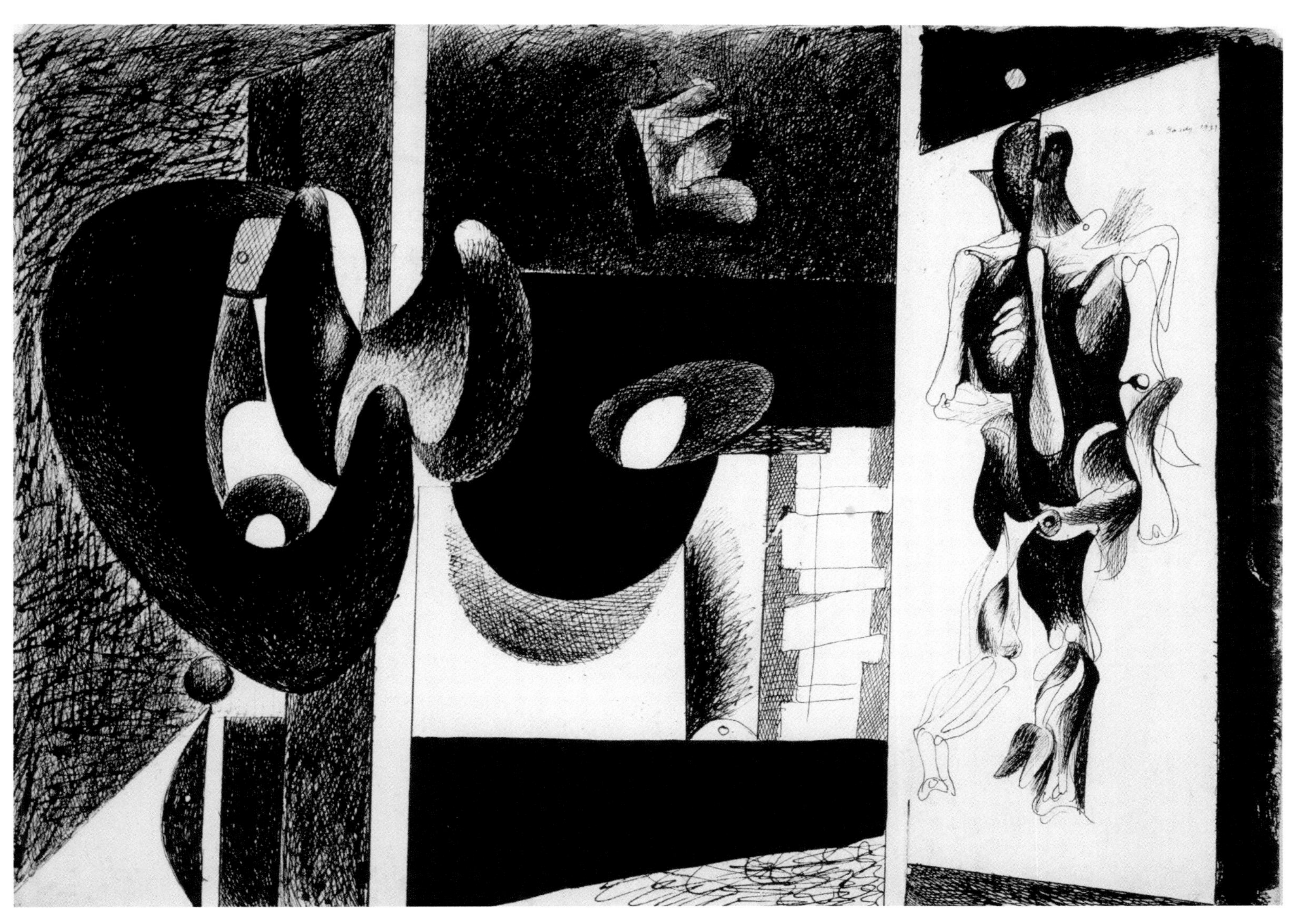

ARSHILE GORKY | American,
born Armenia, 1904–1948
Nighttime, Enigma and Nostalgia, 1931
Ink on paper
Sheet: 21 1/2 x 29 5/8 in. (54.6 x 75.2 cm)
Bequest of Caroline Wiess Law
2004.17

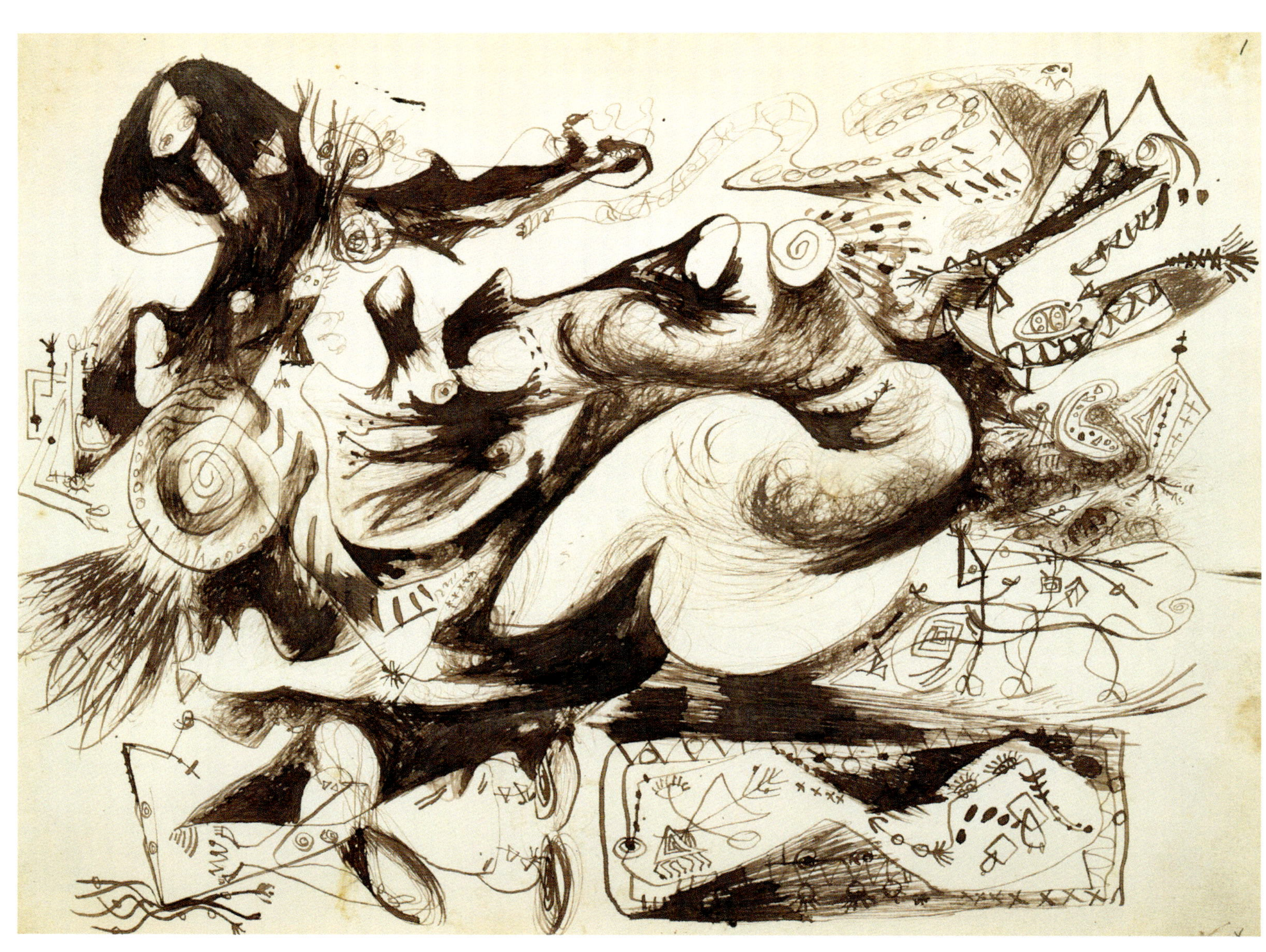

JACKSON POLLOCK | American, 1912–1956
Untitled [O'Connor-Thaw 770], c. 1946–47
From a suite of notebook drawings
Brown ink on paper
8 7/8 x 11 7/8 in. (22.5 x 30.2 cm)
Museum purchase funded by
Caroline Wiess Law
96.1752.1

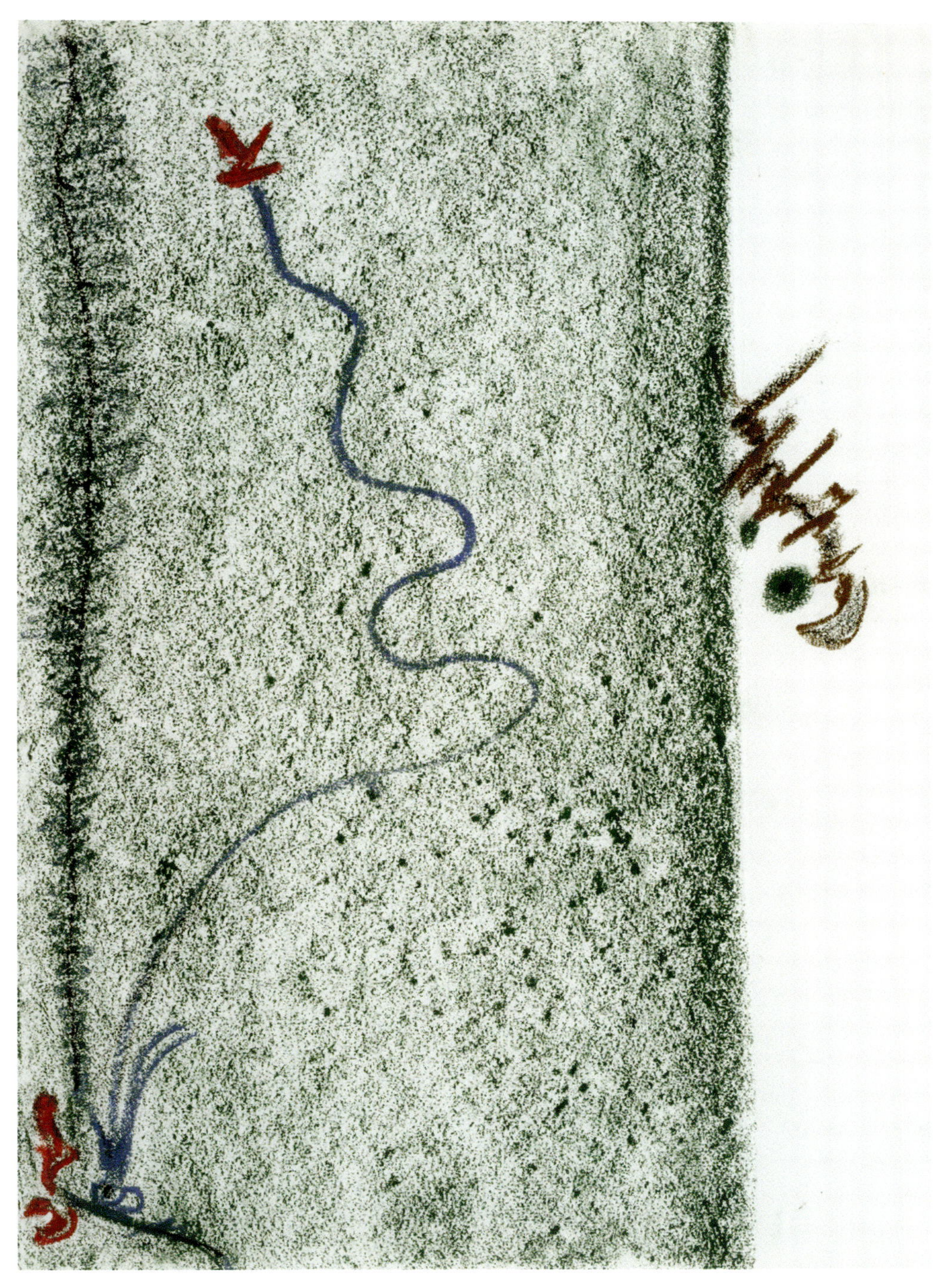

BARNETT NEWMAN | American, 1905–1970
Untitled, 1944
Crayon on paper
Sheet: 21 1/2 x 29 5/8 in. (54.6 x 75.2 cm)
Museum purchase funded by the
Alvin S. Romansky Prints and Drawings
Accessions Endowment Fund and
Max and Isabell Smith Herzstein
2001.3

PABLO PICASSO | Spanish, 1881–1973
Portrait de Françoise, en costume tailleur
(Portrait of Françoise, dressed in a suit), c. 1946
Drypoint
Plate: 27 1/4 x 19 3/8 in. (69.2 x 49.2 cm)
Sheet: 29 x 22 1/4 in. (73.7 x 56.5 cm)
Museum purchase funded by the Museum Collectors
96.853

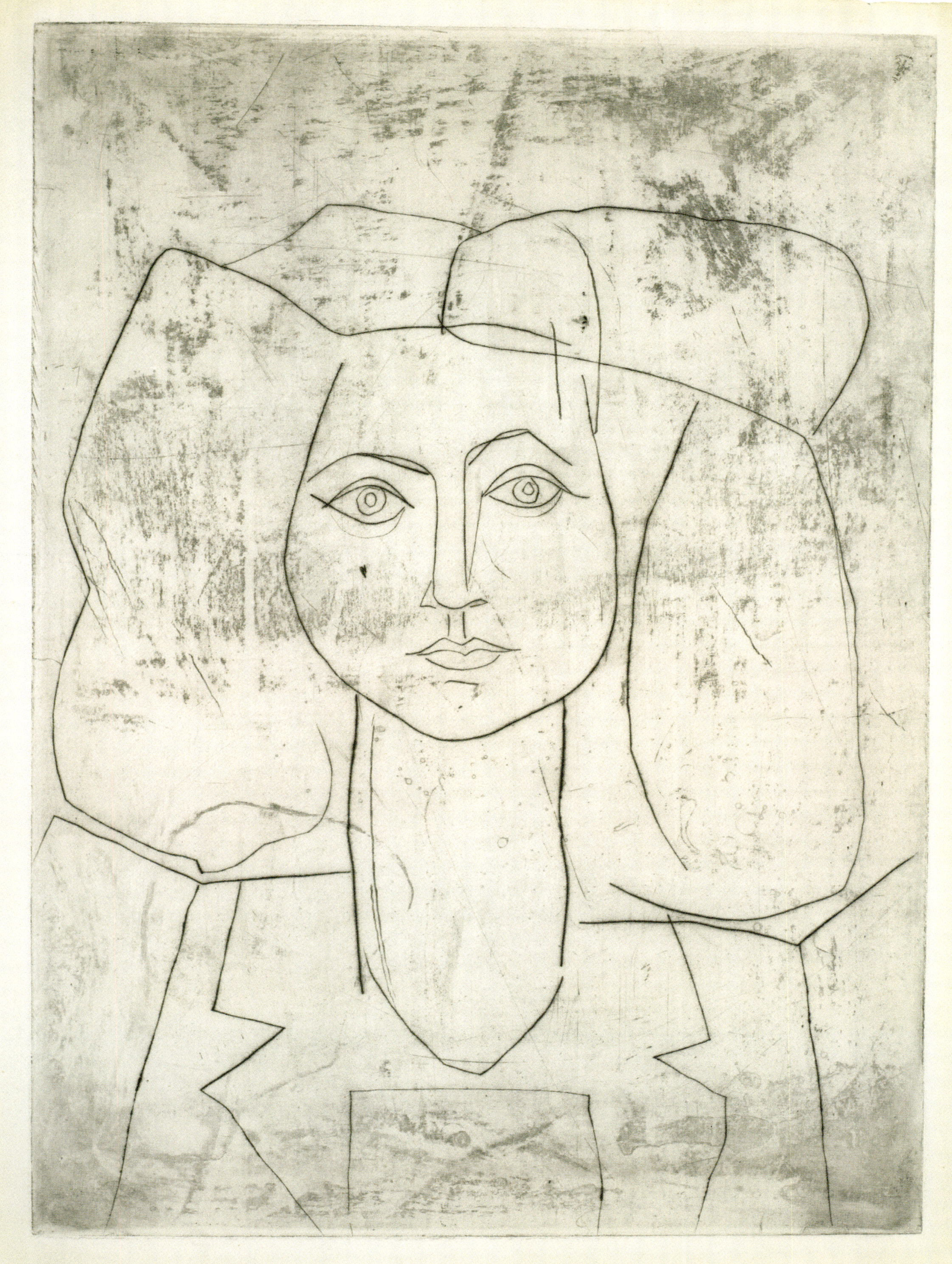

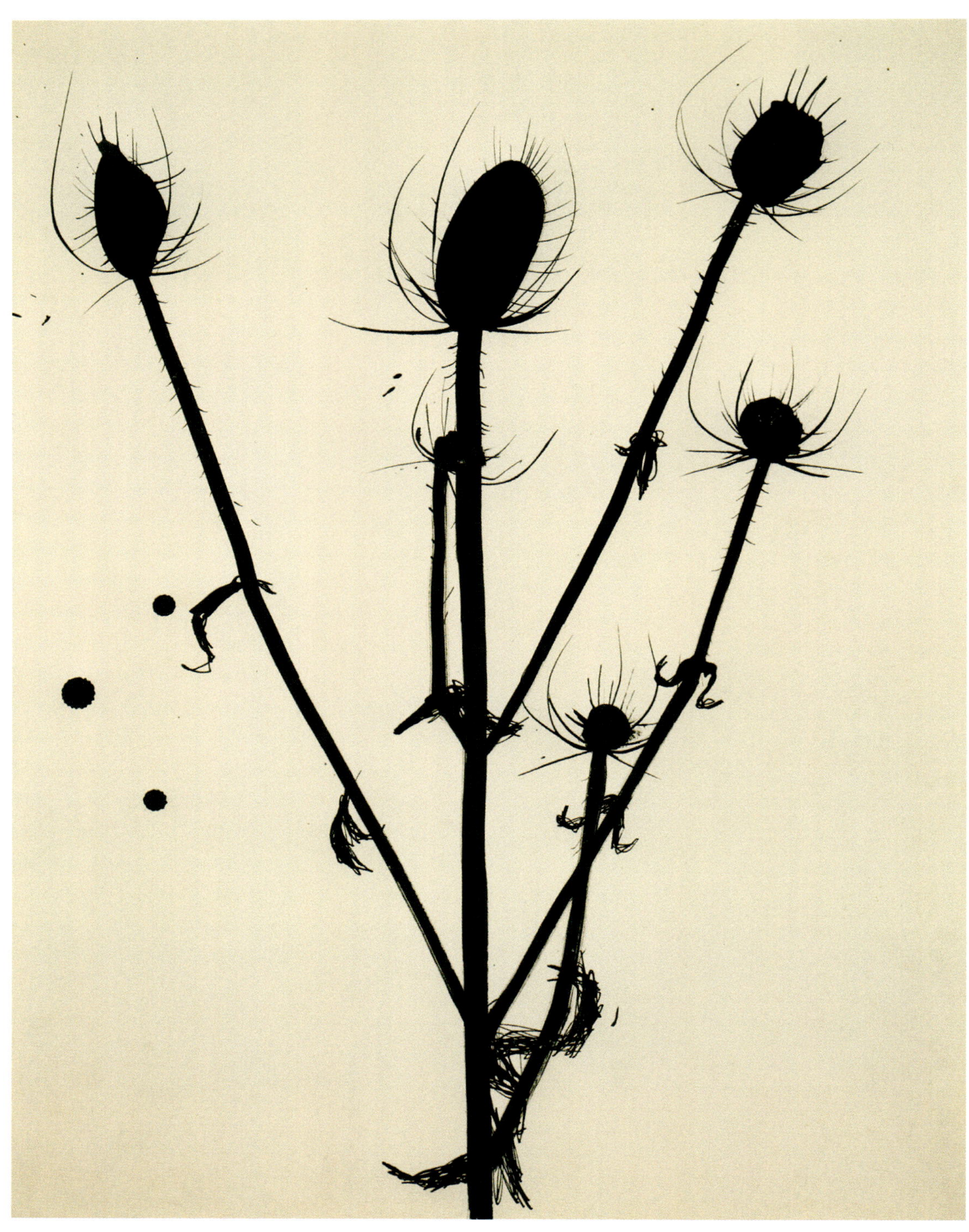

ELLSWORTH KELLY | American, born 1923
Teasel, 1949
Brush and ink with dry stylus on paper
Sheet: 22 1/8 x 17 in. (56.2 x 43.2 cm)
Museum purchase funded by
The Brown Foundation, Inc.
98.46

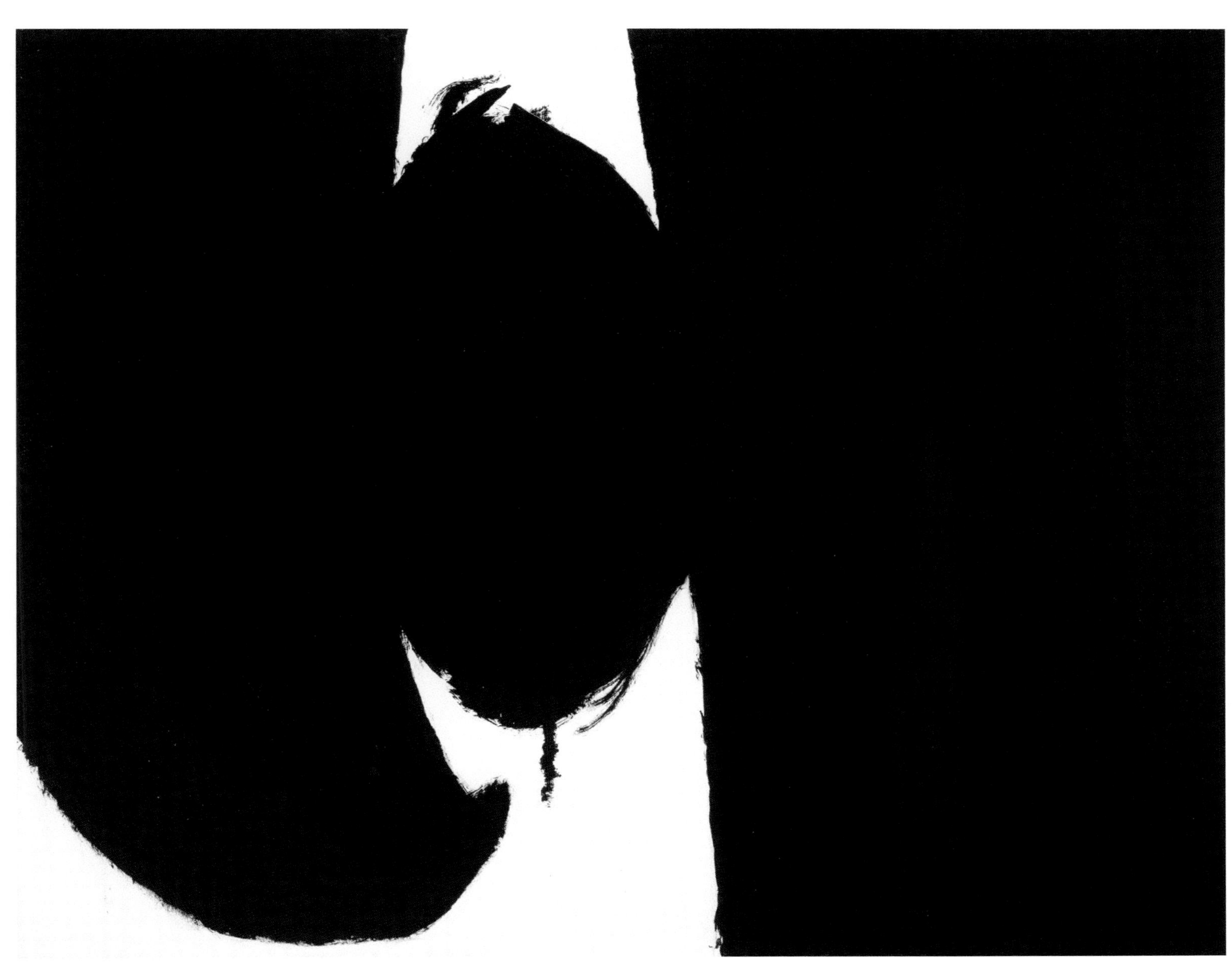

ROBERT MOTHERWELL | American, 1915–1991
Elegy Study, 1958
Oil on paper
22 7/8 x 28 7/8 in. (58.1 x 73.3 cm)
Bequest of Caroline Wiess Law
2004.47

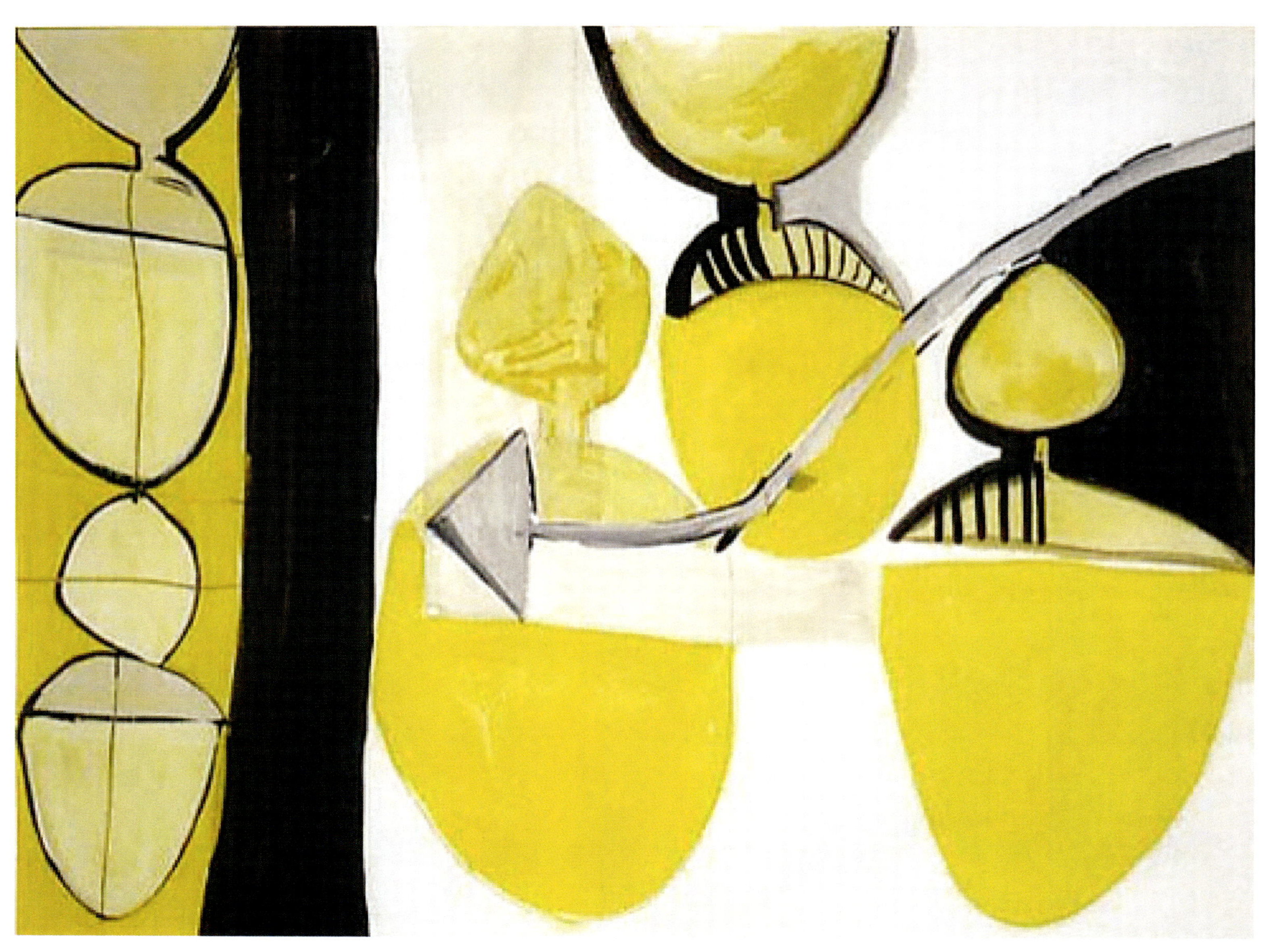

EVA HESSE | American, born Germany, 1936–1970
Untitled, 1964
Gouache, ink, watercolor, and graphite on paper
19 1/2 x 25 1/2 in. (49.5 x 64.8 cm)
Museum purchase funded by the
Caroline Wiess Law Accessions Endowment Fund
98.529

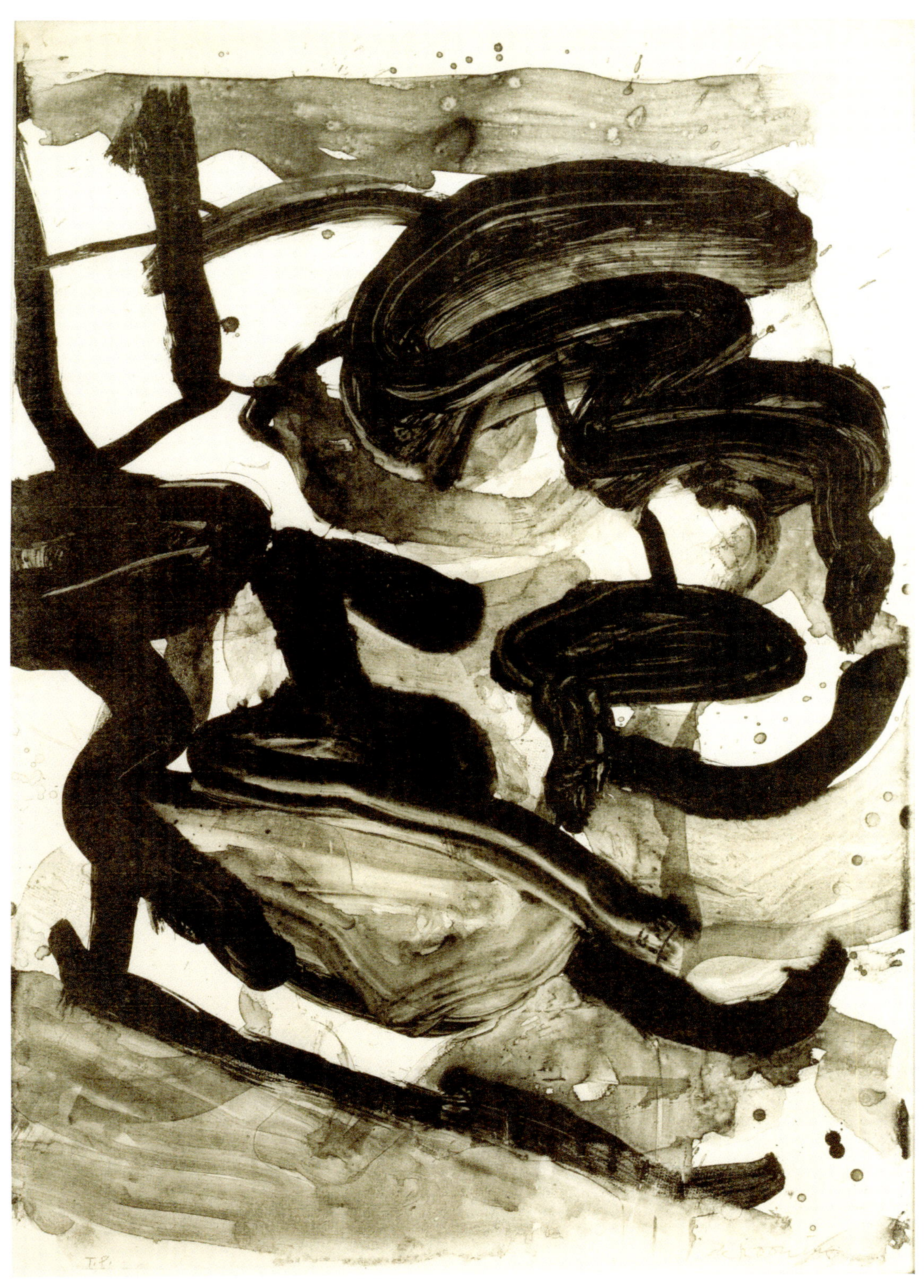

WILLEM DE KOONING | American,
born Netherlands, 1904–1997
Untitled (Large Sumi Brushstrokes), 1970
Lithograph, trial proof
Image: 51 1/2 x 36 in. (130.8 x 91.4 cm)
Gift of Mr. and Mrs. Meredith Long
91.1864

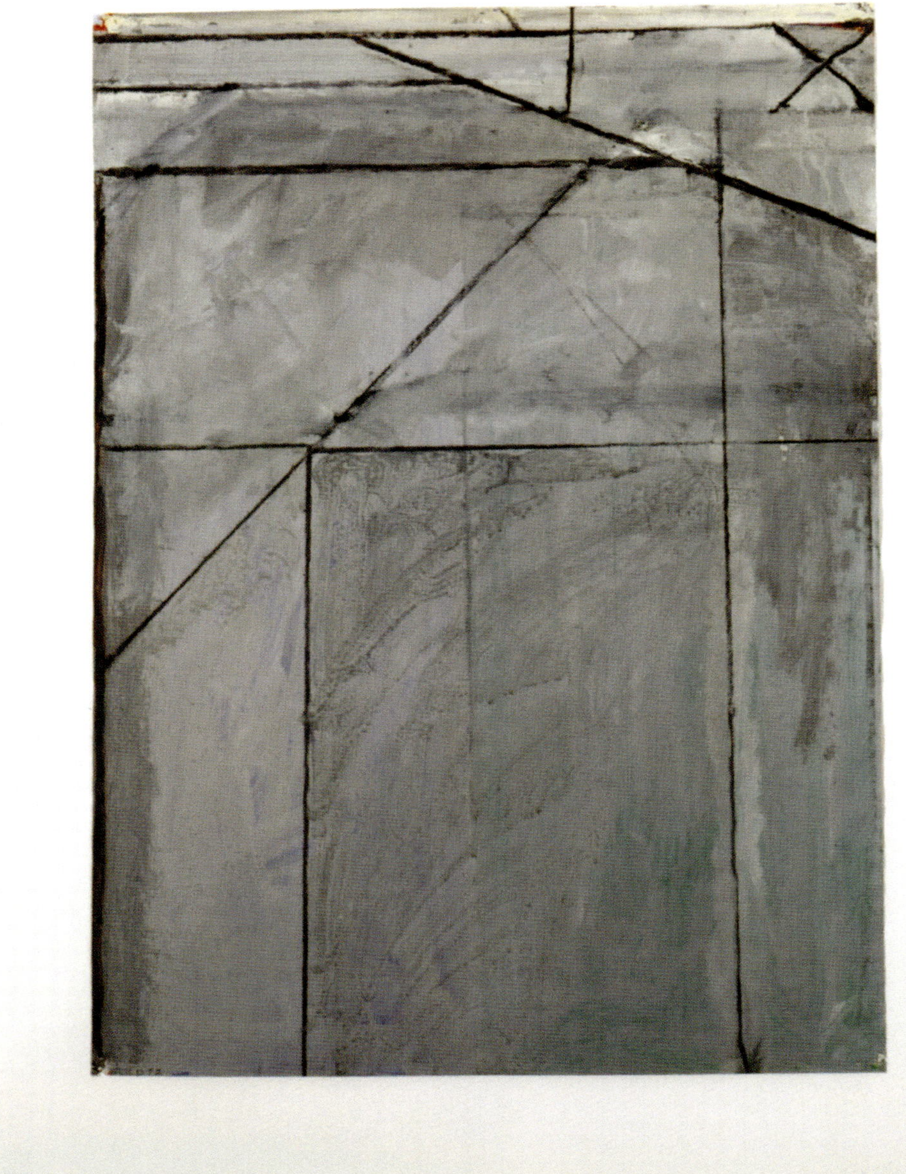

RICHARD DIEBENKORN | American, 1922–1993
Untitled, 1972
A: acrylic and gouache on paper, B: wash and
pasted paper on paper, C: acrylic, charcoal,
and pasted paper on paper
.A, left drawing: 24 15/16 x 17 15/16 in. (63.4 x 45.6 cm)
.B, center drawing: 24 7/8 x 17 7/8 in. (63.2 x 45.5 cm)
.C, right drawing: 24 7/8 x 17 7/8 in. (63.2 x 45.5 cm)
Museum purchase funded by the
Caroline Wiess Law Accessions Endowment Fund
and an anonymous donor
94.109.A–.C

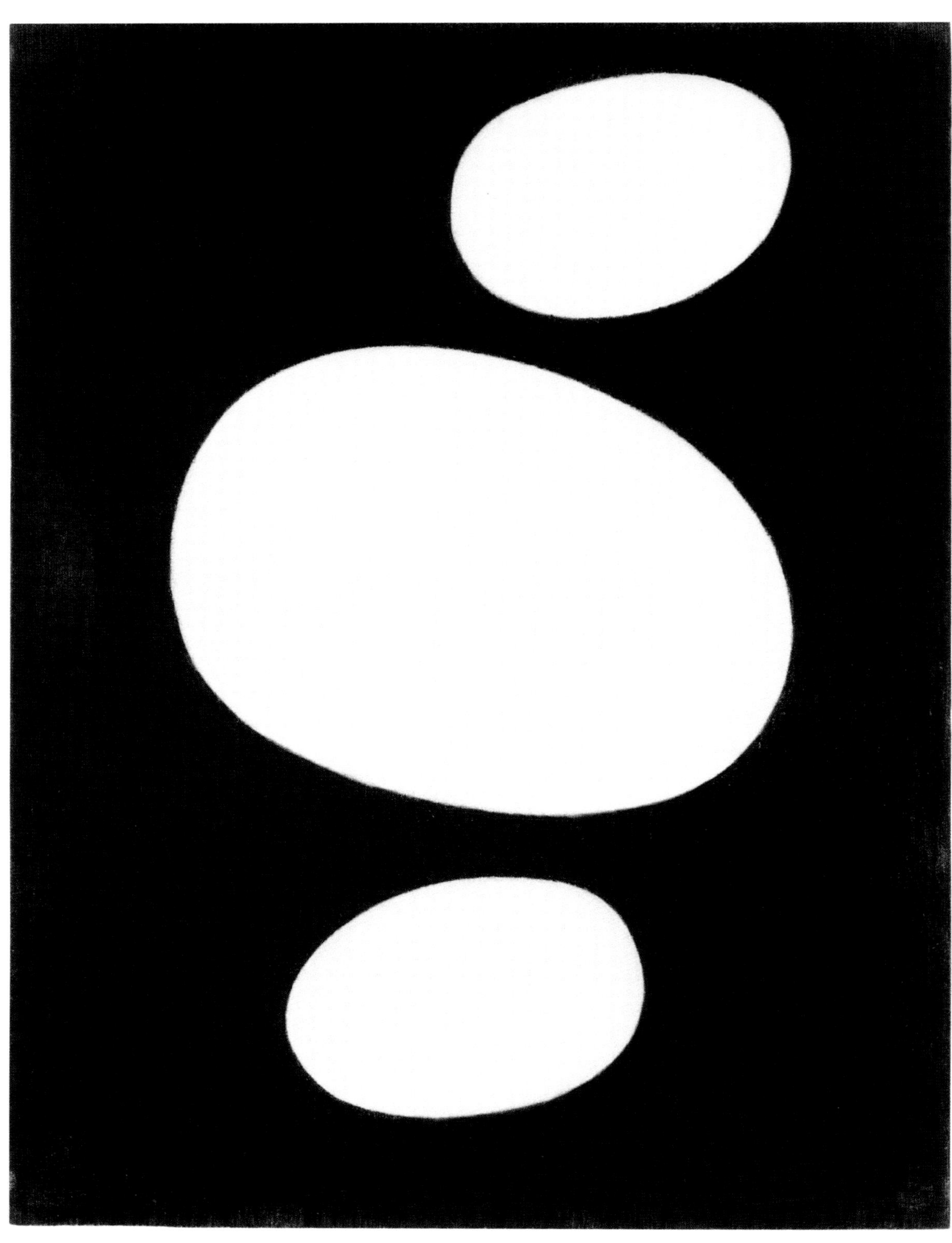

MYRON STOUT | American, 1908–1987
Untitled, 1956
Charcoal on paper
25 1/8 x 18 7/8 in. (63.8 x 48 cm)
Museum purchase funded by
the Caroline Wiess Law
Accessions Endowment Fund
95.44

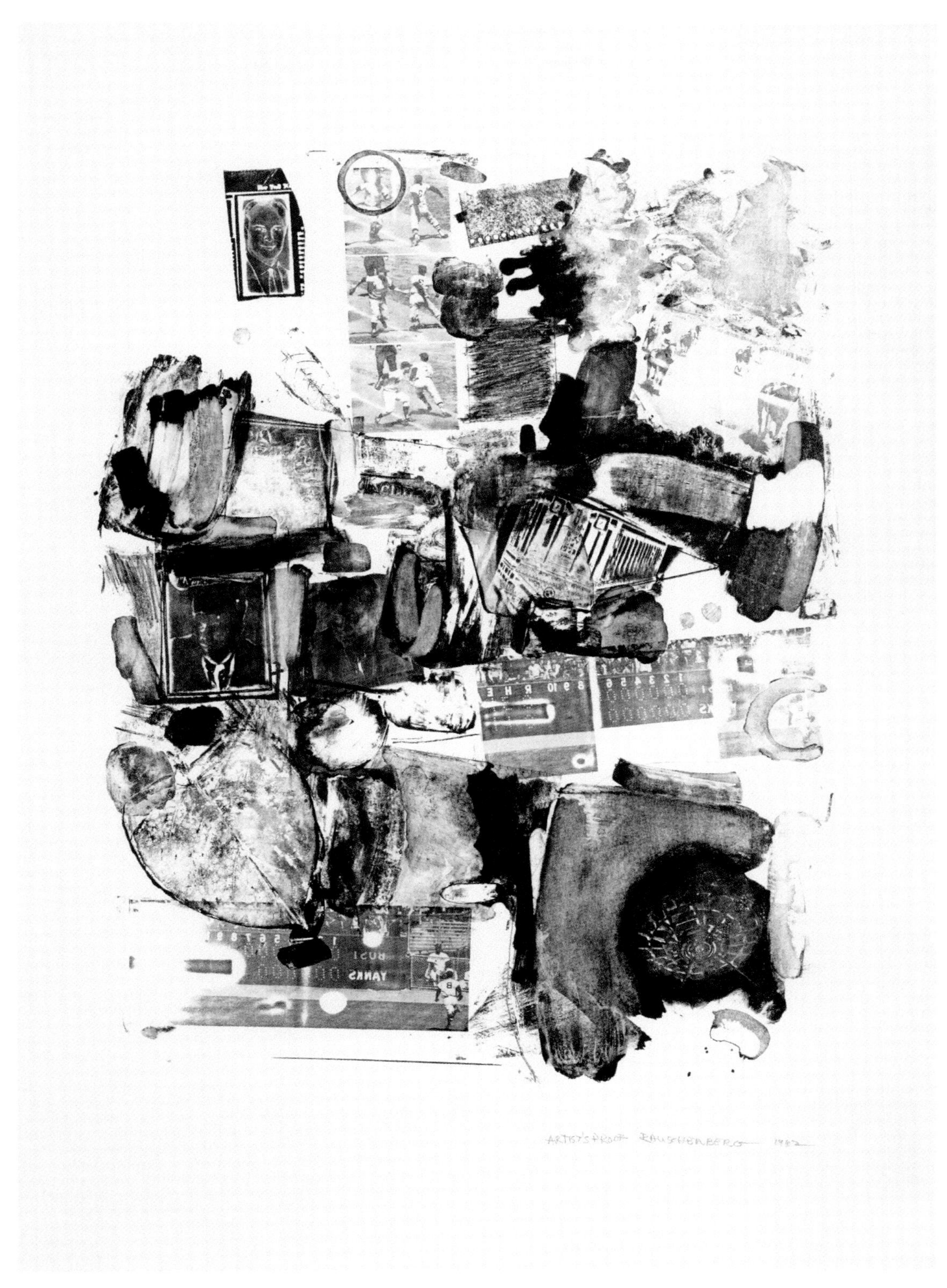

ROBERT RAUSCHENBERG | American, 1925–2008
Urban, 1962
Lithograph
Sheet: 41 3/8 x 29 3/4 in. (105.2 x 75.6 cm)
Gift of Barbara Rose
79.136

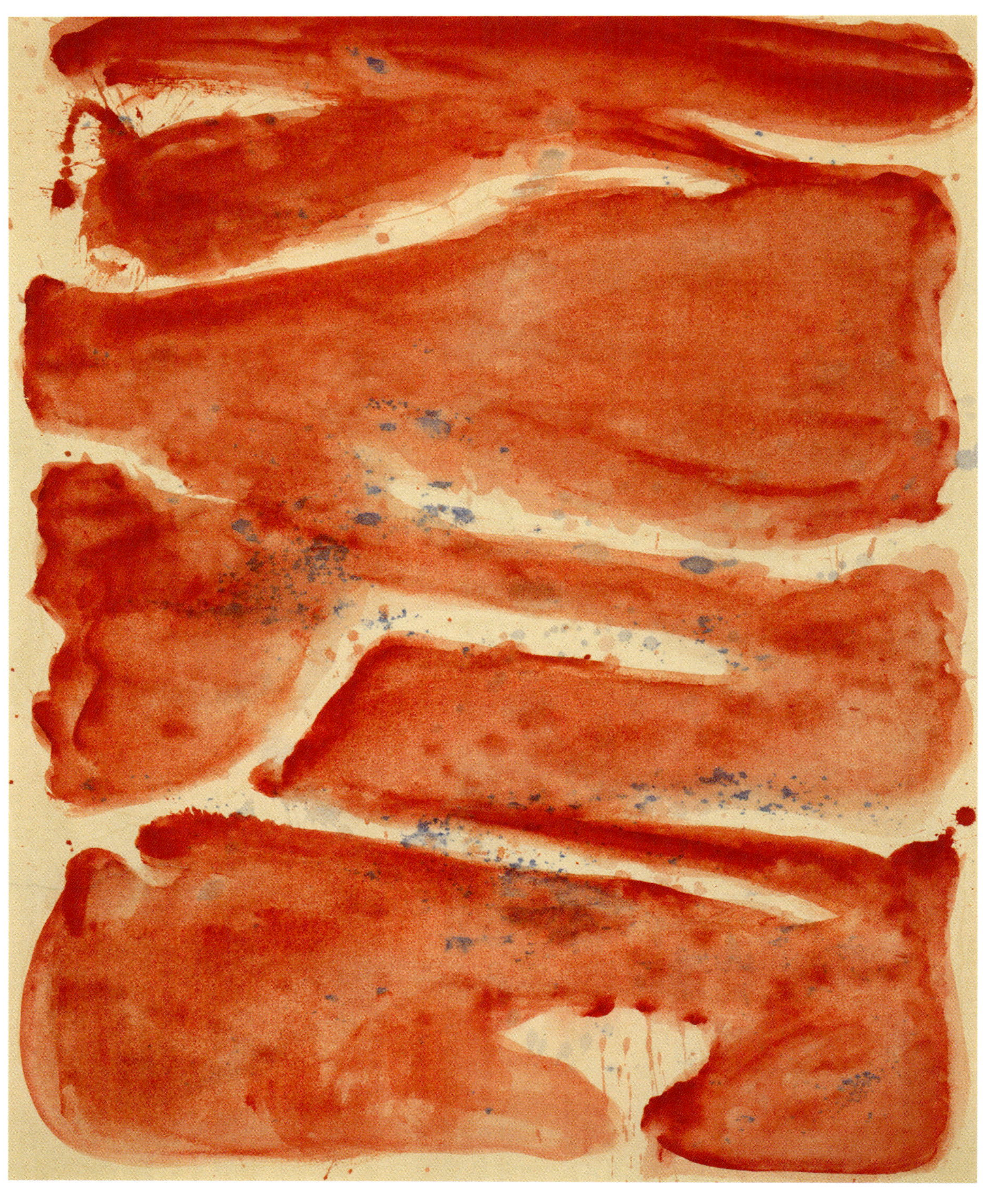

SAM FRANCIS | American, 1923–1994
Untitled (SF 61-1030), 1961
Watercolor on newsprint
21 1/4 x 17 in. (54 x 43.2 cm)
Museum purchase funded by the
Caroline Wiess Law Accessions
Endowment Fund
98.214

JASPER JOHNS | American, born 1930
Cicada, 1979
Watercolor, graphite, and crayon on paper
Overall: 43 x 28 3/4 in. (109.2 x 73 cm)
Museum purchase funded by
the Caroline Wiess Law
Accessions Endowment Fund
2005.35

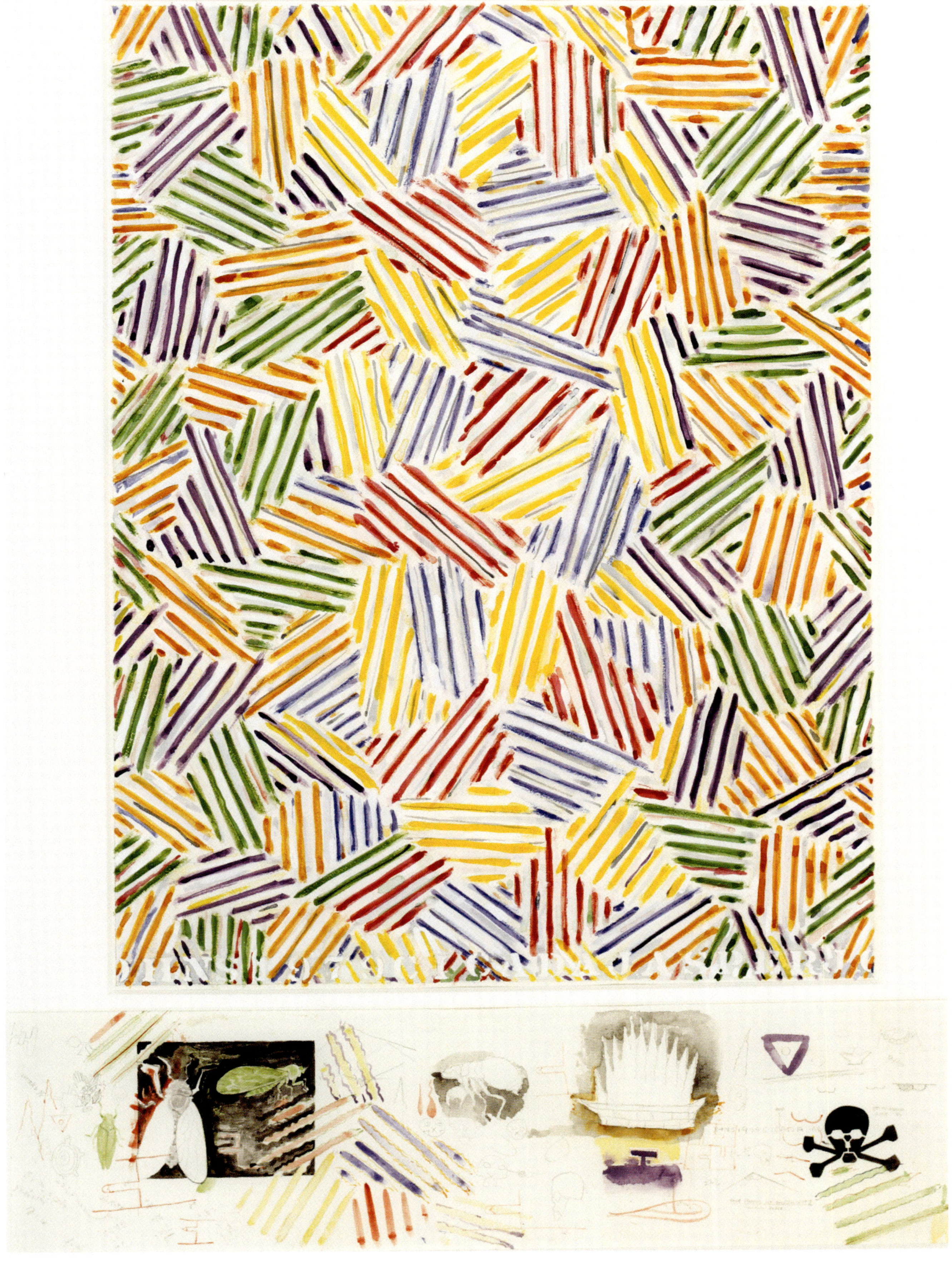

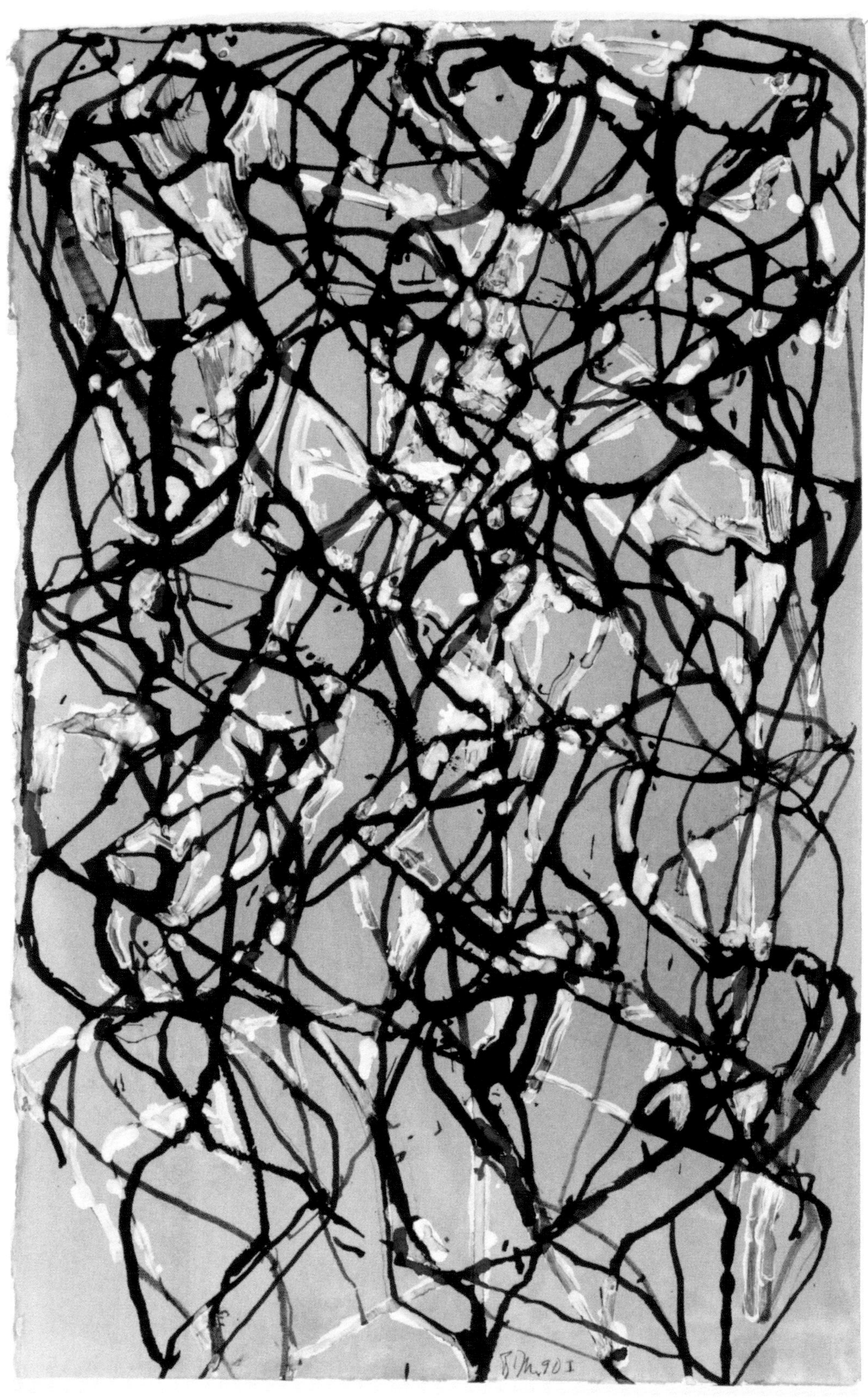

BRICE MARDEN | American, born 1938
Hydra, Summer 1990, I of V, 1990
Ink and gouache on paper
14 x 8 1/2 in. (35.6 x 21.6 cm)
Museum purchase funded by
the Charles Engelhard Foundation
in honor of Louisa Stude Sarofim
91.308

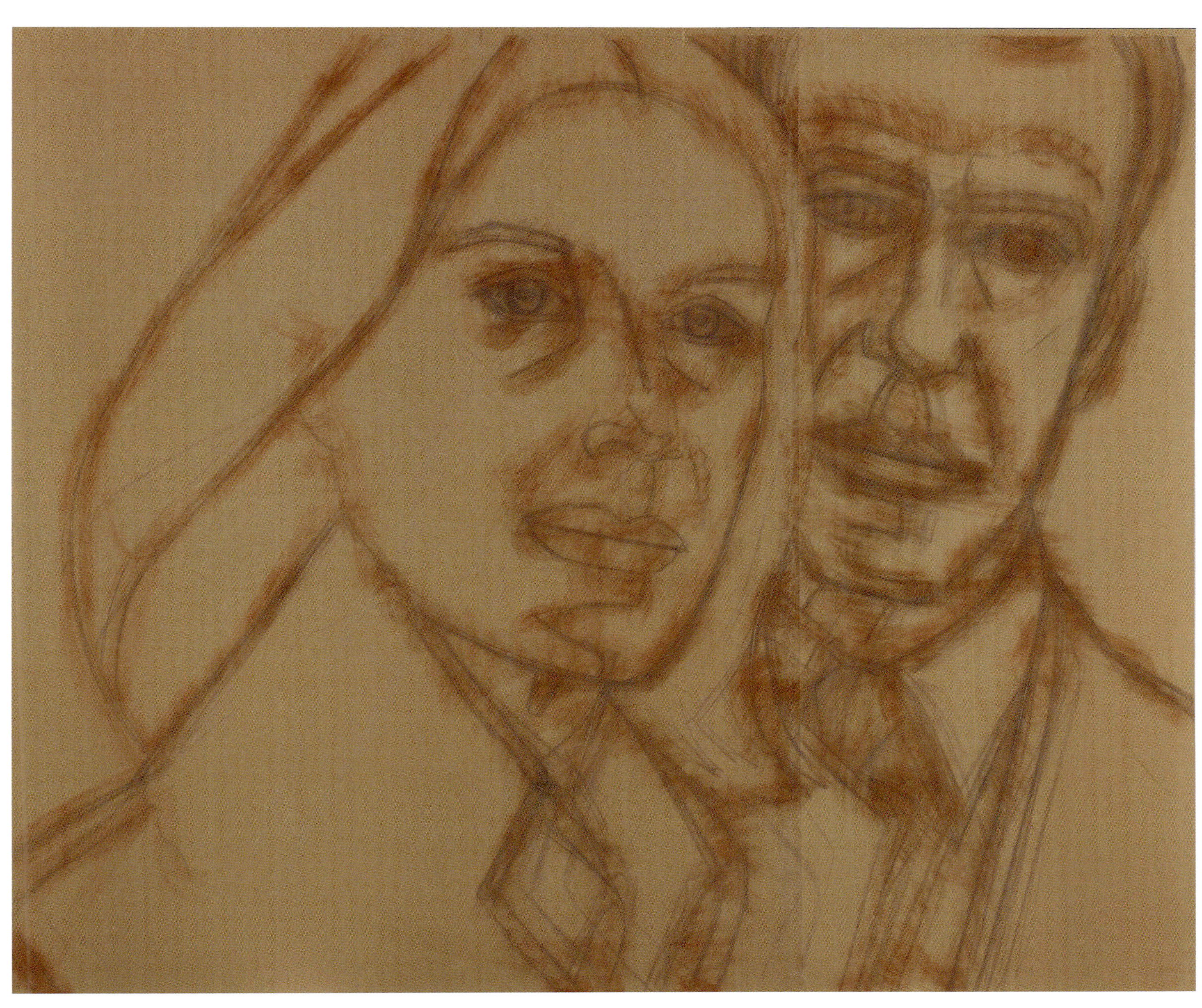

ALEX KATZ | American, born 1927
Ada & Alex, 1980
Charcoal on paper with pouncing and pigment
60 5/8 x 72 in. (154 x 182.9 cm)
Gift of the artist in honor of Barry Walker
2007.104

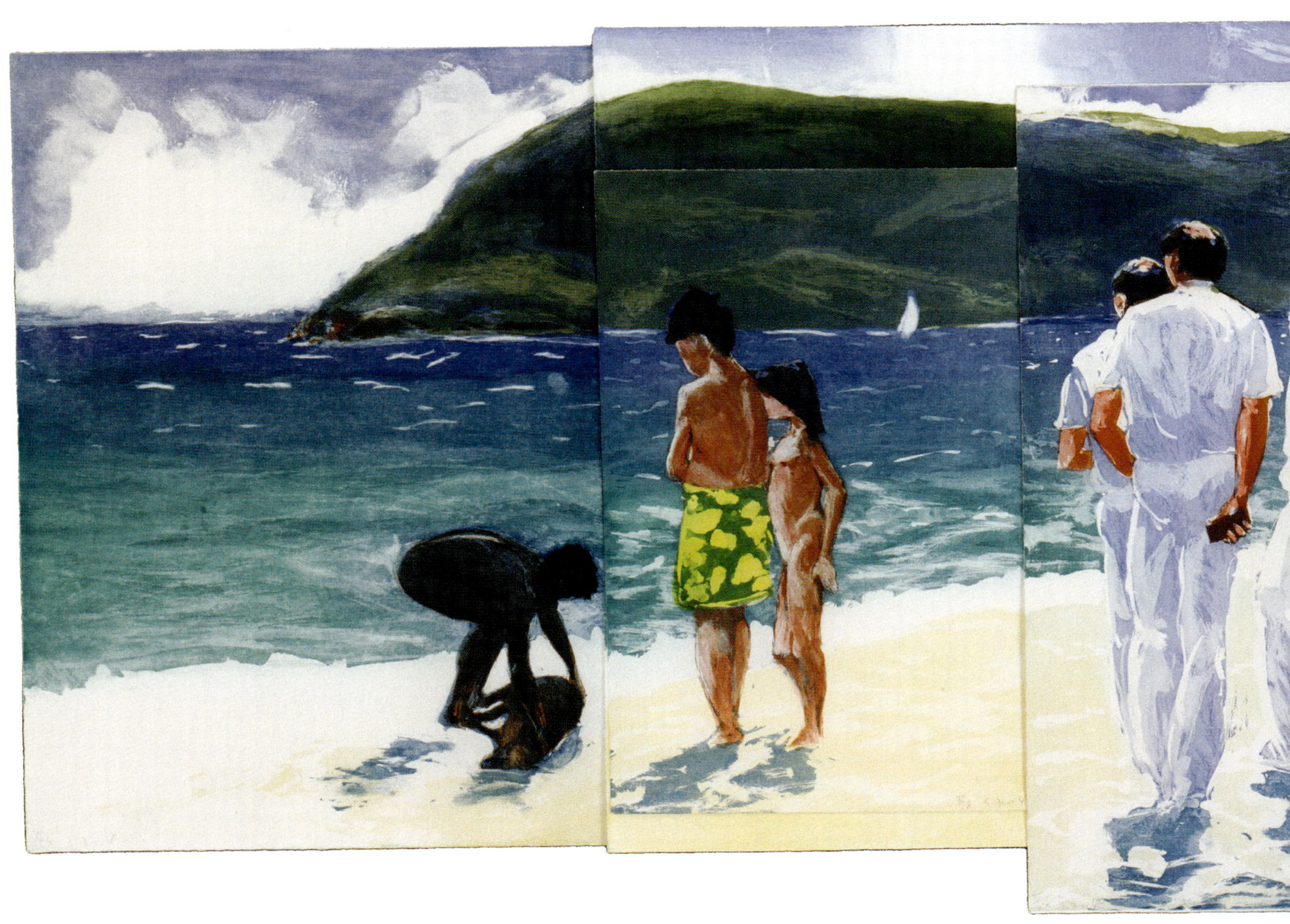

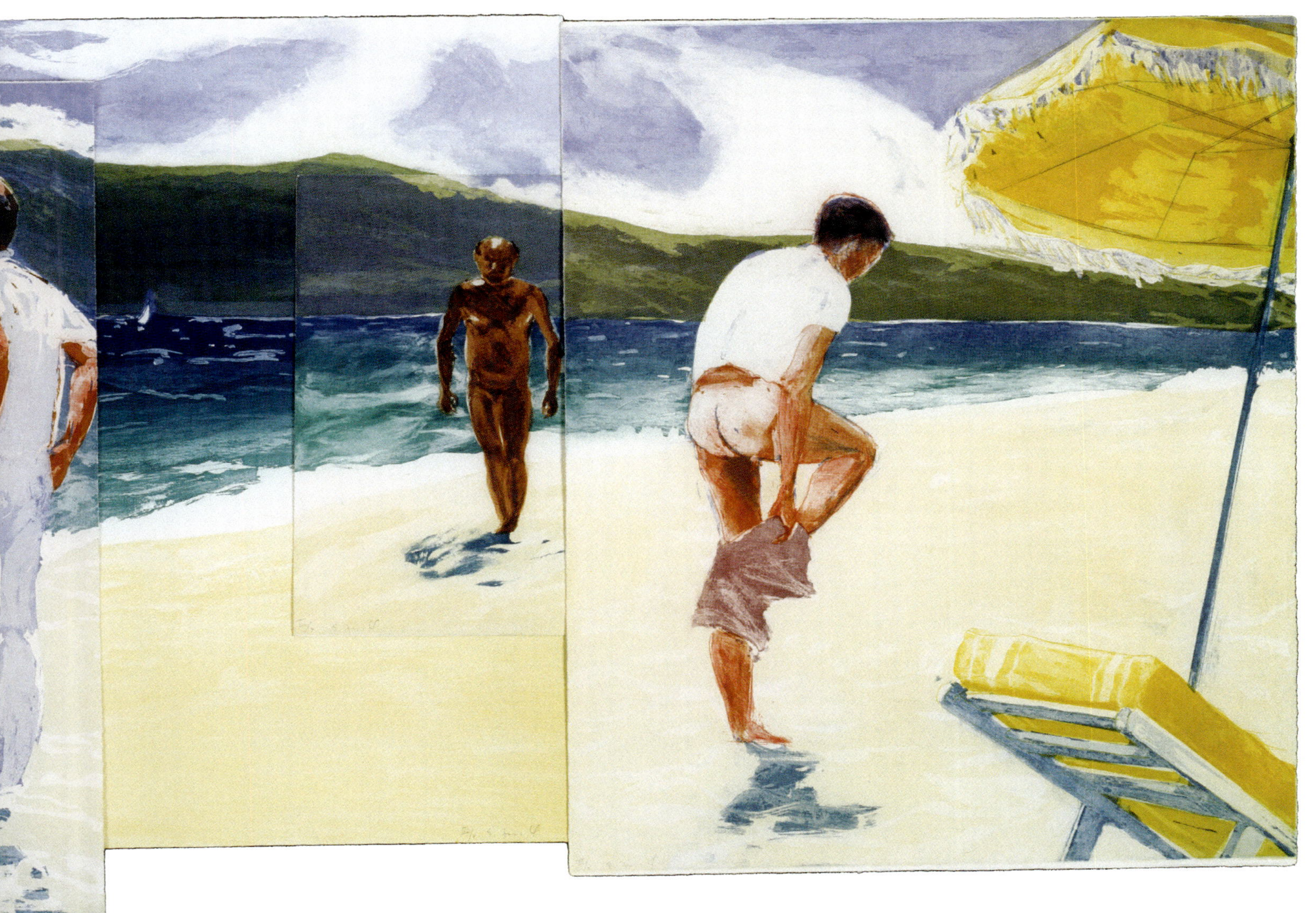

ERIC FISCHL | American, born 1948
Published by Peter Blum Edition/Blumarts, Inc.,
New York
Year of the Drowned Dog, 1983
(.1) Plate/sheet: 17 9/16 x 11 3/16 in. (44.6 x 28.4 cm)
(.2) Plate/sheet: 12 9/16 x 9 5/8 in. (31.9 x 24.4 cm)
(.3) Plate/sheet: 22 11/16 x 11 5/16 in. (57.6 x 28.7 cm)
(.4) Plate/sheet: 23 5/16 x 19 1/2 in. (59.2 x 49.5 cm)
(.5) Plate/sheet: 21 13/16 x 16 13/16 in. (55.4 x 42.7 cm)
(.6) Plate/sheet: 22 7/16 x 34 11/16 in. (57 x 88.1 cm)
Composite image of 6 intaglio prints in colors
The Peter Blum Edition Archive, 1980–1994,
Museum purchase funded by the
Alice Pratt Brown Museum Fund
96.20.1–.6

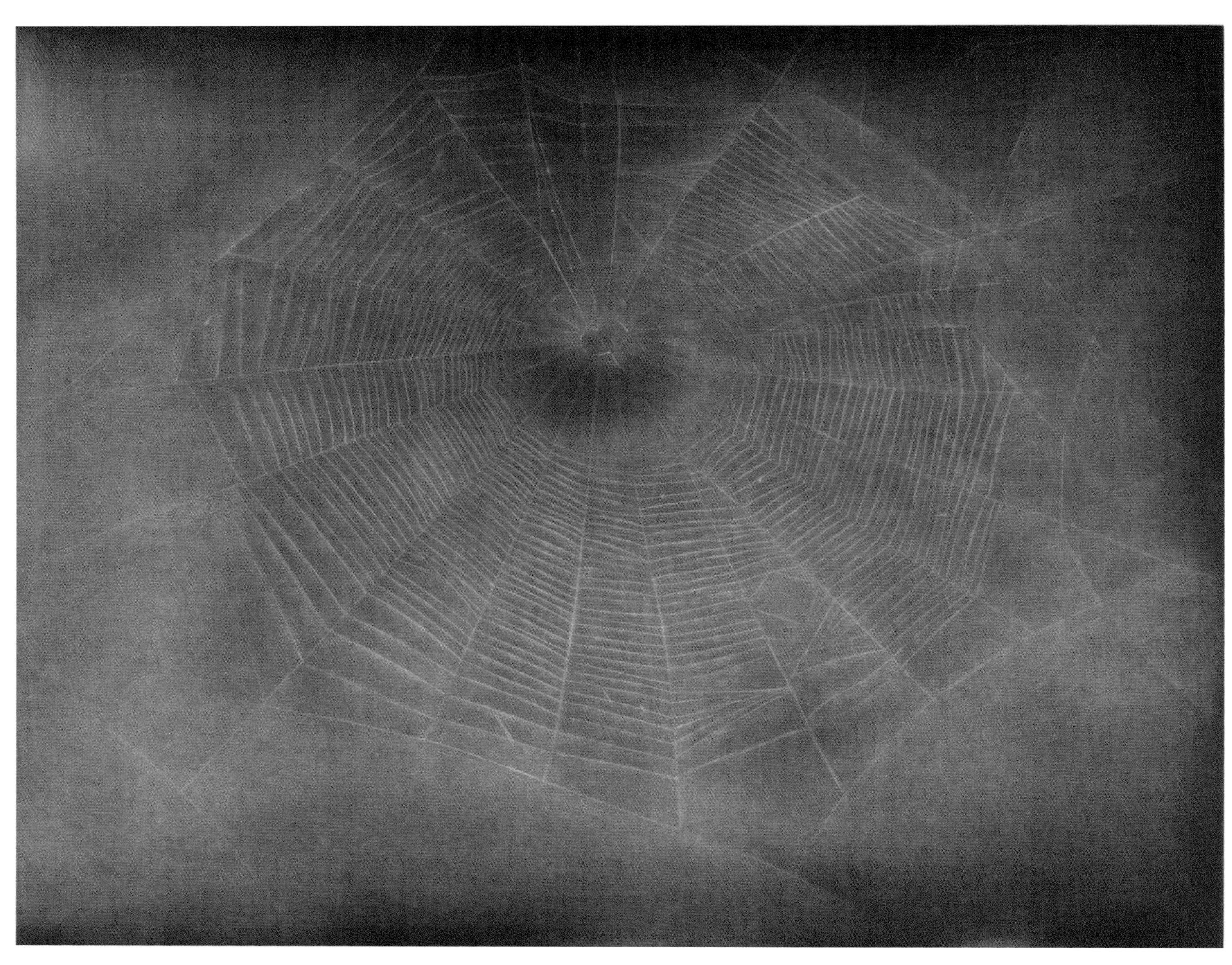

VIJA CELMINS | American, born Latvia, 1939
Untitled (Web 3), 2002
Aquatint with burnishing, scraping, and drypoint
Plate: 15 x 19 in. (38.1 x 48.3 cm)
Sheet: 20 1/8 x 24 1/8 in. (51.1 x 61.3 cm)
Museum purchase funded by
the Alice Pratt Brown Museum Fund
2008.12

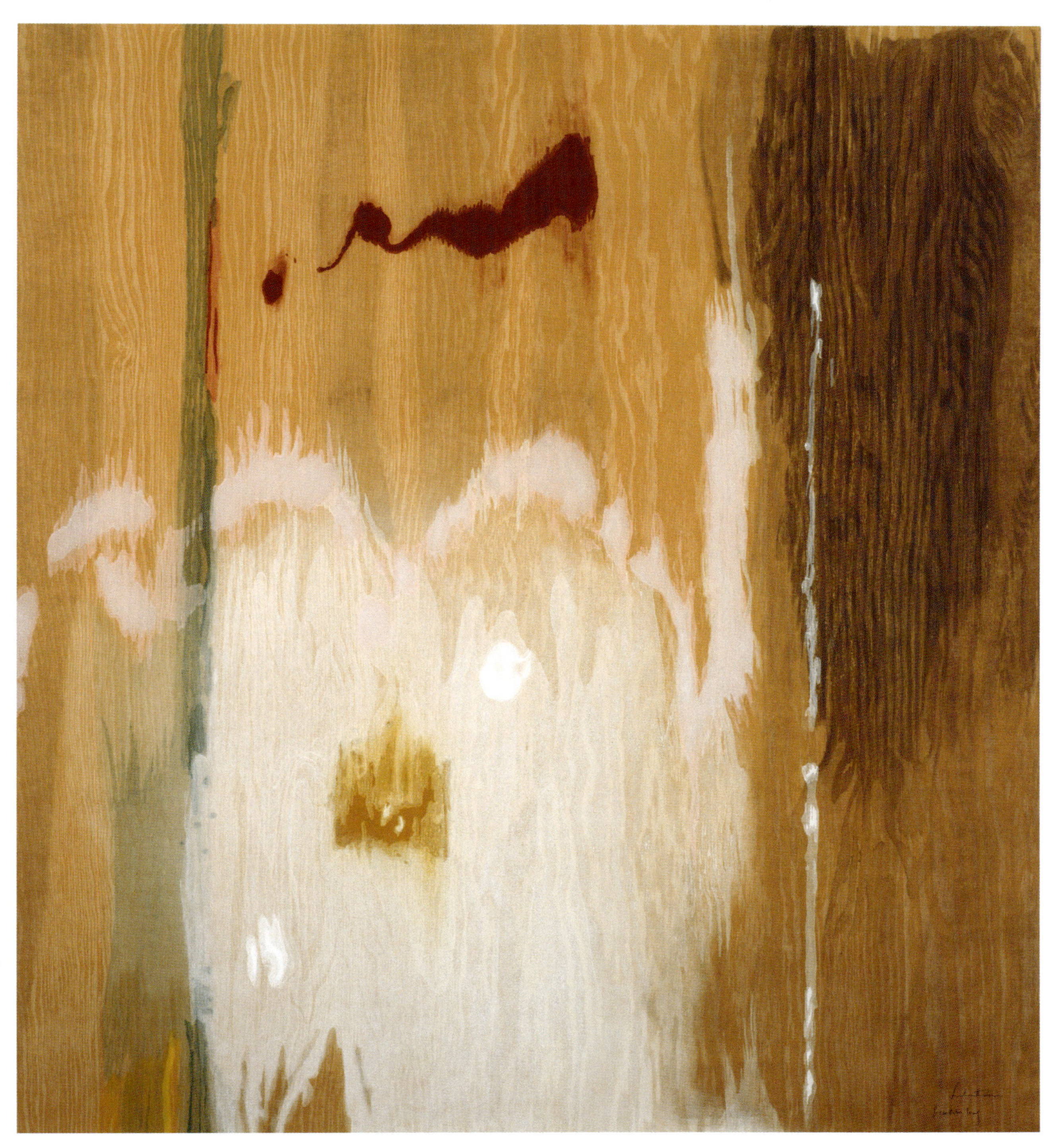

HELEN FRANKENTHALER | American, 1928–2011
Carved by Yasuyuki Shibata,
Published by Tyler Graphics Ltd.
Tales of Genji VI, 1998
From *Tales of Genji*
Woodcut, presentation proof
Sheet: 47 3/8 x 42 3/8 in. (120.3 x 107.6 cm)
Gift of the artist
98.537

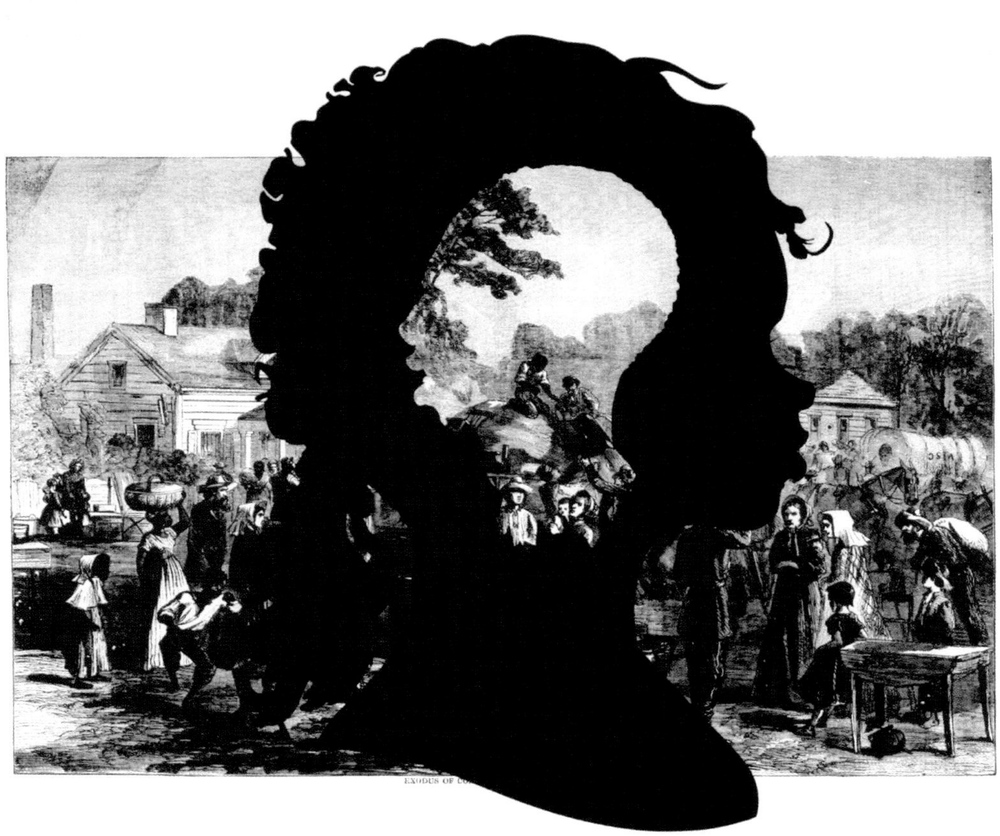

KARA WALKER | American, born 1969
Published by Sikkema Jenkins & Co.
*Harper's Pictorial History of the Civil War
(Annotated): Exodus of Confederates from Atlanta,*
2005
Lithograph and screenprint
Sheet: 39 x 53 in. (99.1 x 134.6 cm)
Museum purchase funded by Mike Ballases,
David Fine, Robert M. Hopson II, Philip J. John, Jr.,
John P. Kotts, Bill Porter, Thomas A. Roupe, and
the Sarofim Foundation in honor of Meredith J.
Long at "One Great Night in November, 2006"
2006.646.1

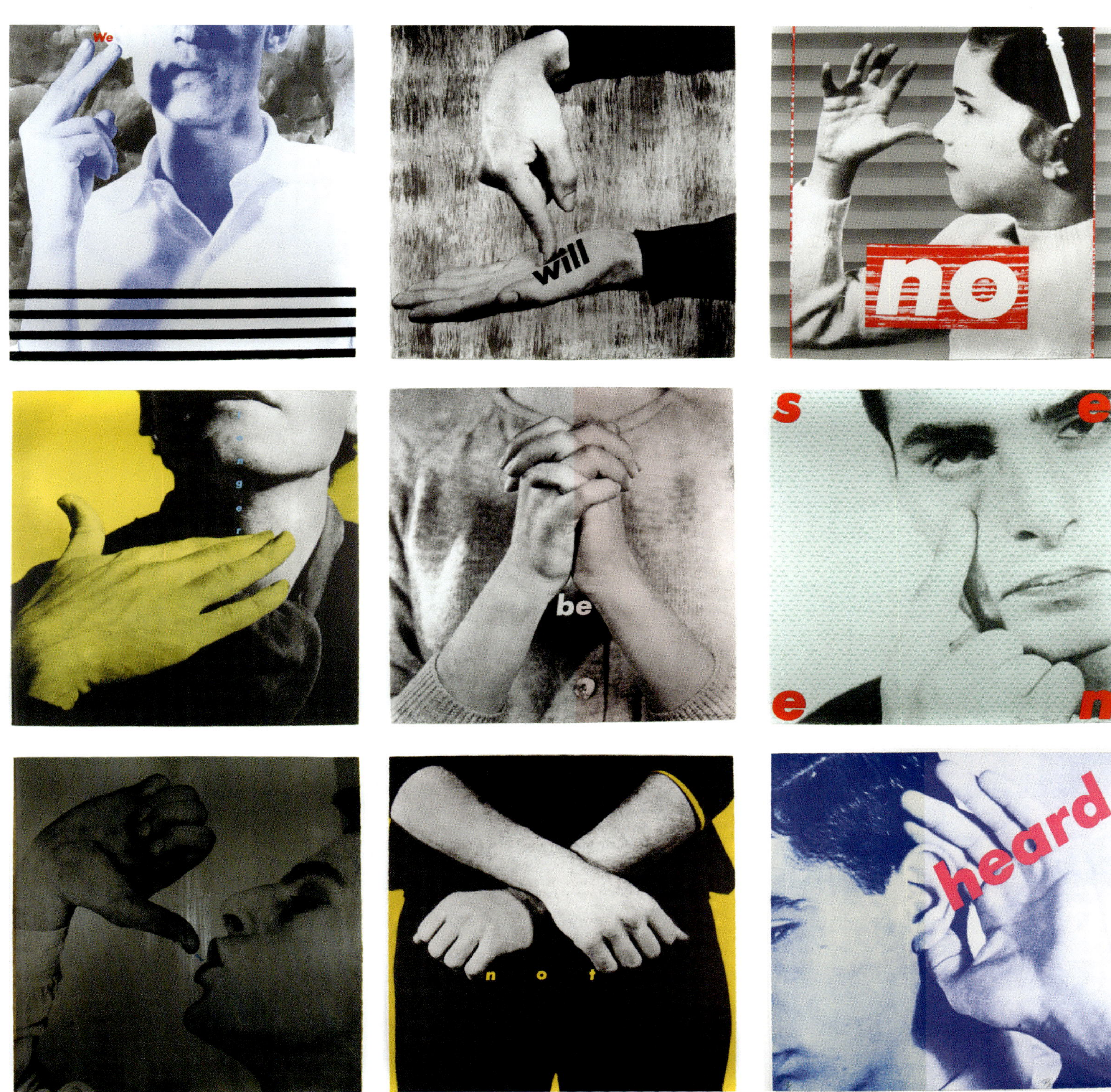

BARBARA KRUGER | American, born 1945
Untitled, 1985
Portfolio of 9 photolithographs with
screenprints in colors
.B, .C title and colophon page:
20 5/8 x 20 5/8 in. (52.4 x 52.4 cm)
Portfolio case (.A):
21 9/16 x 21 9/16 x 1 7/16 in. (54.8 x 54.8 x 3.7 cm)
The Peter Blum Edition Archive, 1980–1994,
Museum purchase funded by
the Alice Pratt Brown Museum Fund
96.27.A–.I

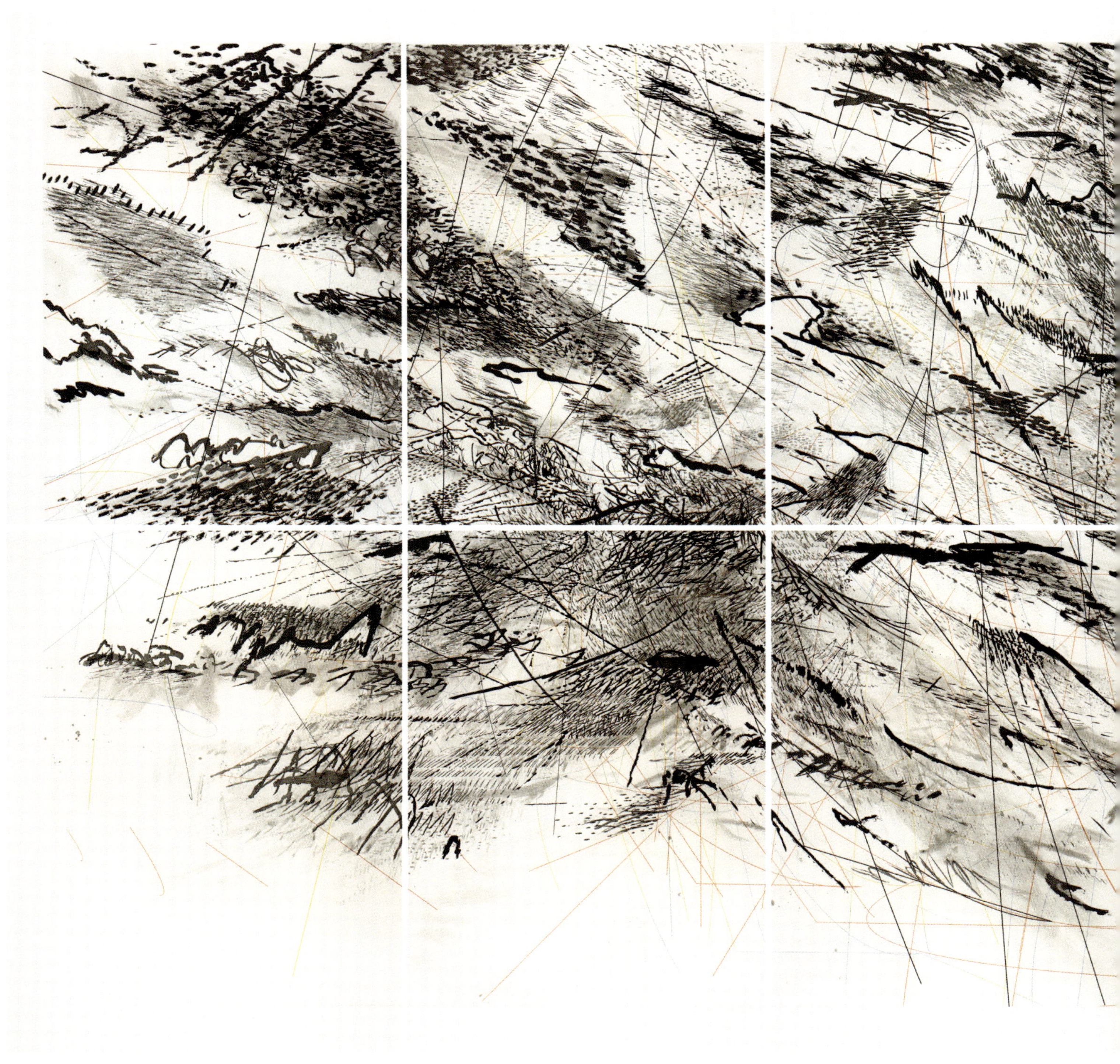

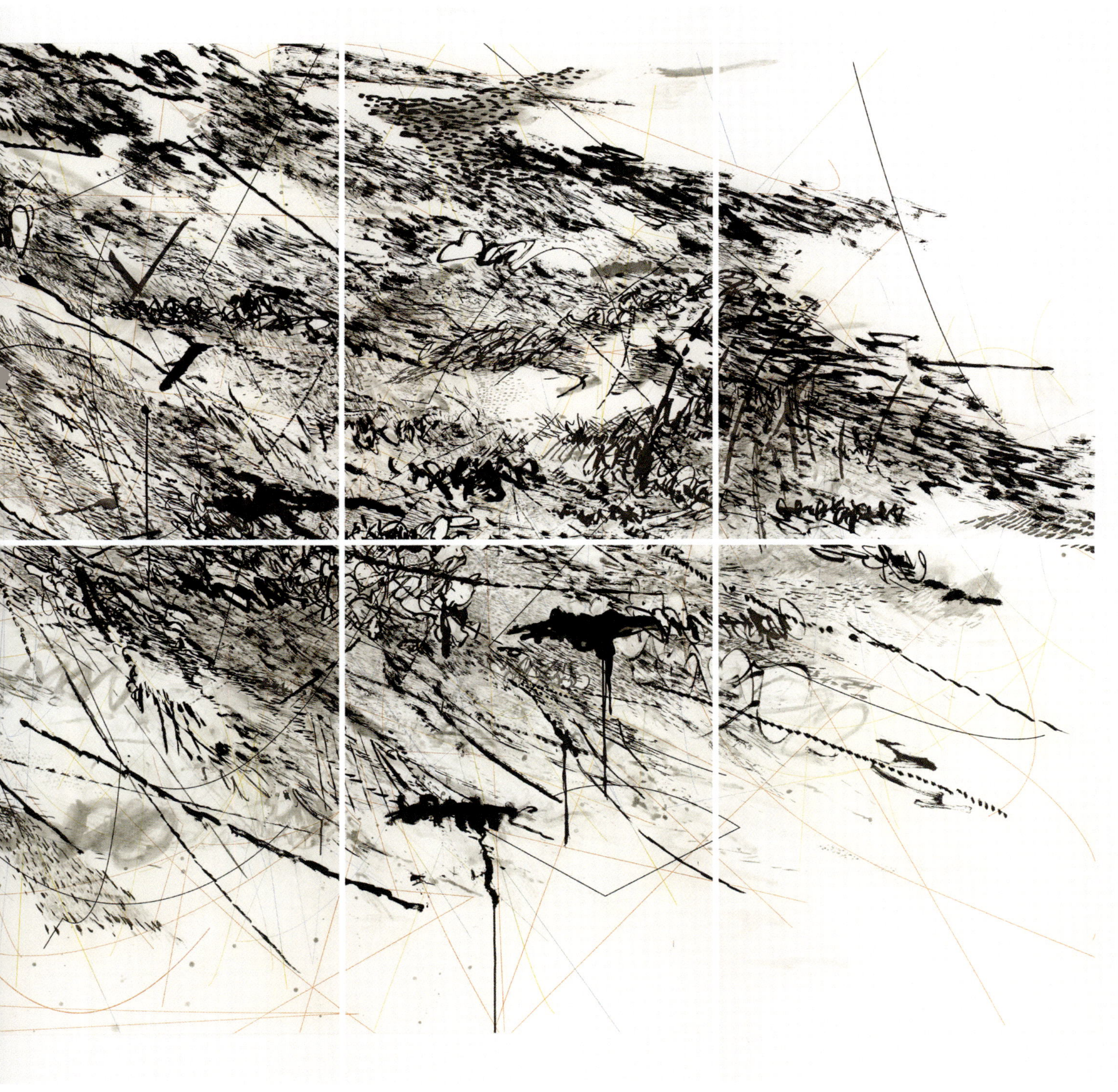

JULIE MEHRETU | American, born Ethiopia, 1970
Auguries, 2010
12-panel aquatint with spit bite in colors
Overall: 87 x 180 in. (221 x 457.2 cm)
Museum purchase, with additional funds provided by
Mr. and Mrs. Rodney Margolis, in their honor; and by Melissa and
Albert Joseph Grobmyer IV/Puffer-Sweiven, L.P.; Charles B.
and Jean G. Smith; Anne S. and Peter H. Brown; Lester Marks in memory
of Peter C. Marzio; Mr. and Mrs. William Shiffick; Bettie Cartwright
and Colin Kennedy; bequests of Eva K. Kitchen and Robert H. Wilson, Jr.;
and the estate of Sue Rowan Pittman
2011.474.A–.L

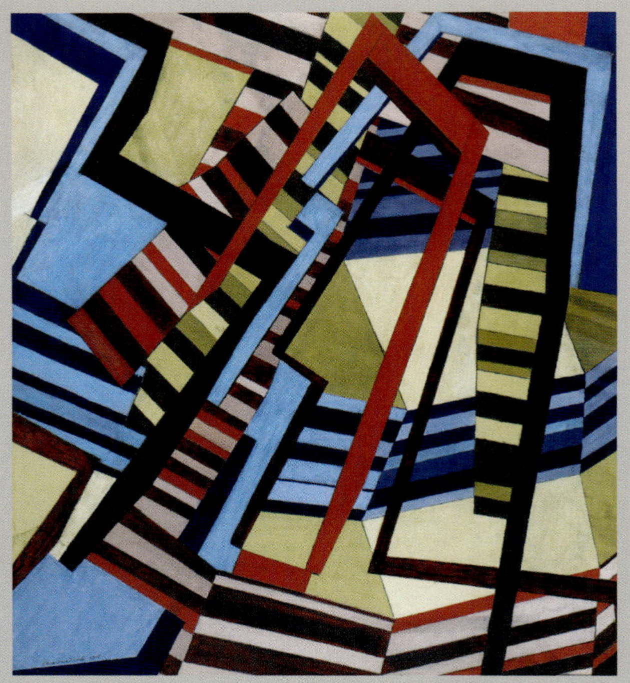

CONSTRUCTIVISM AND ITS LEGACY

One of the most formally and conceptually innovative artistic movements of the twentieth century, Constructivism relied on geometry and the precise organization of autonomous visual elements (lines, planes, circles, squares) in visually engaging compositions constructed from simple, everyday materials such as metal, plastic, or wood. Clarity, simplicity, and economy of means served as the grounding principles of artworks that eschewed traditional media of sculpture and painting in favor of objectively assembled structures that sought to bridge the divide between art and life.

From seminal Russian Constructivist photography and De Stijl furniture to Brazilian Constructivism and American Minimalist sculpture, the following pages illustrate the richness and depth—across media, chronology, and geography—of Constructivism and its legacy in the Museum's collections of modern and contemporary art.

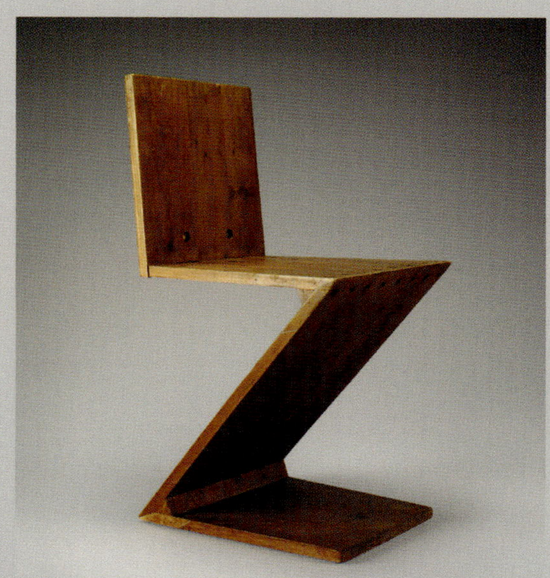

EDWARD ALEXANDER WADSWORTH | English, 1889–1949
Enclosure, 1915
Gouache, ink, pencil, and painted paper on paper
27 15/16 x 21 9/16 in. (70.9 x 54.7 cm)
Museum purchase funded by
The Brown Foundation, Inc.
77.277

LUÍS SACILOTTO | Brazilian, born 1924
Concreção 6045 [Concretion 6045], 1960
Painted iron
12 1/4 x 35 1/2 x 15 1/2 in. (31.1 x 90.2 x 39.4 cm)
The Adolpho Leirner Collection of Brazilian
Constructive Art, Museum purchase funded by
the Caroline Wiess Law Accessions Endowment Fund
2007.24

GERRIT RIETVELD | Dutch, 1888–1964
"Zig-Zag" Chair, designed 1932, made c. 1940
Pine
Overall: 30 3/4 x 14 3/4 x 15 3/4 in. (78.1 x 37.5 x 40 cm)
The American Institute of Architects, Houston Design
Collection, Museum purchase funded by friends of
Anderson Todd and S. I. Morris in their honor, and by
the Decorative Arts Endowment
2007.1791

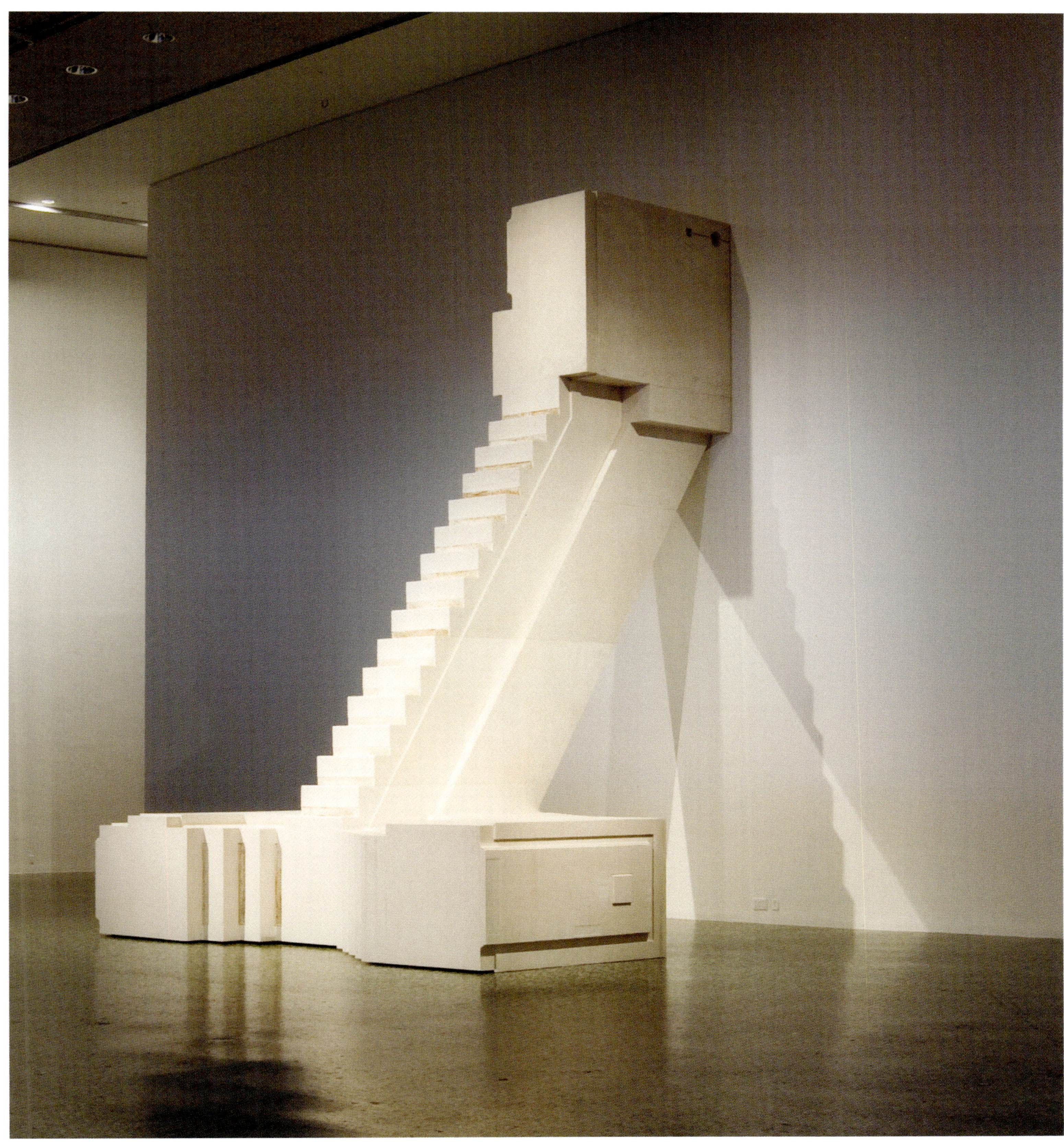

RACHEL WHITEREAD | British, born 1963
Untitled (Fire Escape), 2002
Plaster, fiberglass resin, and wood
Overall: 289 3/4 x 215 3/8 x 236 3/8 in.,
6172.9lb. (736 x 547.1 x 600.4 cm, 2800kg)
Museum purchase funded by
the Caroline Wiess Law
Accessions Endowment Fund
2008.535

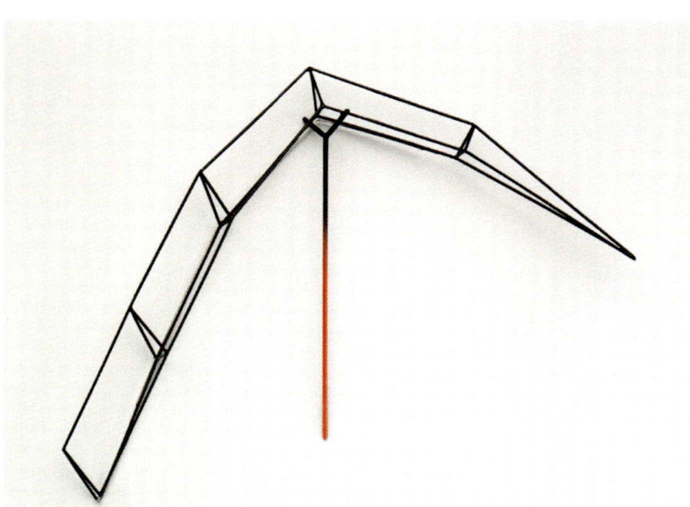

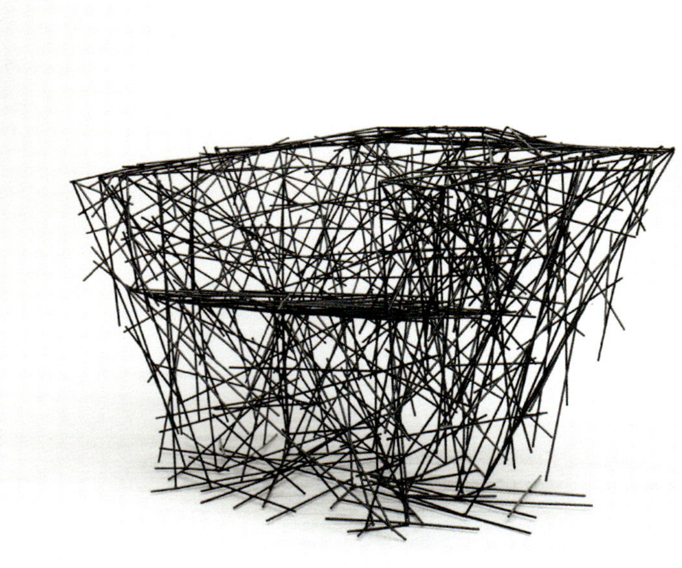

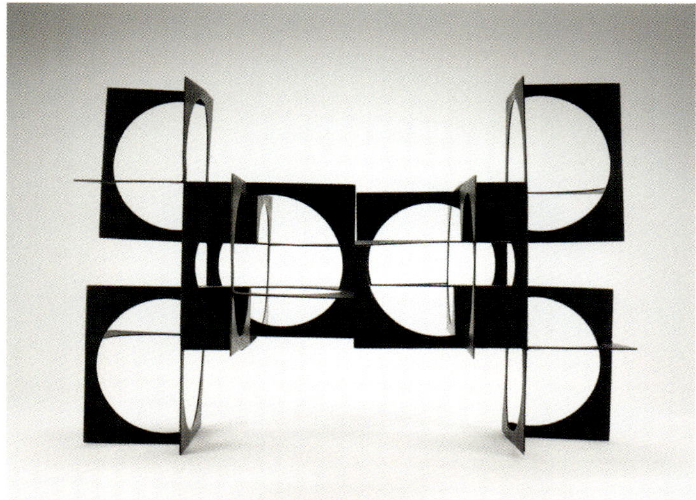

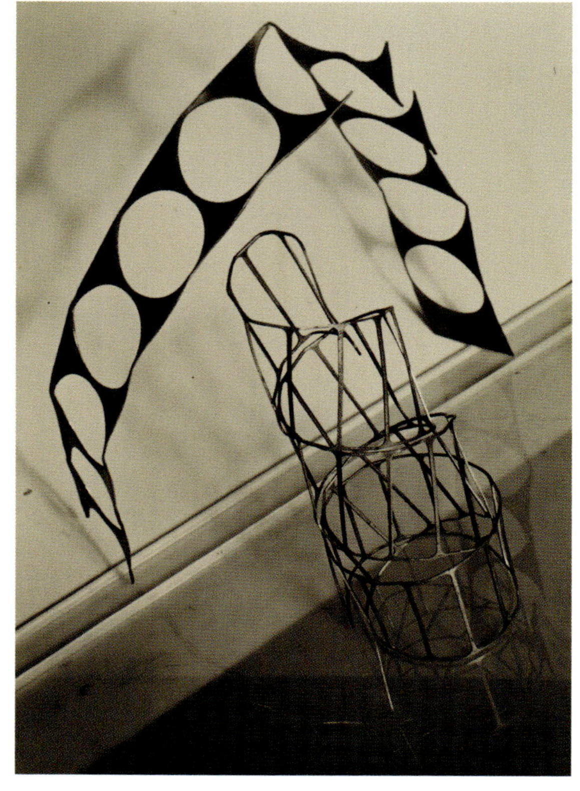

Top:
GEORG DOBLER | German, born 1952
"Salvatore" Brooch, 1985
Steel wire and acrylic lacquer
5 x 6 1/2 x 1/4 in. (12.7 x 16.5 x .6 cm)
Helen Williams Drutt Collection,
Gift of the Caroline Wiess Law Foundation
2002.3720

FRANZ WEISSMANN | Austrian, 1914–2006
Ponte [Bridge], 1958
Painted iron
18 5/8 x 18 5/8 x 26 5/8 in. (47.3 x 47.3 x 67.6 cm)
The Adolpho Leirner Collection of
Brazilian Constructive Art,
Museum purchase funded by
the Caroline Wiess Law Accessions
Endowment Fund
2005.1040

Top:
DESIGNED BY
FERNANDO CAMPANA | Brazilian, born 1961
and HUMBERTO CAMPANA | Brazilian, born 1953
MADE BY ESTUDIO CAMPANA
Poltronoa Ferro Preto [Black Iron Chair],
designed 2004, made 2011
From the series *Iron*
Stainless steel with epoxy paint
Overall: 32 1/2 x 49 x 37 1/2 in. (82.6 x 124.5 x 95.3 cm)
Museum purchase funded by
the Design Council, 2011
2011.545

JAROMÍR FUNKE | Czech, 1896–1945
Composition, c. 1924
Gelatin silver print
Image: 11 1/2 x 8 1/16 in. (29.2 x 20.5 cm)
Sheet: 11 1/2 x 8 1/16 in. (29.2 x 20.5 cm)
Museum purchase funded by
the Caroline Wiess Law Accessions
Endowment Fund,
The Manfred Heiting Collection
2002.1108

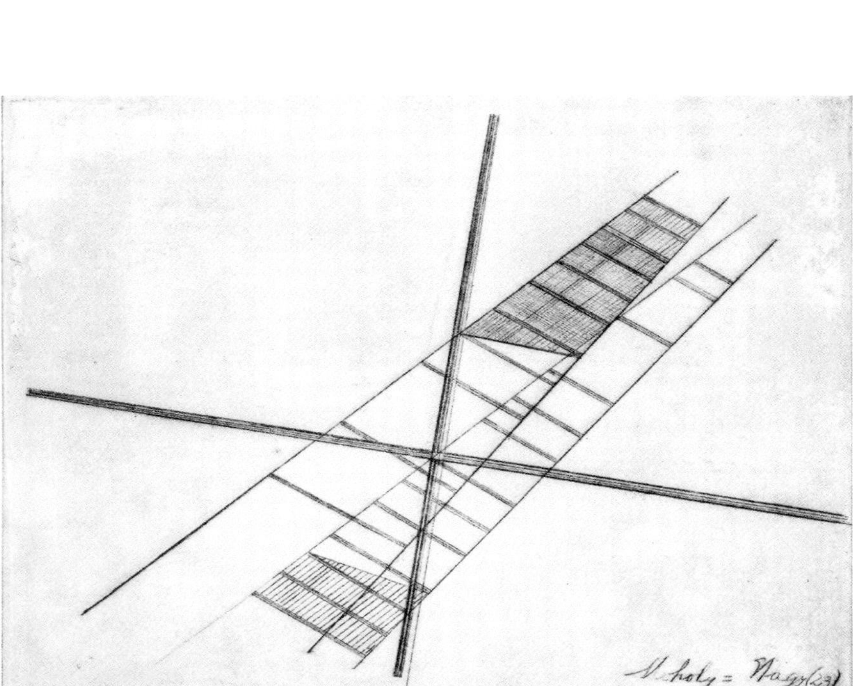

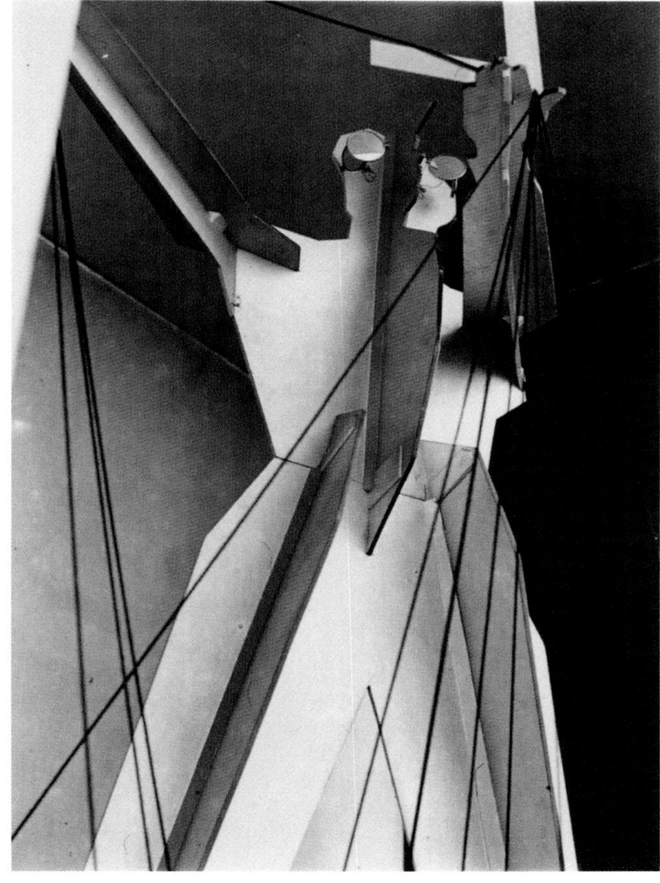

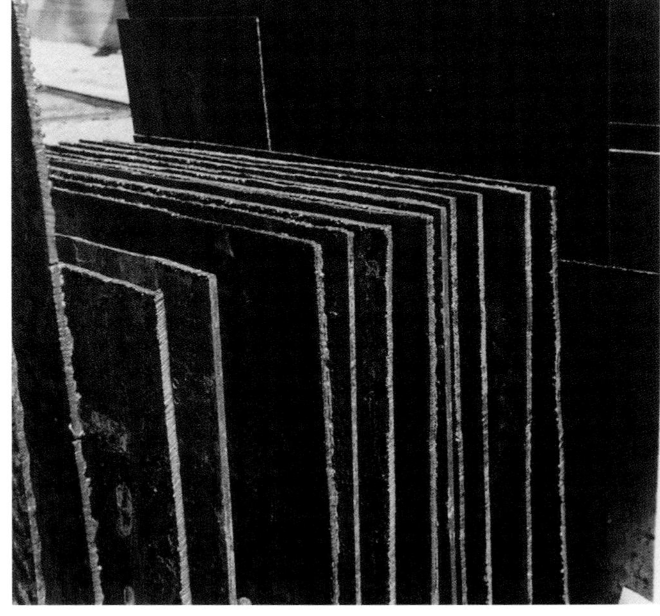

LÁSZLÓ MOHOLY-NAGY | American,
born Austria-Hungary, 1895–1946
Untitled, 1923
Etching with drypoint
Plate: 5 7/8 x 7 13/16 in. (14.9 x 19.8 cm)
Sheet: 11 1/8 x 15 1/2 in. (28.3 x 39.4 cm)
Museum purchase funded by
the Alvin S. Romansky Prints and Drawings
Accessions Endowment Fund
2009.1317

Top:
EL LISSITZKY | Russian, 1890–1941
Sculpture at Pressa, Cologne, 1928
Gelatin silver print
Sheet: 4 3/8 x 3 1/8 in. (11.1 x 7.9 cm)
Image: 4 5/8 x 3 5/16 in. (11.7 x 8.4 cm)
Museum purchase funded by
the Alice Pratt Brown Museum Fund
91.240

LEO MATIZ | Colombian, 1917–1998
Abstracción [Abstraction], 1947
Gelatin silver print
Image: 10 x 10 in. (25.4 x 25.4 cm)
Museum purchase funded by
the Caribbean Art Fund and
the Caroline Wiess Law Accessions
Endowment Fund
2012.308

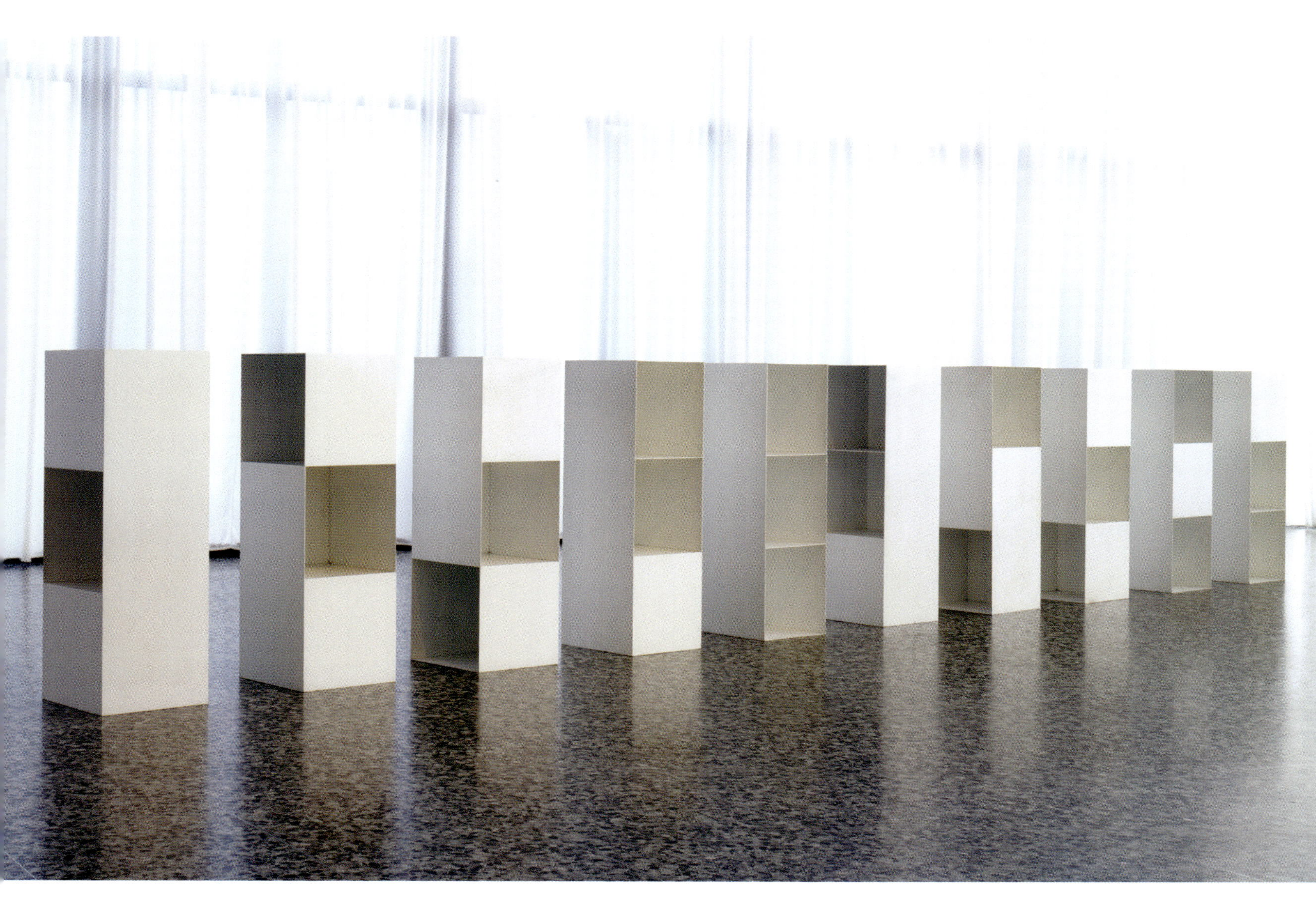

SOL LEWITT | American, 1928–2007
333, 1967
Baked white enamel on steel, 10 units
Overall (each unit): 54 x 18 x 18 in. (137.2 x 45.7 x 45.7 cm)
Gift of Donald Judd
77.332

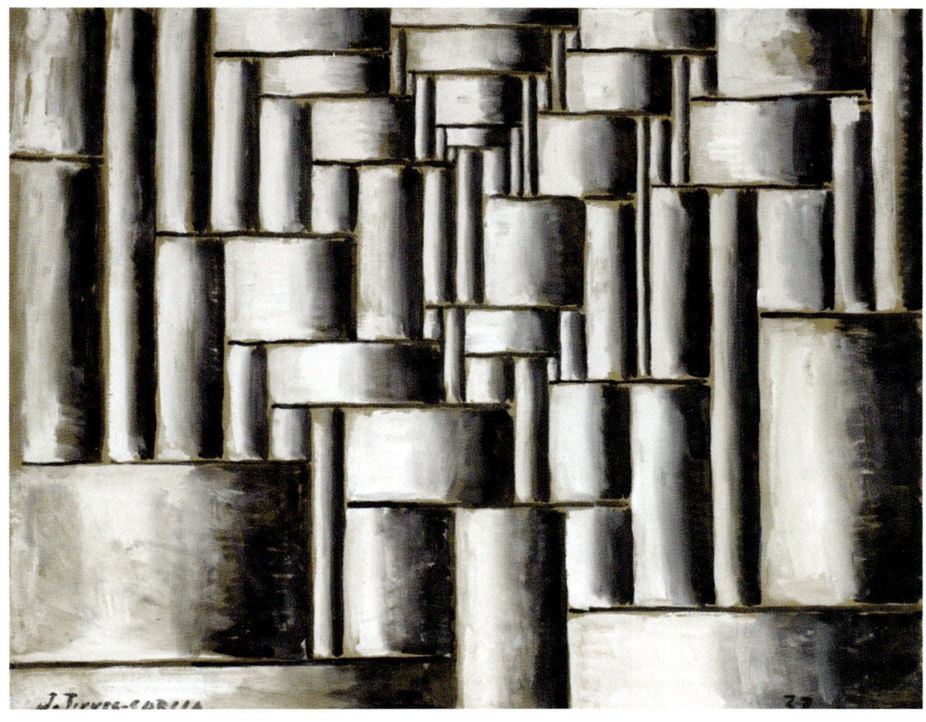

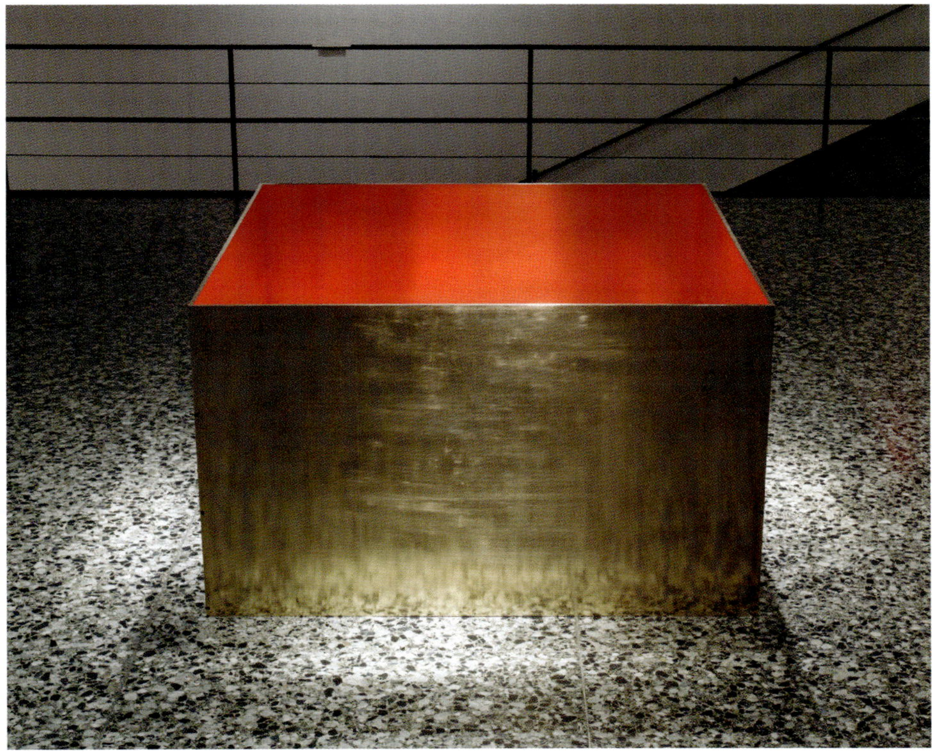

JOAQUÍN TORRES-GARCÍA | Uruguayan, 1874–1949
Composición abstracta tubular
[Abstract Tubular Composition], 1937
Tempera on board marouflé
32 x 39 3/4 in. (81.3 x 101 cm)
Museum purchase funded by the
Alice Pratt Brown Museum Fund
2002.326

DONALD JUDD | American, 1928–1994
Untitled, 1975
Brass, painted aluminum
36 1/8 x 60 x 60 in. (91.8 x 152.4 x 152.4 cm)
Museum commission funded by the National
Endowment for the Arts and matched by
The Brown Foundation, Inc.
75.370

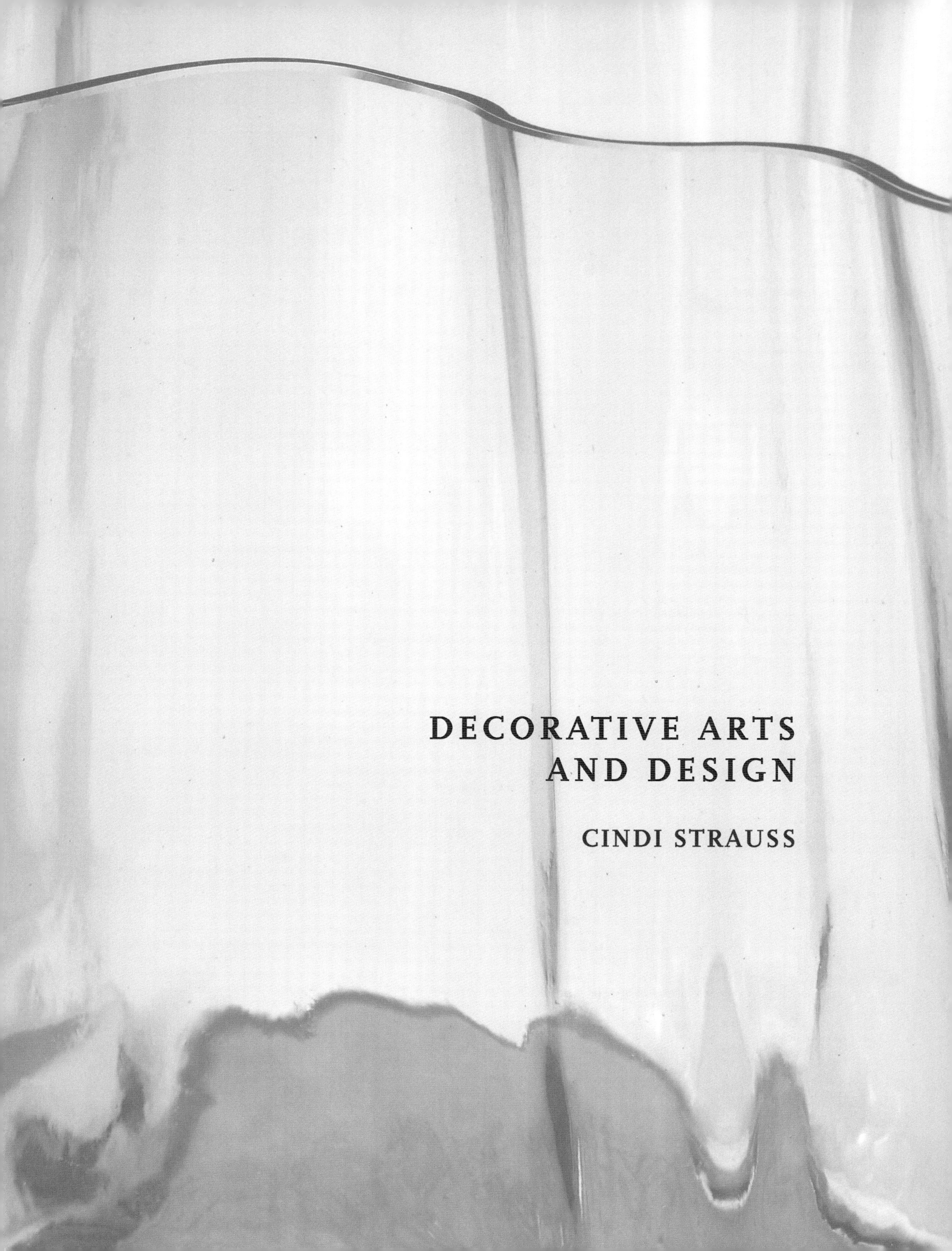

DECORATIVE ARTS AND DESIGN

CINDI STRAUSS

The holdings of the Museum's Decorative Arts and Design Department date to the seventeenth century. Since 1998, the department's focus has been largely on developing its twentieth- and twenty-first-century collections. With an emphasis on singular decorative arts, and contemporary craft, the collections contain ceramics, glass, fiber art, furniture, industrial design, jewelry, lighting, metalwork, and turned and sculpted wood by established masters as well as emerging artists and designers.

After fifteen years of extensive collection-building in these media, the Museum now has strength in a number of international decorative arts and design movements of the period, including early modern German and Viennese furniture and metalwork; American Arts and Crafts furniture, ceramics, and silver; European and American design of the 1920s–50s; Scandinavian glass, ceramics, textiles, and furniture of the 1920s–70s; Italian design of the 1950s–80s (with a particular emphasis on the work of Ettore Sottsass); and contemporary design by established and emerging designers such as Ron Arad, Sebastian Brajkovic, Fernando and Humberto Campana, Hella Jongerius, Joris Laarman, Ingo Maurer, and Marcel Wanders. Seminal works in the collection include Gerrit Rietveld's *Red/Blue Chair* (c. 1920); Tiffany and Co.'s *Cigar Humidor* (1925); a Ludwig Mies van der Rohe *Barcelona Chair* from the second year of production (1931); an early *Chaise Longue* (1933–37) by Le Corbusier, Pierre Jeanneret, and Charlotte Perriand; Ettore Sottsass's *Ceramics of Darkness* (1963); Gaetano Pesce's *Pratt Chair Prototype* (1982); Ron Arad's *Narrow Paparadelle Chair* (1998); and Joris Laarman's *Bone Chair Rocker* (2008).

A major collaboration with the Houston chapter of the American Institute of Architects that began in 2000 has resulted in the addition to the collections of more than forty significant objects designed by architects. This partnership, the only one of its kind in the United States, has drawn attention to the role architects have played in the design field since the late nineteenth century, and has resulted in the acquisition of works by seminal practitioners such as Alvar Aalto, Gae Aulenti, Peter Behrens, Andrea Branzi, Marcel Breuer, Sir Norman Foster, Josef Hoffmann, William Lescaze, Gerrit Rietveld, Eliel Saarinen, and Louis Sullivan, to name a few.

In recent years the Museum has taken a leading role in promoting contemporary craft through its acquisitions, educational programs, catalogues, and exhibitions. Four important collection acquisitions, the Carol Straus Collection of Fiber Arts (2001); the Helen Williams Drutt Collection of Contemporary Jewelry (2002); the Garth Clark and Mark Del Vecchio Collection of Modern and Contemporary Ceramics (2007); and the Leatrice and Melvin Eagle Collection of Contemporary Craft (2010), have created opportunities for groundbreaking scholarship and exhibitions. Additional significant gifts to the Museum of contemporary glass and turned and sculpted wood have also contributed to the Museum's profile as a national leader in the field.

As the Decorative Arts and Design Department looks to the future of galleries in the new Museum building, objects and collections such as those highlighted in the following pages will be central to its presentation. The department continues to seek out masterworks by artists and designers that will enhance the public's understanding of the field as well as the larger realm of modern and contemporary art.

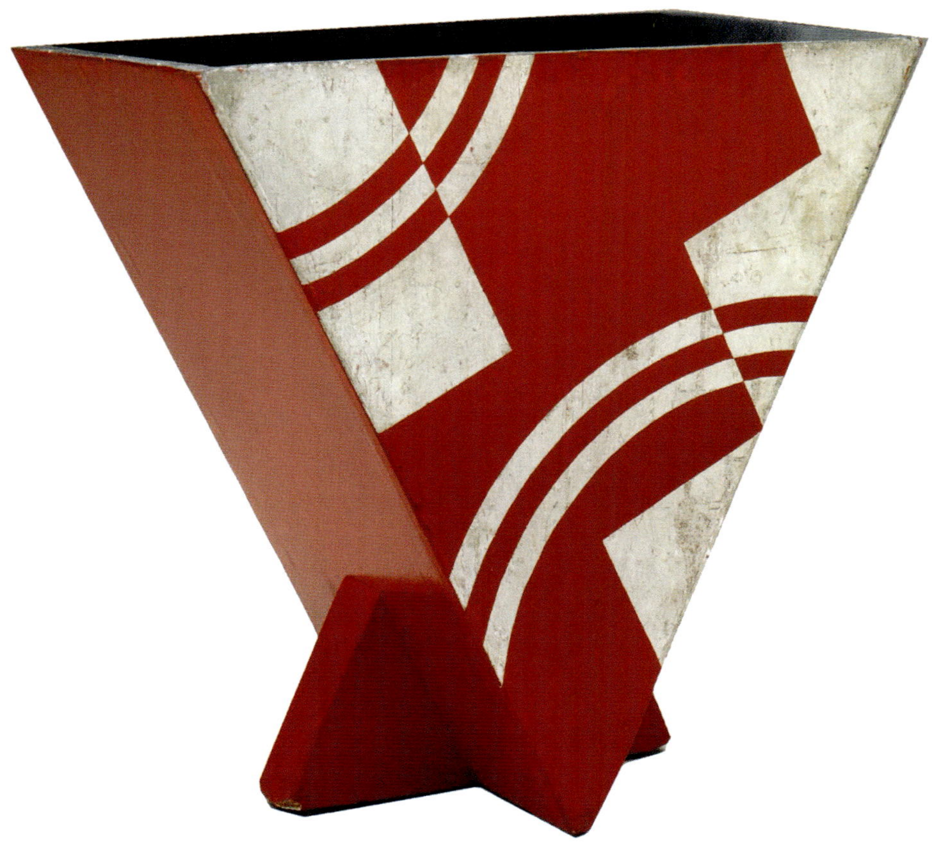

DONALD DESKEY | American, 1894–1989
Waste Basket, c. 1928
Wood, paint, and silver leaf
Overall: 14 x 14 x 8 in. (35.6 x 35.6 x 20.3 cm)
Museum purchase funded by
the Design Council, 2002
2002.2800

GERRIT RIETVELD | Dutch, 1888–1964
Red/Blue Chair, c. 1920
Beech with stain
Overall: 33 3/4 x 26 x 33 in. (85.7 x 66 x 83.8 cm)
Museum purchase funded by
the Caroline Wiess Law Accessions Endowment
Fund
2013. 244

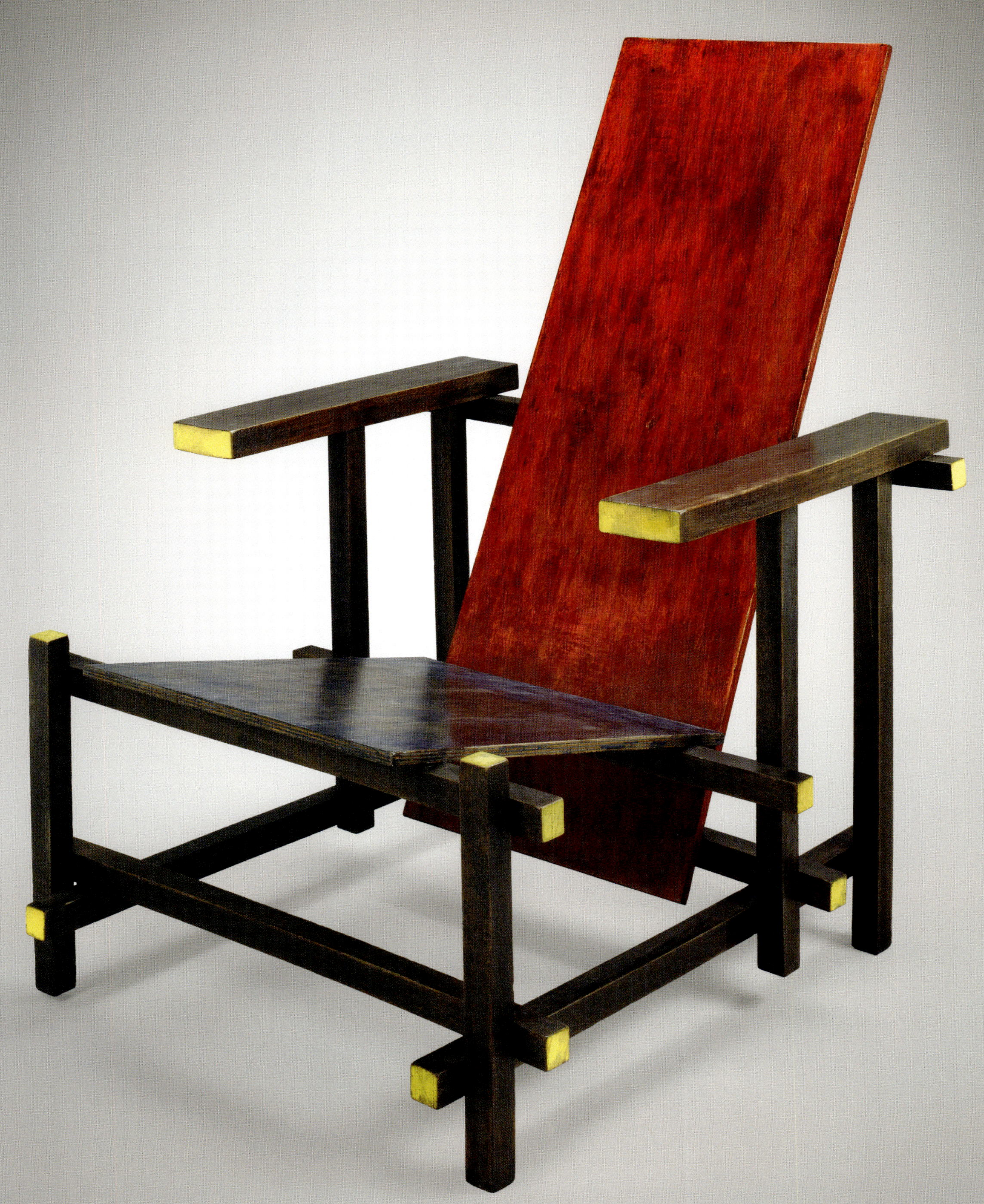

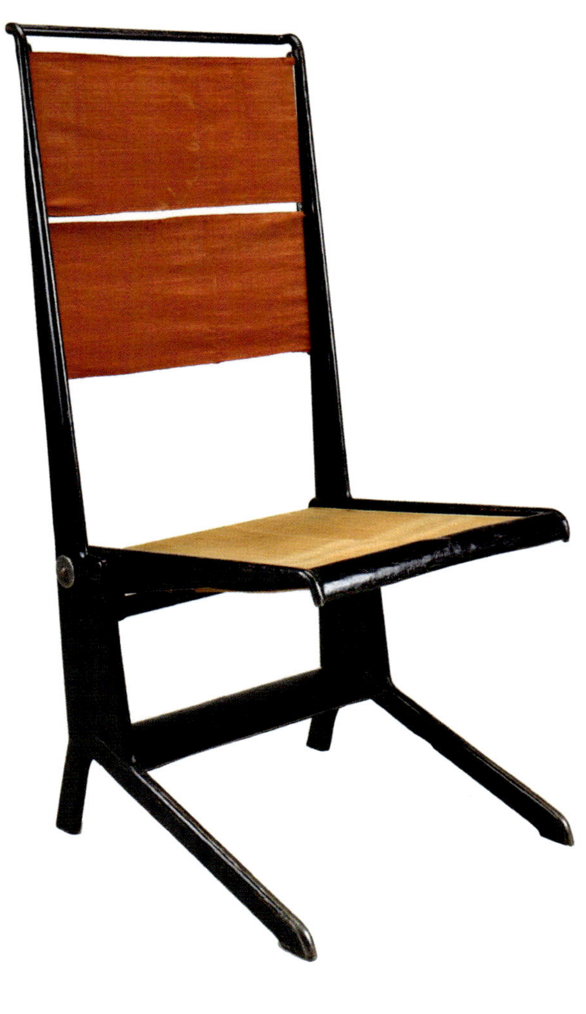

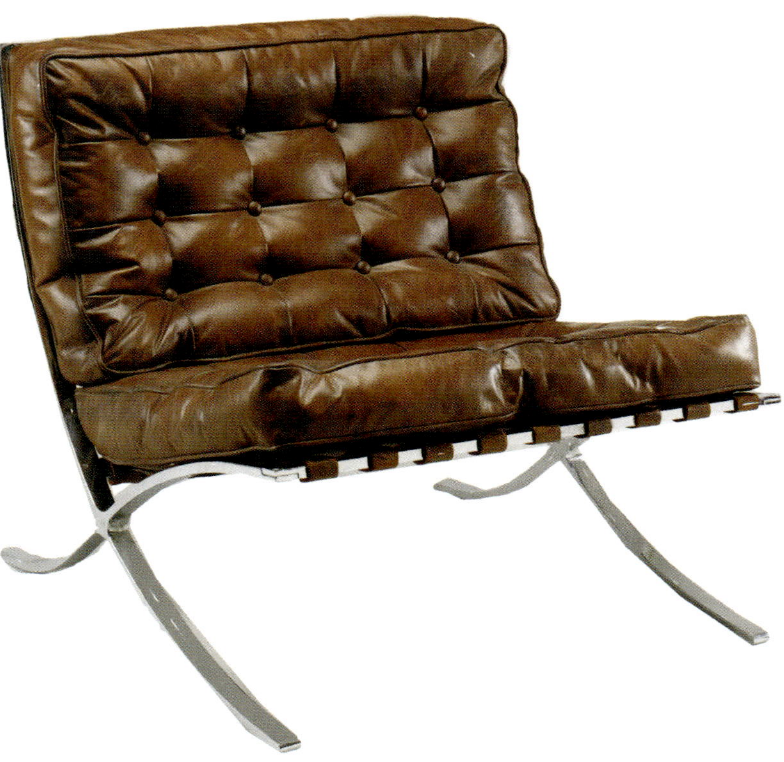

DESIGNED BY JEAN PROUVÉ | French, 1901–1984
Made by Les Ateliers, Jean Prouvé
Folding Chair, designed c. 1924–28, made 1929
Tubular steel and linen canvas
40 1/4 x 17 1/2 x 18 5/8 in. (102.9 x 44.4 x 47.3 cm)
Museum purchase funded by
J. Brian and Varina Eby, by exchange
97.192

DESIGNED BY
LUDWIG MIES VAN DER ROHE | German, 1886–1969
Made by Berliner Metallgewerbe Josef Müller
"Barcelona," Model MR 90 Chair, 1929–30
Bent, chromed flat steel and leather
28 3/4 x 29 1/8 x 29 15/16 in. (73 x 74 x 76 cm)
Museum purchase funded by
J. Brian and Varina Eby, by exchange
97.354

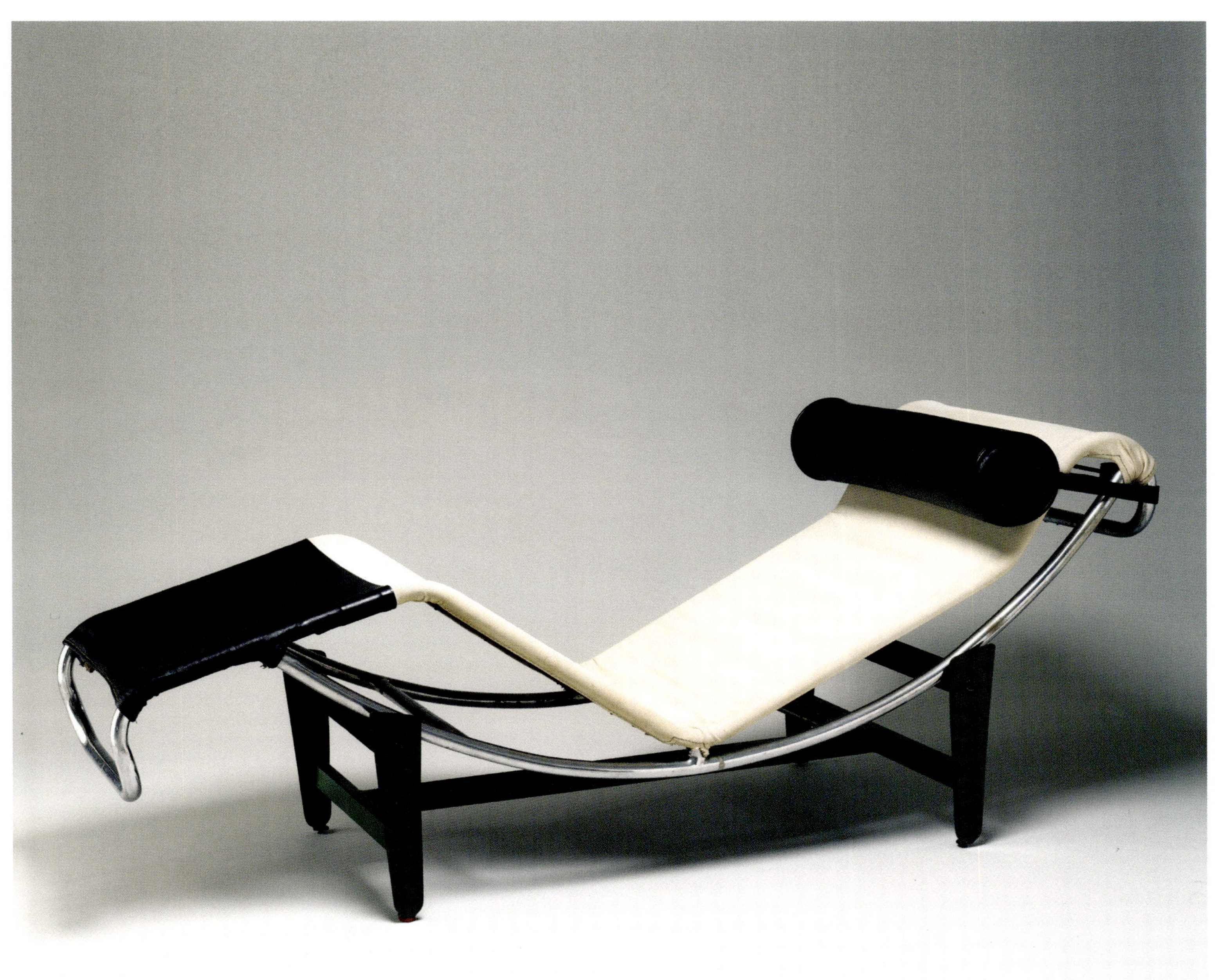

DESIGNED BY
LE CORBUSIER | French, born Switzerland, 1887–1965
PIERRE JEANNERET | Swiss, 1896–1967
CHARLOTTE PERRIAND | French, 1903–99
Manufactured by Embru-Werke AG,
Rüti, Switzerland
Chaise Longue 2072, designed 1928–29,
made c. 1933–37
Bent chromed steel, iron, leather, canvas, and rubber
Overall assembled: 26 x 21 1/4 x 63 in. (66 x 54 x 160.02 cm)
.A, chaise: 14 x 63 x 21 1/2 in. (35.56 x 160.02 x 54.61 cm)
.B, base: 12 7/16 x 21 x 37 1/4 in. (31.59 x 53.34 x 94.62 cm)
.C, pillow: 5 1/4 x 5 1/4 x 22 1/4 in. (13.34 x 13.34 x 56.52 cm)
Museum purchase funded by The Brown Foundation, Inc.
in memory of Sally Walsh
92.190.A,.B,.C

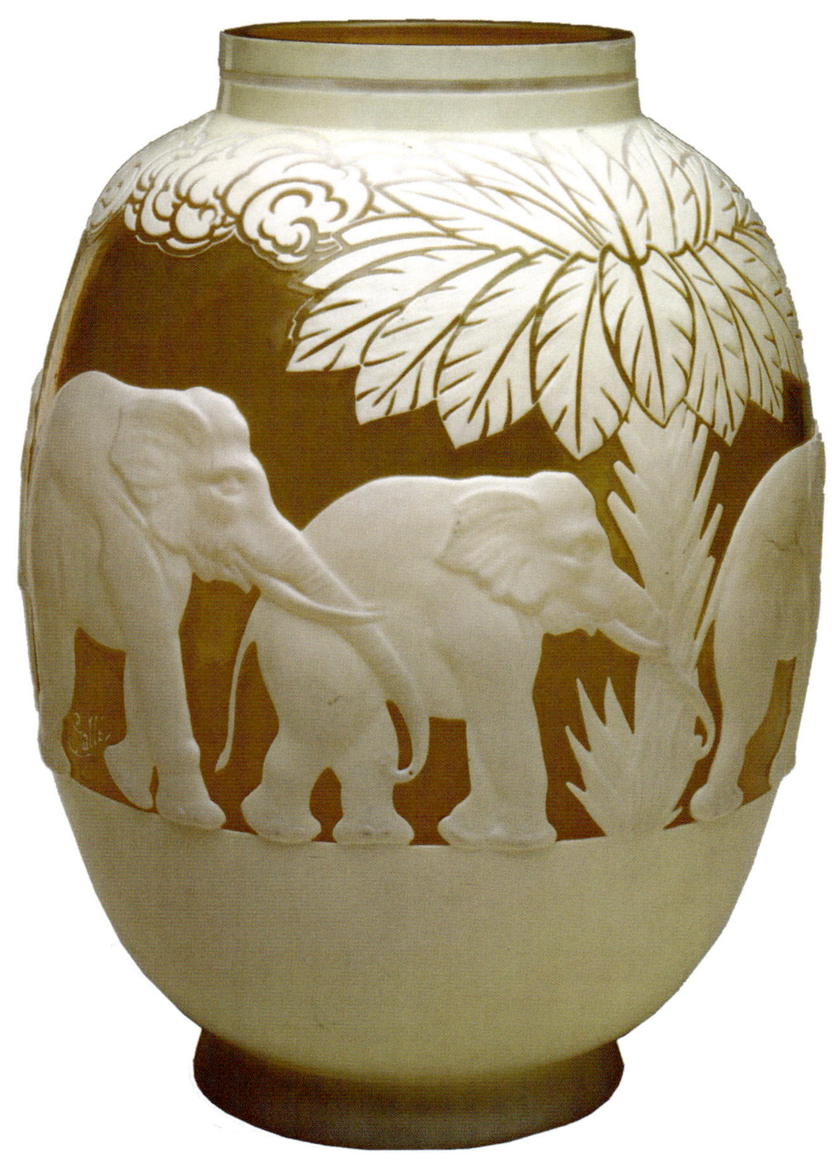

EMILE GALLÉ | French, 1846–1904
Elephant Vase, 1918–31
Molded, carved and overlaid glass
Overall: 15 1/8 x 11 1/4 in. diameter (38.4 x 28.6 cm)
Gift of J. Brian and Varina Eby
73.94

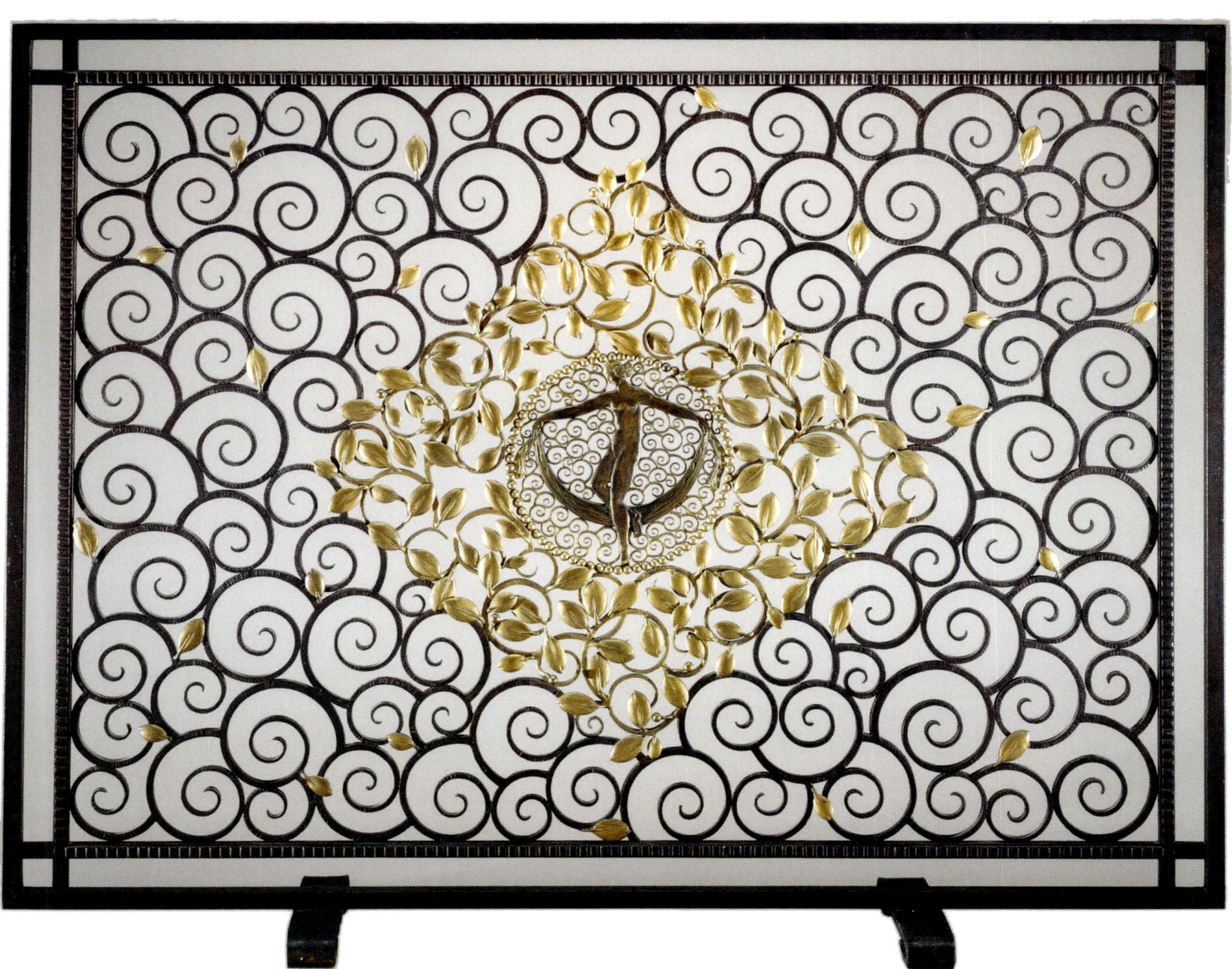

EDGAR BRANDT | French, 1880–1960
Firescreen, c. 1925
Wrought iron and gilding
37 1/4 x 48 3/16 x 9 in. (94.6 x 122.4 x 22.9 cm)
Museum purchase funded by
the Design Council, 2001
2001.257

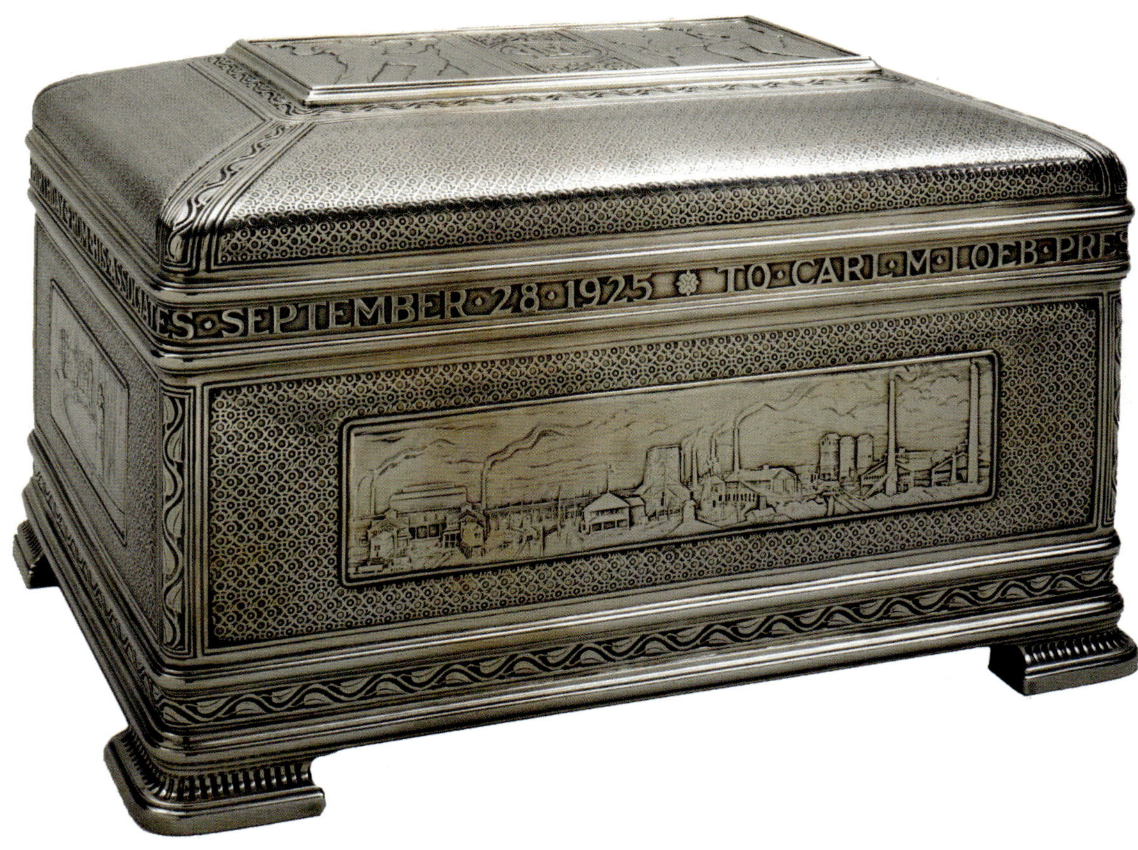

TIFFANY & CO., NEW YORK | Established 1837
Cigar Humidor, 1925
Sterling silver
Overall: 8 5/8 x 14 3/8 x 10 1/4 in. (21.8 x 36.6 x 26 cm)
Museum purchase funded by
"One Great Night in November, 1987"
87.267.A,.B

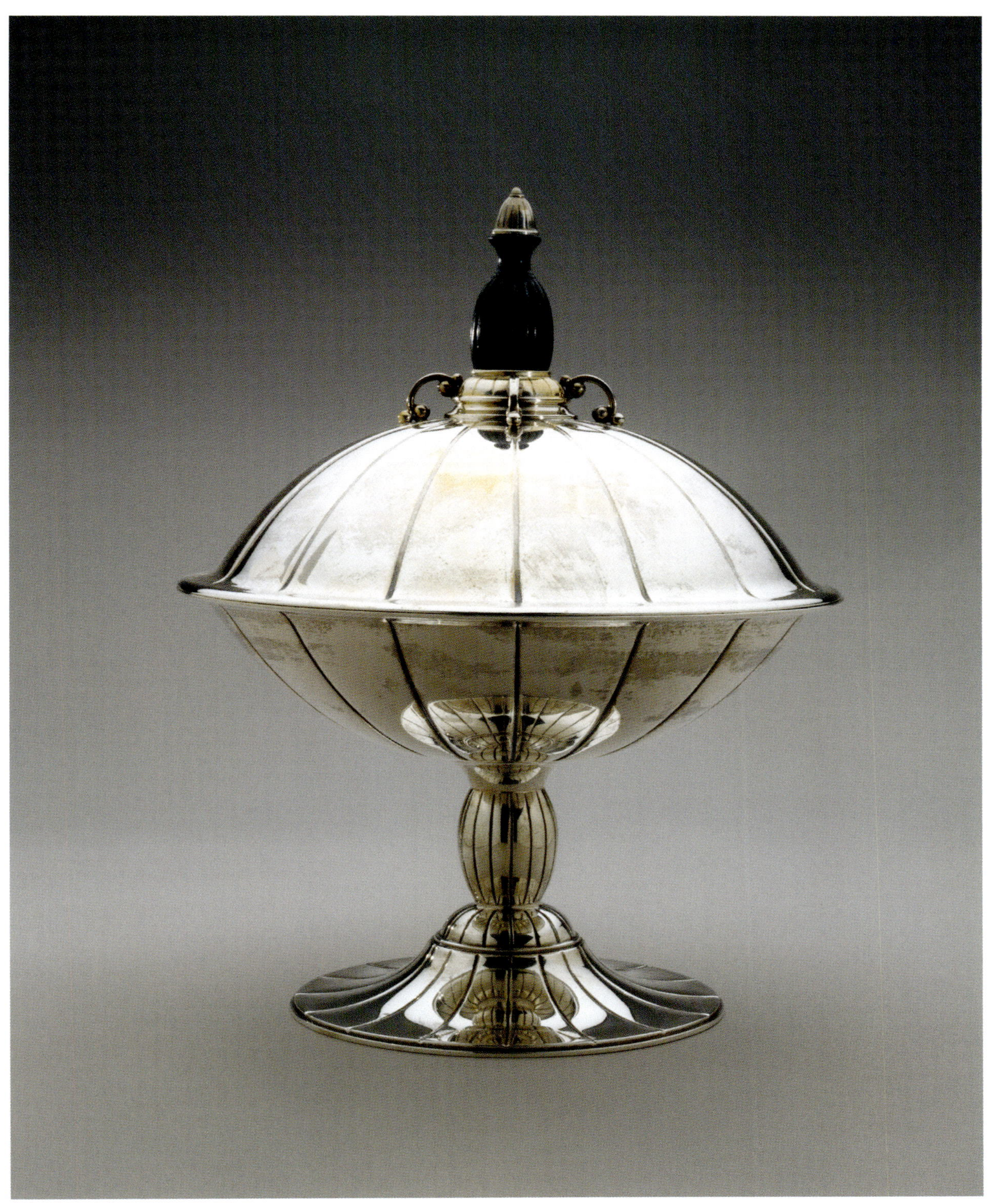

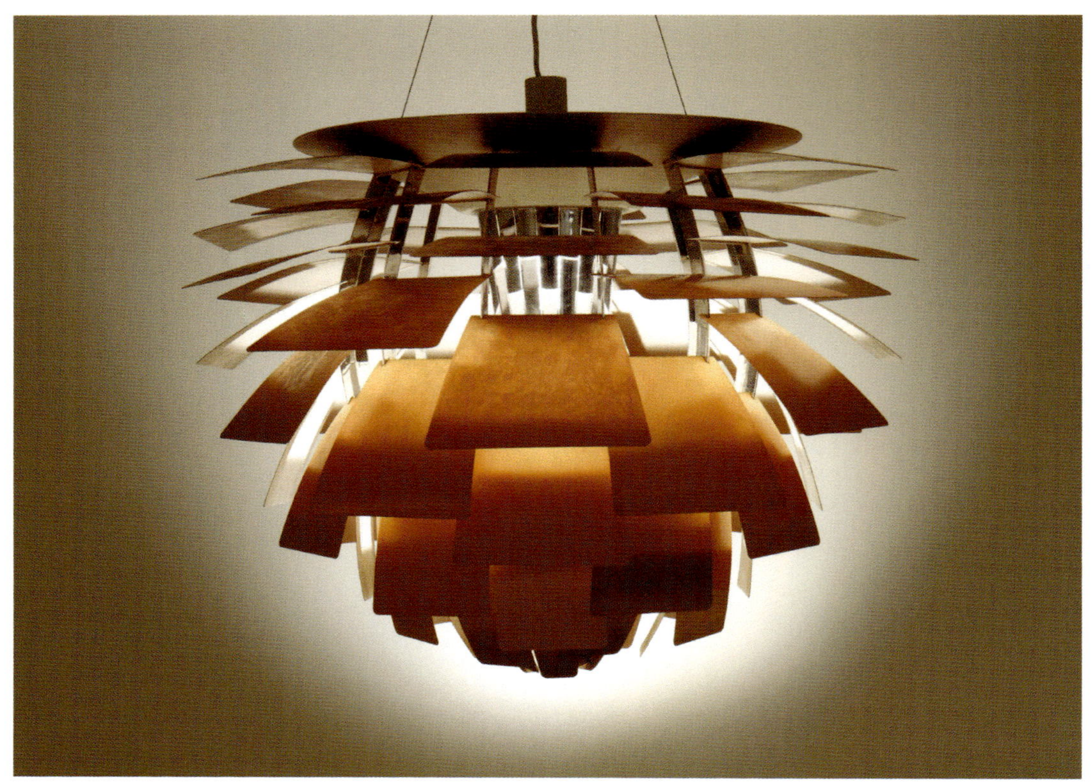

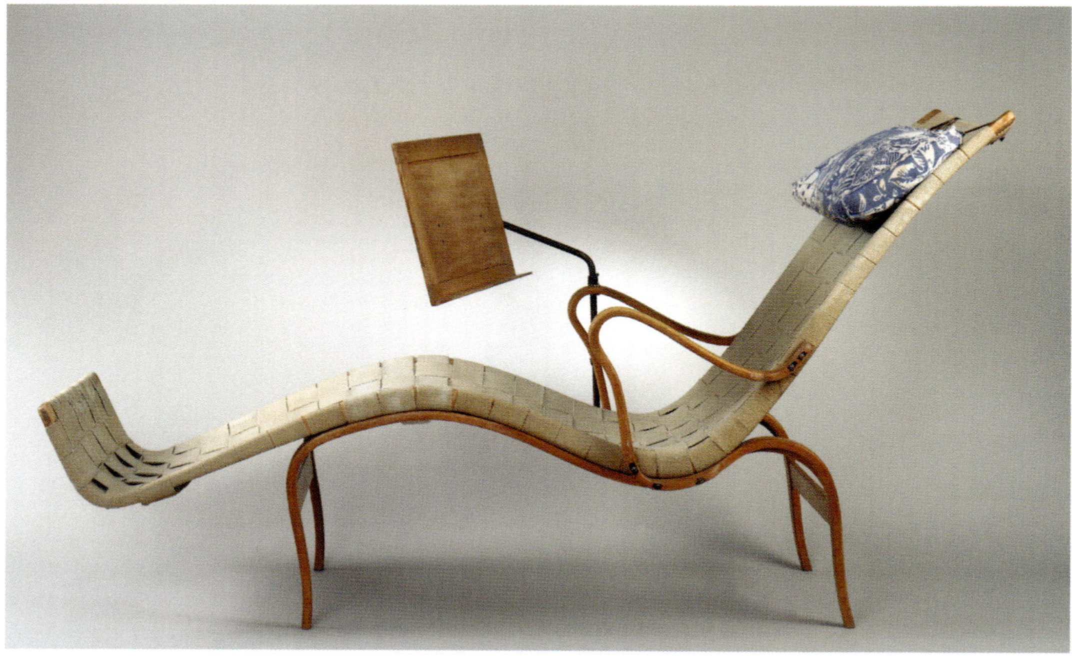

DESIGNED BY POUL HENNINGSEN | Danish, 1894–1967
MANUFACTURED BY LOUIS POULSEN & CO.
"PH Artichoke" Lamp, 1958
Copper, steel, and enameled metal
27 1/8 x 33 1/8 in. diameter (68.9 x 84.1 cm)
Museum purchase funded by
the Design Council, 2000
2000.202

DESIGNED BY BRUNO MATHSSON | Swedish, 1904–1998
MANUFACTURED BY FIRMA KARL MATHSSON
PILLOW FABRIC DESIGNED BY JOSEF FRANK
Chaise Longue, 1942
Beech, jute, cotton, leather, and metal
37 3/8 x 67 x 24 3/4 (94.9 x 170.2 x 62.9)
99.238.A-.D

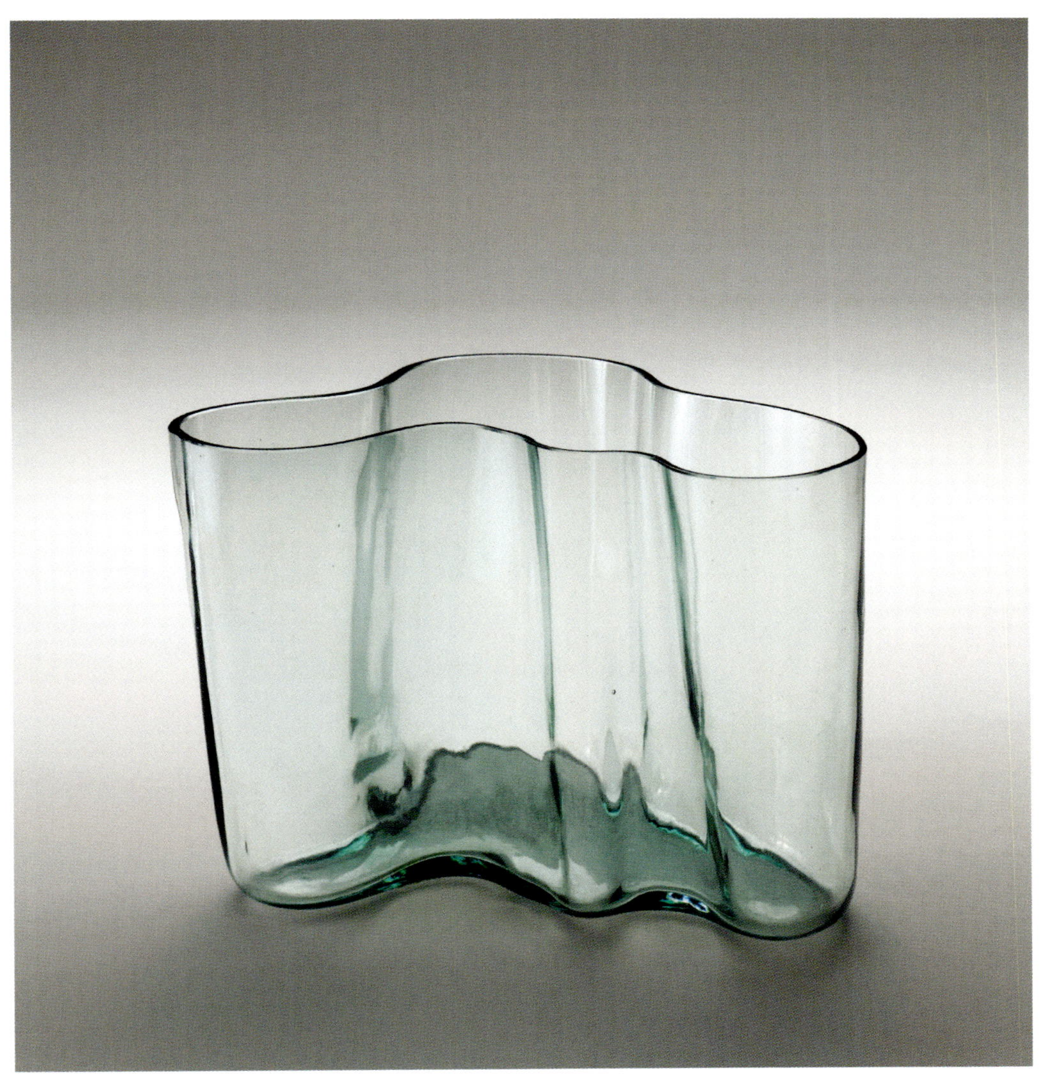

ALVAR AALTO | Finnish, 1898–1976
Made by Karhula-Iittala
Vase, 1937
Glass
Overall: 5 5/8 x 8 1/2 x 7 1/4 in. (14.3 x 21.6 x 18.4 cm)
The American Institute of Architects, Houston Design
Collection, Museum purchase funded by friends of
Arthur Jones, in his honor
2010.2251

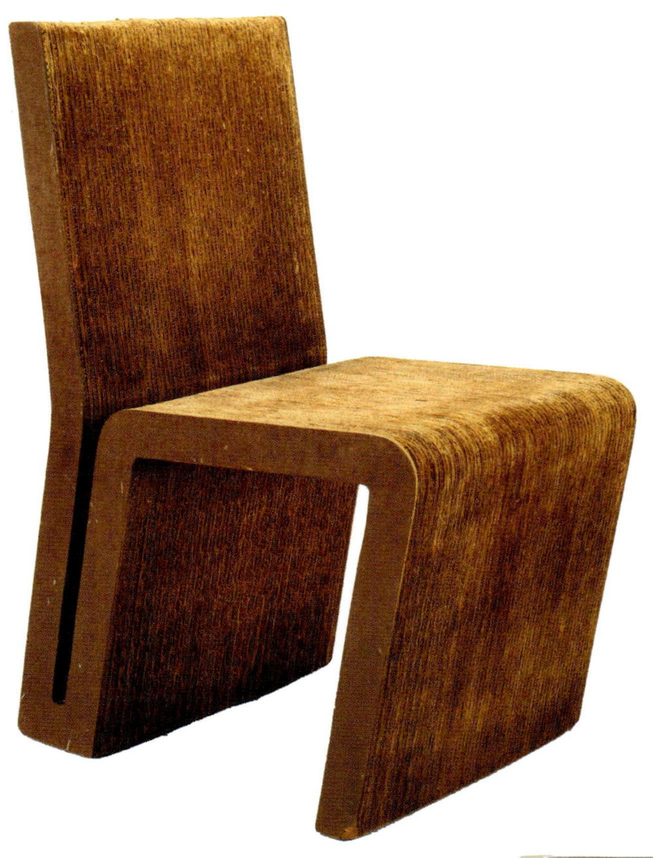

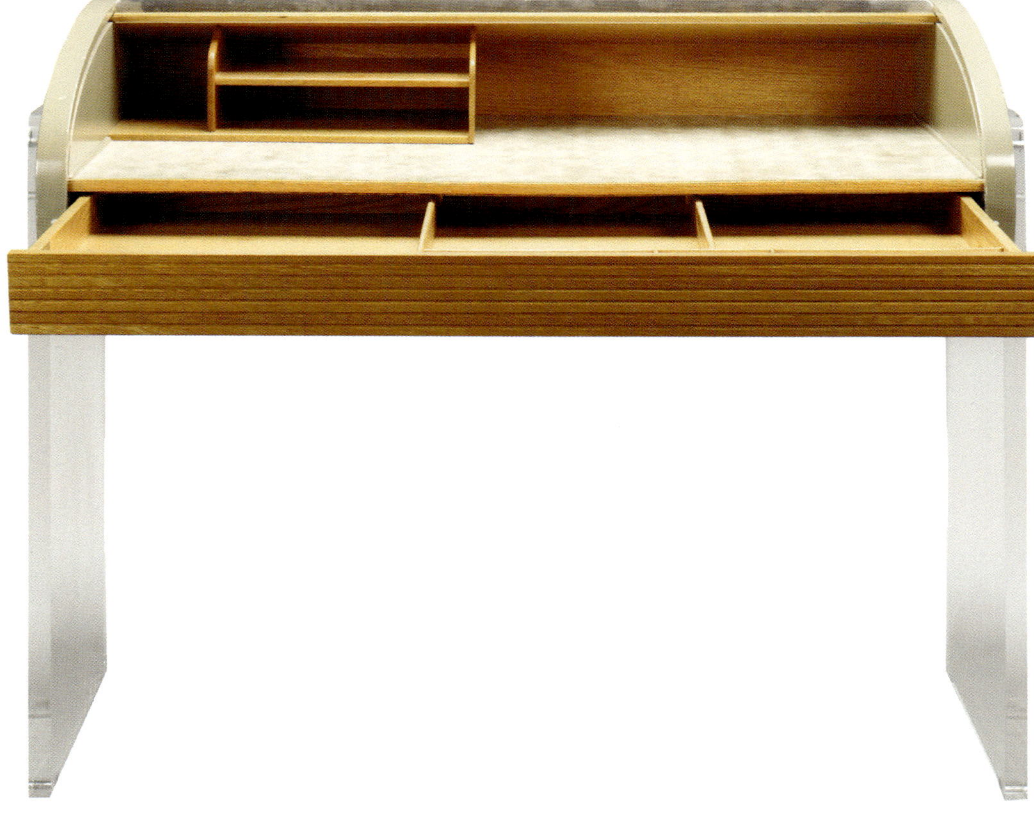

DESIGNED BY FRANK GEHRY | American, born Canada, 1929
IN COLLABORATION WITH ROBERT IRWIN | American, born 1928
Made by Jack Brogan
Easy Edges Dining Chair Prototype, c. 1970–72
Overall: 32 1/2 x 20 x 16 3/16 in. (82.6 x 50.8 x 41.1 cm)
Corrugated box material and pressed fiber
Museum purchase funded by Mrs. David M. Carmichael,
Michael W. Dale, Susan Garwood, Mrs. Jack Lapin,
Mrs. Rodney H. Margolis, Katsy Mullendore Mecom,
Sue Rowan Pittman, the Cyvia and Melvyn Wolff Family
Foundation, Mr. and Mrs. Jimmy Younger, and
Nina and Michael Zilkha
96.609

VLADIMIR KAGAN | American, born Germany, 1927
Manufactured by Vladimir Kagan Designs
Roll Top Desk, c. 1965
Wood, acrylic, metal, and laminate
Overall: 35 x 44 1/8 x 23 1/2 in. (88.9 x 112.1 x 59.7 cm)
Museum purchase funded by
the John R. Eckel, Jr. Foundation
2011.444

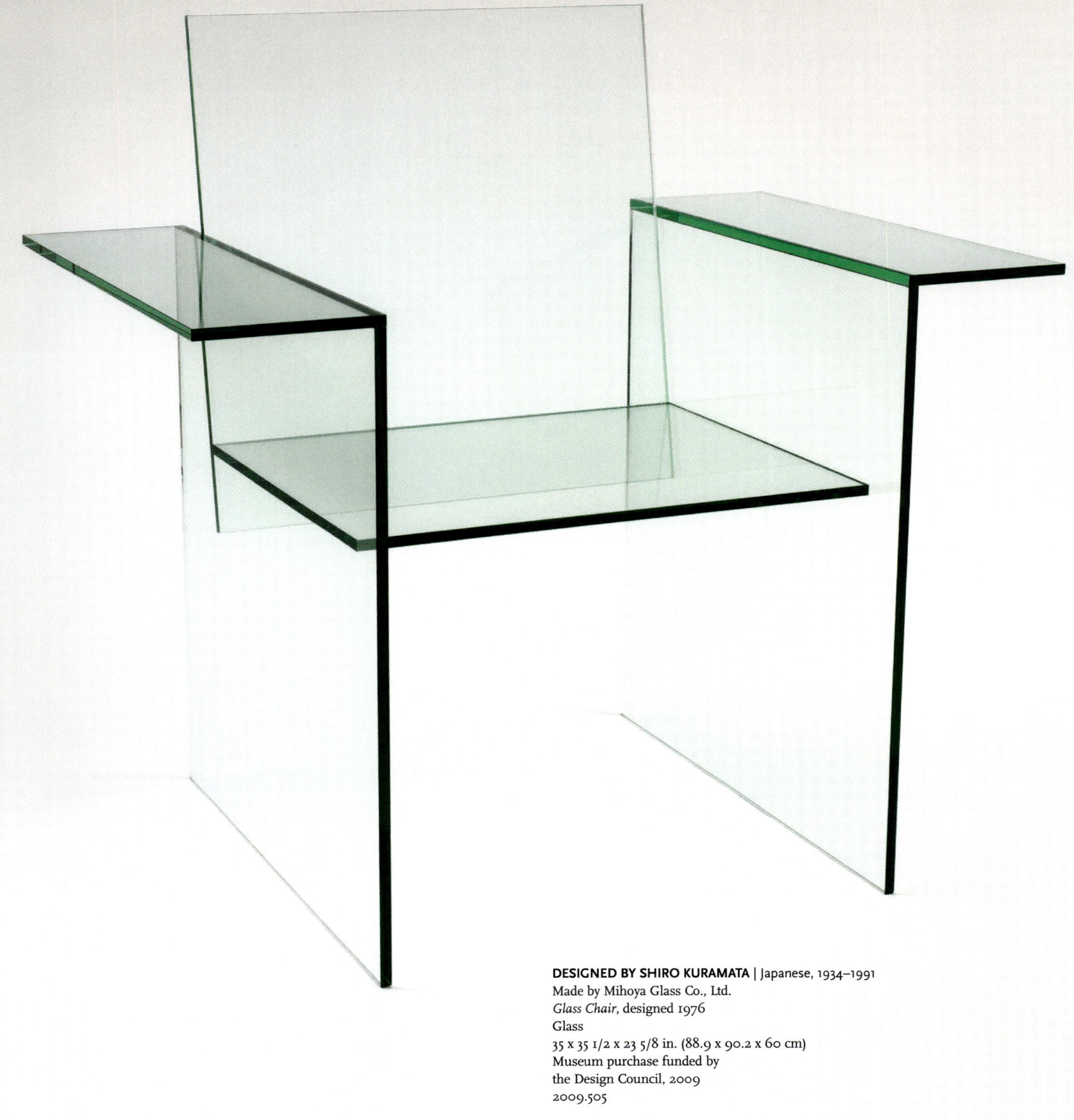

DESIGNED BY SHIRO KURAMATA | Japanese, 1934–1991
Made by Mihoya Glass Co., Ltd.
Glass Chair, designed 1976
Glass
35 x 35 1/2 x 23 5/8 in. (88.9 x 90.2 x 60 cm)
Museum purchase funded by
the Design Council, 2009
2009.505

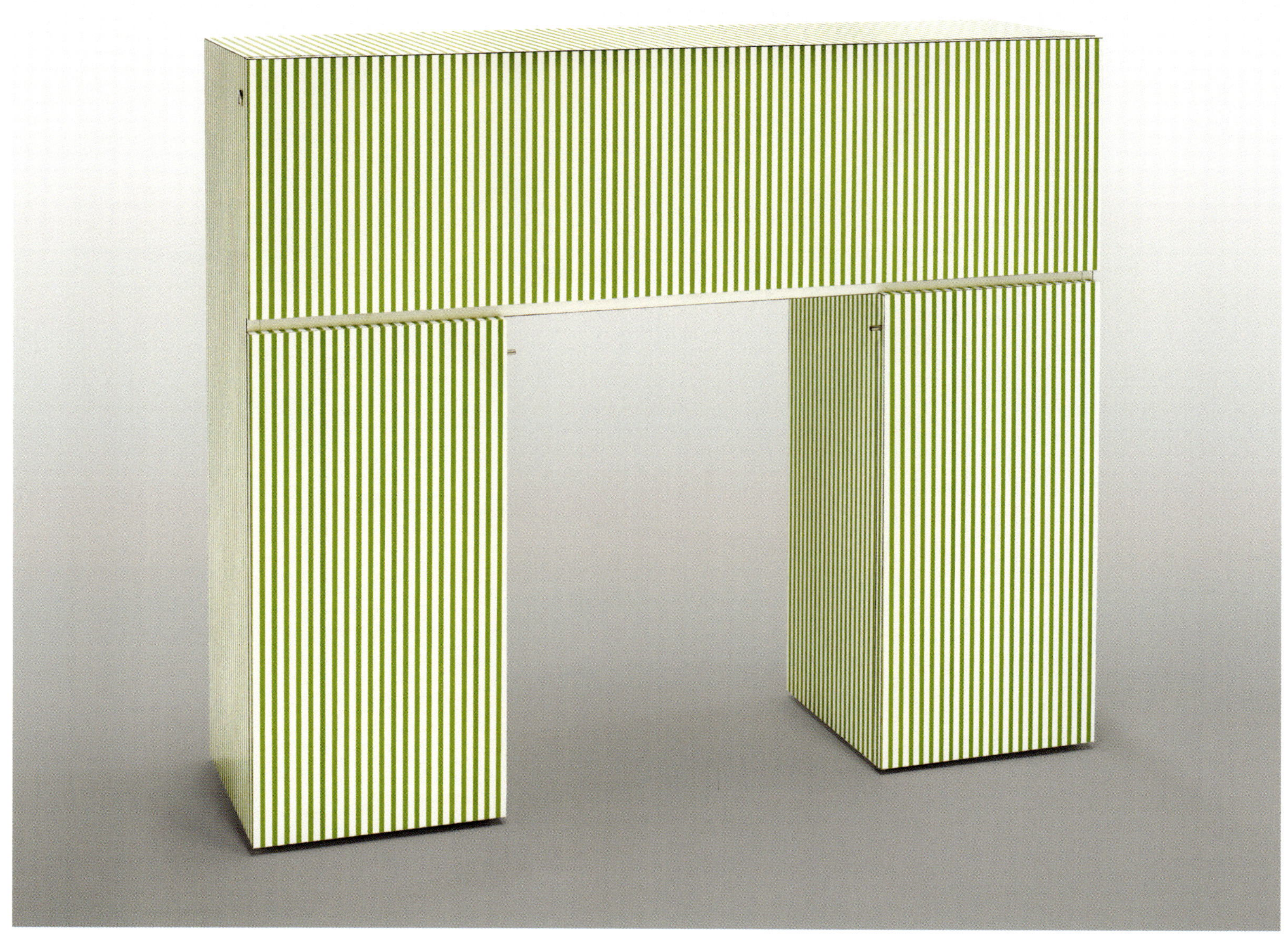

ETTORE SOTTSASS | Italian, born Austria, 1917–2007
"Nefertiti" Desk, 1968
Laminated wood
Overall: 43 1/4 x 49 3/4 x 13 15/16 in. (109.9 x 126.4 x 35.4 cm)
Open (desk top): 27 in. (68.6 cm)
Open (cabinet door): 27 3/8 in. (69.5 cm)
Museum purchase funded by
the Caroline Wiess Law Accessions Endowment Fund,
and by various donors in memory of Peter C. Marzio
2011.1038

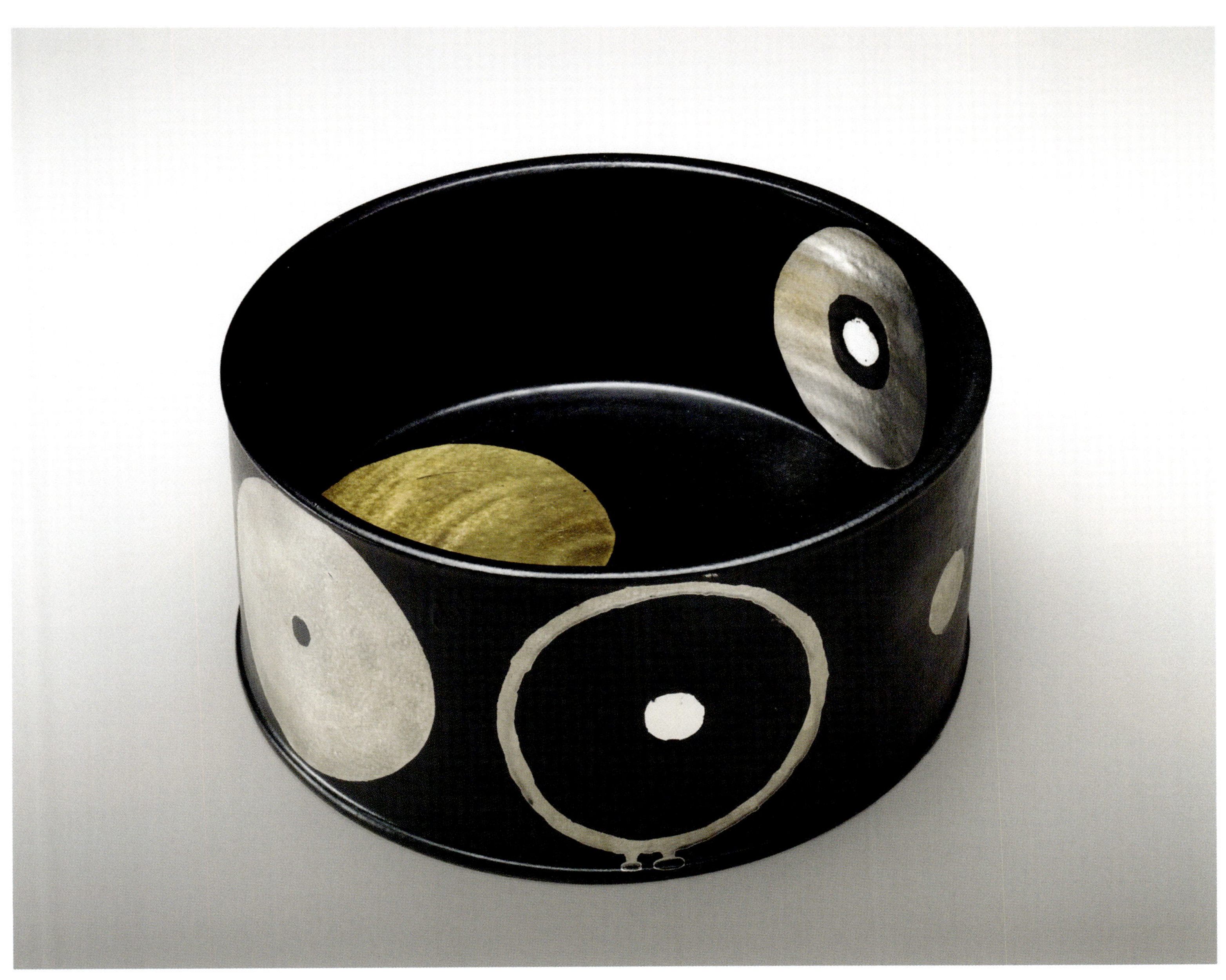

ETTORE SOTTSASS | Italian, born Austria, 1917–2007
Vase, 1963
From the series Ceramiche delle Tenebre
(Ceramics of Darkness)
Ceramic
4 3/8 x 9 1/2 in. diameter (11.1 x 24.1 cm)
Museum purchase funded by
Bill and Sara Morgan in memory
of Peter C. Marzio
2011.713

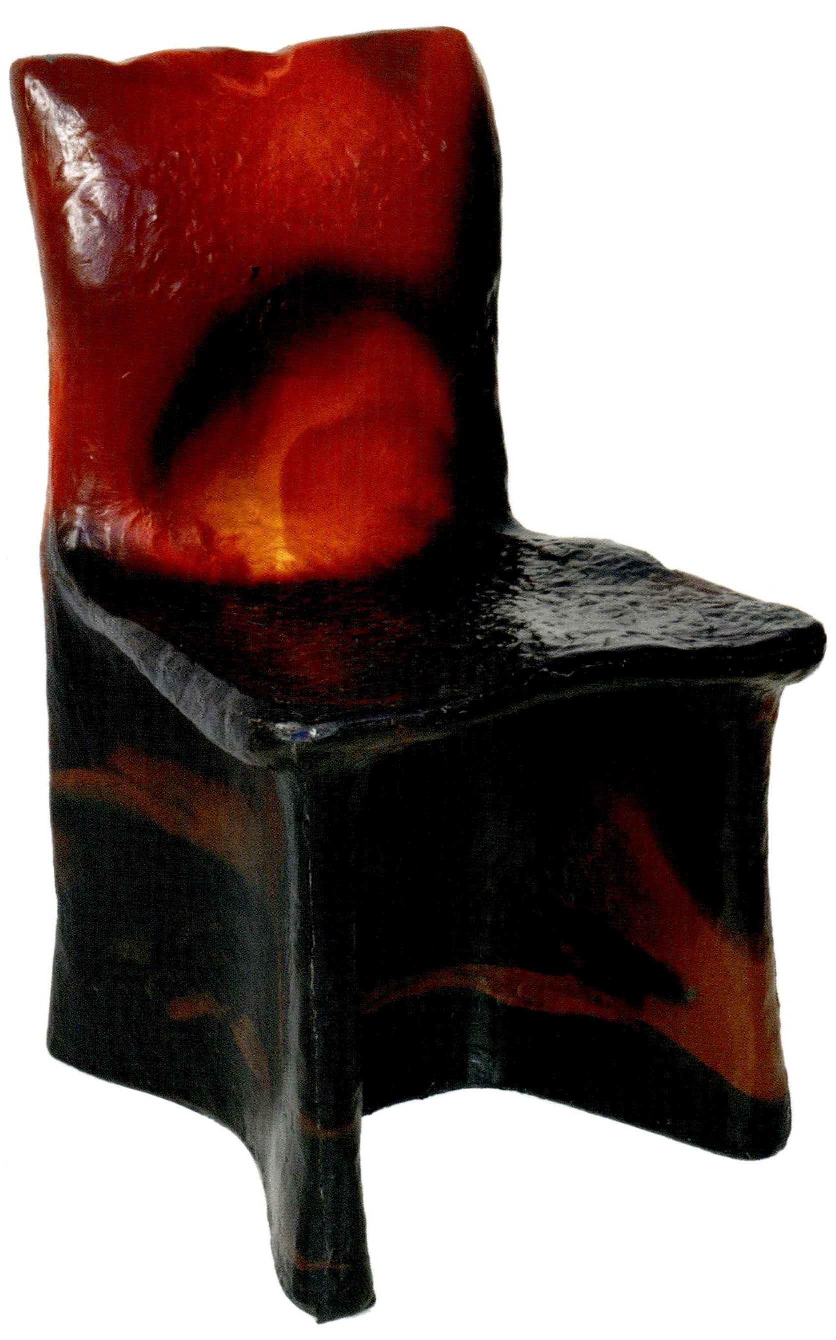

GAETANO PESCE | Italian, born 1939
Pratt Chair Prototype, 1982
Polyurethane
34 5/8 x 18 1/4 x 20 1/4 in. (87.9 x 46.4 x 51.4 cm)
Museum purchase funded
by Nina and Michael Zilkha
98.41

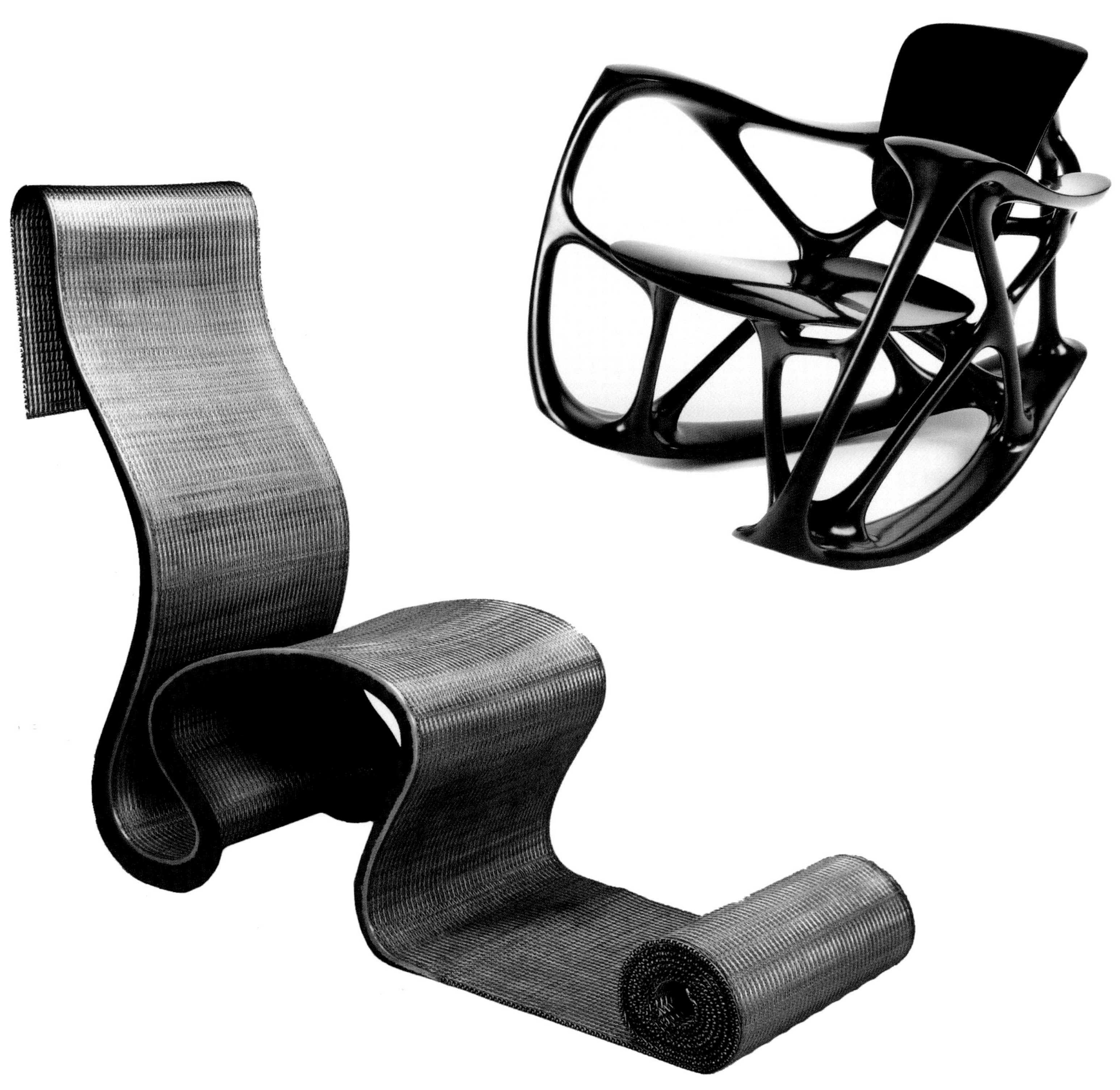

RON ARAD | Israeli, born 1951
Made at Ron Arad Studio
Narrow Paparadelle Chair, designed 1992,
made 1994
Stainless steel and steel
Overall: 42 x 16 x 118 1/8 in. (106.7 x 40.6 x 300 cm)
Other (bottom of base to end of roll,
when displayed, approx.): 44 in. (111.8 cm)
Museum purchase funded by
the Sealy Family Trust, by exchange
98.525

DESIGNED BY JORIS LAARMAN | Dutch, born 1979
Bone Rocker, 2008
Black marble resin
Overall: 30 x 32 x 40 in. (76.2 x 81.3 x 101.6 cm)
Museum purchase funded by
the Mary Kathryn Lynch Kurtz
Charitable Lead Trust
2009.507

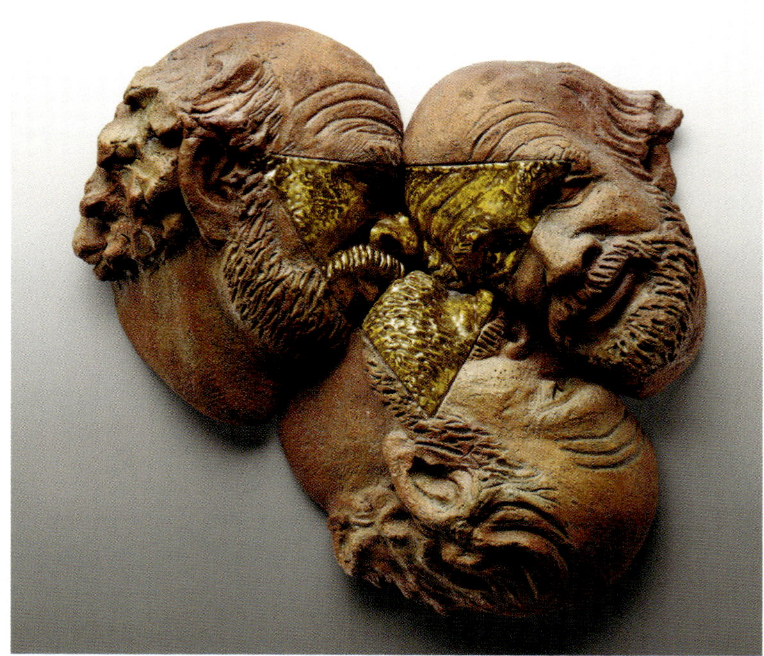

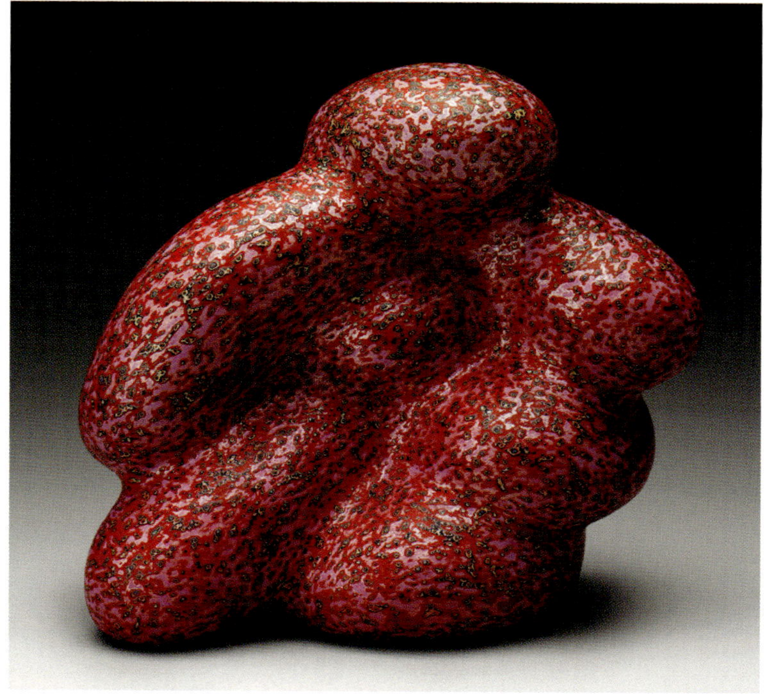

ROBERT ARNESON | American, 1930–1992
Golden Triangle/Us Guys, 1991
Earthenware
Overall: 20 x 23 x 5 in. (50.8 x 53.3 x 12.7 cm)
The Leatrice S. and Melvin B. Eagle Collection,
Museum purchase funded by
Leatrice and Melvin Eagle
2011.970

KEN PRICE | American, 1935–2012
Sag, 2007
Painted ceramic
Overall: 6 1/2 x 6 7/8 x 5 1/8 in. (16.5 x 17.5 x 13 cm)
The Leatrice S. and Melvin B. Eagle Collection,
Museum purchase funded by the
Caroline Wiess Law Accessions
Endowment Fund
2010.2110

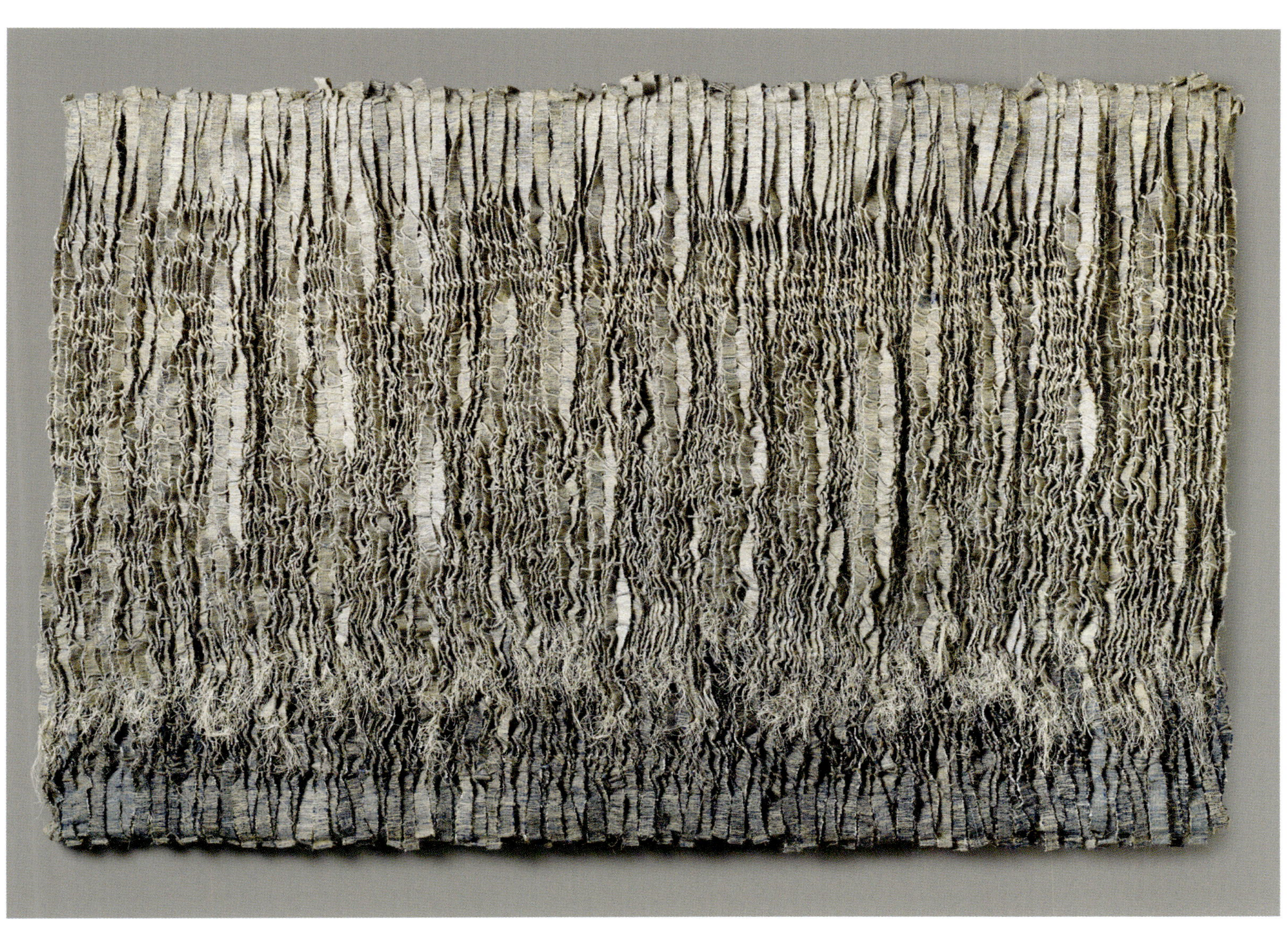

OLGA DE AMARAL | Colombian, born 1932
Riscos y Tiempo, 1985
Fiber
Overall: 47 x 75 in. (119.4 x 190.5 cm)
The Leatrice S. and Melvin B. Eagle Collection,
Gift of Leatrice and Melvin Eagle
2010.2262

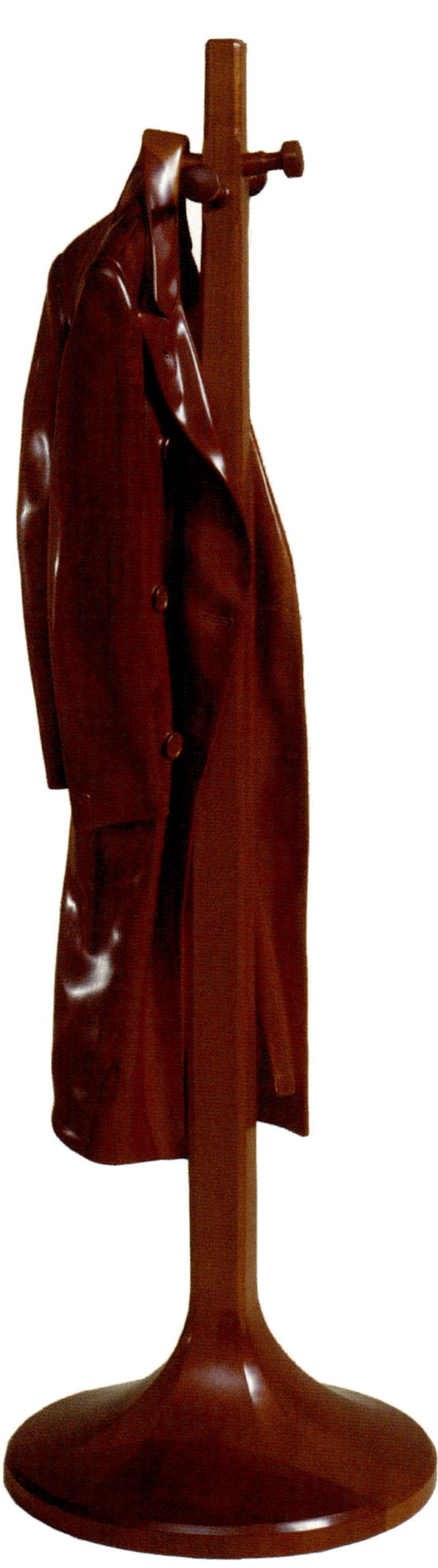

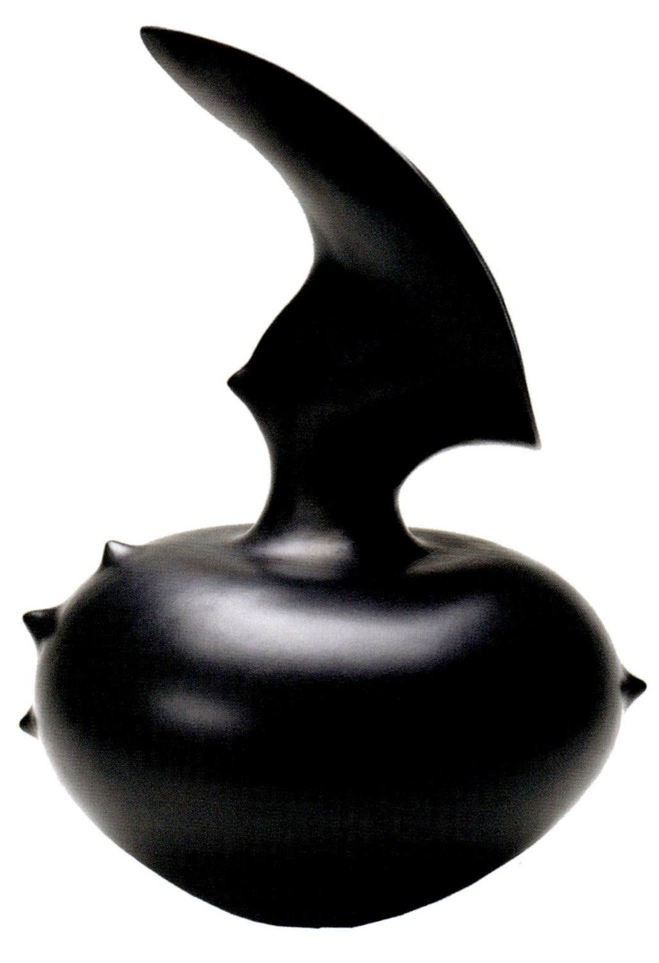

WENDELL CASTLE | American, born 1932
Coat Rack with Trench Coat, 1978
Honduran mahogany
Overall: 75 x 22 7/8 x 21 1/2 in.
(190.5 x 58.1 x 54.6 cm)
Museum purchase funded by
Roy M. Huffington, Inc. and anonymous donors
84.299

MAGDALENE ODUNDO | Kenyan, born 1950
Vase, 1995
Red clay
Overall: 16 3/4 x 13 x 12 1/2 in. (42.6 x 33 x 31.7 cm)
Museum purchase funded by
Helena Woolworth McCann and
the Winfield Foundation, by exchange
96.803

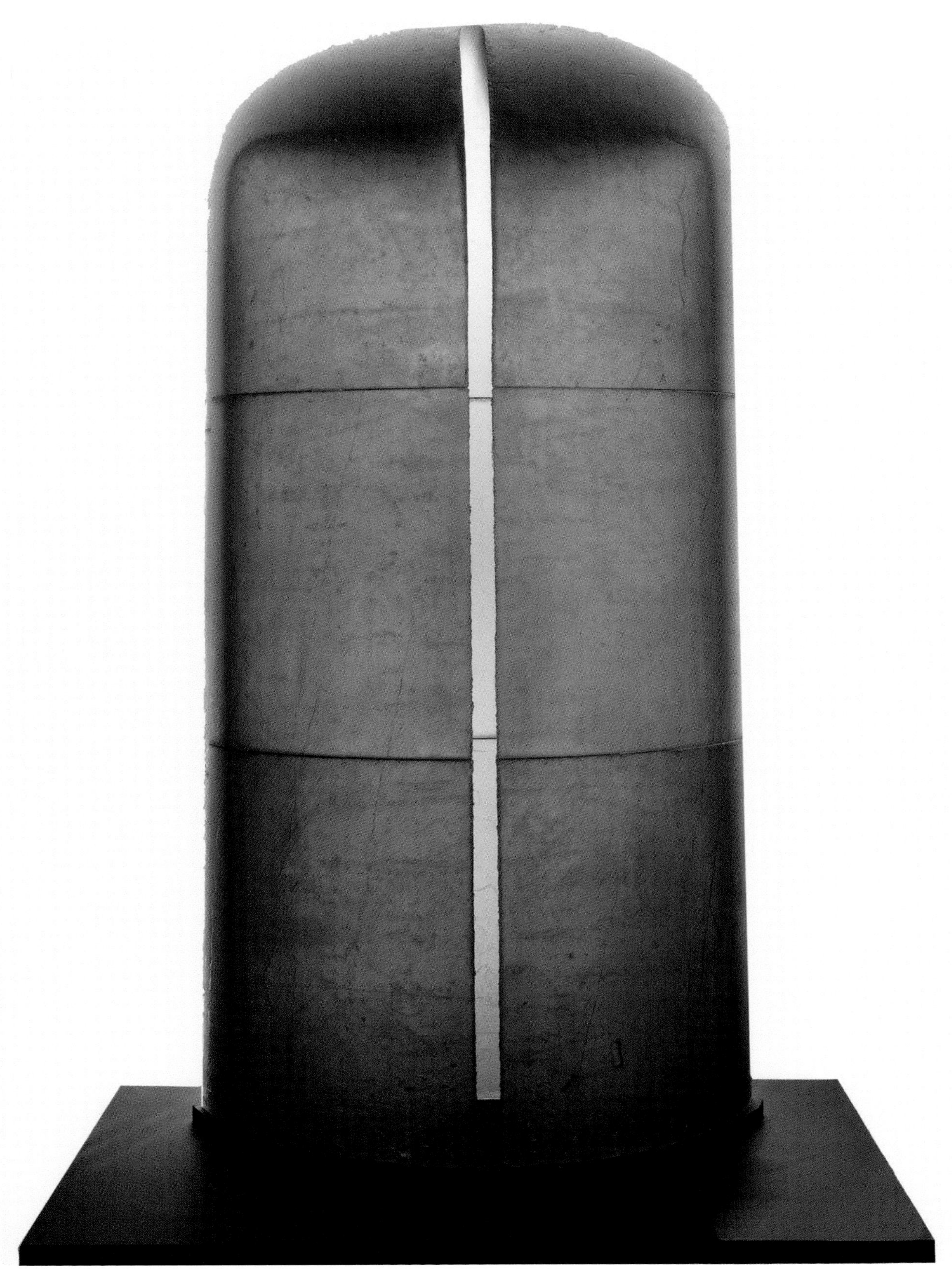

STANISLAV LIBENSKÝ | Czech, 1921–2002
JAROSLAVA BRYCHTOVÁ | Czech, 1924
Imprint of an Angel I, 1998–99
Cast glass
Overall: 92 x 43 1/2 x 17 in. (233.7 x 110.5 x 43.2 cm)
Bottom: 29 11/16 x 43 1/2 x 17 in. (75.4 x 110.5 x 43.2 cm)
Center: 28 1/4 x 42 3/4 x 13 1/2 in. (71.7 x 108.6 x 34.3 cm)
Top: 35 1/2 in. (90.2 cm)
Museum purchase funded by the estate of Roger Ager,
Liberty, Texas; Heller Gallery, New York, NY;
Dr. Frances M. Davis Ryan and Neil F. Ryan; Neal and Judi
Grossman of Illuminata Gallery; Steve Laedtke; Richard H.
Moiel and Katherine S. Poeppel; Barbara and Mark Paull;
the Susan Vaughan Foundation; and various other donors
2002.45

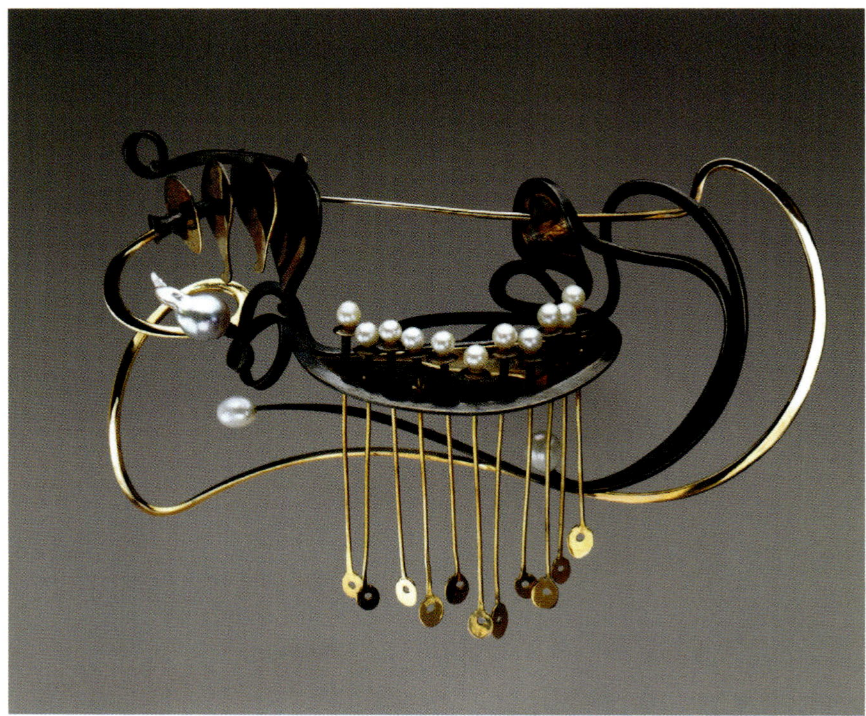

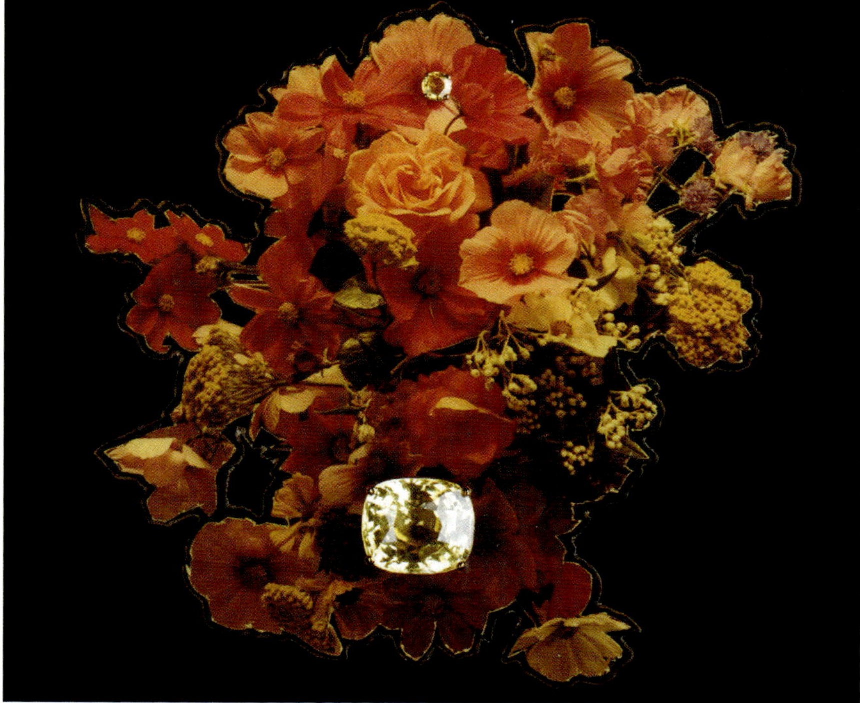

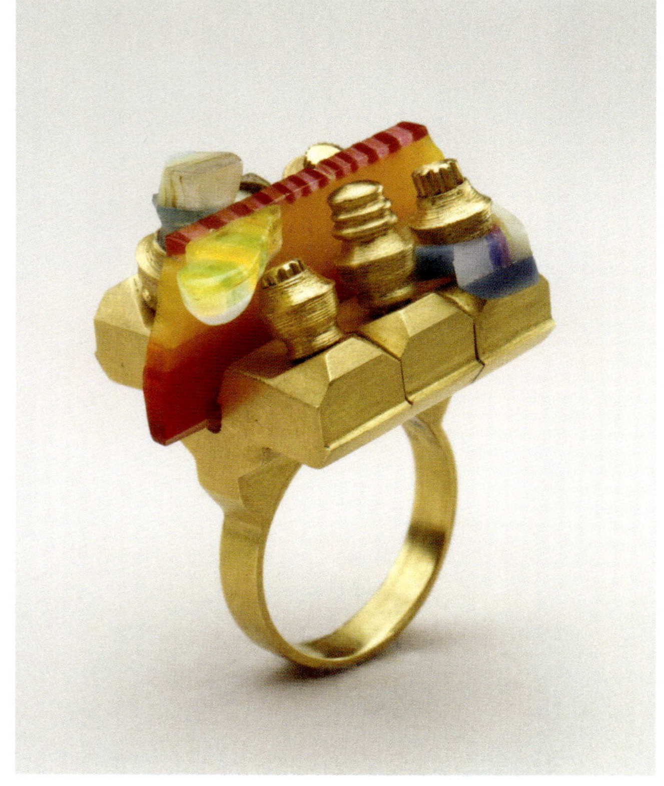

ALBERT PALEY | American, born 1944
Brooch, 1969
14k gold, sterling silver, and freshwater
and baroque pearls
Overall: 3 1/4 x 5 1/4 x 1 1/2 in.
(8.3 x 13.3 x 3.8 cm)
Helen Williams Drutt Collection,
Museum purchase funded by
Mr. and Mrs. John W. Mecom, Jr.,
by exchange
2002.4000

GIJS BAKKER | Dutch, born 1942
Bouquet Brooch, 1988
PVC, print, and yellow sapphires
4 x 3 3/4 x 3/4 in. (10.2 x 9.5 x 1.9 cm)
Helen Williams Drutt Collection,
gift of the Caroline Wiess Law Foundation
2002.3605

CLAUS BURY | German, born 1946
Ring, 1970
Gold and acrylic
7/8 x 1 1/2 x 1 1/2 in. (2.2 x 3.8 x 3.8 cm)
Helen Williams Drutt Collection,
funded by the Mary Kathryn Lynch Kurtz
Charitable Lead Trust
2002.3661

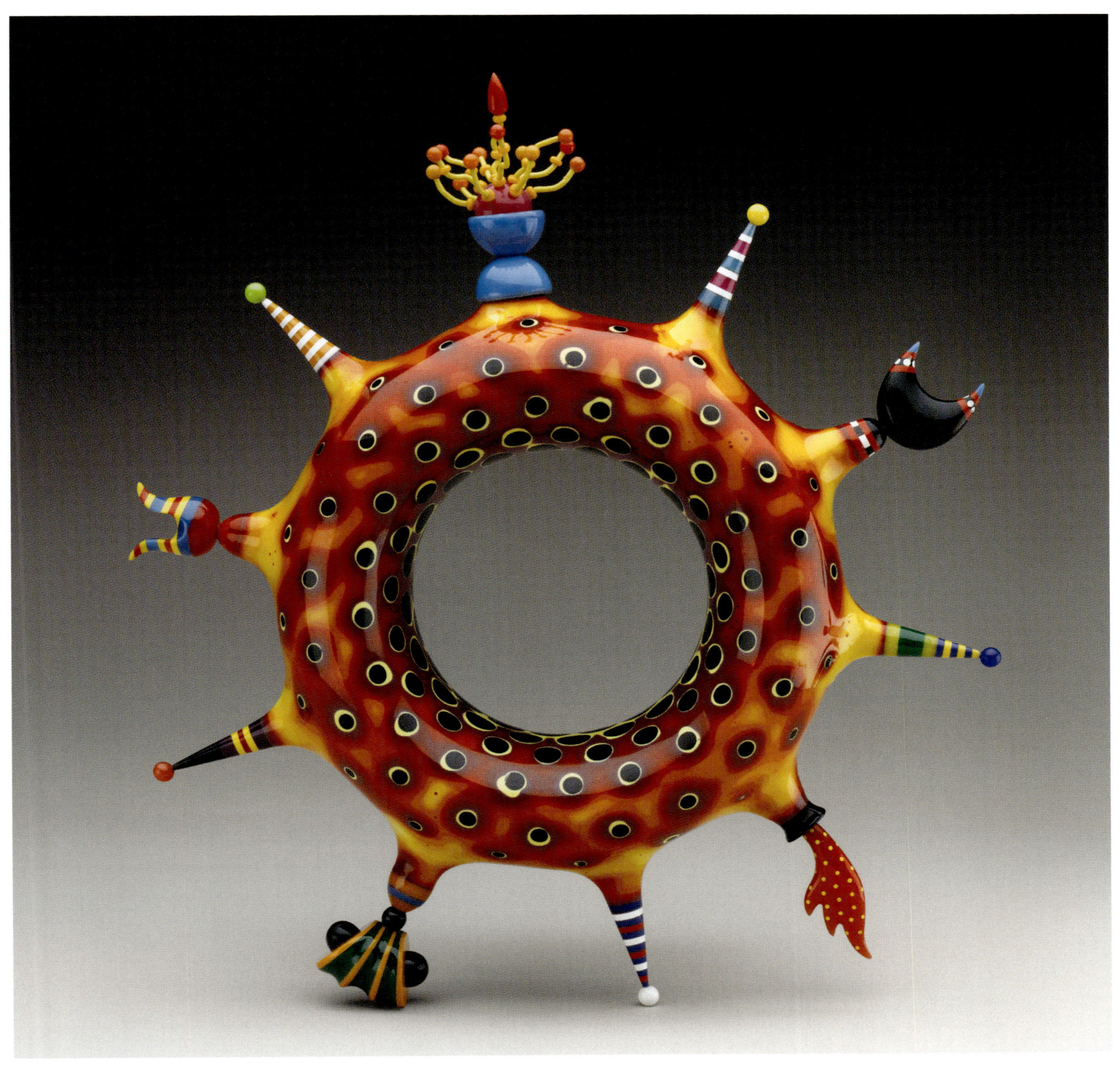

PETER CHANG | British, born 1944
Bracelet, 1992
Acrylic, PVC, and found objects
8 1/2 x 8 1/2 x 2 in. (21.6 x 21.6 x 5.1 cm)
Helen Williams Drutt Collection,
Museum purchase funded by
the Morgan Foundation
2002.3685

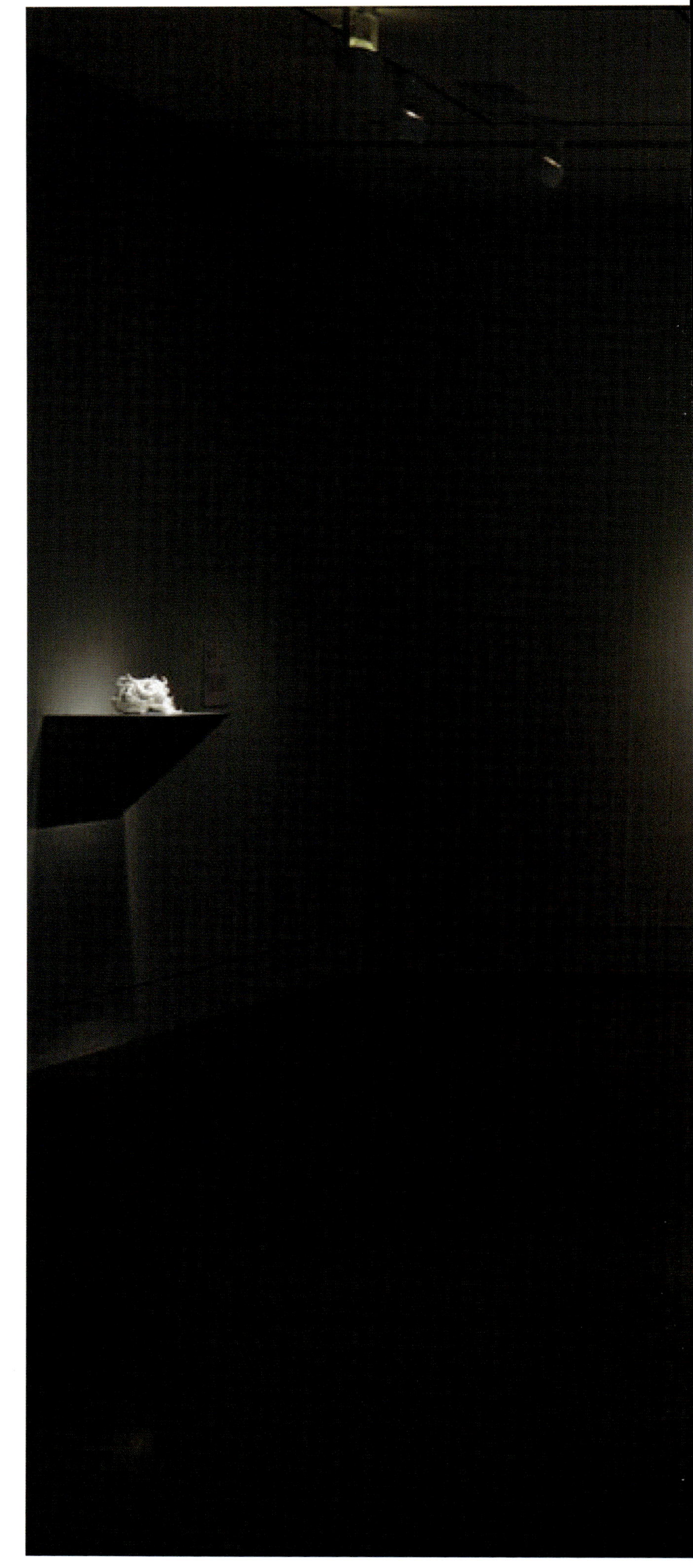

AOKI KATSUYO | Japanese, born 1972
Read the Story (Over the Hill), 2005;
Read the Story (Dark Grove), 2005; and
Tell the Story, 2005
Porcelain
61 3/8 x 46 1/2 x 6 5/8 in. (156 x 118.1 x 16 cm);
61 3/8 x 46 1/2 x 6 5/8 in. (156 x 118.1 x 16 cm);
74 x 11 3/8 x 11 3/8 in. (188 x 29 x 29 cm)
Garth Clark and Mark Del Vecchio Collection,
Museum purchase funded by
the Caroline Wiess Law Accessions Endowment Fund
2007.751.1.A–.F

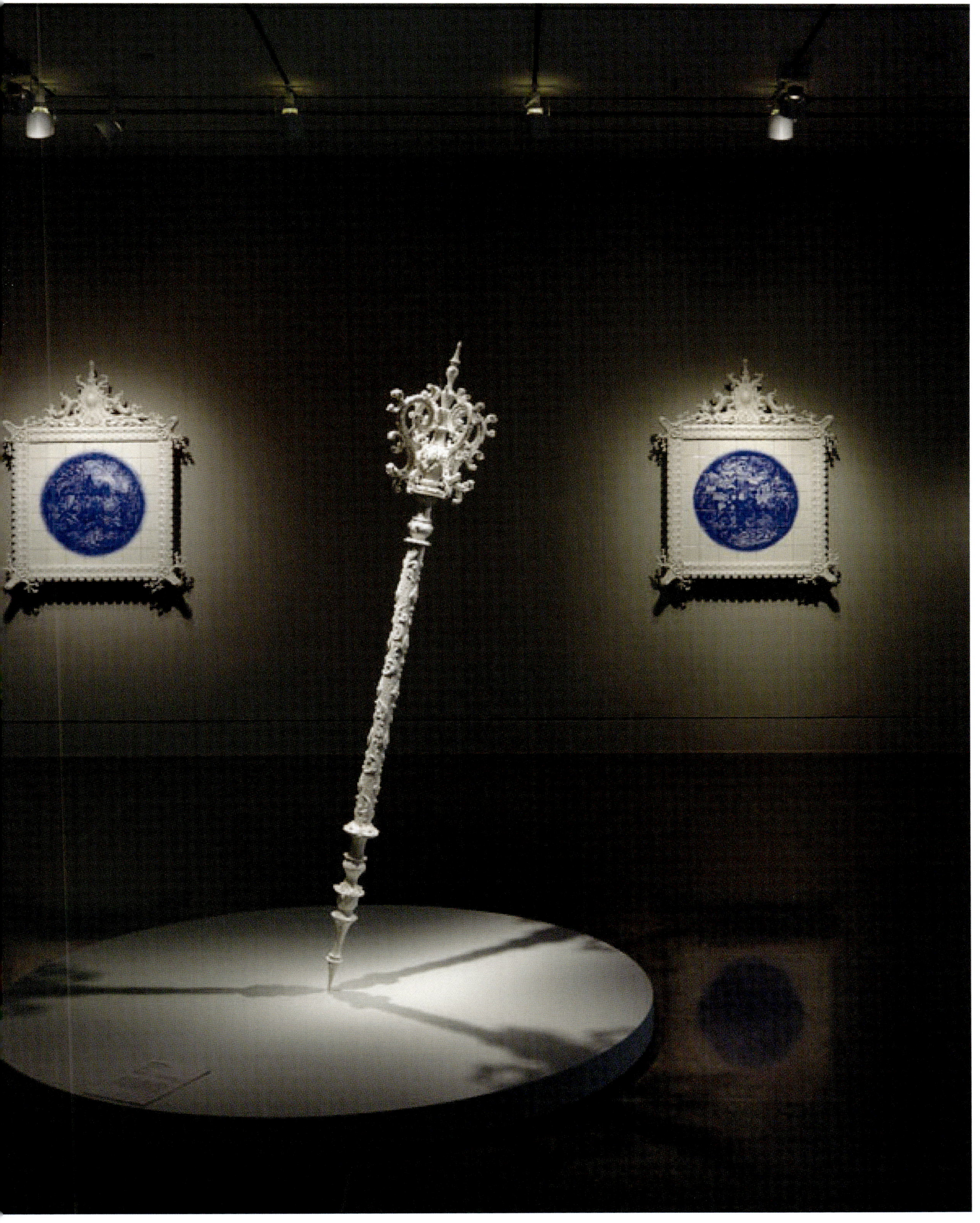

POP ART AND
POPULAR CULTURE

Irreverent, genre-bending, and at times satirical, Pop art mirrored the radical social and economic changes that swept across the world in the 1950s and 1960s. Borrowing freely from comic strips, commercial design, religious icons, cinema, rock and roll, the cult of celebrity, and the bold, seductive graphics of billboards, Pop art also embraced Post-Modernism's challenge to authority.

Claes Oldenburg captured the visceral aspect of Pop when he declared: "I am for an art that takes its form from the lines of life itself, that twists and extends and accumulates and spits and drips, and is heavy and coarse and blunt and sweet and stupid as life itself."

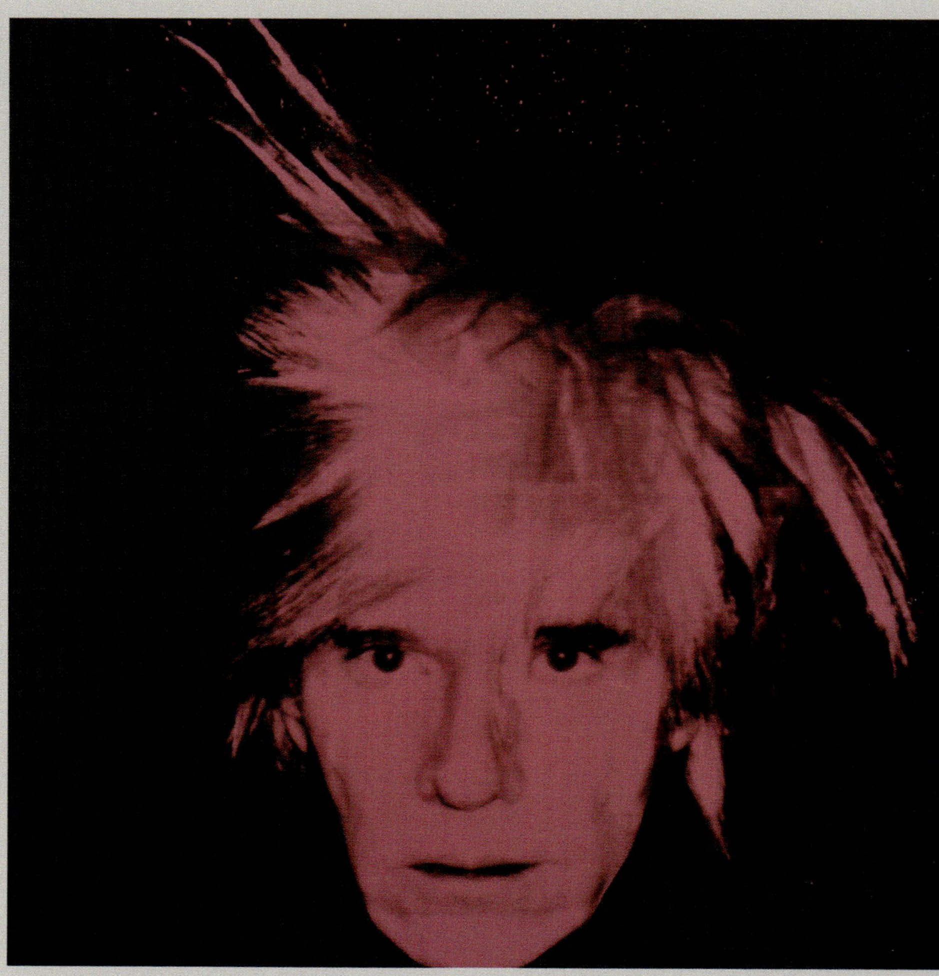

ANDY WARHOL | American, 1928–1987
Self-Portrait, 1986
Acrylic screenprint on canvas
Overall: 80 x 80 in. (203.2 x 203.2 cm)
Museum purchase funded by
the Charles Engelhard Foundation
in honor of Linda L. Cathcart,
Director of the Contemporary Arts
Museum from 1979–1987
88.34

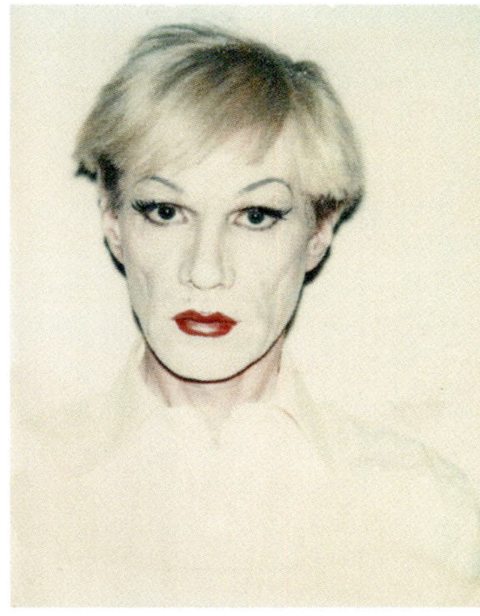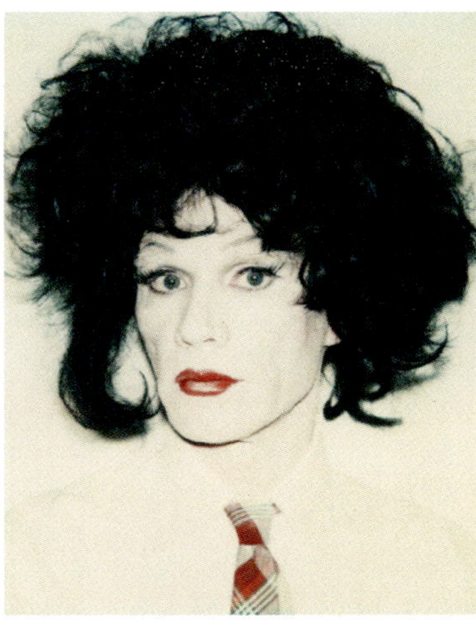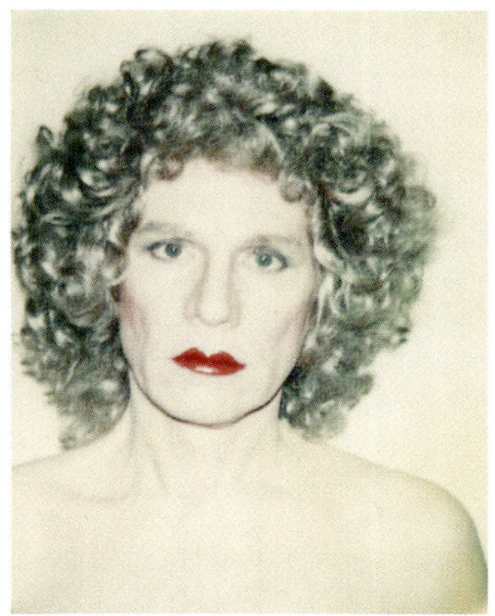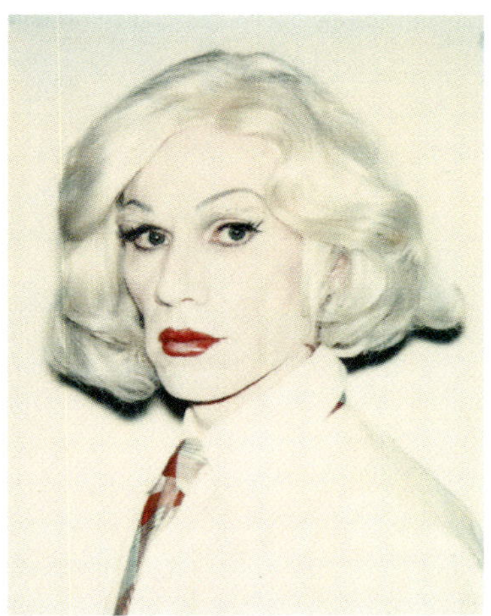

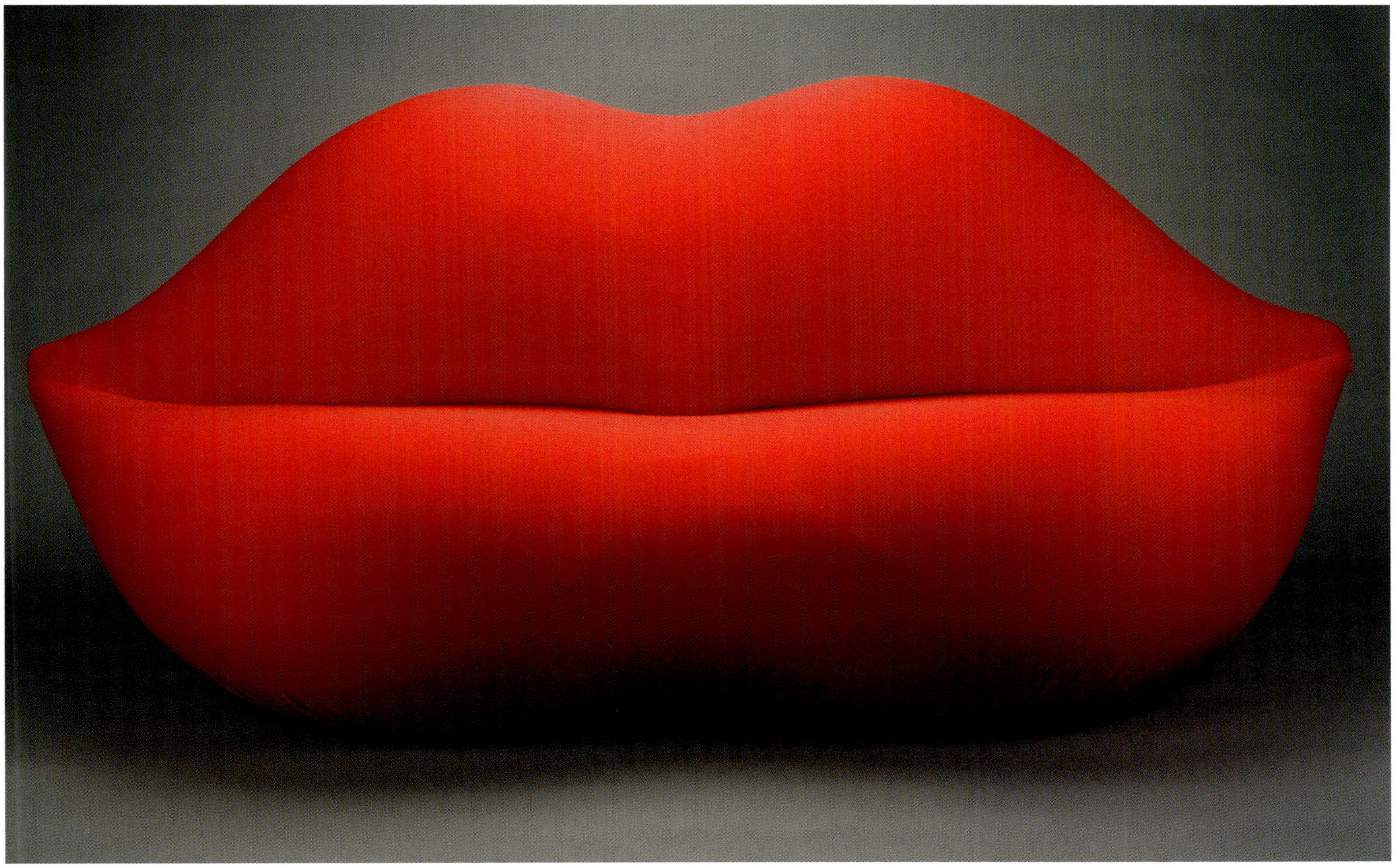

ANDY WARHOL | American, 1928–1987
Self-Portrait in Drag (regular wig), 1981
Self-Portrait in Drag (black wig), 1981–82
Self-Portrait in Drag (blond curly wig), 1981–82
Self-Portrait in Drag (blond wig), 1981–82
Dye diffusion transfer prints
Each sheet: 4 1/4 x 3 3/8 in. (10.8 x 8.6 cm)
Museum purchase
92.199.1–.4

DESIGNED BY STUDIO 65, TURIN, ITALY, | Established 1965
MADE BY GUFRAN
Bocca [Lips], after 1972
Polyurethane, metal, and upholstery
Overall: 33 x 82 3/4 x 32 in. (83.8 x 210.2 x 81.3 cm)
Museum purchase funded by friends of Susan Lapin
96.1749

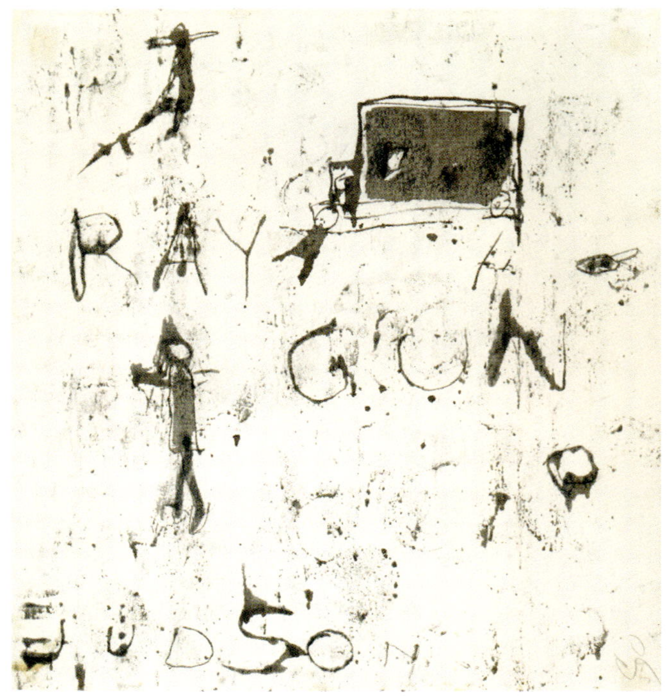

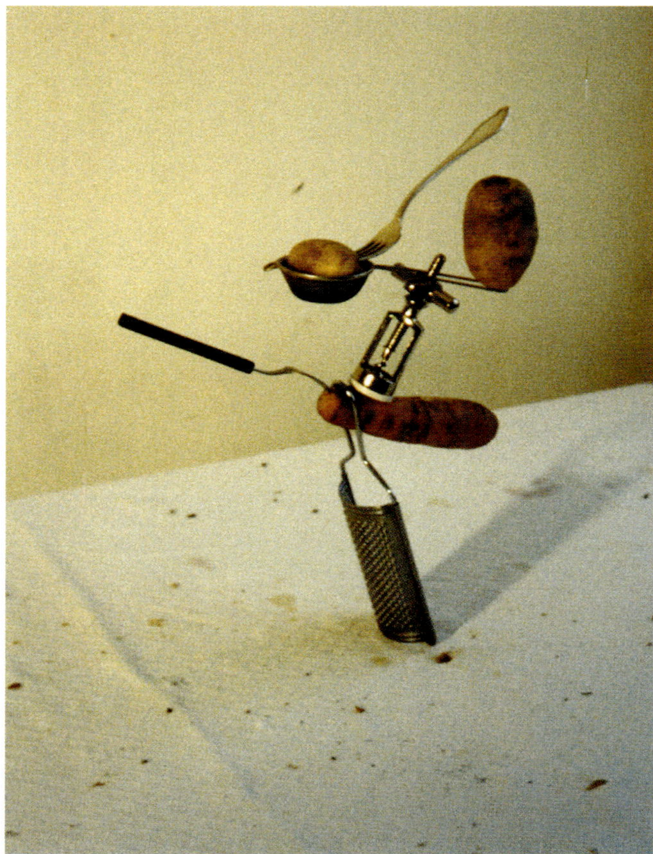

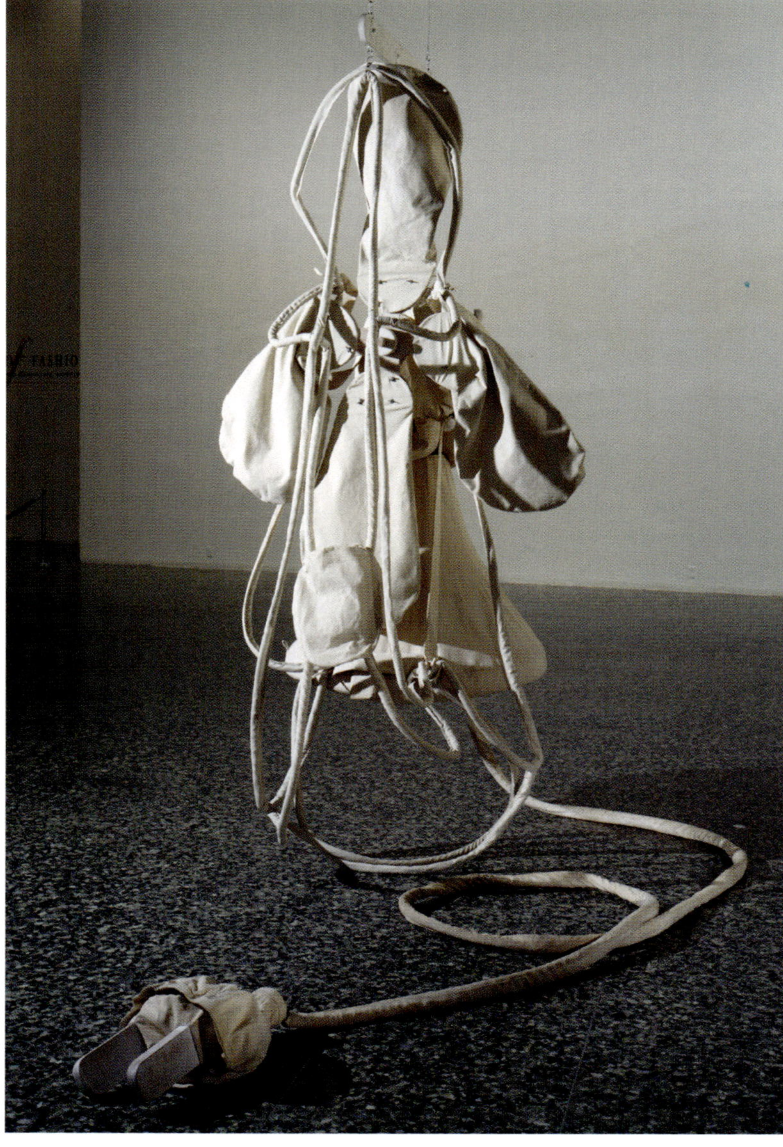

CLAES OLDENBURG | American,
born Sweden, 1929
Ray Gun, 1959
Transfer drawing (monotype)
Image/sheet: 13 13/16 x 12 7/8 in.
(35.1 x 32.7 cm)
Museum purchase funded by
the Alvin S. Romansky Prints and Drawings
Accessions Endowment Fund
2001.401

FISCHLI & WEISS,
PETER FISCHLI | Swiss, born 1952
DAVID WEISS | Swiss, 1946–2012
Nuclear Family, 1987
Chromogenic print, ed. #3/3
Image: 15 3/4 x 11 3/4 in. (40 x 29.9 cm)
Museum purchase funded by
the Charles Engelhard Foundation,
Stephen D. and Karen Susman, and
Max and Isabell Smith Herzstein
97.155

CLAES OLDENBURG | American, born Sweden, 1929
Giant Soft Fan - Ghost Version, 1967
Canvas, wood, and polyurethane foam
120 x 59 x 64 in. (304.8 x 149.9 x 162.6 cm)
Gift of D. and J. de Menil
67.18

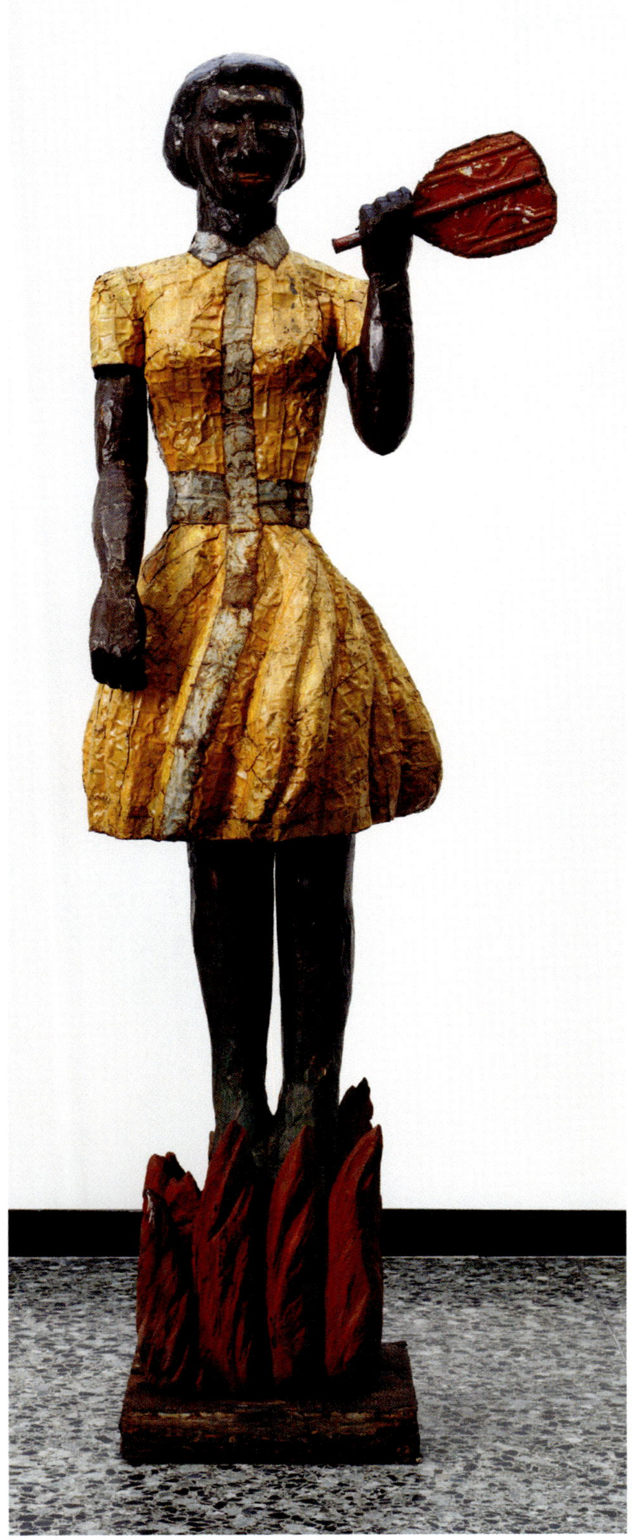

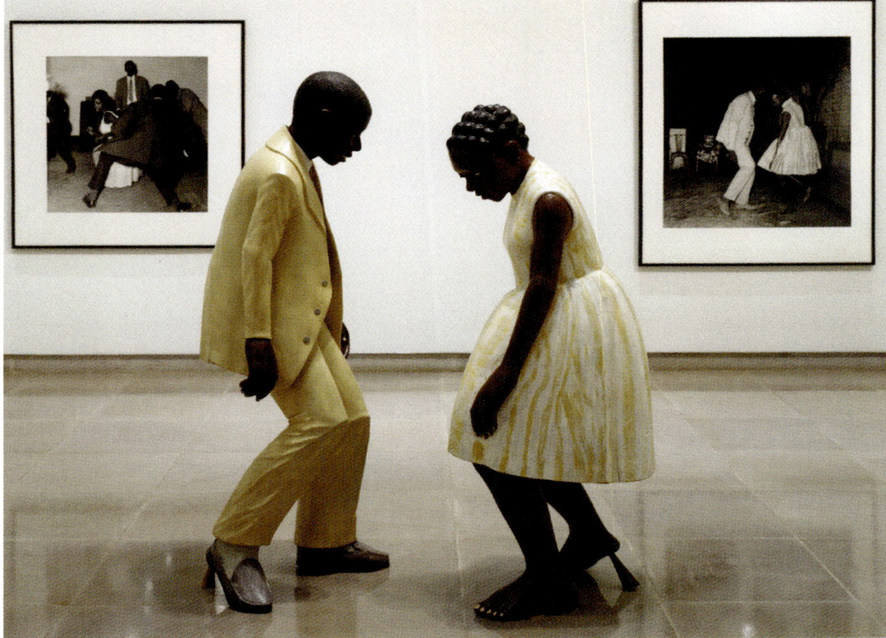

ALISON SAAR | American, born 1956
Fanning the Fire II, 1989
Lead and painted tin nailed over
wooden armature
Overall: 97 x 30 x 22 in. (246.4 x 76.2 x 55.9 cm)
.A: 52 1/4 x 30 x 22 in. (132.7 x 76.2 x 55.9 cm)
.B: 41 1/2 x 18 7/8 x 15 3/4 in. (105.4 x 47.9 x 40 cm)
Gift of Jeanne and Michael Klein in honor of the
African American Art Advisory Association
97.210.A, .B

COULIBALY SIAKA PAUL | Ivoirian, born 1964
Dancing Man
(Bent knees and slouching shoulders), 1999
Dancing Woman
(Shoulders slouching forward, right heel raised), 1999
From the exhibition *Clubs of Bamako*
Polychromed wood
99.232: 67 x 25 x 25 in. (170.2 x 63.5 x 63.5 cm)
99.233: 63 x 25 x 27 in. (160 x 63.5 x 68.6 cm)
Museum purchase funded by Nina and Michael Zilkha
99.232 and 99.232.

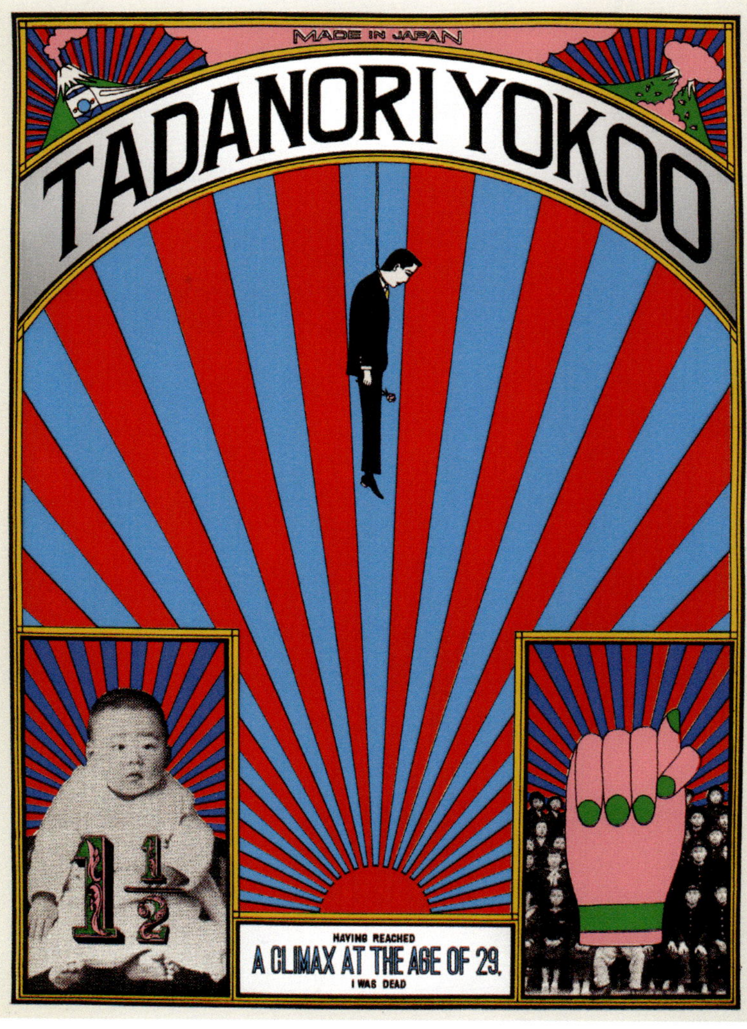

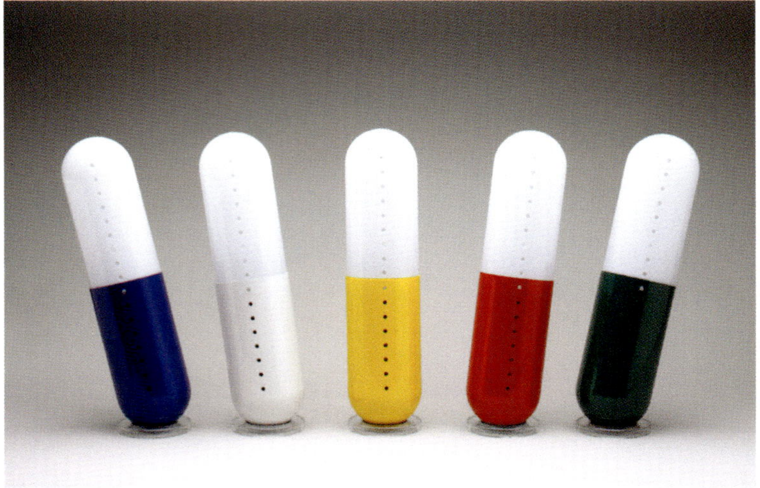

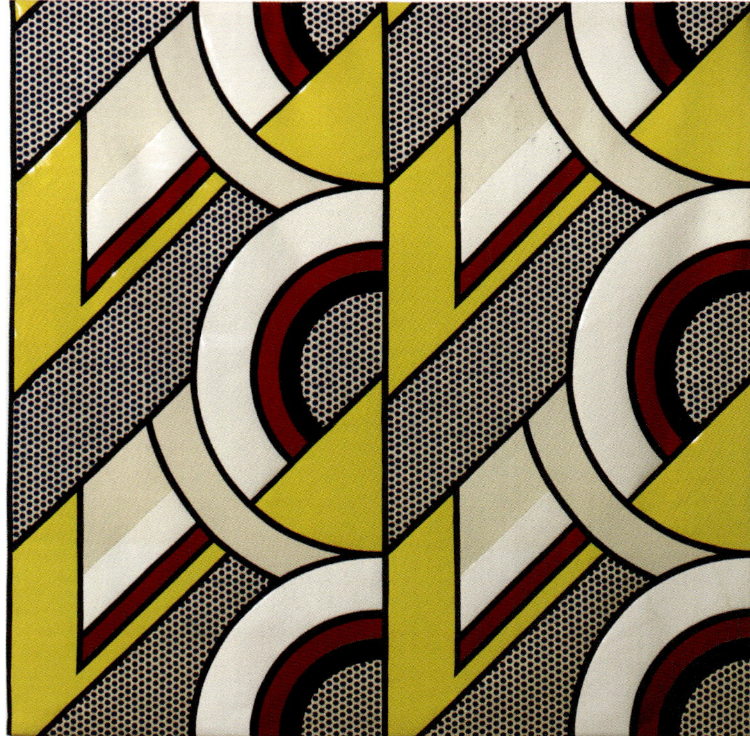

TANADORI YOKOO | Japanese, born 1936
Tanadori Yokoo, 1965
Screenprint
Image: 39 3/8 x 27 3/4 in. (100.1 x 70.5 cm)
Gift of an anonymous donor
2005.182

DESIGNED BY CESARE CASATI | Italian, born 1936
and EMANUELE PONZIO | Italian, born 1923
MANUFACTURED BY PONTEUR
Pillo Series Complet, 1968
PVC plastic and acrylic
Overall: 21 1/2h x 5 1/2 dia. in. (54.6 x 14 cm)
Museum purchase funded by
the Design Council, 2002
2002.2801.1–.5

ROY LICHTENSTEIN | American, 1923–1997
Published by Multiples, Inc., New York
Modular Banner (Modern Painting Banner),
1970
Felt and vinyl backed with linen backing,
edition 23/30
96 x 96 in. (243.8 x 243.8 cm)
Bequest of Edward R. Broida
2007.608

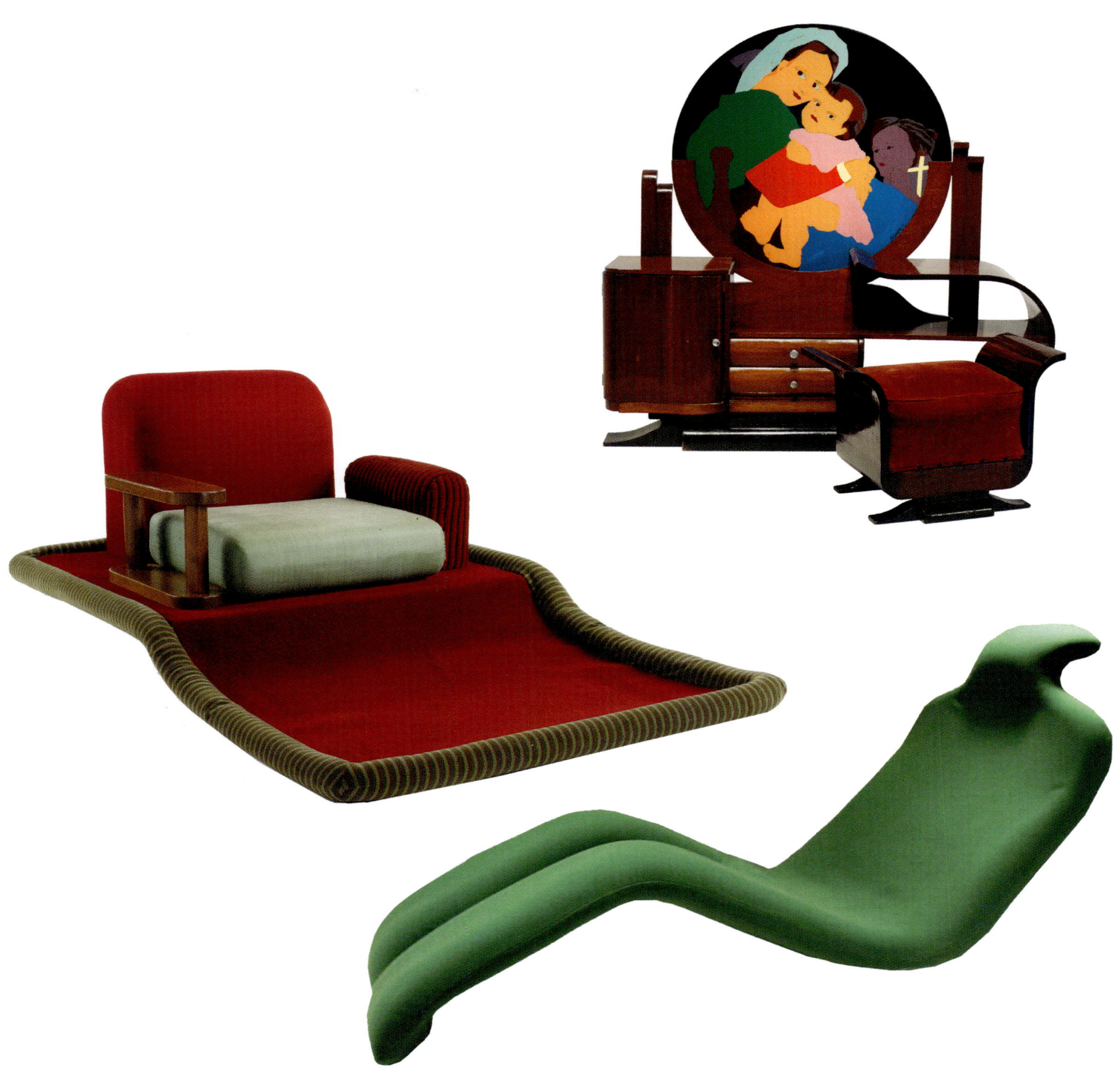

DESIGNED BY ETTORE SOTTSASS | Italian, born Austria, 1917–2007
MANUFACTURED BY POLTRONOVA
Tappeto Volante [Flying Carpet], 1972
Stained beechwood, stretch-jersey fabric,
velvet, and carpeting
25 1/2 x 42 1/2 x 71 1/4 in. (64.8 x 108 x 181 cm)
Museum purchase funded by
the Caroline Wiess Law Accessions
Endowment Fund
2009.506

BEATRIZ GONZÁLEZ | Colombian, born 1938
Gratia plena (peinador)
[Full of grace (Vanity)], 1971
Enamel on metal sheet joint on wood furniture
Overall: 59 x 59 1/16 x 15 in. (150 x 150 x 38 cm)
Museum purchase funded by the 2007
Latin American Experience Gala and Auction
2007.1294

DESIGNED BY OLIVIER MOURGUE | French, born 1939
MANUFACTURED BY AIRBORNE INTERNATIONAL,
MONTREUIL-SOUS-BOIS
"Bouloum" Chaise Lounge, c. 1968
Plastic, polyurethane, and nylon upholstery
26 x 54 x 25 1/4 in. (66.0 x 137.2 x 64.1 cm)
Museum purchase funded by
the Roger Ager Collection, Liberty, Texas
2000.128

© Colette Urbajtel/Archivo Manuel Álvarez Bravo, S.C.: p. 124
© Olga de Amaral: p. 211
© Estate of Diane Arbus: p. 131
© 2013 Estate of Alexander Archipenko/Artists Rights Society (ARS), New York: p. 157
© Estate of Robert Arneson/Licensed by VAGA, New York, New York: p. 210
Art © Figge Art Museum, successors to the Estate of Nan Wood Graham/Licensed by VAGA, New York, NY: p. 159
Art © Alberto Giacometti Estate/Licensed by VAGA and ARS, New York, NY: p. 43
Art © Robert Rauschenberg Foundation/Licensed by VAGA, New York, NY: p. 57
Art © Robert Rauschenberg Foundation and ULAE/ Licensed by VAGA, New York, NY Published by Universal Limited Art Editions: p. 173
© 2013 Artists Rights Society (ARS), New York / ADAGP, Paris: pp. 38, 49, 84, 96, 110, 111, 150–51
© 2013 Artists Rights Society (ARS), New York/ Beeldrecht, Amsterdam: p. 214
© 2013 Artists Rights Society (ARS), New York/ DACS, London: pp. 58–59
© 2013 Artists Rights Society (ARS), New York /c/o Pictoright Amsterdam: pp. 186, 195
© 2013 Artists Rights Society (ARS), New York/SIAE, Rome: p. 48
© 2013 Artists Rights Society (ARS), New York /SOMAAP, Mexico City: p. 79
© 2013 Artists Rights Society (ARS), New York/VG Bild-Kunst, Bonn: p. 133
© Paul Astbury: p. 145
© John Baldessari: p. 139
© Lewis Baltz: p. 137
© Alfredo Barbini: p. 73
© Barford Sculptures Ltd: p. 56
© Estate of William Baziotes: p. 109
© Bernhard and Hilla Becher: p. 136
© José Antonio Berni: pp. 89, 143
© Lee Bontecou: p. 49
© Estate of Edgar Brandt/Artists Rights Society (ARS), New York: p. 199
© James Brown: p. 109
© Christopher Bucklow: p. 74
© Claus Bury: p. 214
© Estate of Harry Callahan, courtesy Pace/MacGill Gallery, New York: p. 118
© Estudio Campana: p. 188
© Wendell Castle, Inc.: p. 212
© Nick Cave: p. 66
© Vija Celmins: p. 180
© Peter Chang: p. 215
© "The World of Lygia Clark" Cultural Association, http://www.lygiaclark.org.br: p. 82
© Analivia Cordeiro: p. 83
© 2013 Carlos Cruz-Diez /Artists Rights Society (ARS), New York / ADAGP, Paris: pp. 72; 92–93
© Imogen Cunningham Trust: p. 122
© Dedalus Foundation, Inc. /Licensed by VAGA, New York, NY: p. 167
© 2002 Estate of Willem de Kooning/Artists Rights Society (ARS), New York: p. 169
© The Estate of Richard Diebenkorn: pp. 170–71
© Juan Carlos Distéfano: p. 85
© Do Ho Suh: p. 67
© Georg Dobler: p. 188
© Eggleston Artistic Trust, courtesy Cheim & Read, New York: p. 134
© Bohumil Eliá : p. 75
© Walker Evans Archive, The Metropolitan Museum of Art: p. 125
© Monir Farmanfarmaian: p. 71
© Magdalena Fernández: pp. 98–99
© León Ferrari: p. 94
© Dan Fischer: p. 152
© Eric Fischl: pp. 178–79
© Fischli & Wiess: p. 220

© 2013 Sam Francis Foundation, California /Artists Rights Society (ARS), NY: p. 174
© Robert Frank; Courtesy of Pace/MacGill Gallery, New York: p. 130
© 2013 Helen Frankenthaler/Artists Rights Society (ARS), New York: p. 181
© Fundación Pan Klub - Museo Xul Solar: p. 78
© Estate of Jaromír Funke: pp. 123, 188
© Fundación Gego: p. 95
© 2013 Frank Gehry /Artists Rights Society (ARS), New York: p. 204
© Nan Goldin: p. 60
© Beatriz González: pp. 86, 223
© 2004 Julio Gonzalez /Artists Rights Society (ARS), New York /ADAGP, Paris: p. 113
© 2013 The Arshile Gorky Foundation/The Artists Rights Society (ARS), New York: pp. 112, 161
© Adolph and Esther Gottlieb Foundation/Licensed by VAGA, New York, NY: p. 47
© Hatakeyama Naoya, courtesy Taka Ishii Gallery: pp. 140–41
© Estate of Robert Heinecken: p. 145
© Estate of Eva Hesse: p. 169
© Hiroshi Sugimoto: p. 70
© 2013 Renate, Hans and Maria Hofmann Trust /Artists Rights Society (ARS), New York: p. 73
© Alfredo Jaar: p. 101
© Doug Jeck: p. 152
© 2013 Estate of Luis A. Jimenez, Jr. /Artists Rights Society (ARS), New York: p. 88
© Jasper Johns/Licensed by VAGA, New York, NY: pp. 54–55, 175
© Estate of Ray Johnson: p. 145
© Judd Foundation. Licensed by VAGA, New York, NY: p. 191
© 2006 Katsuyo Aoki: pp. 216–17
© Alex Katz/ Licensed by VAGA, New York, NY: p. 177
© Ellsworth Kelly: p. 166
© Estate of André Kertész/Higher Pictures: p. 120
© Anselm Kiefer: pp. 58–59
© Nancy Reddin Kienholz: p. 144
© 2013 The Franz Kline Estate /Artists Rights Society (ARS), New York: p. 46
© Gyula Kosice: pp. 75, 90–91
© Barbara Kruger: p. 183
© Joris Laarman: p. 109
© Stoney Lamar: p. 112
© Charles LeDray: p. 144
© Lee Bul: p. 70
© Sherrie Levine and Joost van Oss: pp. 62–63
© Estate of Sol LeWitt /Artists Rights Society (ARS), New York: p. 190
© Stanislav Libensky Estate: p. 213
© Estate of Roy Lichtenstein: p. 222
© Ole Lislerud: p. 153
© 2013 Richard Long /Artists Rights Society (ARS), New York
© 2013 Man Ray Trust/Artists Rights Society (ARS), NY/ADAGP, Paris: p. 132
© 2013 Brice Marden /Artists Rights Society (ARS), New York: p. 176
© Teresa Margolles: pp. 106–7
© Estate of Leo Matiz: p. 189
© 2010 Julie Mehretu and Gemini G.E.L. LLC: pp. 184–85
© Cildo Meireles, courtesy Galerie Lelong, New York: p. 100
© Bruce Metcalf: p. 113
© Estate of Ludwig Mies van der Rohe /Artists Rights Society (ARS), New York: p. 196
© 2013 Successió Miró / Artists Rights Society (ARS), New York /ADAGP, Paris: pp. 43, 160
© Richard Misrach: p. 135
© 2013 Estate of Laszlo Moholy-Nagy/Artists Rights Society (ARS), New York: pp. 71, 121, 189
© 2013 Mondrian/Holtzman Trust c/o HCR International Virginia: p. 39
© Vik Muniz/ Licensed by VAGA, New York, NY: p. 152
© Oscar Muñoz: p. 152
© Estate of Alice Neel: p. 57
© Estate of Barnett Newman /Artists Rights Society (ARS), New York: p. 163

© Luis Felipe Noé: p. 87
© Estate of Kenneth Noland/Licensed by VAGA, New York, NY: p. 51
© Magdalene Odundo: p. 212
© Cesar and Claudio Oiticica: p. 83
© Okanoue Toshiko: p. 145
© 2012 The Georgia O'Keeffe Foundation /Artists Rights Society (ARS), New York: p. 117
© Claes Oldenburg: p. 220
© Judy Onofrio: p. 144
© Estate of Alejandro Otero: p. 80
© Albert Paley: p. 214
© Gaetano Pesce: p. 208
© Irving Penn and Condé Nast Publications, Inc.: p. 126
© 2013 Die Photographische Sammlung /SK Stiftung Kultur-August Sander Archiv, Cologne / ARS, NY: p. 127
© 2013 Estate of Pablo Picasso /Artists Rights Society (ARS), New York: pp. 40–41, 50, 165
© 2013 The Pollock-Krasner Foundation /Artists Rights Society (ARS), New York: pp. 44–45, 162
© Ken Price: pp. 109, 210
© 2013 Estate of Jean Prouvé /Artists Rights Society (ARS), New York /ADAGP, Paris: p. 196
© Walid Raad, courtesy Paula Cooper Gallery, New York: p. 138
© Miguel Angel Rios: p. 104
© Estate of Rhod Rothfuss: p. 80
© Ed Ruscha: pp. 62–63
© Alison Saar: p. 221
© Valter Sacilotto: p. 186
© 2013 Estate of Niki de Saint-Phalle /Artists Rights Society (ARS), New York /ADAGP, Paris: p. 142 (Schendel) TK: p. 97
© Cindy Sherman, courtesy of the artist and Metro Pictures: p. 119
© 2013 Yinka Shonibare MBE. All Rights Reserved, Artists Rights Society (ARS), New York / DACS, London: p. 61
© Coulibaly Siaka Paul: p. 221
© Estate of David Smith/ Licensed by VAGA, New York, NY: p. 111
© Estate of W. Eugene Smith / Black Star: p. 128
© 2013 Estate of Jesús Rafael Soto /Artists Rights Society (ARS), New York / ADAGP, Paris: p. 81
© Ettore Sottsass: pp. 206, 207, 209
© Estate of Richard Stankiewicz: p. 111
© Philippe Starck: p. 108
© Jennifer Steinkamp, courtesy the artist and Lehmann Maupin Gallery, New York: p. 65
© 2013 Frank Stella/ Artists Rights Society (ARS), New York: p. 52
© Estate of Myron Stout: p. 172
© Paul Strand Archives, Aperture Foundation, Inc.: p. 116
© Tadanori Yokoo: p. 222
© Javier Téllez, courtesy the artist and Galerie Peter Kilchmann, Zurich: p. 105
© Tomatsu Shomei: p. 129
© Copyright 2013 Alejandra, Aurelio, and Claudio Torres: p. 191
© 1989, Tunga. Image Courtesy of the artist and Luhring Augustine: pp. 102–3
© James Turrell: pp. 68–69, 71
© Gregorio Vardanega: p. 75
© Estate of Jorge de la Vega: p. 142
© Bill Viola: p. 74
© Estate of Edward Alexander Wadsworth: p. 186
© Fred Wilson, courtesy Pace Gallery: p. 64
© Kara Walker, courtesy of Sikkema Jenkins & Co, New York: p. 182
© 2013 The Andy Warhol Foundation for the Visual Arts, Inc. /Artists Rights Society (ARS), New York: pp. 218, 219
© Waltraud Weissmann: p. 188
© Rachel Whiteread: p. 187

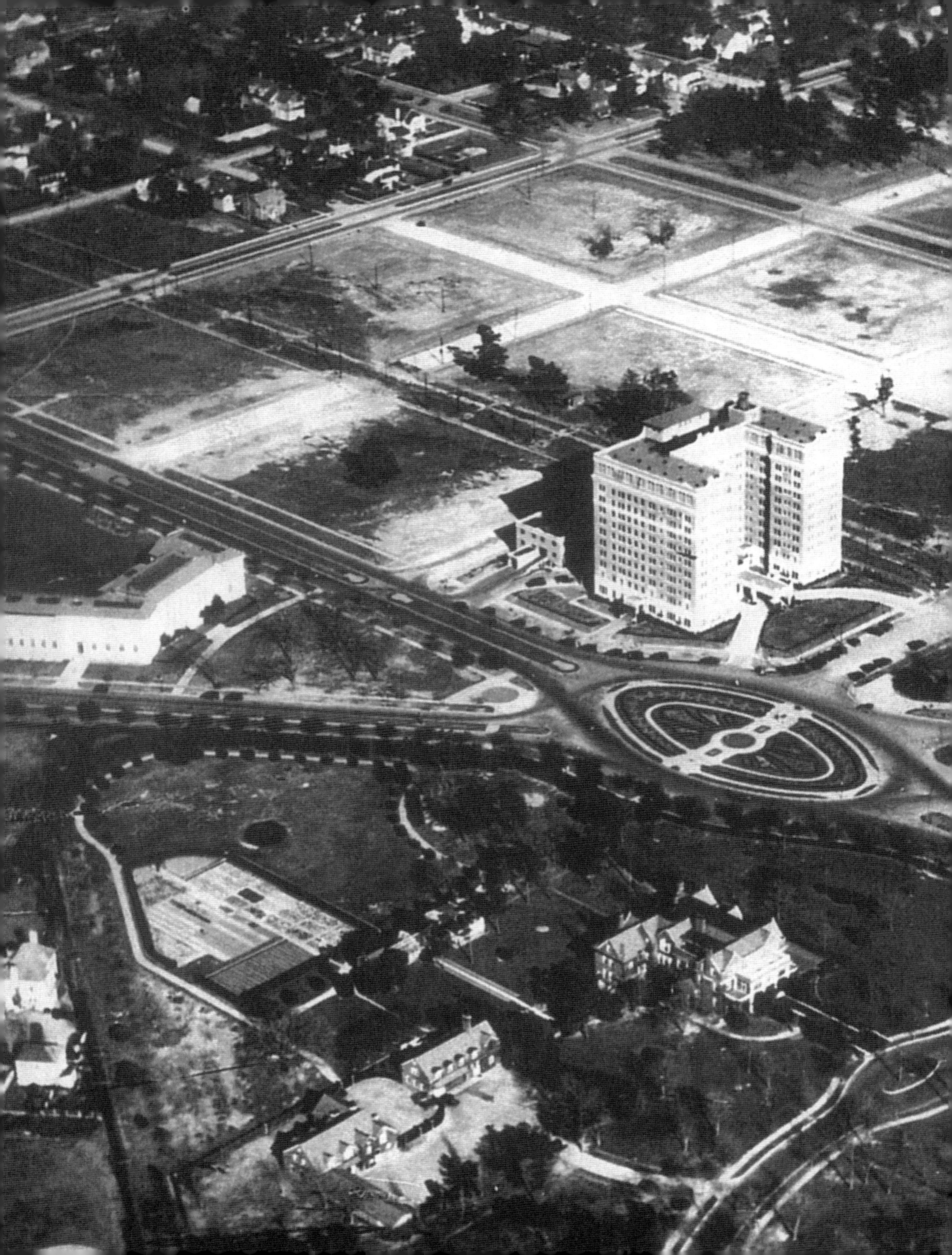